Selected Essays from

"The Tatler,"

"The Spectator,"

and

"The Guardian"

Joseph Addison and Richard Steele

Selected Essays from
"The Tatler,"
"The Spectator,"
and
"The Guardian"

Edited by Daniel McDonald

The Bobbs-Merrill Company, Inc.
Indianapolis and New York

© 1973 by The Bobbs-Merrill Company, Inc.
Printed in the United States of America
Library of Congress Catalog Card Number 73–177472
First Printing
Designed by Starr Atkinson

Contents

The Tatler

The Spectator

Contents

The Guardian

Preface

The editor preparing a collection of Addison-Steele essays necessarily faces questions concerning his text. He can reprint the papers as they appeared in the original folio half-sheets, or he can take his text from the first octavo or the first duodecimo collections, which contain authorial revisions. The octavo editions appeared first and were issued to subscribers; then duodecimo printings were offered to the general public. I have chosen to use the first collected editions, i.e., the octavo editions of *The Spectator* (1712–1715) and *The Guardian* (1714). I have, however, used the first duodecimo reprint of *The Tatler* (1710–1711) because the title page declares it to be "revised and corrected by the Author." While the present text is not identical with that of the folio sheets which circulated through London, it can be argued that it represents the final form in which the authors wished to leave their work.

Except for correcting obvious printing errors, I have not changed the punctuation, capitalization, or spelling of the original text.

The selection—which omits the *Tatlers, Spectators,* and *Guardians* contributed by other authors—attempts to balance the contributions of Steele and Addison, and to include their best and most representative papers. Many have rarely appeared in collected editions. And though I am sure to have left out someone's favorite essays, I take much pleasure in having included my own.

The annotation, is extensive; I like to think it will be found useful rather than intrusive. By statistical necessity, a text with 2100 footnotes contains more than several factual errors. As these come to light, I hope readers will recall Addison's indulgence toward "a pardonable Inadvertency."

My debt to previous editors of these essays is both immense and obvious. I am grateful to Donald F. Bond of the University of Chicago for counsel concerning choice of text and to John C. Stephens, Jr., of Emory University for assistance in choosing essays from *The Guardian*. I am forever indebted to Miss Marte Shaw of the Houghton Library at Harvard for her good offices. I must acknowledge the help of four colleagues (John Edward Hardy and Willene Schaefer Hardy, University of Missouri at St. Louis; Nen Allen Park, Ohio University; and Charles Harwell, University of South Alabama) and of two long-suffering students (Miss Lillie Howard and Mr. Barry Nowlin). I thank my wife Irene for her unfailing encouragement and tolerance.

Daniel McDonald

University of South Alabama
March, 1971

Introduction

Joseph Addison's and Richard Steele's journals—*The Tatler,
The Spectator,* and *The Guardian*—spanned the period from
April 1709 to September 1714 and climaxed the development of
a relatively new literary form, the periodical essay. Though prose
discussions on general or personal subjects had long existed, Montaigne's *Essais* (1580) had established the word "essay" and popularized the easy, discursive form. The word came into English
with the publication of Francis Bacon's *Essayes* (1597), in which
discourses on truth, morality, and the human condition tended
to be formal and eloquent rather than casual and familiar. Related to such allied forms as the prose epistle, the character, the
dialogue, and the pamphlet, the essay developed throughout the
seventeenth century and achieved distinction in the works of Sir
William Cornwallis, Abraham Cowley, John Dryden, and Sir William Temple. In their writings, the essay became a vehicle for personal reflection, social criticism, anecdote, literary judgment, and
entertainment. By 1709, when Addison and Steele joined in writing *The Tatler,* the form was well suited to serve, not the severe
scholar, but the broadly educated man of letters who wished to
comment briefly and casually on a wide range of subjects.

The development of the essay was necessarily related to the
growth of the English newspaper. It can be argued that no real
newspaper existed until the appearance in 1645 of *The Oxford
Gazette* (later *The London Gazette*), a paper that—under the
Licensing Act of 1647—had a monopoly on printed news. Consequently other periodicals arose which supplemented news items
with informative comment on popular subjects. Sir Roger L'Estrange's *The Observator* (1681–1687) offered question-answer
dialogue to treat current problems and to castigate Whigs and
Dissenters. John Dunston's *The Athenian Gazette* (1691–1697)
—later *The Athenian Mercury*—printed news along with paragraphs answering readers' questions on marriage, literature, theology, and popular science. Other journals appealed to more special-

ized interests. Jean de la Crose's *History of Learning* (1691–1694) reviewed learned works concerning theology, classical literature, and archeology. Peter Motteux' *The Gentleman's Journal* (1692–1694) presented news and reviews of current publications, along with short stories, fables, poems, and essays. Ned Ward's *London Spy* (1698–1700) and Tom Brown's *Amusements Serious and Comical* (1700) offered pungent descriptions of London tourist-spots, coffee-houses, prisons, low-taverns, etc., and appealed to the masses. All of these periodicals, with their wide range of interests, contributed to the shaping of *The Tatler*.

The English newspaper was given new life in 1695 when the Licensing Act was allowed to lapse, and several new journals appeared. These routinely combined current news with sharp political commentary. Abel Roper's *The Post Boy* (1695–1736) and Jean de Fonvive's *The Post-Man* (1695–1730) were Tory papers; George Ridpath's *Flying Post* (1695–1731) and Samuel Buckley's *The Daily Courant* (1702–1735) were Whig. *The Observator* (1702–1712) with its dialogue presentation was revived by John Tutchin and converted into a Whig journal. *The Rehearsal* (1704–1709) was begun by Charles Leslie to make the necessary Tory response. By 1709, there were at least eighteen London newspapers, issuing some fifty numbers a week.

The most illustrious predecessor of *The Tatler*, Daniel Defoe's *A Review of the Affairs of France* (1704–1713), though it supported the Whig cause, was particularly notable for its political and religious moderation. The *Review* was in the main a serious journal on political and economic subjects, but Defoe was always provocative and sometimes moralizing and amusing. For a time he included in his paper a section called "Advice from the Scandalous Club" wherein he criticized drunkenness, duelling, the Mohocks, and romantic gallantry. This combination of news, political moderation, wit, and social comment helped establish the form of the topical essay and thus mold the audience for *The Tatler*.

In May 1709, when Addison's first contribution was published in the eighteenth issue of Steele's new periodical *The Tatler*, the men were beginning perhaps the most fruitful collaboration in English literature as well as continuing a personal relationship which had existed for some twenty-three years.

The two had met while attending school at London's Charter-house, and the friendship had grown during their years at Oxford. While Steele left school to serve in the army and later to gain notice as a London dramatist and man of letters, Addison stayed on as a don at Magdalen, later leaving Oxford to make a grand tour of the continent and to establish himself in a diplomatic career. Their friendship continued in London, and both men were admitted to the Kit-Cat Club, an influential circle of Whig statesmen and wits. Probably their first collaboration occurred in 1705 when Addison helped Steele revise his new comedy *The Tender Husband* and then contributed the Prologue to it. Both men won office in the Whig government. When in 1707 Steele became editor of the *London Gazette*—the official voice of the Whig ministry—Addison was already an undersecretary of state and was thus able to supply private information for his friend's use. Steele, then, was already a well-known journalist, and Addison a rising statesman, when the first *Tatler* appeared.

The Tories came into power in 1710, and since both Addison and Steele lost their political appointments (though Steele did remain Commissioner of Stamps) they had more time for literary journalism. The vast majority of their periodical essays—*Tatlers, Spectators,* and *Guardians*—were written during the time of the 1710–1714 Tory ministry. The collaboration continued until political differences (Steele did not think Addison was a zealous enough Whig) terminated *The Guardian.* Thereafter they published separately—Steele castigating government policies and spokesmen in *The Englishmen* and other journals, and Addison chiding social and political folly in the revived *Spectator* and *The Freeholder.* Their association ended when they disputed querulously (Steele in *The Plebeian,* Addison in *The Old Whig*) over the 1719 Peerage Bill.

Nevertheless, during the five years of their collaboration, Addison and Steele produced over 900 essays, many of them of outstanding quality. They won broad and continuing acclaim for their vivid depictions of the social life of the period and for the wit and insight animating their literary, social, and moral criticism. In an age of vigorous political controversy, they counseled and, by and large, practiced moderation. To the new upper-middle class public which associated "wit" with the dissolute and disdainful tendencies of the Restoration court, they were able "to enliven Morality with Wit, and to temper Wit with Morality." They employed the devices of satire and sentiment to scorn fashionable vices and to affirm traditional virtues. Writing for a generally unlettered audience, they discoursed on medicine, aesthetics, theology, science, literature, and economics.

Their papers circulated widely and spawned imitations. Collected editions of *The Spectator* sold better than did the original half-sheets, and the essays were read with attention and delight throughout the century. Dr. Johnson, in a famous line, recommended that one who wished to master an English style, familiar yet elegant, "must give his days and nights to the volumes of Addison." And it is known that many young men—among them Benjamin Franklin in Boston—taught themselves to write by imitating *The Spectator*. The *London Journal* shows twenty-one year old James Boswell reading regularly from the essays. As he reflected on his own buffoonery and dissipation, Boswell felt their chastening influence and wrote: "I felt strong dispositions to be a Mr. Addison."

Nineteenth- and twentieth-century responses to the essays tend to be more critical. They appraise the authors both as men and as artists. And they question the continuing relevance of *The Tatler, The Spectator,* and *The Guardian.*

As Addison and Steele moved from their boyhood friendship through their careers as popular journalists, successful dramatists, and Whig statesmen, their histories were parallel in many respects. But their personal characters were so opposite that critics who praise one man have often felt obliged to disparage the other. Neither man has lacked advocates. Nineteenth-century critics—Thomas Macaulay, Lucy Aiken, Alexandre Beljame—tended to favor Addison. Macaulay extolled him as a man of genius, taste, and moral stature, one who "enrich[ed] our literature with compositions which will live as long as the English language." Victorian descriptions of Steele—his strong passions, his weak principles, and his infinite capacity for drinking, gaming, and indebtedness—sometimes make him seem like an adolescent whom the mature Addison rightly patronized and vainly sought to correct. Modern critics—C. S. Lewis, Bonamy Dobrée, T. S. Eliot—are more apt to praise Steele for his honest emotion, his ready compassion, and his human vulnerability. They disparage Addison for his prudential dispassion and smug complacency. (The story of his having summoned his son-in-law to his deathbed to "see in what peace a Christian can die," is often invoked as summary comment.) C. S. Lewis cites Addison's "vague religious sensibility, the insistence on what came later to be called Good Form, the playful condescension towards women, the untroubled belief in the beneficence of commerce"; and he concludes sharply, "If he is not at present the most hated of our writers, that can only be because he is so little read."

Routinely, such judgments reveal as much about the critic as they do about Addison or Steele. Commonly, they are big with oversimplification. One writer describes Steele as "much of the rake and a little of the swindler." Another maintains that Addison "calculating, ungenerous, and prudent . . . never stumbled in his progress to financial competence, a late marriage to a dowager countess, and a successful political career." Such judgments are misleading, and they are also irrelevant. What is important today are the essays; for the modern reader, the personal qualities of the authors are significant only as they are manifested in the essays.

The contrary characters of Addison and Steele can indeed be deduced from their papers. One can see, for example, that Steele had the zeal and enterprise to begin the periodicals. *The Tatler* and *The Guardian* were well established before Addison began contributing to them. One can recognize the shifting quality of Steele's enthusiasms. When his interest waned or changed its object, he could end a series abruptly. He wrote *Tatler* No. 271, terminating the journal, without notifying Addison. He concluded *The Guardian* so that he could, within a week, undertake a new publication. Steele's quick energies led him to produce a number of papers—*The Englishman, The Lover, The Reader, Town-Talk, The Plebeian,* and *The Theatre*—some of which were notably short-lived.

Addison, more organized and more resolute, was involved in both beginning and ending two journals. *The Spectator* began carefully—establishing the speaker, his club, his audience, and his purpose—and enjoyed a long life. It ended gradually as one club member after another either died or left London. (Thirty-eight issues appeared after the death of Sir Roger.) *The Freeholder,* the

political journal intended to justify the reign of Hanover to Englishmen, was occasioned by the 1715 Jacobite uprising. Addison
began the series "in the very Crisis of the late Rebellion" and carried it through fifty-five numbers until the rebels were put down
and further papers would, he felt, merely seem "Insults of the successful over their defeated Enemies."

Steele's unlimited ambition and limited resolution led him, in
his journals, to set up forms and characters which he did not later
employ, and to promise essays which he never produced. He announced that each *Tatler* would contain several essays written
from different coffee-houses, but he was apparently unable to
maintain this format. He established such characters as Bickerstaff (the Tatler), Pacolet, the Club at the Trumpet, the members
of the Spectator Club, Nestor Ironside, and my Lady Lizard; but
he did relatively little to shape essays around them. He had the
Spectator promise papers on "our most applauded Plays" (No.
65), on the education of boys (No. 66), on his investigations into
"the Haunts of Beauty and Gallantry" (No. 266), on "the Methods of acquiring Riches" (No. 450), etc., but the essays never appeared. With characteristic self-mockery, Steele—in *Spectator* No.
509—offered a letter from Hezekiah Thrift reminding him of his
unfulfilled promises.

Paradoxically, though Steele could always establish journals,
create characters, and promise a variety of specific essays, he often
found himself at a loss to write anything at all. As early as *Tatler*
No. 12, he admitted, "When a man has engaged to keep a Stage
Coach, he is obliged, whether he has Passengers or not, to set out;
thus it fares with us weekly Historians." Consequently, his essays
return again and again to the same subjects: gaming, duelling,
gallantry, etc. Regularly they make use of contributed material.
Of Steele's 251 *Spectators*, no less than 162 contain either letters
or contributed writing. When in *Spectator* No. 142 he published several of his own letters to his wife, one senses an act of
desperation. Such collected material, it should be noted, often
produced fine papers. Steele knew good letters when he saw them,
and he edited them skilfully. His own frequent inability to fulfill
the promises and possibilities of his journals reflects his bustling
life, his shifting enthusiasms, and—to a degree—his intellectual
limitations.

Addison seemed to have little difficulty either in finding material or in executing his announced plans. He promised series of essays on true and false wit, on *Paradise Lost,* on the pleasures of the imagination, etc.; and he produced the papers as scheduled. (Why he did not write further·visions of Mirzah, particularly after the first proved so popular, remains a mystery.) Addison never seemed at a loss for subjects, as he published essays on medicine, economics, superstition, astronomy, music, and criticism, as well as on the broad spectrum of social folly. Only 50 of his 276 *Spectators* contained letters or other contributed material. He declared in *Spectator* No. 131 that his problem in London was not finding topics, but choosing them, that as he wrote on one subject, many others crossed his mind. When he concluded *The Freeholder,* because the occasion for it was gone, he noted, "It would not be difficult to continue a Paper of this kind."

Steele's quick nature and hasty manner of writing are evident from particular flaws in his essays. In *Tatler* No. 181, for example, he wrote from his own biography, making little effort to tailor it to Bickerstaff, the nominal author. In *Spectator* No. 110, he quoted Sir Roger concerning the vices of "Men of fine Parts," then continued the paper in a way which leaves it unclear whether Sir Roger or the Spectator is speaking. In essays on particular plays (e.g., *Tatler* No. 167, *Spectator* No. 65), he quotes lines from memory. In *Guardian* No. 94, he misquotes a passage from *Timon of Athens,* then credits it to Ben Jonson. Though such errors come easily to anyone who writes for a deadline, it is noteworthy that there are few such examples in Addison's work. Steele's carelessness, however, sometimes produced lucky effects: It is doubtful that he would have published *Guardian* No. 40—Pope's ironic praise of Ambrose Philips' *Pastorals*—if he had read much of the paper before handing it on to the printer.

More than anything else, Steele's essays reflect his humanity. They give the sense of his being an emotionally involved citizen of this world. Where Addison defined true honor and formulated proofs of God's existence, Steele wrote angry attacks on fornication, gaming, and obscene plays. Where Addison showed the Spectator weeping with joy over the blessings of the Royal Exchange, Steele depicted the Tatler weeping over the death of his father and his first love. Where Addison generally fulfilled his promise "never to draw a faulty Character which does not fit at least a Thousand People," Steele—passionately involved in political controversy—described particular characters who were more or less easily identifiable as the Bishop of Exeter, Mrs. Mary de la Rivière Manley, Robert Harley, Jonathan Swift, etc. When Addison, very rarely, alluded to a real person (e.g., Dr. Titus Oates, in *Spectator* No. 57, is Henry Sacheverell, the celebrated Tory preacher), his tone is gentle. By contrast, Steele, in a signed letter to *The Guardian,* could refer to Mrs. Manley, an author of *The Examiner,* as sounding like "an exasperated Mistress" (No. 53), then later make mock reparation to the lady by "begging her Pardon that I never lay with her" (No. 63).

If Steele's angry and personal comments offended people at the time of their publication, Addison's capacity for discretion and reserve has offended readers ever since. In treating religion, morality, and politics—subjects which seem to call for an emotional commitment—Addison wrote with cool dispassion. Where Steele confessed being raised above this world and its secular interests on hearing "I know that my Redeemer liveth," Addison recommended the virtue of faith and explained the nature of "Infinitude." Where Steele raged against duellists and procurers as evil creatures, Addison dismissed atheists as fools. In the concluding issue of *The Tatler,* Steele admitted that, on matters of church and state, "I could not be cold enough to conceal my Opinion." And later, when Queen Anne was dying, the succession was in doubt, and fundamental political issues were at stake, Steele produced intemperately partisan essays in *The Guardian*. At the same time, Addison—with admirable wit and resolute discretion—lectured his female readers about tuckers, gaming, and the misuse of time.

Even Addison's best wit had elements of stuffiness and calculation in it. There is a condescending note in the way he addresses himself to "the Fair Sex" and "the Blanks of Society"—a note perceptible in essays on many subjects. He wrote almost all of the admired papers on Sir Roger de Coverley, but it is known that he considered the old knight his personal property and became petulant when others wrote of him. (See *Spectator* No. 410, n. 20.) And even when Addison was most amusing, one senses he was being amusing for a reason. Much is implicit in his admission in *Spectator* No. 179: "I must confess, were I left to my self, I should rather aim at Instructing than Diverting; but if we will be useful to the World, we must take it as we find it."

Of course, anyone who reads a body of Addison-Steele essays will recognize that both men are more interesting and complex than any description which stereotypes them. Nevertheless, the stereotypes have some validity; and the reader who has recognized Steele's emotional honesty and Addison's disciplined prudence, may well concur with Leigh Hunt's famous opinion: "I love Steele with all his faults better than Addison with all his essays." But this, it is important to notice, combines a personal with a literary judgment. Whichever author one prefers, it cannot be doubted that Addison produced the finer essays. His best papers, treating a broad range of subjects, possess an intelligence, insight, and finish that Steele could rarely achieve. Collections of *Tatler-Spectator* essays routinely include two or three papers by Addison for every one by Steele. Editors are frustrated trying to decide which Steele essays to include and which Addison essays to omit.

But even if one agrees with Virginia Woolf that "the essays of Addison are perfect essays," it remains to be asked if either he or Steele is worth reading today. Do they have anything of real significance to offer the general reader who is little interested in the political and social history of Queen Anne's reign, in neoclassicism, or in the development of the novel? In short, are not the essays both trivial and dated?

Modern readers have complained of the superficial character of Addison's and Steele's writing. The moral statements rarely went beyond routine injunctions against drunkenness, jealousy, gaming, and sloth. The religious counsel tended to emphasize the folly of freethinkers and the vanity of churchgoers. And the social commentary inexorably returned to coffee-house pedants (posing as poets, critics, political insiders), beaux (taking snuff, pursuing widows, exaggerating their gallantry), and coquettes (wearing hoop skirts, discarding the tucker, and practicing with their fans). Thus even when the papers were current, Lady Mary Montagu dismissed them as trivial, and Jonathan Swift protested, "I will not meddle with the Spectator, let him fair-sex it to the world's end."

It can be objected, of course, that *The Tatler*, *The Spectator*, and *The Guardian* were not written for Swift, Lady Mary, or for any learned audience. They were journals addressed to a new reading public, mainly upper-class women and the increasing number of men and women becoming rich and leisured through commercial success. The Spectator sought to bring "philosophy out of Closets and Libraries, Schools and Colleges, to dwell in Clubs and Assemblies, at Tea-Tables and in Coffee-Houses." To persuade the public both to buy and to read their papers, the authors had to base their "Lucubrations" on areas of current interest.

Because of this emphasis on popular contemporary subjects, many of the Addison-Steele essays may now seem hopelessly out of date. References to Whigs, the Pretender, bear-baiting, Drury Lane, younger sons, etc., mean little to the general reader. Virginia Woolf, in her essay on Addison, recognizes the problem. "Any historian can explain," she writes, "but it is always a misfortune to have to call in the services of any historian." Citing essays concerning silver garters, tulip roots, coffee-house politicians, little muffs, and critics talking of the unities, she concludes, "As it is, we can only feel that these counsels are addressed to ladies in hoops and gentlemen in wigs—a vanished audience which has learnt its lesson and gone its way and the preacher with it. We can only smile and marvel and perhaps admire the clothes."

Such criticism may mistake externals for essentials. Anyone who sits down to read a number of Addison-Steele papers will find that a great many are entertaining and meaningful exactly because they are not out of date, and that some are outstanding examples of literary art.

The twentieth-century reader can find much of contemporary relevance in *The Tatler, The Spectator,* and *The Guardian.* The papers were addressed to a large body of upper-middle class citizens who read a good deal but without discernment and with little appreciation of an intellectual or literary tradition. This group has not died; it has flourished. There still exists a popular audience which favors prurient comedies, tragedies reeking of gore and cliché, and juvenile romance novels; which only pretends to enjoy opera and which keeps books largely for show; which relishes gothic creations and the many forms of false wit. There still exist dubious authorities offering to guide this audience: critics who, though they rarely discuss the unities, are just as narrow and irascible as Sir Timothy Tittle; scholars who are immensely knowledgeable about book titles and who provide endless variant reading of old texts; metaphysical authors whose "wit" borders on the incomprehensible; religious zealots who offer puritan and scholastic counsel that no one follows; advertisers who employ doubletalk; and pedants who discourse with confident ignorance about politics, war, law, and the town.

Many of the political, social, and religious topics in Addison's and Steele's essays are in reality dated only in externals. Queen Anne and the Jacobites are gone, but politics remains an area for rumor, slogans, fear, libel, self-righteousness, and petty controversy over obscure policies. Hoop skirts and snuff boxes are out of fashion, but social interests have changed little through the years. Courtship remains an occasion for ambition, false hopes, and romantic pretensions; and marriage, the scene for vain wives, outraged husbands, and spoiled children. Modern society is not without its gamesters, drunks, wags, coarse talkers, and tedious story-tellers; coquettes and beaux continue, in modern forms, to emphasize dress, pose, and equipage. And one would be naive to imagine that belief in quacks, lottery systems, and astrology have disappeared. The character of religious belief may have changed since the Spectator's day, but there remain large numbers of Christians who affirm redemption and an after-life and who scorn atheism, worldliness, and the Pope. In many ways, then, the world which Addison and Steele described has changed little.

No one can claim that *The Tatler, The Spectator,* and *The Guardian* are literature of the highest rank. Nevertheless, many of the essays are very fine indeed, revealing an impressive degree of sense, wit, and insight. Only the most recalcitrant critic, it seems to me, can fail to respond to Steele's papers on the death of Betterton, on obvious and digressive talkers, on the moral character of money; to Addison's essays on quack doctors, on Ned Softly's poetry, on Westminster Abbey, on modes of argument; or to a number of other papers of equal quality. The emphasis in most of the papers is on man's social role and on the values of common sense and restraint. While the social world rarely occasions the cry of the heart or the compelling insights which attend man's solitary communion with himself, it is the world in which he spends almost his entire life. And in that sphere, restraint and common sense remain decisive virtues.

Chronology

	Contemporary History	Contemporary Literature	Richard Steele	Joseph Addison
1641	Charles I on throne since 1625.			
1642	Civil wars begin. Edgehill battle.			
1643	Louis XIV becomes king of France.	Browne's *Religio Medici*.		
1644	Parliamentary forces victorious at Marston Moor.	Milton's *Areopagitica*.		
1645	The Battle of Naseby.			
1647		Cowley's *The Mistress*.		
1649	Charles I executed. England declared a commonwealth.			
1651		Hobbes' *Leviathan*.		
1653	Oliver Cromwell becomes Lord Protector.			
1657		Cowley's *Davideis*.		

Year			
1658	Cromwell dies. His son Richard becomes Lord Protector.		
1660	Charles II restored to the throne.		
1661	Oliver Cromwell and regicides disinterred and hanged.		
1662	Act of Uniformity passed. Royal Society chartered.	Howard's *The Committee.*	
1663		Milton's *Paradise Lost* completed.	
1665	The London plague.	Dryden's *The Indian Emperor.*	
1666	The Great Fire of London.	Boileau's *Satires.*	
1669	The Royal Exchange built.		
1671		Buckingham's *The Rehearsal.*	
1672			Born in Dublin, March 12, son of an attorney.
1674		Boileau's *Art Poétique.*	Born in Milston, England, May 1.

Chronology (continued)

	Contemporary History	Contemporary Literature	Richard Steele	Joseph Addison
1676		Etherege's The Man of Mode. Wycherley's The Plain Dealer.		
1677	Mary, daughter of James Stuart, weds William of Orange.		(?) Steele's father dies.	
1678	Titus Oates and the Popish Plot.	Butler's Hudibras completed.	Educated in Dublin by his uncle, Henry Gascoigne.	
1681		Roscommon's translation of Horace's Art of Poetry.		
1682		Dryden's Mac Flecknoe. Otway's Venice Preserved.		
1683	Rye House Plot discovered.			His father, Lancelot Addison, appointed Dean of Lichfield. Joseph attends school at Lichfield.
1684			Sent to school at London's Charterhouse.	His mother, Jane Addison, dies.
1685	Charles II dies. His Catholic brother becomes James II. Louis XIV revokes Edict of Nantes, sending Protestant refugees to England.			

Year	Events	Publications		
1686				Enters the Charterhouse. Meets Steele.
1687	James issues first Declaration of Indulgence, suspending many laws.	Newton's *Principia Mathematica*.		Sent to Queen's College, Oxford. May have shared a room with Henry Sacheverell.
1688	A son born to James II seems to perpetuate the Catholic reign. Following a popular uprising, William of Orange lands to take the crown. James and his family flee to France.			Obtains a scholarship at Magdalen College.
1689	William and Mary called to throne by Convention Parliament. Act of Toleration passed. War of the League of Augsburg begins against France.	Locke's *Essay Concerning Human Understanding*.	Enters Christ's Church, Oxford.	
1690	William defeats Irish forces of Stuarts at the Boyne.			
1691			Made postmaster at Merton College.	
1692	English forces defeated at Steenkirk, in Spanish Netherlands. Salem witch trials in America.		Leaves Oxford without a degree. Enlists in the Second Troop of Life Guards, which thereafter serves in Flanders.	

Chronology (continued)

	Contemporary History	Contemporary Literature	Richard Steele	Joseph Addison
1693			On garrison duty with the Second Troop at Whitehall.	Awarded M.A. Writes a poem *To Mr. Dryden.* Growing reputation for Latin verse.
1694	Queen Mary dies; reign of William III begins. Bank of England founded.		Serves with the Second Troop in the Low Countries, then returns to London.	Translates Virgil's fourth *Georgic.* Writes *An Account of the Greatest English Poets,* a poem dedicated to Henry Sacheverell.
1695		Congreve's *Love for Love.*	Writes *The Procession: A Poem on Her Majesties Funeral,* dedicated to Lord Cutts. Joins the Coldstream Guards.	Writes poem *To the King.*
1697	Treaty of Ryswick ends war. Augustus II becomes King of Poland.	Dryden's translation of *The Aeneid.*	Commissioned ensign in Lord Cutts' Company.	Writes Latin poem on the peace of Ryswick. Also *An Essay on Virgil's Georgics.*
1698	East India Company founded.	Collier's *A Short View of the Immorality and Profaneness of the English Stage.*		Admitted a Fellow of Magdalen College.
1699		Garth's *The Dispensary.*	During this period, fathers one—perhaps two—illegitimate children. Loses money investing in alchemical project.	Leaves Oxford, begins travels on Continent.

1700	Clement XI becomes Pope.	Congreve's *The Way of the World*.	Captain in the Coldstream Guards. Wounds Captain Kelly in a duel. Writes a poem in *Commendatory Verses* defending Addison against criticism of Sir Richard Blackmore.	In France, visits Boileau and Père Malebranche.
1701	James II dies in France. Louis XIV recognizes his son James (thereafter called the Pretender) as rightful king. Act of Settlement assures Protestant succession in England through house of Hanover. War of Spanish Succession begins.	Defoe's *The True-Born Englishman*.	Publishes *The Christian Hero: An Argument Proving that no Principles but those of Religion are Sufficient to make a Great Man*. His comedy *The Funeral or Grief à la Mode* opens at Drury Lane.	Writes *Letter from Italy*, a rhyming epistle addressed to Lord Halifax.
1702	King William dies. Queen Anne comes to throne.	*Daily Courant* begins publishing.	Leaves Guards, becomes Captain of Foot in Lord Lucas's regiment, assigned to garrison Landguard Fort against French privateers and possible invasion.	
1703			His comedy *The Lying Lover; or The Ladies' Friendship* opens at Drury Lane.	Lancelot Addison dies.
1704	Marlborough wins Battle of Blenheim.	Swift's *A Tale of a Tub*. Cibber's *The Careless Husband*. Defoe begins *The Review*.	Admitted to the Kit-Cat Club, a gathering of Whig wits and statesmen.	Returns to England. Takes seat in Kit-Cat Club. Is made Commissioner of Appeals. Writes *The Campaign*, a poem celebrating Marlborough's victory at Blenheim.

Chronology (continued)

	Contemporary History	Contemporary Literature	Richard Steele	Joseph Addison
1705	English victory at Ramillies.	Philips' *The Splendid Shilling*. The opera *Arsinoe, Queen of Cyprus* first presented at Drury Lane.	Leaves the army. Weds Margaret Ford Stretch, a widow of property. His comedy *The Tender Husband; or The Accomplished Fools* opens at Drury Lane.	Writes Prologue to *The Tender Husband*. Publishes *Remarks on Several Parts of Italy*.
1706			Is prosecuted for debt. Becomes Gentleman-waiter to Prince George. His first wife dies.	Made Undersecretary of State. With Lord Halifax, makes state visit to Hanover.
1707	Union of England and Scotland.	Farquhar's *The Beaux' Stratagem*.	Appointed Gazetteer for the Whig ministry. Weds Mary Scurlock.	His opera *Rosamond* produced at Drury Lane. Performs duties as Undersecretary. Lodges with Steele during the summer.
1708	Marlborough and Prince Eugene win at Oudenarde. Abortive Jacobite invasion sets off from Dunkirk.	Swift's *The Bickerstaff Papers*.		Made chief Secretary to Earl of Wharton, Lord-Lieutenant of Ireland. Writes essay *The Present State of the War*.
1709	Charles XII of Sweden defeated by Russians at Poltava.	Pope's *Pastorals*. Philips' *Pastorals*. Mrs. Manley's *Atalantis*.	Birth of his daughter Elizabeth. Begins publishing *The Tatler*. Is arrested for debt.	Made godfather to Steele's daughter. In Ireland from April to September. Contributes essays to *The Tatler*.
1710	Dr. Sacheverell impeached for preaching divine right. Tories elected to power.	*The Examiner* appears. Swift's *Description of a City Shower* (printed in *Tatler* No. 238).	Made Commissioner of the Stamp Office. Loses Gazetteership with fall of Whig government.	Elected to Parliament. Publishes five numbers of *The Whig Examiner*. Loses Irish Secretaryship with fall of Whigs.

1711	Marlborough removed from command, accused of embezzlement. South Sea Company founded.	Pope's *Essay on Criticism.* Swift's *The Conduct of the Allies.*	*Tatler concludes January 2. The Spectator begins March 1.*	Joins Steele in producing *The Spectator.*
1712	A stamp tax imposed on publications.	Philips' *The Distressed Mother.* Pope's *The Rape of the Lock.*	*Writes An Englishman's Thanks to the Duke of Marlborough. Terminates The Spectator.*	Acts as leader of Whig wits at Button's Coffee House.
1713	Treaty of Utrecht ends the war.		*Publishes The Guardian (March 12). Resigns as Commissioner of Stamps. Elected to Parliament. Writes The Importance of Dunkirk Considered. Concludes The Guardian; begins The Englishman (October 6).*	Buys an estate in Warwickshire. *Cato: A Tragedy* opens at Drury Lane. Contributes to *The Guardian.* Writes Whig pamphlet *The Late Trial and Conviction of Count Tariff.*
1714	Queen Anne dies. George I becomes king. Whigs return to power.		*Writes political pamphlets, including The Crisis. Expelled from Parliament for his political writings. Publishes The Lover (February 25–May 27) and The Reader (April 22–May 10). Writes Mr. Steele's Apology for Himself and His Writings. Appointed manager of Drury Lane Theater.*	Revives *The Spectator* (June 18–December 20). Contributes to *The Lover.* Reappointed Secretary to the Irish Government.
1715	The Fifteen Rebellion: James Stuart invades Scotland. Louis XIV dies.	Pope's *Iliad* (I–IV).	*Reenters Parliament. Knighted by King George. Revives The Englishman (July 11–November 21). Writes Town Talk and Letter from the Earl of Mar to the King.*	Writes *To Sir Godfrey Kneller,* a poem praising King George. Appointed Commissioner for Trade and Colonies. Begins *The Freeholder* (December 23).
1716			*Made Commissioner of Forfeited Estates for Scotland.*	His comedy *The Drummer* performed at Drury Lane. Weds the Countess of Warwick.

Chronology (continued)

	Contemporary History	Contemporary Literature	Richard Steele	Joseph Addison
1717			Travels to Scotland as a Commissioner.	Appointed Secretary of State.
1718			Lady Steele dies during pregnancy.	Resigns Secretaryship because of illness.
1719		Defoe's *Robinson Crusoe* (Part I).	Publishes *The Plebeian* and *A Letter to the Earl of O[xfor]d* to help defeat the Peerage Bill.	Birth of a daughter, Charlotte. Writes *The Old Whig* supporting the Peerage Bill against Steele's attacks. Dies (June 17).
1720	Charles Edward Stuart ("the Young Pretender") born. The South Sea Bubble bursts.		Writes *The Theatre* (January 2–April 5). Loses managership of Drury Lane.	
1721	Robert Walpole comes to power, serves until 1742.		Again becomes manager of Drury Lane.	Posthumous works: *Dialogue upon the Usefulness of Ancient Medals. Of the Christian Religion.*
1722		Defoe's *Moll Flanders.*	Reenters Parliament. His Comedy *The Conscious Lovers* performed at Drury Lane.	
1726		Swift's *Gulliver's Travels.*	Retires to Wales. Suffers a stroke. Works on an unfinished comedy.	
1727	George I dies. His son becomes George II.			
1729			Dies in Wales (September 1).	

The TATLER.

By *Isaac Bickerstaff* Esq;

—— *Nugis addere Pondus.* **H.**

From *Thursday August* 24. to *Saturday August* 26. 1710.

From my own Apartment, August 25.

NATURE is full of Wonders; every Atom is a standing Miracle, and endowed with such Qualities, as could not be impressed on it by a Power and Wisdom less than Infinite. For this Reason, I would not discourage any Searches that are made into the most minute and trivial Parts of the Creation. However, since the World abounds in the noblest Fields of Speculation, it is, methinks, the Mark of a little Genius to be wholly conversant among Insects, Reptiles, Animalcules, and those trifling Rarities that furnish out the Apartment of a Virtuoso.

There are some Men whose Heads are so oddly turned this Way, that tho' they are utter Strangers to the common Occurrences of Life, they are able to discover the Sex of a Cockle, or describe the Generation of a Mite, in all its Circumstances. They are so little versed in the World, that they scarce know a Horse from an Ox; but at the same Time will tell you, with a great deal of Gravity, That a Flea is a Rhinoceros, and a Snail an Hermaphrodite. I have known one of these whimsical Philosophers who has set a greater Value upon a Collection of Spiders than he would upon a Flock of Sheep, and has sold his Coat off his Back to purchase a Tarantula.

I would not have a Scholar wholly unacquainted with these Secrets and Curiosities of Nature; but certainly the Mind of Man, that is capable of so much higher Contemplations, should not be altogether fixed upon such mean and disproportioned Objects. Observations of this Kind are apt to alienate us too much from the Knowledge of the World, and to make us serious upon Trifles, by which Means they expose Philosophy to the Ridicule of the Witty, and Contempt of the Ignorant. In short, Studies of this Nature should be the Diversions, Relaxations, and Amusements; not the Care, Business, and Concern of Life.

It is indeed wonderful to consider, that there should be a Sort of learned Men who are wholly employed in gathering together the Refuse of Nature, if I may call it so, and hoarding up in their Chests and Cabinets such Creatures as others industriously avoid the Sight of. One does not know how to mention some of the most precious Parts of their Treasure, without a Kind of an Apology for it. I have been shown a Beetle valued at 20 Crowns, and a Toad at an Hundred: But we must take this for a general Rule, That whatever appears trivial or obscene in the common Notions of the World, looks grave and philosophical in the Eye of a Virtuoso.

To show this Humour in its Perfection, I shall present my Reader with the Legacy of a certain Virtuoso, who laid out a considerable Estate in natural Rarities and Curiosities, which upon his Death-Bed he bequeathed to his Relations and Friends in the following Words:

The Will of a Virtuoso.

I *Nicholas Gimcrack* being in sound Health of Mind, but in great Weakness of Body, do by this my Last Will and Testament bestow my Worldly Goods and Chattels in Manner following:

Imprimis, To my dear Wife,
 One Box of Butterflies,
 One Drawer of Shells,
 A Female Skeleton,
 A dried Cockatrice.

Item, To my Daughter *Elizabeth,*
 My Receipt for preserving dead Caterpillars:
 As also my Preparations of Winter *May-Dew,* and Embrio Pickle.

Item, To my little Daughter *Fanny,*
 Three Crocodile's Eggs.
And upon the Birth of her First Child, if she marries with her Mother's Consent,
 The Nest of an Humming-Bird.

Item, To my eldest Brother, as an Acknowledgment for the Lands he has vested in my Son *Charles,* I bequeath
 My last Year's Collection of Grashoppers.

Item,

Item, To his Daughter *Susanna*, being his only Child, I bequeath my

    English Weeds pasted on Royal Paper.
    With my large Folio of *Indian* Cabbage.

Item, To my learned and worthy Friend Dr. *Johannes Elserickius*, Professor in Anatomy, and my Associate in the Studies of Nature, as an eternal Monument of my Affection and Friendship for him, I bequeath

    My Rat's Testicles, and
    Whale's Pizzle;

To him and his Issue Male; and in Default of such Issue in the said Dr. *Elserickius*, then to return to my Executor and his Heirs for ever.

Having fully provided for my Nephew *Isaac*, by making over to him some Years since

    A Horned *Scarabæus*,
    The Skin of a Rattle-Snake, and
    The Mummy of an *Egyptian* King,

I make no further Provision for him in this my Will.

My eldest Son *John* having spoken disrespectfully of his little Sister whom I keep by me in Spirits of Wine, and in many other Instances behaved himself undutifully towards me, I do disinherit and wholly cut off from any Part of this my Personal Estate, by giving him a Single Cockle-Shell.

To my Second Son *Charles* I give and bequeath all my Flowers, Plants, Minerals, Mosses, Shells, Pebbles, Fossils, Beetles, Butterflies, Caterpillars, Grashoppers, and Vermin, not above specified : As also all my Monsters, both wet and dry, making the said *Charles* whole and sole Executor of this my Last Will and Testament ; he paying, or causing to be paid, the aforesaid Legacies within the Space of Six Months after my Decease. And I do hereby revoke all other Wills whatsoever by me formerly made.

ADVERTISEMENT.

Whereas an ignorant Upstart in Astrology has publickly endeavoured to perswade the World that he is the late John Partridge, *who died the* 28th *of March,* 1708 ; *These are to cert fie all whom it may concern, That the true* John Partridge *was not only dead at that Time, but continues so to this present Day.*

    Beware of Counterfeits, for such are Abroad.

TWenty Freehold Tenements to be sold, lying in Wapping, and a Brew-house and Dwelling-house, with all Brewing Utensils, in a good Place for Trade, in Penning-street near Ratcliff Highway, to be lett, or the Lease (being a-bout 30 Years to come) to be sold ; and a new Brick House, with a Cow-house, Stable, and Home-stall, with other Ground or without, lying in Mile-End Old Town, to be lett ; and a Horse-Mill, and other Materials for Old Spanish, to be sold, Enquire at the Union Coffee-house at King Edward's Stairs in Wapping.

The Tatler

The Tatler appeared in 271 issues from April 12, 1709, to January 2, 1711. Printed on both sides of a folio half-sheet, it was published every Tuesday, Thursday, and Saturday "for the Convenience of the Post," i.e., the post-coaches which left London on those days for different parts of the country. The first four issues were distributed free; after that each cost one penny.

The paper was established by Steele, who wrote at least two-thirds of the essays. Addison wrote parts of Nos. 18, 20, and 24 but did not become a regular contributor until No. 75. Overall, he wrote or collaborated in some eighty-two papers. Other contributors included William Harrison, Jonathan Swift, Heneage Twysden, John Hughes, Samuel Fuller, Nicholas Rowe, and Matthew Prior.

Although *The Tatler* was published anonymously, the nominal author was Isaac Bickerstaff, a character created by Swift some sixteen months earlier to ridicule the pretensions of John Partridge, a widely read astrologer and almanac maker. On the appearance of Partridge's annual almanac *Merlinus Liberatus,* Swift had produced a parallel volume *Predictions for the Year 1708. . . . By Isaac Bickerstaff, Esq.* wherein he forecast that Partridge would die on March 29. He followed this, on March 30, with an *Elegy* announcing the astrologer's death and, a few days later, with *The Accomplishment of the First of Mr. Bickerstaff's Predictions.* In the flurry of publications which followed, Partridge insisted he was alive, and the wits of the town commented on circumstances relating to his death.

Thus Isaac Bickerstaff was already a popular figure when Steele, with Swift's permission, made him the spokesman of the *Tatler* papers. But, though the Partridge-is-dead joke continued through essays No. 1, 7, 11, 36, 96, 118, 124, and 216, Steele did little to develop the character of his narrator. Bickerstaff's guardian angel is introduced in No. 13; his medical and astrological gifts are discussed in No. 23; his genealogy is given in No. 75; and his life and habits are treated in No. 89. His role as Censor of Great

Britain is defined in No. 144 and, as such, he presides first over a Court of Justice and later over a Court of Honour. The large majority of the essays, however, make no reference to Isaac Bickerstaff at all; he is simply the voice of the author. Indeed, in certain papers (e.g., No. 181) it is difficult to tell whether Steele or Bickerstaff is speaking.

The declared purpose of *The Tatler* was to treat news, politics, literature, manners, and morals so that the readers "may be instructed, after their Reading, what to think." The original plan was for one paper to discuss several subjects, each written from an appropriate chocolate or coffee house. But, as advertising encroached on space and as Steele became involved in other projects, he found it easier to make each paper a single essay and to range the essays over a variety of topics. While it is probably true that Steele's papers tended to emphasize social subjects (duelling, fashion, the theater, etc.) and Addison's to treat literary and moral issues (atheism, silence, Tom Folio, a future state, etc.), the generalization is more applicable to *The Spectator* than it is to *The Tatler*. The papers praising the ministry, the Duke of Marlborough, and the prosecution of the war were almost invariably Steele's.

The early *Tatlers* carried news reports. As Gazetteer for the Whig ministry, Steele had access to the latest political and military dispatches. But, probably because he had to write such news three times a week for *The Gazette,* his reports of "foreign and domestic News" soon became quite brief and finally disappeared altogether. The last report from St. James's Coffee-House appeared in *Tatler* No. 210. Steele's Whig sympathies, however, were clear from the first essay, which scorned peace offers from France, to his final paper, which acknowledged that on matters of church and state he "could not be cold enough to conceal my Opinion."

It has been argued that such opinions led to the termination of the papers, that with the election of a Tory ministry, Steele lost his position as Gazetteer and was told he could keep his office as Commissioner of Stamps only if he stopped publishing *The Tatler.* Whatever the cause, Steele, without consulting Addison, wrote a final essay concluding the publication. When the first issue of *The Spectator* appeared two months later, it carried a promise of political neutrality—a promise which, by and large, it kept.

The Tatler, No. 1

Isaac Bickerstaff, Esq.

[S t e e l e]

Quicquid agunt Homines nostri Farrago Libelli.[1]

Tuesday, April 12, 1709.

Tho' the other Papers which are published for the Use of the good People of England, *have certainly very wholsom Effects, and are laudable in their particular Kinds, they do not seem to come up to the main Design of such Narrations, which I humbly presume, should be principally intended for the Use of politick Persons, who are so publick-spirited as to neglect their own Affairs to look into Transactions of State. Now these Gentlemen, for the most Part, being Men of strong Zeal, and weak Intellects; It is both a Charitable and Necessary Work to offer something, whereby such worthy and well-affected Members of the Commonwealth may be instructed, after their Reading,* what to think; *which shall be the End and Purpose of this my Paper: Wherein I shall from Time to Time Report and Consider all Matters of what Kind soever that shall occur to Me, and publish such my Advices and Reflections every* Tuesday, Thursday, *and* Saturday *in the Week,*[2] *for the Convenience of the Post. I resolved also to have something which may be of Entertainment to the Fair Sex, in Honour of whom I have taken the Title of this Paper. I therefore earnestly*

---

[1] Juvenal *Satires* I. 85–86: "All the doings of mankind shall form the motley subject of my page." This motto was repeated through the first forty numbers in the original folio half-sheets.

[2] On these days the post left London for various parts of the country.

desire all Persons, without Distinction, to take it in for the present
Gratis, and hereafter at the Price of One Penny, forbidding all
Hawkers to take more for it at their Peril. And I desire all Persons
to consider, that I am at a very great Charge for proper Materials
for this Work, as well as that before I resolved upon it, I had set-
tled a Correspondence in all Parts of the Known and Knowing
World. And forasmuch as this Globe is not trodden upon by meer
Drudges of Business only, but that Men of Spirit and Genius are
justly to be esteemed as considerable Agents in it, we shall not
upon a Dearth of News, present you with musty Foreign Edicts, or
dull Proclamations, but shall divide our Relation of the Passages
which occur in Action or Discourse throughout this Town as well
as elsewhere, under such Dates of Places as may prepare you for
the Matter you are to expect, in the following Manner:

All Accounts of Gallantry, Pleasure, *and* Entertainment, *shall*
be under the Article of White's Chocolate-house; Poetry, *under*
that of Will's Coffee-house; Learning, *under the Title of* Graecian; Foreign *and* Domestick News, *you will have from* St. James's
Coffee-house; *and what else I have to offer on any other Subject,*
shall be dated from my own Apartment.[3]

I once more desire my Reader to consider, That as I cannot
keep an ingenious Man to go daily to Will's, *under Twopence each*
Day merely for his Charges; to White's, *under Sixpence; nor to*
the Graecian, *without allowing him some Plain* Spanish,[4] *to be as*
able as others at the Learned Table; and that a good Observer can-
not speak with even Kidney[5] *at* St. James's *without clean Linnen.*
I say, these Considerations will, I hope, make all Persons willing
to comply with my Humble Request (when my Gratis Stock *is ex-*
hausted) of a Penny a-piece; especially since they are sure of some
proper Amusement, and that it is impossible for me to want

---

[3] Just as contemporary newspapers dated foreign and domestic news from
particular cities, Steele dated his town news from the coffee-house or chocolate-
house most appropriate to it: White's Chocolate-house was the rendezvous of
those concerned with court society and with gaming; Will's Coffee-house, of
wits, poets, and dramatists; the Grecian, of lawyers and scholars; and St. James's
Coffee-house, of Whig statesmen and men of fashion.

[4] This could refer to Spanish wine or to Spanish snuff.

[5] Humphrey Kidney, headwaiter at St. James's Coffee-house.

Means to entertain 'em, having besides the Force of my own Parts,[6] *the Power of Divination, and that I can, by casting a Figure, tell you all that will happen before it comes to pass.*[7]

But this last Faculty I shall use very sparingly, and speak but of few Things 'till they are passed, for fear of divulging Matters which may offend our Superiors.[8]

White's Chocolate-house, April 7.

The deplorable Condition of a very pretty Gentleman, who walks here at the Hours when Men of Quality first appear, is what is very much lamented. His History is, That on the 9th of *September* 1705, being in his One and twentieth Year, he was washing his Teeth at a Tavern-Window in *Pall-mall*, when a fine Equipage[9] passed by, and in it a young Lady who looked up at him; away goes the Coach, and the young Gentleman pulled off his Night-cap, and instead of rubbing his Gums, as he ought to do out of the Window till about Four a Clock, sits him down, and spoke not a Word till Twelve at Night; after which, he began to enquire, If any Body knew the Lady—the Company asked, What Lady? But he said no more 'till they broke up at Six in the Morning. All the ensuing Winter he went from Church to Church every Sunday, and from Playhouse to Playhouse every Night in the Week, but could never find the Original of the Picture which dwelt in his Bosom. In a Word, his Attention to any Thing but his Passion, was utterly gone. He has lost all the Money he ever played for, and been confuted in every Argument he has enter'd upon since the Moment he first saw her. He is of a Noble Family, has naturally a very good Air, and is of a frank, honest Temper: But this Passion has so extremely mauled him, that his Features are set and uninformed, and his whole Visage is deaden'd by a long Absence of Thought. He never appears in any Alacrity, but when raised by Wine; at which Time he is sure to come hither, and throw away

6 Natural abilities.

7 Bickerstaff, an astrologer, can read the future. See Introduction, p. 3.

8 In the original issue, this introduction was repeated with *Tatlers* No. 2 and No. 3.

9 A horse-drawn carriage, probably with attending servants.

a great deal of Wit on Fellows, who have no Sense further than just to observe, That our poor Lover has most Understanding when he is drunk, and is least in his Senses when he is sober.

Will's Coffee-house, April 8.

On *Thursday* last was acted, for the Benefit of Mr. *Betterton*,[10] the Celebrated Comedy, called *Love for Love*.[11] Those excellent Players, Mrs. *Barry*, Mrs. *Bracegirdle*, and Mr. *Dogget*, though not at present concerned in the House, acted on that Occasion. There has not been known so great a Concourse of Persons of Distinction as at that Time; the Stage it self was cover'd with Gentlemen and Ladies, and when the Curtain was drawn, it discovered even there a very splendid Audience. This unusual Encouragement, which was given to a Play for the Advantage of so great an Actor, gives an undeniable Instance, That the true Relish for Manly Entertainments and Rational Pleasures is not wholly lost. All the Parts were acted to Perfection; the Actors were careful of their Carriage, and no one was guilty of the Affectation to insert Witticisms of his own,[12] but a due Respect was had to the Audience, for encouraging this accomplish'd Player. It is not now doubted but Plays will revive, and take their usual Place in the Opinion of Persons of Wit and Merit, notwithstanding their late Apostacy in Favour of Dress and Sound. This Place[13] is very much altered since Mr. *Dryden* frequented it; where you used to see *Songs, Epigrams,* and *Satyrs,* in the Hands of every Man you met, you have now only a Pack of Cards; and instead of the Cavils about the Turn of the Expression, the Elegance of the Style, and the like, the Learned now dispute only about the Truth of the Game. But however, the Company is altered, all have shewn a

---

[10] Thomas Betterton (1635–1710), the celebrated tragedian, whose death is lamented in *Tatler* No. 167.

[11] In this performance of William Congreve's drama (1695), Mrs. Elizabeth Barry played the role of Mrs. Frail; Mrs. Anne Bracegirdle performed Angelica; and Mr. Thomas Doggett played Ben.

[12] See *Tatler* No. 89, which criticizes this practice.

[13] I.e., Will's Coffee-house.

great Respect for Mr. *Betterton:* And the very Gaming Part of this House have been so much touched with a Sense of the Uncertainty of Humane Affairs, (which alter with themselves every Moment) that in this Gentleman, they pitied *Mark Anthony* of *Rome, Hamlet* of *Denmark, Mithridates* of *Pontus, Theodosius* of *Greece,* and *Henry* the Eighth of *England.* It is well known, he has been in the Condition of each of those illustrious Personages for several Hours together, and behaved himself in those high Stations, in all the Changes of the Scene, with suitable Dignity. For these Reasons, we intend to repeat this Favour to him on a proper Occasion, lest he who can instruct us so well in personating Feigned Sorrows, should be lost to us by suffering under Real Ones. The town is at present in very great Expectation of seeing a Comedy now in Rehearsal,[14] which is the 25th Production of my Honoured Friend Mr. *Thomas D'Urfey;* who, besides his great Abilities in the Dramatick, has a peculiar Talent in the Lyrick Way of Writing, and that with a Manner wholly new and unknown to the Ancient *Greeks* and *Romans,* wherein he is but faintly imitated in the Translations of the Modern *Italian* Opera's.

St. James's Coffee-house, April 11.[15]

Letters from the *Hague* of the 16th say, That Major-General *Cadogan*[16] was gone to *Brussels,* with Orders to disperse proper Instructions for assembling the whole Force of the Allies in *Flanders* in the Beginning of the next Month. The late Offers concerning Peace, were made in the Style of Persons who think themselves upon equal Terms: But the Allies have so just a Sense of their

14 *Modern Prophets* by Thomas D'Urfey (1653–1723) was produced in 1709.

15 As official Gazetteer for the Whig ministry, Steele had access to the latest military and political news. But dispatches from St. James's Coffee-house appeared less and less frequently as the paper progressed. Regularly, the reports reflected the Whig view that, despite the interest of the French and of the English Tories in a negotiated settlement, the war should be prosecuted until the existing French-Spanish alliance could no longer threaten English interests.

16 William, First Earl Cadogan (1675–1726), served as a lieutenant under Marlborough.

present Advantages, that they will not admit of a Treaty, except *France* offers what is more suitable to her present Condition. At the same Time we make Preparations, as if we were alarmed by a greater Force than that which we are carrying into the Field. Thus this Point seems now to be argued Sword in Hand. This was what a great General[17] alluded to, when being asked the Names of those who were to be Plenipotentiaries for the ensuing Peace; answered, with a serious Air, *There are about an Hundred Thousand of us.* Mr. *Kidney,* who has the Ear of the greatest Politicians that come hither, tells me, There is a Mail come in to Day with Letters, dated *Hague, April* 19. *N. S.*[18] which say, a Design of bringing Part of our Troops into the Field at the latter End of this Month, is now altered to a Resolution of marching towards the Camp about the 20th of the next. There happened t'other Day, in the Road of *Scheveling,* an Engagement[19] between a Privateer of *Zealand,* and one of *Dunkirk.* The *Dunkirker,* carrying 33 Pieces of Cannon, was taken and brought into the *Texel.* It is said, the Courier of Monsieur *Rouille*[20] is returned to him from the Court of *France.* Monsieur *Vendosme*[21] being reinstated in the Favour of the Dutchess of *Burgundy,* is to command in *Flanders.*

Mr. *Kidney* added, That there were Letters of the 17th from *Ghent,* which give an Account, that the Enemy had formed a Design to surprize two Battalions of the Allies which lay at *Alost;* but those Battalions received Advice of their March, and retired to *Dendermond.* Lieutenant-General *Wood*[22] appeared on this Occasion at the Head of 5000 Foot, and 1000 Horse, upon which the Enemy withdrew, without making any further Attempt.

[17] John Churchill, First Duke of Marlborough (1650–1722), commander of English forces on the continent.

[18] New Style, i.e., the date according to the Gregorian calendar, then in use on the continent. England retained the Julian calendar, which was eleven days ahead, until 1752.

[19] Presumably this report of the capture of a French armed ship in a North Sea battle, was part of the Hague dispatches of April 19.

[20] A merchant employed by Louis XIV to negotiate peace terms with the Dutch.

[21] Louis Joseph, Duc de Vendóme (1654–1712), French military leader.

[22] General Cornelius Wood (1636–1712) served under Marlborough.

From my own Apartment.

I am very sorry I am obliged to trouble the Publick with so much Discourse upon a Matter which I at the very first mentioned as a Trifle, *viz.* the Death of Mr. *Partridge,*[23] under whose Name there is an *Almanack* come out for the Year 1709. In one Page of which it is asserted by the said *John Partridge,* That he is still living, and not only so, but that he was also living some Time before, and even at the Instant when I writ of his Death. I have in another Place, and in a Paper by it self, sufficiently convinced this Man that he is dead, and if he has any Shame, I don't doubt but that by this Time he owns it to all his Acquaintance: For tho' the Legs and Arms, and whole Body of that Man may still appear and perform their animal Functions; yet since, as I have elsewhere observed, his Art is gone, the Man is gone. I am, as I said, concerned, that this little Matter should make so much Noise; but since I am engaged, I take my self obliged in Honour to go on in my Lucubrations,[24] and by the Help of these Arts of which I am Master, as well as my Skill in Astrological Speculations, I shall, as I see Occasion, proceed to confute other dead Men, who pretend to be in Being, that they are actually deceased. I therefore give all Men fair Warning to mend their Manners, for I shall from Time to Time print Bills of Mortality;[25] and I beg the Pardon of all such who shall be named therein, if they who are good for Nothing shall find themselves in the Number of the Deceased.

23 John Partridge (1644–1715), a well known astrologer and quack. See Introduction, p. 3.

24 Nightly studies.

25 Papers issued by the London Company of Parish Clerks, giving the weekly number of christenings and deaths.

The Tatler, No. 18

From Thursd. May 19. to Saturd. May 21. 1709.

[Steele and Addison][1]

From my own Apartment, May 20.

It is observed too often, that Men of Wit do so much employ their Thoughts upon fine[2] Speculations, that Things useful to Mankind are wholly neglected; and they are busy in making Emendations upon some Encliticks[3] in a *Greek* Author, while obvious Things, that every Man may have use for, are wholly overlooked. It would be an happy Thing, if such as have real Capacities for Publick Service, were employed in Works of general Use; but because a Thing is every Body's Business, it is no Body's Business: This is for Want[4] of publick Spirit. As for my Part, who am only a Student, and a Man of no great Interest, I can only remark Things, and recommend the Correction of 'em to higher Powers. There is an Offence I have a Thousand Times lamented, but fear I shall never see remedy'd; which is, That in a Nation where Learning is so frequent as in *Great Britain,* there should be so many gross Errors as there are in the very Directions of Things, wherein Accuracy is necessary for the Conduct of Life. This is notoriously observed by all Men of Letters when they first come to Town (at which Time they are usually curious that Way) in the Inscriptions on Sign-Posts. I have Cause to know this Matter as

---

[1] The speculations on signs and on the plight of newswriters are usually credited to Addison, his first contribution to the periodical.

[2] Subtle or abstract.

[3] Words without independent accent, which are pronounced as part of the preceding word, e.g., *man* in *layman.*

[4] Lack.

well as any Body; for I have (when I went to Merchant-Taylor's School) suffered Stripes[5] for spelling after the Signs I observed in my Way; tho' at the same Time, I must confess, staring at those Inscriptions first gave me an Idea and Curiosity for Medals; in which I have since arrived at some Knowledge.[6] Many a Man has lost his Way and his Dinner by this general Want of Skill in Orthography: For, considering that the Painters are usually so very bad, that you cannot know the Animal under whose Sign you are to live that Day,[7] How must the Stranger be misled, if it be wrong spelled, as well as ill painted? I have a Cousin now in Town, who has answered under[8] *Batchelor* at *Queen*'s College, whose Name is *Humphrey Mopstaff:* (He is a Kin to us by his Mother.) This young Man going to see a Relation in *Barbekin,* wandered a whole Day by the Mistake of one Letter, for it was written, *This is the B E E R,* instead of, *This is the B E A R.* He was set right at last, by enquiring for the House, of a Fellow who could not read, and knew the Place mechanically, only by having been often drunk there. But, in the Name of Goodness, let us make our Learning of Use to us, or not. Was not this a Shame, that a Philosopher should be thus directed by a Cobler? I'll be sworn, if it were known how many have suffered in this Kind by false Spelling since the Union,[9] this Matter would not long lie thus. What makes these Evils the more insupportable, is, That they are so easily amended, and nothing done in it. But it is so far from that; that the Evil goes on in other Arts as well as Orthography. Places are confounded, as well for want of proper Distinctions, as Things for Want of true Characters.[10] Had I not come by the other Day very early in the Morning, there might have been Mischief done; for a worthy *North-Britain* was swearing at *Stocks-market,* that they would not

5 Strokes applied with a rod or lash.

6 Addison's *Remarks on Several Parts of Italy* (1705) said much about medals. His *Dialogue on Medals* was published posthumously.

7 Inns were commonly named after animals (The Bear, The Lion, etc.) and carried appropriate signs. Addison, who here is using the language of astrology, returned to the subject of signs in *Spectator* No. 28.

8 Earned the degree of.

9 England and Scotland were united politically in 1707.

10 Correct or legible lettering.

let him in at his Lodgings; but I knowing the Gentleman, and observing him look often at the King on Horseback, and then double his Oaths, that he was sure he was right, found he mistook that for *Charing-Cross,* by the Erection of the like Statue in each Place.[11] I grant, private Men[12] may distinguish their Abodes as they please; as one of my Acquaintance who lives at *Marybone,* has put a good Sentence of his own Invention upon his Dwelling-place, to find out where he lives: He is so near *London,* that his Conceit is this, *The Country in Town;* or, *The Town in the Country;* for you know, if they are both in one, they are all one. Besides that, the Ambiguity is not of great Consequence; if you are safe at the Place, 'tis no Matter if you do not distinctly know where to say the Place is. But to return to the Orthography of Publick Places: I propose, That every Tradesman in the Cities of *London* and *Westminster,* shall give me Sixpence a Quarter for keeping their Signs in Repair, as to the Grammatical Part; and I will take into my House a *Swiss* Count of my Acquaintance,[13] who can remember all their Names without Book, for Dispatch sake, setting up the Head of the said Foreigner for my Sign; the Features being strong, and fit for hanging high.

St. James's Coffee-house, May 20.

This Day a Mail arrived from *Holland,* by which there are Advices from *Paris,* That the Kingdom of *France* is in the utmost Misery and Distraction. The Merchants of *Lions* have been at Court, to remonstrate their great Sufferings by the Failure of their Publick Credit; but have received no other Satisfaction, than Promises of a sudden Peace; and that their Debts will be made good by Funds out of the Revenue, which will not answer, but in

[11] Though both the Market and Charing-Cross had statues showing an English king on horseback conquering an enemy, there was little cause for confusion. One statute was of white marble; the other, of brass.

[12] Private citizens, as opposed to merchants and others who would commonly distinguish their buildings with a sign.

[13] John James Heidegger (1659?–1749), who became chief director of the opera house. *Tatler* No. 12 described him as a surgeon who creates male sopranos. Here the reference is to the notable ugliness of his face.

case of the Peace which is promised. In the mean Time, the Cries of the common People are loud for Want of Bread, the Gentry have lost all Spirit and Zeal for their Country, and the King himself seems to languish under the Anxiety of the pressing Calamities of the Nation, and retires from hearing those Grievances which he hath not Power to redress. Instead of Preparations for War, and the Defence of their Country, there is nothing to be seen but evident Marks of a general Despair. Processions, Fastings, Publick Mournings, and Humiliations, are become the sole Employments of a People, who were lately the most vain and gay of any in the Universe.[14]

The Pope has written to the *French* King on the Subject of a Peace, and his Majesty has answered in the lowliest Terms, That he entirely submits his Affairs to Divine Providence, and shall soon show the World, that he prefers the Tranquillity of his People to the Glory of his Arms, and Extent of his Conquests.

Letters from the *Hague* of the 24th say, That his Excellency the Lord *Townshend*[15] delivered his Credentials on that Day to the States-General, as Plenipotentiary from the Queen of *Great-Britain;* as did also Count *Zinzendorf,* who bears the same Character from the Emperor.

Prince *Eugene*[16] intended to set out the next Day for *Brussels,* and his Grace the Duke of *Marlborough* on the *Tuesday* following. The Marquis *de Torcy*[17] talks daily of going, but still continues here. The Army of the Allies is to assemble on the 7th of the next Month at *Helchin;* though 'tis generally believed, that the Preliminaries to a Treaty are fully adjusted.[18]

The Approach of a Peace strikes a Pannick thro' our Armies,

14 Though France was at this time suffering the effects of a long and continuing war, Steele's description does show a measure of Whig excess.

15 Charles, Viscount Townshend (1674–1738), here acting as diplomatic agent to the legislature of the Netherlands.

16 Francois Eugene, Prince of Savoy (1663–1736), the leading Continental general in the War of the Spanish Succession.

17 J. B. Colbert, Marquis de Torcy (1665–1746), a leading French diplomat. See *Spectator* No. 305.

18 Peace negotiations subsequently broke down, owing largely to the uncompromising terms of the Allies.

tho' that of a Battle could never do it, and they almost repent of
their Bravery, that made such hast to humble themselves and the
French King. The Duke of *Marlborough,* tho' otherwise the greatest General of the Age, has plainly shown himself unacquainted
with the Arts of Husbanding[19] a War. He might have grown as
old as the Duke of *Alva,* or Prince *Waldeck,* in the *Low-Countries,*
and yet have got Reputation enough every Year for any reasonable Man: For the Command of General in *Flanders* hath been
ever looked upon as a Provision for Life. For my Part, I can't see
how his Grace can answer it to the World, for the great Eagerness
he hath shown to send a Hundred Thousand of the bravest Fellows in *Europe* a begging. But the private Gentlemen of the Infantry will be able to shift for themselves; a brave Man can never
starve in a Country stock'd with Hen-roosts. *There is not a Yard
of Linnen,* says my honoured Progenitor, Sir *John Falstaff, in my
whole Company; but as for that,* says this worthy Knight, *I am in
no great Pain, we shall find Shirts on every Hedge.*[20] There is another Sort of Gentlemen whom I am much more concerned for,
and that is, the ingenious Fraternity of which I have the Honour
to be an unworthy Member; I mean the *News Writers* of *Great
Britain,* whether *Post-Men* or *Post-Boys,* or by what other Name
or Title soever dignified or distinguished.[21] The Case of these
Gentlemen is, I think, more hard than that of the Soldiers, considering that they have taken more Towns, and fought more Battels. They have been upon Parties and Skirmishes, when our Armies have lain still; and given the General Assault to many a
Place, when the Besiegers were quiet in their Trenches. They
have made us Masters of several strong Towns many Weeks before
our Generals could do it; and compleated Victories, when our
greatest Captains have been glad to come off with a drawn Battle.
Where Prince *Eugene* has slain his Thousands, *Boyer*[22] has slain

19 Conserving.
20 The passage is loosely paraphrased from Shakespeare's *Henry IV, Part I,*
Act 4, sc. 2.
21 The *Post Boy* was a Tory paper published by Abel Roper; the *Flying
Post,* a Whig journal published by George Ridpath. The *Post-Man,* written by
Jean de Fonvive, was considered by Tories to be a Whig periodical.
22 Abel Boyer (1667–1729).

his Ten Thousands. This Gentleman can indeed be never enough commended for his Courage and Intrepidity during this whole War: He has laid about him with an inexpressible Fury, and like the offended *Marius* of Ancient *Rome* made such Havock among his Countrymen, as must be the Work of two or three Ages to repair. It must be confess'd, the Redoubted Mr. *Buckley*[23] has shed as much Blood as the former; but I cannot forbear saying, (and I hope it will not look like Envy) that we regard our Brother *Buckley* as a kind of *Drawcansir*,[24] who spares neither Friend or Foe: But generally kills as many of his own Side as the Enemy's. It is impossible for this ingenious Sort of Men to subsist after a Peace: Every one remembers the Shifts they were driven to in the Reign of King *Charles* the Second, when they could not furnish out a single Paper of News, without lighting up a Comet in *Germany,* or a Fire in *Moscow.* There scarce appeared a Letter without a Paragraph on an Earthquake. Prodigies were grown so familiar, that they had lost their Name, as a great Poet of that Age has it. I remember Mr. *Dyer,*[25] who is justly look'd upon by all the Fox-hunters[26] in the Nation as the greatest Statesman our Country has produced, was particularly famous for dealing in Whales; insomuch that in Five Months Time (for I had the Curiosity to examine his Letters on that Occasion) he brought Three into the Mouth of the River *Thames,* besides Two Porpusses and a Sturgeon. The judicious and wary Mr. *I. Dawks*[27] hath all along been the Rival of this great Writer, and got himself a Reputation from Plagues and Famines, by which, in those Days, he destroyed as great Mul-

23 Samuel Buckley (d. 1741), printer of the *London Gazette,* the *Daily Courant,* and—subsequently—the *Spectator.*

24 In Buckingham's *The Rehearsal* (1671), Drawcansir is described as "a fierce hero, that frights his mistress, snubs up kings, baffles armies, and does what he will, without regard to numbers, good manners, or justice." He is a parody of Almanzor, the hero of Dryden's *The Conquest of Granada.*

25 John Dyer (d. 1715) was the Jacobite author of *Dyer's Letter,* a paper of doubtful credit. In Addison's play *The Drummer* (1716), the steward Vellum is led to believe his master is still living "because the news of his death was first published in Dyer's Letter."

26 The rural gentry, who generally favored the Tory view. In *Spectator* No. 127, Sir Roger de Coverly is shown reading and relishing *Dyer's Letter.*

27 Ichabod Dawks (1661–1730), author of *Dawks's News-Letter.*

titudes, as he has lately done by the Sword. In every Dearth of News, *Grand Cairo* was sure to be unpeopled.[28]

It being therefore visible, that our Society will be greater Sufferers by the Peace than the Soldiery it self; insomuch that the *Daily Courant*[29] is in Danger of being broken, my Friend *Dyer* of being reformed, and the very best of the whole Band of being reduced to Half-pay; Might I presume to offer any Thing in the Behalf of my distressed Brethren, I would humbly move, That an Appendix of proper Apartments furnished with Pen, Ink, and Paper, and other Necessaries of Life, should be added to the Hospital of *Chelsea*,[30] for the Relief of such decay'd News-Writers as have serv'd their Country in the Wars; and that for their Exercise, they should compile the Annals of their Brother Veterans, who have been engaged in the same Service, and are still obliged to do Duty after the same Manner.

I cannot be thought to speak this out of an Eye to any private Interest; for, as my chief Scenes of Action are Coffee houses, Playhouses, and my own Apartment, I am in no need of Camps, Fortifications, and Fields of Battle, to support me; I don't call out for Heroes and Generals to my Assistance. Though the Officers are broken, and the Armies disbanded, I shall still be safe as long as there are Men or Women, or Politicians, or Lovers, or Poets, or Nymphs, or Swains, or Cits,[31] or Courtiers in Being.

[28] I.e., Egypt had to endure plague or pestilence.
[29] A daily newspaper begun in 1702 by Samuel Buckley.
[30] Chelsea Hospital, founded in 1682, for old soldiers.
[31] Mean-spirited merchants. See the description of Avaro in *Tatler* No. 25.

The Tatler, No. 25

From Saturday June 4. to Tuesday June 7. 1709.

[S t e e l e]

White's Chocolate house, June 6.

A Letter from a young Lady, written in the most passionate Terms, wherein she laments the Misfortune of a Gentleman, her Lover, who was lately wounded in a Duel, has turned my Thoughts to that Subject, and enclined me to examine into the Causes which precipitate Men into so fatal a Folly. And as it has been proposed to treat of Subjects of Gallantry[1] in the Article from hence, and no one Point in Nature is more proper to be consider'd by the Company who frequent this Place[2] than that of Duels, it is worth our Consideration to examine into this Chimaerical groundless Humour,[3] and to lay every other Thought aside, till we have strip'd it of all its false Pretences to Credit and Reputation amongst Men.

But I must confess, when I consider what I am going about, and run over in my Imagination all the endless Crowd of Men of Honour[4] who will be offended at such a Discourse; I am undertaking, methinks, a Work worthy an invulnerable Hero in Romance, rather than a private Gentleman with a single Rapier: But

---

[1] Amorous adventures.

[2] I.e., White's Chocolate-house, where gambling was common and quarrels often arose.

[3] Fanciful attitude, notion.

[4] Men willing to defend their reputation ("honour") in a duel. Because of the character of such individuals, the phrase "man of honour" often expressed an ironical meaning.

as I am pretty well acquainted by great Opportunities with the
Nature of Man, and know of a Truth, that all Men fight *against
their Will,* the Danger vanishes, and Resolution rises upon this
Subject. For this Reason I shall talk very freely on a Custom which
all Men wish exploded, though no Man has Courage enough to
resist it.

But there is one unintelligible Word which I fear will extremely perplex my Dissertation; and I confess to you I find very
hard to explain, which is, the Term *Satisfaction.* An honest Country Gentleman had the Misfortune to fall into Company with
Two or Three modern Men of Honour, where he happened to be
very ill treated; and one of the Company being conscious of his
Offence, sends a Note to him in the Morning, and tells him, He
was ready to give him Satisfaction. This is fine Doing (says the
plain Fellow). Last Night he sent me away cursedly out of Humour, and this Morning he fancies it would be a Satisfaction to be
run through the Body.

As the Matter at present stands, it is not to do handsome Actions denominates a Man of Honour; it is enough if he dares to
defend ill Ones. Thus you often see a common Sharper[5] in Competition with a Gentleman of the first Rank; though all Mankind
is convinced, that a fighting Gamester is only a Pick-pocket with
the Courage of an Highway-Man. One cannot with any Patience
reflect on the unaccountable Jumble of Persons and Things in this
Town and Nation, which occasions very frequently, that a brave
Man falls by a Hand below that of the common Hangman, and
yet his Executioner escapes the Clutches of the Hangman for doing it. I shall therefore hereafter consider, how the bravest Men
in other Ages and Nations have behaved themselves upon such
Incidents as we decide by Combat; and show, from their Practice,
that this Resentment neither has its Foundation from true Reason, or solid Fame; but is an Imposture, made up of Cowardice,
Falshood, and Want of Understanding. For this Work, a good
History of Quarrels would be very edifying to the Publick, and I
apply my self to the Town for Particulars and Circumstances
within their Knowledge, which may serve to embellish the Dis-

5 A low-born gambler.

sertation with proper Cuts.[6] Most of the Quarrels I have ever
known, have proceeded from some valiant Coxcomb's persisting
in the Wrong, to defend some prevailing Folly, and preserve himself from the Ingenuity[7] of owning a Mistake.

By this Means it is called, *Giving a Man Satisfaction,* to urge
your Offence against him with your Sword; which puts me in
Mind of *Peter's* Order to the Keeper, in *The Tale of a Tub: If you
neglect to do all this, damn you and your Generation for ever; and
so we bid you heartily farewel.*[8] If the Contradiction in the very
Terms of one of our Challenges were as well explained, and turn'd
into downright *English,* would it not run after this Manner?

> *"Sir,*
> Your extraordinary Behaviour last Night, and the Liberty you were
> pleased to take with me, makes me this Morning give you this, to tell
> you, because you are an ill-bred Puppy, I will meet you in *Hide* Park
> an Hour hence; and because you want both Breeding and Humanity,
> I desire you would come with a Pistol in your Hand, on Horseback,
> and endeavour to shoot me through the Head; to teach you more
> Manners. If you fail of doing me this Pleasure, I shall say, You are a
> Rascal on every Post in Town:[9] And so, Sir, if you will not injure me
> more, I shall never forgive what you have done already. Pray Sir, do
> not fail of getting every Thing ready, and you will infinitely oblige,
>
> > *Sir,*
> > *Your most Obedient,*
> > *Humble Servant,* &c."[10]

From my own Apartment, June 6.

Among the many Employments I am necessarily put upon by
my Friends, that of giving Advice is the most unwelcome to me;

6 Woodcuts or engravings on copper plates, with which he can illustrate his
book on the history of quarrels. The pun is intentional.

7 The honorable candor.

8 In Swift's satire (1704), Peter represents the Roman Church. The slightly
misquoted passage satirizes the arbitrary character of papal proclamations.

9 Should one refuse to accept a challenge, his adversary would commonly
publish the fact of his cowardice.

10 Steele, who fought a duel in 1700, had criticized the practice in *The
Christian Hero* (1701). He went on to satirize duelling in *Tatlers* No. 26, 28, 29,
31, 38, and 39.

and indeed, I am forced to use a little Art in the Matter; for some People will ask Counsel of you, when they have already acted what they tell you is still under Deliberation. I had almost lost a very good Friend t'other Day, who came to know how I liked his Design to marry such a Lady. I answered, By no Means; and I must be positive against it, for very solid Reasons, which are not proper to communicate. Not proper to communicate! (said he with a grave Air) I will know the Bottom of this. I saw him moved, and knew from thence he was already determined; therefore evaded it by saying, To tell you the Truth, dear *Frank,* Of all Women living, I would have her my self. *Isaac,* said he, Thou art too late, for we have been both one these two Months.

I learned this Caution by a Gentleman's consulting me formerly about his Son. He railed at his damn'd Extravagance, and told me, In a very little Time, he would beggar him by the exorbitant Bills which came from *Oxford*[11] every Quarter. *Make the Rogue bite upon the Bridle,*[12] say I, *pay none of his Bills, it will but encourage him to further Trespasses.* He look'd plaguy sowr at me. His Son soon after sent me up a Paper of Verses, forsooth, in Print, on the last publick Occasion;[13] upon which, he is convinced the Boy has Parts,[14] and a Lad of Spirit is not to be too much cramp'd in his Maintenance, lest he take ill Courses. Neither Father nor Son can ever since endure the Sight of me.

These Sort of People ask Opinions, only out of the Fulness of their Heart on the Subject of their Perplexity, and not from a Desire of Information.

There is nothing so easy as to find out which Opinion the Person in Doubt has a Mind to; therefore the sure Way is to tell him, that is certainly to be chosen. Then you are to be very clear and positive; leave no Handle for Scruple. Bless me! Sir, there's no Room for a Question. This rivets you into his Heart; for you at once applaud his Wisdom, and gratify his Inclination. However, I had too much Bowels to be insincere to a Man who came Yester-

---

11 The University of Oxford.

12 A riding image meaning hold him in.

13 The boy had published a poem celebrating a public occasion, e.g., the Queen's birthday, the Lord-Mayor's day, etc.

14 Natural abilities.

day to know of me, With which of two eminent Men in the City he should place his Son? Their Names are *Paulo* and *Avaro*.[15] This gave me much Debate with my self, because not only the Fortune of the Youth, but his Virtue also, depended upon this Choice. The Men are equally wealthy; but they differ in the Use and Application of their Riches, which you immediately see upon entring their Doors.

The Habitation of *Paulo* has at once the Air of a Nobleman and a Merchant. You see the Servants act with Affection to their Master, and Satisfaction in themselves: The Master meets you with an open Countenance, full of Benevolence and Integrity: Your Business is dispatched with that Confidence and Welcome which always accompanies honest Minds: His Table is the Image of Plenty and Generosity, supported by Justice and Frugality. After we had dined here, our Affair was to visit *Avaro:* Out comes an aukward Fellow with a careful Countenance; Sir, Would you speak with my Master? May I crave your Name? After the first Preambles, he leads us into a noble Solitude, a great House that seem'd uninhabited; but from the End of the spacious Hall moves towards us *Avaro,* with a suspicious Aspect, as if he believed us Thieves; and as for my Part, I approached him as if I knew him a Cut-purse.[16] We fell into Discourse of his noble Dwelling, and the Great Estate all the World knew he had to enjoy in it: And I, to plague him, fell a commending *Paulo*'s Way of Living. *Paulo,* answered *Avaro,* is a very good Man; but we who have smaller Estates, must cut our Coat according to our Cloth. Nay, says I, Every Man knows his own Circumstance best; you are in the Right, if you han't wherewithal. He look'd very sowr; (for it is, you must know, the utmost Vanity of a mean-spirited rich Man to be contradicted, when he calls himself Poor.) But I was resolved to vex him, by consenting to all he said; the main Design of which was, that he would have us find out, he was one of the wealthiest Men in *London,* and lived like a Beggar. We left him, and took a Turn on the Change.[17] My Friend was ravished with *Avaro:* This (said

---

[15] These were probably two real London merchants of the day.
[16] A pickpocket.
[17] Walked along toward the stock exchange.

he) is certainly a sure Man. I contradicted him with much Warmth, and summed up their different Characters as well as I could. This *Paulo* (said I) grows wealthy by being a common Good; *Avaro,* by being a general Evil: *Paulo* has the Art, *Avaro* the Craft of Trade. When *Paulo* gains, all Men he deals with are the better: Whenever *Avaro* profits, another certainly loses. In a Word, *Paulo* is a Citizen, and *Avaro* a Cit.[18] I convinced my Friend, and carried the young Gentleman the next Day to *Paulo,* where he will learn the Way both to gain, and enjoy a good Fortune. And tho' I cannot say, I have, by keeping him from *Avaro,* saved him from the Gallows, I have prevented his deserving it every Day he lives: For with *Paulo* he will be an honest Man, without being so for Fear of the Law; as with *Avaro,* he would have been a Villain within the Protection of it.

St. James's Coffee-house, June 6.

We hear from *Vienna* of the 1st Instant, That Baron *Imoff,* who attended her Catholick Majesty with the Character of Envoy from the Duke of *Wolfembuttel,* was returned thither. That Minister brought an Account, That Major-General *Stanhope,*[19] with the Troops which embarked at *Naples,* was returned to *Barcelona.* We hear from *Berlin,* by Advices of the 8th Instant, That his *Prussian* Majesty had received Intelligence from his Minister at *Dresden,* that the King of *Denmark* desired to meet his Majesty at *Magdeburg.* The King of *Prussia* has sent Answer, That his present Indisposition will not admit of so great a Journey; but has sent the King a very pressing Invitation to come to *Berlin* or *Potsdam.* These Advices say, That the Minister of the King of *Sweden* has produced a Letter from his Master to the King of *Poland,* dated from *Batitzau* the 30th of *March, O. S.*[20] wherein he acquaints him, that he has been successful against the *Muscovites* in all the Occasions which have happened since his March into their

---

[18] See *Tatler* No. 18, n. 31. This distinction expresses a notably Whig viewpoint: that a merchant could indeed act like a gentleman, even though some regrettably did not.

[19] James, afterwards 1st Earl of Stanhope (1673–1721), an Allied general.

[20] Old Style. See *Tatler* No. 1, n. 18.

Country. Great Numbers have revolted to the *Swedes* since General *Mazeppa*[21] went over to that Side; and as many as have done so, have taken solemn Oaths to adhere to the Interests of his *Swedish* Majesty.

Advices from the *Hague* of the 14th Instant, *N. S.* say, That all Things tended to a vigorous and active Campagne; the Allies having strong Resentments against the late Behaviour of the Court of *France*; and the *French* using all possible Endeavours to animate their Men to defend their Country against a victorious and exasperated Enemy. Monsieur *Rouillé* had passed through *Brussels* without visiting either the Duke of *Marlborough* or Prince *Eugene,* who were both there at that Time. The States have met, and publickly declared their Satisfaction in the Conduct of their Deputies during the whole Treaty. Letters from *France* say, That the Court is resolved to put all to the Issue of the ensuing Campagne.[22] In the mean Time, they have ordered the Preliminary Treaty to be published, with Observation upon each Article, in order to quiet the Minds of the People, and perswade them, that it has not been in the Power of the King to procure a Peace, but to the Diminution of his Majesty's Glory, and the Hazard of his Dominions. His Grace the Duke of *Marlborough* and Prince *Eugene* arrived at *Ghent* on *Wednesday* last, where, at an Assembly of all the General Officers, it was thought proper, by Reason of the great Rains which have lately fallen, to defer forming a Camp, or bringing the Troops together; but as soon as the Weather would permit, to march upon the Enemy with all Expedition.

21 Ivan Stepanovich Mazeppa (1640?–1709), Ukrainian general, who sought to gain the independence of the Ukraine by intriguing with Poland and Sweden.

22 I.e., to make a final military effort, employing all possible strength, that it might conclude the war on the best possible terms.

The Tatler, No. 60

From Thursd. Aug. 25. to Saturd. Aug. 27. 1709.

[S t e e l e]

White's Chocolate house, August 26.

To proceed regularly in the History of my Worthies,[1] I ought to give you an Account of what has passed from Day to Day in this Place;[2] but a young Fellow of my Acquaintance has so lately been rescued out of the Hands of the Knights of the Industry, that I rather chuse to relate the Manner of his Escape from 'em, and the uncommon Way which was used to reclaim him, than to go on in my intended Diary.

You are to know then, that *Tom Wildair* is a Student of the *Inner Temple*,[3] and has spent his Time, since he left the University for that Place, in the common Diversions of Men of Fashion; that is to say, in Whoring, Drinking, and Gaming. The Two former Vices he had from his Father; but was led into the last by the Conversation of a Partizan of the *Mirmidons*,[4] who had Chambers near him. His Allowance from his Father was a very plentiful one for a Man of Sense, but as scanty for a modern Fine Gentleman.

---

[1] In *Tatler* No. 59, Steele promised an essay on gambling: "I shall in my future Accounts of our modern Heroes and Wits vulgarly called *Sharpers,* imitate the Method of [Aesop]; and think, I cannot represent those Worthies more naturally than under the Shadow of a Pack of Dogs . . ."

[2] White's Chocolate-house.

[3] London residence of students of civil law.

[4] Steele discussed gamblers in *Tatler* No. 56: "I find, all Times have had of this People; *Homer,* in his excellent Heroic Poem, calls them *Myrmidons,* who were a Body who kept among themselves, and had nothing to lose; therefore never spared either *Greek* or *Trojan,* when they fell in their way, upon a Party."

His frequent Losses had reduced him to so necessitous a Condition, that his Lodgings were always haunted by impatient Creditors, and all his Thoughts employed in contriving low Methods
to support himself, in a Way of Life from which he knew not how
to retreat, and in which he wanted Means to proceed. There is
never wanting some good-natur'd Person to send a Man an Account of what he has no Mind to hear; therefore many Epistles
were conveyed to the Father of this Extravagant, to inform him
of the Company, the Pleasures, the Distresses, and Entertainments, in which his Son passed his Time. The old Fellow received
these Advices with all the Pain of a Parent, but frequently consulted his Pillow to know how to behave himself on such important Occasions, as the Welfare of his Son, and the Safety of his
Fortune. After many Agitations of Mind, he reflected, That Necessity was the usual Snare which made Men fall into Meanness,
and that a liberal Fortune generally made a liberal and honest
Mind; he resolved therefore to save him from his Ruin, by giving
him Opportunities of tasting what it is to be at Ease, and enclosed
to him the following Order upon Sir *Tristram Cash:*

> "Sir,
>   *Pray pay to Mr.* Tho. Wildair, *or Order, the Sum of One Thou-*
> *sand Pounds, and place it to the Account of*
>   *Yours,* Humphrey Wildair."

Tom. was so astonished at the Receipt of this Order, that
though he knew it to be his Father's Hand, and that he had always large Sums at Sir *Tristram's*;[5] yet a Thousand Pounds was a
Trust of which his Conduct had always made him appear so little
capable, that he kept his Note by him, till he writ to his Father
the following Letter:

> "Honoured Father,
>   *I have received an Order under your Hand for a Thousand Pounds,*
> *in Words at Length, and I think I could swear it is your Hand. I have*
> *looked it over and over Twenty Thousand Times. There is in plain*
> *Letters, T,H,O,U,S,A,N,D; and after it, the Letters, P,O,U,N,D,S. I*

5 This is perhaps a reference to Sir Francis Child (d. 1713), the founder of
a banking-house, later elected Lord Mayor.

have it still by me, and shall, I believe, continue reading it till I hear from you."

The old Gentleman took no Manner of Notice of the Receipt of his Letter; but sent him another Order for Three Thousand Pounds more. His Amazement on this second Letter was unspeakable. He immediately double-lock'd his Door, and sate down carefully to reading and comparing both his Orders. After he had read 'em till he was half mad, he walked Six or Seven Turns in his Chamber, then opens his Door, then locks it again; and to examine throughly this Matter, he locks his Door again, puts his Table and Chairs against it; then goes into his Closet, and locking himself in, read his Notes over again about Nineteen Times, which did but increase his Astonishment. Soon after, he began to recollect many Stories he had formerly heard of Persons who had been possessed with Imaginations and Appearances which had no Foundation in Nature, but had been taken with sudden Madness in the Midst of a seeming clear and untainted Reason. This made him very gravely conclude he was out of his Wits; and with a Design to compose himself, he immediately betakes him to his Night cap, with a Resolution to sleep himself into his former Poverty and Senses. To Bed therefore he goes at Noon-Day, but soon rose again, and resolved to visit Sir *Tristram* upon this Occasion. He did so, and dined with the Knight, expecting he would mention some Advice from his Father about paying him Money; but no such Thing being said, Look you, Sir *Tristram,* (said he) you are to know, that an Affair has happened, which————Look you, (says *Tristram*) I know Mr. *Wildair,* you are going to desire me to advance; but the late Call of the Bank, where I have not yet made my last Payment, has obliged me————[6] *Tom* interrupted him, by showing him the Bill of a Thousand Pounds. When he had looked at it for a convenient Time, and as often surveyed *Tom*'s Looks and Countenance; Look you, Mr. *Wildair,* a Thousand Pounds————Before he could proceed, he shows him the Order for Three Thousand more————Sir *Tristram* examined the Orders at the Light, and finding at the writing the Name, there was

[6] Thinking that Tom seeks a loan, Sir Tristram prudently begins claiming he has no money to lend.

a certain Stroke in one Letter, which the Father and he had agreed should be to such Directions as he desired might be more immediately honour'd, he forthwith pays the Money. The Possession of Four Thousand Pounds gave my young Gentleman a new Train of Thoughts: He began to reflect upon his Birth, the great Expectations he was born to, and the unsuitable Ways he had long pursued. Instead of that unthinking Creature he was before, he is now provident, generous, and discreet. The Father and Son have an exact and regular Correspondence, with mutual and unreserved Confidence in each other. The Son looks upon his Father as the best Tenant he could have in the Country,[7] and the Father finds the Son the most safe Banker he could have in the City.

Will's Coffee-house, August 26.

There is not any Thing in Nature so extravagant, but that you will find one Man or other that shall practice or maintain it; otherwise, *Harry Spondee* could not have made so long an Harangue as he did here this Evening, concerning the Force and Efficacy of well-applied Nonsense. Among Ladies, he positively averr'd, it was the most prevailing Part of Eloquence; and had so little Complaisance[8] as to say, a Woman is never taken by her Reason, but always by her Passion. He proceeded to assert, the Way to move that, was only to astonish her. I know (continued he) a very late Instance of this; for being by Accident in the next Room to *Strephon,* I could not help over-hearing him as he made Love to a certain great Lady's Woman.[9] The true Method in your Application to one of this second Rank of Understanding, is not to elevate and surprize, but rather to elevate and amaze. *Strephon* is a perfect Master in this Kind of Perswasion: His Way is, to run over with a soft Air a Multitude of Words, without Meaning or Connexion, but such as do each of 'em apart give a pleasing Idea, though they have nothing to do with each other as he assembles 'em. After the common Phrases of Salutation, and making his En-

---

[7] I.e., as caretaker of the estate he will someday inherit.
[8] The wish to please or oblige. See *Guardian* No. 162.
[9] Servant.

try into the Room, I perceived he had taken the fair Nymph's Hand, and kissing it, said, Witness to my Happiness ye Groves! Be still ye Rivulets! Oh! Woods, Caves, Fountains, Trees, Dales, Mountains, Hills, and Streams! Oh! Fairest, Could you love me? To which I over-heard her answer, with a very pretty Lisp, Oh! *Strephon,* You are a dangerous Creature: Why do you talk these tender Things to me? But you Men of Wit————Is it then possible, said the enamour'd *Strephon,* that she regards my Sorrows? Oh! Pity, thou Balmy Cure to an Heart o'erloaded. If Rapture, Solicitation, soft Desire, and pleasing Anxiety————But still I live in the most afflicting of all Circumstances, Doubt————Cannot my Charmer name the Place and Moment?

> *There all those Joys insatiably to prove,*
> *With which Rich Beauty feeds the Glutton Love.*

Forgive me, Madam, it is not that my Heart is weary of its Chain, but————This incoherent Stuff was answer'd by a tender Sigh, Why do you put your Wit to a weak Woman? *Strephon* saw he had made some Progress in her Heart, and pursued it, by saying that he would certainly wait upon her at such an Hour near *Rosamond*'s Pond;[10] and then————The Sylvian Deities, and Rural Powers of the Place,[11] sacred and inviolable to *Love; Love,*[12] the Mover of all noble Hearts, should hear his Vows repeated by the Streams and Ecchoes. The Assignation was accordingly made. This Style he calls the unintelligible Method of speaking his Mind; and I'll engage, had this Gallant spoken plain *English,* she had never understood him half so readily: For we may take it for granted, That he'll be esteemed as a very cold Lover, who discovers to his Mistress that he is in his Senses.

From my own Apartment, August 26.

The following Letter came to my Hand, with a Request to have the Subject recommended to our Readers, particularly the Smart

---

[10] A lake in St. James's Park, a favorite meeting place of lovers. See Pope's *Rape of the Lock* V. 135–136.

[11] Gods of the woods and forests.

[12] I.e., the god of love.

Fellows,[13] who are desired to repair to Major *Touch-hole*,[14] who can help them to Firelocks that are only fit for Exercise.

Just ready for the Press.

"*Mars Triumphant*, or, *London's Glory:* Being the whole Art of Encampment, with the Method of embattelling Armies, marching them off, posting the Officers, forming hollow Squares, and the various Ways of paying the Salute with the Half-pike; as it was performed by the Train'd-Bands of *London* this Year, One Thousand Seven Hundred and Nine, in that Nursery of *Bellona*[15] the *Artillery-Ground.* Wherein you have a new Method how to form a strong Line of Foot, with large Intervals between each Platon, very useful to prevent the breaking in of Horse. A Civil Way of performing the Military Ceremony; wherein the Major alights from his Horse, and at the Head of his Company salutes the Lieutenant-Colonel; and the Lieutenant-Colonel, to return the Compliment, courteously dismounts, and after the same Manner salutes his Major: Exactly as it was performed, with abundance of Applause, on the 5th of *July* last. Likewise an Account of a new Invention made use of in the Red Regiment to quell mutineering Captains; with several other Things alike useful for the Publick. To which is added, An Appendix by Major *Touch-hole;* proving the Method of Discipline now used in our Armies to be very defective: With an Essay towards an Amendment. Dedicated to the Lieutenant-Colonel of the First Regiment."

Mr. Bickerstaff *has now in the Press*, A Defence of Aukward Fellows against the Class of the Smarts:[16] *With a Dissertation upon the Gravity which becomes weighty Persons. Illustrated by Way of Fable, and a Discourse on the Nature of the Elephant, the Cow, the Dray-Horse, and the Dromedary, which have Motions equally steady and grave. To this is added, A Treatise written by*

---

13 The citizen soldiers were usually merchants and apprentices who assumed military titles and grand manners, far from any scene of combat. The Train-Bands of London were often the objects of wit. In *Tatler* No. 28, Steele reported that "Captain *Crabtree* of *Birching-Lane*, Haberdasher, had drawn a Bill upon Major-General *Maggot*, Cheesemonger in *Thames-street*."

14 Said to be a Mr. Gregory of Thames Street, a major in the Train-Bands.

15 The Roman goddess of war.

16 This would have been a satire on the pretentious gravity of the Puritans.

an *Elephant (according to* **Pliny**) *against receiving Foreigners into the Forrest. Adapted to some present Circumstances. Together with Allusions to such Beasts as declare against the Poor* **Palatines.**[17]

[17] Protestant refugees from Bavaria.

The Tatler, No. 89

From Tuesd. Nov. 1. to Thursd. Nov. 3. 1709.

[S t e e l e]

Rura mihi placeant, riguiq; in Vallibus Amnes,
Flumina Amem Sylvasq; inglorius————[1]

Grecian Coffee-house, November 2.

I have received this short Epistle from an unknown Hand.[2]

"Sir,
I have no more to trouble you with, than to desire you would in your next help me to some Answer to the Inclosed concerning your self. In the mean time I congratulate you upon the Increase of your Fame, which you see has extended it self beyond the Bills of Mortality."[3]

"Sir,
That the Country[4] *is barren of News, has been the Excuse Time out of Mind for dropping a Correspondence with our Friends in* London; *as if it were impossible out of a Coffee-house to write an agreeable Letter. I am too ingenuous to endeavour at the covering of my Negligence with so common an Excuse. Doubtless, amongst Friends bred as we have been, to the Knowledge of Books as well as Men, a Letter dated from a Garden, a Grotto, a Fountain, a Wood, a Meadow, or the Banks of a River, may be more entertaining, than one from* Tom's,

---

1 Virgil *Georgics* 2. 485–486: "May the country with its stream-fed valleys, its rivers and woodlands, be my humble love."

2 In *Tatler* No. 112, Steele identified the author of this letter as "an old Friend of mine." He may have been Richard Parker, Vicar of Embleton, in Northumberland.

3 I.e., your essays are more discussed than the weekly sheets announcing births and deaths. See *Tatler* No. 1, n. 25.

4 Here, the rural areas.

Will's, White's, or St. James's.[5] *I promise therefore to be frequent for the future in my rural Dates[6] to you: But for fear you should, from what I have said, be induced to believe I shun the Commerce of Men, I must inform you, That there is a fresh Topick of Discourse[7] lately risen amongst the Ingenious in our Part of the World, and is become the more fashionable for the Ladies giving into it. This we owe to* Isaac Bickerstaff, *who is very much censured by some, and as much justified by others. Some criticise his Style, his Humour and his Matter; others admire the whole Man: Some pretend, from the Informations of their Friends in Town, to decipher the Author; and others confess they are lost in their Guesses. For my Part, I must own my self a professed Admirer of the Paper, and desire you to send me a compleat Set, together with your Thoughts of the 'Squire,[8] and his Lucubrations."*

There is no Pleasure like that of receiving Praise from the Praise-worthy; and I own it a very solid Happiness, that these my Lucubrations are approved by a Person of so fine a Tast as the Author of this Letter, who is capable of enjoying the World in the Simplicity of its natural Beauties. This Pastoral Letter,[9] if I may so call it, must be written by a Man who carries his Entertainment wherever he goes, and is undoubtedly one of those happy Men who appear far otherwise to the Vulgar. I dare say, he is not envied by the Vicious, the Vain, the Frolick, and the Loud; but is continually blessed with that strong and serious Delight which flows from a well-taught and liberal Mind. With great Respect to Country Sports, I may say, this Gentleman could pass his Time agreeably, if there were not a Hare or a Fox in his Country.[10] That calm and elegant Satisfaction which the Vulgar call Melancholy, is the true and proper Delight of Men of Knowledge and Virtue.

[5] Tom's Coffee-house was situated in Russell Street. For the others, see *Tatler* No. 1, n. 3.

[6] Letters.

[7] I.e., the *Tatler* essays, which were published anonymously.

[8] Bickerstaff.

[9] A pun. This usually means a letter from a pastor to his congregation, or from a bishop to his diocese.

[10] See *Tatler* No. 18, n. 26. The term "fox-hunter" was often pejorative, describing the kind of crude, irrational individual best portrayed in Fielding's Squire Western.

What we take for Diversion, which is a kind of forgetting our selves, is but a mean Way of Entertainment, in Comparison of that which is considering, knowing, and enjoying our selves. The Pleasures of ordinary People are in their Passions; but the Seat of this Delight is in the Reason and Understanding. Such a Frame of Mind raises that sweet Enthusiasm which warms the Imagination at the Sight of every Work of Nature, and turns all around you into Picture and Landskip. I shall be ever proud of Advices from this Gentleman; for I profess writing News from the learned as well as the busie World.

As for my Labours,[11] which he is pleased to enquire after, if they can but wear one Impertinence out of humane Life, destroy a single Vice, or give a Morning's Chearfulness to an honest Mind; in short, if the World can be but one Virtue the better, or in any Degree less vicious, or receive from them the smallest Addition to their innocent Diversions, I shall not think my Pains, or indeed my Life, to have been spent in vain.

Thus far as to my Studies. It will be expected I should in the next Place give some Account of my Life. I shall therefore, for the Satisfaction of the present Age, and the Benefit of Posterity, present the World with the following Abridgment of it.

It is remarkable, that I was bred by Hand, and eat nothing but Milk till I was a Twelve-month old; from which Time, to the 8th Year of my Age, I was observed to delight in Pudding and Potatoes; and indeed I retain a Benevolence for that Sort of Food to this Day. I do not remember that I distinguish my self in any Thing at those Years, but by my great Skill at Taw,[12] for which I was so barbarously used, that it has ever since given me an Aversion to Gaming. In my Twelfth Year, I suffered very much for Two or Three false Concords.[13] At Fifteen, I was sent to the University, and stayed there for some Time; but a Drum passing by, (being a Lover of Musick) I listed my self for a Soldier.[14] As Years came on, I began to examine Things, and grew discontented at

[11] His *Tatler* essays.

[12] A game involving marbles.

[13] This could mean false friendships.

[14] In a number of instances, here and elsewhere, Bickerstaff's biography parallels Steele's.

the Times. This made me quit the Sword, and take to the Study of the Occult Sciences, in which I was so wrap'd up, that *Oliver Cromwell* had been buried, and taken up again,[15] Five Years before I heard he was dead. This gave me first the Reputation of a Conjurer, which has been of great Disadvantage to me ever since, and kept me out of all Publick Employments. The greater Part of my later Years has been divided between *Dick*'s Coffee-house, the *Trumpet* in *Sheer-Lane,* and my own Lodgings.[16]

From my own Apartment, Nov. 2.

The Evil of unseasonable Visits has been complained of to me with much Vehemence by Persons of both Sexes; and I am desired to consider this very important Circumstance, that Men may know how to regulate their Conduct in an Affair which concerns no less than Life it self. For to a rational Creature, it is almost the same Cruelty to attack his Life, by robbing him of so many Moments of his Time, or so many Drops of his Blood. The Author of the following Letter has a just Delicacy in this Point, and hath put it into a very good Light.

"*Mr.* Bickerstaff,　　　　　　　　　　　　　　　　　　　　Octob. 29.
I am very much afflicted with the Gravel,[17] which makes me sick and peevish. I desire to know of you, if it be reasonable that any of my Acquaintance should take Advantage over me at this Time, and afflict me with long Visits, because they are idle, and I am confined. Pray Sir, reform the Town in this Matter. Men never consider whether the sick Person be disposed for Company, but make their Visits to humour themselves. You may talk upon this Topick, so as to oblige all Persons afflicted with Chronical Distempers, among which I reckon Visits.

---

[15] Oliver Cromwell (1599–1658), Lord protector of England, died of tertian ague and was buried in Westminster Abbey in 1658. His body and those of other regicides were disinterred and hanged on gallows in 1661.

[16] Dick's Coffee-house was situated in Fleet Street. The Trumpet was a public house in Sheer Lane. (Bickerstaff's associates at the Trumpet are described in *Tatler* No. 132.) As *The Tatler* progressed, the papers tended to be composed, not of several essays dated from different coffee-houses, but of a single essay dated either "From my own Apartment" or from "Sheer Lane."

[17] Kidney stones.

Don't think me a sowr Man, for I love Conversation and my Friends;
but I think one's most intimate Friend may be too familiar; and that
there are such Things as unseasonable Wit, and painful Mirth."

It is with some so hard a Thing to employ their Time, that it is
a great good Fortune when they have a Friend indisposed, that
they may be punctual in preplexing him, when he is recover'd
enough to be in that State which cannot be called Sickness or
Health; when he is too well to deny Company, and too ill to receive them. It is no uncommon Case, if a Man is of any Figure or
Power in the World, to be congratulated into a Relapse.

Will's Coffee-house, Nov. 2.

I was very well pleased this Evening, to hear a Gentleman express a very becoming Indignation against a Practice which I my
self have been very much offended at. There is nothing (said he)
more ridiculous, than for an Actor to insert Words of his own in
the Part he is to act, so that it is impossible to see the Poet for the
Player: You'l have *Pinkethman* and *Bullock*[18] helping out *Beau-*
mont and *Fletcher*. It puts me in Mind (continued he) of a Collection of antique Statues which I once saw in a Gentleman's Possession, who employ'd a neighbouring Stone-Cutter to add Noses,
Ears, Arms, or Legs, to the maimed Works of *Phidias* or *Praxit-*
eles.[19] You may be sure this Addition disfigured the Statues much
more than Time had. I remember a *Venus*, that by the Nose he
had given her, looked like Mother *Shipton*;[20] and a *Mercury*, with
a Pair of Legs that seemed very much swelled with a Dropsy.

I thought the Gentleman's Observations very proper; and he
told me, I had improved his Thought, in mentioning on this Occasion those wise Commentators who had filled up the Hemi-
sticks[21] of *Virgil;* particularly that notable Poet, who, to make the

18 William Penkethman (1692–1724) and William Bullock (1657?–1740?)
were popular comic actors.

19 Greek sculptors of the Periclean age.

20 A seventeenth-century prophetess said to have foretold the death of
Wolsey, Cromwell, and others. She existed only in legend.

21 Half a poetic verse. Among the commentators said to have improved
Virgil was Joannes des Peyrareda, a gentleman of Aquitaine.

Aeneid more perfect, carried on the Story to *Lavinia*'s Wedding.[22]
If the proper Officer will not condescend to take Notice of these
Absurdities, I shall my self, as a Censor of the People, animadvert
upon such Proceedings.

[22] Mapheus Vegius of Lodi (1407–1458) added a thirteenth book to the
Aeneid, which described the marriage of Aeneas and Lavinia.

The Tatler, No. 111

From Thursd. Dec. 22. to Saturd. Dec. 24. 1709.

[Addison][1]

Procul O! Procul este Profani! Virg.[2]

Sheer-Lane, December 23.

The Watchman, who does me particular Honours, as being the chief Man in the Lane, gave so very great a Thump at my Door last Night, that I awakened at the Knock, and heard my self complimented with the usual Salutation of, *Good morrow Mr. Bickerstaff, Good morrow my Masters all.* The Silence and Darkness of the Night, disposed me to be more than ordinarily serious; and as my Attention was not drawn out among exterior Objects, by the Avocations of Sense, my Thoughts naturally fell upon my self. I was considering, amidst the Stilness of the Night, What was the proper Employment of a Thinking Being? What were the Perfections it should propose to it self? And, What the End it should aim at? My Mind is of such a particular Cast, that the Falling of a Shower of Rain, or the Whistling of Wind, at such a Time, is apt to fill my Thoughts with something awful and solemn. I was in this Disposition, when our Bellman[3] began his Midnight Homily (which he has been repeating to us every Winter Night for these Twenty Years) with the usual Exordium:

Oh! mortal Man, thou that art born in Sin!

---

[1] Though (according to Tickell) Steele assisted in this paper, it is usually credited to Addison.

[2] Virgil *Aeneid* 6. 258: "Keep off, keep off, you unsanctified ones."

[3] The town crier, who commonly voiced moral sentiments.

Sentiments of this Nature, which are in themselves just and reasonable, however debased by the Circumstances that accompany them, do not fail to produce their natural Effect in a Mind that is not perverted and depraved by wrong Notions of Gallantry, Politeness, and Ridicule. The Temper which I now found my self in, as well as the Time of the Year, put me in Mind of those Lines in *Shakespeare,* wherein, according to his agreeable Wildness of Imagination, he has wrought a Country Tradition into a beautiful Piece of Poetry. In the Tragedy of *Hamlet,* where the Ghost vanishes upon the Cock's Crowing, he[4] takes Occasion to mention its Crowing all Hours of the Night about *Christmas* Time, and to insinuate a Kind of religious Veneration for that Season.

> *It faded on the Crowing of the Cock.*
> *Some say, That ever 'gainst that Season comes*
> *Wherein our Saviour's Birth is celebrated,*
> *The Bird of Dawning singeth all Night long;*
> *And then, say they, no Spirit dares walk abroad:*
> *The Nights are wholesome, then no Planets strike,*
> *No Fairy takes, no Witch has Power to charm;*
> *So hallowed, and so gracious is the Time.*

This admirable Author, as well as the best and greatest Men of all Ages, and of all Nations, seems to have had his Mind throughly seasoned with Religion, as is evident by many Passages in his Plays, that would not be suffered by a modern Audience; and are therefore certain Instances,[5] that the Age he lived in had a much greater Sense of Virtue than the present.

It is indeed a melancholy Reflection to consider, That the *British* Nation, which is now at a greater Height of Glory for its Councils and Conquests than it ever was before, should distinguish it self by a certain Looseness of Principles, and a Falling off from those Schemes of Thinking, which conduce to the Happiness and Perfection of humane Nature. This Evil comes upon us from the Works of a few solemn Blockheads, that meet together with the Zeal and Seriousness of Apostles, to extirpate common Sense, and

---

[4] The antecedent is Shakespeare. The speech is that of Marcellus in *Hamlet,* act 1, sc. 1.

[5] Demonstrable examples.

propagate Infidelity. These are the Wretches, who, without any Show of Wit, Learning, or Reason, publish their crude Conceptions with an Ambition of appearing more wise than the rest of Mankind, upon no other Pretence, than that of dissenting from them.[6] One gets by Heart a Catalogue of Title Pages and Editions; and immediately to become conspicuous, declares that he is an Unbeliever. Another knows how to write a Receipt, or cut up a Dog, and forthwith argues against the Immortality of the Soul. I have known many a little Wit, in the Ostentation of his Parts, rally the Truth of the Scripture, who was not able to read a Chapter in it. These poor Wretches talk Blasphemy for want of Discourse, and are rather the Objects of Scorn or Pity, than of our Indignation; but the grave Disputant, that reads and writes, and spends all his Time in convincing himself and the World, that he is no better than a Brute, ought to be whipped out of a Government, as a Blot to a civil Society, and a Defamer of Mankind. I love to consider an Infidel, whether distinguished by the Title of Deist,[7] Atheist, or Free-Thinker, in Three different Lights, in his Solitudes, his Afflictions, and his last Moments.

A wise Man, that lives up to the Principles of Reason and Virtue, if one considers him in his Solitude, as taking in the System of the Universe, observing the mutual Dependence and Harmony, by which the whole Frame of it hangs together, beating down his Passions, or swelling his Thoughts with magnificent Idea's of Providence, makes a nobler Figure in the Eye of an intelligent Being, than the greatest Conqueror amidst all the Pomps and Solemnities of a Triumph. On the contrary, there is not a more ridiculous Animal[8] than an Atheist in his Retirement. His Mind is incapable of Rapture or Elevation: He can only consider himself as an insignificant Figure in a Landskip, and wandring up and

[6] Regularly Addison satirized atheists as being ignorant rather than wicked. See *Tatler* No. 158.

[7] Deists advocated natural religion based on human reason, denying that the Creator participated in the temporal course of events. Because they rejected revelation, they were often classed with atheists and freethinkers.

[8] This imagery is intended to show that, if the atheist is correct in his belief, he is proclaiming himself to be nothing more than an animal. He is equated with a beast wandering in the field.

down in a Field or a Meadow, under the same Terms as the meanest Animals about him, and as subject to as total a Mortality as
they, with this Aggravation, That he is the only one amongst 'em
who lies under the Apprehension of it.

In Distresses, he must be of all Creatures the most helpless and
forlorn; he feels the whole Pressure of a present Calamity, without being relieved by the Memory of any Thing that is passed, or
the Prospect of any Thing that is to come. Annihilation is the
greatest Blessing that he proposes to himself, and an Halter or a
Pistol the only Refuge he can fly to. But if you would behold one
of these Gloomy Miscreants in his poorest Figure, you must consider him under the Terrors, or at the Approach, of Death.

About Thirty Years ago I was a Shipboard with one of these
Vermin, when there arose a brisk Gale, which could frighten no
Body but himself. Upon the Rowling of the Ship he fell upon his
Knees, and confessed to the Chaplain, that he had been a vile
Atheist, and had denied a Supreme Being ever since he came to[9]
his Estate. The good Man was astonished, and a Report immediately ran thro' the Ship, That there was an Atheist upon the Up-
per-Deck. Several of the common Seamen, who had never heard
the Word before, thought it had been some strange Fish; but they
were more surprised when they saw it was a Man, and heard out
of his own Mouth, That he never believed till that Day that there
was a God. As he lay in the Agonies of Confession, one of the honest Tarrs whispered to the Boatswain, That it would be a good
Deed to heave him over Board. But we were now within Sight of
Port, when of a sudden the Wind fell, and the Penitent relapsed,
begging all of us that were present, as we were Gentlemen, not to
say any Thing of what had passed.

He had not been ashore above Two Days, when one of the
Company began to rally him upon his Devotion on Shipboard,
which the other denied in so high Terms, that it produced the
Lie[10] on both Sides, and ended in a Duel. The Atheist was run

---

[9] Inherited.

[10] A common feature of quarrels preceding a duel was the phrase "You
lie." This was considered a direct attack on one's honor, and either a man responded by challenging a duel or he bore the reputation of a coward. See
Spectator No. 99 and n. 6.

through the Body, and after some Loss of Blood, became as good a Christian as he was at Sea, till he found that his Wound was not mortal. He is at present one of the Free-Thinkers of the Age, and now writing a Pamphlet against several received Opinions concerning the Existence of Fairies.

As I have taken upon me to censure the Faults of the Age and Country which I live in, I should have thought my self inexcusable to have passed over this Crying one, which is the Subject of my present Discourse. I shall therefore from Time to Time give my Countrymen particular Cautions against this Distemper of the Mind, that is almost become fashionable, and by that Means more likely to spread. I have somewhere either read or heard a very memorable Sentence, That a Man would be a most insupportable Monster, should he have the Faults that are incident to his Years, Constitution, Profession, Family, Religion, Age, and Country; and yet every Man is in Danger of them all.[11] For this Reason, as I am an old Man, I take particular Care to avoid being covetous, and telling long Stories: As I am Cholerick, I forbear not only Swearing, but all Interjections of Fretting, as Pugh! Pish! and the like. As I am a Layman, I resolve not to conceive an Aversion for a wise and a good Man, because his Coat is of a different Colour from mine. As I am descended of the ancient Family of the *Bickerstaffs,* I never call a Man of Merit an Upstart. As a Protestant, I do not suffer my Zeal so far to transport me, as to name the Pope and the Devil together. As I am fallen into this degenerate Age, I guard my self particularly against the Folly I have been now speaking of. And as I am an *Englishman,* I am very cautious not to hate a Stranger, or despise a poor *Palatine.*[12]

[11] This paragraph is more meaningful if one remembers that, during most of the preceding century, England had been subject to war, revolution, religious persecution, political calumny, etc.

[12] See *Tatler* No. 60, n. 17.

The Tatler, No. 132

From Thursd. Feb. 9. to Saturd. Feb. 11. 1709.

[Steele]

Habeo Senectuti magnam Gratiam, quae mihi Sermonis aviditatem auxit, Potionis & Cibi sustulil. Tull de Sen.[1]

Sheer-Lane, February 10.

After having applied my Mind with more than ordinary Attention to my Studies, it is my usual Custom to relax and unbend it in the Conversation of such as are rather easy than shining Companions. This I find particularly necessary for me before I retire to Rest, in order to draw my Slumbers upon me by Degrees, and fall asleep insensibly. This is the particular Use I make of a Set of heavy[2] honest Men, with whom I have passed many Hours with much Indolence, though not with great Pleasure. Their Conversation is a kind of Preparative for Sleep: It takes the Mind down from its Abstractions, leads it into the familiar Traces of Thought, and lulls it into that State of Tranquility, which is the Condition of a thinking Man when he is but half awake. After this, my Reader will not be surprised to hear the Account which I am about to give of a Club of my own Contemporaries,[3] among whom I pass Two or Three Hours every Evening. This I look upon as taking my first Nap before I go to Bed. The Truth of it is, I should

---

[1] Cicero *De Senectute* 46: "I am much beholden to old age, which has increased my eagerness for conversation in proportion as it has lessened my appetites of hunger and thirst."

[2] Dull, slow-witted.

[3] The Club—with members paralleling Sir Roger de Coverly, Captain Sentry, and Will Honeycomb—bears an obvious resemblance to the Spectator Club which was created a year later.

think my self unjust to Posterity, as well as to the Society at the *Trumpet*,[4] of which I am a Member, did not I in some Part of my Writings give an Account of the Persons among whom I have passed almost a Sixth Part of my Time for these last Forty Years. Our Club consisted originally of Fifteen; but partly by the Severity of the Law in arbitrary Times,[5] and partly by the natural Effects of old Age, we are at present reduced to a Third Part of that Number: In which however we have this Consolation, That the best Company is said to consist of Five Persons. I must confess, besides the aforementioned Benefit which I meet with in the Conversation of this select Society, I am not the less pleased with the Company, in that I find my self the greatest Wit among them, and am heard as their Oracle in all Points of Learning and Difficulty.

Sir *Jeoffrey Notch*, who is the oldest of the Club, has been in Possession of the Right Hand Chair Time out of Mind, and is the only Man among us that has the Liberty of stirring the Fire. This our Foreman is a Gentleman of an ancient Family, that came to a great Estate some Years before he had Discretion, and run it out in Hounds, Horses, and Cock-fighting; for which Reason he looks upon himself as an honest worthy Gentleman who has had Misfortunes in the World, and calls every thriving Man a pitiful Upstart.

Major *Matchlock* is the next Senior, who served in the last Civil Wars, and has all the Battles by Heart. He does not think any Action in *Europe* worth talking of since the Fight of *Marston Moor;*[6] and every Night tells us of his having been knock'd off his Horse at the Rising of the *London* 'Prentices;[7] for which he is in great Esteem amongst us.

Honest old *Dick Reptile* is the Third of our Society: He is a good natured indolent Man, who speaks little himself, but laughs

4 See *Tatler* No. 89, n. 16.

5 See *Tatler* No. 111, n. 11.

6 The battle in Yorkshire (July, 1644) in which the Royalists were routed by Parliamentarian forces.

7 In July 1647, London apprentices, carrying a petition, forced their way into the House of Commons. One can appreciate the aged character of the Club by recognizing that Major Matchlock is recalling events which occurred sixty-five years earlier.

at our Jokes, and brings his young Nephew along with him, a Youth of Eighteen Years old, to show him good Company, and give him a Tast of the World. This young Fellow sits generally silent; but whenever he opens his Mouth, or laughs at any Thing that passes, he is constantly told by his Uncle, after a jocular Manner, "Ay, ay, *Jack,* you young Men think us Fools; but we old Men know you are."

The greatest Wit of our Company, next to my self, is a Bencher[8] of the neighbouring Inn, who in his Youth frequented the Ordinaries[9] about *Charing-Cross,* and pretends to have been intimate with *Jack Ogle.*[10] He has about Ten Distichs of *Hudibras*[11] without Book, and never leaves the Club till he has applied them all. If any modern Wit be mentioned, or any Town Frolick spoken of, he shakes his Head at the Dulness of the present Age, and tells us a Story of *Jack Ogle.*

For my own Part, I am esteemed among them, because they see I am something respected by others, though at the same Time I understand by their Behaviour, that I am considered by them as a Man of a great deal of Learning, but no Knowledge of the World; insomuch that the Major sometimes, in the Height of his Military Pride, calls me the Philosopher: And Sir *Jeoffrey* no longer ago than last Night, upon a Dispute what Day of the Month it was then in *Holland,*[12] pulled his Pipe out of his Mouth, and cried, What does the Scholar say to it?

Our Club meets precisely at Six a Clock in the Evening; but I did not come last Night till Half an Hour after Seven, by which Means I escaped the Battle of *Naseby,*[13] which the Major usually begins at about Three Quarters after Six; I found also, that my

8 One of the senior members of the Inns of Court, who form for each Inn a self-elective body.

9 Taverns or eating houses.

10 A famous gentleman of the previous century, given to duels, pranks, and general extravagance. He served in a troop of foot guards, under the Duke of Monmouth.

11 Samuel Butler's famous poem (1663, 1664, 1678) satirizing the puritans. A distich is a strophic unit of two lines.

12 See *Tatler* No. 1, n. 18.

13 Naseby is a village in Northamptonshire, site of Cromwell's victory over the royalists in June, 1645.

good Friend, the Bencher, had already spent Three of his Distichs, and only waiting an Opportunity to hear a Sermon spoken of, that he might introduce the Couplet where *a-Stick* rhimes to *Ecclesiastick*.[14] At my Entrance into the Room, they were naming a red Petticoat and a Cloak, by which I found that the Bencher had been diverting them with a Story of *Jack Ogle*.[15]

I had no sooner taken my Seat, but Sir *Jeoffrey*, to show his good Will towards me, gave me a Pipe of his own Tobacco, and stirred up the Fire. I look upon it as a Point of Morality, to be obliged by those who endeavour to oblige me; and therefore in Requital for his Kindness, and to set the Conversation a going, I took the best Occasion I could, to put him upon telling us the Story of old *Gantlett*, which he always does with very particular Concern. He traced up his Descent on both Sides for several Generations,[16] describing his Diet and Manner of Life, with his several Battles, and particularly that in which he fell. This *Gantlett* was a Game-Cock, upon whose Head the Knight in his Youth had won Five Hundred Pounds, and lost Two Thousand. This naturally set the Major upon the Account of *Edge-hill* Fight,[17] and ended in a Duel of *Jack Ogle*'s.

Old *Reptile* was extremely attentive to all that was said, tho' it was the same he had heard every Night for these Twenty Years, and upon all Occasions, winked upon his Nephew to mind what passed.

This may suffice to give the World a Tast of our innocent Conversation, which we spun out till about Ten of the Clock, when my Maid came with a Lanthorn to light me Home.[18] I could not

14 *Hudibras,* part I, canto I, lines 11–12.

15 Having pawned his trooper's cloak, Jack Ogle once appeared in a review with his landlady's red petticoat rolled up behind him. The Duke of Monmouth detected the substitution and gave order to "cloak all." Ogle, with some hesitation, complied, declaring that although he had no cloak, he would petticoat with the best of them.

16 In *The Conscious Lovers* (1722), Steele ridicules Sir John Bevil's excessive concern for family status, by having Mr. Sealand give the genealogy of his game-cocks. (act 4, sc. 2.)

17 The first battle of the Civil War, October 23, 1642.

18 London streets were poorly lighted and it was unsafe to walk them in the dark.

but reflect with my self as I was going out upon the talkative Humour of old Men, and the little Figures which that Part of Life makes in one who cannot employ this natural Propensity in Discourses which would make him venerable. I must own, it makes me very melancholy in Company, when I hear a young Man begin a Story; and have often observed, That one of a Quarter of an Hour long in a Man of Five and twenty, gathers Circumstances every Time he tells it, till it grows into a long *Canterbury* Tale of two Hours by that Time he is Threescore.

The only Way of avoiding such a trifling and frivolous old Age, is, to lay up in our Way to it such Stores of Knowledge and Observation as may make us useful and agreeable in our declining Years. The Mind of Man in a long Life will become a Magazine of Wisdom or Folly, and will consequently discharge it self in something impertinent or improving. For which Reason, as there is nothing more ridiculous than an old trifling Story-Teller, so there is nothing more venerable than one who has turned his Experience to the Entertainment and Advantage of Mankind.

In short, we who are in the last Stage of Life, and are apt to indulge our selves in Talk, ought to consider, if what we speak be worth being heard, and endeavour to make our Discourse like that of *Nestor,* which *Homer* compares to the Flowing of Honey for its Sweetness.[19]

I am afraid I shall be thought guilty of this Excess I am speaking of, when I cannot conclude without observing, that *Milton* certainly thought of this Passage in *Homer,* when in his Description of an eloquent Spirit, he says, *His Tongue drop'd Manna.*[20]

---

[19] Homer *Iliad* 1. 249.

[20] In *Paradise Lost* 2. 112–114, Milton describes Belial:

> "But all was false and hollow; though his tongue
> Dropped manna, and could make the worse appear
> The better reason . . ."

Clearly, Steele did not intend to consider the whole of the quotation.

The Tatler, No. 133

From Saturd. Feb. 11. to Tuesd. Feb. 14. 1709.

[Addison]

Dum Tacent, Clamant. Tull.[1]

Sheer-Lane, February 13.

Silence is sometimes more significant and sublime than the most noble and most expressive Eloquence, and is on many Occasions the Indication of a great Mind. Several Authors have treated of Silence as a Part of Duty and Discretion, but none of them have considered it in this Light. *Homer* compares the Noise and Clamour of the *Trojans* advancing towards the Enemy, to the Cackling of Cranes when they invade an Army of Pigmies.[2] On the contrary, he makes his Countrymen and Favourites, the *Greeks,* move forward in a regular determined March, and in the Depth of Silence. I find in the Accounts which are given us of some of the more *Eastern* Nations, where the Inhabitants[3] are disposed by their Constitutions and Climates to higher Strains of Thought, and more elevated Raptures than what we feel in the *Northern* Regions of the World, That Silence is a Religious Exercise among them. For when their publick Devotions are in the greatest Fervour, and their Hearts lifted up as high as Words can raise them, there are certain Suspensions of Sound and Motion for a Time, in which the Mind is left to it self, and supposed to swell with such secret Conceptions as are too big for Utterance. I have my self been wonderfully delighted with a Master-Piece of Musick,

1 Cicero: "Their silence pleads aloud."
2 Homer *Iliad* 3. 3.
3 Presumably, oriental mystics.

when in the very Tumult and Ferment of their Harmony, all the
Voices and Instruments have stopped short on a sudden, and after
a little Pause recovered themselves again as it were, and renewed
the Concert in all its Parts. Methoughts this short Interval of Silence has had more Musick in it than any the same Space of Time
before or after it. There are Two Instances of Silence in the Two
greatest Poets that ever wrote, which have something in them as
sublime as any of the Speeches in their whole Works. The First is
that of *Ajax,* in the Eleventh Book of the *Odyssy.*[4] *Ulysses,* who
had been the Rival of this great Man in his Life, as well as the
Occasion of his Death, upon meeting his Shade in the Region of
departed Heroes, makes his Submission to him with an Humility
next to Adoration, which the other passes over with dumb sullen
Majesty, and such a Silence, as (to use the Words of *Longinus*) had
more Greatness in it than any Thing he could have spoken.[5]

The next Instance I shall mention is in *Virgil,* where the Poet,
doubtless, imitates this Silence of *Ajax* in that of *Dido;*[6] though I
do not know that any of his Commentators have taken Notice of
it. *Aeneas* finding among the Shades of despairing Lovers, the
Ghost of her who had lately died for him, with the Wound still
fresh upon her, addresses himself to her with expanded Arms,
Floods of Tears, and the most passionate Professions of his own
Innocence as to what had happen'd; all which *Dido* receives with
the Dignity and Disdain of a resenting Lover, and an injured
Queen; and is so far from vouchsafing him an Answer, that she
does not give him a single Look. The Poet represents her as turning away her Face from him while he spoke to her; and after having kept her Eyes for some time upon the Ground, as one that
heard and contemned his Protestations, flying from him into the
Grove of Myrtle, and into the Arms of another,[7] whose Fidelity
had deserved her Love.

I have often thought our Writers of Tragedy have been very
defective in this Particular, and that they might have given great
Beauty to their Works, by certain Stops and Pauses in the Repre-

---

4 Homer *Odyssey* 11. 543–567.
5 Longinus *On the Sublime* 9. 2–3.
6 Virgil *Aeneid* 6.469–471.
7 Sychaeus, Dido's husband, who died before she met Aeneas.

sentation of such Passions, as it is not in the Power of Language to express. There is something like this in the last Act of *Venice Preserved*,[8] where *Pierre* is brought to an infamous Execution, and begs of his Friend,[9] as a Reparation for past Injuries, and the only Favour he could do him, to rescue him from the Ignominy of the Wheel[10] by stabbing him. As he is going to make this dreadful Request, he is not able to communicate it, but withdraws his Face from his Friend's Ear, and bursts into Tears. The melancholy Silence that follows hereupon, and continues till he has recovered himself enough to reveal his Mind to his Friend, raises in the Spectators a Grief that is inexpressible, and an Idea of such a complicated Distress in the Actor, as Words cannot utter. It would look as ridiculous to many Readers to give Rules and Directions for proper Silences, as for *Penning a Whisper:* But it is certain, that in the Extremity of most Passions, particularly Surprise, Admiration, Astonishment; nay, Rage it self; there is nothing more graceful than to see the Play stand still for a few Moments, and the Audience fixed in an agreeable Suspence during the Silence of a skilful Actor.

But Silence never shows it self to so great an Advantage, as when it is made the Reply to Calumny and Defamation, provided that we give no just Occasion for them. One might produce an Example of it in the Behaviour of one in whom it appear'd in all its Majesty, and one, whose Silence, as well as his Person, was altogether Divine.[11] When one considers this Subject only in its Sublimity, this great Instance could not but occur to me; and since I only make Use of it to show the highest Example of it, I hope I do not offend in it. To forbear replying to an unjust Reproach, and overlook it with a generous, or (if possible) with an entire Neglect of it, is one of the most heroick Acts of a great Mind. And I must confess, when I reflect upon the Behaviour of some of the greatest Men in Antiquity, I do not so much admire them that they deserved the Praise of the whole Age they lived in, as because they contemned the Envy and Detraction of it.

8 A tragedy (1682) by Thomas Otway (1652–1685). The incident occurs in act V, sc. 3.

9 Jaffeir.

10 The torture rack used for stretching a victim.

11 The reference is, of course, to Jesus Christ.

All that is incumbent on a Man of Worth, who suffers under so ill a Treatment, is to lie by for some Time in Silence and Obscurity, till the Prejudice of the Times be over, and his Reputation cleared. I have often read with a great deal of Pleasure a Legacy of the famous Lord *Bacon*,[12] one of the greatest Genius's that our own or any Country has produced: After having bequeathed his Soul, Body, and Estate, in the usual Form, he adds, "My Name and Memory I leave to Foreign Nations, and to my Countrymen, after some Time be passed over."

At the same Time that I recommend this Philosophy to others, I must confess, I am so poor a Proficient in it my self, that if in the Course of my Lucubrations it happens, as it has done more than once, that my Paper is duller than in Conscience it ought to be, I think the Time an Age till I have an Opportunity of putting out another, and growing famous again for Two Days.

I must not close my Discourse upon Silence, without informing my Reader, That I have by me an elaborate Treatise on the *Aposiopesis*[13] call'd an *Et caetera,* it being a Figure much used by some learned Authors, and particularly by the great *Littleton,* who, as my Lord Chief Justice *Coke* observes, had a most admirable Talent at an *&c.*[14]

ADVERTISEMENT

To oblige the Pretty Fellows, and my Fair Readers,[15] I have thought fit to insert the whole Passage above-mentioned relating to *Dido,* as it is translated by Mr. *Dryden.*[16]

> *Not far from thence, the mournful Fields appear;*
> *So call'd, from Lovers that inhabit there.*
> *The Souls, whom that unhappy Flame invades,*

[12] Sir Francis Bacon (1561–1626), English philosopher and statesman. See *Tatler* No. 267.

[13] The leaving of a thought incomplete. There are amusing implications in mentioning this "elaborate Treatise" in an essay on the sublimity of silence.

[14] In the preface to his *Institutes of the Laws of England; of a Commentary upon Littleton* (1628), Sir Edward Coke (1552–1634) writes, "Certain it is, that there is never a period, nor (for the most part) a word, nor an &c., but affordeth excellent matter of learning."

[15] The beaux and the fashionable ladies, who tended to be bright, witty, and unlettered.

[16] Dryden's translation of the *Aeneid* appeared in 1697.

In secret Solitude, and Myrtle Shades,
Make endless Moans, and pining with Desire,
Lament too late their unextinguish'd Fire.
Here Procris, Eryphile *here, he found*
Baring her Breast, yet bleeding with the Wound
Made by her Son. He saw Pasiphae *there,*
With Phaedra's *Ghost, a foul incestuous Pair;*
There Laodamia *with* Evadne *moves:*
Unhappy both, but loyal in their Loves.
Caeneus, *a Woman once, and once a Man;*
But ending in the Sex she first began.
Not far from these, Phoenician Dido *stood;*
Fresh from her Wound, her Bosom bath'd in Blood.
Whom, when the Trojan *Hero hardly knew,*
Obscure in Shades, and with a doubtful View,
(Doubtful as he who runs thro' dusky Night,
Or thinks he sees the Moon's uncertain Light:)
With Tears he first approach'd the sullen Shade;
And, as his Love inspir'd him, thus he said:
Unhappy Queen! Then is the common Breath
Of Rumour true, in your reported Death;
And I, alas, the Cause! By Heav'n, I vow
And all the Pow'rs that rule the Realms below,
Unwilling I forsook your friendly State,
Commanded by the Gods, and forc'd by Fate.
Those Gods, that Fate, whose unresisted Might,
Have sent me to these Regions, void of Light,
Thro' the vast Empire of eternal Night.
Nor dar'd I to presume, that, press'd with Grief,
My Flight should urge you to this dire Relief.
Stay, stay your Steps, and listen to my Vows;
'Tis the last Interview that Fate allows!
In vain he thus attempts her Mind to move,
With Tears and Pray'rs, and late repenting Love.
Disdainfully she look'd, then turning round;
But fix'd her Eyes unmov'd upon the Ground;
And, what he says, and swears, regards no more,
Than the deaf Rocks, when the loud Billows roar.
But whirl'd away, to shun his hateful sight,
Hid in the Forrest, and the Shades of Night.
Then sought Sicheus *thro' the shady Grove,*
Who answer'd all her Cares, and equal'd all **her Love.**

The Tatler, No. 155

From Tuesday April 4. to Thursday April 6. 1710.

[Addison]

—*Aliena Negotia curat Excussus propriis*—Hor.[1]

From my own Apartment, April 5.

There lived some Years since within my Neighbourhood a very grave Person, an Upholsterer,[2] who seemed a Man of more than ordinary Application to Business. He was a very early Riser, and was often abroad Two or Three Hours before any of his Neighbours. He had a particular Carefulness in the knitting of his Brows, and a kind of Impatience in all his Motions, that plainly discovered he was always intent on Matters of Importance. Upon my Enquiry into his Life and Conversation, I found him to be the greatest Newsmonger in our Quarter; that he rose before Day to read the *Post-Man*;[3] and that he would take Two or Three Turns to the other End of the Town before his Neighbours were up, to see if there were any *Dutch* Mails[4] come in. He had a Wife and several Children; but was much more inquisitive to know what passed in *Poland* than in his own Family, and was in greater Pain and Anxiety of Mind for King *Augustus*'s Welfare[5] than that

1 Horace *2 Satires* 3. 19: "He looks after other people's business after having been flung overboard from his own."

2 The original of the political upholsterer (who also appears in *Tatlers* No. 160, 178, and 232) is said to have been an Edward Arne, of Covent Garden.

3 See *Tatler* No. 18, n. 21.

4 News—particularly of political and military events—from the continent.

5 Augustus II (1670–1733), King of Poland from 1697, was deposed by King Charles XII of Sweden but was restored to the throne after Charles's defeat at Poltava in 1709 by Peter the Great.

of his nearest Relations. He looked extremely thin in a Dearth of News, and never enjoyed himself in a Westerly Wind.[6] This indefatigable kind of Life was the Ruin of his Shop; for about the Time that his Favourite Prince left the Crown of *Poland*, he broke[7] and disappeared.

This Man and his Affairs had been long out of my Mind, till about Three Days ago, as I was walking in St. *James*'s Park, I heard some body at a Distance hemming after me: And who should it be but my old Neighbour the Upholsterer? I saw he was reduced to extreme Poverty, by certain shabby Superfluities in his Dress: For notwithstanding that it was a very sultry Day for the Time of the Year, he wore a loose great Coat and a Muff, with a long Campaign-Whig[8] out of Curl; to which he had added the Ornament of a Pair of black Garters buckled under the Knee. Upon his coming up to me, I was going to enquire into his present Circumstances; but was prevented by his asking me, with a Whisper, Whether the last Letters brought any Accounts that one might rely upon from *Bender?*[9] I told him, None that I heard of; and asked him, Whether he had yet married his eldest Daughter? He told me, No. But pray, says he, tell me sincerely, What are your Thoughts of the King of *Sweden?* For tho' his Wife and Children were starving, I found his chief Concern at present was for this great Monarch. I told him, That I looked upon him as one of the first Heroes of the Age. But pray, says he, do you think there is any Thing in the Story of his Wound? And finding me surprised at the Question, Nay, says he, I only propose it to you. I answered, That I thought there was no Reason to doubt of it. But why in the Heel, says he, more than in any other Part of the Body? Because, says I, the Bullet chanced to light there.

This extraordinary Dialogue was no sooner ended, but he began to launch out into a long Dissertation upon the Affairs of the

6 News from Europe came on sailing ships, which required an east wind.

7 Went bankrupt.

8 A full, curled wig imported from France at the time of Marlborough's campaigns.

9 The Turkish city to which Charles XII (1682–1718) fled after his defeat at Poltava. (See Johnson's *The Vanity of Human Wishes*, lines 191–222.) At Poltava, Charles received a musket ball in the heel.

North; and after having spent some Time on them, he told me, He was in a great Perplexity how to reconcile the *Supplement* with the *English-Post,*[10] and had been just now examining what the other Papers say upon the same Subject.[11] The *Daily-Courant,* says he, has these Words, *We have Advices from very good Hands, That a certain Prince has some Matters of great Importance under Consideration.* This is very mysterious; but the *Post-Boy* leaves us more in the Dark, for he tells us, *That there are private Intimations of Measures taken by a certain Prince, which Time will bring to Light.* Now the *Post-Man,* says he, who uses to be very clear, refers to the same News in these Words; *The late Conduct of a certain Prince affords great Matter of Speculation.* This certain Prince, says the Upholsterer, whom they are all so cautious of naming, I take to be—Upon which, tho' there was no body near us, he whispered something in my Ear, which I did not hear, or think worth my while to make him repeat.

We were now got to the upper End of the *Mall,* where were Three or Four very odd Fellows sitting together upon the Bench. These I found were all of them Politicians, who used to Sun themselves in that Place every Day about Dinner-Time. Observing them to be Curiosities in their Kind, and my Friend's Acquaintance, I sat down among them.

The chief Politician of the Bench was a great Asserter of Paradoxes. He told us, with a seeming Concern, That by some News he had lately read from *Muscovy,*[12] it appeared to him that there was a Storm gathering in the Black Sea, which might in Time do Hurt to the Naval Forces of this Nation. To this he added, That for his Part, he could not wish to see the Turk driven out of *Europe,* which he believed could not but be prejudicial to our Woollen Manufacture. He then told us, That he looked upon those ex-

---

[10] *The Supplement* was a Tory paper published from 1708 to 1712. *The English Post* was a paper edited by Richard Burton (1632?–1725?) under the pseudonym Nathaniel Crouch. For the other newspapers mentioned, see *Tatler* No. 18, notes 21 and 29.

[11] The political speculation here, like the "Paradoxes" and the "Discourse at length" which follow, mean about as much to the modern reader as they do to Bickerstaff.

[12] The name of the principality of Moscow applied to Russia generally.

traordinary Revolutions which had lately happened in these Parts of the World, to have risen chiefly from Two Persons who were not much talked of; and those, says he, are Prince *Menzikoff*,[13] and the Dutchess of *Mirandola*.[14] He back'd his Assertions with so many broken Hints, and such a Show of Depth and Wisdom, that we gave our selves up to his Opinions.

The Discourse at length fell upon a Point which seldom escapes a Knot[15] of true-born *Englishmen*, Whether in Case of a Religious War, the Protestants would not be too strong for the Papists? This we unanimously determined on the Protestant Side. One who sat on my Right Hand, and, as I found by his Discourse, had been in the *West-Indies*, assured us, That it would be a very easie Matter for the Protestants to beat the Pope at Sea; and added, That whenever such a War does break out, it must turn to the Good of the *Leeward* Islands.[16] Upon this, one who sat at the End of the Bench, and, as I afterwards found, was the Geographer of the Company, said, That in case the Papists should drive the Protestants from these Parts of *Europe,* when the worst came to the worst, it would be impossible to beat them out of *Norway* and *Greenland,* provided the Northern Crowns hold together, and the Czar of *Muscovy* stand Neuter.

He further told us for our Comfort, That there were vast Tracts of Land about the Pole, inhabited neither by Protestants nor Papists, and of greater Extent than all the *Roman* Catholick Dominions in *Europe.*

When we had fully discussed this Point, my Friend the Upholsterer began to exert himself upon the present Negotiations of Peace,[17] in which he deposed Princes, settled the Bounds of Kingdoms, and ballanced the Power of *Europe,* with great Justice and Impartiality.

I at length took my Leave of the Company, and was going away; but had not been gone Thirty Yards, before the Upholsterer

---

13 Alexander Menzikoff (1672–1729), Prince of the Russian Empire.

14 Mirandola was a duchy in northeast Italy, which allied itself with France in the war.

15 Group.

16 A northern chain of islands in the West Indies.

17 See *Tatler* No. 18, n. 18.

hemm'd again after me. Upon his advancing towards me, with a Whisper, I expected to hear some secret Piece of News, which he had not thought fit to communicate to the Bench; but instead of that, he desired me in my Ear to lend him Half a Crown. In Compassion to so needy a Statesman, and to dissipate the Confusion I found he was in, I told him, if he pleased, I would give him Five Shillings, to receive Five Pounds of him when the Great Turk was driven out of *Constantinople;* which he very readily accepted, but not before he had laid down to me the Impossibility of such an Event, as the Affairs of *Europe* now stand.[18]

This Paper I design for the particular Benefit of those worthy Citizens who live more in a Coffee-house than in their Shops, and whose Thoughts are so taken up with the Affairs of the Allies, that they forget their Customers.

---

[18] The Upholsterer's wager is a good one. The Ottoman sultans were not driven from Constantinople until 1922.

The Tatler, No. 158

From Tuesd. April 11. to Thursd. April 13. 1710.

[Addison]

Faciunt nae intelligendo, ut nihil intelligant. Ter.[1]

From my own Apartment, April 12.

Tom Folio[2] is a Broker in Learning, employed to get together good Editions, and stock the Libraries of great Men. There is not a Sale of Books begins till *Tom Folio* is seen at the Door. There is not an Auction where his Name is not heard, and that too in the very Nick of Time, in the Critical Moment, before the last decisive Stroke of the Hammer. There is not a Subscription[3] goes forward, in which *Tom* is not privy to the first rough Draught of the Proposals; nor a Catalogue printed, that doth not come to him wet from the Press. He is an universal Scholar, so far as the Title-Page of all Authors, knows the Manuscripts in which they were discovered, the Editions through which they have passed, with the Praises or Censures which they have received from the several Members of the Learned World. He has a greater Esteem for *Aldus* and *Elzevir*,[4] than for *Virgil* and *Horace*. If you talk of

---

[1] Terence, prologue to *Andria* 1. 17: "While they pretend to know more than others, they really know nothing."

[2] The original of Tom Folio is said to be Thomas Rawlinson (1681–1725), a noted book-collector. See *Spectator* No. 542, n. 6.

[3] Books were frequently published by subscription, i.e., people were induced to pay for copies before the book's publication or to promise to purchase a specific number of copies after publication. In 1710–11, an octavo edition of *The Tatler* was published by subscription.

[4] Aldus Manutius (1450?–1515) was a famous Venetian printer of the classics. Elzivir was the name of a family of Dutch printers of the early seventeenth century.

Herodotus, he breaks out into a Panegyrick upon *Harry Steph-
ans.*[5] He thinks he gives you an Account of an Author, when he
tells you the Subject he treats of, the Name of the Editor, and the
Year in which it was printed. Or if you draw him into further Par-
ticulars, he cries up the Goodness of the Paper, extols the Dili-
gence of the Corrector, and is transported with the Beauty of the
Letter. This he looks upon to be sound Learning and substantial
Criticism. As for those who talk of the Fineness of Style, and the
Justness of Thought, or describe the Brightness of any particular
Passages; nay, though they write themselves in the Genius and
Spirit of the Author they admire, *Tom* looks upon them as Men
of superficial Learning, and flashy Parts.[6]

I had Yesterday Morning a Visit from this learned Idiot, (for
that is the Light in which I consider every Pedant) when I discovered in him some little Touches of the Coxcomb, which I had
not before observed. Being very full of the Figure which he makes
in the Republick of Letters, and wonderfully satisfied with his
great Stock of Knowledge, he gave me broad Intimations, that he
did not *believe* in all Points as his Forefathers had done. He then
communicated to me a Thought of a certain Author upon a Passage of *Virgil*'s Account of the Dead, which I made the Subject of
a late Paper.[7] This Thought hath taken very much among Men
of *Tom*'s Pitch and Understanding, though universally exploded
by all that know how to construe *Virgil,* or have any Relish of
Antiquity. Not to trouble my Reader with it, I found upon the
whole, that *Tom* did not believe a future State of Rewards and
Punishments, because *Aeneas,* at his leaving the Empire of the
Dead, passed through the Gate of Ivory, and not through that of
Horn.[8] Knowing that *Tom* had not Sense enough to give up an
Opinion which he had once received, that he might avoid wran-
gling, I told him, That *Virgil* possibly had his Oversights as well
as another Author. Ah! Mr. *Bickerstaff,* says he, you would have

---

[5] Herodotus was a Greek historian of the fifth century, B.C. "Harry Steph-
ans" is a familiar reference to Henri Estienne (1528–1598), a French printer of
the classics, one of a distinguished family of printers.

[6] Natural abilities.

[7] *Tatler* No. 154.

[8] The episode occurs in book 6, lines 893f.

another Opinion of him, if you would read him in *Daniel Heinsius*'s Edition.[9] I have perused him my self several Times in that Edition, continued he; and after the strictest and most malicious Examination, could find but Two Faults in him: One of them is in the *Aeneids,* where there are Two Comma's instead of a Parenthesis; and another in the Third *Georgick,* where you may find a Semicolon turned upside down. Perhaps, said I, these were not *Virgil*'s Thoughts, but those of the Transcriber. I do not design it, says *Tom,* as a Reflection on *Virgil:* On the contrary, I know that all the Manuscripts *reclaim*[10] against such a Punctuation. Oh! Mr. *Bickerstaff,* says he, what would a Man give to see one Simile of *Virgil* writ in his own Hand? I asked him which was the Simile he meant; but was answered, Any Simile in *Virgil.* He then told me all the secret History in the Commonwealth of Learning; of Modern Pieces that had the Names of ancient Authors annex'd to them; of all the Books that were now writing or printing in the several Parts of *Europe;* of many Amendments which are made, and not yet published; and a Thousand other Particulars, which I would not have my Memory burthen'd with for a Vatican.[11]

At length, being fully perswaded that I thoroughly admired him, and looked upon him as a Prodigy of Learning, he took his Leave. I know several of *Tom*'s Class who are professed Admirers of *Tasso*[12] without understanding a Word of *Italian;* and one in particular, that carries a *Pastor-Fido*[13] in his Pocket, in which I am sure he is acquainted with no other Beauty but the Clearness of the Character.[14]

There is another Kind of Pedant, who, with all *Tom Folio*'s Impertinencies, hath greater Super-structures and Embellishments of *Greek* and *Latin,* and is still more insupportable than the other, in the same Degree as he is more learned. Of this Kind very often

[9] Daniel Hensius (1580–1655), a Dutch classical scholar, produced a well-known edition of Virgil in 1636.

[10] Protest.

[11] I.e., the Vatican library.

[12] Torquato Tasso (1544–1595), an Italian Renaissance poet.

[13] A pastoral tragicomedy (1590) by the Italian poet Giovanni Battista Guarini (1538–1612).

[14] Lettering.

are Editors, Commentators, Interpreters, Scholiasts, and Criticks; and in short, all Men of deep Learning without common Sense. These Persons set a greater Value on themselves for having found out the Meaning of a Passage in *Greek,* than upon the Author for having written it; nay, will allow the Passage it self not to have any Beauty in it, at the same Time that they would be considered as the greatest Men of the Age for having interpreted it. They will look with Contempt upon the most beautiful Poems that have been composed by any of their Contemporaries; but will lock themselves up in their Studies for a Twelvemonth together, to correct, publish, and expound, such Trifles of Antiquity as a modern Author would be contemn'd for.[15] Men of the strictest Morals, severest Lives, and the gravest Professions, will write Volumes upon an idle Sonnet that is originally in *Greek* or *Latin;* give Editions of the most Immoral Authors, and spin out whole Pages upon the various Readings of a lewd Expression. All that can be said in Excuse for them, is, That their Works sufficiently show they have no Tast of their Authors; and that what they do in this Kind, is out of their great Learning, and not out of any Levity or Lasciviousness of Temper.

A Pedant of this Nature is wonderfully well described in Six Lines of *Boileau,* with which I shall conclude his Character.

> *Un Pédant enyvré de sa vaine science,*
> *Tout herisse de Grec, tout bouffi d'arrogance,*
> *Et qui de mille Auteurs retenus mot pour mot,*
> *Dans sa tête entassez n'a souvent fait qu'un Sot,*
> *Croit qu'un Livre fait tout, & que sans Aristote*
> *La Raison ne voit goute, & le bon Sens radote.*[16]

---

[15] The same criticism is leveled against the scholar Richard Bentley (1662–1742) by Swift in *The Battle of the Books* (1704) and *A Tale of a Tub* (1704), and by Pope in his *Epistle to Dr. Arbuthnot* (1735).

[16] The passage is from *Satires* (6. 5–10) by Nicolas Boileau-Despréaux (1636–1711), noted French author and critic. This is Wynne's translation:

> Brim-ful of learning see that pedant stride,
> Bristling with horrid Greek, and puffed with pride!
> A thousand authors he in vain has read,
> And with their maxims stuffed his empty head;
> And thinks that, without Aristotle's rule,
> Reason is blind, and common sense a fool.

The Tatler, No. 163

From Saturd. April 22. to Tuesd. April 25. 1710.

[Addison]

Idem Inficeto est inficetior Rure
Simul Poemata attigit; neque idem unquam
Aequé est beatus, ac Poema cum scribit;
Tam quadet in se, tamque se ipse miratur.
Nimirum idem omnes fallimur; neque est quisquam
Quem non in aliqua re videre Suffenum
Possis. — — — Catul. *de Suffeno.*[1]

Will's Coffee-house, April 24.

I yesterday came hither[2] about Two Hours before the Company generally make their Appearance, with a Design to read over all the News-Papers; but upon my sitting down, I was accosted by *Ned Softly,* who saw me from a Corner in the other End of the Room, where I found he had been writing something. Mr. *Bickerstaff,* says he, I observe by a late Paper of yours,[3] that you and I are just of a Humour; for you must know, of all Impertinencies, there is nothing which I so much hate as News. I never read a *Gazette* in my Life; and never trouble my Head about our Armies, whether they win or lose, or in what Part of the World they lie encamped. Without giving me Time to reply, he drew a Paper of Verses out of his Pocket, telling me, That he had something which

---

[1] Catullus *De Suffeno* 22. 14: "And at the same time he is never so happy as when he is writing a poem, he delights in himself and admires himself so much. True enough, we are all under the same delusion, and there is no one whom you may not see to be a Suffenus in one thing or another."

[2] I.e., to Will's.

[3] Probably *Tatler* No. 160, which reported the return of the Upholsterer.

would entertain me more agreeably, and that he would desire my Judgment upon every Line, for that we had Time enough before us till the Company came in.

Ned Softly is a very pretty Poet, and a great Admirer of easy Lines. *Waller*[4] is his Favourite: And as that admirable Writer has the best and worst Verses of any among our great *English* Poets, *Ned Softly* has got all the bad Ones without Book, which he repeats upon Occasion, to show his Reading, and garnish his Conversation. *Ned* is indeed a true *English* Reader, incapable of relishing the great and masterly Strokes of this Art; but wonderfully pleased with the little *Gothick*[5] Ornaments of Epigrammatical Conceits, Turns, Points, and Quibbles, which are so frequent in the most admired of our *English* Poets, and practised by those who want Genius and Strength to represent, after the Manner of the Ancients,[6] Simplicity in its natural Beauty and Perfection.

Finding my self unavoidably engaged in such a Conversation, I was resolved to turn my Pain into a Pleasure, and to divert my self as well as I could with so very odd a Fellow. You must understand, says *Ned,* that the Sonnet I am going to read to you was written upon a Lady, who showed me some Verses of her own making, and is perhaps the best Poet of our Age. But you shall hear it. Upon which he begun to read as follows:

To Mira, *on her incomparable Poems.*

1.

When dress'd in Lawrel Wreaths you shine,
And tune your soft melodious Notes,
You seem a Sister of the Nine,
Or Phoebus *self in Petticoats.*

2.

I fancy, when your Song you sing,
(Your Song you sing with so much Art)
Your Pen was plucked from Cupid's *Wing;*
For ah! it wounds me like his Dart.

---

4 Edmund Waller (1606–1687), English poet known for the smoothness and harmony of his verse.

5 Overelaborated, dated. Addison is criticizing the work of the seventeenth-century "metaphysical" poets.

6 The authors and critics of classical antiquity.

Why, says I, this is a little Nosegay of Conceits, a very Lump of Salt: Every Verse hath something in it that piques; and then the Dart in the last Line is certainly as pretty a Sting in the Tail of an Epigram (for so I think your Criticks call it) as ever entered into the Thought of a Poet. Dear Mr. *Bickerstaff,* says he, shaking me by the Hand, every Body knows you to be a Judge of these Things; and to tell you truly, I read over *Roscommon*'s Translation of *Horace*'s *Art of Poetry*[7] Three several Times, before I sat down to write the Sonnet which I have shown you. But you shall hear it again, and pray observe every Line of it, for not one of them shall pass without your Approbation.

> *When dress'd in Lawrel Wreaths you shine.*

That is, says he, when you have your Garland on; when you are writing Verses. To which I replied, I know your Meaning: A Metaphor! The same, said he, and went on.

> *And tune your soft melodious Notes.*

Pray observe the Gliding of that Verse; there is scarce a Consonant in it: I took Care to make it run upon Liquids. Give me your Opinion of it. Truly, said I, I think it as good as the former. I am very glad to hear you say so, says he; but mind the next.

> *You seem a Sister of the Nine.*

That is, says he, you seem a Sister of the Muses; for if you look into ancient Authors, you will find it was their Opinion, that there were Nine of them. I remember it very well, said I; but pray proceed.

> *Or* Phoebus *self in Petticoats.*

Phoebus, says he, was the God of Poetry. These little Instances, Mr. *Bickerstaff,* show a Gentleman's Reading. Then to take off from the Air of Learning, which *Phoebus* and the Muses have given to this First Stanza, you may observe, how it falls all of a sudden into the Familiar; *in Petticoats!*

> *Or* Phoebus *self in Petticoats.*

---

[7] A blank-verse translation of the *Art of Poetry* (1680) by the fourth Earl of Roscommon (1633–1685).

Let us now, says I, enter upon the Second Stanza. I find the First Line is still a Continuation of the Metaphor.

> *I fancy, when your Song you sing.*

It is very right, says he; but pray observe the Turn of Words in those Two Lines. I was a whole Hour in adjusting of them, and have still a Doubt upon me, Whether in the Second Line it should be *Your Song you sing;* or, *You sing your Song?* You shall hear them both:

> *I fancy, when your Song you sing,*
> *(Your Song you sing with so much Art.)*

OR,

> *I fancy, when your Song you sing,*
> *You sing your Song with so much Art.*

Truly, said I, the Turn is so natural either Way, that you have made me almost giddy with it. Dear Sir, said he, grasping me by the Hand, you have a great deal of Patience; but pray what do you think of the next Verse?

> *Your Pen was pluck'd from Cupid's Wing.*

Think! says I; I think you have made *Cupid* look like a little Goose. That was my Meaning, says he; I think the Ridicule is well enough hit off. But we now come to the last, which sums up the whole Matter:

> *For Ah! it wounds me like his Dart.*

Pray how do you like that *Ah!* Doth it not make a pretty Figure in that Place? *Ah!* It looks as if I felt the Dart, and cried out at being pricked with it.

> *For Ah! it wounds me like his Dart.*

My Friend *Dick Easy,*[8] continued he, assured me, he would rather have written that *Ah!* than to have been the Author of the *Aeneid.* He indeed objected, that I made *Mira's* Pen like a Quill

---

[8] Henry Cromwell (d. 1728) is thought to have been the original both of Dick Easy and of Sir Timothy Tittle, who appears in *Tatler* No. 165.

in one of the Lines, and like a Dart in the other. But as to that—
Oh! as to that, says I,[9] it is but supposing *Cupid* to be like a Por-
cupine, and his Quills and Darts will be the same Thing. He was
going to embrace me for the Hint; but half a Dozen Criticks coming into the Room, whose Faces he did not like, he conveyed the
Sonnet into his Pocket, and whispered me in the Ear, he would
show it me again as soon as his Man[10] had written it over fair.

9 I.e., Bickerstaff.
10 His servant.

The Tatler, No. 165

From Thursd. April 27. to Saturd. April 29. 1710.

[A d d i s o n]

From my own Apartment, April 28.

It has always been my Endeavour to distinguish between Realities and Appearances, and to separate true Merit from the Pretence to it. As it shall ever be my Study to make Discoveries of this Nature in Humane Life, and to settle the proper Distinctions between the Virtues and Perfections of Mankind, and those false Colours and Resemblances of them that shine alike in the Eyes of the Vulgar; so I shall be more particularly careful to search into the various Merits and Pretences of the learned World. This is the more necessary, because there seems to be a general Combination among the Pedants to extol one another's Labours, and cry up one another's Parts; while Men of Sense, either through that Modesty which is natural to them, or the Scorn they have for such trifling Commendations, enjoy their Stock of Knowledge like a hidden Treasure, with Satisfaction and Silence. Pedantry indeed in Learning is like Hypocrisy in Religion, a Form of Knowledge without the Power of it, that attracts the Eyes of the Common People, breaks out in Noise and Show, and finds its Reward not from any inward Pleasure that attends it, but from the Praises and Approbations which it receives from Men.

Of this shallow Species there is not a more importunate, empty, and conceited Animal, than that which is generally known by the Name of a Critick. This, in the common Acceptation of the Word, is one that, without entering into the Sense and Soul of an Author, has a few general Rules, which, like mechanical Instruments, he applies to the Works of every Writer, and as they quadrate[1] with them, pronounces the Author perfect or defective. He is Master of a certain Set of Words, as Unity, Style, Fire, Flegm, Easy, Natural, Turn, Sentiment, and the like; which he varies, compounds, divides, and throws together, in every Part of his Discourse, without any Thought or Meaning. The Marks you may know him by are, an elevated Eye, and dogmatical Brow, a positive Voice, and a Contempt for every Thing that comes out, whether he has read it or not. He dwells altogether in Generals. He praises or dispraises in the Lump. He shakes his Head very frequently at the Pedantry of Universities, and bursts into Laughter when you mention an Author that is not known at *Will's*.[2] He hath formed his Judgment upon *Homer, Horace,* and *Virgil,* not from their own Works, but from those of *Rapin* and *Bossu*.[3] He knows his own Strength so well, that he never dares praise any Thing in which he has not a *French* Author for his Voucher.[4]

With these extraordinary Talents and Accomplishments, Sir *Timothy Tittle*[5] puts Men in Vogue, or condemns them to Obscurity, and sits as Judge of Life and Death upon every Author that appears in Publick. It is impossible to represent the Panges, Agonies, and Convulsions, which Sir *Timothy* expresses in every Feature of his Face, and Muscle of his Body, upon the reading of a bad Poet.

About a Week ago I was engaged at a Friend's of mine in an agreeable Conversation with his Wife and Daughters, when in the Height of our Mirth, Sir *Timothy,* who makes Love to[6] my Friend's eldest Daughter, came in amongst us puffing and blowing as if he had been very much out of Breath. He immediately called

1 Correspond.

2 See *Tatler* No. 1, n. 3.

3 René Rapin (1621–1687) and René Le Bossu (1631–1689) were influential French critics. (The implication of the paragraph is that Sir Timothy cannot read Latin.)

4 To ratify his opinion.

5 See *Tatler* No. 163, n. 8. A "tittle" is the name for any minute object or quantity.

6 Courts.

for a Chair, and desired Leave to sit down, without any further Ceremony. I ask'd him, Where he had been? Whether he was out of Order? He only replied, That he was quite spent, and fell a cursing in Soliloquy. I could hear him cry, *A Wicked Rogue*———— *An Execrable Wretch*————*Was there ever such a Monster*———— The young Ladies upon this began to be affrighted, and asked, Whether any one had hurt him? He answered nothing, but still talked to himself. *To lay the first Scene, says he, in St.* James's Park, *and the last in* Northamptonshire! Is that all, says I? Then I suppose you have been at the Rehearsal of a Play this Morning. *Been!* says he; I have been at *Northampton,* in the *Park,* in a Lady's Bed-Chamber, in a Dining-Room, every where; the Rogue has led me such a Dance————Tho' I could scarce forbear laughing at his Discourse, I told him I was glad it was no worse, and that he was only Metaphorically weary. In short, Sir, says he, the Author has not observed a single Unity in his whole Play;[7] the Scene shifts in every Dialogue; the Villain has hurried me up and down at such a Rate, that I am tired off my Legs. I could not but observe with some Pleasure, that the young Lady whom he made Love to, conceived a very just Aversion towards him, upon seeing him so very passionate in Trifles. And as she had that natural Sense which makes her a better Judge than a Thousand Criticks, she began to rally him upon this foolish Humour. For my Part, says she, I never knew a Play take that was written up to your Rules, as you call them. How Madam! says he, Is that your Opinion? I am sure you have a better Tast. It is a pretty Kind of Magick, says she, the Poets have, to transport an Audience from Place to Place without the Help of a Coach and Horses. I could travel round the World at such a Rate. 'Tis such an Entertainment as an Enchantress finds when she fancies her self in a Wood, or upon a Mountain, at a Feast, or a Solemnity; though at the same Time she has never stirred out of her Cottage. Your Simile, Madam, says Sir *Timothy,* is by no Means just. Pray, says she, let my Similies pass without a Criticism. I must confess, continued she, (for I

---

[7] The Aristotelian unities of time, place, and action, which governed classical drama, were championed by many eighteenth-century critics. Sir Timothy is decrying a dramatist who did not observe unity of place.

found she was resolved to exasperate him) I laughed very heartily at the last New Comedy which you found so much Fault with. But Madam, says he, you ought not to have laughed; and I defy any one to show me a single Rule that you could laugh by. Ought not to laugh! says she: Pray who should hinder me. Madam, says he, there are such People in the World as *Rapin, Dacier,*[8] and several others, that ought to have spoiled your Mirth. I have heard, says the young Lady, That your great Criticks are always very bad Poets: I fancy there is as much Difference between the Works of one and the other, as there is between the Carriage of a Dancing-Master and a Gentleman. I must confess, continued she, I would not be troubled with so fine a Judgment as yours is; for I find you feel more Vexation in a bad Comedy than I do in a deep Tragedy. Madam, says Sir *Timothy,* That is not my Fault, they should learn the Art of Writing. For my Part, says the young Lady, I should think the greatest Art in your Writers of Comedies is to please. To please! says Sir *Timothy;* and immediately fell a laughing. Truly, says she, that is my Opinion. Upon this, he composed his Countenance, looked upon his Watch, and took his Leave.

I hear that Sir *Timothy* has not been at my Friend's House since this notable Conference, to the great Satisfaction of the young Lady, who by this Means has got rid of a very impertinent Fop.[9]

I must confess, I could not but observe, with a great deal of Surprize, how this Gentleman, by his ill Nature, Folly, and Affectation, hath made himself capable of suffering so many imaginary Pains, and looking with such a senseless Severity upon the common Diversions of Life.

8 André Dacier (1651–1722), French classical scholar.
9 A vain and pretentious young man.

The Tatler, No. 167

From Tuesday May 2. to Thursday May 4. 1710.

[Steele]

Segnius irritant Animos dimissa per Aures,
Quam quae sunt Oculis submissa fidelibus.—Hor.[1]

From my own Apartment, May 2.

Having received Notice, That the famous Actor Mr. *Betterton* was to be interred this Evening in the Cloysters near *Westminster-Abbey*,[2] I was resolved to walk thither, and see the last Office done to a Man whom I had always very much admired, and from whose Action I had received more strong Impressions of what is great and noble in Humane Nature, than from the Arguments of the most solid Philosophers, or the Descriptions of the most charming Poets I had ever read. As the rude and untaught Multitude are no Way wrought upon more effectually than by seeing publick Punishments and Executions, so Men of Letters and Education feel their Humanity most forcibly exercised, when they attend the Obsequies[3] of Men who had arrived at any Perfection in Liberal Accomplishments. Theatrical Action is to be esteemed as such, except it be objected, that we cannot call that an Art which cannot be attained by Art. Voice, Stature, Motion, and other Gifts, must be very bountifully bestowed by Nature, or Labour and In-

1 Horace *Ars Poetica* 180: "The mind is less vividly stirred by what enters through the ears than by what is brought before the trusty eyes."

2 See *Tatler* No. 1, n. 10. Betterton died on April 28 and was interred in the cloister at Westminster Abbey on May 2.

3 Funerals.

dustry will but push the unhappy Endeavourer, in that Way, the further off his Wishes.

Such an Actor as Mr. *Betterton* ought to be recorded with the same Respect as *Roscius*[4] among the *Romans*. The greatest Orator has thought fit to quote his Judgment, and celebrate his Life. *Roscius* was the Example to all that would form themselves into proper and winning Behaviour. His Action was so well adapted to the Sentiments he expressed, that the Youth of *Rome* thought they wanted only to be virtuous to be as graceful in their Appearance as *Roscius*. The Imagination took a lovely Impression of what was great and good; and they who never thought of setting up for the Arts of Imitation, became themselves imitable Characters.

There is no Humane Inventions so aptly calculated for the forming a Free-born People as that of a Theatre. *Tully*[5] reports, That the celebrated Player of whom I am speaking[6] used frequently to say, *The Perfection of an Actor is only to become what he is doing.* Young Men, who are too unattentive to receive Lectures, are irresistibly taken with Performances. Hence it is, that I extremely lament the little Relish the Gentry of this Nation have at present for the just and noble Representations in some of our Tragedies. The Opera's,[7] which are of late introduced, can leave no Trace behind them that can be of Service beyond the present Moment. To sing and to dance, are Accomplishments very few have any Thoughts of practising; but to speak justly, and move gracefully, is what every Man thinks he does perform, or wishes he did.

I have hardly a Notion, that any Performer of Antiquity could surpass the Action of Mr. *Betterton* in any of the Occasions in which he has appear'd on our Stage. The wonderful Agony which he appeared in, when he examined the Circumstance of the Hand-

4 Quintus Roscius (126?–62? B.C.), the much-praised Roman actor. Betterton was sometimes called "the British Roscius."

5 Marcus Tullius Cicero (106–43 B.C.), the Roman orator and philosopher, is regularly referred to as "Tully."

6 Roscius.

7 See *Spectator* No. 18.

kerchief in *Othello*;[8] the Mixture of Love that intruded upon his Mind upon the innocent Answers *Desdemona* makes, betrayed in his Gesture such a Variety and Vicissitude of Passions, as would admonish a Man to be afraid of his own Heart, and perfectly convince him, that it is to stab it, to admit that worst of Daggers, Jealousy. Whoever reads in his Closet this admirable Scene, will find that he cannot, except he has as warm an Imagination as *Shakespear* himself, find any but dry, incoherent, and broken Sentences: But a Reader that has seen *Betterton* act it, observes there could not be a Word added; that longer Speeches had been unnatural, nay impossible, in *Othello*'s Circumstances. The charming Passage in the same Tragedy, where he tells the Manner of winning the Affection of his Mistress,[9] was urged with so moving and graceful an Energy, that while I walked in the Cloysters, I thought of him with the same Concern as if I waited for the Remains of a Person who had in real Life done all that I had seen him represent. The Gloom of the Place, and faint Lights before the Ceremony appeared, contributed to the melancholy Disposition I was in; and I began to be extremely afflicted, that *Brutus* and *Cassius* had any Difference; that *Hotspur*'s Gallantry was so unfortunate; and that the Mirth and good Humour of *Falstaff*, could not exempt him from the Grave.[10] Nay, this Occasion in me, who look upon the Distinctions amongst Men to be meerly Scenical,[11] raised Reflections upon the Emptiness of all Humane Perfection and Greatness in general; and I could not but regret, that the Sacred Heads which lie buried in the Neighbourhood of this little Portion of Earth in which my poor old Friend is deposited, are returned to Dust as well as he, and that there is no Difference in the Grave between the Imaginary and the Real Monarch. This made me say of Humane Life it self with *Mackbeth*:

> *To Morrow, to Morrow, and to Morrow,*
> *Creeps in a stealing Pace from Day to Day,*

---

[8] In act 3, sc. 4, when Othello interrogates Desdemona about the handkerchief he believes she has given to Cassio, his speeches are notably short.

[9] Act 1, sc. 3.

[10] The references are to *Julius Caesar*, act 4, sc. 3, to *I Henry IV* act 5, sc. 4, and to *Henry V* act 2, sc. 3.

[11] I.e., part of a universal drama.

> *To the last Moment of recorded Time!*
> *And all our Yesterdays have lighted Fools*
> *To their eternal Night! Out, out short Candle!*
> *Life's but a walking Shadow, a poor Player*
> *That struts and frets his Hour upon the Stage,*
> *And then is heard no more.*[12]

The Mention I have here made of Mr. *Betterton,* for whom I had, as long as I have known any Thing, a very great Esteem and Gratitude for the Pleasure he gave me, can do him no Good; but it may possibly be of Service to the unhappy Woman he has left behind him,[13] to have it known, that this great Tragedian was never in a Scene half so moving, as the Circumstances of his Affairs created at his Departure. His Wife, after the Cohabitation of Forty Years in the strictest Amity, has long pined away with a Sense of his Decay, as well in his Person as his little Fortune; and in Proportion to that, she has her self decayed both in her Health and her Reason. Her Husband's Death, added to her Age and Infirmities, would certainly have determined her Life, but that the Greatness of her Distress has been her Relief, by a present Depravation of her Senses. This Absence of Reason is her best Defence against Age, Sorrow, Poverty, and Sickness. I dwell upon this Account so distinctly, in Obedience to a certain great Spirit who hides her Name,[14] and has by Letter applied to me to recommend to her some Object of Compassion, from whom she may be concealed.

This I think, is a proper Occasion for exerting such heroick Generosity; and as there is an ingenuous Shame in those who have known better Fortune to be reduced to receive Obligations, as well as a becoming Pain in the truly Generous to receive Thanks in this Case; both these Delicacies are preserved; for the Person obliged is as incapable of knowing her Benefactress, as her Benefactress is unwilling to be known by her.

[12] *Macbeth,* act 5, sc. 5. Steele quotes, somewhat inaccurately, from Sir William Davenant's edition of the play.

[13] Maria Saunderson Betterton lost her reason after the death of her husband and died the following year.

[14] Possibly Lady Elizabeth Hastings (1682–1739), who was noted for her charities.

Advertisement

Whereas it has been signified to the Censor,[15] *That under the Pretence that he has encouraged the* Moving Picture,[16] *and particularly admired the* Walking Statue, *some Persons within the Liberties of* Westminster *have vended Walking Pictures, insomuch that the said Pictures have within few Days after Sales by Auction returned to the Habitation of their first Proprietors; that Matter has been narrowly looked into, and Orders are given to* Pacolet[17] *to take Notice of all who are concerned in such Frauds, with Directions to draw their Pictures, that they may be hanged* in Effigie, in Terrorem *of all Auctions for the future.*

[15] From *Tatler* No. 140 on, Bickerstaff referred to himself as the Censor of Great Britain.

[16] *Tatler* No. 127 carried the advertisement: "To be seen daily, at the Duke of Marlborough's Head in Fleet Street, a new Moving Picture, drawn by the best Hand, with great variety of curious Motions and Figures, which form a most agreeable Prospect." The picture is alluded to in *Tatler* No. 129.

[17] Bickerstaff's familiar spirit. Taking the form of a venerable gentleman, he introduces himself in *Tatler* No. 13: "*These Beings are usually called amongst Men,* Guardian-Angels; *and,* Mr. Bickerstaff, *I am to acquaint you, that I am to be yours for some Time to come . . .*"

The Tatler, No. 181

From Saturday June 3. to Tuesday June 6. 1710.

[S t e e l e]

—*Dies, ni fallor, adest, quem semper acerbum,*
Semper honoratum; sic, Dii, voluistis, habebo. Virg.[1]

From my own Apartment, June 5.

There are those among Mankind, who can enjoy no Relish of their Being, except the World is made acquainted with all that relates to them, and think every Thing lost that passes unobserved; but others find a solid Delight in stealing by the Crowd, and modelling their Life after such a Manner, as is as much above the Approbation as the Practice of the Vulgar. Life being too short to give Instances great enough of true Friendship or Good-Will, some Sages have thought it pious to preserve a certain Reverence for the Manes[2] of their deceased Friends, and have withdrawn themselves from the rest of the World at certain Seasons, to commemorate in their own Thoughts such of their Acquaintance who have gone before them out of this Life: And indeed, when we are advanced in Years, there is not a more pleasing Entertainment, than to recollect in a gloomy Moment the many we have parted with that have been dear and agreeable to us, and to cast a melancholy Thought or Two after those with whom, perhaps, we have indulged our selves in whole Nights of Mirth and Jollity. With such Inclinations in my Heart I went to my Closet yesterday in the Evening, and resolved to be sorrowful; upon which Occa-

---

1 Virgil *Aeneid* 5. 49: "If I err not, the day is at hand which I shall keep (such, O Gods, was your will) ever as a day of grief, ever as of honor."
2 Venerated spirits.

sion, I could not but look with Disdain upon my self, that though all the Reasons which I had to lament the Loss of many of my Friends are now as forcible as at the Moment of their Departure, yet did not my Heart swell with the same Sorrow which I felt at that Time; but I could, without Tears, reflect upon many pleasing Adventures I have had with some who have long been blended with common Earth. Though it is by the Benefit of Nature that Length of Time thus blots out the Violence of Afflictions; yet with Tempers too much given to Pleasure, it is almost necessary to revive the old Places of Grief in our Memory, and ponder Step by Step on past Life, to lead the Mind into that Sobriety of Thought which poises the Heart, and makes it beat with due Time, without being quickened with Desire, or retarded with Despair, from its proper and equal Motion. When we wind up a Clock that is out of Order, to make it go well for the future, we do not immediately set the Hand to the present Instant, but we make it strike the Round of all its Hours, before it can recover the Regularity of its Time. Such, thought I, shall be my Method this Evening; and since it is that Day of the Year which I dedicate to the Memory of such in another Life as I much delighted in when living, an Hour or Two shall be sacred to Sorrow and their Memory, while I run over all the melancholy Circumstances of this Kind which have occurred to me in my whole Life.

The first Sense of Sorrow I ever knew was upon the Death of my Father,[3] at which Time I was not quite Five Years of Age; but was rather amazed at what all the House meant, than possessed with a real Understanding why no Body was willing to play with me. I remember I went into the Room where his Body lay, and my Mother sat weeping alone by it. I had my Battledore[4] in my Hand, and fell a beating the Coffin, and calling Papa; for I know not how I had some slight Idea that he was locked up there. My Mother catched me in her Arms, and transported beyond all Patience of the silent Grief she was before in, she almost smothered me in her Embrace, and told me in a Flood of Tears, Papa could not hear me, and would play with me no more, for they were go-

---

[3] Steele's father, Richard Steele (d. 1677?) was a Dublin solicitor.
[4] A small racket used in the game of battledore and shuttlecock.

ing to put him under Ground, whence he could never come to us again. She was a very beautiful Woman, of a noble Spirit, and there was a Dignity in her Grief amidst all the Wildness of her Transport, which, methought, struck me with an Instinct of Sorrow, which, before I was sensible of what it was to grieve, seized my very Soul, and has made Pity the Weakness of my Heart ever since. The Mind in Infancy is, methinks, like the Body in Embrio, and receives Impressions so forcible, that they are as hard to be removed by Reason, as any Mark with which a Child is born is to be taken away by any future Application. Hence it is, that Good-Nature in me is no Merit; but having been so frequently overwhelmed with her Tears before I knew the Cause of any Affliction, or could draw Defences from my own Judgment, I imbibed Commiseration, Remorse, and an unmanly Gentleness of Mind, which has since insnared me into Ten Thousand Calamities, and from whence I can reap no Advantage, except it be, that in such an Humour as I am now in, I can the better indulge my self in the Softnesses of Humanity, and enjoy that sweet Anxiety which arises from the Memory of past Afflictions.[5]

We that are very old,[6] are better able to remember Things which befel us in our distant Youth, than the Passages of later Days. For this Reason it is, that the Companions of my strong and vigorous Years present themselves more immediately to me in this Office of Sorrow. Untimely or unhappy Deaths are what we are most apt to lament, so little are we able to make it indifferent when a Thing happens, though we know it must happen. Thus we groan under Life, and bewail those who are relieved from it. Every Object that returns to our Imagination raises different Passions, according to the Circumstance of their Departure. Who can have lived in an Army,[7] and in a serious Hour reflect upon the many gay and agreeable Men that might long have flourished in the Arts of Peace, and not join with the Imprecations of the Fa-

---

[5] This sentimental character manifests itself throughout Steele's writing.

[6] Though the essay reflects Steele's biography, one must remember that the nominal author is Bickerstaff, who is sixty-four years old. Steele, at this time, was thirty-eight.

[7] Steele joined the Coldstream Guards in 1695 and rose to the rank of Captain.

therless and Widow on the Tyrant[8] to whose Ambition they fell
Sacrifices? But gallant Men, who are cut off by the Sword, move
rather our Veneration than our Pity, and we gather Relief enough
from their own Contempt of Death, to make it no Evil, which was
approached with so much Chearfulness, and attended with so
much Honour. But when we turn our Thoughts from the great
Parts of Life[9] on such Occasions, and instead of lamenting those
who stood ready to give Death to those from whom they had the
Fortune to receive it; I say, when we let our Thoughts wander
from such noble Objects, and consider the Havock which is made
among the Tender and the Innocent, Pity enters with an unmixed
Softness, and possesses all our Souls at once.

Here (were there Words to express such Sentiments with proper
Tenderness) I should record the Beauty, Innocence, and untimely
Death, of the first Object my Eyes ever beheld with Love. The
beauteous Virgin![10] How ignorantly did she charm, how carelesly
excel? Oh Death! Thou hast Right to the Bold, to the Ambitious,
to the High, and to the Haughty, but why this Cruelty to the
Humble, to the Meek, to the Undiscerning, to the Thoughtless?[11]
Nor Age, nor Business, nor Distress, can erase the dear Image from
my Imagination. In the same Week, I saw her dressed for a Ball,
and in a Shrowd. How ill did the Habit of Death become the
Pretty Trifler? I still behold the smiling Earth—A large Train
of Disasters were coming on to my Memory, when my Servant
knocked at my Closet Door, and interrupted me with a Letter,
attended with a Hamper of Wine, of the same Sort with that
which is to be put to Sale on *Thursday* next at *Garraway*'s Coffee-
house.[12] Upon the Receipt of it, I sent for Three of my Friends.
We are so intimate, that we can be Company in whatever State of
Mind we meet, and can entertain each other without expecting al-

8 This could be an allusion to King Louis XIV of France, but, more likely,
the reference is general.

9 I.e., the noble concerns of statesmen, generals, heroes, etc.

10 No specific individual has been identified as the source of this reference.

11 Unsuspecting.

12 Garraway's Coffee-house in Exchange Alley was a principal resort of merchants. With this essay appeared an advertisement offering for sale "46 hogsheads and one half of extraordinary French claret."

ways to rejoice. The Wine we found to be generous and warming, but with such an Heat as moved us rather to be chearful than frol-icksome. It revived the Spirits without firing the Blood. We com-mended it till Two of the Clock this Morning, and having to Day met a little before Dinner, we found, that though we drank Two Bottles a Man, we had much more Reason to recollect than forget what had passed the Night before.[13]

[13] The description of the evening with three friends and a hamper of wine is not unrelated to the essay on death which precedes it.

The Tatler, No. 190

From Saturday June 24. to Tuesday June 27. 1710.

[S t e e l e]

—*Timeo Danaos & Dona ferentes.* Virg.[1]

Sheer-Lane, June 26.

There are some Occasions in Life, wherein Regards to a Man's
self is the most pitiful and contemptible of all Passions; and such
a Time certainly is when the true publick Spirit of a Nation is
run into a Faction against their Friends and Benefactors. I have
hinted heretofore some Things which discover the real Sorrow I
am in at the Observation, that it is now very much so in *Great
Britain,* and have had the Honour to be pelted with several Epistles to expostulate with me on that Subject.[2] Among others, one
from a Person of the Number of those they call *Quakers,* who
seems to admonish me out of pure Zeal and Good-will. But as
there is no Character so unjust as that of talking in Party upon
all Occasions, without Respect to Merit or Worth on the contrary
Side, so there is no Part we can act so justifiable as to speak our
Mind when we see Things urged to Extremity, against all that is
Praise-worthy or valuable in Life, upon general and groundless
Suggestions. But if I have talked too frankly upon such Reflec-
tions, my Correspondent has laid before me, after his Way, the
Error of it in a Manner that makes me indeed thankful for his

---

[1] Virgil *Aeneid* 2. 49: "I distrust the Greeks, even when they offer gifts."

[2] In June, 1710, the Whig ministry was falling out of favor. This led Steele,
in *Tatler* No. 187, into specific political criticism of the Tories; of Doctor Sacheverell, the Tory hero (see *Spectator* No. 37, n. 12); and of the Pretender,
James Stuart. This brought a response from several Tory journals.

Kindness, but the more inclinable to repeat the Imprudence from the Necessity of the Circumstance.

The 23d of the 6th Month,
"Friend *Isaac,*   *which is the Month* June.
   Forasmuch as I love thee, I cannot any longer refrain declaring my Mind unto thee concerning some Things. Thou didst thy self indite the Epistle inferred in one of thy late Lucubrations, as thou wouldst have us call them: For verily thy Friend of Stone,[3] and I speak according to Knowledge, hath no Fingers; and tho' he hath a Mouth, yet speaketh he not therewith; nor yet did that Epistle at all come unto thee from the Mansion-House of the Scarlet Whore.[4] It is plain therefore, that the Truth is not in thee: But since thou wouldst lye, couldst thou not lye with more Discretion? Wherefore shouldst thou insult over the Afflicted, or add Sorrow unto the Heavy of Heart? Truly this Gall proceedeth not from the Spirit of Meekness. I tell thee moreover, the People of this Land be marvelously given to Change; insomuch that it may lightly come to pass, that before thou art many Years nearer to thy Dissolution, thou mayst behold him[5] sitting on a high Place whom thou now laughest to Scorn: And then how wilt thou be glad to humble thy self to the Ground, and lick the Dust of his Feet, that thou mayst find Favour in his Sight? If thou didst meditate as much upon the Word as thou dost upon the prophane Scribblings of the wise Ones of this Generation, thou wouldst have remembered what happened unto *Shimei,* the Son of *Gera* the *Benjamite,* who cursed the good Man *David* in his Distress.[6] *David* pardoned his Transgression, yet was he afterwards taken as in a Snare by the Words of his own Mouth, and fell by the Sword of *Solomon* the chief Ruler. Furthermore, I do not remember to have heard in the Days of my Youth and Vanity, when, like thine, my Conversation was with the Gentiles, that the Men of *Rome,* which is *Babylon,* ever sued unto the

3 Pasquino—an Italian tailor of the fifteenth century, noted for his caustic wit—was humorously declared to be the original of a mutilated statue dug up much later. Bickerstaff began receiving letters from the stone "Pasquin" in *Tatler* No. 129.

4 The Vatican. See Rev. 17.

5 James Stuart.

6 Shimei curses David in 2 Samuel 16: 5–13; he is executed by the command of Solomon—on a related charge—in 1 Kings 2: 8, 36–46. The implication is, of course, that Bickerstaff may have to suffer for his statements, when the new king is settled on the throne.

Men of *Carthage* for Tranquility, as thou dost aver: Neither was *Hannibal,* the Son of *Hamilcar,* called Home by his Countrymen, till these saw the Sword of their Enemies at their Gates; And then was it not Time for him, thinkest thou, to return?[7] It appeareth therefore that thou dost Prophesy backwards; thou dost row one Way, and look another; and indeed in all Things art thou too much a Time-server;[8] yet seemest thou not to consider what a Day may bring forth. Think of this, and take Tobacco.

> *Thy Friend,*
> Aminadab."

If the zealous Writer of the above Letter has any Meaning, it is of too high a Nature to be the Subject of my Lucubrations. I shall therefore wave such high Points, and be as useful as I can to Persons of less Moment than any he hints at. When a Man runs into a little Fame in the World, as he meets with a great deal of Reproach which he does not deserve, so does he also a great deal of Esteem to which he has in himself no Pretentions. Were it otherwise, I am sure no one would offer to put a Law-Case to me: But because I am an Adept in Physick and Astrology, they will needs perswade me that I am no less a Proficient in all other Sciences. However, the Point mentioned in the following Letter is so plain a one, that I think I need not trouble my self to cast a Figure[9] to be able to discuss it.

"*Mr.* Bickerstaff,
It is some Years ago since the Entail of the Estate of our Family was altered, by passing a Fine[10] in Favour of me (who now am in Possession of it) after some others deceased. The Heirs-General, who live beyond Sea, were excluded by this Settlement, and the whole Estate is to pass in a new Channel after me and my Heirs. But several Tenants of the Lordship perswade me to let them hereafter hold their Lands of me according to the old Customs of the Barony, and not oblige them to act by the Limitations of the last Settlement. This,

---

[7] Aminadab is rejecting the suggestion that, if the Tories come to power, they will sue for peace with the French. This is, however, what the Tories did do.

[8] I.e., the astrologer Bickerstaff prophecies falsely in order to retain the favor of the party in power.

[9] Employ astrology.

[10] A compromise involving the conveyance of lands.

they say, will make me more popular among my Dependants, and the ancient Vassals of the Estate, to whom any Deviation from the Line of Succession is always invidious.

Yours, &c."

"*Sir,*   *Sheer-Lane, June* 24.

You have by the Fine a plain Right, in which none else of your Family can be your Competitor; for which Reason, by all Means demand Vassalage upon that Title. The contrary Advice can be given for no other Purpose in Nature but to betray you, and favour other Pretenders, by making you place a Right which is in you only, upon a Level with a Right which you have in common with others. I am

S I R,

Your most Faithful
Servant till Death,
I. B."[11]

There is nothing so dangerous or so pleasing, as Compliments made to us by our Enemies: And my Correspondent tells me, That though he knows several of those who give him this Counsel were at first against passing the Fine in Favour of him; yet is he so touched with their Homage to him, that he can hardly believe they have a Mind to set it aside, in order to introduce the Heirs-General into his Estate.

These are great Evils; but since there is no proceeding with Success in this World, without complying with the Arts of it, I shall use the same Method as my Correspondent's Tenants did with him, in Relation to one whom I never had a Kindness for; but shall, notwithstanding, presume to give him my Advice.

Isaac Bickerstaff *Esq; of* Great Britain, *to* Lewis XIV. *of* France.

"*Sir,*

Your Majesty will pardon me while I take the Liberty to acquaint you, that some Passages written from your Side of the Water do very

11 The letters to and from Bickerstaff refer to the Protestant succession established by the Act of Settlement (1700). Those protesting "any Deviation from the Line of Succession" are the Jacobites, who would prefer to see Queen Anne succeeded by her half-brother, James Stuart, than by her distant cousin, George of Hanover. However, on Anne's death in 1714, George I ascended the throne.

much obstruct your Interests. We take it very unkindly that the Prints of *Paris* are so very partial in Favour of one Set of Men among us, and treat the others as irreconcileable to your Interests. Your Writers are very large in recounting any Thing which relates to the Figure and Power of one Party, but are dumb when they should represent the Actions of the other. This is a trifling Circumstance many here are apt to lay some Stress upon, therefore I thought fit to offer it to your Consideration before you dispatch the next Courier.

I. B."[12]

[12] In denying that the Tory party is working in concert with the French to make peace, Swift—in *Examiner* No. 2—comments on this letter from Bicker-staff: "I protest I know no man in England but him that holds a correspondence with his Christian Majesty."

The Tatler, No. 214

From Saturday Aug. 19. to Tuesday Aug. 22. 1710.

[S t e e l e]¹

— *Soles & aperta Serena*
Prospicere, & certis poteris cognoscere Signis. Virg.²

From my own Apartment, August 21.

In every Party there are Two Sorts of Men, the *Rigid* and the *Supple*. The *Rigid* are an intractable Race of Mortals, who act upon Principle, and will not, forsooth, fall into any Measures that are not consistent with their received Notions of Honour. These are Persons of a stubborn, unpliant Morality, that sullenly adhere to their Friends when they are disgraced and to their Principles, tho' they are exploded.³ I shall therefore give up this stiff-necked Generation to their own Obstinacy, and turn my Thoughts to the Advantage of the *Supple,* who pay their Homage to Places, and not Persons; and without enslaving themselves to any particular Scheme of Opinions, are as ready to change their Conduct in Point of Sentiment, as of Fashion. The well-disciplined Part of a Court are generally so perfect at their Exercise, that you may see a whole Assembly, from Front to Rear, face about at once to a new Man of Power, tho' at the same Time they turn their Backs upon him that brought them thither. The great Hardship these

---

1 The account of the State weather-glass in this paper may be by Addison, who wrote the description of the ecclesiastical thermometer in *Tatler* No. 220.

2 Virgil *Georgics* 1. 393–394: "When rain is past, you can by sure signs foresee fair days and unclouded skies."

3 This ironical essay refers to the imminent fall of the Whig ministry. See *Tatler* No. 190.

complaisant Members of Society are under, seems to be the Want of Warning upon any approaching Change or Revolution; so that they are obliged in a Hurry to tack about with every Wind, and stop short in the Midst of a full Career, to the great Surprize and Derision of their Beholders.

When a Man foresees a decaying Ministry, he has Leisure to grow a Malecontent, reflect upon the present Conduct,[4] and by gradual Murmurs fall off from his Friends into a new Party, by just Steps and Measures. For Want of such Notices, I have formerly known a very well-bred Person refuse to return a Bow of a Man whom he thought in Disgrace, that was next Day made Secretary of State; and another, who after a long Neglect of a Minister, came to his Levee, and made Professions of Zeal for his Service the very Day before he was turned out.

This produces also unavoidable Confusions and Mistakes in the Descriptions of great Mens Parts and Merits. That ancient Lyrick, Mr. *D'Urfey*,[5] some Years ago writ a Dedication to a certain Lord, in which he celebrated him for the greatest Poet and Critick of that Age, upon a Misinformation in *Dyer's* Letter,[6] that his noble Patron was made Lord Chamberlain. In short, innumerable Votes, Speeches, and Sermons, have been thrown away, and turned to no Account, meerly for Want of due and timely Intelligence.[7] Nay it has been known, that a Panegyrick has been half printed off, when the Poet, upon the Removal of the Minister, has been forced to alter it into a Satyr.

For the Conduct therefore of such useful Persons as are ready to do their Country Service upon all Occasions, I have an Engine in my Study, which is a Sort of a Political Barometer, or, to speak

[4] I.e., to criticize the current policies.

[5] Thomas D'Urfey (1653–1723), the English dramatist, dedicated the second part of *Don Quixote* to Charles, Earl of Dorset, in these lines:

> You have, my Lord, a patent from above,
> And can monopolise both wit and love,
> Inspired and blest by Heaven's peculiar care,
> Adored by all the wise and all the fair;
> To whom the world united give this due,
> Best judge of men, and best of poets too.

[6] See *Tatler* No. 18, n. 25.

[7] Information. The pun is probably intentional.

more intelligibly, a State *Weather-Glass,* that, by the rising and
falling of a certain Magical Liquor, presages all Changes and Revolutions in Government, as the common Glass does those of the
Weather. This Weather-Glass is said to have been invented by
Cardan,[8] and given by him as a Present to his great Countryman
and Contemporary *Machiavel,*[9] which (by the Way) may serve to
rectify a received Error in Chronology, that places one of these
some Years after the other. How or when it came into my Hands,
I shall desire to be excused, if I keep to my self; but so it is, that
I have walked by it for the better Part of a Century, to my Safety
at least, if not to my Advantage; and have among my Papers, a
Register of all the Changes that have happened in it from the
Middle of Queen *Elizabeth's* Reign.[10]

In the Time of that Princess, it stood long at *settled Fair.* At
the latter End of King *James* the First, it fell to *Cloudy.* It held
several Years after at *Stormy;* insomuch that at last despairing of
seeing any *Clear* Weather at Home, I follow'd the Royal Exile,
and some Time after finding my Glass rise, returned to my native
Country with the rest of the Loyalists.[11] I was then in Hopes to pass
the Remainder of my Days in *settled Fair:* But alas! during the
greatest Part of that Reign, the *English* Nation lay in a *dead
Calm,* which, as it is usual, was followed by high Winds and Tem-
pests till of late Years: In which, with unspeakable Joy and Satisfaction, I have seen our Political Weather returned to *settled Fair.*
I must only observe, that for all this last Summer my Glass has
pointed at Changeable. Upon- the whole, I often apply to Fortune
Aenaeas's Speech to the Sybil:

8 Jerome Cardan (1501–1576), Italian physician and astrologer.

9 Niccolo Machiavelli (1469–1527), celebrated Florentine statesman whose
political counsels embraced cunning, duplicity, and bad faith. Even without
the magical barometer, Machiavelli was aware of political climates.

10 The register had many changes to record. The period saw the excom-
munication of Elizabeth, the arbitrary rule of the Stuart kings, the Civil War
which led to the beheading of Charles I, puritan repressiveness under Oliver
Cromwell and the Commonwealth, the restoration of Charles II, the revolution which forced James II to flee the throne, the emergence of Whig and
Tory parties, and the continuing and increasingly unpopular wars under William III and Queen Anne.

11 This feature of Bickerstaff's biography is rarely noted.

———— *Non ulla Laborum,*
O Virgo, nova mi Facies inopinave surgit
Omnia praecepi, atq; Animo mecum ante peregi.[12]

The Advantages which have accrued to those whom I have advised in their Affairs, by Virtue of this Sort of Praescience, have been very considerable. A Nephew of mine, who has never put his Money into the Stocks, or taken it out, without my Advice, has in a few Years raised Five hundred Pounds to almost so many Thousands. As for my self, who look upon Riches to consist rather in Content than Possessions, and measure the Greatness of the Mind rather by its Tranquility than its Ambition. I have seldom used my Glass to make my Way in the World, but often to retire from it. This is a By-Path to Happiness, which was first discovered to me by a most pleasing Apothegm of *Pythagoras:*[13] *When the Winds,* says he, *rise, worship the Eccho.* That great Philosopher (whether to make his Doctrines the more venerable, or to guild his Precepts with the Beauty of Imagination, or to awaken the Curiosity of his Disciples; for I will not suppose what is usually said, that he did it to conceal his Wisdom from the Vulgar) has couched several admirable Precepts in remote Allusions and mysterious Sentences. By the Winds in this Apothegm, are meant State-Hurricanes and popular Tumults. When these arise, says he, worship the Eccho; that is, withdraw your self from the Multitude into Deserts, Woods, Solitudes, or the like Retirements, which are the usual Habitations of the Eccho.

[12] Virgil *Aeneid* 6. 103–105: "There is nothing strange or unexpected, O Virgin, in the trials you prophesy. Already, I have forecast and contemplated them all."

[13] Pythagoras (fl. c. 530 B.C.), Greek philosopher and mathematician.

The Tatler, No. 216

From Thursday Aug. 24. to Saturday Aug. 26. 1710.

[Addison]

— *Nugis addere Pondus.*[1]

From my own Apartment, August 25.

Nature is full of Wonders; every Atom is a standing Miracle, and endowed with such Qualities, as could not be impressed on it by a Power and Wisdom less than Infinite. For this Reason, I would not discourage any Searches that are made into the most minute and trivial Parts of the Creation. However, since the World abounds in the noblest Fields of Speculation, it is, methinks, the Mark of a little Genius to be wholly conversant among Insects, Reptiles, Animalcules, and those trifling Rarities that furnish out the Apartment of a Virtuoso.[2]

There are some Men whose Heads are so odly turned this Way, that tho' they are utter Strangers to the common Occurrences of Life, they are able to discover the Sex of a Cockle, or describe the Generation of a Mite, in all its Circumstances. They are so little versed in the World, that they scarce know a Horse from an Ox; but at the same Time will tell you, with a great deal of Gravity, That a Flea is a Rhinoceros, and a Snail an Hermaphrodite. I have known one of these whimsical Philosophers who has set a greater Value upon a Collection of Spiders than he would upon

[1] Horace *Epistles* 1. 19. 42: "Some give weight and importance to trifles."
[2] The collector of trivial specimens was a common object of satire. See Pope's *The Rape of the Lock* 5. 121–122, and *The Dunciad* 4. 397–458.

a Flock of Sheep, and has sold his Coat off his Back to purchase a Tarantula.

I would not have a Scholar wholly unacquainted with these Secrets and Curiosities of Nature; but certainly the Mind of Man, that is capable of so much higher Contemplations, should not be altogether fixed upon such mean and disproportioned Objects. Observations of this Kind are apt to alienate us too much from the Knowledge of the World, and to make us serious upon Trifles, by which Means they expose Philosophy to the Ridicule of the Witty, and Contempt of the Ignorant. In short, Studies of this Nature should be the Diversions, Relaxations, and Amusements; not the Care, Business, and Concern of Life.

It is indeed wonderful to consider, that there should be a Sort of learned Men who are wholly employed in gathering together the Refuse of Nature, if I may call it so, and hoarding up in their Chests and Cabinets such Creatures as others industriously avoid the Sight of. One does not know how to mention some of the most precious Parts of their Treasure, without a Kind of an Apology for it. I have been shown a Beetle valued at Twenty Crowns, and a Toad at an Hundred: But we must take this for a general Rule, That whatever appears trivial or obscene in the common Notions of the World, looks grave and philosophical in the Eye of a Virtuoso.

To show this Humour in its Perfection, I shall present my Reader with the Legacy of a certain Virtuoso, who laid out a considerable Estate in natural Rarities and Curiosities, which upon his Death Bed he bequeathed to his Relations and Friends, in the following Words:

The Will of a Virtuoso.

I *Nicholas Gimcrack*[3] being in sound Health of Mind, but in great Weakness of Body, do by this my Last Will and Testament bestow my Worldly Goods and Chattels in Manner following:

Imprimis,[4] To my dear Wife,[5]

---

[3] A gimcrack is a showy object of little use or value.

[4] First.

[5] *Tatler* No. 221 carries a letter from the widow, Elizabeth Gimcrack, offering to sell a parcel of dried spiders at a bargain.

> One Box of Butterflies,
> One Drawer of Shells,
> A Female Skeleton,
> A dried Cockatrice.

Item,[6] To my Daughter *Elizabeth,*
> My Receipt for preserving dead Caterpillars,
> As also my Preparations of Winter *May*-Dew,
> and Embrio Pickle.

Item, To my little Daughter *Fanny,*
> Three Crocodile's Eggs.

And upon the Birth of her First Child, if she marries with her Mother's Consent,
> The Nest of an Humming-Bird.

Item, To my eldest Brother, as an Acknowledgment for the Lands he has vested in my Son *Charles,* I bequeath
> My last Year's Collection of Grashoppers.

Item, To his Daughter *Susanna,* being his only Child, I bequeath my
> *English* Weeds pasted on Royal Paper.
> With my large Folio of *Indian* Cabbage.

Item, To my learned and worthy Friend Dr. *Johannes Elscrikius,* Professor in Anatomy, and my Associate in the Studies of Nature, as an eternal Monument of my Affection and Friendship for him, I bequeath
> My Rat's Testicles, and
> Whale's Pizzle,

To him and his Issue Male; and in Default of such Issue in the said Dr. *Elscrickius,* then to return to my Executor and his Heirs for ever.

Having fully provided for my Nephew *Isaac,* by making over to him some Years since
> A Horned *Scarabaeus,*[7]
> The Skin of a Rattle-Snake, and
> The Mummy of an *Egyptian* King,

I make no further Provision for him in this my Will.

---

[6] Also.
[7] A large black dung-beetle.

My eldest Son *John* having spoken disrespectfully of his little Sister[8] whom I keep by me in Spirits of Wine, and in many other Instances behaved himself undutifully towards me, I do disinherit, and wholly cut off from any Part of this my Personal Estate, by giving him a single Cockle Shell.

To my Second Son *Charles,* I give and bequeath all my Flowers, Plants, Minerals, Mosses, Shells, Pebbles, Fossils, Beetles, Butterflies, Caterpillars, Grashoppers, and Vermin, not above specified: As also all my Monsters, both wet and dry, making the said *Charles* whole and sole Executor of this my Last Will and Testament; he paying, or causing to be paid, the aforesaid Legacies within the Space of Six Months after my Decease. And I do hereby revoke all other Wills whatsoever by me formerly made.

ADVERTISEMENT

Whereas an ignorant Upstart in Astrology has publickly endeavoured to perswade the World, that he is the late John Partridge,[9] *who died in the* 28th *of March, 1708; These are to certifie all whom it may concern, That the true* John Partridge *was not only dead at that Time, but continues so to this present Day.*

Beware of Counterfeits, for such are Abroad.

8 A fetal specimen.
9 See *Tatler* No. 1, n. 23, and Introduction, p. 3.

The Tatler, No. 220

From Saturday Sept. 2. to Tuesday Sept. 5. 1710.

[Addison]

Insani sanus Nomen ferat, aequus iniqui,
Ultra quam satis est, Virtutem si petat ipsam. Hor.[1]

From my own Apartment, Sept. 4.

Having received many Letters filled with Compliments and Acknowledgments for my late useful Discovery of the Political Barometer,[2] I shall here communicate to the Publick an Account of my Ecclesiastical Thermometer, the latter giving as manifest Prognostications of the Changes and Revolutions in Church, as the former does of those in State, and both of them being absolutely necessary for every prudent Subject who is resolved to keep what he has, and get what he can.

The Church Thermometer, which I am now to treat of, is supposed to have been invented in the Reign of *Henry* the Eighth, about the Time when that Religious Prince put some to Death for owning the Pope's Supremacy, and others for denying Transubstantiation.[3] I do not find, however, any great Use made of this Instrument till it fell into the Hands of a learned and vigilant Priest or Minister, (for he frequently wrote himself both one and

---

[1] Horace *I Epistles* 6. 15–16: "Let the wise man be called mad, the just man corrupt, if they pursue virtue with irrational zeal."

[2] See *Tatler* No. 214.

[3] During the reign of Henry VIII (1509–1547), the transition from the authority of the Church of Rome to that of the Church of England was attended by dogmatic confusion.

the other)[4] who was some Time Vicar of *Bray*.[5] This Gentleman lived in his Vicaridge to a good old Age; and after having seen several Successions of his neighbouring Clergy either burnt or banish'd, departed this Life with the Satisfaction of having never deserted his Flock, and died Vicar of *Bray*. As this Glass was first designed to calculate the different Degrees of Heat in Religion, as it raged in Popery, or as it cooled and grew temperate in the Reformation, it was marked at several Distances, after the Manner our ordinary Thermometer is to this Day, *viz. Extream Hot, sultry Hot, very Hot, Hot, Warm, Temperate, Cold, just Freezing, Frost, hard Frost, great Frost, extream Cold.*

It is well known, that *Toricellius*,[6] the Inventor of the common Weather Glass, made the Experiment in a long Tube which held Thirty two Foot of Water; and that a more modern Virtuoso finding such a Machine altogether unweildy and useless, and considering that Thirty two Inches of Quicksilver weigh'd as much as so many Foot of Water in a Tube of the same Circumference, invented that sizeable Instrument which is now in Use. After this Manner, that I might adapt the Thermometer I am now speaking of to the present Constitution of our Church, as divided into *High* and *Low*,[7] I have made some necessary Variations both in the Tube and the Fluid it contains. In the first Place, I ordered a Tube to be cast in a Planetary Hour, and took Care to seal it Hermetically, when the Sun was in Conjunction with *Saturn*.[8] I then took the proper Precautions about the Fluid, which is a Compound of Two very different Liquors; one of them a Spirit drawn out of a strong heady Wine; the other a particular Sort of Rock

---

[4] I.e., he was a priest when Tory and High Church sentiment prevailed and a minister when Whig and Low Church authorities were in power. There is rich irony in the Vicar's "Satisfaction of having never deserted his Flock."

[5] A small seaport in Ireland.

[6] Evangelista Torricelli (1608–1647), Italian physicist.

[7] High Church and Low Church were unofficial divisions within the Church of England. High Church spokesmen resembled Roman Catholics in their emphasis on the priesthood, the sacraments, and liturgical ceremony. Low Church spokesmen rejected the Catholic heritage of doctrines, rites, and organization, and stressed instead the authority of the Bible and personal religious response.

[8] This is the jargon of an astrologer.

Water, colder than Ice, and clearer than Christal.[9] The Spirit is of a red fiery Colour, and so very apt to ferment, that unless it be mingled with a Proportion of the Water, or pent up very close, it will burst the Vessel that holds it, and fly up in Fume and Smoak. The Water on the contrary is of such a subtle piercing Cold, that unless it be mingled with a Proportion of the Spirits, it will sink through almost every Thing that it is put into, and seems to be of the same Nature as the Water mentioned by *Quintus Curtius*,[10] which, says the Historian, could be contained in nothing but in the Hoof or (as the *Oxford* Manuscript has it) in the Skull of an Ass. The Thermometer is marked according to the following Figure, which I set down at length, not only to give my Reader a clear Idea of it, but also to fill up my Paper.

> *Ignorance.*
> *Persecution.*
> *Wrath.*
> *Zeal.*
> *CHURCH.*
> *Moderation.*
> *Lukewarmness.*
> *Infidelity.*
> *Ignorance.*

The Reader will observe, that the Church is placed in the Middle Point of the Glass, between *Zeal* and *Moderation,* the Situation in which she always flourishes, and in which every good *Englishman* wishes her who is a Friend to the Constitution of his Country. However, when it mounts to *Zeal,* it is not amiss; and when it sinks to *Moderation,* is still in a most admirable Temper. The worst of it is, that when once it begins to rise, it has still an Inclination to ascend, insomuch that it is apt to climb from *Zeal* to *Wrath,* and from *Wrath* to *Persecution,* which always ends in *Ignorance,* and very often proceeds from it. In the same Manner

---

9 Addison establishes as the two elements of religious belief, the "Wine" of emotion and the "Water" of reason.

10 Quintus Curtius (fl. 1st Century, A.D.), Latin biographer of Alexander the Great.

it frequently takes its Progress through the lower Half of the Glass; and when it has a Tendency to fall, will gradually descend from *Moderation* to *Lukewarmness,* and from *Lukewarmness* to *Infidelity,* which very often terminates in *Ignorance,* and always proceeds from it.

It is a common Observation, that the ordinary Thermometer will be affected by the breathing of People who are in the Room where it stands; and indeed, it is almost incredible to conceive how the Glass I am now describing will fall by the Breath of a Multitude crying *Popery;* or on the contrary, how it will rise when the same Multitude (as it sometimes happens) cry out in the same Breath, *The Church is in Danger.*[11]

As soon as I had finished my Glass, and adjusted it to the above-mentioned Scale of Religion, that I might make proper Experiments with it, I carried it under my Cloak to several Coffee-houses, and other Places of Resort about this great City. At St. *James's* Coffee-house, the Liquor stood at *Moderation;* but at *Will's,* to my extream Surprize, it subsided to the very lowest Mark on the Glass. At the *Grecian,* it mounted but just one Point higher; at the *Rainbow,* it still ascended Two Degrees: *Child's* fetched it up to *Zeal,* and other adjacent Coffee-houses to *Wrath.*[12]

It fell into the lower Half of the Glass as I went further into the City, till at length it settled at *Moderation,* where it continued all the Time I staid about the *Change,* as also whilst I passed by the *Bank.* And here I cannot but take Notice, that through the whole Course of my Remarks, I never observed my Glass to rise at the same Time that the Stocks did.[13]

To compleat the Experiment, I prevailed upon a Friend of mine, who works under me in the Occult Sciences, to make a Progress with my Glass through the whole Island of *Great Britain;* and after his Return, to present me with a Register of his Observa-

---

[11] "The Church is in Danger" was a Tory slogan, warning that when Anglican principles were rejected, one might reasonably fear the return of the Commonwealth.

[12] The Rainbow Coffee-house was situated in Fleet Street; Child's was in St. Paul's Churchyard. For the other coffee-houses, see *Tatler* No. 1, n. 3.

[13] I.e., no one became emotional about religious problems while his financial situation was improving.

tions. I guessed beforehand at the Temper of several Places he passed through, by the Characters they have had Time out of Mind. Thus that facetious Divine, Dr. *Fuller*,[14] speaking of the Town of *Banbury* near a Hundred Years ago, tells us, it was a Place famous for Cakes and *Zeal*,[15] which I find by my Glass is true to this Day as to the latter Part of this Description; though I must confess, it is not in the same Reputation for Cakes that it was in the Time of that learned Author; and thus of other Places. In short, I have now by me, digested in an Alphabetical Order, all the Counties, Corporations and Boroughs, in *Great Britain*, with their respective Tempers, as they stand related to my Thermometer: But this I shall keep to my self, because I would by no Means do any Thing that may seem to influence any ensuing Elections.[16]

The Point of Doctrine which I would propagate by this my Invention, is the same which was long ago advanced by that able Teacher *Horace,* out of whom I have taken my Text for this Discourse: We should be careful not to overshoot our selves in the Pursuits even of Virtue. Whether *Zeal* or *Moderation* be the Point we aim at, let us keep Fire out of the one, and Frost out of the other. But alas! the World is too Wise to want such a Precaution. The Terms *High-Church* and *Low-Church,* as commonly used, do not so much denote a Principle, as they distinguish a Party. They are like Words of Battle, that have nothing to do with their original Signification, but are only given out to keep a Body of Men together, and to let them know Friends from Enemies.

I must confess, I have considered with some little Attention the Influence which the Opinions of these great National Sects have upon their Practice; and do look upon it as one of the unaccountable Things of our Times, that Multitudes of honest Gentlemen, who entirely agree in their Lives, should take it in their Heads to differ in their Religion.

[14] Thomas Fuller (1608–1661), English clergyman and biographer.

[15] A play on Sir Toby's line from *Twelfth Night,* act 2, sc. 3: "Dost thou think, because thou art virtuous, there shall be no more cakes and ale?"

[16] Unfortunately for Addison and Steele, the elections went against the Whigs.

The Tatler, No. 229

From Saturday Sept. 23. to Tuesday Sept. 26. 1710.

[A d d i s o n]

~~~~~~~~

Quaesitam Meritis sume Superbiam. Hor.[1]

From my own Apartment, Sept. 25.

The whole Creation preys upon it self: Every living Creature is
inhabited. A Flea has a Thousand invisible Insects that teaze him
as he jumps from Place to Place, and revenge our Quarrels upon
him. A very ordinary Microscope shows us, that a Louse is it self
a very lousy Creature. A Whale, besides those Seas and Oceans in
the several Vessels of his Body, which are filled with innumerable
Shoals of little Animals, carries about it a whole World of Inhabitants; insomuch that, if we believe the Calculations some have
made, there are more living Creatures which are too small for the
naked Eye to behold about the Leviathan, than there are of visible Creatures upon the Face of the whole Earth. Thus every nobler Creature is as it were the Basis and Support of Multitudes
that are his Inferiors.

This Consideration very much comforts me, when I think on
those numberless Vermin[2] that feed upon this Paper, and find
their Sustenance out of it: I mean, the small Wits and Scribblers
that every Day turn a Penny by nibbling at my Lucubrations.
This has been so advantageous to this little Species of Writers,
that, if they do me Justice, I may expect to have my Statue erected

---

1 Horace *Odes* 3. 30. 14: "Accept the proud honor won by thy merits."
2 The biological metaphor is sustained throughout the essay.

in *Grub-street*,[3] as being a common Benefactor to that Quarter.

They say, when a Fox is very much troubled with Fleas, he goes into the next Pool with a little Lock of Wool in his Mouth, and keeps his Body under Water till the Vermin get into it, after which he quits the Wool, and diving, leaves his Tormentors to shift for themselves, and get their Livelihood where they can. I would have these Gentlemen take Care that I do not serve them after the same Manner; for though I have hitherto kept my Temper pretty well, it is not impossible but I may some Time or other disappear; and what will then become of them? Should I lay down my Paper, What a Famine would there be among the Hawkers,[4] Printers, Booksellers, and Authors? It would be like Dr. B——s's[5] dropping his Cloak, with the whole Congregation hanging upon the Skirts of it. To enumerate some of these my doughty Antagonists, I was threatened to be answered Weekly *Tit* for *Tat:* I was undermined by the *Whisperer,* haunted by *Tom Brown's Ghost,* scolded at by a *Female Tatler,*[6] and slandered by another of the same Character, under the Title of *Atalantis.*[7] I have been *annotated, retattled, examined,* and *condoled:*[8] But it being my standing Maxim never to speak ill of the Dead, I shall let these Authors rest in Peace, and take great Pleasure in thinking that I

3 The London street which Doctor Johnson defined as "Much inhabited by writers of small histories, dictionaries, and temporary poems."

4 Vocal street-salesmen.

5 Doctor Daniel Burgess (1645–1713), a dissenting minister whose ranting ("Grace! Regeneration! Sanctification! A new light!") was ridiculed by Steele in *Tatler* No. 66.

6 Among the competing publications, *Tit for Tat* (March 2–March 10, 1710) appeared in five issues. *The Whisperer* (October 11, 1709) and *Gazette à-la-Mode, or Tom Brown's Ghost* (March 12, 1709) were published but once. *The Female Tatler* (July 8, 1709–March 31, 1710) ran to 115 issues.

7 A celebrated book by Mary de la Rivière (1672–1724), which appeared in 1709, offering party scandal and several attacks on Richard Steele.

8 The sentence refers to specific publications: "Annotations upon the Tatler" (1710), "A Condoling Letter to the *Tatler;* on account of the misfortunes of Isaac Bickerstaff, a prisoner in the ——— on suspicion of debt" (September 19, 1710), and the Tory *Examiner* (August 3, 1710–July 26, 1714) which regularly criticized Steele and his writings. Nothing is known of a *Re-Tatler.*

have sometimes been the Means of their getting a Belly-full. When
I see my self thus surrounded by such formidable Enemies, I often
think of the Knight of the *Red Cross* in *Spencer*'s *Den of Error*,[9]
who after he has cut off the Dragon's Head, and left it wallowing
in a Flood of Ink, sees a Thousand monstrous Reptiles making
their Attempts upon him, one with many Heads, another with
none, and all of them without Eyes.

> *The same so sore annoyed has the Knight,*
> *That well nigh choaked with the deadly Stink,*
> *His Forces fail, he can no longer fight;*
> *Whose Courage when the Fiend perceived to shrink,*
> *She poured forth out of her Hellish Sink*
> *Her fruitful cursed Spawn of Serpents small,*
> *Deformed Monsters, foul, and black as Ink;*
> *Which swarming all about his Legs did crawl,*
> *And him encombred sore, but could not hurt at all.*
>
> *As gentle Shepherd in sweet Even-tide,*
> *When ruddy* Phoebus *gins to welk in West,*
> *High on an Hill, his Flock to viewen wide,*
> *Marks which do bite their hasty Supper best;*
> *A Cloud of combrous Gnats do him molest,*
> *All striving to infix their feeble Stings*
> *That from their Noyance he no where can rest;*
> *But with his clownish Hands their tender Wings*
> *He brusheth oft, and oft doth mar their Murmurings.*

If ever I should want such a Fry[10] of little Authors to attend
me, I shall think my Paper in a very decaying Condition. They
are like Ivy about an Oak, which adorns the Tree at the same
Time that it eats into it; or like a great Man's Equipage,[11] that do
Honour to the Person on whom they feed. For my Part, when I
see my self thus attacked, I do not consider my Antagonists as malicious, but hungry, and therefore am resolved never to take any
Notice of them.

---

9 From *The Faerie Queene* (1590) by Edmund Spenser (1552–1599). The
quoted stanzas are from book 1, canto 1, lines 190–207.

10 Spawn, mass of offspring.

11 A horse-drawn carriage with attending servants.

As for those who detract from my Labours without being prompted to it by an empty Stomach, in Return to their Censures I shall take Pains to excel, and never fail to perswade my self, that their Enmity is nothing but their Envy or Ignorance.

Give me Leave to conclude, like an old Man and a Moralist, with a Fable:

The Owls, Bats, and several other Birds of Night, were one Day got together in a thick Shade, where they abused their Neighbours in a very sociable Manner. Their Satyr at last fell upon the Sun, whom they all agreed to be very troublesome, impertinent, and inquisitive. Upon which the Sun, who overheard them, spoke to them after this Manner: Gentlemen, I wonder how you dare abuse one that you know could in an Instant scorch you up, and burn every Mother's Son of you: But the only Answer I shall give you, or the Revenge I shall take of you, is, to *shine on*.[12]

---

[12] *Examiner* No. 11, a response to this essay, is ridiculed by Addison in *Tatler* No. 239.

The Tatler, No. 240

From Thursd. Octob. 19. to Saturd. Octob. 21. 1710.

[Addison]

Ad Populum Phaleras —— Pers.[1]

From my own Apartment, October 20.

I do not remember that in any of my Lucubrations I have touched upon that useful Science of Physick,[2] notwithstanding I have declared my self more than once a Professor of it.[3] I have indeed joined the Study of Astrology with it, because I never knew a Physician recommend himself to the Publick who had not a Sister Art to embellish his Knowledge in Medicine. It has been commonly observed in Compliment to the Ingenious of our Profession, that *Apollo* was God of Verse as well as Physick; and in all Ages the most celebrated Practitioners of our Country were the particular Favourites of the Muses. Poetry to Physick is indeed like the Gilding to a Pill; it makes the Art shine, and covers the Severity of the Doctor with the Agreeableness of the Companion.

The very Foundation of Poetry is good Sense, if we may allow *Horace* to be a Judge of the Art.

Scribendi recte sapere est, & Principium, & Fons.[4]

And if so, we have Reason to believe, that the same Man who writes well can prescribe well, if he has applied himself to the Study of both. Besides, when we see a Man making Profession of

---

1 Persius *Satires* 3. 30: "Appeal to the mob with your trappings."
2 Medicine.
3 E.g., *Tatler* No. 195.
4 Horace *Ars Poetica* 309: "The source and fount of good writing is wisdom."

Two different Sciences, it is natural for us to believe he is no Pretender in that which we are not Judges of when we find him skilful in that which we understand.

Ordinary Quacks and Charlatans are throughly sensible how
necessary it is to support themselves by these collateral Assistances,
and therefore always lay their Claim to some supernumerary Accomplishments which are wholly foreign to their Profession.

About 20 Years ago, it was impossible to walk the Streets without having an Advertisement thrust into your Hand of a Doctor
*who was arrived at the Knowledge of the Green and Red Dragon,
and had discovered the Female Fern Seed.* No Body ever knew
what this meant; but the Green and Red Dragon so amused the
People, that the Doctor lived very comfortably upon them. About
the same Time there was pasted a very hard Word upon every
Corner of the Streets. This, to the best of my Remembrance, was

TETRACHYMAGOGON,

Which drew great Shoals of Spectators about it, who read the Bill
that it introduced with unspeakable Curiosity; and when they
were sick, would have no Body but this learned Man for their
Physician.

I once received an Advertisement of one *who had studied
Thirty Years by Candle-light for the Good of his Countrymen.* He
might have studied Twice as long by Day-light, and never have
been taken Notice of: But Lucubrations[5] cannot be over-valued.
There are some who have gained themselves great Reputation for
Physick by their Birth, as the *Seventh Son of a Seventh Son,*[6] and
others by not being born at all, as the *Unborn Doctor,*[7] who, I
hear, is lately gone the Way of his Patients, having died worth

[5] Bickerstaff usually uses the word in the sense of studied thoughts (see *Tatler* No. 1, n. 24). Here he employs the more literal definition, i.e., study done
at night, by lamplight.

[6] From the time of the ancient Babylonians, Egyptians, and Hebrews, seven
has been accounted a mystic number.

[7] The reference is to "the great Kirleus" who was either John Kirleus or
his father Thomas Kirleus, "a sworn physician in ordinary to King Charles II."
The doctor pretended to extraordinary gifts, by virtue of his having been born
by a cesarean operation. He is mentioned in *Tatlers* No. 14, 41, and 226, and
advertisements proclaiming his daughter's medical gifts appeared in *Spectators*
No. 331 and 341.

Five Hundred Pounds *per Annum,* though he was not *born* to a Halfpenny.

My ingenious Friend Doctor *Saffold,* succeeded my old Contemporary Doctor *Lilly* in the Studies both of Physick and Astrology, to which he added that of Poetry, as was to be seen both upon the Sign where he lived, and in the Bills which he distributed. He was succeeded by Doctor *Case,*[8] who erased the Verses of his Predecessor out of the Sign-Post, and substituted in their Stead Two of his own, which were as follows:

> *Within this Place*
> *Lives Doctor* Case.

He is said to have got more by this Distich,[9] than Mr. *Dryden* did by all his Works. There would be no End of enumerating the several imaginary Perfections and unaccountable Artifices by which this Tribe of Men ensnare the Minds of the Vulgar, and gain Crowds of Admirers. I have seen the whole Front of a Mountebank's Stage from one End to the other faced with Patents, Certificates, Medals, and Great Seals, by which the several Princes of *Europe* have testified their particular Respect and Esteem for the Doctor. Every great Man with a sounding Title has been his Patient. I believe I have seen Twenty Mountebanks that have given Physick to the Czar of *Muscovy*. The Great Duke of *Tuscany* escapes no better. The Elector of *Brandenburg* was likewise a very good Patient.

This great Condescension of the Doctor[10] draws upon him much Good-Will from his Audience; and it is Ten to One, but if any of them be troubled with an aching Tooth, his Ambition will prompt him to get it drawn by a Person who has had so many Princes, Kings, and Emperors, under his Hands.

I must not leave this Subject without observing, that as Physicians are apt to deal in Poetry, Apothecaries endeavour to recommend themselves by Oratory, and are therefore without Controversy the most eloquent Persons in the whole *British* Nation. I

---

8 The three quacks mentioned had comparable qualifications: Thomas Saffold (d. 1691) had practiced as a weaver and a fortune-teller; William Lilly (1602–1681) and John Case, a friend of John Partridge, were astrologers.

9 Couplet.

10 I.e., the willingness of the royal doctor to treat humble people.

would not willingly discourage any of the Arts, especially that of which I am an humble Professor; but I must confess, for the Good of my native Country, I could wish there might be a Suspension of Physick for some Years, that our Kingdom, which has been so much exhausted by the Wars, might have Leave to recruit it self.

As for my self, the only Physick which has brought me safe to almost the Age of Man,[11] and which I prescribe to all my Friends, is Abstinence. This is certainly the best Physick for Prevention, and very often the most effectual against a present Distemper. In short, my *Recipe* is, *Take nothing*.

Were the Body Politick to be physick'd like particular Persons, I should venture to prescribe to it after the same Manner. I remember when our whole Island was shaken with an Earthquake some Years ago, there was an impudent Mountebank who sold Pills which (as he told the Country People) were very good against an Earthquake. It may perhaps be thought as absurd to prescribe a Diet for the allaying Popular Commotions, and National Ferments. But I am verily perswaded, that if in such a Case a whole People were to enter into a Course of Abstinence, and eat nothing but Water-gruel for a Fortnight, it would abate the Rage and Animosity of Parties, and not a little contribute to the Cure of a distracted Nation.[12] Such a Fast would have a natural Tendency to the procuring of those Ends for which a Fast is usually proclaimed. If any Man has a Mind to enter on such a voluntary Abstinence, it might not be improper to give him the Caution of *Pythagoras* in particular:[13]

> *Abstine a Fabis.*
> "Abstain from Beans."

That is, say the Interpreters, Meddle not with Elections, Beans having been made Use of by the Voters among the *Athenians* in the Choice of Magistrates.

---

11 Presumably, 70 years of age. Bickerstaff is 64.

12 Addison did not exaggerate. Winston Churchill (*The Age of Revolution*, 1957) writes of Anne's reign: "All the time controversy ran to extremes. The religious passions of former years now flowed into the channels of political faction. Never was the strife of party groups so hot, so fiercely maintained, or more unscrupulous."

13 See Cicero *De Divinatione* 1. 30. 62; and Horace *Satires* 2. 6. 63.

The Tatler, No. 249

From Thursd. Nov. 9. to Saturday Nov. 11. 1710.

[Addison]

Per varios Casus, per tot Discrimina Rerum,
Tendimus. ———Virg.[1]

From my own Apartment, November 10.

I was last Night visited by a Friend of mine[2] who has an inex-
haustible Fund of Discourse, and never fails to entertain his Company with a Variety of Thoughts and Hints that are altogether
new and uncommon. Whether it were in Complaisance to my
Way of Living, or his real Opinion, he advanced the following
Paradox, That it required much greater Talents to fill up and
become a retired Life, than a Life of Business. Upon this Occasion he rallied very agreeably the busie Men of the Age, who only
valued themselves for being in Motion, and passing through a
Series of trifling and insignificant Actions. In the Heat of his Discourse, seeing a Piece of Money lying on my Table, I defie (says
he) any of these active Persons to produce half the Adventures
that this Twelvepenny-Piece has been engaged in, were it possible
for him to give us an Account of his Life.

My Friend's Talk made so odd an Impression upon my Mind,
that soon after I was a-Bed I fell insensibly into a most unaccountable *Reverie,* that had neither Moral nor Design in it, and cannot be so properly called a Dream as a Delirium.

Methoughts the Shilling that lay upon the Table reared it self

---

1 Virgil *Aeneid* 1. 204: "We move through various events and hazards."
2 Jonathan Swift twice mentions that his "hints" contributed to this essay,
in his *Journal to Stella* (November 30 and December 14, 1710).

upon its Edge, and turning the Face towards me, opened its
Mouth, and in a soft Silver Sound gave me the following Account
of his Life and Adventures:

I was born, says he, on the Side of a Mountain, near a little Village of *Peru*,[3] and made a Voyage to *England* in an Ingot, under
the Convoy of Sir *Francis Drake*.[4] I was, soon after my Arrival,
taken out of my *Indian* Habit, refined, naturalized, and put into
the *British* Mode, with the Face of Queen *Elizabeth* on one Side,
and the Arms of the Country on the other. Being thus equipped,
I found in me a wonderful Inclination to ramble, and visit all the
Parts of the new World into which I was brought. The People
very much favoured my natural Disposition, and shifted me so
fast from Hand to Hand, that before I was Five Years old, I had
travelled into almost every Corner of the Nation. But in the Beginning of my Sixth Year, to my unspeakable Grief, I fell into the
Hands of a miserable old Fellow, who clapped me into an Iron
Chest, where I found Five Hundred more of my own Quality who
lay under the same Confinement. The only Relief we had, was to
be taken out and counted over in the fresh Air every Morning and
Evening. After an Imprisonment of several Years, we heard some
Body knocking at our Chest, and breaking it open with an Hammer. This we found was the old Man's Heir, who, as his Father
lay a dying, was so good as to come to our Release: He separated
us that very Day. What was the Fate of my Companions, I know
not: As for my self, I was sent to the Apothecary's Shop for a Pint
of Sack.[5] The Apothecary gave me to an Herb-Woman, the Herb-
Woman to a Butcher, the Butcher to a Brewer, and the Brewer to
his Wife, who made a Present of me to a Nonconformist Preacher.[6]
After this Manner I made my Way merrily through the World;
for, as I told you before, we Shillings love nothing so much as
travelling. I sometimes fetched in a Shoulder of Mutton, sometimes a Play-Book, and often had the Satisfaction to treat a Tem-

3 I.e., in a Peruvian silver mine.

4 Sir Francis Drake (1540?–1596), the English navigator, plundered the
coasts of Chile and Peru in 1577.

5 A dry, white wine.

6 A protestant who disputed the authority of the Church of England.

plar at a Twelvepenny Ordinary, or carry him with Three Friends to *Westminster-Hall*.[7]

In the Midst of this pleasant Progress which I made from Place to Place, I was arrested by a superstitious old Woman, who shut me up in a greazy Purse, in Pursuance of a foolish Saying, That while she kept a Queen *Elizabeth*'s Shilling about her, she should never be without Money. I continued here a close Prisoner for many Months, till at last I was exchanged for Eight and Forty Farthings.

I thus rambled from Pocket to Pocket till the Beginning of the Civil Wars,[8] when, to my Shame be it spoken, I was employed in raising Soldiers against the King: For being of a very tempting Breadth, a Serjeant made Use of me to inveigle Country Fellows, and list[9] them in the Service of the Parliament.

As soon as he had made one Man sure, his Way was to oblige him to take a Shilling of a more homely Figure, and then practise the same Trick upon another. Thus I continued doing great Mischief to the Crown, till my Officer chancing one Morning to walk Abroad earlier than ordinary, sacrificed me to his Pleasures, and made Use of me to seduce a Milk-Maid. This Wench bent me, and gave me to her Sweetheart, applying more properly than she intended the usual Form of, *To my Love and from my Love*. This ungenerous Gallant[10] marrying her within few Days after, pawned me for a Dram of Brandy, and drinking me out next Day, I was beaten flat with an Hammer, and again set a running.

After many Adventures, which it would be tedious to relate, I was sent to a young Spendthrift, in Company with the Will of his deceased Father. The young Fellow, who I found was very extravagant, gave great Demonstrations of Joy at the receiving the Will; but opening it, he found himself disinherited and cut off from the Possession of a fair Estate, by Vertue of my being made a Present

---

[7] I.e., to treat a law student to a meal at an inn or to pay his coach fare.

[8] 1642. See Chronology, p. xxii.

[9] Enlist. Rural men were sometimes treated by a recruiting officer who persuaded them to accept a coin. Then they were told that this constituted enlistment in the army. See Farquhar's *The Recruiting Officer* 2.: 3.

[10] Lover. The word is used ironically when applied to a low-born person.

to him.[11] This put him into such a Passion, that after having taken me in his Hand, and cursed me, he squirred[12] me away from him as far as he could fling me. I chanced to light in an unfrequented Place under a dead Wall, where I lay undiscovered and useless, during the Usurpation of *Oliver Cromwell.*

About a Year after the King's Return,[13] a poor Cavalier that was walking there about Dinner-Time fortunately cast his Eye upon me, and, to the great Joy of us both, carried me to a Cook's-Shop, where he dined upon me, and drank the King's Health. When I came again into the World, I found that I had been happier in my Retirement than I thought, having probably by that Means escaped wearing a monstrous Pair of Breeches.[14]

Being now of great Credit and Antiquity, I was rather looked upon as a Medal than an ordinary Coin; for which Reason a Gamester laid hold of me, and converted me to a Counter,[15] having got together some Dozens of us for that Use. We led a melancholy Life in his Possession, being busy at those Hours wherein Current Coin is at rest, and partaking the Fate of our Master, being in a few Moments valued at a Crown, a Pound, or a Sixpence, according to the Situation in which the Fortune of the Cards placed us. I had at length the good Luck to see my Master break,[16] by which Means I was again sent Abroad under my primitive Denomination of a Shilling.

I shall pass over many other Accidents of less Moment, and hasten to that fatal Catastrophe when I fell into the Hands of an Artist[17] who conveyed me under Ground, and with an unmerciful Pair of Sheers cut off my Titles, clipped my Brims, retrenched my

---

[11] A person left a single shilling (or today, a single dollar) is thought to have no legal recourse against the will which disinherits him.

[12] Threw away with a jerk.

[13] Charles II was restored to the throne in 1660.

[14] The commonwealth coin bore two shields—one for England and one for Ireland. These resembled a pair of breeches and were so designated in popular speech.

[15] A gambling chip.

[16] Become bankrupt.

[17] An outlaw who salvaged silver by trimming the edges of coins.

Shape, rubbed me to my inmost Ring, and, in short, so spoiled and pillaged me, that he did not leave me worth a Groat. You may think what a Confusion I was in to see my self thus curtailed and disfigured. I should have been ashamed to have shown my Head, had not all my old Acquaintance been reduced to the same shameful Figure, excepting some few that were punched through the Belly.[18] In the midst of this general Calamity, when every Body thought our Misfortune irretrievable, and our Case desperate, we were thrown into the Furnace together, and (as it often happens with Cities rising out of a Fire) appeared with greater Beauty and Lustre than we could ever boast of before. What has happened to me since the Change of Sex[19] which you now see, I shall take some other Opportunity to relate. In the mean Time I shall only repeat Two Adventures, as being very extraordinary, and neither of them having ever happened to me above once in my Life. The First was, my being in a Poet's Pocket, who was so taken with the Brightness and Novelty of my Appearance, that it gave Occasion to the finest Burlesque Poem in the *British* Language, entituled from me, *The Splendid Shilling*.[20] The Second Adventure, which I must not omit, happened to me in the Year 1703, when I was given away in Charity to a blind Man; but indeed this was by a Mistake, the Person who gave me having heedlesly thrown me into the Hat among a Pennyworth of Farthings.

[18] Old silver coins were worn as ornaments.

[19] If a picture of Queen Anne replaced that of Queen Elizabeth, there would be no change of sex. Presumably, the shilling had already been recast in the form of one of the English kings.

[20] John Philips (1676–1709) published the *Splendid Shilling*, a Miltonic burlesque, in 1705.

The Tatler, No. 257

From Tuesday Nov. 28. to Thursday Nov. 30. 1710.

[S t e e l e   a n d   A d d i s o n]

In nova fert Animus mutatas dicere Formas
Corpora: Dii, Caeptis (nam vos mutastis & illas)
Aspirate meis. —— Ovid. Met.[1]

From my own Apartment, Nov. 29.

Every Nation is distinguished by Productions that are peculiar to it. *Great Britain* is particularly fruitful in Religions, that shoot up and flourish in this Climate more than in any other. We are so famous Abroad for our great Variety of Sects and Opinions, that an ingenious Friend of mine, who is lately returned from his Travels, assures me, there is a Show at this Time *carried* up and down in *Germany,* which represents all the Religions of *Great Britain* in Waxwork. Notwithstanding that the Pliancy of the Matter[2] in which the Images are wrought makes it capable of being moulded into all Shapes and Figures, my Friend tells me, that he did not think it possible for it to be twisted and tortured into so many skrew'd Faces and wry Features as appeared in several of the Figures that composed the Show. I was indeed so pleased with the Design of the *German* Artist, that I begged my Friend to give me an Account of it in all its Particulars, which he did after the following Manner:

I have often, says he, been present at a Show of Elephants, Camels, Dromedaries, and other strange Creatures, but I never saw so

1 Ovid *Metamorphoses* 1. 1–3: "I will write of bodies changed to new forms. You gods, from whom these miracles did spring, assist me in this task."
2 The wax.

113

great an Assembly of Spectators as were met together at the Opening of this great Piece of Wax work. We were all placed in a large Hall, according to the Price that we had paid for our Seats: The Curtain that hung before the Show was made by a Master of Tapestry, who had woven it in the Figure of a monstrous *Hydra*[3] that had several Heads, which brandished out their Tongues, and seemed to hiss at each other. Some of these Heads were large and entire; and where any of them had been lopped away, there sprouted up several in the Room of them; insomuch that for one Head cut off, a Man might see Ten, Twenty, or an Hundred of a smaller Size, creeping through the Wound. In short, the whole Picture was nothing but Confusion and Bloodshed. On a sudden, says my Friend, I was startled with a Flourish of many Musical Instruments that I had never heard before, which was followed by a short Tune, (if it might be so called) wholly made up of Jars and Discords. Among the rest, there was an Organ, a Bagpipe, a Groaning-Board, a Stentorophonick-Trumpet,[4] with several Wind Instruments of a most disagreeable Sound, which I do not so much as know the Name of. After a short Flourish, the Curtain was drawn up, and we were presented with the most extraordinary Assembly of Figures that ever entered into a Man's Imagination. The Design of the Workman was so well expressed in the dumb Show[5] before us, that it was not hard for an *Englishman* to comprehend the Meaning of it.

The principal Figures were placed in a Row, consisting of Seven Persons. The middle Figure,[6] which immediately attracted the Eyes of the whole Company, and was much bigger than the rest, was formed like a Matron, dressed in the Habit of an elderly Woman of Quality in Queen *Elizabeth*'s Days. The most remarkable Parts of her Dress, was the Beaver[7] with the Steeple Crown,

---

[3] A snake with many heads, which grew again as quickly as they were cut off.

[4] A groaning board is a board made of elm which was thought to give out a groaning sound when a hot iron was applied to it. A stentorophonic trumpet is a megaphone.

[5] A drama without words.

[6] Representing the Anglican Church.

[7] A hat made of beaver fur.

the Scarf that was darker than Sable, and the Lawn[8] Apron that
was whiter than Ermin. Her Gown was of the richest black Velvet,
and just upon her Heart studded with large Diamonds of an in-
estimable Value, disposed in the Form of a Cross. She bore an inexpressible Chearfulness and Dignity in her Aspect; and though
she seemed in Years, appeared with so much Spirit and Vivacity,
as gave her at the same Time an Air of old Age and Immortality.
I found my Heart touched with so much Love and Reverence at
the Sight of her, that the Tears ran down my Face as I looked
upon her; and still the more I looked upon her, the more my
Heart was melted with the Sentiments of Filial Tenderness and
Duty. I discovered every Moment something so charming in this
Figure, that I could scarce take my Eyes off it. On its Right Hand
there sat the Figure of a Woman[9] so covered with Ornaments, that
her Face, her Body, and her Hands, were almost entirely hid under them. The little you could see of her Face was painted; and
what I thought very odd, had something in it like Artificial Wrinkles;[10] but I was the less surprised at it, when I saw upon her Forehead an old-fashioned Tower of grey Hairs. Her Head-Dress rose
very high by Three several Stories or Degrees;[11] her Garments had
a Thousand Colours in them, and were embroidered with Crosses
in Gold, Silver and Silk: She had nothing on, so much as a Glove
or a Slipper, which was not marked with this Figure; nay; so su-
perstitiously fond did she appear of it, that she sat cross-legged. I
was quickly sick of this tawdry Composition of Ribands, Silks and
Jewels, and therefore cast my Eye on a Dame which was just the
Reverse of it. I need not tell my Reader, that the Lady before
described was *Popery,* or that she I am now going to describe is
Presbytery. She sat on the Left Hand of the venerable Matron, and
so much resembled her in the Features of her Countenance, that
she seemed her Sister; but at the same Time that one observed a
Likeness in her Beauty, one could not but take Notice, that there

8 Fine linen.
9 Representing Roman Catholicism. The description of Popery and Presbytery which follows, closely parallels Swift's satire in *A Tale of a Tub* (1704).
10 The Roman Church liked to proclaim its antiquity.
11 The Pope's tiara, with its three crowns, represents his jurisdiction in
Heaven, Earth, and Hell.

was something in it sickly and splenatick. Her Face had enough to discover the Relation,[12] but it was drawn up into a peevish Figure, sowred with Discontent, and overcast with Melancholy. She seemed offended at the Matron for the Shape of her Hat, as too much resembling the tripple Coronet of the Person who sate by her. One might see likewise, that she dissented from the white Apron and the Cross; for which Reasons she had made her self a plain, homely Dowdy, and turned her Face towards the Sectaries[13] that sat on her Left Hand, as being afraid of looking upon the Matron, lest she should see the Harlot[14] by her.

On the Right Hand of *Popery* sat *Judaism,* represented by an old Man embroidered with Phylacteries,[15] and distinguished by many Typical Figures, which I had not Skill enough to unriddle. He was placed among the Rubbish of a Temple; but instead of weeping over it, (which I should have expected from him) he was counting out a Bag of Money upon the Ruins of it.[16]

On his Right Hand was *Deism,*[17] or *Natural Religion.* This was a Figure of an half-naked aukward Country Wench, who with proper Ornaments and Education would have made an agreeable and beautiful Appearance; but for Want of those Advantages, was such a Spectacle, as a Man would blush to look upon.

I have now, continued my Friend, given you an Account of those who were placed on the Right Hand of the Matron, and who, according to the Order in which they sat, were *Deism, Judaism,* and *Popery.* On the Left Hand, as I told you, appeared *Presbytery.* The next to her was a Figure[18] which somewhat puzzled me: It was that of a Man looking, with Horror in his Eyes, upon

12 Resemblance.

13 I.e., the wax figures representing other sects.

14 See *Tatler* No. 190, n. 4.

15 Small leather boxes, containing the Hebrew texts, bound to the head and arm during prayer.

16 The suggestion is that Jews were neglecting their religious traditions—symbolized by the Temple, which was destroyed in 75 A.D.—in pursuing their commercial interests.

17 See *Tatler* No. 111, n. 7.

18 Anabaptism, which first became prominent in Germany in 1521, denied the validity of infant baptism. This explains the aversion to water (hydrophobia) and to the silver basin.

a Silver Bason filled with Water. Observing something in his Countenance that looked like Lunacy, I fancied at first that he was to express that kind of Distraction which the Physicians call the *Hydro-Phobia;* but considering what the Intention of the Show was, I immediately recollected my self, and concluded it to be *Anabaptism.*

The next Figure was a Man that sat under a most profound Composure of Mind: He wore an Hat whose Brims were exactly parallel with the Horizon: His Garment had neither Sleeve nor Skirt, nor so much as a superfluous Button. What they called his Cravat, was a little Piece of white Linen quilled[19] with great Exactness, and hanging below his Chin about Two Inches. Seeing a Book in his Hand, I asked our Artist what it was, who told me it was the *Quakers* Religions,[20] upon which I desired a Sight of it. Upon Perusal, I found it to be nothing but a new-fashioned Grammar, or an Art of abridging ordinary Discourse. The Nouns were reduced to a very small Number, as the *Light, Friend, Babylon.* The principal of his Pronouns was *Thou;* and as for You, Ye, and Yours, I found they were not looked upon as Parts of Speech in this Grammar. All the Verbs wanted the Second Person Plural; the Participles ended all in *ing* or *ed,* which were marked with a particular Accent. There were no Adverbs besides *Yea* and *Nay.* The same Thrift was observed in the Prepositions. The Conjunctions were only *Hem!* and *Ha!* and the Interjections brought under the Three Heads of Sighing, Sobbing, and Groaning.

There was at the End of the Grammar a little Nomenclature, called, *The Christian Man's Vocabulary,* which gave new Appellations, or (if you will) Christian Names to almost every Thing in Life.[21] I replaced the Book in the Hand of the Figure, not without admiring the Simplicity of its Garb, Speech, and Behaviour.

Just opposite to this Row of Religions, there was a Statue dressed in a Fool's Coat, with a Cap of Bells upon his Head, laugh-

19 Folded.

20 The Society of Friends, an evangelical religious body having no definite creed and no regular ministry, was founded by George Fox (1624–1691) in the mid-seventeenth century. The group's more familiar name came from Fox's injunction to "quake and tremble at the word of the Lord."

21 See *Guardian* No. 116, n. 14.

ing and pointing at the Figures that stood before him. This Ideot is supposed to say in his Heart what *David's* Fool[22] did some Thousands of Years ago, and was therefore designed as a proper Representative of those among us who are called Atheists and Infidels by others, and Free-Thinkers by themselves.

There were many other Groupes of Figures which I did not know the Meaning of; but seeing a Collection of both Sexes turning their Backs upon the Company, and laying their Heads very close together, I enquired after their Religion, and found that they called themselves the *Philodelphians,*[23] or the Family of Love.

In the opposite Corner there sat another little Congregation of strange Figures, opening their Mouths as wide as they could gape, and distinguished by the Title of the *Sweet Singers of Israel.*[24]

I must not omit, that in this Assembly of Wax there were several Pieces that moved by Clockwork, and gave great Satisfaction to the Spectators. Behind the Matron there stood one of these Figures, and behind *Popery* another, which, as the Artist told us, were each of them the Genius[25] of the Person they attended. That behind *Popery* represented *Persecution,* and the other *Moderation.* The first of these moved by secret Springs towards a great Heap of dead Bodies that lay piled upon one another at a considerable Distance behind the principal Figures. There were written on the Foreheads of these dead Men several hard Words, as *Prae-Adamites, Sabbatarians, Camaronians, Muggletonians, Brownists, Independants, Masonites, Camisars,* and the like.[26] At the Approach of *Persecution,* it was so contrived, that as she held up her Bloody Flag, the whole Assembly of dead Men, like those in the

22 The figure is Atheism. See Ps. 14:1: "The fool hath said in his heart, 'There is no God.' "

23 A religious sect founded in London in 1652.

24 A puritan sect which flourished in Edinburgh during the late seventeenth century.

25 Spirit or characteristic.

26 Listed are a number of small protestant sects which flourished during the seventeenth century, but which had few followers by 1710. The implication of the following lines is that such sects can exist only in times of persecution.

Rehearsal,[27] started up and drew their Swords. This was followed by great Clashings and Noise, when, in the Midst of the Tumult, the Figure of *Moderation* moved gently towards this new Army, which upon her holding up a Paper in her Hand, inscribed, *Liberty of Conscience,* immediately fell into a Heap of Carcasses, remaining in the same quiet Posture that they lay at first.

[27] See *Tatler* No. 18, n. 24. In the drama (act 2, sc. 5), Bayes tells the actors that after they fall dead, they must rise dancing.

The Tatler, No. 259

From Saturday Dec. 2. to Tuesday Dec. 5. 1710.

[S t e e l e   a n d   A d d i s o n]

——— *Vexat Censura Columbas.*   Juv.[1]

A Continuation of the Journal of the Court of Honour,[2] *held in* Sheer-Lane *on* Monday *the 27th of* November, *before* Isaac Bickerstaff *Esq; Censor of* Great Britain.

Elizabeth Makebate,[3] of the Parish of St. *Catherine's,* Spinster, was indicted for surreptitiously taking away the Hassock[4] from under the Lady *Grave-Airs,* between the Hours of Four and Five, on *Sunday* the 26th of *November.* The Prosecutor deposed, That as she stood up to make a Courtesie to a Person of Quality in a neighbouring Pew, the Criminal conveyed away the Hassock by Stealth, insomuch that the Prosecutor[5] was obliged to sit all the

---

1 Juvenal *Satires* 2. 63: "Censure condemns the dove."

2 The Court is established in *Tatler* No. 250: "As I last Year presided over a Court of Justice, it is my Intention this Year to set myself at the Head of a Court of Honour. . . . I intend to sit myself in it as President, with several Men of Honour on my Right Hand, and Women of Virtue on my Left, as my Assistants. . . . Having given this public Notice of my Court, I must further add, that I intend to open it on this Day Sevennight, being *Monday* the Twentieth Instant; and do hereby invite all such as have suffered Injuries and Affronts, that are not to be redressed by the common Laws of the Land, whether they be short Bows, cold Salutations, supercilious Looks, unreturned Smiles, distant Behaviour, or forced Familiarity . . ."

3 A makebate is a breeder of quarrels.

4 A kneeling hassock.

5 Through all the Court of Honour essays (*Tatlers* No. 253, 256, 259, 262, and 265) the plaintiff is called "the Prosecutor" and the defendant "the Criminal."

while she was at Church, or to say her Prayers in a Posture that
did not become a Woman of her Quality. The Prisoner pleaded
Inadvertency; and the Jury were going to bring it in Chance-med-
ley,[6] had not several Witnesses been produced against the said
Elizabeth Makebate, that she was an old Offender, and a Woman
of a bad Reputation. It appeared in particular, that on the *Sunday* before she had detracted from a new Petticoat of Mrs. *Mary
Doelittle,* having said in the Hearing of several credible Witnesses, that the said Petticoat was scowred,[7] to the great Grief and
Detriment of the said *Mary Doelittle.* There were likewise many
Evidences produced against the Criminal, that though she never
failed to come to Church on *Sunday,* she was a most notorious
Sabbath-Breaker, and that she spent her whole Time, during Divine Service, in disparaging other People's Cloaths, and whisper-
ing to those who sat next her. Upon the whole, she was found
guilty of the Indictment, and received Sentence to ask Pardon of
the Prosecutor upon her bare Knees, without either Cushion or
Hassock under her, in the Face of the Court.

   N. B.[8] As soon as the Sentence was executed on the Criminal,
which was done in open Court with the utmost Severity, the first
Lady of the Bench on Mr. *Bickerstaff's* Right Hand stood up, and
made a Motion to the Court, That whereas it was impossible for
Women of Fashion to dress themselves before the Church was half
done, and whereas many Confusions and Inconveniencies did arise
thereupon, it might be lawful for them to send a Footman, in order to keep their Places, as was usual in other polite and well regulated Assemblies.[9] The Motion was ordered to be entered in the
Books, and considered at a more convenient Time.

   Charles Cambrick, Linendraper, in the City of *Westminster,*
was indicted for speaking obscenely to the Lady *Penelope Touch-
wood.* It appeared, That the Prosecutor and her Woman going in
a Stage-Coach from *London* to *Brentford,* where they were to be

   [6] I.e., to rule the event an accident.
   [7] Scrubbed. The implication is that the petticoat was not new, as Mrs. Doelittle claimed.
   [8] *Nota bene,* note well.
   [9] Servants were commonly sent to the theater to keep seats for their
employers.

met by the Lady's own Chariot, the Criminal and another of his
Acquaintance travelled with them in the same Coach, at which
Time the Prisoner talked Bawdy for the Space of Three Miles and
a half. The Prosecutor alledged, That over-against *the Old Fox* at
Knightsbridge he mentioned the Word Linen; That at the further
End of *Kensington* he made Use of the Term Smock; and that before he came to *Hammersmith,* he talked almost a Quarter of an
Hour upon Wedding-Shifts. The Prosecutor's Woman confirmed
what her Lady had said, and added further, That she had never
seen her Lady in so great a Confusion, and in such a Taking,[10] as
she was during the whole Discourse of the Criminal. The Prisoner
had little to say for himself, but that he talked only in his own
Trade, and meant no Hurt by what he said. The Jury however
found him guilty, and represented by their Forewoman, That
such Discourses were apt to sully the Imagination, and that by a
Concatenation of Idea's, the Word Linen implied many Things
that were not proper to be stirred up in the Mind of a Woman
who was of the Prosecutor's Quality, and therefore gave it as their
Verdict, That the Linendraper should lose his Tongue. Mr. *Bickerstaff* said, he thought the Prosecutor's Ears were as much to
blame as the Prisoner's Tongue, and therefore gave Sentence as
follows: That they should both be placed over-against one another in the Midst of the Court, there to remain for the Space of
one Quarter of an Hour, during which Time, the Linendraper
was to be gagged, and the Lady to hold her Hands close upon both
her Ears, which was executed accordingly.

Edward Callicoat was indicted as an Accomplice to *Charles
Cambrick,* for that he the said *Edward Callicoat* did, by his Silence and his Smiles, seem to approve and abet the said *Charles
Cambrick* in every Thing he said. It appeared, That the Prisoner
was Foreman of the Shop to the aforesaid *Charles Cambrick,* and
by his Post obliged to smile at every Thing that the other should
be pleased to say: Upon which he was acquitted.

Josias Shallow was indicted in the Name of Dame *Winifred,*
sole Relict of *Richard Dainty* Esq. for having said several Times
in Company, and in the Hearing of several Persons there present,

---

10 In such agitation.

That he was extremely obliged to the Widow *Dainty,* and that he should never be able sufficiently to express his Gratitude. The Prosecutor urged, That this might blast her Reputation, and that it was in Effect a boasting of Favours which he had never received. The Prisoner seemed to be much astonished at the Construction which was put upon his Words, and said, That he meant nothing by them, but that the Widow had befriended him in a Lease, and was very kind to his younger Sister. The Jury finding him a little weak in his Understanding, without going out of the Court, brought in their Verdict *Ignoramus.*

Ursula Goodenough was accused by the Lady *Betty Wou'dbe,* for having said, That she the Lady *Betty Wou'dbe* was painted. The Prisoner brought several Persons of good Credit to witness to her Reputation, and proved by undeniable Evidences, that she was never at the Place where the Words were said to have been uttered. The Censor[11] observing the Behaviour of the Prosecutor, found Reason to believe that she had indicted the Prisoner for no other Reason but to make her Complexion be taken Notice of, which indeed was very fresh and beautiful: He therefore asked the Offender with a very stern Voice, How she could presume to spread so groundless a Report? And whether she saw any Colours in the Lady *Wou'dbe*'s Face that could procure Credit to such a Falshood? Do you see (says he) any Lillies or Roses in her Cheeks, any Bloom, any Probability?————The Prosecutor not able to bear such Language any longer, told him, That he talked like a blind old Fool, and that she was asham'd to have entertained any Opinion of his Wisdom: But she was soon put to Silence, and sentenced to wear her Mask[12] for Five Months, and not to presume to show her Face till the Town should be empty.

Benjamin Buzzard Esq; was indicted for having told the Lady *Everbloom* at a publick Ball, That she looked very well for a Woman of her Years. The Prisoner not denying the Fact, and persisting before the Court that he looked upon it as a Compliment, the Jury brought him in *Non Compos Mentis.*[13]

[11] I.e., Bickerstaff.

[12] The mask was worn by ladies of quality for some years after the Restoration; by 1710, its use was associated with prostitutes.

[13] Of unsound mind.

The Court then adjourned to Monday *the* 11*th Instant.*

Copia Vera,

Charles Lillie.[14]

---

[14] Charles Lillie, a perfumer at the corner of Beaufort-Buildings in the Strand, was an agent for the sale of *The Tatler* and, later, of *The Spectator*. He is specified as clerk of both the earlier Court of Justice and of the present Court of Honour.

The Tatler, No. 267

From Thursd. Dec. 21. to Saturday Dec. 23. 1710.

[Addison]

Qui Genus humanum Ingenio superavit, & omnes
Restinxit Stellas, exortus uti Aerius Sol. Lucr.[1]

From my own Apartment, December 22.

I have heard, that it is a Rule among the Conventuals[2] of several Orders in the Romish Church, to shut themselves up at a certain Time of the Year, not only from the World in general, but from the Members of their own Fraternity, and to pass away several Days by themselves in settling Accounts between their Maker and their own Souls, in cancelling unrepented Crimes, and renewing their Contracts of Obedience for the future. Such stated Times for particular Acts of Devotion, or the Exercise of certain religious Duties, have been enjoined in all civil Governments, whatever Deity they worshipped, or whatever Religion they professed. That which may be done at all Times, is often totally neglected and forgotten, unless fixed and determined to some Time more than another; and therefore, though several Duties may be suitable to every Day of our Lives, they are most likely to be performed if some Days are more particularly set apart for the Practice of them. Our Church[3] has accordingly instituted several Seasons of Devotion, when Time, Custom, Prescription, and

---

[1] Lucretius *De Rerum Natura* 3. 1043: "He whose intellect surpassed humanity, who outshone others as the risen sun extinguishes the stars."

[2] Convent members.

[3] The Church of England.

(if I may so say) the Fashion it self, call upon a Man to be serious and attentive to the great End of his Being.

I have hinted in some former Papers,[4] that the greatest and wisest of Men in all Ages and Countries, particularly in *Rome* and *Greece,* were renowned for their Piety and Virtue. It is now my Intention to show how those in our own Nation, that have been unquestionably the most eminent for Learning and Knowledge, were likewise the most eminent for their Adherence to the Religion of their Country.

I might produce very shining Examples from among the Clergy; but because Priestcraft[5] is the common Cry of every cavelling empty Scribbler, I shall show, that all the Laymen who have exerted a more than ordinary Genius in their Writings, and were the Glory of their Times, were Men whose Hopes were filled with Immortality, and the Prospect of future Rewards, and Men who lived in a dutiful Submission to all the Doctrines of Revealed Religion.

I shall in this Paper only instance Sir *Francis Bacon,*[6] a Man who for the Greatness of Genius, and Compass of Knowledge, did Honour to his Age and Country; I could almost say to Humane Nature it self. He possessed at once all those extraordinary Talents which were divided amongst the greatest Authors of Antiquity. He had the sound, distinct, comprehensive Knowledge of *Aristotle,* with all the beautiful Lights, Graces and Embellishments, of *Cicero.* One does not know which to admire most in his Writings, the Strength of Reason, Force of Style, or Brightness of Imagination.

This Author has remarked in several Parts of his Works, that a thorough Insight into Philosophy[7] makes a good Believer, and that a Smattering in it naturally produces such a Race of despicable Infidels as the little profligate Writers of the present Age,

4 *Tatler* No. 152 considers Homer's depiction of "a future State," and No. 154 discusses Virgil's description.

5 Because of the puritan repressiveness under the Commonwealth, it was fashionable to reject any religious or moral injunction as "priestcraft."

6 English philosopher and statesman (1561–1626).

7 I.e., scientific and liberal studies.

whom (I must confess) I have always accused to my self, not so much for their Want of Faith as their Want of Learning.[8]

I was infinitely pleased to find among the Works of this extraordinary Man a Prayer of his own composing, which, for the Elevation of Thought, and Greatness of Expression, seems rather the Devotion of an Angel than a Man. His principal Fault seems to have been the Excess of that Virtue which covers a Multitude of Faults.[9] This betrayed him to so great an Indulgence towards his Servants, who made a corrupt Use of it, that it strip'd him of all those Riches and Honours which a long Series of Merits had heaped upon him.[10] But in this Prayer, at the same Time that we find him prostrating himself before the great Mercy-Seat, and humbled under Afflictions which at that Time lay heavy upon him, we see him supported by the Sense of his Integrity, his Zeal, his Devotion, and his Love to Mankind, which give him a much higher Figure in the Minds of Thinking Men, than that Greatness had done from which he was fallen. I shall beg Leave to write down the Prayer it self, with the Title to it, as it was found among his Lordship's Papers, written in his own Hand; not being able to furnish my Reader with an Entertainment more suitable to this solemn Time.[11]

A PRAYER OR PSALM MADE BY MY LORD BACON, CHANCELLOR OF ENGLAND.

"Most gracious Lord God, my merciful Father; from my Youth up my Creator, my Redeemer, my Comforter. Thou, O Lord, foundest and searchest the Depths and Secrets of all Hearts; Thou acknowledgest the Upright of Heart; Thou judgest the Hypocrite; Thou ponderest Men's Thoughts and Doings as in a Ballance; Thou measurest their Intentions as with a Line; Vanity and crooked Ways cannot be hid from Thee.

Remember, O Lord! how thy Servant hath walked before thee; re-

8 See *Tatlers* No. 111 and No. 158.

9 I Pet. 4:8: "Charity shall cover a multitude of sins."

10 Bacon, who became Lord Chancellor of England in 1618, was found guilty of bribery and corrupt dealing in chancery suits in 1621 and was banished from parliament and court. He was later pardoned.

11 Christmas.

member what I have first sought, and what hath been principal in my Intentions. I have loved thy Assemblies, I have mourned for the Divisions of thy Church, I have delighted in the Brightness of thy Sanctuary. This Vine[12] which thy Right Hand hath planted in this Nation, I have ever prayed unto Thee, that it might have the first and the latter Rain, and that it might stretch her Branches to the Seas, and to the Floods. The State and Bread of the Poor and Oppressed have been precious in mine Eyes; I have hated all Cruelty and Hardness of Heart; I have (though in a despised Weed)[13] procured the Good of all Men. If any have been my Enemies, I thought not of them, neither hath the Sun almost set upon my Displeasure; but I have been as a Dove, free from Superfluity of Maliciousness. Thy Creatures have been my Books, but thy Scriptures much more. I have sought Thee in the Courts, Fields and Gardens, but I have found Thee in thy Temples.

Thousands have been my Sins, and Ten Thousands my Transgressions, but thy Sanctifications have remained with me, and my Heart (through thy Grace) hath been an unquenched Coal upon thine Altar.

O Lord, my Strength! I have since my Youth met with Thee in all my Ways, by thy Fatherly Compassions, by thy comfortable Chastisements, and by thy most visible Providence. As thy Favours have increased upon me, so have thy Corrections; so as Thou hast been always near me, O Lord! And ever as my Worldly Blessings were exalted, so secret Darts from Thee have pierced me; and when I have ascended before Men, I have descended in Humiliation before Thee. And now when I thought most of Peace and Honour, thy Hand is heavy upon me, and hath humbled me according to thy former loving Kindness, keeping me still in thy Fatherly School, not as a Bastard, but as a Child. Just are thy Judgments upon me for my Sins, which are more in Number than the Sands of the Sea, but have no Proportion to thy Mercies; for what are the Sands of the Sea? Earth, Heavens, and all these, are nothing to thy Mercies. Besides my innumerable Sins, I confess before Thee, that I am Debtor to Thee for the gracious Talent of thy Gifts and Graces, which I have neither put into a Napkin, nor put it (as I ought) to Exchangers,[14] where it might have made

[12] The Church of England.

[13] The man wearing the garb of the Lord Chancellor necessarily made many enemies.

[14] I.e., he neither saved them nor invested them profitably. Bacon was alluding to the parable of the talents in Matt. 25:14–29.

best Profit, but mispent it in Things for which I was least fit: So I may truly say, my Soul hath been a Stranger in the Course of my Pilgrimage. Be merciful unto me, O Lord, for my Saviour's Sake, and receive me unto thy Bosom, or guide me in thy Ways."

The Tatler, No. 271

From Saturday Dec. 30. to Tuesday Jan. 2. 1710.

[Steele]

The Printer having informed me, that there are as many of these Papers printed as will make Four Volumes, I am now come to the End of my Ambition in this Matter, and have nothing further to say to the World, under the Character of *Isaac Bickerstaff*.[1] This Work has indeed for some Time been disagreeable to me, and the Purpose of it wholly lost by my being so long understood as the Author.[2] I never designed in it to give any Man any secret Wound by my Concealment, but spoke in the Character of an old Man, a Philosopher, an Humorist, an Astrologer, and a Censor, to allure my Reader with the Variety of my Subjects, and insinuate, if I could, the Weight of Reason with the Agreeableness of Wit. The general Purpose of the whole has been to recommend Truth, Innocence, Honour, and Virtue, as the chief Ornaments of Life; but I considered, that Severity of Manners[3] was absolutely necessary to him who would censure others, and for that Reason, and that only, chose to talk in a Mask. I shall not carry my Humility so far as to call my self a vicious Man; but at the same Time must confess, my Life is at best but pardonable. And with no greater Character than this, a Man would make but an indifferent Progress in attacking prevailing and fashionable Vices, which Mr.

---

[1] Swift's *Journal to Stella* (January 2, 1711) noted: "Steele's last *Tatler* came out today. You will see it before this comes to you, and how he takes leave of the world. He never told so much as Addison of it, who was surprised as much as I; but, to say the truth, it was time, for he grew cruel dull and dry."

[2] The essays were published anonymously.

[3] Exemplary moral standards.

Bickerstaff has done with a Freedom of Spirit that would have lost both its Beauty and Efficacy, had it been pretended to by Mr. *Steele.*

As to the Work it self, the Acceptance it has met with is the best Proof of its Value; but I should err against that Candour which an honest Man should always carry about him, if I did not own, that the most approved Pieces in it were written by others, and those which have been most excepted against[4] by my self. The Hand[5] that has assisted me in those noble Discourses upon the Immortality of the Soul, the glorious Prospects of another Life, and the most sublime Idea's of Religion and Virtue, is a Person who is too fondly my Friend ever to own them; but I should little deserve to be his, if I usurped the Glory of them. I must acknowledge at the same Time, that I think the finest Strokes of Wit and Humour in all Mr. *Bickerstaff*'s Lucubrations are those for which he is also beholden to him.

As for the Satyrical Parts of these Writings, those against the Gentlemen who profess Gaming[6] are the most licentious; but the main of them I take to come from losing Gamesters, as Invectives against the Fortunate; for in very many of them, I was very little else but the Transcriber.[7] If any have been more particularly marked at, such Persons may impute it to their own Behaviour, (before they were touched upon) in publickly speaking their Resentment against the Author, and professing they would support any Man who should insult him. When I mention this Subject, I hope Major-General *Davenport,* Brigadier *Bisset,* and my Lord *Forbes,*[8] will accept of my Thanks for their frequent good Offices, in professing their Readiness to partake any Danger that should befal me in so just an Undertaking, as the Endeavour to banish

4 Most objected to.

5 Joseph Addison.

6 *Tatlers* No. 56, 57, 59, 62, 65, 66, 68, 70, etc.

7 I.e., the "Satyrical Parts" were either written by losing gamesters or were transcribed by Steele from their conversation.

8 Major-General Sherington Davenport, Brigadier Andrew Bisset, and George, Lord Forbes were military friends of Steele, who had publicly faced down a group of cardsharpers at St. James's Coffee-house when they threatened to attack him.

Fraud and Couzenage from the Presence and Conversation of Gentlemen.

But what I find is the least excusable Part of all this Work is, That I have, in some Places in it, touched upon Matters which concern both the Church and State.[9] All I shall say for this is, That the Points I alluded to are such as concerned every Christian and Freeholder[10] in *England;* and I could not be cold enough to conceal my Opinion on Subjects which related to either of those Characters. But Politicks apart. I must confess, it has been a most exquisite Pleasure to me to frame Characters of Domestick Life, and put those Parts of it which are least observed into an agreeable View; to enquire into the Seeds of Vanity and Affectation, to lay before my Readers the Emptiness of Ambition: In a Word, to trace Humane Life through all its Mazes and Recesses, and show much shorter Methods than Men ordinarily practise, to be happy, agreeable, and great.

But to enquire into Men's Faults and Weaknesses has something in it so unwelcome, that I have often seen People in Pain to act[11] before me, whose Modesty only make them think themselves liable to Censure. This, and a Thousand other nameless Things, have made it an irksome Task to me to personate Mr. *Bickerstaff* any longer; and I believe it does not often happen, that the Reader is delighted where the Author is displeased.

All I can now do for the further Gratification of the Town, is to give them a faithful Index and Explication of Passages and Allusions, and sometimes of Persons intended in the several scattered Parts of the Work. At the same Time, the succeeding Volumes[12] shall discover which of the whole have been written by me, and which by others, and by whom, as far as I am able, or permitted.[13]

Thus I have voluntarily done what I think all Authors should do when call'd upon. I have published my Name to my Writings,

9 I.e., political issues.
10 Landowner.
11 Afraid to behave naturally.
12 I.e., the four volumes of the collected *Tatler* papers.
13 Steele did this in his preface to Volume I.

and given my self up to the Mercy of the Town (as *Shakespear* expresses it) with all my Imperfections on my Head.[14] The indulgent Readers

> *Most Obliged,*
> *Most Obedient,*
> *Humble Servant,*
> Richard Steele.

[14] *Hamlet,* act 1, sc. 5.

The SPECTATOR.

——Equitis quoq; jam migravit ab aure voluptas
Omnis ad incertos oculos & gaudia vana. Hor.

Wednesday, March 21. 1711.

IT is my Design in this Paper to deliver down to Posterity a faithful Account of the Italian Opera, and of the gradual Progress which it has made upon the English Stage: For there is no Question but our great Grand-children will be very curious to know the Reason why their Forefathers used to sit together like an Audience of Foreigners in their own Country, and to hear whole Plays acted before them in a Tongue which they did not understand.

Arsinoe was the first Opera that gave us a Taste of Italian Musick. The great Success which this Opera met with, produced some Attempts of forming Pieces upon Italian Plans, that should give a more natural and reasonable Entertainment than what can be met with in the elaborate Trifles of that Nation. This alarm'd the Poetasters and Fidlers of the Town, who were used to deal in a more ordinary Kind of Ware; and therefore laid down an establish'd Rule, which is receiv'd as such to this very Day, *That nothing is capable of being well set to Musick, that is not Nonsense.*

This Maxim was no sooner receiv'd, but we immediately fell to translating the Italian Operas; and as there was no great Danger of hurting the Sense of those extraordinary Pieces, our Authors would often make Words of their own that were entirely foreign to the Meaning of the Passages which they pretended to translate; their chief Care being to make the Numbers of the English Verse answer to those of the Italian, that both of them might go to the same Tune. Thus the famous Song in *Camilla,*

Barbara si t'intendo, &c.

Barbarous Woman, yes, I know your Meaning,

which expresses the Resentments of an angry Lover, was translated into that English Lamentation

Frail are a Lover's Hopes, &c.

And it was pleasant enough to see the most refined Persons of the British Nation dying away and languishing to Notes that were filled with a Spirit of Rage and Indignation. It happen'd also very frequently, where the Sense was rightly translated, the necessary Transposition of Words that were drawn out of the Phrase of one Tongue into that of another, made the Musick appear very absurd in one Tongue that was very natural in the other. I remember an Italian Verse that ran thus Word for Word,

And turn'd my Rage into Pity;

which the English for Rhime sake translated,

And into Pity turn'd my Rage.

By this Means the soft Notes that were adapted to Pity in the Italian, fell upon the Word Rage in the English; and the angry Sounds that were turn'd to Rage in the Original, were made to express Pity in the Translation. It oftentimes happen'd likewise, that the finest Notes in the Air fell upon the most insignificant Words in the Sentence. I have known the Word *And* pursu'd through the whole Gamut, have been entertain'd with many a melodious *The,* and have heard the most beautiful Graces Quavers and Divisions bestow'd upon *Then, For,* and *From;* to the eternal Honour of our English Particles.

The next Step to our Refinement, was the introducing of Italian Actors into our Opera; who sung their Parts in their own Language, at the same Time that our Countrymen perform'd theirs in our native Tongue. The King or Hero of the Play generally spoke in Italian, and his Slaves answer'd him in English: The Lover frequently made his Court, and gain'd the Heart of his Princess in a Language which she did not understand. One would have thought it very difficult to have carry'd on Dialogues after this Manner, without an Interpreter between the Persons that convers'd together; but this was the State of the English Stage for about three Years.

At length the Audience grew tir'd of understanding Half the Opera, and therefore to ease themselves intirely of the Fatigue of Thinking, have so order'd it at Present that the whole Opera is perform'd in an unknown Tongue. We no longer under-

understand the Language of our own Stage ; insomuch that I have often been afraid, when I have seen our Italian Performers chattering in the Vehemence of Action, that they have been calling us Names, and abusing us among themselves ; but I hope, since we do put such an entire Confidence in them, they will not talk against us before our Faces, though they may do it with the same Safety as if it was behind our Backs. In the mean Time I cannot forbear thinking how naturally an Historian, who writes Two or Three hundred Years hence, and does not know the Taste of his wise Fore-fathers, will make the following Reflection, *In the Beginning of the Eighteenth Century the Italian Tongue was so well understood in England, that Opera's were acted on the publick Stage in that Language.*

One scarce knows how to be serious in the Confutation of an Absurdity that shews itself at the first Sight. It does not want any great Measure of Sense to see the Ridicule of this monstrous Practice ; but what makes it the more astonishing, it is not the Taste of the Rabble, but of Persons of the greatest Politeness, which has establish'd it.

If the Italians have a Genius for Musick above the English, the English have a Genius for other Performances of a much higher Nature, and capable of giving the Mind a much nobler Entertainment. Would one think it was possible (at a Time when an Author lived that was able to write the *Phædra* and *Hippolitus*) for a People to be so stupidly fond of the Italian Opera, as scarce to give a Third Days Hearing to that admirable Tragedy? Musick is certainly a very agreeable Entertainment, but, if it would take the entire Possession of our Ears, if it would make us incapable of hearing Sense, if it would exclude Arts that have a much greater Tendency to the Refinement of humane Nature : I must confess I would allow it no better Quarter than *Plato* has done, who banishes it out of his Commonwealth.

At present, our Notions of Musick are so very uncertain, that we do not know what it is we like, only, in general, that we are transported with any thing that is not English : So it be of a foreign Growth,let it be Italian, French,or High-Dutch, it is the same thing.In short, our English Musick is quite rooted out, and nothing yet planted in its stead.

When a Royal Palace is burnt to the Ground, every Man is at Liberty to present his Plan for a new one ; and tho' it be but indifferently put together, it may furnish several Hints that may be of Use to a good Architect. I shall take the same Liberty in a following Paper, of giving my Opinion upon the Subject of Musick, which I shall lay down only in a problematical Manner to be considered by those who are Masters in the Art.

ADVERTISEMENTS.

LONDON: Printed for *Sam. Buckley*, at the *Dolphin* in *Little-Britain*; and Sold by *A. Baldwin* in *Warwick-Lane*; where Advertisements are taken in; as also by *Charles Lillie*, Perfumer, at the Corner of *Beauford-Buildings* in the *Strand.*

C

The Spectator

The Spectator appeared in two separate series. The first 555 issues were published six times a week (Monday through Saturday) from March 1, 1711, to December 6, 1712; the next 80 numbers, three times a week (Monday, Wednesday, and Friday) from July 18 to December 20, 1714. The original paper cost one penny, but with the stamp tax imposed in August, 1712, the price was raised to twopence. Thereafter the circulation, which had been running at about 3000 copies a day, was cut by half.

Because the papers were published anonymously and because many utilized contributions or were written in collaboration, it is difficult to credit the several authors. The most obvious clues are the terminal initials which appeared with the first series of *Spectators*. It is clear that Addison wrote the essays signed with a *C, L, I,* or *O;* that Steele wrote those ending in *R* or *T;* and that Eustace Budgell wrote those signed with an *X*. It is less easy, however, to establish authorship for the papers that appeared with a *Z* or *Q* or those that in both series were unsigned. In the definitive edition of *The Spectator* (Oxford, 1965), Donald Bond credits Addison with 276 essays, Steele with 251, Budgell with 29, Thomas Tickell with 26, and John Hughes with 7, assigning the remaining numbers to Henry Martyn, Alexander Pope, Henry Carey, Rev. Thomas Parnell, Laurence Eusden, Richard Ince, Henry Grove, John Byrom, Zachary Pearce, and Lady Mary Montagu.

Appearing two months after the final issue of *The Tatler, The Spectator* was in many ways a continuation of the earlier journal. Both were printed on folio half-sheets, with two columns on each side and with advertising taking up part of the second page. Where Isaac Bickerstaff had planned various essays from different coffee-houses in each issue, the Spectator offered one subject for each paper but indicated he would obtain his material from Will's, Child's, St. James's, the Grecian, the Cocoa-Tree, Jonathan's, and the theaters. Where the Tatler had sought to teach his readers "what to think," the Spectator addressed individuals who were either idle or "altogether unfurnished with Ideas" and promised "to enliven Morality with Wit, and to temper Wit with Morality." Bickerstaff's Club at the Trumpet—with its country squire, its old soldier, and its elderly beau—seems the original from which the Spectator Club developed.

It seems evident that Addison and Steele collaborated on *Spectators* No. 1 and 2, and intended to employ the Club members as spokesmen for "the most conspicuous Classes of Mankind." Besides the taciturn Spectator, the group includes Sir Roger de Coverly, a country squire with fixed Tory views; the Templar, a law-student whose main interest is the theater; Sir Andrew Freeport, a successful Whig merchant; Captain Sentry, a retired army officer; Will Honeycomb, a Restoration beau in his declining years; and an elderly and infirm clergyman. In *Spectator* No. 34, readers were assured "that there is no Rank or Degree among them who have not their Representative in this Club."

But with the exception of Sir Roger, and perhaps of Will Honeycomb, no member of the Club was particularly developed as a character or much employed as a spokesman. Bits of biographical information about the Spectator can be pieced together through the essays, but he shows little of the humanity or singularity that sometimes characterized Bickerstaff. (In the second series of *The Spectator*, he makes much of the fact that he is going to begin talking, but thereafter he says little.) The Templar says almost nothing about art or law until his "Farewell Essay" (No. 541). Sir Andrew expresses Whig sentiments regarding trade (No. 174) and about charity (No. 232) but beyond this does little besides retire to the country (No. 549). Though the papers say much about military matters, Captain Sentry only once discusses army life (No. 152). The clergyman provides spiritual counsel in four essays (Nos. 27, 103, 186, and 513) and thereafter is announced to be dead (No. 550).

Only the depictions of Will Honeycomb and Sir Roger de Coverly seem to fulfill the intentions implicit in *Spectator* No. 2. Honeycomb appears often in the papers, accompanying the Spectator, lying about the past, reading love letters, pursuing rich widows, offering essays on "those dear confounded Creatures *Women*" (Nos. 499 and 511), and finally marrying a farmer's daughter. Though he never emerges beyond a one-dimensional figure, he exists as a witty comment on Restoration values. Sir Roger, a more fully developed character, makes many memorable appearances. He is seen acting as a country host, reminiscing about the widow, performing as justice of the quorum, attending church, visiting Westminster Abbey, commenting on *The Distressed Mother,* and being duped by gypsies. In such scenes, he reveals the qualities of charity, naiveté, eccentricity, and common sense, which make him one of the enduring characterizations in English literature.

The subjects discussed in *The Tatler* (duelling, marriage, old age, female extravagance, etc.) continued in *The Spectator,* but there were notable additions. Through the papers, particular areas were given more serious and lengthy consideration, either as recurring themes or as part of a planned series. Addison produced important essays on criticism, discoursing on English tragedy (Nos. 39, 40, 42, and 44), true and false wit (Nos. 58–63), *Paradise Lost* (eighteen papers between Nos. 267 and 369), and the pleasures of the imagination (Nos. 411–421). He wrote most of the Sir Roger papers, providing them with a degree of continuity. And regularly he gave his Saturday essay to religious subjects: superstition, eternity, prayer, faith, death, the idea of God.

While various themes and forms recurred in Steele's papers as well, his range was smaller. He protested the sexual immorality which was evident in the town, reflected in common conversation, and depicted on the stage. He offered criticism of particular plays: *Sir Fopling Flutter* (No. 65), *The Scornful Lady* (No. 270), *The Distressed Mother* (No. 290), and Terence's *The Self-Tormentor* (No. 502). He wrote memorable tales: Inkle and Yarico (No. 11), Laetitia and Daphne (No. 33), Cynthio and Flavia (No. 398), Will Trap and Jack Stint (No. 448), etc. And he made successful use of letters—generally on social topics—both those he wrote himself and those contributed by others. In general, he kept the promise of *Spectator* No. 1 to remain neutral on political issues.

Though the series continued through 635 numbers, Steele's last *Spectator* was No. 555; Addison's, No. 600.

The Spectator, No. 1

Thursday, March 1, 17$\frac{10}{11}$.

[Addison]

Non fumum ex fulgore, sed ex fumo dare lucem
Cogitat, ut speciosa dehinc miracula promat. Hor.[1]

I have observed, that a Reader seldom peruses a Book with Pleasure, 'till he knows whether the Writer of it be a black[2] or a fair Man, of a mild or cholerick Disposition, Married or a Batchelor, with other Particulars of the like nature, that conduce very much to the right understanding of an Author. To gratifie this Curiosity, which is so natural to a Reader, I design this Paper, and my next, as Prefatory Discourses to my following Writings, and shall give some Account in them of the several Persons that are engaged in this Work. As the chief Trouble of Compiling, Digesting, and Correcting will fall to my Share, I must do my self the Justice to open the Work with my own History.

I was born to a small Hereditary Estate, which, according to the Tradition of the Village where it lies, was bounded by the same Hedges and Ditches in *William* the Conqueror's Time that it is at present, and has been delivered down from Father to Son whole and entire, without the Loss or Acquisition of a single Field or Meadow, during the Space of six hundred Years. There runs a Story in the Family, that when my Mother was gone with Child of me about three Months, she dreamt that she was brought to Bed of a Judge: Whether this might proceed from a Law-Suit

---

[1] Horace *Ars Poetica* 143–144: "He plans to give, not smoke after flame, but light after the smoke, that he may set forth striking and marvelous stories."

[2] Dark in complexion.

which was then depending[3] in the Family, or my Father's being a Justice of the Peace, I cannot determine; for I am not so vain as to think it presaged any Dignity that I should arrive at in my future Life, though that was the Interpretation which the Neighbourhood put upon it. The Gravity of my Behaviour at my very first Appearance in the World, and all the Time that I sucked, seemed to favour my Mother's Dream: For, as she has often told me, I threw away my Rattle before I was two Months old, and would not make use of my Coral[4] till they had taken away the Bells from it.

As for the rest of my Infancy, there being nothing in it remarkable, I shall pass it over in Silence. I find, that, during my Nonage, I had the Reputation of a very sullen Youth, but was always a Favourite of my School-Master, who used to say, *that my Parts*[5] *were solid and would wear well.* I had not been long at the University, before I distinguished my self by a most profound Silence: For during the Space of eight Years, excepting in the publick Exercises of the College,[6] I scarce uttered the Quantity of an hundred Words; and indeed do not remember that I ever spoke three Sentences together in my whole Life. Whilst I was in this Learned Body I applied my self with so much Diligence to my Studies, that there are very few celebrated Books, either in the Learned[7] or the Modern Tongues, which I am not acquainted with.

Upon the Death of my Father I was resolved to travel into Foreign Countries, and therefore left the University, with the Character of an odd unaccountable Fellow, that had a great deal of Learning, if I would but show it. An insatiable Thirst after Knowledge carried me into all the Countries of *Europe,* in which there was any thing new or strange to be seen; nay, to such a Degree was my Curiosity raised, that having read the Controversies of some great Men concerning the Antiquities of *Egypt,* I made

---

3 In progress.
4 Teething ring.
5 Natural abilities.
6 Scholastic disputations required to qualify for a degree.
7 I.e., Greek and Latin.

a Voyage to *Grand Cairo*,[8] on purpose to take the Measure of a Pyramid; and as soon as I had set my self right in that Particular, returned to my Native Country with great Satisfaction.

I have passed my latter Years in this City,[9] where I am frequently seen in most publick Places, tho' there are not above half a dozen of my select Friends that know me; of whom my next Paper shall give a more particular Account. There is no Place of general Resort, wherein I do not often make my Appearance; sometimes I am seen thrusting my Head into a Round of Politicians at *Will's*, and listning with great Attention to the Narratives that are made in those little Circular Audiences. Sometimes I smoak a Pipe at *Child's*; and whilst I seem attentive to nothing but the *Post-Man*,[10] over-hear the Conversation of every Table in the Room. I appear on *Sunday* Nights at St. *James*'s Coffee-House, and sometimes join the little Committee of Politicks in the Inner Room, as one who comes there to hear and improve. My Face is likewise very well known at the *Grecian,* the *Cocoa-Tree,* and in the Theatres both of *Drury-Lane* and the *Hay-Market*. I have been taken for a Merchant upon the *Exchange*[11] for above these ten Years, and sometimes pass for a *Jew* in the Assembly of Stock-Jobbers at *Jonathan*'s.[12] In short, where-ever I see a Cluster of People I always mix with them, though I never open my Lips but in my own Club.

Thus I live in the World, rather as a Spectator of Mankind, than as one of the Species; by which means I have made my self a Speculative Statesman, Soldier, Merchant and Artizan, without ever medling with any Practical Part in Life. I am very well versed

8 The visit to Cairo (mentioned in Nos. 8, 17, 46, 69, 101, 159, and 604) may be a reference to John Greaves, a professor of astronomy at Oxford, who took the measurements of the pyramids in 1638–39.

9 London.

10 See *Tatler* No. 18, n. 21.

11 Presumably, the Royal Exchange. See *Spectator* No. 69.

12 Jonathan's Coffee-house in Change Alley served as a stock exchange. The Cocoa-Tree, a chocolate-house in St. James's Street, had a Tory clientele. For Will's, St. James's, and the Grecian, see *Tatler* No. 1, n. 3. For Child's, see *Tatler* No. 220, n. 12.

in the Theory of an Husband, or a Father, and can discern the Errors in the Oeconomy, Business and Diversion of others, better than those who are engaged in them; as Standers-by discover Blots,[13] which are apt to escape those who are in the Game. I never espoused any Party with Violence, and am resolved to observe an exact Neutrality between the Whigs and Tories, unless I shall be forced to declare my self by the Hostilities of either Side.[14] In short, I have acted in all the Parts of my Life as a Looker-on, which is the Character I intend to preserve in this Paper.

I have given the Reader just so much of my History and Character, as to let him see I am not altogether unqualified for the Business I have undertaken. As for other Particulars in my Life and Adventures, I shall insert them in following Papers, as I shall see occasion. In the mean time, when I consider how much I have seen, read and heard, I begin to blame my own Taciturnity; and since I have neither Time nor Inclination to communicate the Fulness of my Heart in Speech, I am resolved to do it in Writing; and to Print my self out, if possible, before I Die. I have been often told by my Friends, that it is Pity so many useful Discoveries which I have made, should be in the Possession of a Silent Man. For this Reason therefore, I shall publish a Sheet-full of Thoughts every Morning, for the Benefit of my Contemporaries; and if I can any way contribute to the Diversion or Improvement of the Country in which I live, I shall leave it, when I am summoned out of it, with the secret Satisfaction of thinking that I have not Lived in vain.

There are three very material Points which I have not Spoken to in this Paper, and which, for several important Reasons, I must keep to my self, at least for some Time: I mean, an Account of my Name, my Age, and my Lodgings. I must confess I would gratifie my Reader in any thing that is reasonable; but as for these three Particulars, though I am sensible they might tend very much to the Embellishment of my Paper, I cannot yet come to a Resolu-

[13] In backgammon, a vulnerable piece.
[14] One of the reasons given for terminating *The Tatler* two months earlier, was its failure to maintain such neutrality. (See *Tatler* No. 271.) In general, the Spectator keeps his promise.

tion of communicating them to the Publick. They would indeed draw me out of that Obscurity which I have enjoyed for many Years, and expose me in Publick Places to several Salutes and Civilities, which have been always very disagreeable to me; for the greatest Pain I can suffer, is the being talked to, and being stared at. It is for this Reason likewise, that I keep my Complexion and Dress as very great Secrets; tho' it is not impossible but I may make Discoveries of both, in the Progress of the Work I have undertaken.

After having been thus particular upon my self, I shall in to-Morrow's Paper give an Account of those Gentlemen who are concerned with me in this Work. For, as I have before intimated, a Plan of it is laid and concerted (as all other Matters of Importance are) in a Club. However, as my Friends have engaged me to stand in the Front, those who have a mind to correspond with me, may direct their Letters *To the Spectator,* at Mr. *Buckley*'s in *Little Britain*.[15] For I must further acquaint the Reader, that tho' our Club meets only on *Tuesdays* and *Thursdays,* we have appointed a Committee to sit every Night, for the Inspection of all such Papers as may contribute to the Advancement of the Publick Weal.   C[16]

[15] A street of printers and booksellers near Aldersgate. For Buckley, see *Tatler* No. 18, n. 23.

[16] The terminal letters were clues to authorship. The essays signed *C, L, I,* and *O* were Addison's; those signed *R* and *T,* Steele's. Other contributors were noted by different letters. See headnote to *The Spectator,* p. 137, and essays No. 221 and 555.

The Spectator, No. 2

Friday, March 2.

[S t e e l e]

‿͜⁀

————*Ast Alii sex*
Et plures uno conclamant ore.————Juv.[1]

The first of our Society is a Gentleman of *Worcestershire,* of antient Descent, a Baronet, his Name Sir Roger de Coverly. His great Grandfather was Inventor of that famous Country-Dance which is call'd after him.[2] All who know that Shire, are very well acquainted with the Parts and Merits of Sir Roger. He is a Gentleman that is very singular in his Behaviour, but his Singularities proceed from his good Sense, and are Contradictions to the Manners of the World, only as he thinks the World is in the wrong. However, this Humour creates him no Enemies, for he does nothing with Sourness or Obstinacy; and his being unconfined to Modes and Forms, makes him but the readier and more capable to please and oblige all who know him. When he is in Town he lives in *Soho-Square.*[3] It is said he keeps himself a Batchelor by reason he was crossed in Love, by a perverse beautiful Widow of the next County to him. Before this Disappointment, Sir Roger was what you call a fine Gentleman,[4] had often supped with my

---

[1] Juvenal *Satires* 7. 167–68: "So six or more cry with one voice."

[2] A 1684 tract refers to a tune called *Roger of Cauverley,* which later became associated with a country dance. In *Tatler* No. 34, it is called *Roger de Caubley.*

[3] A fashionable suburban neighborhood west of the City.

[4] The term "fine gentleman"—as used here and later in the description of Will Honeycomb—has elements of irony.

Lord *Rochester* and Sir *George Etherege*,[5] fought a Duel upon his first coming to Town, and kick'd Bully *Dawson*[6] in a publick Coffee-house for calling him Youngster. But being ill used by the above-mentioned Widow, he was very serious for a Year and a half; and though, his Temper being naturally jovial, he at last got over it, he grew careless of himself, and never dressed afterwards; he continues to wear a Coat and Doublet[7] of the same Cut that were in Fashion at the Time of his Repulse, which, in his merry Humours, he tells us, has been in and out twelve Times since he first wore it. 'Tis said Sir Roger grew humble in his Desires after he had forgot this cruel Beauty, insomuch that it is reported he has frequently offended in Point of Chastity with Beggars and Gypsies: But this is look'd upon by his Friends rather as Matter of Raillery[8] than Truth. He is now in his Fifty sixth Year, cheerful, gay, and hearty, keeps a good House both in Town and Country; a great Lover of Mankind; but there is such a mirthful Cast in his Behaviour, that he is rather beloved than esteemed: His Tenants grow rich, his Servants look satisfied, all the young Women profess Love to him, and the young Men are glad of his Company: When he comes into a House he calls the Servants by their Names, and talks all the way up Stairs to a Visit. I must not omit that Sir Roger is a Justice of the *Quorum;* that he fills the Chair at a Quarter-Session[9] with great Abilities, and three Months ago gain'd universal Applause by explaining a Passage in the Game-Act.[10]

The Gentleman next in Esteem and Authority among us, is

5 John Wilmot, Earl of Rochester (1647–1680), was a Restoration poet and celebrated rake. Sir George Etherege (1634–1691), a friend of Lord Rochester, was the author of *The Man of Mode* (1676), the drama Steele criticized in *Spectators* No. 65 and No. 75.

6 A noted sharper, swaggerer, and debauchee.

7 An inner garment which served as lining for an outer one.

8 Good-natured ridicule.

9 A court of limited jurisdiction held four times a year by country justices of the peace.

10 To prevent poaching, game-laws restricted the right of shooting to landowners worth 100 pounds a year. Since the act was not in any way complicated, this passage gently ridicules Sir Roger.

another Batchelor, who is a Member of the *Inner-Temple;*[11] a
Man of great Probity, Wit, and Understanding; but he has chosen
his Place of Residence rather to obey the Direction of an old hu-
moursom Father, than in Pursuit of his own Inclinations. He was
placed there to study the Laws of the Land, and is the most learned
of any of the House in those of the Stage. *Aristotle* and *Longinus*
are much better understood by him than *Littleton* or *Cooke.*[12]
The Father sends up every Post Questions relating to Marriage-
Articles, Leases, and Tenures, in the Neighbourhood; all which
Questions he agrees with an Attorney to answer and take care of
in the Lump: He is studying the Passions themselves, when he
should be inquiring into the Debates among Men which arise
from them. He knows the Argument of each of the Orations of
Demosthenes and *Tully,*[13] but not one Case in the Reports of our
own Courts. No one ever took him for a Fool, but none, except his
intimate Friends, know he has a great deal of Wit. This Turn
makes him at once both disinterested and agreeable: As few of his
Thoughts are drawn from Business, they are most of them fit for
Conversation. His Taste of Books is a little too just[14] for the Age
he lives in; he has read all, but approves of very few. His Familiarity with the Customs, Manners, Actions, and Writings of the
Antients,[15] makes him a very delicate Observer of what occurs to
him in the present World. He is an excellent Critick, and the
Time of the Play is his Hour of Business; exactly at five he passes
thro' *New-Inn,* crosses thro' *Russel-Court,* and takes a Turn at
Will's 'till the Play begins; he has his Shooes rubbed and his Perriwig powder'd at the Barber's as you go into the *Rose.*[16] It is for
the Good of the Audience when he is at a Play, for the Actors have
an Ambition to please him.

The Person of next Consideration, is Sir Andrew Freeport, a

[11] London residence of students of civil law.
[12] Sir Thomas Littleton (1402–1481) and Sir Edward Coke (1552–1634) were
legal authorities. See *Tatler* No. 133, n. 14.
[13] The most famous Greek and Roman orators. See *Tatler* No. 167, n. 5.
[14] Severe, rigorous.
[15] The classical authorities of Greece and Rome.
[16] The Rose Tavern, near Drury Lane Theater.

Merchant of great Eminence in the City[17] of *London*. A Person
of indefatigable Industry, strong Reason, and great Experience.
His Notions of Trade are noble and generous, and (as every rich
Man has usually some sly Way of Jesting, which would make no
great Figure were he not a rich Man) he calls the Sea the *British
Common*. He is acquainted with Commerce in all its Parts, and
will tell you that it is a stupid and barbarous Way to extend Dominion by Arms; for true Power is to be got by Arts and Industry.
He will often argue, that if this Part of our Trade were well cultivated, we should gain from one Nation; and if another, from
another. I have heard him prove, that Diligence makes more lasting Acquisitions than Valour, and that Sloth has ruined more
Nations than the Sword. He abounds in several frugal Maxims,
among which the greatest Favourite is, "A Penny saved is a Penny
got." A General Trader of good Sense, is pleasanter Company
than a general Scholar; and Sir Andrew having a natural unaffected Eloquence, the Perspicuity of his Discourse gives the same
Pleasure that Wit would in another Man. He has made his Fortunes himself; and says that *England* may be richer than other
Kingdoms, by as plain Methods as he himself is richer than other
Men; tho' at the same Time I can say this of him, that there is not
a Point in the Compass but blows home a Ship in which he is an
Owner.

Next to Sir Andrew in the Club-room sits Captain Sentry, a
Gentleman of great Courage, good Understanding, but invincible
Modesty. He is one of those that deserve very well, but are very
awkard at putting their Talents within the Observation of such
as should take Notice of them. He was some Years a Captain, and
behaved himself with great Gallantry[18] in several Engagements
and at several Sieges; but having a small Estate of his own, and
being next Heir to Sir Roger, he has quitted a Way of Life in
which no Man can rise suitably to his Merit, who is not something of a Courtier as well as a Soldier. I have heard him often

17 I.e., the central section, the business district.
18 The descriptions of Captain Sentry and Will Honeycomb illustrate the
two senses of the word "gallantry." See *Tatler* No. 25, n. 1.

lament, that in a Profession where Merit is placed in so conspicuous a View, Impudence should get the Better of Modesty. When
he has talked to this Purpose I never heard him make a sour Expression, but frankly confess that he left the World because he
was not fit for it. A strict Honesty and an even regular Behaviour,
are in themselves Obstacles to him that must press through
Crowds, who endeavour at the same End with himself, the Favour
of a Commander. He will however in his way of Talk excuse Generals, for not disposing according to Mens Desert, or enquiring
into it: For, says he, that great Man who has a Mind to help me,
has as many to break through to come at me, as I have to come at
him: Therefore he will conclude, that the Man who would make
a Figure,[19] especially in a military Way, must get over all false
Modesty, and assist his Patron against the Importunity of other
Pretenders, by a proper Assurance in his own Vindication. He
says it is a civil Cowardice to be backward in asserting what you
ought to expect, as it is a military Fear to be slow in attacking
when it is your Duty. With this Candour does the Gentleman
speak of himself and others. The same Frankness runs through all
his Conversation. The military Part of his Life has furnish'd him
with many Adventures, in the Relation of which he is very agreeable to the Company; for he is never over-bearing, though accustomed to command Men in the utmost Degree below him; nor
ever too obsequious, from an Habit of obeying Men highly above
him.

But that our Society may not appear a Set of Humourists[20] unacquainted with the Gallantries and Pleasures of the Age, we have
among us the gallant Will. Honeycomb, a Gentleman who according to his Years should be in the Decline of his Life, but having ever been very careful of his Person, and always had a very
easie Fortune, Time has made but very little Impression, either
by Wrinkles on his Forehead, or Traces in his Brain. His Person
is well turn'd, of a good Height. He is very ready at that sort of
Discourse with which Men usually entertain Women. He has all

[19] Achieve prominence.
[20] Individuals subject to "humors" or fancies, whimsical or capricious
persons.

his Life dressed very well, and remembers Habits as others do Men. He can smile when one speaks to him, and laughs easily. He knows the History of every Mode, and can inform you from which of the *French* King's Wenches our Wives and Daughters had this Manner of curling their Hair, that Way of placing their Hoods; whose Frailty was covered[21] by such a Sort of Petticoat, and whose Vanity to shew her Foot made that part of the Dress so short in such a Year. In a word, all his Conversation and Knowledge has been in the female World: As other Men of his Age will take notice to you what such a Minister said upon such and such an Occasion, he will tell you when the Duke of *Monmouth*[22] danced at Court such a Woman was then smitten, another was taken with him[23] at the Head of his Troop in the *Park*. In all these important Relations, he has ever about the same time received a kind Glance or a Blow of a Fan from some celebrated Beauty, Mother of the present Lord such-a-one. If you speak of a young Commoner[24] that said a lively thing in the House, he starts up, "He has good Blood in his Veins, *Tom Mirabell*[25] begot him, the Rogue cheated me in that Affair; that young Fellow's Mother used me more like a Dog than any Woman I ever made Advances to." This way of Talking of his very much enlivens the Conversation among us of a more sedate Turn; and I find there is not one of the Company, but my self, who rarely speak at all, but speaks of him as of that Sort of Man who is usually called a well-bred fine Gentleman. To conclude his Character, where Women are not concern'd, he is an honest worthy Man.

I cannot tell whether I am to account him whom I am next to speak of, as one of our Company; for he visits us but seldom, but when he does it adds to every Man else a new Enjoyment of himself. He is a Clergyman, a very philosophick Man, of general Learning, great Sanctity of Life, and the most exact good Breed-

---

21 I.e., whose pregnancy was concealed.

22 The Duke (1649–1685), the natural son of Charles II, was portrayed as Absalom in Dryden's *Absalom and Achitophel* (1681).

23 Was smitten on seeing him.

24 A member of the House of Commons.

25 Presumably, a reference to the hero of Congreve's *The Way of the World* (1700).

ing. He has the Misfortune to be of a very weak Constitution, and consequently cannot accept of such Cares and Business as Preferments in his Function[26] would oblige him to: He is therefore among Divines what a Chamber-Counsellor[27] is among Lawyers. The Probity of his Mind, and the Integrity of his Life, create him Followers, as being eloquent or loud advances others. He seldom introduces the Subject he speaks upon; but we are so far gone in Years, that he observes, when he is among us, an Earnestness to have him fall on some divine Topick, which he always treats with much Authority, as one who has no Interests in this World, as one who is hastening to the Object of all his Wishes, and conceives Hope from his Decays and Infirmities. These are my ordinary Companions.   R

[26] Advancement in his profession.
[27] A lawyer who gives counsel but does not appear in court.

The Spectator, No. 3

Saturday, March 3.

[Addison]

Quoi quisque ferè studio devinctus adhaeret:
Aut quibus in rebus multùm sumus antè morati:
Atque in quâ ratione fuit contenta magis mens;
In somnis eadem plerumque videmur obire.

Lucr. L. 4.[1]

In one of my late Rambles, or rather Speculations, I looked into the great Hall where the Bank is kept,[2] and was not a little pleased to see the Directors, Secretaries, and Clerks, with all the other Members of that wealthy Corporation, ranged in their several Stations, according to the Parts they act in that just and regular Oeconomy. This revived in my Memory the many Discourses which I had both read and heard concerning the Decay of Publick Credit,[3] with the Methods of restoring it, and which, in my Opinion, have always been defective, because they have always been made with an Eye to separate Interests, and Party Principles.

The Thoughts of the Day gave my Mind Employment for the whole Night, so that I fell insensibly into a kind of Methodical Dream, which dispos'd all my Contemplations into a Vision or Allegory, or what else the Reader shall please to call it.

---

1 Lucretius *De Rerum Natura* 4. 962–965: "In dreams, we encounter those things we most enjoyed and contemplated in the past."

2 The Directors of the Bank of England had their offices in a room known as the Hall in Grocer's Hall.

3 Many Whigs feared that the election of a Tory majority among the directors of the Bank might bring on the restoration of James III, the repudiation of government debts contracted since the revolution, and a decline in public credit.

Methoughts I returned to the Great Hall, where I had been the Morning before, but, to my Surprize, instead of the Company that I left there, I saw towards the upper end of the Hall, a beautiful Virgin, seated on a Throne of Gold. Her Name (as they told me) was *Publick Credit*. The Walls, instead of being adorn'd with Pictures and Maps, were hung with many Acts of Parliament written in Golden Letters. At the Upper end of the Hall was the *Magna Charta,* with the Act of Uniformity on the right Hand, and the Act of Toleration on the left.[4] At the Lower end of the Hall was the Act of Settlement,[5] which was placed full in the Eye of the Virgin that sat upon the Throne. Both the Sides of the Hall were covered with such Acts of Parliament as had been made for the Establishment of Publick Funds. The Lady seemed to set an unspeakable Value upon these several Pieces of Furniture, insomuch that she often refreshed her Eye with them, and often smiled with a Secret Pleasure, as she looked upon them; but, at the same time, showed a very particular Uneasiness, if she saw any thing approaching that might hurt them. She appeared indeed infinitely timorous in all her Behaviour: And, whether it was from the Delicacy of her Constitution, or that she was troubled with Vapours, as I was afterwards told by one who I found was none of her Well-wishers, she changed Colour, and startled at every thing she heard.[6] She was likewise (as I afterwards found) a greater Valetudinarian than any I had ever met with, even in her own Sex, and subject to such Momentary Consumptions, that in the twinkling of an Eye, she would fall away from the most florid Complexion, and the most healthful State of Body, and wither into a Skeleton. Her Recoveries were often as sudden as her De-

[4] The Act of Uniformity (1662) made obligatory the use of the Book of Common Prayer in the Church of England; the Act of Toleration (1689) guaranteed freedom of worship to Protestant nonconformists. Here, the balancing of the two represents the middle-of-the-road policy which the Whigs claimed to practice.

[5] The Act of Settlement (1701) established the Protestant succession to the British throne, voiding the claim of James Stuart, the son of James II and the half-brother of Queen Anne.

[6] Even rumors of change in public affairs might significantly change the state of public credit. The "vapours," also called the spleen, was a nervous condition which manifest itself in depression or fanciful notions.

cays, insomuch that she would revive in a Moment out of a wasting Distemper, into a Habit[7] of the highest Health and Vigour.

I had very soon an Opportunity of observing these quick Turns and Changes in her Constitution. There sat at her Feet a Couple of Secretaries, who received every Hour Letters from all Parts of the World, which the one or the other of them was perpetually reading to her; and, according to the News she heard, to which she was exceedingly attentive, she changed Colour, and discovered many Symptoms of Health or Sickness.

Behind the Throne was a prodigious Heap of Bags of Mony, which were piled upon one another so high that they touched the Ceiling. The Floor, on her right Hand and on her left, was covered with vast Sums of Gold that rose up in Pyramids on either side of her: But this I did not so much wonder at, when I heard, upon Enquiry, that she had the same Virtue in her Touch, which the Poets tell us a *Lydian* King[8] was formerly possess'd of; and that she could convert whatever she pleas'd into that precious Metal.

After a little Dizziness, and confused Hurry of Thought, which a Man often meets with in a Dream, methoughts the Hall was alarm'd, the Doors flew open, and there enter'd half a dozen of the most hideous Phantoms that I had ever seen (even in a Dream) before that Time. They came in two by two, though match'd in the most dissociable Manner, and mingled together in a kind of Dance. It would be tedious to describe their Habits and Persons, for which Reason I shall only inform my Reader that the first Couple were Tyranny and Anarchy, the second were Bigotry and Atheism, the third the Genius[9] of a Common-Wealth and a young Man of about twenty two Years of Age,[10] whose Name I could not learn. He had a Sword in his right Hand, which in the Dance he often brandished at the Act of Settlement; and a Citizen, who stood by me, whisper'd in my Ear, that he saw a Spunge in his left Hand. The Dance of so many jarring Natures, put me in Mind

[7] Condition. Usually, as later in this essay, the word means dress.

[8] Midas, legendary king of Phrygia.

[9] Spirit.

[10] James Francis Edward Stuart (1688–1766), the Pretender, who with his "Spunge" would wipe out (repudiate) government debts.

of the Sun Moon and Earth, in the *Rehearsal*,[11] that danced together for no other end but to eclipse one another.

The Reader will easily suppose, by what has been before said, that the Lady on the Throne would have been almost frighted to Distraction, had she seen but any one of these Spectres; what then must have been her Condition when she saw them all in a Body? She fainted and dyed away at the Sight.

> *Et neq; jam color est misto candore rubori;*
> *Nec Vigor, & Vires, & quae modo visa placebant;*
> *Nec Corpus remanet*——Ov. Met. Lib. 3.[12]

There was as great a Change in the Hill of Mony Bags, and the Heaps of Mony, the former shrinking, and falling into so many empty Bags, that I now found not above a tenth part of them had been filled with Mony. The rest that took up the same Space, and made the same Figure as the Bags that were really filled with Mony, had been blown up with Air, and called into my Memory the Bags full of Wind, which *Homer* tells us his Hero receiv'd as a Present from *Aeolus*.[13] The great Heaps of Gold, on either side the Throne, now appeared to be only Heaps of Paper,[14] or little Piles of notched Sticks, bound up together in Bundles, like *Bath-Faggots*.[15]

Whilst I was lamenting this sudden Desolation that had been made before me, the whole Scene vanished: In the Room of the frightful Spectres, there now enter'd a second Dance of Apparitions very agreeably matched together, and made up of very amiable Phantoms. The first Pair was Liberty with Monarchy at her

---

[11] In Buckingham's *The Rehearsal* (act 5, sc. 1), Luna, Sol, and Earth dance together on the stage. See *Tatler* No. 18, n. 24.

[12] Ovid *Metamorphoses* 3. 491–493: "No longer has [she] that ruddy color mixing with the white, no longer that vigor and strength, and all that lately was so pleasing to behold; hardly does [her] body remain . . ." (In the original, the passage described Narcissus.)

[13] Homer *Odyssey* 10. 19. Odysseus, returning to Ithaca, visited the island of Aeolus, the god of the winds, and took away a bagful of various winds to help him on his journey.

[14] Currency notes issued by the Bank of England.

[15] The notched sticks were Exchequer "tallies" used for keeping accounts; "Bath faggots" were bundles of split firewood.

right Hand: The second was Moderation leading in Religion; and the third a Person whom I had never seen,[16] with the Genius of *Great Britain*. At their first Entrance the Lady revived, the Bags swell'd to their former Bulk, the Piles of Faggots and Heaps of Paper changed into Pyramids of Guineas: And for my own part I was so transported with Joy, that I awaked, tho', I must confess, I would fain have fallen asleep again to have closed my Vision, if I could have done it.[17]   C

[16] The Elector of Hanover, afterward George I. It was a common Whig complaint that he had never been invited to visit England.

[17] It is difficult to square this essay with Addison's promise of political neutrality, printed two days earlier.

The Spectator, No. 10

Monday, March 12.

[Addison]

Non aliter quam qui adverso vix flumine lembum
Remigiis subigit: si brachia forte remisit,
Atque illum in praeceps prono rapit alveus amni. Virg.[1]

It is with much Satisfaction that I hear this great City inquiring Day by Day after these my Papers, and receiving my Morning Lectures with a becoming Seriousness and Attention. My Publisher tells me, that there are already Three thousand of them distributed every Day: So that if I allow Twenty Readers to every Paper, which I look upon as a modest Computation, I may reckon about Threescore thousand Disciples in *London* and *Westminster*,[2] who I hope will take care to distinguish themselves from the thoughtless Herd of their ignorant and unattentive Brethren. Since I have raised to my self so great an Audience, I shall spare no Pains to make their Instruction agreeable, and their Diversion useful. For which Reasons I shall endeavour to enliven Morality with Wit, and to temper Wit with Morality, that my Readers may, if possible, both Ways find their Account in the Speculation of the Day. And to the End that their Virtue and Discretion may not be short transient intermitting Starts of Thought, I have resolved to refresh their Memories from Day to Day, till I have recovered them out of that desperate State of Vice and Folly into which the

---

[1] Virgil *Georgics* 1. 201–203: "If one, whose oars can scarcely force his skiff against the current, should by chance slacken his arms, the boat sweeps him headlong down the stream."

[2] Addison's computation may be wishful, but there is no doubting the immediate success of *The Spectator*. See headnote to *The Spectator*, p. 137.

Age is fallen. The Mind that lies fallow but a single Day, sprouts up in Follies that are only to be killed by a constant and assiduous Culture. It was said of *Socrates,* that he brought Philosophy down from Heaven, to inhabit among Men;[3] and I shall be ambitious to have it said of me, that I have brought Philosophy out of Closets[4] and Libraries, Schools and Colleges, to dwell in Clubs and Assemblies, at Tea-Tables and in Coffee-Houses.

I would therefore in a very particular Manner recommend these my Speculations to all well regulated Families, that set apart an Hour in every Morning for Tea and Bread and Butter; and would earnestly advise them for their Good to order this Paper to be punctually served up, and to be looked upon as a Part of the Tea Equipage.

Sir *Francis Bacon*[5] observes, that a well-written Book, compared with its Rivals and Antagonists, is like *Moses*'s Serpent, that immediately swallow'd up and devoured those of the *Aegyptians.* I shall not be so vain as to think, that where the *Spectator* appears, the other publick Prints will vanish; but shall leave it to my Reader's Consideration, whether, Is it not much better to be let into the Knowledge of ones self, than to hear what passes in *Muscovy* or *Poland;*[6] and to amuse our selves with such Writings as tend to the wearing out of Ignorance, Passion, and Prejudice, than such[7] as naturally conduce to inflame Hatreds, and make Enmities irreconcileable?

In the next Place, I would recommend this Paper to the daily Perusal of those Gentlemen whom I cannot but consider as my good Brothers and Allies, I mean the Fraternity of Spectators who live in the World without having any thing to do in it; and either by the Affluence of their Fortunes, or Laziness of their Disposi-

---

3 Socrates was so described in Cicero's *Tusculan Disputations* 5. 4. 10.

4 Private rooms.

5 See *Tatler* No. 267, n. 6. Bacon's *The Advancement of Learning* (2, Introduction) alludes to events in Exod. 7:10–12.

6 In *Tatler* No. 155, the Upholsterer is "more inquisitive to know what passed in Poland than in his own Family," and his colleague in St. James's Park creates political paradoxes out of "some News he had lately read from Muscovy."

7 I.e., partisan political tracts.

tions, have no other Business with the rest of Mankind, but to look upon them. Under this Class of Men are comprehended all contemplative Tradesmen, titular Physicians, Fellows of the Royal Society,[8] Templers that are not given to be contentious, and Statesmen that are out of Business; in short, every one that considers the World as a Theatre, and desires to form a right Judgment of those who are the Actors on it.

There is another Set of Men that I must likewise lay a Claim to, whom I have lately[9] called the Blanks of Society, as being altogether unfurnish'd with Ideas, till the Business and Conversation of the Day has supplied them. I have often consider'd these poor Souls with an Eye of great Commiseration, when I have heard them asking the first Man they have met with, whether there was any News stirring? and by that Means gathering together Materials for thinking. These needy Persons do not know what to talk of, 'till about twelve a Clock in the Morning; for by that Time they are pretty good Judges of the Weather, know which Way the Wind sits, and whether the *Dutch* Mail[10] be come in. As they lie at the Mercy of the first Man they meet, and are grave or impertinent all the Day long, according to the Notions which they have imbibed in the Morning, I would earnestly entreat them not to stir out of their Chambers till they have read this Paper, and do promise them that I will daily instil into them such sound and wholesom Sentiments, as shall have a good Effect on their Conversation for the ensuing twelve Hours.

But there are none to whom this Paper will be more useful, than to the Female World.[11] I have often thought there has not been sufficient Pains taken in finding out proper Employments and Diversions for the Fair ones. Their Amusements seem contrived for them rather as they are Women, than as they are reasonable Creatures; and are more adapted to the Sex than to the Species. The Toilet is their great Scene of Business, and the right adjusting of their Hair the principal Employment of their Lives.

---

8 Addison criticized amateur scientists in *Tatlers* No. 119, 216, 221, and 236.

9 I.e., in *Spectator* No. 4, by Steele.

10 See *Tatler* No. 155, n. 4.

11 Steele wrote in *Tatler* No. 1: "I resolved also to have something which may be of Entertainment to the Fair Sex, in Honour of whom I have taken the Title of this Paper."

The sorting of a Suit of Ribbons, is reckon'd a very good Morning's Work; and if they make an Excursion to a Mercer's or a Toy-shop,[12] so great a Fatigue makes them unfit for any thing else all the Day after. Their more serious Occupations are Sowing and Embroidery, and their greatest Drudgery the Preparation of Jellies and Sweet-meats. This, I say, is the State of ordinary Women; tho' I know there are Multitudes of those of a more elevated Life and Conversation, that move in an exalted Sphere of Knowledge and Virtue, that join all the Beauties of the Mind to the Ornaments of Dress, and inspire a kind of Awe and Respect, as well as Love, into their Male-Beholders. I hope to encrease the Number of these by Publishing this daily Paper, which I shall always endeavour to make an innocent if not an improving Entertainment, and by that Means at least divert the Minds of my Female Readers from greater Trifles. At the same Time, as I would fain give some finishing Touches to those which are already the most beautiful Pieces in human Nature, I shall endeavour to point out all those Imperfections that are the Blemishes, as well as those Virtues which are the Embellishments, of the Sex. In the mean while I hope these my gentle Readers, who have so much Time on their Hands, will not grudge throwing away a Quarter of an Hour in a Day on this Paper, since they may do it without any Hindrance to Business.

I know several of my Friends and Well-wishers are in great Pain for me, lest I should not be able to keep up the Spirit of a Paper which I oblige my self to furnish every Day: But to make them easie in this Particular, I will promise them faithfully to give it over as soon as I grow dull. This I know will be Matter of great Raillery to the small Wits; who will frequently put me in mind of my Promise, desire me to keep my Word, assure me that it is high Time to give over, with many other little Pleasantries of the like Nature, which Men of a little smart Genius cannot forbear throwing out against their best Friends, when they have such a Handle given them of being witty. But let them remember that I do hereby enter my Caveat[13] against this Piece of Raillery.   C

---

12 A mercer sold dry-goods; a toy-shop, trinkets and small ornamental articles.

13 A warning enjoining one from certain acts or practices.

The Spectator, No. 18

Wednesday, March 21.

[Addison]

————*Equitis quoque jam migravit ab aure voluptas*
Omnis ad incertos oculos & gaudia vana. Hor.[1]

It is my Design in this Paper to deliver down to Posterity a faithful Account of the *Italian* Opera, and of the gradual Progress which it has made upon the *English* Stage:[2] For there is no question but our great Grand-children will be very curious to know the Reason why their Forefathers used to sit together like an Audience of Foreigners in their own Country, and to hear whole Plays acted before them in a Tongue which they did not understand.

Arsinoe[3] was the first Opera that gave us a Taste of *Italian* Musick. The great Success this Opera met with, produced some Attempts of forming Pieces upon *Italian* Plans, which should give a more natural and reasonable Entertainment than what can be met with in the elaborate Trifles of that Nation. This alarmed the Poetasters[4] and Fidlers of the Town, who were used to deal in a more ordinary kind of Ware; and therefore laid down an estab-

---

[1] Horace *Epistles* 2. 1. 187–188: "Now even the nobility find their pleasure, not in hearing good sense, but in the vain joys of the wandering eye."

[2] The amazing popularity of Italian opera in England was regularly criticized by English wits. Steele ridiculed opera as early as *Tatler* No. 4, and Addison had already satirized it in *Spectators* No. 5 and 13.

[3] *Arsinoe, Queen of Cyprus* was first produced in January, 1705, at Drury Lane Theater. Peter Motteaux's libretto was based on an Italian work by Tomaso Stanzani.

[4] Inferior or would-be poets.

lished Rule, which is received as such to this Day, *That nothing is capable of being well set to Musick, that is not Nonsense.*

This Maxim was no sooner received, but we immediately fell to translating the *Italian* Opera's; and as there was no great Danger of hurting the Sense of those extraordinary Pieces, our Authors would often make Words of their own which were entirely foreign to the Meaning of the Passages they pretended to translate; their chief Care being to make the Numbers[5] of the *English* Verse answer to those of the *Italian,* that both of them might go to the same Tune. Thus the famous Song in *Camilla,*[6]

> *Barbara si t' intendo, &c.*
> *Barbarous Woman, yes, I know your Meaning.*

which expresses the Resentments of an angry Lover, was translated into that *English* Lamentation,

> *Frail are a Lover's Hopes,* &c.

And it was pleasant enough to see the most refined Persons of the *British* Nation dying away and languishing to Notes that were filled with a Spirit of Rage and Indignation. It happened also very frequently, where the Sense was rightly translated, the necessary Transposition of Words which were drawn out of the Phrase of one Tongue into that of another, made the Musick appear very absurd in one Tongue that was very natural in the other. I remember an *Italian* Verse that ran thus Word for Word,

> *And turn'd my Rage into Pity;*

which the *English* for Rhime sake translated,

> *And into Pity turn'd my Rage.*

By this means the soft Notes that were adapted to *Pity* in the *Italian,* fell upon the Word *Rage* in the *English;* and the angry Sounds that were tuned to *Rage* in the Original, were made to ex-

---

5 Metrics.

6 *Camilla,* based on an episode from the *Aeneid,* was written by Antonio Bononcini in 1696. It was performed with an English libretto by Owen Swiney at Drury Lane in March, 1706, and became the most successful Italian opera in England.

press *Pity* in the Translation. It oftentimes happened likewise, that the finest Notes in the Air fell upon the most insignificant Words in the Sentence. I have known the Word *And* pursued through the whole Gamut, have been entertained with many a melodious *The,* and have heard the most beautiful Graces, Quavers and Divisions bestowed upon *Then, For,* and *From;* to the eternal Honour of our *English* Particles.[7]

The next Step to our Refinement, was the introducing of *Italian* Actors into our Opera; who sung their Parts in their own Language, at the same time that our Countrymen performed theirs in our native Tongue. The King or Hero of the Play generally spoke in *Italian,* and his Slaves answered him in *English:* The Lover frequently made his Court, and gained the Heart of his Princess, in a Language which she did not understand. One would have thought it very difficult to have carried on Dialogues after this manner, without an Interpreter between the Persons that convers'd together; but this was the State of the *English* Stage for about three Years.

At length the Audience grew tired of understanding Half the Opera, and therefore to ease themselves intirely of the Fatigue of Thinking, have so ordered it at present that the whole Opera is performed in an unknown Tongue. We no longer understand the Language of our own Stage; insomuch that I have often been afraid, when I have seen our *Italian* Performers chattering in the Vehemence of Action, that they have been calling us Names, and abusing us among themselves; but I hope, since we do put such an entire Confidence in them, they will not talk against us before our Faces, though they may do it with the same Safety as if it were behind our Backs. In the mean time, I cannot forbear thinking how naturally an Historian who writes two or three hundred Years hence, and does not know the Taste of his wise Forefathers, will make the following Reflection, *In the Beginning of the Eighteenth Century the* Italian *Tongue was so well understood in* England, *that Opera's were acted on the publick Stage in that Language.*

One scarce knows how to be serious in the Confutation of an

[7] Minor units of speech.

Absurdity that shews it self at the first Sight. It does not want any great measure of Sense to see the Ridicule of this monstrous Practice; but what makes it the more astonishing, it is not the Taste of the Rabble, but of Persons of the greatest Politeness,[8] which has established it.

If the *Italians* have a Genius for Musick above the *English,* the *English* have a Genius for other Performances of a much higher Nature, and capable of giving the Mind a much nobler Entertainment. Would one think it was possible (at a Time when an Author lived that was able to write the *Phaedra* and *Hippolitus*)[9] for a People to be so stupidly fond of the *Italian* Opera, as scarce to give a third Day's Hearing[10] to that admirable Tragedy? Musick is certainly a very agreeable Entertainment, but if it would take the entire Possession of our Ears, if it would make us incapable of hearing Sense, if it would exclude Arts that have a much greater Tendency to the Refinement of human Nature; I must confess I would allow it no better Quarter than *Plato* has done, who banishes it out of his Common-wealth.[11]

At present, our Notions of Musick are so very uncertain, that we do not know what it is we like; only, in general, we are transported with any thing that is not *English:* So it be of a foreign Growth, let it be *Italian, French,* or *High-Dutch,* it is the same thing. In short, our *English* Musick is quite rooted out, and nothing yet planted in its stead.

When a Royal Palace is burnt to the Ground, every Man is at Liberty to present his Plan for a new one; and though it be but indifferently put together, it may furnish several Hints that may be of Use to a good Architect. I shall take the same Liberty in a following Paper,[12] of giving my Opinion upon the Subject of Musick; which I shall lay down only in a problematical Manner, to be considered by those who are Masters in the Art.   C

8 Refined elegance.

9 This tragedy, written by Edmund Smith (1672–1710), was produced at the Haymarket in April, 1707. Addison wrote the prologue.

10 Traditionally, the dramatist was paid with the proceeds of the third performance of his play. Smith's tragedy ran through four performances.

11 Plato *The Republic* 398C–399C.

12 *Spectator* No. 29.

The Spectator, No. 20

Friday, March 23.

[Steele]

⁓

———Κύνὸς ὄμματ᾽ ἔχων———Hom.[1]

Among the other hardy Undertakings which I have proposed
to my self, that of the Correction of Impudence is what I have
very much at Heart. This in a particular Manner is my Province
as Spectator;[2] for it is generally an Offence committed by the Eyes,
and that against such[3] as the Offenders would perhaps never have
an Opportunity of injuring any other Way. The following Letter
is a Complaint of a young Lady, who sets forth a Trespass of this
Kind, with that Command of her self as befits Beauty and Innocence, and yet with so much Spirit as sufficiently expresses her Indignation. The whole Transaction is performed with the Eyes;
and the Crime is no less than employing them in such a Manner,
as to divert the Eyes of others from the best Use they can make
of them, even looking up to Heaven.

"*Sir,*
    There never was (I believe) an acceptable Man, but had some awk-
ard Imitators. Ever since the Spectator appeared, have I remarked a
kind of Men, whom I chuse to call *Starers;* that without any regard to
Time, Place, or Modesty, disturb a large Company with their impertinent Eyes. Spectators make up a proper Assembly for a Puppet-

---

[1] Homer *Iliad* 1. 225: "Having dog's eyes."

[2] In essay No. 1, the Spectator declared, "In short, I have acted in all the
Parts of my Life as a Looker-on, which is the Character I intend to preserve in
this paper."

[3] Such individuals.

Show or a Bear-Garden;[4] but devout Supplicants and attentive Hearers, are the Audience one ought to expect in Churches. I am, Sir, Member of a small pious Congregation near one of the North Gates of this City; much the greater Part of us indeed are Females, and used to behave our selves in a regular attentive Manner, till very lately one whole Isle[5] has been disturbed with one of these monstrous Starers: He's the Head taller than any one in the Church; but for the greater Advantage of exposing himself, stands upon a Hassock,[6] and commands the whole Congregation, to the great Annoyance of the devoutest Part of the Auditory; for what with Blushing, Confusion, and Vexation, we can neither mind the Prayers nor Sermon. Your Animadversion[7] upon this Insolence, would be a great Favour to,

> Sir,
> Your most humble Servant,
> S. C."

I have frequently seen of this Sort of Fellows; and do not think there can be a greater Aggravation of an Offence, than that it is committed where the Criminal is protected by the Sacredness of the Place which he violates.[8] Many Reflections of this sort might be very justly made upon this kind of Behaviour, but a *Starer* is not usually a Person to be convinced by the Reason of the thing; and a Fellow that is capable of shewing an impudent Front before a whole Congregation, and can bear being a publick Spectacle, is not so easily rebuked as to amend by Admonitions. If therefore my Correspondent does not inform me, that within seven Days after this Date the Barbarian does not at least stand upon his own Legs only, without an Eminence,[9] my Friend *Will. Prosper*[10] has promised to take an Hassock opposite to him, and stare

---

[4] The bear gardens offered a variety of grisly spectacles: men combating with swords and daggers; bears and bulls tormented with fireworks and set on by wild dogs; etc. (Steele discussed such events in *Spectator* No. 436.) The spectators here, like those at the popular puppet shows, were often low and unruly.

[5] Aisle.

[6] A kneeling hassock. See *Tatler* No. 259, n. 4.

[7] Adverse criticism.

[8] Formerly refugees from the law, invoking the right of sanctuary, could resort to a church and be immune from arrest.

[9] I.e., a hassock.

[10] In *Spectator* No. 19, Steele described Will Prosper as a kind of nemesis:

against him in Defence of the Ladies. I have given him Directions, according to the most exact Rules of Opticks, to place himself in such a manner that he shall meet his Eyes where-ever he throws them: I have Hopes that when *Will.* confronts him, and all the Ladies, in whose Behalf he engages him, cast kind Looks and Wishes of Success at their Champion, he will have some Shame, and feel a little of the Pain he has so often put others to, of being out of Countenance.

It has indeed been Time out of Mind generally remarked, and as often lamented, that this Family of Starers have infested pub-lick Assemblies: And I know no other Way to obviate so great an Evil, except, in the Case of fixing their Eyes upon Women, some Male Friend will take the Part of such as are under the Oppression of Impudence, and encounter the Eyes of the Starers where-ever they meet them. While we suffer our Women to be thus impu-dently attacked, they have no Defence, but in the End to cast yielding Glances at the Starers: And in this Case, a Man who has no Sense of Shame has the same Advantage over his Mistress, as he who has no Regard for his own Life has over his Adversary.[11] While the Generality of the World are fettered by Rules, and move by proper and just Methods; he who has no Respect to any of them, carries away the Reward due to that Propriety of Behav-iour, with no other Merit, but that of having neglected it.

I take an impudent Fellow to be a sort of Outlaw in Good-breeding, and therefore what is said of him no Nation or Person can be concerned for. For this Reason, one may be free[12] upon him. I have put my self to great Pains in considering this prevail-ing Quality which we call Impudence, and have taken notice that it exerts it self in a different Manner, according to the different Soils wherein such Subjects of these Dominions, as are Masters of it, were born. Impudence in an *English-man* is sullen and inso-lent; in a *Scotch-man* it is untractable and rapacious; in an *Irish-man* absurd and fawning: As the Course of the World now runs,

---

he seeks out envious men and tells them of the good fortune which has occured to others.

11 I.e., in a battle or a duel.

12 Criticize freely.

the impudent *English-man* behaves like a surly Landlord, the *Scot* like an ill-received Guest, and the *Irish-man* like a Stranger who knows he is not welcome. There is seldom any thing entertaining either in the Impudence of a *South* or *North Briton;*[13] but that of an *Irish-man* is always Comick:[14] A true and genuine Impudence is ever the Effect of Ignorance, without the least Sense of it: The best and most successful Starers now in this Town, are of that Nation; they have usually the Advantage of the Stature mentioned in the above Letter of my Correspondent, and generally take their Stands in the Eye of Women of Fortune: Insomuch that I have known one of them, three Months after he came from Plough, with a tolerable good Air lead out a Woman from a Play, which[15] one of our own Breed, after four Years at *Oxford,* and two at the *Temple,* would have been afraid to look at.

I cannot tell how to account for it, but these People have usually the Preference to our own Fools, in the Opinion of the sillier Part of Womankind. Perhaps it is that an *English* Coxcomb is seldom so obsequious as an *Irish* one; and when the Design of pleasing is visible, an Absurdity in the Way toward it is easily forgiven.

But those who are downright impudent, and go on without Reflection that they are such; are more to be tolerated, than a Set of Fellows among us who profess Impudence with an Air of Humour, and think to carry off the most inexcusable of all Faults in the World, with no other Apology than saying in a gay Tone, *I put an impudent Face upon the Matter.*[16] No; no Man shall be allowed the Advantages of Impudence, who is conscious that he is such: If he knows he is impudent, he may as well be otherwise; and it shall be expected that he blush, when he sees he makes another do it. For nothing can attone for the Want of Modesty; without which Beauty is ungraceful, and Wit detestable.   R

13 I.e., an Englishman or a Scotchman.

14 Steele himself was born in Ireland and had a generous share of impudence.

15 The pronoun refers to the well-born woman, not to the play.

16 In *Spectator* No. 6, Sir Roger maintains, ". . . for the Loss of publick and private Virtue, we are beholden to your Men of Parts forsooth; it is with them no matter what is done, so it is done with an Air."

The Spectator, No. 26

Friday,[1] March 30.

[A d d i s o n]

Pallida mors aequo pulsat pede pauperum tabernas
Regumque turres. O beate Sexti,
Vitae summa brevis spem nos vetat inchoare longam.
Jam te premet nox, fabulaeque manes,
Et domus exilis Plutonia————Hor.[2]

When I am in a serious Humour, I very often walk by my self in *Westminster* Abby;[3] where the Gloominess of the Place, and the Use to which it is applied, with the Solemnity of the Building, and the Condition[4] of the People who lye in it, are apt to fill the Mind with a kind of Melancholy, or rather Thoughtfulness, that is not disagreeable. I Yesterday pass'd a whole Afternoon in the Church-yard, the Cloysters, and the Church, amusing[5] my self with the Tomb-stones and Inscriptions that I met with in those several Regions of the Dead.[6] Most of them recorded nothing else of the buried Person, but that he was born upon one Day and died

---

[1] Appropriately, this paper appeared on Good Friday.

[2] Horace *Odes* 1. 4. 13–17: "Impartially, pale death knocks at the hut of the poor and the towers of the rich. Fortunate Sextus. The span of life forbids us to entertain long hope. Soon night will cover you, and the storied infernal regions, and the cheerless house of Pluto."

[3] The Gothic church in Westminster, London—burial place of kings, nobles, churchmen, poets, and military heroes.

[4] Rank or quality, though a double meaning is probably intended.

[5] Bemusing.

[6] Specifically, "the Church-yard, the Cloysters, and the Church." However a reference to the after-life is fairly clear. In *Tatler* No. 152, Addison mentioned the voyage of Ulysses "to the Regions of the Dead."

upon another: The whole History of his Life being comprehended
in those two Circumstances, that are common to all Mankind. I
could not but look upon these Registers of Existence, whether of
Brass or Marble, as a kind of Satyr[7] upon the departed Persons;
who had left no other Memorial of them, but that they were born
and that they died. They put me in mind of several Persons mentioned in the Battels of Heroic Poems, who have sounding[8] Names
given them, for no other Reason but that they may be killed, and
are celebrated for nothing but being knocked on the Head.

Γλαῦκόν τε Μέδοντά τε Θερσιλοχόν τε. Hom.

Glaucumque, Medontaque, Thersilochumque. Vir.[9]

The Life of these Men is finely described in Holy Writ by *the
Path of an Arrow,* which is immediately closed up and lost.[10]

Upon my going into the Church, I entertained my self with[11]
the digging of a Grave; and saw in every Shovel-full of it that was
thrown up, the Fragment of a Bone or Skull intermixt with a kind
of fresh mouldering Earth that some time or other had a Place in
the Composition of an human Body. Upon this, I began to consider with my self what innumerable Multitudes of People lay
confused together under the Pavement of that ancient Cathedral;
how Men and Women, Friends and Enemies, Priests and Soldiers,
Monks and Prebendaries,[12] were crumbled amongst one another,
and blended together in the same common Mass; how Beauty,
Strength, and Youth, with Old-age, Weakness, and Deformity, lay
undistinguished in the same promiscuous Heap of Matter.

After having thus surveyed this great Magazine[13] of Mortality,
as it were, in the Lump; I examined it more particularly by the
Accounts which I found on several of the Monuments which are

---

7 Satire.

8 Impressive, high-sounding.

9 "Glaucus and Medon and Thersilochus" were heroes lost in the Trojan
War. They are mentioned in the *Iliad* 17. 216, and in the *Aeneid* 6. 483.

10 From the Apocrypha, Wisdom of Solomon 5:12–13.

11 Reflected upon.

12 Canons, ecclesiastical dignitaries who occupy a special stall in the choir.

13 Storehouse.

raised in every Quarter of that ancient Fabrick.[14] Some of them were covered with such extravagant Epitaphs, that, if it were possible for the dead Person to be acquainted with them, he would blush at the Praises which his Friends have bestowed upon him. There are others so excessively modest, that they deliver the Character of the Person departed in *Greek* or *Hebrew,* and by that means are not understood once in a Twelve-month. In the Poetical Quarter,[15] I found there were Poets who had no Monuments, and Monuments which had no Poets. I observed indeed that the present War had filled the Church with many of these uninhabited Monuments, which had been erected to the Memory of Persons whose Bodies were perhaps buried in the Plains of *Blenheim,*[16] or in the Bosom of the Ocean.

I could not but be very much delighted with several modern Epitaphs, which are written with great Elegance of Expression and Justness of Thought, and therefore do Honour to the Living as well as to the Dead. As a Foreigner is very apt to conceive an Idea of the Ignorance or Politeness[17] of a Nation from the Turn of their publick Monuments and Inscriptions, they should be submitted to the Perusal of Men of Learning and Genius before they are put in Execution. Sir *Cloudesly Shovel's*[18] Monument has very often given me great Offence: Instead of the brave rough *English* Admiral, which was the distinguishing Character of that plain gallant Man, he is represented on his Tomb by the Figure of a Beau, dress'd in a long Perriwig, and reposing himself upon Velvet Cushions under a Canopy of State. The Inscription is answerable[19] to the Monument; for instead of celebrating the many remarkable Actions he had performed in the Service of his Country,

14 Structure.

15 The burial place of the great English poets, located in the southern end of the south transept of Westminster. Addison is buried in Westminster Abbey.

16 The great English victory in the War of the Spanish Succession won August 13, 1704. An estimated 670 British soldiers were killed in the Bavarian battle.

17 Refinement.

18 The British admiral (1650–1707) who was drowned in the wreck of his ship off the Scilly Isles.

19 Appropriate.

it acquaints us only with the Manner of his Death, in which it was impossible for him to reap any Honour. The *Dutch,* whom we are apt to despise for want of Genius, shew an infinitely greater Taste of Antiquity and Politeness in their Buildings and Works of this nature, than what we meet with in those of our own Country. The Monuments of their Admirals, which have been erected at the publick Expence, represent them like themselves; and are adorned with rostral Crowns[20] and naval Ornaments, with beautiful Festoons of Sea-weed, Shells, and Coral.

But to return to our Subject. I have left the Repository of our *English* Kings for the Contemplation of another Day,[21] when I shall find my Mind disposed for so serious an Amusement. I know that Entertainments of this nature are apt to raise dark and dismal Thoughts in timorous Minds, and gloomy Imaginations; but for my own part, though I am always serious,[22] I do not know what it is to be melancholy; and can therefore take a View of Nature in her deep and solemn Scenes, with the same Pleasure as in her most gay and delightful ones. By this means I can improve my self with those Objects, which others consider with Terror. When I look upon the Tombs of the Great, every Emotion of Envy dies in me; when I read the Epitaphs of the Beautiful, every inordinate Desire goes out; when I meet with the Grief of Parents upon a Tomb-stone, my Heart melts with Compassion; when I see the Tomb of the Parents themselves, I consider the Vanity of grieving for those whom we must quickly follow: When I see Kings lying by those who deposed them, when I consider rival Wits placed Side by Side, or the holy Men that divided the World with their Contests and Disputes,[23] I reflect with Sorrow and Astonishment on the little Competitions, Factions, and Debates of Mankind. When I read the several Dates of the Tombs, of some that died Yesterday, and some six hundred Years ago, I consider that great Day when we shall all of us be Contemporaries, and make our Appearance together.   C

20 Crowns adorned with figures of ships' prows, originally awarded to the person who first boarded an enemy ship.

21 Addison returned to the subject in *Spectator* No. 329.

22 See *Spectator* No. 1.

23 There is a hint of irony in this description.

The Spectator, No. 34

Monday, April 9.

[A d d i s o n]

———————

———————*parcit*
Cognatis maculis similis fera———Juv.[1]

The Club of which I am a Member, is very luckily composed of such Persons as are engaged in different Ways of Life, and deputed as it were out of the most conspicuous Classes of Mankind: By this Means I am furnished with the greatest Variety of Hints and Materials, and know every thing that passes in the different Quarters and Divisions, not only of this great City,[2] but of the whole Kingdom. My Readers too have the Satisfaction to find, that there is no Rank or Degree among them who have not their Representative in this Club, and that there is always some Body present who will take Care of their respective Interests, that nothing may be written or published to the Prejudice or Infringement of their just Rights and Privileges.

I last Night sate very late in Company with this select Body of Friends, who entertained me with several Remarks which they and others had made upon these my Speculations, as also with the various Success which they had met with among their several Ranks and Degrees of Readers. Will. Honeycomb told me, in the softest manner he could, That there were some Ladies (but for your Comfort, says Will. they are not those of the most Wit) that were offended at the Liberties I had taken with the Opera and the

---

[1] Juvenal *Satires* 15. 159–160: "Wild beasts spare animals spotted like themselves."

[2] London. The word is later used in a specialized sense.

Puppet-Show:[3] That some of them were likewise very much surprised, that I should think such serious Points as the Dress and Equipage of Persons of Quality, proper Subjects for Raillery.

He was going on, when Sir Andrew Freeport took him up short, and told him, that the Papers he hinted at had done great Good in the City,[4] and that all their Wives and Daughters were the better for them: And further added, that the whole City thought themselves very much obliged to me for declaring my generous Intentions to scourge Vice and Folly as they appear in a Multitude, without condescending to be a Publisher of particular Intreagues and Cuckoldoms.[5] In short, says Sir Andrew, if you avoid that foolish beaten Road of falling upon Aldermen and Citizens, and employ your Pen upon the Vanity and Luxury of Courts, your Paper must needs be of general Use.

Upon this my Friend the Templer told Sir Andrew, That he wondered to hear a Man of his Sense talk after that manner; that the City had always been the Province for Satyr; and that the Wits of King *Charles*'s Time jested upon nothing else during his whole Reign.[6] He then shewed, by the Examples of *Horace, Juvenal, Boileau*,[7] and the best Writers of every Age, that the Follies of the Stage and Court had never been accounted too sacred for Ridicule, how great soever the Persons might be that patroniz'd them. But after all, says he, I think your Raillery has made too great an Excursion, in attacking several Persons of the Inns of Court;[8] and I do not believe you can shew me any Precedent for your Behaviour in that Particular.

My good Friend Sir Roger de Coverly, who had said nothing all this while, began his Speech with a Pish! and told us, That he wondered to see so many Men of Sense so very serious upon Fool-

3 For the opera, see *Spectator* No. 18, n. 2; for the puppet show, *Spectator* No. 20, n. 4. The puppet shows had been discussed in paper No. 14.

4 The business district.

5 A cuckold is a husband said to have sprouted horns because his wife is unfaithful. The Spectator promised to avoid such gossip in essay No. 16.

6 Restoration comedy regularly satirized the merchant. Sir Jasper Fidget, the "grave man of business" in Wycherley's *The Country Wife* (1675) is probably the most notable example.

7 See *Tatler* No. 158, n. 16. Boileau had died only a month earlier.

8 Practice of the law was discussed in *Spectator* No. 21.

eries. Let our good Friend, says he, attack every one that deserves it: I would only advise you, Mr. Spectator, applying himself to me, to take Care how you meddle with Country Squires: They are the Ornaments of the *English* Nation; Men of good Heads and sound Bodies! and let me tell you, some of them take it ill of you, that you mention Fox-hunters with so little Respect.[9]

Captain Sentry spoke very sparingly on this Occasion. What he said was only to commend my Prudence in not touching upon the Army, and advised me to continue to act discreetly in that Point.

By this time I found every Subject of my Speculations was taken away from me, by one or other of the Club; and began to think my self in the Condition of the good Man that had one Wife who took a Dislike to his grey Hairs, and another to his black, till by their picking out what each of them had an Aversion to, they left his Head altogether bald and naked.[10]

While I was thus musing with my self, my worthy Friend the Clergyman, who, very luckily for me, was at the Club that Night, undertook my Cause. He told us, that he wondered any Order of Persons should think themselves too considerable to be advis'd: That it was not Quality, but Innocence, which exempted Men from Reproof: That Vice and Folly ought to be attacked where-ever they could be met with, and especially when they were placed in high and conspicuous Stations of Life. He further added, That my Paper would only serve to aggravate the Pains of Poverty, if it chiefly exposed those who are already depress'd, and in some measure turned into Ridicule, by the Meanness of their Conditions and Circumstances. He afterwards proceeded to take Notice of the great Use this Paper might be of to the Publick, by reprehending those Vices which are too trivial for the Chastisement of the Law, and too fantastical for the Cognizance of the Pulpit. He then advised me to prosecute my Undertaking with Chearfulness; and assured me, that whoever might be displeased with me, I should be approved by all those whose Praises do Honour to the Persons on whom they are bestowed.

9 See *Tatler* No. 18, n. 26 and *Tatler* No. 89, n. 10. Sir Roger's statement is more a warning than a criticism: up to this time, *The Spectator* had said almost nothing about fox-hunters.

10 Aesop *Fable* 162.

The whole Club pays a particular Deference to the Discourse of this Gentleman, and are drawn into what he says, as much by the candid ingenuous Manner with which he delivers himself, as by the Strength of Argument and Force of Reason which he makes use of. Will. Honeycomb immediately agreed, that what he had said was right; and that for his Part, he would not insist upon the Quarter which he had demanded for the Ladies. Sir Andrew gave up the City with the same Frankness. The Templer would not stand out; and was followed by Sir Roger and the Captain: Who all agreed that I should be at Liberty to carry the War into what Quarter I pleased; provided I continued to combat with Criminals in a Body, and to assault the Vice without hurting the Person.

This Debate, which was held for the Good of Mankind, put me in mind of that which the *Roman* Triumvirate were formerly engaged in, for their Destruction.[11] Every Man at first stood hard for his Friend, till they found that by this Means they should spoil their Proscription: And at length, making a Sacrifice of all their Acquaintance and Relations, furnished out a very decent Execution.

Having thus taken my Resolutions to march on boldly in the Cause of Virtue and good Sense, and to annoy their Adversaries in whatever Degree or Rank of Men they may be found: I shall be deaf for the future to all the Remonstrances that shall be made to me on this Account. If *Punch* grows extravagant,[12] I shall reprimand him very freely: If the Stage becomes a Nursery of Folly and Impertinence, I shall not be afraid to animadvert upon it. In short, If I meet with any thing in City, Court, or Country, that shocks Modesty or good Manners, I shall use my utmost Endeavours to make an Example of it. I must however intreat every particular Person, who does me the Honour to be a Reader of this Paper, never to think himself, or any one of his Friends or Enemies, aimed at in what is said: For I promise him, never to draw a faulty Character which does not fit at least a Thousand Peo-

---

[11] The Second Triumvirate—Octavius, Antony, and Lepidus—having taken power considered a list of hostile or suspected persons and debated which should be executed. (Plutarch *Life of Antony* 19. 2; *Life of Cicero* 46. 4.)

[12] This puppet-show hero often discussed political and moral questions and employed intemperate language.

ple;[13] or to publish a single Paper, that is not written in the Spirit
of Benevolence, and with a Love to Mankind.   C

[13] This seems a reasonable refutation of those critics who claim that each
member of the Spectator Club had a specific real-life counterpart, e.g., that
Sir Roger was Sir John Packington, that Sir Andrew was Sir Gilbert Heathcote,
that Captain Sentry was Steele, etc.

The Spectator, No. 37

Thursday, April 12.

[A d d i s o n]

————*Non illa colo calathisve Minervae*
Foemineas assueta manus.————Virg.[1]

Some Months ago, my Friend Sir Roger being in the Country, enclosed a Letter to me, directed to a certain Lady whom I shall here call by the Name of *Leonora,* and as it contained Matters of Consequence, desired me to deliver it to her with my own Hand. Accordingly I waited upon her Ladyship pretty early in the Morning, and was desired by her Woman to walk into her Lady's Library, till such time as she was in a Readiness to receive me. The very Sound of a *Lady's Library* gave me a great Curiosity to see it; and, as it was some time before the Lady came to me, I had an Opportunity of turning over a great many of her Books, which were ranged together in a very beautiful Order. At the End of the *Folio's* (which were finely bound and gilt) were great Jars of *China* placed one above another in a very noble piece of Architecture. The *Quarto's* were separated from the *Octavo's* by a pile of smaller Vessels, which rose in a delightful Pyramid.[2] The *Octavo's* were bounded by Tea Dishes of all Shapes, Colours and Sizes, which were so disposed on a wooden Frame, that they looked like one continued Pillar indented with the finest Strokes of Sculpture, and stained with the greatest Variety of

[1] Virgil *Aeneid* 1. 805–806: "She never having accustomed her woman's hands to the distaff or the work-baskets of Minerva."

[2] The books of different sizes (a *folio* is twice as large as a *quarto;* a *quarto* twice the size of an *octavo*) were combined with the useless pieces of china it was then fashionable to collect, to make an architectural display.

Dyes. That Part of the Library which was designed for the Reception of Plays and Pamphlets, and other loose Papers, was enclosed in a kind of Square, consisting of one of the prettiest Grotesque Works[3] that ever I saw, and made up of Scaramouches, Lions, Monkies, Mandarines, Trees, Shells, and a thousand other odd Figures in *China* Ware. In the midst of the Room was a little Japan Table,[4] with a Quire of gilt Paper upon it, and on the Paper a Silver Snuff-box made in the shape of a little Book. I found there were several other Counterfeit Books upon the upper Shelves, which were carved in Wood, and served only to fill up the Number, like Faggots in the Muster of a Regiment.[5] I was wonderfully pleased with such a mixt kind of Furniture, as seemed very suitable both to the Lady and the Scholar, and did not know at first whether I should fancy my self in a Grotto, or in a Library.

Upon my looking into the Books, I found there were some few which the Lady had bought for her own use, but that most of them had been got together, either because she had heard them praised, or because she had seen the Authors of them.[6] Among

[3] Painted or sculptured pieces representing human and animal forms fantastically interwoven with foliage and flowers. Among the figures are Scaramouche, the stock character from Italian farce, and Chinese mandarins.

[4] A lacquered table.

[5] Persons hired temporarily to fill a deficiency on the roll of a company or regiment.

[6] Leonora's library includes books collected for edification, for reference, for pleasure, and for show. Though she was aware the books looked impressive on her shelves, the lady probably read all or parts of William Sherlock's *A Practical Discourse concerning Death* (1689); the English version (1682) of the *Quinze joies de mariage;* Father Malebranche's *Recherche de la vérité,* which was translated into English in 1694; the Marquis of Halifax's *The Lady's New-Years Gift; or, Advice to a Daughter* (1688); Richard Allestree's *The Ladies Calling* (1673); Richard Steele's *The Christian Hero* (1701); Jeremy Taylor's *The Rule and Exercise of Holy Living* (1650) and *The Rule and Exercise of Holy Dying* (1651), and the prayer book. She certainly consulted the reference books: Nicolas Culpeper's *A Directory for Midwives* (1651); Anthony Fert's *A Discourse or Explications of the Grounds of Dancing;* the dictionary, probably *Cocker's English Dictionary* (1704); and the spelling book. Leonora relished the works of romantic literature: La Calprenède's *Cassandra* (1642–1645) and *Cleopatra* (1647); Honoré d'Urfé's *L'Astrée* (1607–1627); Madeleine de Scudéry's

several that I examined, I very well remember these that follow.

> *Ogleby*'s *Virgil.*
> *Dryden*'s *Juvenal.*
> *Cassandra.*
> *Cleopatra.*
> *Astraea.*
> Sir *Isaac Newton*'s Works.
> *The Grand Cyrus:* With a Pin stuck in one of the middle Leaves.
> *Pembroke*'s *Arcadia.*
> *Lock* of Human Understanding: With a Paper of Patches[7] in it.
> A Spelling Book.
> A Dictionary for the Explanation of hard Words.
> *Sherlock* upon Death.
> The fifteen Comforts of Matrimony.
> Sir *William Temple*'s Essays.[8]
> Father *Malbranche*'s *Search after Truth,* translated into *English.*
> A Book of Novels.
> The Academy of Compliments.
> *Culpepper*'s Midwifery.
> The Ladies Calling.

Artamène ou le grand Cyrus (1649–1653) and *Clélie* (1654–1660); Sir Philip Sidney's *The Countesse of Pembrokes Arcadia* (1590); Thomas D'Urfey's *Tales Tragical and Comical* (1704); Mrs. Mary Manley's *Secret Memoirs and Manners of several Persons of Quality of both Sexes, from the new Atalantis . . .* (1709); and the book of novels. Assuredly she read the books reporting sensational events: *The Speech of Henry Sacheverell D.D. upon his Impeachment . . .* (1710); and *The Arraignment, Tryal and Conviction of Robert Fielding, Esq; for Felony, in Marrying her Grace the Dutchess of Cleveland, his first Wife, Mrs. Mary Wadsworth, being then alive* (1708). But it is probable Baker's *A Chronicle of the Kings of England from the Time of the Romans Government . . .* (1643); John Ogilby's translation of Virgil (1649, 1650, 1654); Dryden's translation of Juvenal (1693); and Sir Roger L'Estrange's *Seneca's Morals, by way of Abstract* were kept largely for appearance. "All the Classick Authors in Wood" and "A Set of *Elzivers* by the same hand"—i.e., carved by the same hand—were demonstrably so.

7 Bits of black silk worn on the faces of fashionable ladies, either to conceal blemishes or to heighten the whiteness of their complexions. See *Spectator* No. 81.

8 Sir William Temple (1628–1699), English diplomat and author, wrote the essay *Of Ancient and Modern Learning* (1690), which led to the intellectual controversy that finally produced Swift's *The Battle of the Books* (1704).

Tales in Verse by Mr. *Durfey:* Bound in Red Leather, gilt on the Back, and doubled down in several Places.

All the Classick Authors in Wood.

A Set of *Elzivers*[9] by the same Hand.

Clelia: Which opened of it self in the Place that describes two Lovers in a Bower.

Baker's Chronicle.

Advice to a Daughter.

The New *Atalantis,* with a Key to it.[10]

Mr. *Steele's* Christian Heroe.

A Prayer Book: With a Bottle of *Hungary* Water[11] by the Side of it.

Dr. *Sacheverell's* Speech.[12]

Fielding's Tryal.

Seneca's Morals.

Taylor's holy Living and Dying.

La Ferte's Instructions for Country Dances.

I was taking a Catalogue in my Pocket-Book[13] of these, and several other Authors, when *Leonora* entred, and upon my presenting her with the Letter from the Knight, told me, with an unspeakable Grace, that she hoped Sir Roger was in good Health: I answered *Yes,* for I hate long Speeches, and after a Bow or two retired.

Leonora was formerly a celebrated Beauty, and is still a very lovely Woman. She has been a Widow for two or three Years, and being unfortunate in her first Marriage, has taken a Resolution never to venture upon a second. She has no Children to take care of, and leaves the Management of her Estate to my good Friend Sir Roger. But as the Mind naturally sinks into a kind of Leth-

9 See *Tatler* No. 158, n. 4.

10 See *Tatler* No. 229, n. 7. The book reported scandalous incidents involving prominent Whigs but used false names, hence the need for a key.

11 A mixture of wine, lavender, and rosemary used both as a medicine and a cosmetic.

12 Henry Sacheverell (1674?–1714), a Tory preacher tried for seditious libel in 1710, became a national hero and contributed to the fall of the Whig ministry. *Spectator* No. 57 describes a lady who has pictures of him throughout her room.

13 A pocket tablet.

argy, and falls asleep, that is not agitated by some Favourite Pleasures and Pursuits, *Leonora* has turned all the Passions of her Sex,
into a Love of Books and Retirement. She converses chiefly with
Men, (as she has often said her self) but it is only in their Writings; and admits of very few Male-Visitants, except my Friend Sir
Roger, whom she hears with great Pleasure, and without Scandal.
As her Reading has lain very much among Romances, it has given
her a very particular Turn of Thinking, and discovers it self even
in her House, her Gardens, and her Furniture. Sir Roger has entertained me an Hour together with a Description of her Country-Seat,[14] which is situated in a kind of Wilderness, about an
hundred Miles distant from *London,* and looks like a little en-
chanted Palace. The Rocks about her are shaped into Artificial
Grottoes, covered with Woodbines and Jessamines. The Woods
are cut into shady Walks, twisted into Bowers, and filled with
Cages of Turtles.[15] The Springs are made to run among Pebbles,
and by that means taught to murmur very agreeably. They are
likewise collected into a beautiful Lake, that is inhabited by a
Couple of Swans, and empties it self by a little Rivulet which runs
through a green Meadow, and is known in the Family by the
Name of *The Purling Stream.*[16] The Knight likewise tells me,
that this Lady preserves her Game better than any of the Gentlemen in the Country; not (says Sir Roger) that she sets so great a
Value upon her Partridges and Pheasants, as upon her Larks and
Nightingales. For she says that every Bird which is killed in her
Ground will spoil a Consort,[17] and that she shall certainly miss
him the next Year.

When I think how odly this Lady is improved by Learning, I
look upon her with a mixture of Admiration and Pity. Amidst

[14] Estate.

[15] Turtle-doves.

[16] *Spectator* No. 414 gave Addison's views on landscape gardening: ". . . our
English Gardens are not so entertaining to the Fancy as those in *France* and
Italy, where we see a large Extent of Ground covered over with an agreeable
mixture of Garden and Forest, which represent every where an artificial Rude-
ness, much more charming than that Neatness and Elegancy which we meet
with in those of our own country."

[17] Concert.

these innocent Entertainments which she has formed to her self, how much more Valuable does she appear than those of her Sex, who employ themselves in Diversions that are less Reasonable, though more in Fashion? What Improvements would a Woman have made, who is so susceptible of Impressions from what she reads, had she been guided to such Books as have a tendency to enlighten the Understanding and rectifie the Passions, as well as to those which are of little more use than to divert the Imagination?

But the manner of a Lady's employing her self usefully in Reading shall be the Subject of another Paper, in which I design to recommend such particular Books as may be proper for the Improvement of the Sex.[18] And as this is a Subject of a very nice Nature, I shall desire my Correspondents to give me their Thoughts upon it.   C

[18] Addison's recommendations appear in *Spectator* No. 92.

The Spectator, No. 40[1]

Monday, April 16.

[Addison]

Ac ne forte putes me, quae facere ipse recusem,
Cum recte tractent alii, laudare maligne;
Ille per extentum funem mihi posse videtur
Ire Poeta, meum qui pectus inaniter angit,
Irritat, mulcet, falsis terroribus implet,
Ut magus; & modo me Thebis, modo ponit Athenis. Hor.[2]

The *English* Writers of Tragedy are possessed with a Notion, that when they represent a virtuous or innocent Person in Distress, they ought not to leave him till they have delivered him out of his Troubles, or made him triumph over his Enemies. This Error they have been led into by a ridiculous Doctrine in Modern Criticism, that they are obliged to an equal[3] Distribution of Rewards and Punishments, and an impartial Execution of Poetical Justice. Who were the first that established this Rule I know not; but I am sure it has no Foundation in Nature, in Reason, or in

---

1 *Spectator* No. 39 introduced Addison's papers on tragedy: ". . . that I may contribute something towards the Improvement of English Tragedy, I shall take Notice, in this and in other following Papers, of some particular Parts in it that seem liable to Exception." He treats the subject in essays No. 39, 40, 42, and 44.

2 Horace *Epistles* 2. 1. 208–213: "And lest, perchance, you think that I grudgingly praise when others are handling well what I myself decline to do; it seems to me that that poet is able to walk a tight rope, who with airy nothings wrings my heart, inflames it, soothes it, fills it with false fears, like a wizard, and sets me down now in Thebes, now in Athens."

3 Just, honorable.

the Practice of the Ancients.[4] We find that Good and Evil happen alike to all Men on this Side the Grave; and as the principal Design of Tragedy is to raise Commiseration and Terror in the Minds of the Audience, we shall defeat this great End, if we always make Virtue and Innocence happy and successful. Whatever Crosses and Disappointments a good Man suffers in the Body of the Tragedy, they will make but small Impression on our Minds, when we know that in the last Act he is to arrive at the End of his Wishes and Desires. When we see him engaged in the Depth of his Afflictions, we are apt to comfort our selves, because we are sure he will find his Way out of them; and that his Grief, how great soever it may be at present, will soon terminate in Gladness. For this Reason the ancient Writers of Tragedy treated Men in their Plays, as they are dealt with in the World, by making Virtue sometimes happy and sometimes miserable, as they found it in the Fable[5] which they made choice of, or as it might affect their Audience in the most agreeable Manner. *Aristotle* considers the Tragedies that were written in either of these Kinds, and observes, That those which ended unhappily, had always pleased the People, and carried away the Prize in the publick Disputes of the Stage, from those that ended happily.[6] Terror and Commiseration leave a pleasing Anguish in the Mind; and fix the Audience in such a serious Composure of Thought, as is much more lasting and delightful than any little transient Starts of Joy and Satisfaction. Accordingly we find, that more of our *English* Tragedies have succeeded, in which the Favourites of the Audience sink under their Calamities, than those in which they recover themselves out of them. The best Plays of this Kind are the *Orphan, Venice preserved, Alexander the Great, Theodosius, All for Love, Oedipus, Oroonoko, Othello, &c.*[7] *King Lear* is an admirable Tragedy

4 See *Spectator* No. 2, n. 15.

5 Story.

6 *Poetics* 13. 4–6.

7 *The Orphan* (1680) and *Venice Preserved* (1682) were by Thomas Otway (1652–1685). *Alexander the Great* (1677) and *Theodosius* (1680) were by Nathaniel Lee (1649?–1692). *All for Love* (1678) was by John Dryden (1631–1700). *Oroonoko* (1696) was by Thomas Southerne (1660–1746). *Oedipus* (1678), by Lee and Dryden, provides the quotations which conclude this essay.

of the same Kind, as *Shakespear* wrote it; but as it is reformed according to the chymerical Notion of Poetical Justice,[8] in my humble Opinion it has lost half its Beauty. At the same time I must allow, that there are very noble Tragedies which have been framed upon the other Plan, and have ended happily; as indeed most of the good Tragedies, which have been written since the starting of the above-mentioned Criticism, have taken this Turn: As the *Mourning Bride, Tamerlane, Ulysses, Phaedra* and *Hyppolitus,*[9] with most of Mr. *Dryden's.* I must also allow, that many of *Shakespear's,* and several of the celebrated Tragedies of Antiquity, are cast in the same Form. I do not therefore dispute against this way of writing Tragedies, but against the Criticism that would establish this as the only Method; and by that Means would very much cramp the *English* Tragedy, and perhaps give a wrong Bent to the Genius of our Writers.

The Tragi-Comedy, which is the Product of the *English* Theatre, is one of the most monstrous Inventions that ever entered into a Poet's Thoughts. An Author might as well think of weaving the Adventures of *Aeneas* and *Hudibras*[10] into one Poem, as of writing such a motly Piece of Mirth and Sorrow. But the Absurdity of these Performances is so very visible, that I shall not insist upon it.

The same Objections which are made to Tragi-Comedy, may in some Measure be applied to all Tragedies that have a double Plot in them; which are likewise more frequent upon the *English* Stage, than upon any other: For though the Grief of the Audience, in such Performances, be not changed into another Passion, as in Tragi-Comedies; it is diverted upon another Object, which weakens their Concern for the principal Action, and breaks the Tide of Sorrow, by throwing it into different Channels. This Inconvenience, however, may in a great Measure be cured, if not wholly removed, by the skilful Choice of an Under-Plot, which

8 At this time, *King Lear* was usually offered in the adaptation of Nahum Tate (1672–1710).

9 *The Mourning Bride* (1697) was by William Congreve (1670–1729); *Tamerlane* (1702) and *Ulysses* (1705) were by Nicholas Rowe (1674–1718); and *Phaedra and Hippolitus* was by Edmund Smith (1672–1710).

10 See *Tatler* No. 132, n. 11.

may bear such a near Relation to the principal Design, as to contribute towards the Completion of it, and be concluded by the same Catastrophe.[11]

There is also another Particular, which may be reckoned among the Blemishes, or rather the false Beauties, of our *English* Tragedy: I mean those particular Speeches which are commonly known by the Name of *Rants*. The warm and passionate Parts of a Tragedy, are always the most taking with the Audience; for which Reason we often see the Players pronouncing, in all the Violence of Action, several Parts of the Tragedy which the Author writ with great Temper,[12] and designed that they should have been so acted. I have seen *Powell*[13] very often raise himself a loud Clap by this Artifice. The Poets that were acquainted with this Secret, have given frequent Occasion for such Emotions in the Actor, by adding Vehemence to Words where there was no Passion, or inflaming a real Passion into Fustian. This hath filled the Mouths of our Heroes with Bombast;[14] and given them such Sentiments, as proceed rather from a Swelling than a Greatness of Mind. Unnatural Exclamations, Curses, Vows, Blasphemies, a Defiance of Mankind, and an Outraging of the Gods, frequently pass upon the Audience for tow'ring Thoughts, and have accordingly met with infinite Applause.

I shall here add a Remark, which I am afraid our Tragick Writers may make an ill use of. As our Heroes are generally Lovers, their Swelling and Blustring upon the Stage very much recommends them to the fair Part of their Audience. The Ladies are wonderfully pleased to see a Man insulting Kings, or affronting the Gods, in one Scene, and throwing himself at the Feet of his Mistress in another. Let him behave himself insolently towards the Men, and abjectly towards the Fair One, and it is ten to one but he proves a Favourite of the Boxes. *Dryden* and *Lee,* in several of their Tragedies, have practised this Secret with good Success.[15]

---

11 One year later, Addison's tragedy *Cato* illustrated this effect.

12 Restraint.

13 George Powell (d. 1717), actor and dramatist.

14 The words *rant, fustian,* and *bombast* have essentially the same meaning.

15 The most notable hero of this type is Almanzor in Dryden's *The Conquest of Granada* (1670). See *Tatler* No. 18, n. 24.

But to shew how a *Rant* pleases beyond the most just and natural Thought that is not pronounced with Vehemence, I would desire the Reader, when he sees the Tragedy of *Oedipus,* to observe how quietly the Hero is dismissed at the End of the third Act, after having pronounced the following Lines, in which the Thought is very natural, and apt to move Compassion.

> *To you, good Gods, I make my last Appeal,*
> *Or clear my Virtues, or my Crimes reveal.*
> *If in the Maze of Fate I blindly run,*
> *And backward trod those Paths I sought to shun;*
> *Impute my Errors to your own Decree:*
> *My Hands are guilty, but my Heart is free.*

Let us then observe with what Thunder-claps of Applause he leaves the Stage, after the Impieties and Execrations at the End of the fourth Act; and you will wonder to see an Audience so cursed and so pleased at the same Time.

> *O that as oft I have at* Athens *seen,*
>   [Where, by the way, there was no Stage till many Years after
>   *Oedipus.*]
> *The Stage arise, and the big Clouds descend;*
> *So now, in very deed, I might behold*
> *This pond'rous Globe, and all you marble Roof,*
> *Meet, like the Hands of* Jove, *and crush Mankind.*
> *For all the Elements,* &c.

ADVERTISEMENT

Having spoken of Mr. Powell, *as sometimes raising himself Applause from the ill Taste of an Audience; I must do him the Justice to own, that he is excellently formed for a Tragaedian, and, when he pleases, deserves the Admiration of the best Judges; as I doubt not but he will in the* Conquest of Mexico,[16] *which is acted for his own Benefit To-morrow Night.*   C

---

[16] In *Spectator* No. 41, Dryden's play is advertised by its better known title *The Indian Emperor* (1665).

The Spectator, No. 41

Tuesday, April 17.

[S t e e l e]

⎯⎯⎯*Tu non inventa reperta es.* Ovid.[1]

Compassion for the Gentleman who writes the following Letter, should not prevail upon me to fall upon[2] the Fair Sex, if it were not that I find they are frequently Fairer than they ought to be. Such Impostures are not to be tolerated in Civil Society; and I think his Misfortune ought to be made publick, as a Warning for other Men always to Examine into what they Admire.

"*Sir,*

Supposing you to be a Person of general Knowledge, I make my Application to you on a very particular Occasion. I have a great Mind to be rid of my Wife, and hope, when you consider my Case, you will be of Opinion I have very just Pretensions to a Divorce. I am a mere Man of the Town,[3] and have very little Improvement, but what I have got from Plays. I remember in *The Silent Woman,*[4] the Learned Dr. *Cutberd,* or Dr. *Otter* (I forget which) makes one of the Causes of Separation to be *Error Personae,* when a Man marries a Woman, and finds her not to be the same Woman whom he intended to marry, but another. If that be Law, it is, I presume, exactly my Case. For you are to know, Mr. Spectator, that there are Women who do not let their Husbands see their Faces till they are married.

1 Adapted from Ovid *Metamorphoses* 1. 654–655: "Undiscovered, you are discovered."

2 Criticize.

3 See the description of Will Honeycomb and his like, in *Spectator* No. 105.

4 In Ben Jonson's *Epicoene, or the Silent Woman* (1609), Captain Otter tells Cutbeard, the barber, that *error personae* is cause for "a lawful divorce": "If you contract yourself to one person, thinking her another" (act 5, sc. 3).

"Not to keep you in Suspense, I mean plainly, that part of the Sex who paint. They are some of them so exquisitely skilful this Way, that give them but a tolerable Pair of Eyes to set up with, and they will make Bosom, Lips, Cheeks, and Eyebrows, by their own Industry. As for my Dear,[5] never Man was so inamour'd as I was of her fair Forehead, Neck and Arms, as well as the bright Jett of her Hair; but to my great Astonishment, I find they were all the Effect of Art: Her Skin is so tarnished with this Practice, that when she first wakes in a Morning, she scarce seems young enough to be the Mother of her whom I carried to Bed the Night before. I shall take the Liberty to part with her by the first Opportunity, unless her Father will make her Portion[6] suitable to her real, not her assumed, Countenance. This I thought fit to let him and her know by your Means. I am,

Sir,

Your most Obedient Humble Servant."

I cannot tell what the Law, or the Parents of the Lady will do for this Injured Gentleman, but must allow he has very much Justice on his side. I have indeed very long observed this Evil, and distinguished those of our Women who wear their own, from those in borrowed Complexions, by the *Picts* and the *British.*[7] There does not need any great Discernment to judge which are which. The *British* have a lively animated Aspect; the *Picts,*[8] though never so Beautiful, have dead uninformed Countenances. The Muscles of a real Face sometimes swell with soft Passion, sudden Surprize, and are flushed with agreeable Confusions, according as the Objects before them, or the Ideas presented to them, affect their Imagination. But the *Picts* behold all things with the same Air, whether they are Joyful or Sad; The same fixed Insensibility appears upon all Occasions. A *Pict,* though she takes all that Pains to invite the Approach of Lovers, is obliged to keep them at a certain Distance; a Sigh in a Languishing Lover, if fetched too near her, would dissolve a Feature; and a Kiss snatched by a Forward one, might transfer the Complexion of the

5 Wife.

6 The financial settlement.

7 The Spectator means that he has thought about and perhaps discussed this distinction between two types of women; he has written nothing on the subject.

8 Natives in ancient Britain, who painted their bodies.

Mistress to the Admirer. It is hard to speak of these false Fair
Ones, without saying something uncomplaisant, but I would only
recommend to them to consider how they like coming into a
Room new Painted; they may assure themselves, the near Approach of a Lady who uses this Practice is much more offensive.

Will. Honeycomb told us, one Day, an Adventure he once had
with a *Pict*. This Lady had Wit, as well as Beauty, at Will; and
made it her Business to gain Hearts, for no other Reason, but to
railly⁹ the Torments of her Lovers. She would make great Advances to insnare Men, but without any manner of Scruple break
off when there was no Provocation. Her Ill-Nature and Vanity
made my Friend very easily Proof against the Charms of her Wit
and Conversation; but her beauteous Form, instead of being
blemished by her Falshood and Inconstancy, every Day increased
upon him,¹⁰ and she had new Attractions every time he saw her.
When she observed Will. irrevocably her Slave, she began to use
him as such, and after many steps toward such a Cruelty, she at
last utterly banished him. The unhappy Lover strove in vain, by
servile Epistles,¹¹ to revoke his Doom; till at length he was forced
to the last Refuge, a round Sum of Mony to her Maid. This corrupt Attendant placed him early in the Morning behind the
Hangings in her Mistress's Dressing-Room. He stood very conve-
niently to observe, without being seen. The *Pict* begins the Face
she designed to wear that Day, and I have heard him protest she
had worked a full half Hour before he knew her to be the same
Woman. As soon as he saw the Dawn of that Complexion, for
which he had so long languished, he thought fit to break from his
Concealment, repeating that of *Cowley*:

> *Th' adorning Thee with so much Art,*
> *Is but a barb'rous Skill;*
> *'Tis like the Pois'ning of a Dart,*
> *Too apt before to kill.*¹²

⁹ Mock.

¹⁰ Attracted him more.

¹¹ Letters or poems emphasizing the lady's fine qualities and his own un-
worthiness.

¹² The quatrain is stanza 4 of "The Waiting Maid," one of the near-hun-
dred poems which comprise *The Mistress, or Several Copies of Love-Verses*
(1647), by Abraham Cowley (1618–1667).

The *Pict* stood before him in the utmost Confusion, with the prettiest Smirk imaginable on the finish'd side of her Face, pale as Ashes on the other. Honeycomb seized all her Gally-pots and Washes, and carried off his Handkerchief full of Brushes, Scraps of *Spanish* Wooll, and Phials of Unguents.[13] The Lady went into the Country; the Lover was cured.

It is certain no Faith ought to be kept with Cheats, and an Oath made to a *Pict* is of it self void. I would therefore exhort all the *British* Ladies to single them out, nor do I know any but *Lindamira* who should be Exempt from Discovery; for her own Complexion is so delicate, that she ought to be allowed the Covering it with Paint, as a Punishment for chusing to be the worst Piece of Art extant, instead of the Masterpiece of Nature. As for my part, who have no Expectations[14] from Women, and consider them only as they are Part of the Species, I do not half so much fear offending a Beauty as a Woman of Sense; I shall therefore produce several Faces[15] which have been in Publick this many Years, and never appeared; it will be a very pretty Entertainment in the Play-house (when I have abolished this Custom) to see so many Ladies, when they first lay it down, *incog.*[16] in their own Faces.

In the mean time, as a Pattern for improving their Charms, let the Sex study the agreeable *Statira.* Her Features are enlivened with the Chearfulness of her Mind, and good Humour gives an Alacrity to her Eyes. She is Graceful without affecting an Air, and Unconcerned without appearing Careless. Her having no manner of Art in her Mind, makes her want none in her Person.

How like is this Lady, and how unlike is a *Pict,* to that Description Dr. *Donne* gives of his Mistress?

> ——*Her pure and eloquent Blood*
> *Spoke in her Cheeks, and so distinctly wrought,*
> *That one would almost say her Body thought.*[17]

[13] Washes were cosmetic lotions; Spanish wool was wool treated with dye and used as a cosmetic; and unguents were salves and ointments.

[14] "Expectations" could refer to a legal inheritance or a romantic prospect.

[15] Publish the names of notorious Picts.

[16] Incognito, i.e., in disguise.

[17] From *Anatomy of the World (The Second Anniversary),* lines 244–246. This is the only reference to John Donne in *The Spectator.*

ADVERTISEMENT

A young Gentlewoman of about Nineteen Years of Age (bred in the Family of a Person of Quality lately deceased) who Paints the Finest Flesh-colour, wants a Place, and is to be heard of at the House of Minheer Grotesque, *a* Dutch *Painter in* Barbican.[18]

N. B. *She is also well skilled in the Drapery-part, and puts on Hoods and mixes Ribbons so as to suit the Colours of the Face with great Art and Success.*   R

[18] This is a continuation of Long Lane in London.

The Spectator, No. 44

Friday, April 20.

[Addison]

Tu quid ego & populus mecum desideret audi. Hor.[1]

Among the several Artifices which are put in Practice by the
Poets to fill the Minds of an Audience with Terror, the first Place
is due to Thunder and Lightning, which are often made use of at
the Descending of a God, or the Rising of a Ghost, at the Vanish-
ing of a Devil, or at the Death of a Tyrant. I have known a Bell
introduced into several Tragedies with good Effect; and have seen
the whole Assembly in a very great Alarm all the while it has been
ringing. But there is nothing which delights and terrifies our *English* Theatre so much as a Ghost, especially when he appears in
a bloody Shirt.[2] A Spectre has very often saved a Play, though he
has done nothing but stalked across the Stage, or rose through a
Cleft of it, and sunk again without speaking one Word. There
may be a proper Season[3] for these several Terrors; and when they
only come in as Aids and Assistances to the Poet, they are not only
to be excused, but to be applauded. Thus the sounding of the
Clock in *Venice preserved,* makes the Hearts of the whole Audi-

---

1 Horace *Ars Poetica* 153: "Now hear what I and the public expect."

2 Steele's *Spectator* No. 36 published a letter of complaint from Salmoneus
of Covent Garden: "I have for many Years last past been Thunderer to the
Play-house; and have not only made as much Noise out of the Clouds as any
Predecessor of mine in the Theatre that ever bore that Character, but also
have descended and spoke on the Stage as the bold Thunder in the *Rehearsal.*
When they got me down thus low, they thought fit to degrade me further, and
make me a Ghost."

3 Occasion.

ence quake; and conveys a stronger Terror to the Mind, than it is possible for Words to do.[4] The Appearance of the Ghost in *Hamlet*[5] is a Master-piece in its kind, and wrought up with all the Circumstances that can create either Attention or Horror. The Mind of the Reader is wonderfully prepared for his Reception, by the Discourses that precede it: His dumb Behaviour at his first Entrance, strikes the Imagination very strongly; but every time he enters, he is still more terrifying. Who can read the Speech with which young *Hamlet* accosts him, without trembling?

> Hor. *Look, my Lord, it comes!*
> Ham. *Angels and Ministers of Grace defend us!*
> *Be thou a Spirit of Health,*[6] *or Goblin damn'd;*
> *Bring with thee Airs from Heav'n, or Blasts from Hell;*
> *Be thy Events wicked or charitable;*
> *Thou com'st in such a questionable Shape*
> *That I will speak to thee. I'll call thee* Hamlet,
> King, Father, Royal *Dane: Oh! Oh! Answer me,*
> *Let me not burst in Ignorance; but tell*
> *Why thy canoniz'd Bones, hearsed in Death,*
> *Have burst their Cearments?*[7] *Why the Sepulchre,*
> *Wherein we saw thee quietly inurn'd,*
> *Hath op'd his ponderous and marble Jaws*
> *To cast thee up again? What may this mean?*
> *That thou dead Coarse again in compleat Steel*
> *Revisit'st thus the Glimpses of the Moon,*
> *Making Night hideous?*

I do not therefore find Fault with the Artifices abovementioned, when they are introduced with Skill, and accompanied by proportionable Sentiments and Expressions in the Writing.

For the moving of Pity, our principal Machine is the Handkerchief; and indeed in our common Tragedies, we should not know very often that the Persons are in Distress by any thing they say, if they did not from time to time apply their Handkerchiefs to

---

[4] In Otway's drama (1682), Jaffeir and Belvidera hear the passing bell which tolls the present execution of Pierre (act 5, sc. 2). Later, "The Ghosts of Jaffeir and Pierre rise together, both bloody" (act 5, sc. 4).

[5] Shakespeare *Hamlet*, act 1, sc. 4.

[6] A blessed spirit.

[7] I.e., why your body, buried with all sacred rites, has shed its grave-clothes and appears in armor.

their Eyes. Far be it from me to think of banishing this Instrument of Sorrow from the Stage; I know a Tragedy could not subsist without it: All that I would contend for, is, to keep it from being misapplied. In a Word, I would have the Actor's Tongue sympathize with his Eyes.

A disconsolate Mother, with a Child in her Hand, has frequently drawn Compassion from the Audience, and has therefore gained a Place in several Tragedies.[8] A Modern Writer, that observed how this had took in other Plays, being resolved to double the Distress, and melt his Audience twice as much as those before him had done, brought a Princess upon the Stage with a little Boy in one Hand and a Girl in the other. This too had a very good Effect. A third Poet, being resolved to out-write all his Predecessors, a few Years ago introduced three Children, with great Success: And, as I am informed, a young Gentleman, who is fully determined to break the most obdurate Hearts, has a Tragedy by him, where the first Person that appears upon the Stage is an afflicted Widow in her Mourning-Weeds,[9] with half a Dozen fatherless Children attending her, like those that usually hang about the Figure of Charity. Thus several Incidents that are beautiful in a good Writer, become ridiculous by falling into the Hands of a bad one.

But among all our Methods of moving Pity or Terror, there is none so absurd and barbarous, and what more exposes us to the Contempt and Ridicule of our Neighbours, than that dreadful butchering of one another, which is so very frequent upon the *English* Stage. To delight in seeing Men stabbed, poisoned, racked, or impaled, is certainly the Sign of a cruel Temper: And as this is often practised before the *British* Audience, several *French* Criticks, who think these are grateful Spectacles to us, take Occasion from them to represent us as a People that delight in Blood.[10] It is indeed very odd, to see our Stage strowed with Carcasses in the last Scene of a Tragedy; and to observe in the Wardrobe of the Play-house several Daggers, Poniards, Wheels, Bowls

---

8 Perhaps a reference to Dryden's *All for Love* (act 3, sc. 1), in which Octavia enters "leading Antony's two little daughters."

9 Mourning dress.

10 Rapin's *Réflexions sur la Poetique d'Aristotle* (1674) discussed the English spirit "which delights in Cruelty." See *Tatler* No. 165, n. 3.

for Poison, and many other Instruments of Death. Murders and Executions are always transacted behind the Scenes in the *French* Theatre; which in general is very agreeable to the Manners of a polite and civilized People: But as there are no Exceptions to this Rule on the *French* Stage, it leads them into Absurdities almost as ridiculous as that which falls under our present Censure. I remember in the famous Play of *Corneille,*[11] written upon the Subject of the *Horatii* and *Curiatii;* the fierce young Hero who had overcome the *Curiatii* one after another (instead of being congratulated by his Sister for his Victory, being upbraided by her for having slain her Lover) in the height of his Passion and Resentment kills her. If any thing could extenuate so brutal an Action, it would be the doing of it on a sudden, before the Sentiments of Nature, Reason, or Manhood could take Place in him. However, to avoid *publick Blood-shed,* as soon as his Passion is wrought to its Height, he follows his Sister the whole length of the Stage, and forbears killing her till they are both withdrawn behind the Scenes. I must confess, had he murder'd her before the Audience, the Indecency might have been greater; but as it is, it appears very unnatural, and looks like killing in cold Blood. To give my Opinion upon this Case; the Fact ought not to have been represented, but to have been told, if there was any Occasion for it.

It may not be unacceptable to the Reader, to see how *Sophocles* has conducted a Tragedy[12] under the like delicate Circumstances. *Orestes* was in the same Condition with *Hamlet* in *Shakespear,* his Mother having murdered his Father, and taken Possession of his Kingdom in Conspiracy with her Adulterer. That young Prince therefore, being determined to revenge his Father's Death upon those who filled his Throne, conveys himself by a beautiful Stratagem into his Mother's Apartment, with a Resolution to kill her. But because such a Spectacle would have been too shocking to the Audience, this dreadful Resolution is executed behind the Scenes: The Mother is heard calling out to her Son for Mercy; and the Son answering her, that she shewed no Mercy to his Father.[13]

---

11 The play is *Horace* (1640) by Pierre Corneille. It concerns the war between the Horatii, three brothers in a Roman clan, and the Curiatii, three brothers from Alba Longa. The sister, Camille, is killed in act 4, sc. 5.

12 *Electra.*

13 Actually, this answer was made by Electra.

After which she shrieks out that she is wounded, and by what follows we find that she is slain. I do not remember that in any of
our Plays there are Speeches made behind the Scenes, though
there are other Instances of this Nature to be met with in those of
the Ancients: And I believe my Reader will agree with me, that
there is something infinitely more affecting in this dreadful Dialogue between the Mother and her Son behind the Scenes, than
could have been in any thing transacted before the Audience.
Orestes immediately after meets the Usurper at the Entrance of
his Palace; and by a very happy Thought of the Poet avoids killing him before the Audience, by telling him that he should live
some Time in his present Bitterness of Soul before he would dispatch him, and by ordering him to retire into that part of the
Palace where he had slain his Father, whose Murther he would
revenge in the very same Place where it was committed. By this
Means the Poet observes that Decency, which *Horace* afterwards
established by a Rule, of forbearing to commit Parricides or unnatural Murthers before the Audience.

> *Nec coram populo natos* Medea *trucidet.*[14]

> *Let not* Medea *draw her murth'ring Knife,*
> *And spill her Childrens Blood upon the Stage.*

The *French* have therefore refined too much upon *Horace*'s Rule,
who never designed to banish all Kinds of Death from the Stage;
but only such as had too much Horror in them, and which would
have a better Effect upon the Audience when transacted behind
the Scenes. I would therefore recommend to my Countrymen the
Practice of the ancient Poets, who were very sparing of their publick Executions, and rather chose to perform them behind the
Scenes, if it could be done with as great an Effect upon the Audience. At the same Time I must observe, that though the devoted
Persons of the Tragedy were seldom slain before the Audience,
which has generally something ridiculous in it, their Bodies were
often produced after their Death, which has always in it something melancholy or terrifying; so that the killing on the Stage

---

[14] Horace *Ars Poetica* 185. The translation of this and of the passage following is by the Earl of Roscommon. See *Tatler* No. 163, n. 7.

does not seem to have been avoided only as an Indecency, but also as an Improbability.

> *Nec pueros coram populo* Medea *trucidet;*
> *Aut humana palam coquat extra nefarius* Atreus;
> *Aut in Avem* Progne *vertatur,* Cadmus *in anguem,*
> *Quodcunq; ostendis mihi sic, incredulus odi.* Hor.

> Medea *must not draw her murth'ring Knife,*
> *Nor* Atreus *there his horrid Feast prepare.*[15]
> Cadmus *and* Progne's *Metamorphosis,*
> *(She to a Swallow turn'd, he to a Snake)*
> *And whatsoever contradicts my Sense,*
> *I hate to see, and never can believe.*

Ld. Roscommon.

I have now gone through the several dramatick Inventions which are made use of by the ignorant Poets to supply the Place of Tragedy, and by the skilful to improve it; some of which I could wish entirely rejected, and the rest to be used with Caution. It would be an endless Task to consider Comedy in the same Light, and to mention the innumerable Shifts that small Wits put in practice to raise a Laugh. *Bullock* in a short Coat, and *Norris* in a long one, seldom fail of this Effect.[16] In ordinary Comedies, a broad and a narrow brim'd Hat are different Characters. Sometimes the Wit of the Scene lies in a Shoulder-Belt, and sometimes in a Pair of Whiskers. A Lover running about the Stage, with his Head peeping out of a Barrel, was thought a very good Jest in King *Charles* the Second's Time; and invented by one of the first Wits of that Age.[17] But because Ridicule is not so delicate as Compassion, and because the Objects that make us laugh are infinitely more numerous than those that make us weep, there is a much greater Latitude for comick than tragick Artifices, and by consequence a much greater Indulgence to be allowed them.   C

---

[15] Atreus murdered the children of his brother and served them to him at a feast.

[16] William Bullock (1657?–1740?) and Henry Norris (1665–1730?) were popular comic actors.

[17] The reference is to the plight of the Frenchman Dufoy in acts 4 and 5 of Etherege's *Comical Revenge, or Love in a Tub* (1664).

The Spectator, No. 46

Monday, April 23.

[A d d i s o n]

Non bene junctarum discordia semina rerum. Ovid.[1]

When I want Materials for this Paper, it is my Custom to go Abroad in quest of Game; and when I meet any proper Subject, I take the first Opportunity of setting down an Hint of it upon Paper. At the same Time I look into the Letters of my Correspondents, and if I find any thing suggested in them that may afford Matter of Speculation, I likewise enter a Minute of it in my Collection of Materials. By this Means I frequently carry about me a whole Sheet-full of Hints, that would look like a Rhapsody of Nonsense to any Body but my self: There is nothing in them but Obscurity and Confusion, Raving and Inconsistency. In short, they are my Speculations in the first Principles, that (like the World in its Chaos[2]) are void of all Light, Distinction and Order.

About a Week since there happened to me a very odd Accident, by Reason of one of these my Papers of Minutes which I had accidentally dropped at *Lloyd*'s Coffee-house,[3] where the Auctions are usually kept. Before I missed it, there were a Cluster of People who had found it, and were diverting themselves with it at one End of the Coffee-house: It had raised so much Laughter among them, before I had observed what they were about, that I had not the Courage to own it. The Boy of the Coffee-house, when they

1 Ovid *Metamorphoses* 1. 9: "The jarring seeds of ill-consorted things."

2 In Greek mythology, the original void.

3 A coffee-house in Lombard Street, known for wine sales and ship-broking business. The house and its auction-pulpit were described in *Tatler* No. 268.

had done with it, carried it about in his Hand, asking every Body if they had dropped a written Paper; but no Body challenging it, he was ordered by those merry Gentlemen who had before perused it, to get up into the Auction-Pulpit, and read it to the whole Room, that if any one would own it they might. The Boy accordingly mounted the Pulpit, and with a very audible Voice read as follows.

Minutes

Sir Roger de Coverly's Country-Seat———Yes, for I hate long Speeches———Query, if a good Christian may be a Conjurer——— *Childermas-day,* Saltseller, House-Dog, Screech-Owl, Cricket,——— Mr. *Thomas Inkle* of *London,* in the good Ship called the *Achilles. Yarico*———*Egrescitque medendo*———Ghosts———The Lady's Library[4]———Lion by Trade a Taylor———Dromedary called *Bucephalus*———Equipage the Lady's *summum bonum*———*Charles Lillie* to be taken Notice of———Short Face a Relief to Envy——— Redundancies in the three Professions———King *Latinus* a Recruit ———Jew devouring an Ham of Bacon———*Westminster-Abby* ———*Grand Cairo*———Procrastination———*April* Fools——— Blue Boars, Red Lyons, Hogs in Armour———Enter a King and two Fidlers *solus*———Admission into the Ugly Club———Beauty, how improveable———Families of true and false Humour———The Parrot's School-Mistress———Face half *Pict* half *British*———No Man to be an Hero of a Tragedy under six Foot———Club of Sighers ———Letters from Flower-Pots, Elbow-Chairs, Tapestry-Figures, Lion, Thunder———The Bell rings to the Puppet-Show———Old Woman with a Beard Married to a Smock-faced[5] Boy———My next Coat to be turn'd up with Blue———Fable of Tongs and Gridiron ———Flower Dyers———The Soldier's Prayer———Thank ye for nothing, says the Gally-Pot———*Pactolus* in Stockings, with golden Clocks to them[6]———Bamboos, Cudgels, Drum-sticks———Slip of

---

4 See *Spectator* No. 37: the Spectator had surveyed the titles in Leonora's library and "was taking a Catalogue in my Pocket-Book of these, and several other Authors" when the lady entered.

5 Pale, smooth-faced.

6 Pactolus, the Lydian river in which Midas bathed, was famed for its golden sands. Clocks are ornamental figures on the sides of stockings. "*Pactolus* in Stockings, with golden Clocks to them" might have produced a witty essay, but it never did.

my Land-lady's eldest Daughter———The black Mare with a Star in
her Forehead———The Barber's Pole———Will. Honeycomb's
Coat-Pocket———*Caesar's* Behaviour and my own in Parallel Circumstances———Poem in Patch-work———*Nulli gravis est percussus
Achilles*[7]———The Female Conventicler———The Ogle-Master.

The reading of this Paper made the whole Coffee-house very
merry; some of them concluded it was written by a Madman, and
others by some Body that had been taking Notes out of the Spectator. One who had the Appearance of a very substantial Citizen,
told us, with several politick Winks and Nods, that he wished
there was no more in the Paper than what was expressed in it:
That for his Part, he looked upon the Dromedary, the Gridiron,
and the Barber's Pole, to signifie something more than what is
usually meant by those Words; and that he thought the Coffee-
man could not do better, than to carry the Paper to one of the
Secretaries of State.[8] He further added, that he did not like the
Name of the outlandish Man with the Golden Clock in his Stockings. A young *Oxford* Scholar, who chanced to be with his Uncle
at the Coffee-house, discovered to us who this *Pactolus* was; and
by that Means turned the whole Scheme of this worthy Citizen
into Ridicule. While they were making their several Conjectures
upon this innocent Paper, I reached out my Arm to the Boy, as he
was coming out of the Pulpit, to give it me; which he did accordingly. This drew the Eyes of the whole Company upon me; but
after having cast a cursory Glance over it, and shook my Head
twice or thrice at the reading of it, I twisted it into a kind of
Match, and litt my Pipe with it. My profound Silence, together
with the Steadiness of my Countenance, and the Gravity of my
Behaviour during this whole Transaction, raised a very loud
Laugh on all Sides of me; but as I had escaped all Suspicion of
being the Author, I was very well satisfied; and applying my self
to my Pipe and the *Post-Man*,[9] took no further Notice of any thing
that passed about me.

---

[7] Juvenal *Satires* 1. 163: "Nobody resents the slaughter of Achilles."

[8] See *Spectator* No. 568 and *Guardian* No. 160, which satirize the citizen
who reads political meaning into everything.

[9] See *Tatler* No. 18, n. 21.

My Reader will find, that I have already made use of above half the Contents of the foregoing Paper; and will easily suppose, that those Subjects which are yet untouched, were such Provisions as I had made for his future Entertainment. But as I have been unluckily prevented by this Accident, I shall only give him the Letters which relate to the two last Hints. The first of them I should not have published, were I not informed that there is many an Husband who suffers very much in his private Affairs by the indiscreet Zeal of such a Partner as is hereafter mentioned; to whom I may apply the barbarous Inscription quoted by the Bishop of *Salisbury*[10] in his Travels; *Dum nimia pia est, facta est impia.*

"Sir,

I am one of those unhappy Men that are plagued with a Gospel-Gossip, so common among Dissenters (especially Friends[11]). Lectures in the Morning, Church-Meetings at Noon, and Preparation-Sermons at Night, take up so much of her Time, 'tis very rare she knows what we have for Dinner, unless when the Preacher is to be at it. With him come a Tribe, all Brothers and Sisters it seems; while others, really such,[12] are deemed no Relations. If at any time I have her Company alone, she is a meer Sermon Pop-gun, repeating and discharging Texts, Proofs, and Applications so perpetually, that however weary I may go to Bed, the Noise in my Head will not let me sleep till towards Morning. The Misery of my Case, and great Numbers of such Sufferers, plead your Pity and speedy Relief; otherwise must expect, in a little Time, to be lectured, preached, and prayed into Want, unless the Happiness of being sooner talked to Death prevent it.

I am, &c.
R. G."

The second Letter, relating to the Ogling Master, runs thus.

"*Mr.* Spectator,

I am an *Irish* Gentleman, that have travelled many Years for my Improvement; during which Time I have accomplished my self in the

---

[10] Gilbert Burnet (1643–1715), Bishop of Salisbury, in a work describing his continental travels, recorded the "barbarous Inscription" at Lyons. Chalmers' translation: "Through too much piety she becomes impious."

[11] Quakers. See *Tatler* No. 257, n. 20.

[12] I.e., her real brothers and sisters.

whole Art of Ogling,[13] as it is at present practised in all the polite Nations of *Europe*. Being thus qualified, I intend, by the Advice of my Friends, to set up for an Ogling-Master. I teach the Church Ogle in the Morning, and the Play-house Ogle by Candle-light. I have also brought over with me a new flying Ogle fit for the Ring;[14] which I teach in the Dusk of the Evening, or in any Hour of the Day by darkning one of my Windows. I have a Manuscript by me called *The compleat Ogler*,[15] which I shall be ready to shew you upon any Occasion: In the mean time, I beg you will publish the Substance of this Letter in an Advertisement, and you will very much oblige,

C   *Your*, &c."

[13] *Ogling* can be defined as the language of the eyes. See *Spectator* No. 20.
[14] A fashionable driving area in Hyde Park.
[15] The allusion to Isaak Walton's treatise on fishing, *The Compleat Angler* (1653) adds a degree of meaning here.

The Spectator, No. 50

Friday, April 27.

[Addison]

Nunquam aliud Natura, aliud Sapientia dicit. Juv.[1]

When the four *Indian* Kings were in this Country about a Twelve-month ago,[2] I often mixed with the Rabble,[3] and followed them a whole Day together, being[4] wonderfully struck with the Sight of every thing that is new or uncommon. I have, since their Departure, employed a Friend to make many Enquiries of their Landlord the Upholsterer, relating to their Manners and Conversation, as also concerning the Remarks which they made in this Country: For, next to the forming a right Notion of such Strangers, I should be desirous of learning what Ideas they have conceived of us.

The Upholsterer finding my Friend very inquisitive about these his Lodgers, brought him some time since a little Bundle of Papers, which he assured him were written by King *Sa Ga Yean Qua Rash Tow,* and, as he supposes, left behind by some mistake. These Papers are now translated, and contain abundance of very odd Observations, which I find this little Fraternity of Kings made

---

[1] Juvenal *Satires* 14. 321: "Nature never says one thing and wisdom another."

[2] In 1710, four Iroquois chiefs had visited London, accompanied by Col. Peter Schuyler and other colonial leaders, to ask Queen Anne for military assistance against the French in Canada. They were lodged at the Two Crowns and Cushions, the residence of an upholsterer, in Covent Garden. Their visit was described in *Tatler* No. 171.

[3] The London lower-class people.

[4] The word *being* can modify "Kings" or "I" or "Rabble." Probably it refers to "Kings."

during their Stay in the Isle of *Great Britain*. I shall present my Reader with a short Specimen of them in this Paper, and may, perhaps, communicate more to him hereafter.[5] In the Article of *London*[6] are the following Words, which without doubt are meant of the Church of St. *Paul*.[7]

"On the most rising Part of the Town there stands a huge House, big enough to contain the whole Nation of which I am King. Our good Brother *E Tow O Koam*, King of the *Rivers*, is of Opinion it was made by the Hands of that great God to whom it is consecrated.[8] The Kings of *Granajah* and of the *Six Nations* believe that it was created with the Earth, and produced on the same Day with the Sun and Moon. But for my own Part, by the best Information that I could get of this Matter, I am apt to think that this prodigious Pile was fashioned into the Shape it now bears by several Tools and Instruments, of which they have a wonderful Variety in this Country. It was probably at first an huge mis-shapen Rock that grew upon the Top of the Hill, which the Natives of the Country (after having cut it into a kind of regular Figure) bored and hollowed with incredible Pains and Industry, till they had wrought in it all those beautiful Vaults and Caverns into which it is divided at this Day. As soon as this Rock was thus curiously[9] scooped to their Liking, a prodigious Number of Hands must have been employed in chipping the Outside of it, which is now as smooth as the Surface of a Pebble; and is in several Places hewn out into Pillars that stand like the Trunks of so many Trees bound about the Top with Garlands of Leaves. It is probable that when this great Work was begun, which must have been many Hundred Years ago, there was some Religion among this People; for they give it the Name of a Temple, and have a Tradition that it was designed for Men to pay their Devotions in. And indeed, there are several Reasons which make us think, that the Natives of this Country had formerly among them some sort of Worship; for they set apart every seventh Day as sacred: But upon my going into one of these holy Houses on that Day, I could not observe any Circumstance of Devotion in their Behaviour: There was indeed a Man in Black who was mounted

5 This tentative promise was never fulfilled.

6 I.e., in his notes concerning London.

7 After thirty-five years in construction, St. Paul's cathedral had just been completed. It was designed by Sir Christopher Wren to replace the building burned in the fire of 1666.

8 I.e., St. Paul.

9 Carefully, painstakingly.

above the rest, and seemed to utter something with a great deal of Vehemence; but as for those underneath him, instead of paying their Worship to the Deity of the Place, they were most of them bowing and curtisying to one another, and a considerable Number of them fast asleep.[10]

"The Queen of the Country[11] appointed two Men to attend us, that had enough of our Language to make themselves understood in some few Particulars. But we soon perceived these two were great Enemies to one another, and did not always agree in the same Story. We could make a Shift[12] to gather out of one of them, that this Island was very much infested with a monstrous Kind of Animals, in the Shape of Men, called *Whigs;* and he often told us, that he hoped we should meet with none of them in our Way, for that if we did, they would be apt to knock us down for being Kings.

"Our other Interpreter used to talk very much of a kind of Animal called a *Tory,* that was as great a Monster as the *Whig,* and would treat us as ill for being Foreigners.[13] These two Creatures, it seems, are born with a secret Antipathy to one another, and engage when they meet as naturally as the Elephant and the Rhinoceros. But as we saw none of either of these Species, we are apt to think that our Guides deceived us with Misrepresentations and Fictions, and amused us with an Account of such Monsters as are not really in their Country.

"These Particulars we made a Shift to pick out from the Discourse of our Interpreters; which we put together as well as we could, being able to understand but here and there a Word of what they said, and afterwards making up the Meaning of it among our selves. The Men of the Country are very cunning and ingenious in handicraft Works; but withal so very idle, that we often saw young lusty raw-boned Fellows carried up and down the Streets in little covered Rooms[14] by a Couple of Porters, who are hired for that Service. Their Dress is likewise very barbarous, for they almost strangle themselves about the Neck, and bind their Bodies with many Ligatures, that we are apt to think are the Occasion of several Distempers among them which our

[10] See *Spectator* No. 407 for Addison's views concerning English preaching. *Spectator* No. 20 by Steele comments about worldly conduct in church.

[11] The Kings had an audience with Queen Anne on April 19, 1710.

[12] Manage.

[13] The Whigs could be accused of hating kings because of their rejection of the Stuart line; the Tories, of hating foreigners, because of their unwillingness to accept George of Hanover.

[14] Sedan chairs.

Country is entirely free from. Instead of those beautiful Feathers with which we adorn our Heads, they often buy up a monstrous Bush of Hair,[15] which covers their Heads, and falls down in a large Fleece below the Middle of their Backs; with which they walk up and down the Streets, and are as proud of it as if it was of their own Growth.

"We were invited to one of their publick Diversions, where we hoped to have seen the great Men of their Country running down a Stag or pitching a Bar,[16] that we might have discovered who were the Persons of the greatest Abilities among them; but instead of that, they conveyed us into an huge Room lighted up with abundance of Candles, where this lazy People sate still above three Hours to see several Feats of Ingenuity performed by others, who it seems were paid for it.

"As for the Women of the Country, not being able to talk with them, we could only make our Remarks upon them at a Distance. They let the Hair of their Heads grow to a great Length; but as the Men make a great Show with Heads of Hair that are none of their own, the Women, who they say have very fine Heads of Hair, tie it up in a Knot, and cover it from being seen. The Women look like Angels, and would be more beautiful than the Sun, were it not for little black Spots[17] that are apt to break out in their Faces, and sometimes rise in very odd Figures. I have observed that those little Blemishes wear off very soon; but when they disappear in one Part of the Face, they are very apt to break out in another, insomuch that I have seen a Spot upon the Forehead in the Afternoon, which was upon the Chin in the Morning."

The Author then proceeds to shew the Absurdity of Breeches and Petticoats,[18] with many other curious Observations, which I shall reserve for another Occasion. I cannot however conclude this Paper without taking Notice, That amidst these wild Remarks there now and then appears something very reasonable. I cannot likewise forbear observing, That we are all guilty in some Measure of the same narrow way of Thinking, which we meet with in this Abstract of the *Indian* Journal; when we fancy the Customs, Dresses, and Manners of other Countries are ridiculous and extravagant, if they do not resemble those of our own.   C

15 A periwig.

16 A common exercise of strength among rural people involved the throwing of a heavy iron bar.

17 See *Spectator* No. 37, n. 7.

18 *Tatler* No. 116 by Addison ridiculed the fashion of wearing huge, sweeping petticoats.

The Spectator, No. 58

Monday, May 7.

[A d d i s o n]

Ut pictura poesis crit————Hor.[1]

Nothing is so much admired, and so little understood, as Wit. No Author that I know of has written professedly upon it; and as for those who make any Mention of it, they only treat on the Subject as it has accidentally fallen in their Way, and that too in little short Reflections, or in general declamatory Flourishes, without entring into the Bottom of the Matter. I hope therefore I shall perform an acceptable Work to my Countrymen, if I treat at large upon this Subject; which I shall endeavour to do in a Manner suitable to it, that I may not incur the Censure which a famous Critick bestows upon one who had written a Treatise upon *the Sublime* in a low groveling Stile.[2] I intend to lay aside a whole Week for this Undertaking, that the Scheme of my Thoughts may not be broken and interrupted; and I dare promise my self, if my Readers will give me a Week's Attention, that this great City will be very much changed for the better by next *Saturday* Night.[3] I shall endeavour to make what I say intelligible to ordinary Capacities; but if my Readers meet with any Paper that in some Parts of it may be a little out of their Reach, I would not have them discouraged, for they may assure themselves the next shall be much clearer.

1 Horace *Ars Poetica* 361: "A poem will be like a picture . . ."
2 Longinus begins his treatise *On the Sublime* by criticizing the Sicilian rhetorician, Caecilius, for writing an argument in an inappropriately humble style.
3 The six essays on wit (Nos. 58–63) ran Monday through Saturday.

As the great and only End of these my Speculations is to banish Vice and Ignorance out of the Territories of *Great Britain,* I shall endeavour as much as possible to establish among us a Taste of polite Writing. It is with this View that I have endeavoured to set my Readers right in several Points relating to Opera's and Tragedies;[4] and shall from Time to Time impart my Notions of Comedy,[5] as I think they may tend to its Refinement and Perfection. I find by my Bookseller that these Papers of Criticism, with that upon Humour, have met with a more kind Reception than indeed I could have hoped for from such Subjects;[6] for which Reason I shall enter upon my present Undertaking with greater Chearfulness.

In this, and one or two following Papers, I shall trace out the History of false Wit, and distinguish the several Kinds of it as they have prevailed in different Ages of the World. This I think the more necessary at present, because I observed there were Attempts on foot last Winter to revive some of those antiquated Modes of Wit that have been long exploded out of the Commonwealth of Letters. There were several Satyrs and Panegyricks handed about in Acrostick,[7] by which Means some of the most arrant undisputed Blockheads about the Town began to entertain ambitious Thoughts, and to set up for polite Authors. I shall therefore describe at length those many Arts of false Wit, in which a Writer does not shew himself a Man of a beautiful Genius, but of great Industry.[8]

The first Species of false Wit which I have met with is very venerable for its Antiquity, and has produced several Pieces which have lived very near as long as the *Iliad* it self: I mean those short

4 The opera was discussed in *Spectators* No. 5, 14, 18, 22, 29, and 31; tragedy in Nos. 39, 40, 42, and 44.

5 These never appeared. In *Spectator* No. 44, Addison, concluding his papers on tragedy, wrote, "It would be an endless Task to consider Comedy in the same Light...."

6 I.e., sales had not fallen off significantly.

7 A composition in which the first letters of every line form a message when taken in order; either middle or terminal letters could, of course, be used as well.

8 Regularly, false wit will be manifest in a work in which meaning is subordinate to qualities of sound or shape or lettering.

Poems printed among the minor *Greek* Poets, which resemble the Figure of an Egg, a Pair of Wings, an Ax, a Shepherd's Pipe, and an Altar.[9]

As for the first, it is a little oval Poem, and may not improperly be called a Scholar's Egg. I would endeavour to hatch it, or, in more intelligible Language, to translate it into *English,* did not I find the Interpretation of it very difficult; for the Author seems to have been more intent upon the Figure of his Poem, than upon the Sense of it.

The Pair of Wings consist of twelve Verses, or rather Feathers, every Verse decreasing gradually in its Measure according to its Situation in the Wing. The Subject of it (as in the rest of the Poems which follow) bears some remote Affinity with the Figure, for it describes a God of Love,[10] who is always painted with Wings.

The Ax methinks would have been a good Figure for a Lampoon, had the Edge of it consisted of the most satyrical Parts of the Work; but as it is in the Original, I take it to have been nothing else but the Posie[11] of an Ax which was consecrated to *Minerva,* and was thought to have been the same that *Epeus*[12] made use of in the building of the *Trojan* Horse; which is a Hint I shall leave to the Consideration of the Criticks. I am apt to think that the Posie was written originally upon the Ax, like those which our modern Cutlers inscribe upon their Knives; and that therefore the Posie still remains in its ancient Shape, though the Ax it self is lost.

The Shepherd's Pipe may be said to be full of Musick, for it is composed of nine different Kinds of Verses, which by their several Lengths resemble the nine Stops[13] of the old musical Instrument, that is likewise the Subject of the Poem.

---

[9] Addison's source was Ralph Winterton's *Poetae Minores Graeci* (1635). The 1677 edition gave examples, in order, of poems shaped like an egg, wings, an axe, a shepherd's pipe, and an altar.

[10] Cupid.

[11] The legend or motto.

[12] Minerva, the Roman goddess of wisdom, is commonly represented in helmet with a coat of mail. Epeus, the principal craftsman among the Greeks, was the builder of the Trojan horse (Virgil *Aeneid* 2. 264).

[13] Holes in the pipe used to regulate musical pitch.

The Altar is inscribed with the Epitaph of *Troilus*[14] the Son of *Hecuba;* which, by the way, makes me believe, that these false Pieces of Wit are much more ancient than the Authors to whom they are generally ascribed; at least I will never be perswaded, that so fine a Writer as *Theocritus*[15] could have been the Author of any such simple Works.

It was impossible for a Man to succeed in these Performances who was not a kind of Painter, or at least a Designer: He was first of all to draw the Out-line of the Subject which he intended to write upon, and afterwards conform the Description to the Figure of his Subject. The Poetry was to contract or dilate it self according to the Mould in which it was cast. In a Word, the Verses were to be cramped or extended to the Dimensions of the Frame that was prepared for them; and to undergo the Fate of those Persons whom the Tyrant *Procrustes*[16] used to lodge in his Iron Bed; if they were too short he stretched them on a Rack, and if they were too long chopped off a Part of their Legs, till they fitted the Couch which he had prepared for them.

Mr. *Dryden* hints at this obsolete kind of Wit in one of the following Verses, in his *Mac Fleckno;*[17] which an *English* Reader cannot understand, who does not know that there are those little Poems abovementioned in the Shape of Wings and Altars.

> ————*Chuse for thy Command*
> *Some peaceful Province in Acrostick Land;*
> *There may'st thou* Wings *display, and* Altars *raise,*
> *And torture one poor Word a thousand Ways.*

This Fashion of false Wit was revived by several Poets of the last Age, and in particular may be met with among Mr. *Herbert*'s Poems;[18] and, if I am not mistaken, in the Translation of *Du*

14 The Trojan prince, son of King Priam and brother of Hector, was killed by Achilles.

15 Witherton's book describes the altar as by Simias of Rhodes, but notes that "according to others," it is by Theocritus.

16 In Greek legend, Procrustes was a robber of Attica, who subjected his victims to this bed of torture.

17 In quoting *Mac Flecknoe* (1682), lines 205–208, Addison has transposed the words "may'st" and "thou" from the original.

18 George Herbert's *The Temple* (1633) contained "The Altar" and "Easter Wings."

Bartas.[19] I do not remember any other Kind of Work among the Moderns which more resembles the Performances I have mentioned, than that famous Picture of King *Charles* I. which has the whole Book of *Psalms* written in the Lines of the Face and the Hair of the Head. When I was last at *Oxford* I perused one of the Whiskers;[20] and was reading the other, but could not go so far in it as I would have done, by reason of the Impatience of my Friends and Fellow-Travellers, who all of them pressed to see such a Piece of Curiosity. I have since heard, that there is now an eminent Writing-Master in Town, who has transcribed all the *Old Testament* in a full-bottomed Perriwig; and if the Fashion should introduce the thick Kind of Wigs which were in Vogue some few Years ago, he promises to add two or three supernumerary[21] Locks that shall contain all the *Apocrypha.*[22] He designed this Wig originally for King *William,*[23] having disposed of the two Books of *Kings* in the two Forks of the Foretop; but that glorious Monarch dying before the Wig was finished, there is a Space left in it for the Face of any one that has a mind to purchase it.

But to return to our ancient Poems in Picture, I would humbly propose, for the Benefit of our modern Smatterers in Poetry, that they would imitate their Brethren among the Ancients in those ingenious Devices. I have communicated this Thought to a young Poetical Lover of my Acquaintance, who intends to present his Mistress with a Copy of Verses made in the Shape of her Fan; and, if he tells me true, has already finished the three first Sticks of it. He has likewise promised me to get the Measure of his Mistress's Marriage-Finger, with a Design to make a Posie in the Fashion of a Ring which shall exactly fit it. It is so very easie to enlarge upon a good Hint, that I do not question but my ingenious Readers will apply what I have said to many other Particulars; and that we shall see the Town filled in a very little time with Poetical Tip-

19 *Divine Weeks and Works* by Guillaume de Salluste, Seigneur du Bartas (1544–1590) was translated by Joshua Sylvester (1563–1618). The translation was printed in 1605 and reprinted many times during the seventeenth century.

20 Such a picture did exist at St. John's College, Oxford.

21 Extra.

22 Old Testament books of doubtful authority.

23 King William III (1689–1694).

pets,[24] Handkerchiefs, Snuff-Boxes, and the like Female-Ornaments. I shall therefore conclude with a Word of Advice to those admirable *English* Authors who call themselves Pindarick Writers,[25] that they would apply themselves to this Kind of Wit without Loss of Time, as being provided better than any other Poets with Verses of all Sizes and Dimensions.   C

[24] Pieces of cloth hanging from a sleeve, cap, or hood.

[25] For Addison and Steele, the word "Pindarick"—reflecting the characteristics of the Greek poet Pindar (c. 522–442 B.C.)—meant disordered and irregular. They criticized such qualities in *Tatler* No. 106 and in *Spectators* No. 147 and 160. The latter essay ridicules "Men following Irregularities by Rule, and by the little Tricks of Art straining after the most unbounded Flights of Nature. . . ."

The Spectator, No. 61

Thursday, May 10.

[Addison]

Non equidem hoc studeo, bullatis ut mihi nugis
Pagina turgescat, dare pondus idonea fumo. Pers.[1]

There is no kind of false Wit which has been so recommended by the Practice of all Ages, as that which consists in a Jingle of Words, and is comprehended under the general Name of *Punning.* It is indeed impossible to kill a Weed, which the Soil has a natural Disposition to produce. The Seeds of Punning are in the Minds of all Men, and tho' they may be subdued by Reason, Reflection, and good Sense, they will be very apt to shoot up in the greatest Genius, that is not broken and cultivated by the Rules of Art.[2] Imitation is natural to us, and when it does not raise the Mind to Poetry, Painting, Musick, or other more noble Arts, it often breaks out in Punns and Quibbles.[3]

Aristotle, in the Eleventh Chapter of his Book of Rhetorick,[4] describes two or three kinds of Punns, which he calls Paragrams, among the Beauties of good Writing, and produces Instances of them out of some of the greatest Authors in the *Greek* Tongue.

---

[1] Persius *Satires* 5. 19–20: "Indeed, I do not take pains that my page swell with childish trifles, fit only to give weight to smoke."

[2] See *Spectator* No. 160, by Addison, which discusses more specifically the distinction between genius and art.

[3] Even the Spectator, finding a page from a religious book under a Christmas pie, could not resist affirming the author's "Piety" (Essay No. 85, by Addison).

[4] Aristotle *Rhetoric* 3. 2. 7. A paragram is a play on words, deriving from the alteration of one or more letters in a word.

Cicero has sprinkled several of his Works with Punns, and in his Book where he lays down the Rules of Oratory,[5] quotes abundance of Sayings as Pieces of Wit, which also upon Examination prove arrant Punns. But the Age in which *the Punn* chiefly flourished, was the Reign of King *James* the First.[6] That learned Monarch was himself a tolerable Punnster, and made very few Bishops or Privy-Counsellors that had not some time or other signalized themselves by a Clinch, or a *Conundrum*.[7] It was therefore in this Age that the Punn appeared with Pomp and Dignity. It had before been admitted into merry Speeches and ludicrous Compositions, but was now delivered with great Gravity from the Pulpit, or pronounced in the most solemn manner at the Council-Table. The greatest Authors, in their most serious Works, made frequent use of Punns. The Sermons of Bishop *Andrews*, and the Tragedies of *Shakespear*,[8] are full of them. The Sinner was punned into Repentance by the former, as in the latter nothing is more usual than to see a Hero weeping and quibbling for a dozen Lines together.

I must add to these great Authorities, which seem to have given a kind of Sanction to this Piece of false Wit, that all the Writers of Rhetorick have treated of Punning with very great Respect, and divided the several kinds of it into hard Names, that are reckoned among the Figures of Speech, and recommended as Ornaments in Discourse. I remember a Country School-master of my Acquaintance told me once, that he had been in Company with a Gentleman whom he looked upon to be the greatest *Paragrammatist* among the Moderns. Upon Enquiry, I found my learned Friend had dined that Day with Mr. *Swan*, the famous Punnster;[9]

5 Cicero *De Oratore* 2. 61–63.

6 King James I, (1603–1625). In *The Dunciad* 4. 174–175, Pope quotes the plea of Dulness: "Oh (cry'd the Goddess) for some pedant Reign, / Some gentle James, to bless the land again!"

7 As used here, the words *Clinch, Conundrum,* and *Quibble* mean simply pun.

8 The point is that sermons and tragedies could be expected to avoid puns. Nevertheless Lancelot Andrews (1555–1626), Bishop of Winchester, and Shakespeare used them.

9 Dryden's *Discourse concerning Satire* (1693) mentions "Honest Mr. Swan" as a noted punster.

and desiring him to give me some Account of Mr. *Swan's* Conversation, he told me that he generally talked in the *Paranomasia,* that he sometimes gave into the *Plocè,* but that in his humble Opinion he shined most in the *Antanaclasis.*[10]

I must not here omit, that a famous University of this Land[11] was formerly very much infested with Punns; but whether or no this might not arise from the Fens and Marshes in which it was situated, and which are now drained, I must leave to the Determination of more skilful Naturalists.

After this short History of Punning, one would wonder how it should be so entirely banished out of the Learned World, as it is at present, especially since it had found a Place in the Writings of the most ancient Polite Authors. To account for this, we must consider, that the first Race of Authors, who were the great Heroes in Writing, were destitute of all Rules and Arts of Criticism; and for that Reason, though they excel later Writers in Greatness of Genius, they fall short of them in Accuracy and Correctness. The Moderns cannot reach their Beauties, but can avoid their Imperfections. When the World was furnished with these Authors of the first Eminence, there grew up another Set of Writers, who gained themselves a Reputation by the Remarks which they made on the Works of those who preceded them. It was one of the Employments of these Secondary Authors, to distinguish the several kinds of Wit by Terms of Art, and to consider them as more or less perfect, according as they were founded in Truth. It is no wonder therefore, that even such Authors as *Isocrates,*[12] *Plato,* and *Cicero,* should have such little Blemishes as are not to be met with in Authors of a much inferior Character, who have written since those several Blemishes were discovered. I do not find that there was a proper Separation made between Punns and true Wit by any of the ancient Authors, except *Quintilian* and *Longinus.*[13]

---

[10] *Paranomasia, Plocè,* and *Antanaclasis* denote different kinds of puns. Only someone as commited to false wit as Mr. Swan would distinguish them.

[11] Cambridge.

[12] Isocrates (436–338 B.C.), Athenian orator and rhetorician. Twenty-one of his orations have been preserved.

[13] Quintilian was a Roman rhetorician of the first century; Longinus, a Greek rhetorician of the third century.

But when this Distinction was once settled, it was very natural for all Men of Sense to agree in it. As for the Revival of this false Wit, it happened about the time of the Revival of Letters;[14] but as soon as it was once detected, it immediately vanished and disappeared. At the same time there is no question, but as it has sunk in one Age and rose in another, it will again recover it self in some distant Period of Time, as Pedantry and Ignorance shall prevail upon Wit and Sense. And, to speak the Truth, I do very much apprehend, by some of the last Winter's Productions, which had their Sets of Admirers, that our Posterity will in a few Years degenerate into a Race of Punnsters: At least, a Man may be very excusable for any Apprehensions of this kind, that has seen *Acrosticks* handed about the Town with great Secresie and Applause; to which I must also add a little *Epigram* called the *Witches Prayer,* that fell into Verse when it was read either backward or forward, excepting only that it Cursed one way and Blessed the other. When one sees there are actually such Pains-takers among our *British* Wits, who can tell what it may end in? If we must Lash one another, let it be with the manly Strokes of Wit and Satyr; for I am of the old Philosopher's Opinion, That if I must suffer from one or the other, I would rather it should be from the Paw of a Lion, than the Hoof of an Ass.[15] I do not speak this out of any Spirit of Party. There is a most crying Dulness on both Sides. I have seen Tory *Acrosticks* and Whig *Anagrams,* and do not quarrel with either of them, because they are *Whigs* or *Tories,* but because they are *Anagrams* and *Acrosticks.*

But to return to Punning. Having pursued the History of a Punn, from its Original to its Downfal, I shall here define it to be a Conceit arising from the use of two Words that agree in the Sound, but differ in the Sense. The only way therefore to try a Piece of Wit, is to translate it into a different Language: If it bears the Test you may pronounce it true; but if it vanishes in the Experiment you may conclude it to have been a Punn. In short, one may say of a Punn as the Country-man described his Nightingale,

[14] The Renaissance.

[15] The story appeared in the *Fables of Aesop* (No. 14), as translated by Sir Roger L'Estrange (1616–1704) in 1692.

that it is *vox & praeterè nihil*,[16] a Sound, and nothing but a
Sound. On the contrary, one may represent true Wit by the Description which *Aristinetus* makes of a fine Woman, When she is
dressed she is Beautiful, when she is *undressed* she is Beautiful:
Or, as *Mercerus* has translated it more Emphatically, *Induitur,
formosa est: Exuitur, ipsa forma est.*[17]   C

---

[16] A frequently quoted line from Plutarch, "Sayings of Spartans," *Moralia*
233A.

[17] From Aristenetus, book 1, letter 1. Some critics have noted that Addison
ends his essay on puns by playing on the words *formosa* (beautiful) and *ipsa
forma* (form or beauty itself).

The Spectator, No. 62

Friday, May 11.

[Addison]

Scribendi recte Sapere est & principium & fons. Hor.[1]

Mr. *Lock* has an admirable Reflection upon the Difference of Wit and Judgment, whereby he endeavours to shew the Reason why they are not always the Talents of the same Person. His Words are as follow: *And hence, perhaps, may be given some Reason of that common Observation, That Men who have a great deal of Wit and prompt Memories, have not always the clearest Judgment, or deepest Reason. For Wit lying most in the Assemblage of Ideas, and putting those together with Quickness and Variety, wherein can be found any Resemblance or Congruity, thereby to make up pleasant Pictures and agreeable Visions in the Fancy; Judgment, on the contrary, lies quite on the other Side, In separating carefully one from another, Ideas wherein can be found the least Difference, thereby to avoid being mis-led by Similitude, and by Affinity to take one thing for another. This is a Way of proceeding quite contrary to Metaphor and Allusion; wherein, for the most Part, lies that Entertainment and Pleasantry of Wit which strikes so lively on the Fancy, and is therefore so acceptable to all People.*[2]

This is, I think, the best and most philosophical Account that I have ever met with of Wit, which generally, though not always, consists in such a Resemblance and Congruity of Ideas as this

---

[1] Horace *Ars Poetica* 309: "Knowledge is the origin and source of writing well."

[2] John Locke, *Essay concerning Human Understanding* (1690), 2. 11. 2.

Author mentions. I shall only add to it, by way of Explanation, That every Resemblance of Ideas is not that which we call Wit, unless it be such an one that gives *Delight* and *Surprize* to the Reader: These two Properties seem essential to Wit, more particularly the last of them. In order therefore that the Resemblance in the Ideas be Wit, it is necessary that the Ideas should not lie too near one another in the Nature of things; for where the Likeness is obvious, it gives no Surprize. To compare one Man's Singing to that of another, or to represent the Whiteness of any Object by that of Milk and Snow, or the Variety of its Colours by those of the Rainbow, cannot be called Wit, unless, besides this obvious Resemblance, there be some further Congruity discovered in the two Ideas that is capable of giving the Reader some Surprize. Thus when a Poet tells us, the Bosom of his Mistress is as white as Snow, there is no Wit in the Comparison; but when he adds, with a Sigh, that it is as cold too, it then grows into Wit.[3] Every Reader's Memory may supply him with innumerable Instances of the same Nature. For this Reason, the Similitudes in Heroick Poets, who endeavour rather to fill the Mind with great Conceptions, than to divert it with such as are new and surprizing, have seldom any thing in them that can be called Wit. Mr. *Lock*'s Account of Wit, with this short Explanation, comprehends most of the Species of Wit, as Metaphors, Similitudes, Allegories, Aenigmas, Mottos, Parables, Fables, Dreams, Visions, dramatick Writings, Burlesque, and all the Methods of Allusion: As there are many other Pieces of Wit (how remote soever they may appear at first Sight from the foregoing Description) which upon Examination will be found to agree with it.

As *true Wit* generally consists in this Resemblance and Congruity of Ideas, *false Wit* chiefly consists in the Resemblance and Congruity sometimes of single Letters, as in Anagrams, Chronograms, Lipograms, and Acrosticks:[4] Sometimes of Syllables, as in

[3] The image appears in Captain Ayloffe's poem "Upon the Constellation of Beauties that were lately seen in Greenwitch-Park," published in 1705.

[4] An *anagram* is a word or phrase made by transposing the letters of another word or phrase; a *chronogram* is an inscription, sentence, or phrase in which certain letters express a date or epoch; a *lipogram* is a composition containing but a single vowel or one avoiding a certain letter altogether. For *acrostic*, see *Spectator* No. 58, n. 7.

Ecchos and Doggerel Rhymes: Sometimes of Words, as in Punns and Quibbles; and sometimes of whole Sentences or Poems, cast into the Figures of *Eggs, Axes* or *Altars:*[5] Nay, some carry the Notion of Wit so far, as to ascribe it even to external Mimickry;[6] and to look upon a Man as an ingenious Person, that can resemble the Tone, Posture, or Face of another.

As *true Wit* consists in the Resemblance of Ideas, and *false Wit* in the Resemblance of Words, according to the foregoing Instances; there is another kind of Wit which consists partly in the Resemblance of Ideas, and partly in the Resemblance of Words; which for Distinction Sake I shall call *mixt Wit*. This Kind of Wit is that which abounds in *Cowley,* more than in any Author that ever wrote. Mr. *Waller* has likewise a great deal of it. Mr. *Dryden* is very sparing in it. *Milton* had a Genius much above it. *Spencer* is in the same Class with *Milton*.[7] The *Italians,* even in their Epic Poetry, are full of it. Monsieur *Boileau,*[8] who formed himself upon the Ancient Poets, has every where rejected it with Scorn. If we look after mixt Wit among the *Greek* Writers, we shall find it no where but in the Epigrammatists. There are indeed some Strokes of it in the little Poem ascribed to *Musaeus,*[9] which by that, as well as many other Marks, betrays it self to be a Modern Composition. If we look into the *Latin* Writers, we find none of this mixt Wit in *Virgil, Lucretius,* or *Catullus;* very little in *Horace,* but a great deal of it in *Ovid,* and scarce any thing else in *Martial.*

Out of the innumerable Branches of *mixt Wit,* I shall chuse one Instance which may be met with in all the Writers of this Class. The Passion of Love in its Nature has been thought to resemble Fire; for which Reason the Words Fire and Flame are made use of to signifie Love. The witty Poets therefore have taken

5 See *Spectator* No. 58, on shaped poetry.

6 Pantomime, impersonation.

7 Addison discussed Waller, Dryden, Milton, Spenser, and Cowley in his poem "An Account of the Greatest English Poets" (1694). Of Cowley, he said: "His turns too closely on the reader press: / He more had pleas'd us, had he pleas'd us less."

8 See *Tatler* No. 158, n. 16.

9 Musaeus' poem "Hero and Leander" was published in Ralph Winterton's *Poetae Minores Graeci* (1635).

an Advantage from the doubtful Meaning of the Word Fire, to make an infinite Number of Witticisms. *Cowley*[10] observing the cold Regard of his Mistress's Eyes, and at the same Time their Power of producing Love in him, considers them as Burning-Glasses made of Ice; and finding himself able to live in the greatest Extremities of Love, concludes the Torrid Zone to be habitable. When his Mistress has read his Letter written in Juice of Lemmon by holding it to the Fire, he desires her to read it over a second time by Love's Flames. When she weeps, he wishes it were inward Heat that distilled those Drops from the Limbeck.[11] When she is absent he is beyond eighty, that is, thirty Degrees nearer the Pole than when she is with him.[12] His ambitious Love is a Fire that naturally mounts upwards; his happy Love is the Beams of Heaven, and his unhappy Love Flames of Hell. When it does not let him sleep, it is a Flame that sends up no Smoak; when it is opposed by Counsel and Advice, it is a Fire that rages the more by the Wind's blowing upon it. Upon the dying of a Tree in which he had cut his Loves, he observes that his written Flames had burnt up and withered the Tree. When he resolves to give over his Passion, he tells us that one burnt like him for ever dreads the Fire. His Heart is an *Aetna*,[13] that instead of *Vulcan*'s Shop encloses *Cupid*'s Forge in it. His endeavouring to drown his Love in Wine, is throwing Oil upon the Fire. He would insinuate to his Mistress, that the Fire of Love, like that of the Sun (which produces so many living Creatures) should not only warm but beget.[14] Love in another Place cooks Pleasure at his Fire. Sometimes the Poet's Heart is frozen in every Breast, and sometimes scorched in every Eye. Sometimes he is drowned in Tears, and burnt in Love, like a Ship set on fire in the Middle of the Sea.

The Reader may observe in every one of these Instances, that the Poet mixes the Qualities of Fire with those of Love; and in

[10] The examples which follow are from *The Mistress*. See *Spectator* No. 41, n. 12.

[11] Alembic, an apparatus used for distillation.

[12] England is situated roughly fifty degrees north of the Equator.

[13] In Roman mythology, this Italian volcano is the site of Vulcan's workshop.

[14] The theory of spontaneous generation held that the sun could produce living creatures out of fertile mud.

the same Sentence speaking of it both as a Passion, and as real Fire, surprizes the Reader with those seeming Resemblances or Contradictions that make up all the Wit in this kind of Writing. Mixt Wit therefore is a Composition of Punn and true Wit, and is more or less perfect as the Resemblance lies in the Ideas or in the Words: Its Foundations are laid partly in Falsehood and partly in Truth: Reason puts in her Claim for one Half of it, and Extravagance for the other. The only Province therefore for this kind of Wit, is Epigram, or those little occasional Poems that in their own Nature are nothing else but a Tissue of Epigrams. I cannot conclude this Head of *mixt Wit,* without owning that the admirable Poet out of whom I have taken the Examples of it, had as much true Wit as any Author that ever writ; and indeed all other Talents of an extraordinary Genius.

It may be expected, since I am upon this Subject, that I should take Notice of Mr. *Dryden's* Definition of Wit; which, with all the Deference that is due to the Judgment of so great a Man, is not so properly a Definition of Wit, as of good Writing in general. Wit, as he defines it, is "a Propriety of Words and Thoughts adapted to the Subject."[15] If this be a true Definition of Wit, I am apt to think that *Euclid* was the greatest Wit that ever set Pen to Paper.[16] It is certain there never was a greater Propriety of Words and Thoughts adapted to the Subject, than what that Author has made use of in his Elements. I shall only appeal to my Reader, if this Definition agrees with any Notion he has of Wit: If it be a true one, I am sure Mr. *Dryden* was not only a better Poet, but a greater Wit than Mr. *Cowley;* and *Virgil* a much more facetious Man than either *Ovid* or *Martial.*[17]

Bouhours,[18] whom I look upon to be the most penetrating of

15 From Dryden's *Apology for Heroic Poetry,* prefixed to *The State of Innocence* (1677). This definition was in no way singular. As often as not, Augustan writers used *wit* to mean simply *good writing.*

16 Euclid (fl. 300 B.C.), the Greek mathematician. Though speaking ironically, Addison introduces the idea expressed in the twentieth century by Edna St. Vincent Millay: "Euclid alone has looked on beauty bare."

17 Addison tries to reject Dryden's definition of *wit* by relating it to *witty* and indicating it makes comic writers of both Dryden and Virgil.

18 Dominique Bouhours (1628–1702), Jesuit and grammarian. The reference is to his *Manière de bien penser dans les ouvrages d'esprit* (1687).

all the *French* Criticks, has taken Pains to shew, That it is impossible for any Thought to be beautiful which is not just, and has not its Foundation in the Nature of things: That the Basis of all Wit is Truth; and that no Thought can be valuable, of which good Sense is not the Ground-work. *Boileau* has endeavoured to inculcate the same Notion in several Parts of his Writings, both in Prose and Verse. This is that natural Way of Writing, that beautiful Simplicity, which we so much admire in the Compositions of the Ancients; and which no Body deviates from, but those who want Strength of Genius to make a Thought shine in its own natural Beauties. Poets who want this Strength of Genius to give that Majestick Simplicity to Nature, which we so much admire in the Works of the Ancients, are forced to hunt after foreign Ornaments, and not to let any Piece of Wit of what Kind soever escape them. I look upon these Writers as *Goths*[19] in Poetry, who, like those in Architecture, not being able to come up to the beautiful Simplicity of the old *Greeks* and *Romans,* have endeavoured to supply its Place with all the Extravagances of an irregular Fancy. Mr. *Dryden* makes a very handsome Observation[20] on *Ovid's* Writing a Letter from *Dido* to *Aeneas,* in the following Words: *"Ovid"* (says he, speaking of *Virgil's* Fiction of *Dido* and *Aeneas*)

"takes it up after him, even in the same Age, and makes an Ancient Heroine of *Virgil's* new-created *Dido;* dictates a Letter for her just before her Death to the ungrateful Fugitive; and, very unluckily for himself, is for measuring a Sword with a Man so much superior in Force to him, on the same Subject. I think I may be Judge of this, because I have translated both. The famous Author of the Art of Love[21] has nothing of his own; he borrows all from a greater Master in his own Profession, and, which is worse, improves nothing which he finds: Nature fails him, and being forced to his old Shift, he has Recourse to Witticism. This passes indeed with his soft Admirers, and gives him the Preference to *Virgil* in their Esteem."

Were not I supported by so great an Authority as that of Mr.

---

[19] The reference is to Gothic architecture common in European cathedrals. Regularly, the Spectator uses *Gothic* as the equivalent of *Pindaric*. See *Spectator* No. 58, n. 25.

[20] From Dryden's *Dedication of the Aeneis* (1697).

[21] Ovid (43 B.C.–17? A.D.).

Dryden, I should not venture to observe, That the Taste of most of our *English* Poets, as well as Readers, is extremely *Gothick.* He quotes Monsieur *Segrais*[22] for a threefold Distinction of the Readers of Poetry: In the first of which he comprehends the Rabble of Readers, whom he does not treat as such with regard to their Quality,[23] but to their Numbers and the Coarseness of their Taste. His Words are as follow:

> "*Segrais* has distinguished the Readers of Poetry, according to their Capacity of judging, into three Classes. [He might have said the same of Writers too, if he had pleased.] In the lowest Form he places those whom he calls *Les Petits Esprits,* such things as are our Upper-Gallery Audience in a Play-house; who like nothing but the Husk and Rind of Wit, prefer a Quibble, a Conceit, an Epigram, before solid Sense and elegant Expression: These are Mob-Readers. If *Virgil* and *Martial* stood for Parliament-Men,[24] we know already who would carry it. But though they make the greatest Appearance in the Field, and cry the loudest, the best on't is they are but a Sort of *French* Huguenots, or *Dutch* Boors,[25] brought over in Herds, but not Naturalized; who have not Lands of two Pounds *per Annum* in *Parnassus,* and therefore are not privileged to Poll.[26] Their Authors are of the same Level, fit to represent them on a Mountebank's Stage, or to be Masters of the Ceremonies in a Bear-Garden?[27] Yet these are they who have the most Admirers. But it often happens, to their Mortification, that as their Readers improve their Stock of Sense (as they may by reading better Books, and by Conversation with Men of Judgment), they soon forsake them."

I must not dismiss this Subject without observing, that as Mr. *Lock* in the Passage above-mentioned has discovered the most

[22] Jean Regnauld de Segrais (1624–1701), French poet. Dryden quoted from the dissertation on Virgil, prefixed to Segrais' translation of the *Aeneid* and the *Georgics.*

[23] Social rank.

[24] I.e., if they were competing candidates for election to Parliament.

[25] French Calvinists or Dutch peasants.

[26] Only owners of freeholds yielding at least two pounds per year could vote in parliamentary elections. Parnassus is, of course, the Greek mountain thought to be the seat of poetry and music.

[27] A mountebank sold quack medicine from a platform. For "Bear-Garden," see *Spectator* No. 20, n. 4.

fruitful Source of Wit, so there is another of a quite contrary Nature to it, which does likewise branch it self out into several Kinds. For not only the *Resemblance* but the *Opposition* of Ideas does very often produce Wit; as I could shew in several little Points, Turns, and Antitheses, that I may possibly enlarge upon in some future Speculation.[28]   C

[28] Addison never returned to the subject, though Steele briefly referred to it in *Spectator* No. 140.

The Spectator, No. 65

Tuesday, May 15.

[S t e e l e]

———————*Demetri, teque, Tigelli,*
Discipularum inter Jubeo plorare cathedras. Hor.[1]

After having at large explained what Wit is, and described the
false Appearances of it, all that Labour seems but an useless Enquiry, without some Time be spent in considering the Application of it. The Seat of Wit, when one speaks as a Man of the Town
and the World, is the Play-house; I shall therefore fill this Paper
with Reflections upon the Use of it in that Place. The Application
of Wit in the Theatre has as strong an Effect upon the Manners of
our Gentlemen, as the Taste of it has upon the Writings of our
Authors.[2] It may, perhaps, look like a very presumptuous Work,
though not Foreign from the Duty of a Spectator, to tax[3] the Writings of such as have long had the general Applause of a Nation:
But I shall always make Reason, Truth, and Nature the Measures
of Praise and Dispraise; if those are for me, the Generality of
Opinion is of no Consequence against me; if they are against me,
the general Opinion cannot long support me.[4]

Without further Preface, I am going to look into some of our

---

[1] Horace *Satires* 1. 10. 90–91: "Demetrius and Tigellius, I bid you go whine
among the easy chairs of your lady pupils."

[2] I.e., just as the taste of the audience affects an author's writing, so an author's writing affects the manners of the audience.

[3] Criticize.

[4] Because common sense is regularly affirmed by the Spectator, it is unusual
for him to criticize "the Generality of Opinion."

most applauded Plays, and see whether they deserve the Figure they at present bear in the Imaginations of Men, or not.[5]

In reflecting upon these Works, I shall chiefly dwell upon that for which each respective Play is most celebrated. The present Paper shall be employed upon Sir *Foplin Flutter*.[6] The received Character of this Play is, That it is the Pattern of Gentile Comedy. *Dorimant* and *Harriot* are the Characters of greatest Consequence, and if these are Low and Mean, the Reputation of the Play is very Unjust.

I will take for granted, that a fine Gentleman should be honest in his Actions, and refined in his Language. Instead of this, our Hero, in this Piece, is a direct Knave in his Designs, and a Clown in his Language. *Bellair* is his Admirer and Friend; in return for which, because he is forsooth a greater Wit than his said Friend, he thinks it reasonable to perswade him to Marry a young Lady, whose Virtue, he thinks, will last no longer than till she is a Wife,[7] and then she cannot but fall to his Share, as he is an irresistible fine Gentleman. The Falshood to Mrs. *Loveit,* and the Barbarity of Triumphing over her Anguish for losing him,[8] is another Instance of his Honesty, as well as his good Nature. As to his fine Language;[9] he calls the Orange Woman, who, it seems, is inclined to grow Fat, *An Over-grown Jade, with a Flasket of Guts before her;* and salutes her with a pretty Phrase of, *How now, Double Tripe?* Upon the Mention of a Country Gentlewoman, whom he knows nothing of, (no one can imagine why) he *will lay his Life she is some awkard, ill-fashioned Country Toad, who not having above four Dozen of Hairs on her Head, has adorned her Baldness with a large white Fruz,*[10] *that she may look Sparkishly in the*

---

[5] Steele seems to have planned a series of essays on "our most applauded Plays," but such never appeared.

[6] Etherege's *The Man of Mode, or Sir Fopling Flutter* (1676).

[7] Dorimant says of Emilia: "She's a discreet maid, and I believe nothing can corrupt her but a husband" (act 1, sc. 1).

[8] The falsehood of his "vows" to Mrs. Loveit is referred to in act 1, sc. 1; his triumphing over her anguish appears in act 5, sc. 1.

[9] The quotations in this essay are sometimes exact, sometimes rough, and sometimes creative paraphrase. Those in this paragraph are all from act 1, sc. 1.

[10] A frizzy arrangement of artificial hair.

Fore-front of the King's Box at an old Play. Unnatural Mixture of senseless Common Place!

As to the Generosity of his Temper, he tells his poor Footman, *If he did not wait better*—he would turn him away, in the insolent Phrase of, *I'll Uncase you.*[11]

Now for Mrs. *Harriot:* She laughs at Obedience to an absent Mother, whose Tenderness *Busie*[12] describes to be very exquisite, for *that she is so pleased with finding* Harriot *again, that she cannot chide her for being out of the Way.* This Witty Daughter, and Fine Lady, has so little Respect for this good Woman, that she Ridicules her Air in taking Leave, and cries, *In what Struggle is my poor Mother yonder? See, see, her Head tottering, her Eyes staring, and her under Lip trembling.*[13] But all this is atoned for, because *she has more Wit than is usual in her Sex, and as much Malice, though she is as wild as you would wish her, and has a Demureness in her Looks that makes it so surprising!*[14] Then to recommend her as a fit Spouse for his Hero, the Poet makes her speak her Sense of Marriage very ingeniously. *I think,* says she, *I might be brought to endure him, and that is all a reasonable Woman should expect in an Husband.*[15] It is, methinks, unnatural that we are not made to understand how she that was bred under a silly pious old Mother, that would never trust her out of her Sight, came to be so Polite.

It cannot be denied, but that the Negligence of every thing, which engages the Attention of the sober and valuable Part of Mankind, appears very well drawn in this Piece: But it is denied,[16] that it is necessary to the Character of a Fine Gentleman, that he should in that manner Trample upon all Order and Decency. As for the Character of *Dorimant,* it is more of a Coxcomb than that of *Foplin.* He says of one of his Companions, that a good Correspondence between them is their mutual Interest. Speaking of

[11] I.e., I'll strip you of your livery (act 1, sc. 1).
[12] Mrs. Harriot's maid. Her speech is from act 3, sc. 3.
[13] Here Steele merges two separate speeches from act 4, sc. 1.
[14] Medley so describes the heroine in act 1, sc. 1.
[15] Act 3, sc. 1.
[16] I do deny.

that Friend,[17] he declares, their being much together *makes the Women think the better of his Understanding, and judge more favourably of my Reputation. It makes him pass upon some for a Man of very good Sense, and me upon others for a very civil Person.*

This whole celebrated Piece is a perfect Contradiction to good Manners, good Sense, and common Honesty; and as there is nothing in it but what is built upon the Ruin of Virtue and Innocence, according to the Notion of Merit in this Comedy, I take the Shooemaker to be, in reality, the Fine Gentleman of the Play: For it seems he is an Atheist, if we may depend upon his Character as given by the Orange-Woman, who is her self far from being the lowest in the Play. She says of a Fine Man, who is *Dorimant*'s Companion,[18] *There is not such another Heathen in the Town, except the Shooe-maker.* His Pretention to be the Hero of the *Drama* appears still more in his own Description of his way of Living with his Lady. *There is,* says he, *never a Man in Town lives more like a Gentleman with his Wife than I do; I never mind her Motions; she never enquires into mine. We speak to one another civilly, hate one another heartily; and because it is Vulgar to Lye and Soak together, we have each of us our several Settle-Bed.*[19] That of *Soaking together* is as good as if *Dorimant* had spoken it himself; and, I think, since he puts human Nature in as ugly a Form as the Circumstance will bear, and is a staunch Unbeliever, he is very much Wronged in having no part of the good Fortune bestowed in the last Act.

To speak plainly of this whole Work, I think nothing but being lost to a Sense of Innocence and Virtue can make any one see this Comedy, without observing more frequent Occasion to move Sorrow and Indignation, than Mirth and Laughter. At the same time I allow it to be Nature, but it is Nature in its utmost Corruption and Degeneracy.   R

[17] Bellair, who is handsome, well-bred, honorable, and not without wit. The quotation is from act 1, sc. 1.

[18] The reference is to Medley (act 1, sc. 1).

[19] Act 1, sc. 1. The shoemaker boasts that he and his wife have individual beds in which to get drunk.

The Spectator, No. 66

Wednesday, May 16.

[S t e e l e]

Motus Doceri gaudet Jonicos
Matura Virgo, & fingitur Artibus
Jam nunc, & incestos amores
De Tenero meditatur Ungui. Hor.[1]

The two following Letters[2] are upon a Subject of very great Importance, tho' expressed without any Air of Gravity.

To the Spectator.

"Sir,

I take the Freedom of asking your Advice in Behalf of a young Country Kinswoman of mine who is lately come to Town, and under my Care for her Education. She is very pretty, but you can't imagine how unformed a Creature it is. She comes to my Hands just as Nature left her, half finished, and without any acquired Improvements. When I look on her I often think of the *Belle Sauvage* mentioned in one of your Papers.[3] Dear Mr. Spectator, help me to make her comprehend

---

1 Horace *Odes* 3. 6. 21–24: "The maiden enjoys learning Grecian dances, and even now trains herself in coquetry, and plans unholy loves, from childhood."

2 The letters are by John Hughes (1677–1720), who contributed half a dozen *Spectators.*

3 *Spectator* No. 28 by Addison offered a letter protesting "that Creatures of jarring and incongruous Natures should be joined together in the same Sign," and citing "the Bell-Savage, which is the Sign of a savage Man standing by a Bell . . ." The writer continues, "I was formerly very much puzzled upon the Conceit of it, till I accidentally fell into the reading of an old Romance translated out of the *French;* which gives an Account of a very beautiful Woman who was found in a Wilderness, and is called in the *French la belle Sauvage. . . .*"

the visible Graces of Speech, and the dumb Eloquence of Motion; for she is at present a perfect Stranger to both. She knows no Way to express her self but by her Tongue, and that always to signifie her Meaning. Her Eyes serve her yet only to see with, and she is utterly a Foreigner to the Language of Looks and Glances.[4] In this I fancy you could help her better than any Body. I have bestowed two Months in teaching her to Sigh when she is not concerned, and to Smile when she is not pleased; and am ashamed to own she makes little or no Improvement. Then she is no more able now to walk, than she was to go[5] at a Year old. By Walking you will easily know I mean that regular but easie Motion, which gives our Persons so irresistible a Grace as if we moved to Musick, and is a kind of disengaged Figure, or, if I may so speak, recitative Dancing. But the want of this I cannot blame in her, for I find she has no Ear, and means nothing by Walking but to change her Place. I could pardon too her Blushing, if she knew how to carry her self in it, and if it did not manifestly injure her Complexion.

"They tell me you are a Person who have seen the World, and are a Judge of fine Breeding; which makes me ambitious of some Instructions from you for her Improvement: Which when you have favoured me with, I shall further advise with you about the Disposal of this fair Forrester in Marriage; for I will make it no Secret to you, that her Person and Education are to be her Fortune.[6]

> *I am, Sir,*
> *Your very Humble Servant,*
> Celimene."

"Sir,

Being employed by *Celimene* to make up and send to you her Letter, I make bold to recommend the Case therein mentioned to your Consideration, because she and I happen to differ a little in our Notions. I, who am a rough Man, am afraid the young Girl is in a fair Way to be spoiled: Therefore pray, Mr. Spectator, let us have your Opinion of this fine thing called *Fine Breeding*;[7] for I am afraid it differs too much from that plain thing called *Good Breeding*.

> *Your most humble Servant.*"

[4] See the letter from the Ogling Master in *Spectator* No. 46.

[5] Walk.

[6] I.e., she is not from a wealthy family.

[7] *Fine Breeding* would refer to the exquisitely refined, socially-oriented education which produces a coquette or a fop.

The general Mistake among us in the Educating our Children, is, That in our Daughters we take Care of their Persons and neglect their Minds; in our Sons, we are so intent upon adorning their Minds, that we wholly neglect their Bodies. It is from this that you shall see a young Lady celebrated and admired in all the Assemblies about Town; when her elder Brother is afraid to come into a Room. From this ill Management it arises, That we frequently observe a Man's Life is half spent before he is taken Notice of; and a Woman in the Prime of her Years is out of Fashion and neglected. The Boy I shall consider upon some other Occasion,[8] and at present stick to the Girl: And I am the more inclined to this, because I have several Letters which complain to me that my Female Readers have not understood me for some Days last past, and take themselves to be unconcerned in the present Turn of my Writings.[9] When a Girl is safely brought from her Nurse, before she is capable of forming one simple Notion of any thing in Life, she is delivered to the Hands of her Dancing-Master; and with a Collar[10] round her Neck, the pretty wild Thing is taught a fantastical Gravity of Behaviour, and forced to a particular Way of holding her Head, heaving her Breast, and moving with her whole Body; and all this under Pain of never having an Husband, if she steps, looks, or moves awry. This gives the young Lady wonderful Workings of Imagination, what is to pass between her and this Husband, that she is every Moment told of, and for whom she seems to be educated. Thus her Fancy is engaged to turn all her Endeavours to the Ornament of her Person, as what must determine her Good and Ill in this Life; and she naturally thinks, if she is tall enough, she is wise enough for any thing for which her Education makes her think she is designed. To make her an agreeable Person is the main Purpose of her Parents; to that is all their Cost, to that all their Care directed; and from this general Folly of Parents we

8 Though *The Spectator* regularly discussed education, a corresponding essay about "The Boy" never appeared.

9 Probably this refers to the papers on true and false wit.

10 The collar, together with a steel backboard and straps, was part of an apparatus worn to straighten the posture and expand the chest.

owe our present numerous Race of Coquets.[11] These Reflections puzzle me, when I think of giving my Advice on the Subject of managing the wild Thing mentioned in the Letter of my Correspondent. But sure there is a middle Way to be followed; the Management of a young Lady's Person is not to be overlooked, but the Erudition of her Mind is much more to be regarded. According as this is managed, you will see the Mind follow the Appetites of the Body, or the Body express the Virtues of the Mind.

Cleomira[12] dances with all the Elegance of Motion imaginable; but her Eyes are so chastised with the Simplicity and Innocence of her Thoughts, that she raises in her Beholders Admiration and good Will, but no loose Hope or wild Imagination. The true Art in this Case is, To make the Mind and Body improve together; and if possible, to make Gesture follow Thought, and not let Thought be employed upon Gesture.　　　　　　　　　　R

[11] A coquette was a young lady who sought, through appearance and manner, to win widespread admiration and attention. The most memorable example is Belinda in Pope's *The Rape of the Lock* (1714).

[12] Steele's *Tatler* No. 61 also concerned the education of women and also mentioned a Cleomira. But she is considerably less admirable than the Cleomira of this paper.

The Spectator, No. 69

Saturday, May 19.

[Addison]

Hic segetes, illic veniunt felicius uvae:
Arborei faetus alibi, atque injussa virescunt
Gramina. Nonne vides, croceos ut Tmolus odores,
India mittit ebur, molles sua thura Sabaei?
At Chalybes nudi ferrum, virosaque Pontus
Castorea, Eliadum palmas Epirus equarum?
Continuo has leges aeternaque faedera certis
Imposuit Natura locis————Vir.[1]

There is no Place in the Town which I so much love to frequent as the *Royal Exchange.*[2] It gives me a secret Satisfaction, and, in some measure, gratifies my Vanity, as I am an *Englishman,* to see so rich an Assembly of Country-men and Foreigners consulting together upon the private Business of Mankind, and making this Metropolis a kind of *Emporium* for the whole Earth. I must confess I look upon High-Change[3] to be a great Council, in which

---

[1] Virgil *Georgics* 1. 54–61: "Here corn, there grapes come more easily; elsewhere the seedlings of trees, and unbidden grasses grow green. Do you not see how Tmolus sends us the scent of saffron, India ivory, the soft Sabaeans their incense? And the naked Chalybes give us iron, Pontus the strong-smelling beaver's oil, and Epirus the Olympian victories of her mares? From the first, Nature laid these laws and eternal covenants on certain lands."

[2] The Royal Exchange was built in 1669 to replace the original building destroyed in the great fire of 1666. The two-story, quadrangle structure, situated between Cornhill and Threadneedle Street, had within a paved court adorned by statues of English kings.

[3] The full assemblage of merchants at the busiest time of the day.

all considerable Nations have their Representatives. Factors[4] in
the Trading World are what Ambassadors are in the Politick
World; they negotiate Affairs, conclude Treaties, and maintain a
good Correspondence between those wealthy Societies of Men that
are divided from one another by Seas and Oceans, or live on the
different Extremities of a Continent. I have often been pleased to
hear Disputes adjusted between an Inhabitant of *Japan* and an
Alderman of *London,* or to see a Subject of the *Great Mogul* entering into a League with one of the *Czar* of *Muscovy.*[5] I am infinitely delighted in mixing with these several Ministers of Commerce, as they are distinguished by their different Walks and
different Languages: Sometimes I am justled among a Body of
Armenians': Sometimes I am lost in a Crowd of *Jews;* and sometimes make one in a Groupe of *Dutch-men.* I am a *Dane, Swede,*
or *Frenchman* at different times, or rather fancy my self like the
old Philosopher,[6] who upon being asked what Country-man he
was, replied, That he was a Citizen of the World.

Though I very frequently visit this busie Multitude of People,
I am known to no Body there but my Friend Sir Andrew,
who often smiles upon me as he sees me bustling in the Croud,
but at the same time connives at my Presence without taking
any further Notice of me. There is indeed a Merchant of
Egypt, who just knows me by sight, having formerly remitted
me some Mony to *Grand Cairo;*[7] but as I am not versed in the
Modern *Coptick,* our Conferences go no further than a Bow and
a Grimace.

This grand Scene of Business gives me an infinite Variety of
solid and substantial Entertainments. As I am a great Lover of
Mankind, my Heart naturally overflows with Pleasure at the sight
of a prosperous and happy Multitude, insomuch that at many
publick Solemnities I cannot forbear expressing my Joy with

4 Agents.

5 The Great Mogul was emperor of the Mohammedan-Tartar empire in
India. Muscovy is Russia.

6 Diogenes the Cynic (412?–323 B.C.), Greek philosopher.

7 See Essay No. 1 concerning the Spectator's visit to Cairo. "Coptick" refers to the language of the ancient Egyptians.

Tears that have stoln down my Cheeks.[8] For this Reason I am wonderfully delighted to see such a Body of Men thriving in their own private Fortunes, and at the same time promoting the Publick Stock; or in other Words, raising Estates for their own Families, by bringing into their Country whatever is wanting, and carrying out of it whatever is superfluous.

Nature seems to have taken a particular Care to disseminate her Blessings among the different Regions of the World, with an Eye to this mutual Intercourse and Traffick among Mankind, that the Natives of the several Parts of the Globe might have a kind of Dependance upon one another, and be united together by their common Interest. Almost every *Degree*[9] produces something peculiar to it. The Food often grows in one Country, and the Sauce in another. The Fruits of *Portugal* are corrected by the Products of *Barbadoes:* The Infusion of a *China* Plant sweetned with the Pith of an *Indian* Cane: The *Philippick* Islands give a Flavour to our *European* Bowls.[10] The single Dress of a Woman of Quality is often the Product of an hundred Climates. The Muff and the Fan come together from the different Ends of the Earth. The Scarf is sent from the Torrid Zone, and the Tippet[11] from beneath the Pole. The Brocade Petticoat rises out of the Mines of *Peru,* and the Diamond Necklace out of the Bowels of *Indostan.*[12]

If we consider our own Country in its natural Prospect, without any of the Benefits and Advantages of Commerce, what a barren uncomfortable Spot of Earth falls to our Share! Natural Historians tell us, that no Fruit grows originally among us, besides Hips and Haws, Acorns and Pig-Nutts, with other Delicacies of the like Nature;[13] That our Climate of it self, and without the

8 This emotional response does not accord with the characteristics of the Spectator already established.

9 Latitude.

10 I.e., the fruits of Portugal are qualified by sugar from the West Indies. Chinese tea is sweetened with Indian sugar. The Philippine Islands also supply sugar cane.

11 Here, a shoulder cape of fur or cloth.

12 India.

13 Since hips and haws are berries of the dog-rose and the hawthorne, and pig nuts are an edible tuberous root, the word *Delicacies* is intended as irony.

Assistances of Art, can make no further Advances towards a Plumb than to a Sloe, and carries an Apple to no greater a Perfection than a Crab: That our Melons, our Peaches, our Figs, our Apricots, and Cherries, are Strangers among us, imported in different Ages, and naturalized in our *English* Gardens; and that they would all degenerate and fall away into the Trash of our own Country, if they were wholly neglected by the Planter, and left to the Mercy of our Sun and Soil. Nor has Traffick more enriched our Vegetable World, than it has improved the whole Face of Nature among us. Our Ships are laden with the Harvest of every Climate: Our Tables are stored with Spices, and Oils, and Wines: Our Rooms are filled with Pyramids of *China,* and adorned with the Workmanship of *Japan*.[14] Our Morning's-Draught comes to us from the remotest Corners of the Earth: We repair our Bodies by the Drugs of *America,* and repose our selves under *Indian* Canopies.[15] My Friend Sir Andrew calls the Vineyards of *France* our Gardens; the Spice-Islands[16] our Hot-Beds; the *Persians* our Silk-Weavers, and the *Chinese* our Potters. Nature indeed furnishes us with the bare Necessaries of Life, but Traffick gives us a great Variety of what is Useful, and at the same time supplies us with every thing that is Convenient and Ornamental. Nor is it the least Part of this our Happiness, that whilst we enjoy the remotest Products of the North and South, we are free from those Extremities of Weather which give them Birth; That our Eyes are refreshed with the green Fields of *Britain,* at the same time that our Palates are feasted with Fruits that rise between the Tropicks.

For these Reasons there are not more useful Members in a Commonwealth than Merchants. They knit Mankind together in a mutual Intercourse of good Offices, distribute the Gifts of Nature, find Work for the Poor, add Wealth to the Rich, and Magnificence to the Great. Our *English* Merchant converts the Tin of his own Country into Gold,[17] and exchanges his Wooll for Rubies. The *Mahometans* are cloathed in our *British* Manufacture, and

[14] See the lady's library in *Spectator* No. 37.
[15] The reference is to drugs such as quinine and to curtains made of muslin or chintz.
[16] The Moluccas islands near New Guinea.
[17] The allusion is to alchemy.

the Inhabitants of the Frozen Zone warmed with the Fleeces of our Sheep.

When I have been upon the *'Change,* I have often fancied one of our old Kings[18] standing in Person, where he is represented in Effigy, and looking down upon the wealthy Concourse of People with which that Place is every Day filled. In this Case, how would he be surprized to hear all the Languages of *Europe* spoken in this little Spot of his former Dominions, and to see so many private Men, who in his Time would have been the Vassals of some powerful Baron, Negotiating like Princes for greater Sums of Mony than were formerly to be met with in the Royal Treasury! Trade, without enlarging the *British* Territories, has given us a kind of additional Empire: It has multiplied the Number of the Rich, made our Landed Estates infinitely more Valuable than they were formerly, and added to them an Accession of other Estates as Valuable as the Lands themselves.[19]   C

[18] There is no reason to believe that the Spectator had any particular king in mind.

[19] Though Addison may not have intended a partisan political tract, this tribute to trade was clearly a Whig statement.

The Spectator, No. 70

Monday, May 21.

[A d d i s o n]

Interdum vulgus rectum videt. Hor.[1]

When I travelled,[2] I took a particular Delight in hearing the Songs and Fables that are come from Father to Son, and are most in vogue among the common People of the Countries through which I passed; for it is impossible that any thing should be universally tasted and approved by a Multitude, tho' they are only the Rabble of a Nation, which hath not in it some peculiar Aptness to please and gratifie the Mind of Man. Human Nature is the same in all reasonable Creatures; and whatever falls in with it, will meet with Admirers amongst Readers of all Qualities and Conditions. *Moliere,* as we are told by Monsieur *Boileau,* used to read all his Comedies to an old Woman who was his House-keeper, as she sat with him at her Work by the Chimney-Corner; and could foretel the Success of his Play in the Theatre, from the Reception it met at his Fire-Side: For he tells us the Audience always followed the old Woman, and never failed to laugh in the same Place.[3]

I know nothing which more shews the essential and inherent Perfection of Simplicity of Thought, above that which I call the Gothick Manner in Writing, than this, that the first pleases all Kinds of Palates, and the latter only such as have formed to them-

---

1 Horace *Epistles,* 2. 1. 63: "At times the crowd sees and judges right."

2 See *Spectator* No. 1.

3 See *Tatler* No. 158, n. 16. The anecdote appears in Boileau's "Critical Reflections on . . . Longinus."

selves a wrong artificial Taste upon little fanciful Authors and Writers of Epigram. *Homer, Virgil,* or *Milton,* so far as the Language of their Poems is understood, will please a Reader of plain common Sense, who would neither relish nor comprehend an Epigram of *Martial,* or a Poem of *Cowley:*[4] So, on the contrary, an ordinary Song or Ballad that is the Delight of the common People, cannot fail to please all such Readers as are not unqualified for the Entertainment by their Affectation or Ignorance; and the Reason is plain, because the same Paintings of Nature which recommend it to the most ordinary Reader, will appear beautiful to the most refined.

The old Song of *Chevy-Chase*[5] is the favourite Ballad of the common People of *England;* and *Ben. Johnson* used to say he had rather have been the Author of it than of all his Works.[6] Sir *Philip Sidney* in his Discourse of Poetry[7] speaks of it in the following Words; *I never heard the old Song of* Piercy *and* Douglas, *that I found not my Heart more moved than with a Trumpet; and yet is sung by some blind Crowder*[8] *with no rougher Voice than rude Stile; which being so evil apparelled in the Dust and Cobweb of that uncivil Age, what would it work trimmed in the gorgeous Eloquence of* Pindar? For my own Part, I am so professed an Admirer of this antiquated Song, that I shall give my Reader a Critick upon it, without any further Apology for so doing.[9]

The greatest Modern Criticks have laid it down as a Rule, That an Heroick Poem should be founded upon some important Precept of Morality, adapted to the Constitution of the Country in

4 This echoes the papers on true and false wit (Nos. 58–63), which were concluded a week earlier.

5 "The Ballad of Chevy Chase" was a revised broadside version of "The Hunting of the Cheviot," a ballad dating before 1549. The poem describes, with great freedom, the Battle of Otterburn (August 19, 1388). The text quoted is Version B in Child (3. 303).

6 Addison is mistaken. Ben Jonson did say something like this about Southwell's "Burning Babe" (*Works,* ed. Herford and Simpson, 1. 137).

7 *An Apology for Poetry* (1595).

8 Celtic musician.

9 The critique required an introductory apology. In an age of literary elegance, ballads were considered rustic and old-fashioned. Addison quotes at length, because many of his readers had never read the poem.

which the Poet writes.[10] *Homer* and *Virgil* have formed their
Plans in this View. As *Greece* was a Collection of many Governments, who suffered very much among themselves, and gave the
Persian Emperor, who was their common Enemy, many Advantages over them by their mutual Jealousies and Animosities, *Homer,* in order to establish among them an Union, which was so
necessary for their Safety, grounds his Poem upon the Discords of
the several *Grecian* Princes who were engaged in a Confederacy
against an *Asiatick* Prince, and the several Advantages which the
Enemy gained by such their Discords. At the Time the Poem we
are now treating of was written, the Dissentions of the Barons,
who were then so many petty Princes, ran very high, whether they
quarrelled among themselves, or with their Neighbours, and produced unspeakable Calamities to the Country: The Poet, to deter
Men from such unnatural Contentions, describes a bloody Battel
and dreadful Scene of Death, occasioned by the mutual Feuds
which reigned in the Families of an *English* and *Scotch* Nobleman. That he designed this for the Instruction of his Poem, we
may learn from his four last Lines, in which, after the Example
of the Modern Tragedians, he draws from it a Precept for the
Benefit of his Readers.

> *God save the King, and bless the Land*
> *In Plenty, Joy, and Peace;*
> *And grant henceforth that foul Debate*
> *'Twixt Noblemen may cease.*

The next Point observed by the greatest Heroic Poets, hath been
to celebrate Persons and Actions which do Honour to their Country: Thus *Virgil*'s Hero was the Founder of *Rome, Homer*'s a
Prince of *Greece;* and for this Reason *Valerius Flaccus* and *Statius,*
who were both *Romans,* might be justly derided for having chosen
the Expedition of the *Golden Fleece* and *the Wars of Thebes,* for
the Subjects of their Epic Writings.[11]

---

[10] The weight of seventeenth-century critical opinion does support this
statement, but Addison's examples show he was principally indebted to René
Le Bossu's *Treatise of the Epick Poem* (1675). See *Tatler* No. 165, n. 3.

[11] The *Argonautica,* an epic poem based on the legend of the golden fleece,
was left unfinished by Valerius Flaccus at the time of his death (ca. 90 A.D.).
The *Thebaid* was an epic written by Publius Papinius Statius (45?–96? A.D.).

The Poet before us, has not only found out an Hero in his own Country, but raises the Reputation of it by several beautiful Incidents. The *English* are the first who take the Field, and the last who quit it. The *English* bring only Fifteen hundred to the Battel, the *Scotch* Two thousand. The *English* keep the Field with Fifty three: The *Scotch* retire with Fifty five: All the rest on each Side being slain in Battel. But the most remarkable Circumstance of this Kind, is the different Manner in which the *Scotch* and *English* Kings receive the News of this Fight, and of the great Mens Deaths who commanded in it.

> *This News was brought to* Edinburgh,
>   *Where* Scotland*'s King did reign,*
> *That brave Earl* Douglas *suddenly*
>   *Was with an Arrow slain.*
>
> *O heavy News, King* James[12] *did say,*
>   Scotland *can Witness be,*
> *I have not any Captain more*
>   *Of such Account as he.*
>
> *Like Tydings to King* Henry *came*
>   *Within as short a Space,*
> *That* Piercy *of* Northumberland
>   *Was slain in* Chevy-Chace.
>
> *Now God be with him, said our King,*
>   *Sith 'twill no better be,*
> *I trust I have within my Realm*
>   *Five hundred as good as he.*
>
> *Yet shall not* Scot *nor* Scotland *say*
>   *But I will Vengeance take,*
> *And be revenged on them all*
>   *For brave Lord* Piercy*'s Sake.*
>
> *This Vow full well the King perform'd*
>   *After on* Humble-down,[13]

---

[12] Though the Battle of Otterburn occurred in 1388, the references are clearly to Henry IV of England (reigned 1399–1413), and James I of Scotland (reigned 1406–1437), as well as to Sir Henry Percy (1364–1403) and Archibald, 4th Earl of Douglas (1372–1424).

[13] The Battle of Humbledon Hill occurred in 1402.

> *In one Day Fifty Knights were slain*
> *With Lords of great Renown.*
>
> *And of the rest of small Account*
> *Did many Thousands dye,* &c.

At the same Time that our Poet shews a laudable Partiality to his Country-men, he represents the *Scots* after a Manner not unbecoming so bold and brave a People.

> *Earl* Douglas *on a milk-white Steed,*
> *Most like a Baron bold,*
> *Rode foremost of the Company*
> *Whose Armour shone like Gold.*

His Sentiments and Actions are every Way suitable to an Hero. One of us two, says he, must dye: I am an Earl as well as your self, so that you can have no Pretence for refusing the Combat: However, says he, 'tis Pity, and indeed would be a Sin, that so many innocent Men should perish for our Sakes; rather let you and I end our Quarrel in single Fight.

> *E'er thus I will out-braved be,*
> *One of us two shall dye;*
> *I know thee well, an Earl thou art,*
> *Lord* Piercy, *so am I.*
>
> *But trust me,* Piercy, *Pity it were,*
> *And great Offence, to kill*
> *Any of these our harmless Men,*
> *For they have done no Ill.*
>
> *Let thou and I the Battel try,*
> *And set our Men aside;*
> *Accurst be he, Lord* Piercy *said,*
> *By whom this is deny'd.*

When these brave Men had distinguished themselves in the Battel and in single Combat with each other, in the Midst of a generous Parly, full of heroic Sentiments, the *Scotch* Earl falls; and with his Dying Words encourages his Men to revenge his Death, representing to them, as the most bitter Circumstance of it, that his Rival saw him fall.

With that there came an Arrow keen
  Out of an English *Bow,*
Which struck Earl Douglas *to the Heart*
  A deep and deadly Blow.

Who never spoke more Words than these,
  Fight on my merry Men all;
For why, my Life is at an End,
  Lord Piercy *sees my Fall.*

Merry Men, in the Language of those Times, is no more than a
chearful Word for Companions and Fellow-Soldiers. A Passage in
the Eleventh Book of *Virgil's Aeneids*[14] is very much to be admired, where *Camilla* in her last Agonies, instead of weeping over
the Wound she had received, as one might have expected from
a Warrior of her Sex, considers only (like the Hero of whom we
are now speaking) how the Battel should be continued after her
Death.

Tum sic exspirans, &c.

A gathering Mist o'erclouds her chearful Eyes
And from her Cheeks the rosie Colour flies.
Then, turns to her, whom, of her Female Train,
She trusted most, and thus she speaks with Pain.
Acca, 'tis past! He swims before my Sight,
Inexorable Death; and claims his Right.
Bear my last Words to Turnus, *fly with Speed,*
And bid him timely to my Charge succeed:
Repel the Trojans, *and the Town relieve:*
Farewel.——— ———

Turnus did not die in so heroic a Manner; tho' our Poet seems
to have had his Eye upon *Turnus*'s Speech in the last Verse,

Lord Piercy *sees my Fall.*

———*Vicisti, & victum tendere palmas*
Ausonii videre ——— ———[15]

14 Virgil *Aeneid* 11. 820f. Camilla is a warrior maiden of the Rutulians, and
Turnus is their leader. Both are killed by Aeneas and the Trojans. (The translation is Dryden's.)

15 *Aeneid* 12. 936–937: "Thou hast conquered, and the Ausonians have
seen me stretch forth my hands."

Earl *Piercy*'s Lamentation over his Enemy is generous, beauti-
ful, and passionate; I must only caution the Reader not to let the
Simplicity of the Stile, which one may well pardon in so old a
Poet, prejudice him against the Greatness of the Thought.

> *Then leaving Life Earl* Piercy *took*
> *The dead Man by the Hand,*
> *And said, Earl* Douglas *for thy Life*
> *Would I had lost my Land.*
>
> *O Christ! My very Heart doth bleed*
> *With Sorrow for thy Sake;*
> *For sure a more renowned Knight*
> *Mischance did never take.*

That beautiful Line *Taking the dead Man by the Hand,* will put
the Reader in Mind of *Aeneas*'s Behaviour towards *Lausus,* whom
he himself had Slain as he came to the Rescue of his aged Father.

> *At vero ut vultum vidit morientis, & ora,*
> *Ora modis Anchisiades, pallentia miris:*
> *Ingemuit, miserans graviter, dextramque tetendit,* &c.[16]
>
> *The pious Prince beheld young* Lausus *dead;*
> *He griev'd, he wept; then grasp'd his Hand, and said,*
> *Poor hapless Youth! What Praises can be paid*
> *To Worth so great———!*

I shall take another Opportunity to consider the other Parts of
this old Song.[17]

                                                            C

---

[16] *Aeneid* 10. 821–823. (Dryden's translation follows.)

[17] Addison returned to the ballad in *Spectator* No. 74. But responses to the
two essays made it clear that many eighteenth-century critics remained un-
convinced.

The Spectator, No. 81

Saturday, June 2, 1711.

[Addison]

Qualis ubi audito venantum murmure Tigris
Horruit in maculas——Statius.[1]

About the middle of last Winter I went to see an *Opera* at the Theatre in the *Hay-Market,* where I could not but take notice of two Parties of very Fine Women, that had placed themselves in the opposite Side-Boxes,[2] and seemed drawn up in a kind of Battle-Array one against another. After a short Survey of them, I found they were *Patched*[3] differently; the Faces, on one Hand,[4] being Spotted on the Right Side of the Forehead, and those upon the other on the Left. I quickly perceived that they cast Hostile Glances upon one another; and that their Patches were placed in those different Situations, as Party-Signals to distinguish Friends from Foes. In the Middle-Boxes, between these two opposite Bodies, were several Ladies who Patched indifferently on both sides of their Faces, and seemed to sit there with no other Intention but to see the *Opera.* Upon Enquiry I found, that the Body of *Amazons*[5] on my Right Hand, were Whigs; and those on my Left, Tories; and that those who had placed themselves in the Middle-Boxes were a Neutral Party, whose Faces had not yet declared themselves. These last, however, as I afterwards found, di-

1 Statius *Thebaid* 2. 128–129: "Like the tigress, at the sound of hunters, when spots appear upon her skin."

2 The women were in the compartments usually occupied by the men.

3 See *Spectator* No. 37, n. 7.

4 I.e., in the boxes on one side.

5 An ancient race of female warriors.

minished daily, and took their Party with one Side or the other; insomuch that I observed in several of them, the Patches which were before dispersed equally, are now all gone over to the Whig or Tory Side of the Face. The Censorious say, That the Men whose Hearts are aimed at are very often the Occasions that one part of the Face is thus Dishonoured, and lyes under a kind of Disgrace, while the other is so much Set off and Adorned by the Owner; and that the Patches turn to the Right or to the Left, according to the Principles of the Man who is most in Favour. But whatever may be the Motives of a few Fantastical Coquets,[6] who do not Patch for the Publick Good, so much as for their own Private Advantage; it is certain, that there are several Women of Honour who Patch out of Principle, and with an Eye to the Interest of their Country. Nay, I am informed, that some of them adhere so stedfastly to their Party, and are so far from Sacrificing their Zeal for the Publick to their Passion for any particular Person, that in a late Draught of Marriage-Articles[7] a Lady has stipulated with her Husband, That, whatever his Opinions are, she shall be at Liberty to Patch on which side she pleases.

I must here take notice, that *Rosalinda,* a Famous Whig Partizan, has most unfortunately a very beautiful Mole on the Tory part of her Forehead; which, being very conspicuous, has occasioned many Mistakes,[8] and given an Handle to her Enemies to misrepresent her Face, as though it had Revolted from the Whig Interest. But whatever this natural Patch may seem to intimate, it is well known that her Notions of Government are still the same. This unlucky Mole however has mis-led several Coxcombs; and, like the hanging out of false Colours,[9] made some of them converse with *Rosalinda* in what they thought the Spirit of her Party, when on a sudden she has given them an unexpected Fire, that has sunk them all at once. If *Rosalinda* is unfortunate in her

6 See *Spectator* No. 66, n. 11.

7 A draft of the marriage settlement spelling out the property, allowances, etc., guaranteed to the wife.

8 The mole is mistaken for a patch.

9 The practice of a vessel which seeks to deceive an enemy by hoisting the flag of the nation to which the enemy belongs or is on friendly terms with.

Mole, *Nigranilla* is as unhappy in a Pimple, which forces her, against her Inclinations, to Patch on the Whig side.[10]

I am told that many Virtuous Matrons, who formerly have been taught to believe that this Artificial Spotting of the Face was unlawful, are now reconciled by a Zeal for their Cause, to what they could not be prompted by a Concern for their Beauty. This way of declaring War upon one another, puts me in mind of what is reported of the Tigress, that several Spots rise in her Skin when she is angry; or as Mr. *Cowley* has imitated the Verses that stand as the Motto of this Paper,

> ———*She Swells with angry Pride,*
> *And calls forth all her Spots on ev'ry side.*[11]

When I was in the Theatre the time abovementioned, I had the Curiosity to count the Patches on both Sides, and found the Tory Patches to be about twenty Stronger than the Whig; but to make amends for this small Inequality, I the next Morning found the whole Puppet-show filled with Faces spotted after the Whiggish manner. Whether or no the Ladies had retreated hither in order to rally their Forces I cannot tell; but the next Night they came in so great a Body to the Opera, that they outnumbered the Enemy.

This Account of Party-Patches will, I am afraid, appear improbable to those who live at a distance from the fashionable World; but as it is a Distinction of a very singular Nature, and what perhaps may never meet with a Parallel, I think I should not have discharged the Office of a faithful Spectator had I not recorded it.

I have, in former Papers,[12] endeavoured to expose this Party-Rage in Women, as it only serves to aggravate the Hatreds and Animosities that reign among Men, and in a great measure deprives the Fair Sex of those peculiar Charms with which Nature has endowed them.

[10] The pimple is so unsightly she must use a patch to conceal it.
[11] Abraham Cowley *Davideis* 3. 403–404.
[12] E.g., *Spectator* No. 57.

When the *Romans* and *Sabines*[13] were at War, and just upon the point of giving Battle, the Women, who were allied to both of them, interposed with so many Tears and Intreaties, that they prevented the mutual Slaughter which threatned both Parties, and united them together in a firm and lasting Peace.

I would recommend this noble Example to our *British* Ladies, at a time when their Country is torn with so many unnatural Divisions, that if they continue, it will be a Misfortune to be born in it. The *Greeks* thought it so improper for Women to interest themselves in Competitions and Contentions, that for this Reason, among others, they forbad them, under Pain of Death, to be present at the *Olympick* Games,[14] notwithstanding these were the Publick Diversions of all *Greece*.

As our *English* Women excel those of all Nations in Beauty, they should endeavour to outshine them in all other Accomplishments proper to the Sex, and to distinguish themselves as tender Mothers and faithful Wives, rather than as furious Partizans. Female Virtues are of a Domestick turn. The Family is the proper Province for Private Women to Shine in. If they must be showing their Zeal for the Publick, let it not be against those who are perhaps of the same Family, or at least of the same Religion or Nation, but against those who are the open, professed, undoubted Enemies of their Faith, Liberty, and Country.[15] When the *Romans* were pressed with a Foreign Enemy, the Ladies voluntarily contributed all their Rings and Jewels to assist the Government under a publick Exigence;[16] which appeared so laudable an Action in the Eyes of their Countrymen, that from thenceforth it was permitted by a Law to pronounce publick Orations at the Funeral of a Woman in Praise of the deceased Person, which till that time was peculiar[17] to Men. Would our *English* Ladies, instead of

---

13 Livy *History of Rome* 1. 13.

14 The athletic games and combats held at Olympia in Elis from about the ninth century B.C. till the fourth century A.D.

15 Presumably a reference to the French, the Spanish, and the Jacobites.

16 During the Second Punic War (218–201 B.C.), the Consul, Marcus Lavinus, proposed such a contribution and the Roman ladies responded enthusiastically.

17 A special privilege reserved.

sticking on a Patch against those of their own Country, shew themselves so truly Publick-spirited as to Sacrifice every one her Necklace against the Common Enemy, what Decrees ought not to be made in favour of them?

Since I am recollecting upon this Subject such Passages as occur to my Memory out of ancient Authors, I cannot omit a Sentence in the Celebrated Funeral Oration of *Pericles,* which he made in Honour of those Brave *Athenians* that were Slain in a Fight with the *Lacedemonians.*[18] After having addressed himself to the several Ranks and Orders of his Countrymen, and shewn them how they should behave themselves in the Publick Cause, he turns to the Female part of his Audience; "And as for you (says he) I shall advise you in very few Words: Aspire only to those Virtues that are peculiar to your Sex; follow your natural Modesty, and think it your greatest Commendation not to be talked of one way or other."   C

[18] Pericles (d. 429 B.C.), the Athenian statesman, made his famous funeral oration to honor all who had fallen in the Peloponnesian War, not those who were killed in one particular battle against the Spartans.

The Spectator, No. 82

Monday, June 4.

[S t e e l e]

———*Caput domina venale sub hasta.* Juv.[1]

Passing under *Ludgate*[2] the other Day I heard a Voice bawling
for Charity, which I thought I had somewhere heard before. Coming near to the Grate, the Prisoner called me by my Name, and
desired I would throw something into the Box: I was out of Countenance[3] for him, and did as he bid me, by putting in half a
Crown. I went away reflecting upon the strange Constitution of
some Men, and how meanly they behave themselves in all Sorts
of Conditions.[4] The Person who begged of me is now, as I take
it, Fifty: I was well acquainted with him till about the Age of
Twenty five; at which Time a good Estate fell to him, by the Death
of a Relation. Upon coming to this unexpected good Fortune, he
ran into all the Extravagancies imaginable; was frequently in
drunken Disputes, broke Drawers[5] Heads, talked and swore loud;
was unmannerly to those above him, and insolent to those below
him. I could not but remark, that it was the same Baseness of
Spirit which worked in his Behaviour in both Fortunes: The same
little Mind was insolent in Riches, and shameless in Poverty. This
Accident made me muse upon the Circumstance of being in Debt

---

1 Juvenal *Satires* 3. 33: "A slave for sale under the authority of the spear."

2 Ludgate Prison, where citizens of London, beneficed clergy, and lawyers
were confined for debt.

3 Embarrassed.

4 The word probably refers both to the degree of birth and to the present
circumstances. See *Spectator* No. 26, n. 4.

5 Persons who draw liquor.

in general, and solve in my Mind what Tempers were most apt to fall into this Errour of Life, as well as the Misfortune it must needs be to languish under such Pressures. As for my self, my natural Aversion to that Sort of Conversation which makes a Figure with the Generality of Mankind, exempts me from any Temptations to Expence;[6] and all my Business lies within a very narrow Compass, which is, only to give an honest Man who takes care of my Estate proper Vouchers for his quarterly Payments to me, and observe what Linnen my Laundress brings and takes away with her once a Week: My Steward brings his Receipt ready for my signing, and I have a pretty Implement[7] with the respective Names of Shirts, Cravats, Handkerchiefs and Stockings, with proper Numbers to know how to reckon with my Laundress. This being almost all the Business I have in the World for the Care of my own Affairs, I am at full Leisure to observe upon what others do, with Relation to their Equipage and Oeconomy.

When I walk the Street, and observe the Hurry about me in this Town,

> *Where with like Haste, tho' different Ways, they run;*
> *Some to undo, and some to be undone.*[8]

I say, when I behold this vast Variety of Persons and Humours, with the Pains they both take for the Accomplishment of the Ends mentioned in the above Verses of *Denham*, I cannot much wonder at the Endeavour after Gain; but am extreamly astonished that Men can be so insensible of the Danger of running into Debt. One would think it impossible a Man who is given to contract Debts should know, that his Creditor has from that Moment in which he transgresses Payment, so much as that Demand comes to in his Debtor's Honour, Liberty and Fortune.[9] One would think he did

6 The circumspect character of the Spectator is totally opposite that of Richard Steele, who was regularly in debt. Though probably sincere, Steele must have intended the essay to be a kind of private joke.

7 An inventory statement.

8 From Sir John Denham's "Cooper's Hill" (1642), lines 31–32.

9 I.e., it seems impossible a man should not know that, from the moment he defaults on a debt, the creditor takes away a portion of his personal honor and can encumber his actions and possessions at will.

not know, that his Creditor can say the worst thing imaginable of him, to wit, *That he is unjust,* without Defamation; and can sieze his Person,[10] without being guilty of an Assault. Yet such is the loose and abandoned Turn of some Mens Minds, that they can live under these constant Apprehensions, and still go on to encrease the Cause of them. Can there be a more low and servile Condition, than to be ashamed, or afraid, to see any one Man breathing? Yet he that is much in debt, is in that Condition with relation to twenty different People. There are indeed Circumstances wherein Men of honest Natures may become liable to Debts, by some unadvised Behaviour in any great Point of their Life, or mortgaging a Man's Honesty as a Security for that of another, and the like; but these Instances are so particular and circumstantiated, that they cannot come within general Considerations: For one such Case as one of these, there are ten, where a Man, to keep up a Farce of Retinue and Grandeur within his own House, shall shrink at the Expectation of surly Demands at his Doors. The Debtor is the Creditor's Criminal, and all the Officers of Power and State whom we behold make so great a Figure, are no other than so many Persons in Authority to make good his Charge against him. Humane Society depends upon his having the Vengeance Law allots him; and the Debtor owes his Liberty to his Neighbour, as much as the Murderer does his Life to his Prince.[11]

Our Gentry are, generally speaking, in debt; and many Families have put it into a kind of Method of being so from Generation to Generation. The Father mortgages when his Son is very young; and the Boy is to marry assoon as he is at Age, to redeem it, and find Portions for his Sisters. This, forsooth, is no great Inconvenience to him;[12] for he may wench, keep a publick Table, or feed Dogs, like a worthy *English* Gentleman, till he has outrun half his Estate, and leave the same Incumbrance upon his First-born; and so on, till one Man of more Vigour[13] than ordinary

---

10 Have him arrested.

11 I.e., under the law, just as the prince can in justice execute the murderer, so the creditor ("his Neighbour") has the right to imprison the debtor.

12 I.e., the son.

13 More stamina for drinking, hunting, and wenching.

goes quite thorough the Estate, or some Man of Sense comes into it, and scorns to have an Estate in Partnership, that is to say, liable to the Demand or Insult of any Man living. There is my Friend Sir Andrew, tho' for many Years a great and general Trader, was never the Defendant in a Law Suit, in all the Perplexity of Business, and the Iniquity of Mankind at present: No one had any Colour for the least Complaint against his Dealings with him.[14] This is certainly as uncommon, and in its Proportion as laudable in a Citizen, as it is in a General never to have suffered a Disadvantage in Fight. How different from this Gentleman is *Jack Truepenny,*[15] who has been an old Acquaintance of Sir Andrew and my self from Boys, but could never learn our Caution. *Jack* has a whorish unresisting good Nature, which makes him incapable of having a Property in any thing. His Fortune, his Reputation, his Time and his Capacity, are at any Man's Service that comes first. When he was at School, he was whipp'd thrice a Week for Faults he took upon him to excuse others; since he came into the Business of the World, he has been arrested twice or thrice a Year for Debts he had nothing to do with but as Surety for others; and I remember when a Friend of his had suffered in the Vice of the Town, all the Physick his Friend took was conveyed to him by *Jack,* and inscribed, "A Bolus or an Electuary for Mr. *Truepenny.*"[16] *Jack* had a good Estate left him, which came to nothing; because he believed all who pretended to Demands upon it.[17] This Easiness and Credulity destroy all the other Merit he has; and he has all his Life been a Sacrifice to others, without ever receiving Thanks or doing one good Action.

I will end this Discourse with a Speech which I heard *Jack* make to one of his Creditors (of whom he deserved gentler Usage) after lying a whole Night in Custody[18] at his Suit.

---

[14] The view that the fox-hunting gentry were commonly in debt and that a trader like Sir Andrew had never been so, was a notably Whig sentiment.

[15] It is reasonably claimed that Steele intended to describe himself, at least partly, in the character of Jack Truepenny.

[16] A bolus is a pill; an electuary, a sweet medicine. The point is that, just as Jack assumed the debts of others, he lets the world think that he, and not his friend, has contracted the venereal disease.

[17] Claimed charges against the estate.

[18] Probably at Ludgate.

"*Sir,*

Your Ingratitude for the many Kindnesses I have done you, shall not make me unthankful for the Good you have done me, in letting me see there is such a Man as you in the World. I am obliged to you for the Diffidence I shall have all the rest of my Life: *I shall hereafter trust no Man so far as to be in his Debt.*"

R

The Spectator, No. 94

Monday, June 18.

[Addison]

—————— —————— ——————*Hoc est*
Vivere bis, vita posse priore frui. Mart.[1]

The last Method which I proposed in my *Saturday*'s Paper,[2] for filling up those empty Spaces of Life which are so tedious and burthensome to idle People, is the employing our selves in the Pursuit of Knowledge. I remember Mr. *Boyle*,[3] speaking of a certain Mineral, tells us, That a Man may consume his whole Life in the Study of it, without arriving at the Knowledge of all its Qualities. The Truth of it is, there is not a single Science, or any Branch of it, that might not furnish a Man with Business for Life, though it were much longer than it is.

I shall not here engage on those beaten Subjects of the Usefulness of Knowledge, nor of the Pleasure and Perfection it gives the Mind, nor on the Methods of attaining it, nor recommend any particular Branch of it, all which have been the Topicks of many other Writers; but shall indulge my self in a Speculation that is more uncommon, and may therefore perhaps be more entertaining.

I have before shewn how the unemployed Parts of Life appear long and tedious, and shall here endeavour to shew how those

1 Martial *Epigrams* 10. 23. 7–8: "To take pleasure in one's past life is to live twice."

2 *Spectator* No. 93. This is referred to again in the third paragraph.

3 Robert Boyle (1627–1691), British physicist and chemist. The quotation is from *Some Considerations Touching upon the Usefulness of Experimental Naturall Philosophy* (1664).

Parts of Life which are exercised in Study, Reading, and the Pursuits of Knowledge, are long but not tedious; and by that Means discover a Method of lengthening our Lives, and at the same Time of turning all the Parts of them to our Advantage. Mr. *Lock* observes,[4]

> "That we get the Idea of Time, or Duration, by reflecting on that Train of Ideas which succeed one another in our Minds: That for this Reason, when we sleep soundly without dreaming, we have no Perception of Time, or the Length of it, whilst we sleep; and that the Moment wherein we leave off to think, till the Moment we begin to think again, seem to have no Distance." To which the Author adds; "And so, I doubt not, but it would be to a waking Man, if it were possible for him to keep only one *Idea* in his Mind, without Variation, and the Succession of others: And we see, that one who fixes his Thoughts very intently on one thing, so as to take but little Notice of the Succession of *Ideas* that pass in his Mind whilst he is taken up with that earnest Contemplation, lets slip out of his Account a good Part of that Duration, and thinks that Time shorter than it is."

We might carry this Thought further, and consider a Man as, on one Side, shortening his Time by thinking on nothing, or but a few things; so, on the other, as lengthening it, by employing his Thoughts on many Subjects, or by entertaining a quick and constant Succession of Ideas. Accordingly Monsieur *Mallebranche,* in his *Enquiry after Truth,*[5] (which was published several Years before Mr. *Lock*'s *Essay on Humane Understanding*) tells us, That it is possible some Creatures may think Half an Hour as long as we do a thousand Years; or look upon that Space of Duration which we call a Minute, as an Hour, a Week, a Month, or an whole Age.

This Notion of Monsieur *Mallebranche,* is capable of some little Explanation from what I have quoted out of Mr. *Lock;* for if our Notion of Time is produced by our reflecting on the Succession of Ideas in our Mind, and this Succession may be infinitely accelerated or retarded, it will follow, that different Beings may

[4] The passage is from John Locke's *An Essay Concerning Human Understanding* (2. 14. 4); the first sentence is a paraphrase, the rest a direct quotation.

[5] Father Nicolas de Malebranche's *Recherche de la Vérité* (1674–1675) was one of the books in Leonora's library in *Spectator* No. 37.

have different Notions of the same Parts of Duration, according as their Ideas, which we suppose are equally distinct in each of them, follow one another in a greater or less Degree of Rapidity.

There is a famous Passage in the *Alcoran,* which looks as if *Mahomet* had been possessed of the Notion we are now speaking of.[6] It is there said, That the Angel *Gabriel* took *Mahomet* out of his Bed one Morning to give him a Sight of all things in the seven Heavens, in Paradise, and in Hell, which the Prophet took a distinct View of; and after having held ninety thousand Conferences with God, was brought back again to his Bed. All this, says the *Alcoran,* was transacted in so small a Space of Time, that *Mahomet,* at his Return, found his Bed still warm, and took up an Earthen Pitcher (which was thrown down at the very Instant that the Angel *Gabriel* carried him away) before the Water was all spilt.

There is a very pretty Story in the *Turkish* Tales which relates to this Passage of that famous Impostor,[7] and bears some Affinity to the Subject we are now upon. A Sultan of *Aegypt,* who was an Infidel, used to laugh at this Circumstance in *Mahomet*'s Life, as what was altogether impossible and absurd: But conversing one Day with a great Doctor in the Law, who had the Gift of working Miracles, the Doctor told him, he would quickly convince him of the Truth of this Passage in the History of *Mahomet,* if he would consent to do what he should desire of him. Upon this the Sultan was directed to place himself by an huge Tub of Water, which he did accordingly; and as he stood by the Tub amidst a Circle of his great Men, the holy Man bid him plunge his Head into the Water, and draw it up again: The King accordingly thrust his Head into the Water, and at the same time found himself at the Foot of a Mountain on a Sea-shore. The King immediately began to rage against his Doctor for this Piece of Treachery and Witchcraft; but at length, knowing it was in vain to be angry, he set himself to think on proper Methods for getting a Livelihood in this strange

[6] Though the journey of Mahomet to Jerusalem appears in the *Koran* (Chapter 17), The Spectator's story is taken from "The History of Chec Chahabeddin," which was one of the *Turkish Tales* published by Jacob Tonson in 1708.

[7] I.e., Mahomet.

Country: Accordingly he applied himself to some People whom he saw at work in a neighbouring Wood; these People conducted him to a Town that stood at a little Distance from the Wood, where after some Adventures he married a Woman of great Beauty and Fortune. He lived with this Woman so long till he had by her seven Sons and seven Daughters: He was afterwards reduced to great Want, and forced to think of plying in the Streets as a Porter for his Livelyhood. One Day as he was walking alone by the Sea-Side, being seized with many melancholy Reflections upon his former and his present State of Life, which had raised a Fit of Devotion in him, he threw off his Cloaths with a Design to wash himself, according to the Custom of the *Mahometans,* before he said his Prayers.

After his first Plunge into the Sea, he no sooner raised his Head above the Water, but he found himself standing by the Side of the Tub, with the great Men of his Court about him, and the holy Man at his Side: He immediately upbraided his Teacher for having sent him on such a Course of Adventures, and betray'd him into so long a State of Misery and Servitude; but was wonderfully surprized when he heard that the State he talked of was only a Dream and Delusion; that he had not stirred from the Place where he then stood; and that he had only dipped his Head into the Water, and immediately taken it out again.

The *Mahometan* Doctor took this Occasion of instructing the Sultan, that nothing was impossible with God; and that *He,* with whom a Thousand Years are but as one Day,[8] can if he pleases make a single Day, nay a single Moment, appear to any of his Creatures as a thousand Years.

I shall leave my Reader to compare these Eastern Fables with the Notions of those two great Philosophers whom I have quoted in this Paper; and shall only, by way of Application, desire him to consider how we may extend Life beyond its natural Dimensions, by applying ourselves diligently to the Pursuits of Knowledge.

The Hours of a wise Man are lengthened by his Ideas, as those of a Fool are by his Passions: The Time of the one is long, because

8 Psalms 90:4

he does not know what to do with it; so is that of the other, because he distinguishes every Moment of it with useful or amusing Thought; or in other Words, because the one is always wishing it away, and the other always enjoying it.

How different is the View of past Life, in the Man who is grown old in Knowledge and Wisdom, from that of him who is grown old in Ignorance and Folly? The latter is like the Owner of a barren Country, that fills his Eye with the Prospect of naked Hills and Plains which produce nothing either profitable or ornamental; the other beholds a beautiful and spacious Landskip, divided into delightful Gardens, green Meadows, fruitful Fields, and can scarce cast his Eye on a single Spot of his Possessions, that is not covered with some beautiful Plant or Flower.   L

The Spectator, No. 99

Saturday, June 23.

[Addison]

——*Turpi secernis Honestum.* Hor.[1]

The Club, of which I have often declar'd my self a Member, were last Night engaged in a Discourse upon that which passes for the chief Point of Honour among Men and Women; and started a great many Hints upon the Subject which I thought were entirely new. I shall therefore methodize the several Reflections that arose upon this Occasion, and present my Reader with them for the Speculation of this Day; after having premised, that if there is any thing in this Paper which seems to differ with any Passage of last *Thursday*'s, the Reader will consider this as the Sentiments of the Club, and the other as my own private Thoughts, or rather those of *Pharamond*.[2]

The great Point of Honour in Men is Courage, and in Women Chastity. If a Man loses his Honour in one Rencounter, it is not impossible for him to regain it in another; a Slip in a Woman's Honour is irrecoverable. I can give no Reason for fixing the Point of Honour to these two Qualities; unless it be that each Sex sets the greatest Value on the Qualification which renders them the most amiable in the Eyes of the contrary Sex. Had Men chosen for themselves, without Regard to the Opinions of the fair Sex, I should believe the Choice would have fallen on Wisdom or Vir-

1 Horace *Satires* 1. 6. 63: "You who know good from bad."

2 In *Spectator* No. 97, Steele published an edict against duels issued by Pharamond, the legendary king of the Franks, said to have ruled from 418 to 428. There are no notable differences between the sentiments of the two papers.

tue; or had Women determined their own Point of Honour, it is probable that Wit or Good-Nature would have carried it against Chastity.

Nothing recommends a Man more to the female Sex than Courage; whether it be that they are pleased to see one who is a Terror to others fall like a Slave at their Feet,[3] or that this Quality supplies their own principal Defect, in guarding them from Insults and avenging their Quarrels, or that Courage is a natural Indication of a strong and sprightly Constitution. On the other Side, nothing makes a Woman more esteemed by the opposite Sex than Chastity; whether it be that we always prize those most who are hardest to come at, or that nothing besides Chastity, with its collateral Attendants, Truth, Fidelity, and Constancy, gives the Man a Property in the Person he loves, and consequently endears her to him above all things.

I am very much pleased with a Passage in the Inscription on a Monument erected in *Westminster* Abby to the late Duke and Dutchess of *Newcastle*,[4] "Her Name was *Margaret Lucas,* youngest Sister to the Lord *Lucas* of *Colchester; a noble Family, for all the Brothers were valiant, and all the Sisters virtuous.*"

In Books of Chivalry, where the Point of Honour is strained to Madness, the whole Story runs on Chastity and Courage. The Damsel is mounted on a white Palfrey, as an Emblem of her Innocence; and, to avoid Scandal, must have a Dwarf for her Page. She is not to think of a Man, till some Misfortune has brought a Knight-Errant to her Relief. The Knight falls in Love, and did not Gratitude restrain her from murdering her Deliverer,[5] would die at her Feet by her Disdain. However, he must waste many Years in the Desart, before her Virgin Heart can think of a Surrender. The Knight goes off, attacks every thing he meets that is bigger and stronger than himself; seeks all Opportunities of being knock'd on the Head; and after seven Year's Rambling returns to his Mistress, whose Chastity has been attacked in the

3 See *Spectator* No. 40. Addison used this idea to explain the popularity of ranting tragedy.

4 William Cavendish, Duke of Newcastle, died in 1677; his wife, in 1680.

5 I.e., killing him through indifference.

mean Time by Giants and Tyrants, and undergone as many Trials as her Lover's Valour.

In *Spain*, where there are still great Remains of this romantick Humour, it is a transporting Favour for a Lady to cast an accidental Glance on her Lover from a Window, tho' it be two or three Stories high; as it is usual for the Lover to assert his Passion for his Mistress, in single Combat with a mad Bull.

The great Violation of the Point of Honour from Man to Man, is giving the Lie.[6] One may tell another he whores, drinks, blasphemes, and it may pass unresented; but to say he lies, tho' but in jest, is an Affront that nothing but Blood can expiate. The Reason perhaps may be, because no other Vice implies a Want of Courage so much as the making of a Lie; and therefore telling a Man he lies, is touching him in the most sensible Part of Honour, and indirectly calling him a Coward. I cannot omit under this Head what *Herodotus*[7] tells us of the ancient *Persians,* That from the Age of five Years to twenty they instruct their Sons only in three things, to manage the Horse, to make use of the Bow, and to speak Truth.

The placing the Point of Honour in this false kind of Courage,[8] has given Occasion to the very Refuse of Mankind, who have neither Virtue nor common Sense, to set up for Men of Honour. An *English* Peer,[9] who has not been long dead, used to tell a pleasant Story of a *French* Gentleman that visited him early one Morning at *Paris,* and after great Professions of Respect, let him know that he had it in his Power to oblige him; which, in short, amounted to this, that he believed he could tell his Lordship the Person's Name who justled him as he came out from the Opera; but before he would proceed, he begged his Lordship that he

---

[6] See *Tatler* No. 111. n. 10. In *Tatler* No. 256, Bickerstaff's Court of Honour treated a sensitive case: Richard Newman was indicted for having used the words "Perhaps it may be so" in a dispute with Major Punto. The Major contended that the word "perhaps" was questioning his veracity and that "it was an indirect Manner of giving him the Lie."

[7] Herodotus *History* 1. 136.

[8] I.e., the courage to give or defend the lie.

[9] This may have been William Cavendish (d. 1707), the first Duke of Devonshire. (This is not the same William Cavendish mentioned earlier in the essay.)

would not deny him the Honour of making him his Second. The *English* Lord, to avoid being drawn into a very foolish Affair, told him that he was under Engagements for his two next Duels to a Couple of particular Friends. Upon which the Gentleman immediately withdrew; hoping his Lordship would not take it ill, if he medled no farther in an Affair from whence he himself was to receive no Advantage.

The beating down this false Notion of Honour, in so vain and lively a People as those of *France,* is deservedly looked upon as one of the most glorious Parts of their present King's Reign.[10] It is Pity but[11] the Punishment of these mischievous Notions should have in it some particular Circumstances of Shame and Infamy; that those who are Slaves to them may see, that instead of advancing their Reputations they lead them to Ignominy and Dishonour.

Death is not sufficient to deter Men, who make it their Glory to despise it; but if every one that fought a Duel were to stand in the Pillory, it would quickly lessen the Number of these imaginary Men of Honour, and put an End to so absurd a Practice.

When Honour is a Support to virtuous Principles, and runs parallel with the Laws of God and our Country, it cannot be too much cherished and encouraged: But when the Dictates of Honour are contrary to those of Religion and Equity, they are the greatest Depravations of human Nature, by giving wrong Ambitions and false Ideas of what is good and laudable; and should therefore be exploded by all Governments, and driven out as the Bane and Plague of human Society.   L

[10] Louis XIV issued a number of edicts against the duel.
[11] I.e., it is to be wished that.

The Spectator, No. 101

Tuesday, June 26.

[Addison]

Romulus, & Liber pater, & cum Castore Pollux,
Post ingentia facta, Deorum in templa recepti;
Dum terras hominumque colunt genus, aspera bella
Componunt, agros assignant, oppida condunt;
Ploravere suis non respondere favorem
Speratum meritis:———Hor.[1]

Censure, says a late ingenious Author, *is the Tax a Man pays to the Publick for being Eminent.*[2] It is a Folly for an eminent Man to think of escaping it, and a Weakness to be affected with it. All the illustrious Persons of Antiquity, and indeed of every Age in the World, have passed through this fiery Persecution. There is no Defence against Reproach, but Obscurity; it is a kind of Concomitant to Greatness, as Satyrs and Invectives were an essential Part of a *Roman* Triumph.[3]

If Men of Eminence are exposed to Censure on one hand, they are as much liable to Flattery on the other. If they receive Reproaches which are not due to them, they likewise receive Praises

---

[1] Horace *Epistles* 2. 1. 5–10: "Romulus, father Liber, Pollux and Castor, who, after performing mighty deeds, were received into the temples of the gods, so long as they cared for the earth and the race of men, settling fierce wars, assigning lands, and founding towns, lamented that the good will they hoped for did not answer to their merits."

[2] From Jonathan Swift's *Thoughts on Various Subjects, Moral and Diverting* (1706).

[3] A ceremonial honoring a general for a decisive victory over a foreign enemy.

which they do not deserve. In a word, the Man in a high Post is never regarded with an indifferent Eye, but always considered as a Friend or an Enemy. For this Reason Persons in great Stations have seldom their true Characters drawn, till several Years after their Deaths. Their personal Friendships and Enmities must cease, and the Parties[4] they were engaged in be at an end, before their Faults or their Virtues can have Justice done them. When Writers have the least Opportunity of knowing the Truth, they are in the best Disposition to tell it.

It is therefore the Privilege of Posterity to adjust the Characters of Illustrious Persons, and to set matters right between those Antagonists who by their Rivalry for Greatness divided a whole Age into Factions. We can now allow *Caesar* to be a great Man, without derogating from *Pompey;* and celebrate the Virtues of *Cato,* without detracting from those of *Caesar.* Every one that has been long dead has a due Proportion of Praise allotted him, in which whilst he lived his Friends were too profuse and his Enemies too sparing.

According to Sir *Isaac Newton*'s Calculations, the last Comet that made its Appearance in 1680, imbibed so much Heat by its Approaches to the Sun, that it would have been two thousand times hotter than red hot Iron, had it been a Globe of that Metal; and that supposing it as big as the Earth, and at the same Distance from the Sun, it would be fifty thousand Years in cooling, before it recover'd its natural Temper.[5] In the like manner, if an *English* Man considers the great Ferment into which our Political World is thrown at present, and how intensely it is heated in all its Parts, he cannot suppose that will cool again in less than three hundred Years.[6] In such a Tract of Time it is possible that the Heats of the present Age may be extinguished, and our several Classes of great Men represented under their proper Characters. Some eminent

[4] I.e., the political parties.

[5] Isaac Newton's *Principia* (1687) argued that the nuclei of comets must consist of solid matter. The particular comet was named after Newton's friend Edmund Halley (1656–1742), who calculated that the celestial body would appear every 76 years. It will reappear in 1986.

[6] See *Tatler* No. 240, n. 12.

Historian may then probably arise that will not write *recentibus odiis*, (as *Tacitus*[7] expresses it,) with the Passions and Prejudices of a Contemporary Author, but make an impartial Distribution of Fame among the Great Men of the present Age.

I cannot forbear entertaining my self very often with the Idea of such an imaginary Historian describing the Reign of *Anne* the First, and introducing it with a Preface to his Reader, that he is now entring upon the most shining Part of the *English* Story. The great Rivals in Fame will be then distinguished according to their respective Merits, and shine in their proper Points of Light. Such an one (says the Historian) though variously represented by the Writers of his own Age, appears to have been a Man of more than ordinary Abilities, great Application, and uncommon Integrity: Nor was such an one (tho' of an opposite Party and Interest) inferior to him in any of these Respects. The several Antagonists who now endeavour to depreciate one another, and are celebrated or traduced by different Parties, will then have the same Body of Admirers, and appear Illustrious in the Opinion of the whole *British* Nation. The Deserving Man, who can now recommend himself to the Esteem of but half his Countrymen, will then receive the Approbations and Applauses of a whole Age.

Among the several Persons that flourish in this Glorious Reign, there is no Question but such a future Historian as the Person of whom I am speaking, will make mention of the Men of Genius and Learning, who have now any Figure in the *British* Nation. For my own part, I often flatter my self with the honourable Mention which will then be made of me; and have drawn up a Paragraph in my own Imagination, that I fancy will not be altogether unlike what will be found in some Page or other of this Imaginary Historian.

It was under this Reign, says he, that the Spectator Published those little Diurnal Essays which are still extant. We know very little of the Name or Person of this Author, except only that he was a Man of a very short Face, extreamly addicted to Silence, and so great a Lover of Knowledge that he made a Voyage to *Grand*

---

[7] Tacitus (55?–117? A.D.), Roman politician and historian. The quotation is from *Annals* 1. 1.

Cairo for no other Reason but to take the Measure of a Pyramid. His chief Friend was one Sir Roger de Coverly, a whimsical Country Knight, and a *Templar* whose Name he has not transmitted to us. He lived as a Lodger at the House of a Widow-Woman, and was a great Humourist[8] in all parts of his Life. This is all we can affirm with any Certainty of his Person and Character. As for his Speculations, notwithstanding the several obsolete Words and obscure Phrases of the Age in which he liv'd, we still understand enough of them to see the Diversions and Characters of the *English* Nation in his time: Not but that we are to make Allowance for the Mirth and Humour of the Author, who has doubtless strained many Representations of things beyond the Truth. For if we interpret his Words in their litteral Meaning, we must suppose that Women of the First Quality used to pass away whole Mornings at a Puppet-Show: That they attested their Principles by their *Patches:* That an Audience would sit out an Evening to hear a Dramatical Performance written in a Language which they did not understand: That Chairs and Flower-Pots were introduced as Actors upon the *British* Stage: That a Promiscuous Assembly of Men and Women were allowed to meet at Midnight in Masques within the Verge of the Court; with many Improbabilities of the like Nature.[9] We must therefore, in these and the like Cases, suppose that these remote Hints and Allusions aimed at some certain Follies which were then in Vogue, and which at present we have not any Notion of. We may guess by several Passages in the *Speculations*,[10] that there were Writers who endeavoured to detract from the Works of this Author; but as nothing of this nature is come down to us, we cannot guess at any Objections that could be made to his Paper. If we consider his Style with that Indulgence which we must shew to old *English* Writers, or if we look into the Variety of his Subjects, with those several Critical Dissertations, Moral Reflections,

[8] See *Spectator* No. 2, n. 20.

[9] See *Spectator* No. 81 for the reference to puppet shows and party patches, and No. 18, for the criticism of opera. Essay No. 22 carried letters from actors who had performed as a chair and a flower-pot; No. 14 discussed masquerades.

[10] *Spectators* No. 19 and No. 79 by Steele are probably referred to here.

The following part of the Paragraph is so much to my Advantage, and beyond any thing I can pretend to, that I hope my Reader will excuse me for not inserting it.   L

The Spectator, No. 105

Saturday, June 30.

[Addison]

—— ——*Id arbitror*
Adprime in vita esse utile, ne quid nimis. Ter. Andr.[1]

My Friend Will. Honeycomb, values himself very much upon what he calls the Knowledge of Mankind, which has cost him many Disasters in his Youth; for Will. reckons every Misfortune that he has met with among the Women, and every Rencounter among the Men, as Parts of his Education; and fancies he should never have been the Man he is, had not he broke Windows,[2] knocked down Constables, disturbed honest People with his Midnight Serenades, and beat up a lewd Woman's Quarters, when he was a young Fellow. The engaging in Adventures of this nature, Will. calls the studying of Mankind; and terms this Knowledge of the Town, the Knowledge of the World. Will. ingenuously confesses, that for half his Life his Head ached every Morning with reading of Men over-night; and at present comforts himself under certain Pains which he endures from time to time, that without them he could not have been acquainted with the Gallantries[3] of the Age. This Will. looks upon as the Learning of a Gentleman, and regards all other kinds of Science as the Accomplishments of one whom he calls a Scholar, a Bookish Man, or a Philosopher.

1 Terence *Andria* 60–61 (altered): "This I judge to be the most useful rule in life: nothing in excess."

2 Window-breaking was a common activity of Restoration rakes. In *Tatler* No. 77 by Steele, when Bickerstaff's parlor windows were shattered by a hurled half-pence, he called it "a generous Piece of Wit."

3 Social adventures.

For these Reasons Will. shines in mixed Company, where he has the Discretion not to go out of his Depth, and has often a certain way of making his real Ignorance appear a seeming one. Our Club however has frequently caught him tripping, at which times they never spare him. For as Will. often insults us with the Knowledge of the Town, we sometimes take our Revenge upon him by our Knowledge of Books.

He was last Week producing two or three Letters which he writ in his Youth to a Coquet Lady. The Raillery of them was natural, and well enough for a meer Man of the Town; but, very unluckily, several of the Words were wrong spelt. Will. laught this off at first as well as he could, but finding himself pushed on all sides, and especially by the *Templer,*[4] he told us, with a little Passion, that he never liked Pedantry in Spelling, and that he spelt like a Gentleman, and not like a Scholar: Upon this Will. had Recourse to his old Topick of shewing the narrow Spiritedness, the Pride, and Ignorance of Pedants; which he carried so far, that upon my retiring to my Lodgings, I could not forbear throwing together such Reflections as occurred to me upon that Subject.

A Man who has been brought up among Books, and is able to talk of nothing else, is a very indifferent Companion, and what we call a Pedant. But, methinks, we should enlarge the Title, and give it every one that does not know how to think out of his Profession, and particular way of Life.

What is a greater Pedant than a meer Man of the Town? Barr him the Play-houses, a Catalogue of the reigning Beauties, and an Account of a few fashionable Distempers[5] that have befallen him, and you strike him Dumb. How many a pretty Gentleman's Knowledge lies all within the Verge of the Court? He will tell you the Names of the Principal Favourites,[6] repeat the shrewd Sayings of a Man of Quality, whisper an Intreague that is not yet blown upon by common Fame;[7] or, if the Sphere of his Observations is a little larger than ordinary, will perhaps enter into all the Inci-

---

[4] The Templar, as literary critic, would be the most concerned about scholarly accuracy.

[5] Presumably venereal.

[6] Men or women who enjoy the particular favor of the monarch.

[7] A piece of gossip not yet current.

dents, Turns, and Revolutions in a Game of Ombre.[8] When he has gone thus far he has shown you the whole Circle of his Accomplishments, his Parts are drained, and he is disabled from any further Conversation. What are these but rank Pedants? and yet these are the Men who value themselves most on their Exemption from the Pedantry of Colleges.

I might here mention the Military Pedant, who always talks in a Camp, and is storming Towns, making Lodgments, and fighting Battels from one end of the Year to the other. Every thing he speaks smells of Gunpowder; if you take away his Artillery from him, he has not a Word to say for himself. I might likewise mention the Law Pedant, that is perpetually putting Cases, repeating the Transactions of *Westminster-Hall,* wrangling with you upon the most indifferent Circumstances of Life, and not to be convinced of the Distance of a Place, or of the most trivial Point in Conversation, but by dint of Argument. The State-Pedant is wrapt up in News, and lost in Politicks. If you mention either of the Kings of *Spain* or *Poland,* he talks very notably;[9] but if you go out of the *Gazette,*[10] you drop him. In short, a meer Courtier, a meer Soldier, a meer Scholar, a meer any thing, is an insipid Pedantick Character, and equally ridiculous.

Of all the Species of Pedants, which I have mentioned, the Book-Pedant is much the most supportable; he has at least an exercised Understanding, and a Head which is full though confused, so that a Man who converses with him may often receive from him hints of things that are worth knowing, and what he may possibly turn to his own Advantage, tho' they are of little use to the Owner. The worst kind of Pedants among Learned Men, are such as are naturally endued with a very small Share of com-

8 A fashionable card-game. To appreciate the reference—as well as Pope's use of the game in *Rape of the Lock*—one must recognize that ombre is a notably uncomplicated game.

9 See *Tatler* No. 155, n. 5, which explains the Upholsterer's concern about "what passed in Poland." Philip V (1683–1746) had been king of Spain since 1700, and the central issue of the continuing war was whether he should remain so.

10 The *London Gazette* was the official publication for the Whig ministry. Steele wrote for the journal from 1707 to October 1710.

mon Sense, and have read a great number of Books without Taste or Distinction.

The Truth of it is, Learning, like Travelling, and all other Methods of Improvement, as it finishes good Sense, so it makes a silly Man ten thousand times more insufferable, by supplying variety of Matter to his Impertinence, and giving him an Opportunity of abounding in Absurdities.

Shallow Pedants cry up one another much more than Men of solid and useful Learning. To read the Titles they give an Editor, or Collator of a Manuscript, you would take him for the Glory of the Common-Wealth of Letters, and the Wonder of his Age; when perhaps upon Examination you find that he has only Rectify'd a *Greek* Particle, or laid out a whole Sentence in proper Commas.[11]

They are obliged indeed to be thus lavish of their Praises, that they may keep one another in Countenance; and it is no wonder if a great deal of Knowledge, which is not capable of making a Man Wise, has a natural Tendency to make him Vain and Arrogant.   L

[11] See Addison's description of Tom Folio and his like in *Tatler* No. 158.

The Spectator, No. 106

Monday, July 2.

[A d d i s o n]

⁂

————*Hinc tibi Copia*
Manabit ad plenum, benigno
Ruris honorum opulenta cornu. Hor.[1]

Having often received an Invitation from my Friend Sir Roger de Coverly to pass away a Month with him in the Country, I last Week accompanied him thither, and am settled with him for some Time at his Country-house, where I intend to form several of my ensuing Speculations.[2] Sir Roger, who is very well acquainted with my Humour, lets me rise and go to Bed when I please, dine at his own Table or in my Chamber as I think fit, sit still and say nothing without bidding me be merry. When the Gentlemen of the Country come to see him, he only shews me at a Distance: As I have been walking in his Fields I have observed them stealing a Sight of me over an Hedge, and have heard the Knight desiring them not to let me see them, for that I hated to be stared at.

I am the more at Ease in Sir Roger's Family, because it consists of sober and staid Persons; for as the Knight is the best Master in the World, he seldom changes his Servants; and as he is beloved by all about him, his Servants never care for leaving him: By this Means his Domesticks are all in Years, and grown old with their Master. You would take his Valet de Chambre for his Brother, his Butler is grey-headed, his Groom is one of the gravest Men that I

[1] Horace *Odes* 1. 17. 14–16: "Here the rich wealth of the glories of the field will, from bounteous horn, flow abundantly for you."

[2] The Spectator's visit extended through the month of July, as was reported in Essays No. 106–132. All but seven are by Addison.

have ever seen, and his Coachman has the Looks of a Privy-Counsellor.[3] You see the Goodness of the Master even in the old Housedog, and in a grey Pad[4] that is kept in the Stable with great Care and Tenderness out of Regard to his past Services, tho' he has been useless for several Years.

I could not but observe with a great deal of Pleasure the Joy that appeared in the Countenances of these ancient Domesticks upon my Friend's Arrival at his Country-Seat. Some of them could not refrain from Tears at the Sight of their old Master; every one of them press'd forward to do something for him, and seemed discouraged if they were not employed. At the same Time the good old Knight, with a Mixture of the Father and the Master of the Family, tempered the Enquiries after his own Affairs with several kind Questions relating to themselves. This Humanity and Goodnature engages every Body to him, so that when he is pleasant upon any of them, all his Family are in good Humour, and none so much as the Person whom he diverts himself with: On the Contrary, if he coughs, or betrays any Infirmity of old Age, it is easy for a Stander-by to observe a secret Concern in the Looks of all his Servants.

My worthy Friend has put me under the particular Care of his Butler, who is a very prudent Man, and, as well as the rest of his Fellow-Servants, wonderfully desirous of pleasing me, because they have often heard their Master talk of me as of his particular Friend.

My chief Companion, when Sir Roger is diverting himself in the Woods or the Fields, is a very venerable Man, who is ever with Sir Roger, and has lived at his House in the Nature[5] of a Chaplain above thirty Years. This Gentleman is a Person of good Sense and some Learning, of a very regular Life and obliging Conversation: He heartily loves Sir Roger, and knows that he is very much in the old Knight's Esteem; so that he lives in the Family rather as a Relation than a Dependant.

---

[3] A groom is one having charge of a gentleman's horses. A privy-counsellor is a member of the sovereign's highest council, therefore presumably a person of wisdom and discretion.

[4] A horse ridden with a pad, or stuffed saddle; an easy-paced riding horse.

[5] Capacity.

I have observed in several of my Papers, that my Friend Sir
Roger, amidst all his good Qualities, is something of an Humourist;[6] and that his Virtues, as well as Imperfections, are as it were
tinged by a certain Extravagance, which makes them particularly
his, and distinguishes them from those of other Men. This Cast of
Mind, as it is generally very innocent in it self, so it renders his
Conversation highly agreeable, and more delightful than the same
Degree of Sense and Virtue would appear in their common and
ordinary Colours. As I was walking with him last Night, he ask'd
me how I liked the good Man whom I have just now mentioned?
and without staying for my Answer, told me, That he was afraid
of being insulted with Latin and Greek at his own Table; for
which Reason, he desired a particular Friend of his at the University to find him out a Clergyman rather of plain Sense than
much Learning, of a good Aspect, a clear Voice, a sociable Temper, and, if possible, a Man that understood a little of Back-Gam-
mon.[7] My Friend, says Sir Roger, found me out this Gentleman,
who, besides the Endowments required of him, is, they tell me, a
good Scholar though he does not shew it. I have given him the
Parsonage of the Parish; and because I know his Value, have settled upon him a good Annuity for Life. If he out-lives me, he
shall find that he was higher in my Esteem than perhaps he thinks
he is. He has now been with me thirty Years; and though he does
not know I have taken Notice of it, has never in all that Time
asked any thing of me for himself, tho' he is every Day sollicting
me for something in Behalf of one or other of my Tenants his
Parishioners. There has not been a Law-Suit in the Parish since
he has lived among them: If any Dispute arises, they apply themselves to him for the Decision; if they do not acquiesce in his Judgment, which I think never happened above once, or twice at most,
they appeal to me. At his first settling with me, I made him a
Present of all the good Sermons which have been printed in *English,* and only begged of him that every *Sunday* he would pronounce one of them in the Pulpit. Accordingly, he has digested[8]

---

[6] I.e., one subject to humours or fancies, a capricious individual.

[7] A game played on a double board, in which the throwing of dice deter-
mines the moves of the pieces.

[8] Arranged or classified.

them into such a Series, that they follow one another naturally, and make a continued System of practical Divinity.

As Sir Roger was going on in his Story, the Gentleman we were talking of came up to us; and upon the Knight's asking him who preached to Morrow (for it was *Saturday* Night) told us, the Bishop of St. *Asaph* in the Morning, and Doctor *South* in the Afternoon.[9] He then shewed us his List of Preachers for the whole Year, where I saw with a great deal of Pleasure Archbishop *Tillotson;* Bishop *Saunderson,* Doctor *Barrow,* Doctor *Calamy,*[10] with several living Authors who have published Discourses of Practical Divinity. I no sooner saw this venerable Man in the Pulpit, but I very much approved of my Friend's insisting upon the Qualifications of a good Aspect and a clear Voice; for I was so charmed with the Gracefulness of his Figure and Delivery, as well as with the Discourses he pronounced, that I think I never passed any Time more to my Satisfaction. A Sermon repeated after this Manner, is like the Composition of a Poet in the Mouth of a graceful Actor.

I could heartily wish that more of our Country-Clergy would follow this Example; and instead of wasting their Spirits in laborious Compositions of their own, would endeavour after a handsome Elocution, and all those other Talents that are proper to enforce what has been penned by greater Masters. This would not only be more easy to themselves, but more edifying to the People.[11]   L

[9] The Bishop of St. Asaph was probably William Fleetwood (1656–1723), a prominent Whig figure. Doctor Robert South (1634–1716) was a popular preacher during the reign of Charles II. Doctor South was praised in *Tatler* No. 61 and quoted in *Tatlers* No. 205 and 211.

[10] John Tillotson (1630–1694) was Archbishop of Canterbury from 1691; Steele quoted from one of his sermons in *Spectator* No. 103. Robert Saunderson (1587–1663) was chaplain to Charles I and, thereafter, Bishop of Lincoln; his strong Tory views would please Sir Roger. Doctor Isaac Barrow (1630–1677) was a distinguished mathematician and preacher. Doctor Edward Calamy (1600–1666) was a leading Presbyterian.

[11] The practice of reading sermons was, in fact, fairly common in eighteenth-century country churches.

The Spectator, No. 108

Wednesday, July 4.

[Addison]

Gratis anhelans, multa agendo nihil agens. Phaed.[1]

As I was Yesterday Morning walking with Sir Roger before his House, a Country-Fellow brought him a huge Fish, which, he told him, Mr. *William Wimble* had caught that very Morning; and that he presented it, with his Service,[2] to him, and intended to come and dine with him. At the same Time he delivered a Letter, which my Friend read to me assoon as the Messenger left him.

"*Sir* Roger,
I Desire you to accept of a Jack,[3] which is the best I have caught this Season. I intend to come and stay with you a Week, and see how the Perch bite in the *Black River*.[4] I observed, with some Concern, the last Time I saw you upon the Bowling-Green,[5] that your Whip wanted a Lash to it: I will bring half a Dozen with me that I twisted last Week, which I hope will serve you all the Time you are in the Country. I have not been out of the Saddle for six Days last past, having been at *Eaton* with Sir *John*'s eldest Son. He takes to his Learning hugely.[6]

> I am,
> Sir,
> *Your humble Servant,*
> Will. Wimble."[7]

[1] Phaedrus *Fables* 2. 5. 3: "Puffing hard and, in doing much, doing nothing."
[2] With his compliments, his good will.
[3] A pike.
[4] Presumably Blackwater River in Essex.
[5] A field on which the popular game of bowls was played.
[6] I.e., with a keen appetite.
[7] Will Wimble, who may have been modeled after Thomas Morecraft (d.

This extraordinary Letter, and Message that accompanied it, made me very curious to know the Character and Quality of the Gentleman who sent them; which I found to be as follows; *Will. Wimble* is younger Brother to a Baronet,[8] and descended of the ancient Family of the *Wimbles*. He is now between Forty and Fifty; but being bred to no Business and born to no Estate, he generally lives with his elder Brother as Superintendant of his Game. He hunts a Pack of Dogs better than any Man in the Country, and is very famous for finding out a Hare. He is extremely well versed in all the little Handicrafts of an idle Man: He makes a *May*-fly to a Miracle; and furnishes the whole Country with Angle-Rods.[9] As he is a good-natur'd officious Fellow, and very much esteemed upon Account of his Family, he is a welcome Guest at every House, and keeps up a good Correspondence among all the Gentlemen about him. He carries a Tulip-Root[10] in his Pocket from one to another, or exchanges a Puppy between a couple of Friends that live perhaps in the opposite Sides of the County. *Will.* is a particular Favourite of all the young Heirs, whom he frequently obliges with a Net that he has weaved, or a Setting-dog that he has *made*[11] himself: He now and then presents a Pair of Garters of his own knitting to their Mothers or Sisters; and raises a great deal of Mirth among them, by enquiring as often as he meets them *how they wear?* These Gentleman-like Manufactures and obliging little Humours, make *Will.* the Darling of the Country.

1741), recalls Mr. Thomas Gules of *Tatler* No. 256, a younger brother who "had chosen rather to starve like a Man of Honour than do anything beneath his Quality."

[8] Traditionally, the oldest son inherited the estate of his father, and younger sons either went into the professions (law, medicine, religion) or were dependent on the generosity of their relatives. The letter referred to Sir John's eldest son, and the following paragraph notes that Will is a favorite of "all the young Heirs," i.e., eldest sons.

[9] I.e., he makes and distributes fishing lures and poles.

[10] With the introduction of Dutch fashions by King William, there arose a craze for growing tulips, which had not yet abated. *Tatler* No. 218 by Addison comments on the fashion.

[11] Trained.

Sir Roger was proceeding in the Character of him, when we saw him make up to us,[12] with two or three Hazle-twigs in his Hand that he had cut in Sir Roger's Woods, as he came through them, in his Way to the House. I was very much pleased to observe on one Side the hearty and sincere Welcome with which Sir Roger received him, and on the other the secret Joy which his Guest discovered at Sight of the good old Knight. After the first Salutes were over, *Will.* desired Sir Roger to lend him one of his Servants to carry a Set of Shuttlecocks[13] he had with him in a little Box to a Lady that liv'd about a Mile off, to whom it seems he had promised such a Present for above this half Year. Sir Roger's Back was no sooner turn'd, but honest *Will.* began to tell me of a large Cock-Pheasant that he had sprung[14] in one of the neighbouring Woods, with two or three other Adventures of the same Nature. Odd and uncommon Characters are the Game that I look for,[15] and most delight in; for which Reason I was as much pleased with the Novelty of the Person that talked to me, as he could be for his Life[16] with the springing of a Pheasant, and therefore listned to him with more than ordinary Attention.

In the Midst of his Discourse the Bell rung to Dinner, where the Gentleman I have been speaking of had the Pleasure of seeing the huge Jack, he had caught, served up for the first Dish in a most sumptuous Manner. Upon our sitting down to it he gave us a long Account how he had hooked it, played with it, foiled it, and at length drew it out upon the Bank, with several other Particulars that lasted all the first Course. A Dish of Wild-fowl that came afterwards furnished Conversation for the rest of the Dinner, which concluded with a late Invention of *Will*'s for improving the Quail Pipe.[17]

Upon withdrawing into my Room after Dinner, I was secretly

12 I.e., Sir Roger was describing him when we saw him approach.

13 Pieces of cork, stuck round with feathers, struck back and forth in battledore or badminton.

14 Flushed out, caused to fly from its place of concealment.

15 Addison repeated this hunting metaphor in *Spectator* No. 131: "My greatest Difficulty in the Country is to find Sport, and in Town to chuse it."

16 As if he were a prisoner, pleading in court for his life.

17 A pipe or reed used for decoying quail.

touched with Compassion towards the honest Gentleman that had dined with us; and could not but consider with a great deal of Concern, how so good an Heart and such busy Hands were wholly employed in Trifles; that so much Humanity should be so little beneficial to others, and so much Industry so little advantageous to himself. The same Temper of Mind and Application to Affairs might have recommended him to the publick Esteem, and have raised his Fortune in another Station of Life. What Good to his Country or himself might not a Trader or Merchant have done with such useful tho' ordinary Qualifications?

Will. Wimble's is the Case of many a younger Brother of a great Family, who had rather see their Children starve like Gentlemen, than thrive in a Trade or Profession that is beneath their Quality. This Humour fills several Parts of *Europe* with Pride and Beggary. It is the Happiness of a trading Nation, like ours, that the younger Sons, tho' uncapable of any liberal Art or Profession,[18] may be placed in such a Way of Life, as may perhaps enable them to vie with the best of their Family: Accordingly we find several Citizens that were launched into the World with narrow Fortunes, rising by an honest Industry to greater Estates than those of their elder Brothers. It is not improbable but *Will.* was formerly tried at Divinity, Law, or Physick; and that finding his Genius[19] did not lie that Way, his Parents gave him up at length to his own Inventions: But certainly, however improper he might have been for Studies of a higher Nature, he was perfectly well turned for the Occupations of Trade and Commerce. As I think this is a Point which cannot be too much inculcated, I shall desire my Reader to compare what I have here written with what I have said in my Twenty first Speculation.[20]   L

---

[18] Referring to the areas cited below: "Divinity, Law, or Physick."

[19] Gifts, capacities.

[20] In *Spectator* No. 21, Addison wrote: "I am sometimes very much troubled, when I reflect upon the three great Professions of Divinity, Law and Physick; how they are each of them over-burdened with Practitioners, and filled with Multitudes of Ingenious Gentlemen that starve one another. . . . A well-regulated Commerce is not, like Law, Physick or Divinity, to be overstocked with Hands; but, on the contrary, flourishes by Multitudes, and gives Employments to all its Professors." This is a notably Whig sentiment.

The Spectator, No. 112

Monday, July 9.

[Addison]

Ά'θανάτους μὲν πρῶτα θεους, νόμῳ ὡς διάκειται, τιμα————Pyth.[1]

I am always very well pleased with a Country *Sunday;* and think, if keeping holy the Seventh Day were only a human[2] Institution, it would be the best Method that could have been thought of for the polishing and civilizing of Mankind. It is certain the Country-People would soon degenerate into a kind of Savages and Barbarians, were there not such frequent Returns of a stated Time,[3] in which the whole Village meet together with their best Faces, and in their cleanliest Habits, to converse with one another upon indifferent Subjects, hear their Duties explained to them, and join together in Adoration of the supreme Being. *Sunday* clears away the Rust of the whole Week, not only as it refreshes in their Minds the Notions of Religion, but as it puts both the Sexes upon appearing in their most agreeable Forms, and exerting all such Qualities as are apt to give them a Figure[4] in the Eye of the Village. A Country-Fellow distinguishes himself as much in the *Church-yard,* as a Citizen does upon the *Change;*[5] the whole Parish-Politicks being generally discuss'd in that Place either after Sermon or before the Bell rings.

My Friend Sir Roger being a good Church-man, has beautified

---

[1] Pythagoras *Carmina Aurea* 1–2: "And first honor the immortal gods, holding it as a law."

[2] I.e., not divine.

[3] A regular succession of Sundays.

[4] A good appearance.

[5] See *Spectator* No. 69.

285

the Inside of his Church with several Texts of his own chusing:[6]
He has likewise given a handsome Pulpit-Cloth, and railed in the
Communion-Table at his own Expence.[7] He has often told me,
that at his coming to his Estate he found his Parishioners very
irregular; and that in order to make them kneel and join in the
Responses, he gave every one of them a Hassock[8] and a Common-
prayer Book; and at the same Time employed an itinerant Sing-
ing-Master, who goes about the Country for that Purpose, to instruct them rightly in the Tunes of the Psalms; upon which they
now very much value themselves, and indeed out-do most of the
Country Churches that I have ever heard.[9]

As Sir Roger is Landlord to the whole Congregation, he keeps
them in very good Order, and will suffer no Body to sleep in it
besides himself; for if by Chance he has been surprized into a short
Nap at Sermon, upon recovering out of it he stands up and looks
about him, and if he sees any Body else nodding, either wakes
them himself, or sends his Servant to them. Several other of the
old Knight's Particularities break out upon these Occasions:
Sometimes he will be lengthening out a Verse in the Singing-
Psalms, half a Minute after the rest of the Congregation have done
with it; sometimes, when he is pleased with the Matter of his Devotion,[10] he pronounces *Amen* three or four times to the same
Prayer; and sometimes stands up when every Body else is upon
their Knees, to count the Congregation, or see if any of his Tenants are missing.

I was Yesterday very much surprized to hear my old Friend, in
the Midst of the Service, calling out to one *John Matthews* to
mind what he was about, and not disturb the Congregation. This
John Matthews it seems is remarkable for being an idle Fellow,
and at that Time was kicking his Heels for his Diversion. This
Authority of the Knight, though exerted in that odd Manner

---

[6] The Ten Commandments and other selections of religious text commonly
decorated the walls of English churches and chapels.

[7] At this time, the communion table was not always in the Sanctuary, therefore not railed in. A mild pun may be intended in this sentence.

[8] A kneeling hassock.

[9] This accolade can refer either to their tone or to their volume.

[10] The sentiments of the prayer.

which accompanies him in all Circumstances of Life, has a very good Effect upon the Parish, who are not polite[11] enough to see any thing ridiculous in his Behaviour; besides that, the general good Sense and Worthiness of his Character, make his Friends observe these little Singularities as Foils[12] that rather set off than blemish his good Qualities.

Assoon as the Sermon is finished, no Body presumes to stir till Sir Roger is gone out of the Church. The Knight walks down from his Seat in the Chancel[13] between a double Row of his Tenants, that stand bowing to him on each Side; and every now and then enquires how such an one's Wife, or Mother, or Son, or Father do whom he does not see at Church; which is understood as a secret Reprimand to the Person that is absent.

The Chaplain has often told me, that upon a Catechizing-day,[14] when Sir Roger has been pleased with a Boy that answers well, he has ordered a Bible to be given him next Day for his Encouragement; and sometimes accompanies it with a Flitch of Bacon[15] to his Mother. Sir Roger has likewise added five Pounds a Year to the Clerk's Place; and that he may encourage the young Fellows to make themselves perfect in the Church-Service, has promised upon the Death of the present Incumbent, who is very old, to bestow it according to Merit.

The fair Understanding between Sir Roger and his Chaplain, and their mutual Concurrence in doing Good, is the more remarkable, because the very next Village is famous for the Differences and Contentions that rise between the Parson and the 'Squire, who live in a perpetual State of War. The Parson is always preaching at the 'Squire, and the 'Squire to be revenged on the Parson never comes to Church. The 'Squire has made all his Tenants Atheists and Tithe-Stealers;[16] while the Parson instructs

11 Refined, polished.

12 A foil is one quality which serves as contrast to another.

13 The part of the church lying east of the nave and including the choir and sanctuary.

14 When children are questioned on their Biblical knowledge.

15 A side of pork, salted and cured.

16 A tithe is the 10 percent of a person's income that is due to the church. Tenants who do not attend services do not pay the tax due from them; hence, they are "Tithe-Stealers."

them every *Sunday* in the Dignity of his Order, and insinuates to them in almost every Sermon, that he is a better Man than his Patron. In short, Matters are come to such an Extremity, that the 'Squire has not said his Prayers either in publick or private this half Year; and that the Parson threatens him, if he does not mend his Manners, to pray for him in the Face of the whole Congregation.

Feuds of this Nature, though too frequent in the Country, are very fatal to the ordinary People; who are so used to be dazled with Riches, that they pay as much Deference to the Understanding of a Man of an Estate, as of a Man of Learning; and are very hardly brought to regard any Truth, how important soever it may be, that is preached to them, when they know there are several Men of five hundred a Year who do not believe it.   L

The Spectator, No. 113

Tuesday, July 10.

[S t e e l e]

————*Haerent infixi Pectore vultus.* Virg.[1]

In my first Description of the Company in which I pass most of my Time,[2] it may be remembered that I mentioned a great Affliction which my Friend Sir Roger had met with in his Youth, which was no less than a Disappointment in Love. It happened this Evening, that we fell into a very pleasing Walk[3] at a Distance from his House: As soon as we came into it, "It is," quoth the good old Man, looking round him with a Smile, "very hard, that any Part òf my Land should be settled upon one who has used me so ill as the perverse Widow did; and yet I am sure I could not see a Sprig of any Bough of this whole Walk of Trees, but I should reflect upon her and her Severity. She has certainly the finest Hand of any Woman in the World. You are to know this was the Place wherein I used to muse upon her; and by that Custom I can never come into it, but the same tender Sentiments revive in my Mind, as if I had actually walked with that beautiful Creature under these Shades. I have been Fool enough to carve her Name on the Bark of several of these Trees; so unhappy is the Condition of Men in Love, to attempt the removing of their Passion by the Methods which serve only to imprint it deeper. She has certainly the finest Hand of any Woman in the World."

Here followed a profound Silence; and I was not displeased to

1 Virgil *Aeneid* 4. 4: "His features remain fixed within her bosom."
2 See *Spectator* No. 2.
3 I.e., we came to a lovely wooded walking-area.

observe my Friend falling so naturally into a Discourse, which I had ever before taken Notice he industriously avoided. After a very long Pause, he entered upon an Account of this great Circumstance in his Life, with an Air which I thought raised my *Idea* of him above what I had ever had before;[4] and gave me the Picture of that chearful Mind of his, before it received that Stroke which has ever since affected his Words and Actions. But he went on as follows.

"I came to[5] my Estate in my Twenty second Year, and resolved to follow the Steps of the most worthy of my Ancestors, who have inhabited this Spot of Earth before me, in all the Methods of Hospitality and good Neighbourhood, for the Sake of my Fame;[6] and in Country Sports and Recreations, for the Sake of my Health. In my Twenty third Year I was obliged to serve as Sheriff of the County; and in my Servants, Officers, and whole Equipage,[7] indulged the Pleasure of a young Man (who did not think ill of his own Person) in taking that publick Occasion of shewing my Figure and Behaviour to Advantage. You may easily imagine to your self what Appearance I made, who am pretty tall, rid well, and was very well dressed, at the Head of a whole County, with Musick before me, a Feather in my Hat, and my Horse well bitted. I can assure you I was not a little pleased with the kind Looks and Glances I had from all the Balconies and Windows, as I rode to the Hall where the Assizes[8] were held. But when I came there, a beautiful Creature in a Widow's Habit sat in Court, to hear the Event of a Cause concerning her Dower.[9] This commanding Creature (who was born for Destruction[10] of all who behold her) put on such a Resignation in her Countenance, and bore the Whispers of all around the Court with such a pretty Uneasiness, I warrant

[4] Gave me a fuller insight into his character.

[5] Inherited.

[6] Reputation.

[7] The handsome procession as he rode to serve in court.

[8] Periodical sessions of the superior court in the various counties of England.

[9] The widow seeks to retain the wealth she brought to her husband in marriage, against the suit of "the next Heir to her Husband." She is the defendant; he, the plaintiff.

[10] A common hyperbole.

you, and then recovered her self from one Eye to another, till she was perfectly confused by meeting something so wistful in all she encountered, that at last, with a Murrain[11] to her, she casts her bewitching Eye upon me. I no sooner met it, but I bowed like a great surprized Booby; and knowing her Cause to be the first which came on, I cried, like a captivated Calf as I was, Make Way for the Defendant's Witnesses. This sudden Partiality made all the County immediately see the Sheriff also was become a Slave to the fine Widow. During the Time her Cause was upon Trial, she behaved her self, I warrant you, with such a deep Attention to her Business, took Opportunities to have little Billets handed to her Counsel, then would be in such a pretty Confusion, occasioned, you must know, by acting before so much Company, that not only I but the whole Court was prejudiced in her Favour; and all that the next Heir to her Husband had to urge, was thought so groundless and frivolous, that when it came to her Counsel to reply, there was not half so much said as every one besides in the Court thought he could have urged to her Advantage.[12] You must understand, Sir, this perverse Woman is one of those unaccountable Creatures that secretly rejoyce in the Admiration of Men, but indulge themselves in no further Consequences. Hence it is that she has ever had a Train of Admirers, and she removes from her Slaves in Town to those in the Country, according to the Seasons of the Year. She is a reading Lady, and far gone in the Pleasures of Friendship: She is always accompanied by a Confident, who is Witness to her daily Protestations against our Sex, and consequently a Bar to her first Steps towards Love, upon the Strength of her own Maxims and Declarations.

"However, I must needs say this accomplished Mistress of mine has distinguished me above the rest, and has been known to declare Sir Roger de Coverley was the tamest and most human of all the Brutes in the Country.[13] I was told she said so by one who

11 Literally, a plague infecting domestic animals and plants. Here, it metaphorically continues the "Destruction" hyperbole.

12 Following this line, Sir Roger ends the courtroom discussion and pursues a general description.

13 For discussion of "Fox-hunters," see *Tatler* No. 18, n. 26 and *Tatler* No. 89, n. 10.

thought he rallied me; but upon the Strength of this slender Encouragement of being thought least detestable, I made new Liveries,[14] new paired my Coach-Horses, sent them all to Town to be
bitted, and taught to throw their Legs well, and move altogether,
before I pretended to cross the Country and wait upon her. As
soon as I thought my Retinue suitable to the Character of my Fortune and Youth, I set out from hence to make my Addresses. The
particular Skill of this Lady has ever been to inflame your Wishes,
and yet command Respect. To make her Mistress of this Art, she
has a greater Share of Knowledge, Wit, and good Sense, than is
usual even among Men of Merit. Then she is beautiful beyond
the Race of Women. If you won't let her go on[15] with a certain
Artifice with her Eyes, and the Skill of Beauty, she will arm her
self with her real Charms, and strike you with Admiration instead
of Desire. It is certain that if you were to behold the whole
Woman, there is that Dignity in her Aspect, that Composure in
her Motion, that Complacency in her Manner, that if her Form
makes you hope, her Merit makes you fear. But then again, she is
such a desperate Scholar, that no Country-Gentleman can approach her without being a Jest. As I was going to tell you, when
I came to her House I was admitted to her Presence with great
Civility; at the same Time she placed her self to be first seen by
me in such an Attitude, as I think you call the Posture of a Picture,[16] that she discovered new Charms, and I at last came towards
her with such an Awe as made me speechless. This she no sooner
observed but she made her Advantage of it, and began a Discourse
to me concerning Love and Honour,[17] as they both are followed
by Pretenders, and the real Votaries to them. When she discussed
these Points in a Discourse, which I verily believe was as learned
as the best Philosopher in *Europe* could possibly make, she asked
me whether she was so happy as to fall in with my Sentiments on
these important Particulars. Her Confident sat by her, and upon

[14] New uniforms for the servants.

[15] Defeat you. The sentence employs a military metaphor.

[16] I.e., an advantageous pose.

[17] The two are personified as ruling deities, with both real and pretended
devotees.

my being in the last Confusion and Silence, this malicious Aide of hers turning to her says, I am very glad to observe Sir Roger pauses upon this Subject, and seems resolved to deliver all his Sentiments upon the Matter when he pleases to speak. They both kept their Countenances, and after I had sat half an Hour meditating how to behave before such profound Casuists, I rose up and took my Leave. Chance has since that Time thrown me very often in her Way, and she as often has directed a Discourse to me which I do not understand. This Barbarity has kept me ever at a Distance from the most beautiful Object my Eyes ever beheld. It is thus also she deals with all Mankind, and you must make Love to her, as you would conquer the Sphinx, by posing her.[18] But were she like other Women, and that there were any talking to her, how constant must the Pleasure of that Man be, who could converse with a Creature————But, after all, you may be sure her Heart is fixed on some one or other; and yet I have been credibly informed; but who can believe half that is said! After she had done speaking to me, she put her Hand to her Bosom and adjusted her Tucker.[19] Then she cast her Eyes a little down, upon my beholding her too earnestly. They say she sings excellently: Her Voice in her ordinary Speech has something in it inexpressibly sweet. You must know I dined with her at a publick Table the Day after I first saw her, and she helpd me to some Tansy[20] in the Eye of all the Gentlemen in the Country: She has certainly the finest Hand of any Woman in the World. I can assure you, Sir, were you to behold her, you would be in the same Condition; for as her Speech is Musick, her Form is Angelick. But I find I grow irregular while I am talking of her; but indeed it would be Stupidity to be unconcerned at such Perfection. Oh the excellent Creature, she is as inimitable to all Women, as she is inaccessible to all Men!"

18 In Greek legend, the city of Thebes was devastated by the Sphinx, a monster who could be exorcised only by the man able to answer a particular riddle. Oedipus answered it, freed the city, and became its king.

19 A piece of cloth attached to the neck of a lady's gown. See *Guardians* No. 100 and 116, which protest the discontinued use of the tucker.

20 A pudding or cake flavored with the juice of tansy, a bitter herb.

I found my Friend begin to rave,[21] and insensibly led him towards the House, that we might be joined by some other Company; and am convinced that the Widow is the secret Cause of all that Inconsistency which appears in some Parts of my Friend's Discourse; tho' he has so much Command of himself as not directly to mention her, yet according to that[22] of *Martial*, which one knows not how to render in English, *Dum tacet hanc loquitur*.[23] I shall end this Paper with that whole Epigram, which represents with much Humour my honest Friend's Condition.

> *Quicquid agit, Rufus, nihil est, nisi Naevia Rufo,*
> *Si gaudet, si flet, si tacet, hanc loquitur:*
> *Caenat, propinat, poscit, negat, annuit, una est*
> *Naevia: Si non sit Naevia, mutus erit.*
> *Scriberet hesterna Patri cum Luce Salutem.*
> *Naevia lux, inquit, Naevia numen, ave.*[24]

> *Let* Rufus *weep, rejoice, stand, sit, or walk,*
> *Still he can nothing but of* Naevia *talk:*
> *Let him eat, drink, ask Questions, or dispute,*
> *Still he must speak of* Naevia, *or be mute.*
> *He writ to his Father, ending with this Line,*
> *I am, my Lovely* Naevia, *ever thine.*

R

[21] To say that Sir Roger grows "irregular" and begins to "rave" means only that his praise of the widow has become emotional and too long.

[22] That passage.

[23] Roughly, "While he is silent, he is speaking of her."

[24] Martial *Epigrams* 1. 68. 1–6.

The Spectator, No. 117

Saturday, July 14.

[A d d i s o n]

————*Ipsi sibi somnia fingunt.* Virg.[1]

There are some Opinions in which a Man should stand Neuter, without engaging his Assent to one side or the other. Such a hovering Faith as this, which refuses to settle upon any Determination, is absolutely necessary in a Mind that is careful to avoid Errors and Prepossessions. When the Arguments press equally on both sides in Matters that are indifferent to us, the safest Method is to give up our selves to neither.

It is with this Temper of Mind that I consider the Subject of Witchcraft. When I hear the Relations[2] that are made from all Parts of the World, not only from *Norway* and *Lapland,* from the *East* and *West Indies,* but from every particular Nation in *Europe,* I cannot forbear thinking that there is such an Intercourse and Commerce with Evil Spirits, as that which we express by the Name of Witchcraft. But when I consider that the ignorant and credulous Parts of the World abound most in these Relations, and that the Persons among us who are supposed to engage in such an Infernal Commerce are People of a weak Understanding and crazed Imagination,[3] and at the same time reflect upon the many Impostures and Delusions of this Nature that have been detected in all Ages, I endeavour to suspend my Belief till I hear more certain Accounts than any which have yet come to my

1 Virgil *Eclogues* 8. 108: "They fashion their own dreams."

2 Reports, stories.

3 A reference to those persons, mentioned again at the end of the essay, who confessed to being witches.

Knowledge. In short, when I consider the Question, Whether
there are such Persons in the World as those we call Witches? my
Mind is divided between the two opposite Opinions; or rather
(to speak my Thoughts freely) I believe in general that there is,
and has been such a thing as Witchcraft; but at the same time can
give no Credit to any Particular Instance of it.[4]

I am engaged in this Speculation, by some Occurrences that I
met with Yesterday, which I shall give my Reader an Account of
at large. As I was walking with my Friend Sir Roger by the side
of one of his Woods, an old Woman applied her self to me for my
Charity. Her Dress and Figure put me in mind of the following
Description in *Otway*.[5]

> *In a close Lane as I pursu'd my Journey,*
> *I spy'd a wrinkled* Hag, *with Age grown double,*
> *Picking dry Sticks, and mumbling to her self.*
> *Her Eyes with scalding Rheum[6] were gall'd and red;*
> *Cold Palsy shook her Head; her Hands seem'd wither'd;*
> *And on her crooked Shoulders had she wrapp'd*
> *The tatter'd Remnants of an old striped Hanging,*
> *Which serv'd to keep her Carcass from the Cold:*
> *So there was nothing of a-piece about her.*
> *Her lower Weeds[7] were all o'er coarsly patch'd*
> *With diff'rent-colour'd Rags, black, red, white, yellow,*
> *And seem'd to speak Variety of Wretchedness.*

As I was musing on this Description, and comparing it with
the Object before me, the Knight told me, that this very old
Woman had the Reputation of a Witch all over the Country,[8]

[4] Though witchcraft had lost much of its hold on the minds of educated
people, belief still prevailed in many quarters. Addison's essay appeared several months before the celebrated trial of Jane Wenham, an English woman
who was condemned to death for witchcraft. The Salem witch trials in the
United States had occurred only twenty years earlier.

[5] From Otway's *The Orphan* (1680), act 2. Addison omits one line from the
original quotation.

[6] A serous or mucous discharge from the eyes.

[7] Garments.

[8] There follow the usual charges made against witches: that they conversed
with the devil, flew on broomsticks, were shaken at the sight of a cross, worshipped the devil by reciting holy prayers backwards, made their neighbors
vomit pins, and performed all manner of local mischief.

that her Lips were observed to be always in Motion, and that there was not a Switch about her House which her Neighbours did not believe had carried her several hundreds of Miles. If she chanced to stumble, they always found Sticks or Straws that lay in the Figure of a Cross before her. If she made any Mistake at Church, and cryed *Amen* in a wrong Place, they never failed to conclude that she was saying her Prayers backwards. There was not a Maid in the Parish that would take a Pin of her, though she should offer a Bag of Money with it. She goes by the Name of *Moll White,* and has made the Country ring with several imaginary Exploits which are palmed upon her. If the Dairy Maid does not make her Butter come so soon as she would have it, *Moll White* is at the bottom of the Churn. If a Horse sweats in the Stable, *Moll White* has been upon his Back. If a Hare makes an unexpected Escape from the Hounds, the Huntsman curses *Moll White.* Nay, (says Sir Roger) I have known the Master of the Pack, upon such an Occasion, send one of his Servants to see if *Moll White* had been out that Morning.

This Account raised my Curiosity so far, that I begged my Friend Sir Roger to go with me into her Hovel, which stood in a solitary Corner under the side of the Wood. Upon our first entring Sir Roger winked to me, and pointed at something that stood behind the Door, which upon looking that way I found to be an old Broomstaff. At the same time he whispered me in the Ear to take notice of a Tabby Cat[9] that sat in the Chimney-Corner, which, as the Knight told me, lay under as bad a Report as *Moll White* her self; for besides that *Moll* is said often to accompany her in the same Shape, the Cat is reported to have spoken twice or thrice in her Life, and to have played several Pranks above the Capacity of an ordinary Cat.

I was secretly concerned to see Human Nature in so much Wretchedness and Disgrace, but at the same time could not forbear smiling to hear Sir Roger, who is a little puzzled about the old Woman, advising her as a Justice of Peace to avoid all Communication with the Devil, and never to hurt any of her Neigh-

---

[9] Traditionally, witches were attended by familiars, diabolical agents who both served them and threatened them when they showed signs of failing in their evil duties. Commonly, familiars took the form of cats, dogs, toads, etc.

bours Cattle. We concluded our Visit with a Bounty,[10] which was
very acceptable.

In our Return home Sir Roger told me, that old *Moll* had been
often brought before him for making Children spit Pins, and
giving Maids the Night-Mare; and that the Country People would
be tossing her into a Pond and trying Experiments with her every
Day,[11] if it was not for him and his Chaplain.

I have since found, upon Enquiry, that Sir Roger was several
times staggered with the Reports that had been brought him concerning this old Woman, and would frequently have bound her
over to the County Sessions, had not his Chaplain with much ado
perswaded him to the contrary.

I have been the more particular in this Account, because I hear
there is scarce a Village in *England* that has not a *Moll White* in
it. When an old Woman begins to doat, and grow chargeable to
a Parish,[12] she is generally turned into a Witch, and fills the
whole Country with extravagant Fancies, imaginary Distempers,
and terrifying Dreams. In the mean time, the poor Wretch that is
the innocent Occasion of so many Evils begins to be frighted at
her self, and sometimes confesses secret Commerces and Familiarities that her Imagination forms in a delirious old Age. This frequently cuts off Charity from the greatest Objects of Compassion,
and inspires People with a Malevolence towards those poor de-
crepid Parts of our Species, in whom Human Nature is defaced
by Infirmity and Dotage.   L

---

[10] A gift of money.

[11] A number of experiments were thought to reveal the witch: one could
see if she bore a "witch's mark" on her body, if she was able to recite the Lord's
Prayer without error or suspicious pause, or if she could float on water. The
last test was based on the idea that water was a pure element which would refuse to receive one who had renounced her baptism.

[12] Becomes the subject of community charity.

The Spectator, No. 122

Friday, July 20.

[Addison]

Comes jucundus in via pro vehiculo est. Publ. Syr. Frag.[1]

A man's first Care should be to avoid the Reproaches of his own Heart; his next, to escape the Censures of the World: If the last interferes with the former, it ought to be entirely neglected; but otherwise, there cannot be a greater Satisfaction to an honest Mind, than to see those Approbations which it gives itself seconded by the Applauses of the Publick: A Man is more sure of his Conduct, when the Verdict which he passes upon his own Behaviour is thus warranted, and confirmed by the Opinion of all that know him.

My worthy Friend Sir Roger is one of those who is not only at Peace within himself, but beloved and esteemed by all about him. He receives a suitable Tribute for his universal Benevolence to Mankind, in the Returns of Affection and Good-will, which are paid him by every one that lives within his Neighbourhood. I lately met with two or three odd Instances of that general Respect which is shewn to the good old Knight. He would needs carry *Will. Wimble* and my self with him to the County-Assizes:[2] As we were upon the Road *Will. Wimble* joyned a couple of plain Men[3] who rid before us, and conversed with them for some Time; dur-

[1] Publlilius Syrus *Sententiae* 116: "A pleasant companion is as good as a coach."

[2] Court sessions.

[3] I.e., ordinary country-men, as opposed to fine gentlemen of the town. Will Wimble is introduced in *Spectator* No. 108.

ing which my Friend Sir Roger acquainted me with their Characters.

The first of them, says he, that has a Spaniel by his Side, is a Yeoman of about an hundred Pounds a Year, an honest Man: He is just within the Game-Act, and qualified to kill an Hare or a Pheasant:[4] He knocks down a Dinner with his Gun twice or thrice a Week; and by that Means lives much cheaper than those who have not so good an Estate as himself. He would be a good Neighbour if he did not destroy so many Partridges: In short, he is a very sensible Man; shoots flying;[5] and has been several Times Foreman of the Petty-Jury.[6]

The other that rides along with him is *Tom Touchy,* a Fellow famous for *taking the Law* of every Body. There is not one in the Town where he lives that he has not sued at a Quarter-Sessions.[7] The Rogue had once the Impudence to go to Law with the *Widow*.[8] His Head is full of Costs, Damages, and Ejectments:[9] He plagued a couple of honest Gentlemen so long for a Trespass in breaking one of his Hedges, till he was forced to sell the Ground it enclosed to defray the Charges of the Prosecution: His Father left him fourscore Pounds a Year; but he has *cast* and been cast[10] so often, that he is not now worth thirty. I suppose he is going upon the old Business of the Willow-Tree.[11]

As Sir Roger was giving me this Account of *Tom Touchy, Will. Wimble* and his two Companions stopped short till we came up to them. After having paid their Respects to Sir Roger, *Will.* told him that Mr. *Touchy* and he must appeal to him upon a Dispute

---

4 See *Spectator* No. 2, n. 10.

5 I.e., he is not so unsportsmanlike as to shoot a bird while it is sitting in a tree or on the ground.

6 A jury that sits in court to give a verdict on cases tried, unlike a grand jury which decides beforehand whether a case should be sent to trial at all.

7 See *Spectator* No. 2, n. 9.

8 Sir Roger's attitude toward the Widow's legal adversaries was expressed in *Spectator* No. 113.

9 Dispossessions.

10 Won and lost in court.

11 The reference to "the old Business of the Willow-Tree" makes the description realistic. No allusion to a real event or to an event mentioned in other *Spectators* seems intended.

that arose between them. *Will.* it seems had been giving his Fellow Travellers an Account of his angling one Day in such a Hole; when *Tom Touchy,* instead of hearing out his Story, told him, that Mr. such an One, if he pleased, might *take the Law of him* for fishing in that Part of the River. My Friend Sir Roger heared them both, upon a round Trot;[12] and after having paused some Time told them, with the Air of a Man who would not give his Judgment rashly, that *much might be said on both Sides.* They were neither of them dissatisfied with the Knight's Determination, because neither of them found himself in the Wrong by it: Upon which we made the best of our Way to the Assizes.

The Court was sat before Sir Roger came, but notwithstanding all the Justices had taken their Places upon the Bench, they made Room for the old Knight at the Head of them; who for his Reputation in the Country took Occasion to whisper in the Judge's Ear, That *he was glad his Lordship had met with so much good Weather in his Circuit.*[13] I was listening to the Proceedings of the Court with much Attention, and infinitely pleased with that great Appearance and Solemnity which so properly accompanies such a publick Administration of our Laws; when, after about an Hour's Sitting, I observed to my great Surprize, in the Midst of a Trial, that my Friend Sir Roger was getting up to speak. I was in some Pain for him, till I found he had acquitted himself of two or three Sentences, with a Look of much Business and great Intrepidity.

Upon his first Rising the Court was hushed, and a general Wisper ran among the Country-People that Sir Roger *was up.* The Speech he made was so little to the Purpose, that I shall not trouble my Readers with an Account of it; and I believe was not so much designed by the Knight himself to inform the Court, as to give him a Figure in my Eye,[14] and keep up his Credit in the Country.

I was highly delighted, when the Court rose, to see the Gentle-

12 While riding at a brisk pace.

13 Though the Knight says little of importance, those in court would reasonably assume he is making some crucial statement to the chief justice. This, of course, is the impression Sir Roger wants to give.

14 To show the Spectator he was a man of eminence in the area.

men of the Country gathering about my old Friend, and striving who should compliment him most; at the same Time that the ordinary People gazed upon him at a Distance, not a little admiring his Courage, that was not afraid to speak to the Judge.

In our Return home we met with a very odd Accident; which I cannot forbear relating, because it shews how desirous all who know Sir Roger are of giving him Marks of their Esteem. When we were arrived upon the Verge of his Estate, we stopped at a little Inn to rest our selves and our Horses. The Man of the House[15] had it seems been formerly a Servant in the Knight's Family; and to do Honour to his old Master, had some Time since, unknown to Sir Roger, put him[16] up in a Sign-post before the Door; so that *the Knight's Head* had hung out upon the Road about a Week before he himself knew any thing of the Matter. As soon as Sir Roger was acquainted with it, finding that his Servant's Indiscretion proceeded wholly from Affection and Good-will, he only told him that he had made him too high a Compliment; and when the Fellow seemed to think that could hardly be, added with a more decisive Look, That it was too great an Honour for any Man under a Duke; but told him at the same time that it might be altered with a very few Touches, and that he himself would be at the Charge of it.[17] Accordingly they got a Painter by the Knight's Directions to add a Pair of Whiskers to the Face, and by a little Aggravation of the Features to change it into the *Saracen's Head.*[18] I should not have known this Story, had not the Innkeeper upon Sir Roger's alighting told him in my Hearing, That his Honour's Head was brought back last Night with the Alterations that he had ordered to be made in it. Upon this my Friend with his usual Chearfulness related the Particulars above-mentioned, and ordered the Head to be brought into the Room. I could not forbear discovering greater Expressions of Mirth than ordinary upon the Appearance of this monstrous Face, under which, notwithstanding it was made to frown and stare in a most

[15] The Innkeeper.

[16] I.e., put an image of Sir Roger's head.

[17] He would pay for its being altered.

[18] The attempt was to change Sir Roger's benign face into that of a fierce Arab warrior.

extraordinary Manner, I could still discover a distant Resemblance of my old Friend. Sir Roger, upon seeing me laugh, desired me to tell him truly if I thought it possible for People to know him in that Disguise. I at first kept my usual Silence; but upon the Knight's conjuring me to tell him whether it was not still more like himself than a *Saracen*, I composed my Countenance in the best Manner I could, and replied, *That much might be said on both Sides*.

These several Adventures, with the Knight's Behaviour in them, gave me as pleasant a Day as ever I met with in any of my Travels.   L

The Spectator, No. 126

Wednesday, July 25.

[Addison]

Tros Rutulusve fuat nullo discrimine habebo. Virg.[1]

In my Yesterday's Paper[2] I proposed, that the honest Men of all Parties should enter into a Kind of Association for the Defence of one another and the Confusion of their common Enemies. As it is designed this neutral Body should act with a Regard to nothing but Truth and Equity, and divest themselves of the little Heats and Prepossessions that cleave to Parties of all Kinds, I have prepared for them the following Form[3] of an Association, which may express their Intentions in the most plain and simple Manner.

> *We whose Names are hereunto subscribed do solemnly declare, that we do in our Consciences believe two and two make four; and that we shall adjudge any Man whatsoever to be our Enemy who endeavours to perswade us to the contrary. We are likewise ready to maintain, with the Hazard of all that is near and dear to us, that six is less than seven in all Times and all Places; and that ten will not be more three Years hence than it is at present. We do also firmly declare, that it is our Resolution as long as we live to call black black, and white white. And we shall upon all Occasions oppose such Per-*

---

1 Virgil *Aeneid* 10. 108: "Trojans and Rutulians are the same to me."

2 In *Spectator* No. 125, Addison wrote: "A furious Party Spirit, when it rages in its full Violence, exerts it self in Civil War and Blood-shed; and when it is under its greatest Restraints naturally breaks out in Falshood, Detraction, Calumny, and a partial Administration of Justice. In a word, It fills a Nation with Spleen and Rancour, and extinguishes all the Seeds of Good-nature, Compassion and Humanity."

3 Manifesto.

sons that upon any Day of the Year shall call black white, or white
black, with the utmost Peril of our Lives and Fortunes.

Were there such a Combination of honest Men, who without
any Regard to Places would endeavour to extirpate all such furious Zealots as would sacrifice one half of their Country to the
Passion and Interest of the other; as also such infamous Hypo-
crites, that are for promoting their own Advantage, under Colour
of the publick Good; with all the profligate immoral Retainers to
each Side, that have nothing to recommend them but an implicit
Submission to their Leaders; we should soon see that furious
Party-Spirit extinguished, which may in Time expose us to the
Derision and Contempt of all the Nations about us.

A Member of this Society, that would thus carefully employ
himself in making Room for Merit, by throwing down the worthless and depraved Part of Mankind from those conspicuous Stations of Life to which they have been sometimes advanced, and
all this without any Regard to his private Interest, would be no
small Benefactor to his Country.

I remember to have read in *Diodorus Siculus*[4] an Account of a
very active little Animal, which I think he calls the *Ichneumon,*
that makes it the whole Business of his Life to break the Eggs of
the Crocodile, which he is always in search after. This Instinct is
the more remarkable, because the *Ichneumon* never feeds upon
the Eggs he has broken, nor any other Way finds his Account in
them. Were it not for the incessant Labours of this industrious
Animal, *Aegypt,* says the Historian, would be over-run with Croc-
odiles; for the *Aegyptians* are so far from destroying those pernicious Creatures, that they worship them as Gods.

If we look into the Behaviour of ordinary Partizans, we shall
find them far from resembling this disinterested Animal; and
rather acting after the Example of the wild *Tartars,*[5] who are am-

---

4 *The historical Library of Diodorus the Sicilian* was translated by B. Booth
in 1700. The Ichneumon, a mongoose-like creature, is discussed in book I,
chapter 3.

5 The allusion here is to *Hudibras* 1. 2. 23–26:

> So a wilde *Tartar* when he spies
> A man that's handsome, valiant, wise,
> If he can kill him, thinks t'inherit
> His Wit, his Beauty, and his Spirit.

bitious of destroying a Man of the most extraordinary Parts and Accomplishments,[6] as thinking that upon his Decease the same Talents, whatever Post they qualified him for, enter of Course into his Destroyer.

As in the whole Train of my Speculations, I have endeavoured as much as I am able to extinguish that pernicious Spirit of Passion and Prejudice, which rages with the same Violence in all Parties, I am still the more desirous of doing some Good in this Particular, because I observe that the Spirit of Party reigns more in the Country than in the Town. It here contracts a kind of Brutality and rustick Fierceness, to which Men of a politer Conversation are wholly Strangers. It extends it self even to the Return of the Bow and the Hat; and at the same Time that the Heads of Parties preserve towards one another an outward Show of good Breeding, and keep up a perpetual Intercourse of Civilities, their Tools that are dispersed in these outlying Parts will not so much as mingle together at a Cock-Match.[7] This Humour fills the Country with several periodical Meetings of Whig Jockeys and Tory Fox-hunters;[8] not to mention the innumerable Curses, Frowns, and Whispers it produces at a Quarter-Sessions.[9]

I do not know whether I have observed in any of my former Papers,[10] that my Friends Sir Roger de Coverley and Sir Andrew Freeport are of different Principles, the first of them inclined to the *landed* and the other to the *money'd* Interest. This Humour is so moderate in each of them, that it proceeds no farther than to an agreeable Raillery, which very often diverts the rest of the Club. I find however that the Knight is a much stronger Tory in the Country than in Town, which, as he has told me in my Ear, is absolutely necessary for the keeping up his Interest. In all our

6 This reference, like later that in Will Wimble's stories of "a certain great Man," is presumably to the Duke of Marlborough, who had been suspended and harshly criticized by the Tory ministry and its spokesmen.

7 I.e., while the heads of parties, who reside in the cities, act civilly toward one another, their rural followers observe no such restraint.

8 See *Tatler* No. 18, n. 26.

9 See *Spectator* No. 2, n. 9.

10 If not directly stated, this fact was implicit in *Spectators* No. 2, 82, and 109.

Journey from *London* to his House we did not so much as bait at a Whig Inn; or if by Chance the Coachman stopped at a wrong Place, one of Sir Roger's Servants would ride up to his Master full Speed, and whisper to him that the Master of the House was against such an one in the last Election. This often betrayed as into hard Beds and bad Cheer;[11] for we were not so inquisitive about the Inn as the Inn-keeper; and provided our Landlord's Principles were sound, did not take any Notice of the Staleness of his Provisions. This I found still the more inconvenient, because the better the Host was, the worse generally were his Accomodations; the Fellow knowing very well, that those who were his Friends would take up with coarse Diet and an hard Lodging. For these Reasons, all the while I was upon the Road I dreaded entering into an House of any one that Sir Roger had applauded for an honest Man.

Since my Stay at Sir Roger's in the Country, I daily find more Instances of this narrow Party-Humour. Being upon the Bowling-Green[12] at a neighbouring Market-Town the other Day, (for that is the Place where the Gentlemen of one Side meet once a Week) I observed a Stranger among them of a better Presence and genteeler Behaviour than ordinary; but was much surprized, that notwithstanding he was a very fair *Bettor*,[13] no Body would take him up. But upon Enquiry I found, that he was one who had given a disagreeable Vote in a former Parliament, for which Reason there was not a Man upon that Bowling-Green who would have so much Correspondence with him as to win his Money of him.

Among other Instances of this Nature I must not omit one which concerns my self. *Will. Wimble* was the other Day relating several strange Stories that he had picked up no Body knows where of a certain great Man; and upon my staring at him, as one that was surprized to hear such things in the Country which had never been so much as whispered in the Town, *Will.* stopped short in the Thread of his Discourse, and after Dinner asked my

---

11 Provisions or hospitality.

12 See *Spectator* No. 108, n. 5.

13 I.e., one offering honest and reasonable wagers.

Friend Sir Roger in his Ear if he was sure that I was not a Fanatick.[14]

It gives me a serious Concern to see such a Spirit of Dissention in the Country; not only as it destroys Virtue and common Sense, and renders us in a Manner Barbarians towards one another, but as it perpetuates our Animosities, widens our Breaches, and transmits our present Passions and Prejudices to our Posterity. For my own Part, I am sometimes afraid that I discover the Seeds of a Civil War in these our Divisions;[15] and therefore cannot but bewail, as in their first Principles, the Miseries and Calamities of our Children.   C

[14] Though the term could apply to anyone with excessive devotion to a cause, it more commonly described the nonconformist given to religious enthusiasm and could be extended to include anyone with Whig sympathies.

[15] Brief civil uprisings did occur in 1715 and 1745.

The Spectator, No. 130

Monday, July 30.

[A d d i s o n]

————*Semperque recentes*
Convectare juvat praedas, & vivere rapto. Virg.[1]

As I was Yesterday riding out in the Fields with my Friend Sir
Roger, we saw at a little Distance from us a Troop of Gypsies.[2]
Upon the first Discovery of them, my Friend was in some Doubt
whether he should not exert the *Justice of the Peace*[3] upon such
a Band of lawless Vagrants; but not having his Clerk[4] with him,
who is a necessary Counsellour on these Occasions, and fearing
that his Poultry might fare the worse for it, he let the Thought
Drop: But at the same Time gave me a particular Account of the
Mischiefs they do in the Country, in stealing Peoples Goods and
spoiling their Servants.[5] If a stray Piece of Linnen hangs upon an
Hedge, says Sir Roger, they are sure to have it; if a Hog loses his
Way in the Fields, it is ten to one but he becomes their Prey;[6] our
Geese cannot live in Peace for them; if a Man prosecutes them
with Severity, his Hen-roost is sure to pay for it: They generally

1 Virgil *Aeneid* 7. 748–749: "It is ever their delight to bear away fresh booty,
and to live on plunder."
2 The name derives from the assumption that they were Egyptians.
3 Exercise his powers as justice of the peace, i.e., arrest them.
4 The clerk of a justice of the peace was trained in the law and gave advice
on doubtful cases like this one.
5 As references to servant-maids and to the dairy-maid and the butler make
clear, the servants become excited with the fortune-telling, the promise of
sweethearts, etc., and grow inefficient.
6 I.e., nine times out of ten, the gypsies will steal him.

straggle into these Parts about this Time of the Year; and set the Heads of our Servant-Maids so agog for Husbands, that we do not expect to have any Business done, as it should be, whilst they are in the Country. I have an honest Dairy-Maid who crosses their Hands with a Piece of Silver every Summer; and never fails being promised the handsomest young Fellow in the Parish for her Pains. Your Friend the Butler has been Fool enough to be seduced by them; and though he is sure to lose a Knife, a Fork, or a Spoon every Time his Fortune is told him, generally shuts himself up in the Pantry with an old Gypsie for above half an Hour once in a Twelve-month. Sweet-hearts are the things they live upon, which they bestow very plentifully upon all those that apply themselves to them. You see now and then some handsome young Jades among them: The Sluts have often very white Teeth and black Eyes.

Sir Roger observing that I listned with great Attention to his Account of a People who were so entirely new to me, told me, That if I would[7] they should tell us our Fortunes. As I was very well pleased with the Knight's Proposal, we rid up and communicated our Hands to them. A *Cassandra*[8] of the Crew, after having examined my Lines very diligently, told me, That I loved a pretty Maid in a Corner, that I was a good Woman's Man,[9] with some other Particulars which I do not think proper to relate. My Friend Sir Roger alighted from his Horse, and exposing his Palm to two or three that stood by him, they crumpled it into all Shapes, and diligently scanned every Wrinkle that could be made in it; when one of them who was older and more Sun-burnt than the rest, told him, That he had a Widow in his Line of Life:[10] Upon which the Knight cryed, Go, go,[11] you are an idle Baggage; and at

---

[7] If I wished it done.

[8] In Greek legend, Cassandra, daughter of Priam and Hecuba, possessed the gift of prophecy. Because Cassandra was always correct in her predictions but never believed, there may be some irony in the reference here.

[9] *Spectator* No. 156 by Steele gives a fuller definition of "the Woman's Man."

[10] The life-line runs in the curve from the ball of the forefinger across the whole palm of the hand.

[11] A friendly expression of disbelief, like "Go on with you."

the same time smiled upon me. The Gypsie finding he was not displeased in his Heart, told him, after a further Enquiry into his Hand, that his True-love was constant, and that she should dream of him to Night. My old Friend cryed pish, and bid her go on. The Gypsie told him that he was a Batchelour, but would not be so long; and that he was dearer to some Body than he thought: The Knight still repeated, She was an idle Baggage, and bid her go on. Ah Master says the Gypsie, that roguish Leer of yours makes a pretty Woman's Heart ake; you ha'n't that Simper about the Mouth for Nothing[12]—The uncouth Gibberish with which all this was uttered, like the Darkness of an Oracle,[13] made us the more attentive to it. To be short, the Knight left the Money with her that he had crossed her Hand with, and got up again on his Horse.

As we were riding away, Sir Roger told me, that he knew several sensible People who believed these Gypsies now and then foretold very strange things; and for Half an Hour together appeared more jocund than ordinary. In the Height of his good Humour, meeting a common Beggar upon the Road who was no Conjuror, as he went to relieve him he found his Pocket was pickt: That being a Kind of Palmistry[14] at which this Race of Vermin are very dexterous.

I might here entertain my Reader with Historical Remarks on this idle profligate People, who infest all the Countries of *Europe,* and live in the Midst of Governments in a kind of Commonwealth by themselves. But instead of entering into Observations of this Nature, I shall fill the remaining part of my Paper with a Story which is still fresh in *Holland,* and was printed in one of our Monthly Accounts about twenty Years ago.

"As the *Trekschuyt,* or Hackney-boat,[15] which carries Passengers from *Leiden* to *Amsterdam,* was putting off, a Boy running along the Side of the Canal, desir'd to be taken in; which the Master of the Boat

12 I.e., that wicked smile shows your amorous nature.

13 The prophecies of the Greek Oracle were delivered in a mysterious and ambiguous form.

14 The term, which usually relates to reading a man's future from the lines of his hand, here refers to pocket-picking.

15 A hackney-boat was one offered for hire, like a hackney-coach.

refused, because the Lad had not quite Money enough to pay the usual Fare. An eminent Merchant being pleased with the Looks of the Boy, and secretly touched with Compassion towards him, paid the Money for him, and ordered him to be taken on board. Upon talking with him afterwards, he found that he could speak readily in three or four Languages, and learned upon further Examination that he had been stolen away when he was a Child by a Gypsy, and had rambled ever since with a Gang of those Strolers up and down several Parts of *Europe*. It happened that the Merchant, whose Heart seems to have inclined towards the Boy by a secret kind of Instinct, had himself lost a Child some Years before. The Parents, after a long Search for him, gave him for drowned in one of the Canals with which that Country abounds; and the Mother was so afflicted at the Loss of a fine Boy, who was her only Son, that she died for Grief of it. Upon laying together all Particulars, and examining the several Moles and Marks by which the Mother used to describe the Child when he was first missing, the Boy proved to be the Son of the Merchant, whose Heart had so unaccountably melted at the Sight of him. The Lad was very well peased to find a Father, who was so rich, and likely to leave him a good Estate; the Father, on the other Hand, was not a little delighted to see a Son return to him, whom he had given for lost, with such a Strength of Constitution, Sharpness of Understanding, and Skill in Languages."

Here the printed Story leaves off; but if I may give Credit to Reports, our Linguist[16] having received such extraordinary Rudiments towards a good Education, was afterwards trained up in every thing that becomes a Gentleman; wearing off by little and little all the vicious Habits and Practices that he had been used to in the Course of his Peregrinations: Nay, it is said, that he has since been employed in foreign Courts upon National Business, with great Reputation to himself and Honour to those who sent him, and that he has visited several Countries as a publick Minister, in which he formerly wandered as a Gypsy.   C

[16] I.e., the son raised as a gypsy.

The Spectator, No. 138

Wednesday, August 8.

[S t e e l e]

Utitur in re non Dubia testibus non necessariis. Tull.[1]

One meets now and then with Persons who are extreamly learned and knotty in Expounding clear Cases. *Tully*[2] tells us of an Author that spent some Pages to prove that Generals could not perform the Great Enterprizes which have made them so Illustrious, if they had not had Men. He asserted also, it seems, that a Minister[3] at home, no more than a Commander abroad, could do any thing without other Men were his Instruments and Assistants. On this Occasion he produces the Example of *Themistocles, Pericles, Cyrus,* and *Alexander*[4] himself, whom he denies to have been capable of effecting what they did, except they had been followed by others. It is pleasant enough to see such Persons contend without Opponents, and triumph without Victory.

The Author above-mention'd by the Orator,[5] is placed for ever in a very ridiculous Light, and we meet every Day in Conversation such as deserve the same kind of Renown for troubling those with whom they Converse with the like Certainties. The Persons that

---

[1] Cicero *De Officiis* 2. 5. 16: "He calls in unnecessary witnesses, in a matter not in doubt."

[2] See *Tatler* No. 167, n. 5. The substance of the paragraph is drawn from *De Officiis* 2. 5.

[3] A minister of state.

[4] Themistocles (527?–460? B.C.) and Pericles (d. 429 B.C.) were Athenian statesmen. Cyrus the Great (600?–529 B.C.) was king of Persia. Alexander the Great (356–323 B.C.) was king of Macedonia and conquerer of the East.

[5] I.e., by Cicero.

I have always thought to deserve the highest Admiration in this kind are your ordinary Story-tellers, who are most religiously careful of keeping to the Truth in every particular Circumstance of a Narration, whether it concern the main end, or not. A Gentleman whom I had the Honour to be in Company with the other Day, upon some Occasion that he was pleas'd to take, said, He remember'd a very pretty Repartee made by a very Witty Man in King *Charles*'s time upon the like Occasion. I remember (said he, upon entring into the Tale) much about the time of *Oates*'s Plot,[6] that a Cousin-German of mine and I were at the *Bear* in *Holborn:* No, I am out, it was at the *Cross Keys;* but *Jack Thomson* was there,[7] for he was very great with[8] the Gentleman who made the Answer. But I am sure it was spoken somewhere thereabouts, for we drank a Bottle in that Neighbourhood every Evening: But no matter for all that, the thing is the same; but———

He was going on to settle the Geography of the Jest when I left the Room, wondering at this odd turn of Head which can play away its Words, with uttering nothing to the purpose, still observing its own Impertinences, and yet proceeding in them. I do not question but he inform'd the rest of his Audience, who had more Patience than I, of the Birth and Parentage, as well as the Collateral Alliances of his Family who made the Repartee, and of him who provoked him to it.

It is no small Misfortune to any who have a just value for their Time, when this Quality of being so very Circumstantial, and careful to be exact, happens to shew it self in a Man whose Quality[9] obliges them to attend his Proofs, that it is now Day, and the like. But this is augmented when the same Genius gets into Au-

---

[6] In 1678, Titus Oates (1649–1705), a former Anglican minister, concocted the famous Popish Plot, charging that Roman Catholics planned to assassinate Charles II, place his brother (later James II) on the throne, and turn the country over to the Jesuits. The story, though false, was widely believed and led to the execution of some thirty-five persons.

[7] Holborn is a borough of London; the Bear and the Cross Keys are presumably coffee-houses; Jack Thomson is simply a vague name. The point is that all this data is irrelevant. So, consequently, is this footnote.

[8] A near acquaintance of.

[9] In the space of three lines, Steele uses the word "Quality" in two different senses. In the first use, it means simply "characteristic" as does the word "Genius" below. In the second, it refers to "high social rank."

thority, as it often does. Nay, I have known it more than once ascend the very Pulpit. One of this sort taking it in his Head to be a great Admirer of Dr. *Tillotson* and Dr. *Beveridge*,[10] never fail'd of proving out of these great Authors things which no Men living would have denied him upon his own single Authority. One Day resolving to come to the point in hand, he said, According to that excellent Divine,[11] I will enter upon the Matter, or in his Words in his fifteenth Sermon of the Folio Edition, Page 160,

> *I shall briefly explain the Words, and then consider the Matter contained in them.*

This honest Gentleman needed not, one would think, strain his Modesty so far as to alter his design of *Entring into the Matter*, to that of *Briefly explaining*. But so it was, that he would not even be contented with that Authority, but added also the other Divine to strengthen his Method, and told us, With the Pious and Learned Dr. *Beveridge*, Page 4th of his 9th Volume, *I shall endeavour to make it as plain as I can from the Words which I have now read, wherein for that Purpose we shall consider*—This Wiseacre[12] was reckoned by the Parish, who did not understand him, a most Excellent Preacher, but that he read too much, and was so Humble that he did not trust enough to his own Parts.

Next to these ingenious Gentlemen, who argue for what no body can deny them, are to be ranked a sort of People who do not indeed attempt to prove insignificant things, but are ever labouring to raise Arguments with you about Matters you will give up to them without the least Controversy. One of these People told a Gentleman who said he saw Mr. such a one go this Morning at nine a Clock towards the *Gravel-Pits*, Sir, I must beg your Pardon for that, for tho' I am very loath to have any Dispute with you, yet I must take the Liberty to tell you it was nine when I saw him at St. *James*'s.[13] When Men of this Genius are pretty far gone in

---

[10] William Beveridge (1637–1708) was Bishop of St. Asaph. For Doctor Tillotson, see *Spectator* No. 106, n. 10.

[11] I.e., Bishop Tillotson.

[12] Here, the term applies to an intellectual pretender.

[13] The Gravel-Pits were at Kensington; St. James's probably refers to the coffee-house, though it might mean St. James Street.

Learning they will put you to prove[14] that Snow is White, and when you are upon that Topick can say that there is really no such thing as Colour in Nature; in a Word, they can turn what little Knowledge they have, into a ready Capacity of raising Doubts; into a Capacity of being always frivolous and always unanswerable. It was of two Disputants of this impertinent and laborious kind that the Cynick said, *One of these Fellows is Milking a Ram, and the other holds the Pail.*

Advertisement.

The Exercise of the Snuff-Box,[15] *according to the most fashionable Airs and Motions, in opposition to the Exercise of the Fan, will be Taught with the best plain or perfum'd Snuff, at* Charles Lillie's,[16] *Perfumer, at the Corner of* Bauford-Buildings *in the* Strand, *and Attendance given for the benefit of the young Merchants about the Exchange for two Hours every Day at Noon, except* Saturdays, *at a Toy-Shop near* Garraway's *Coffee-house.*[17] *There will be likewise Taught* The *Ceremony of the Snuff-Box, or Rules for offering Snuff to a Stranger, a Friend, or a Mistress, according to the Degrees of Familiarity or Distance; with an Explanation of the Careless, the Scornful, the Politick, and the Surly Pinch, and the Gestures proper to each of them.*

N. B. The Undertaker[18] *does not question but in a short time to have form'd a Body of Regular Snuff-Boxes ready to meet and make Head against all the Regiment of Fans which have been lately Disciplin'd, and are now in Motion.*   T

---

[14] I.e., they will urge you to contend.

[15] *Spectator* No. 134 by Steele carried a petition from Benjamin Easie, complaining of a charming lady who mortified a number of gentlemen with the dextrous handling of her fan, and urging that a course be established wherein gentlemen "be taught to manage our Snuff-Boxes in such a manner as we may be an equal Match for her." *Spectator* No. 102 by Addison described "an Academy for the training up of young Women in the *Exercise of the Fan . . .*"

[16] See *Tatler* No. 259, n. 14.

[17] See *Tatler* No. 181, n. 12.

[18] I.e., the advertiser undertaking the project.

The Spectator, No. 142

Monday, August 13.

[S t e e l e]

———*Irrupta tenet Copula*———Hor.[1]

The following Letters being Genuine,[2] and the Images of a
Worthy Passion, I am willing to give the old Lady's Admonition
to my self,[3] and the Representation of her own Happiness, a Place
in my Writings.

"*Mr.* Spectator,   *August* 9, 1711.
I am now in the Sixty seventh Year of my Age, and read you with
Approbation; but methinks you do not strike at the Root of the greatest Evil in Life, which is the false Notion of Gallantry[4] in Love. It is,
and has long been, upon a very ill foot; but I who have been a Wife
Forty Years, and was bred in a way that has made me ever since very
happy, see through the Folly of it.[5] In a Word, Sir, when I was a
young Woman, all who avoided the Vices of the Age were very carefully educated, and all Phantastical Objects were turned out of our
Sight. The Tapistry Hangings, with the great and venerable Simplic-

---

1 Horace *Odes* 1. 13. 18: "An unbroken bond unites them."

2 The letters are indeed genuine. They were addressed by Steele to his second wife, Mary Scurlock ("dear Prue") and were written four years previously,
not forty. The letters are not in their original sequence and were somewhat
altered before publication. The final letter, which may have been composed
for this essay, is nevertheless accepted by scholars as a genuine letter from
Steele to his wife.

3 I.e., the Spectator.

4 See *Tatler* No. 25, n. 1., and *Spectator* No. 2, n. 18.

5 I.e., *Gallantry* which should denote virtuous love and noble dedication,
has long been ill-defined, but the writer can see the folly of the amorous ar-
rangements and intrigues which the word now is used to describe.

ity of the Scripture Stories, had better Effects than now the Loves of *Venus* and *Adonis,* or *Bacchus* and *Ariadne* in your fine present Prints.[6] The Gentleman I am Married to made Love to me in Rapture, but it was the Rapture of a Christian and a Man of Honour, not a Romantick Hero, or a Whining Coxcomb: This put our Life upon a right Basis: To give you an Idea of our Regard one to another, I enclose to you several of his Letters writ Forty Years ago, when my Lover; and one writ t'other Day, after so many Years Cohabitation.

> *Your Servant,*
> Andromache."

"*Madam,*   *August* 7, 1671.
If my Vigilance and ten thousand Wishes for your Welfare and Repose could have any force, you last Night slept in Security, and had every good Angel in your Attendance. To have my Thoughts ever fix'd on you, to live in constant Fear of every Accident to which Human Life is liable, and to send up my hourly Prayers to avert 'em from you; I say, Madam, thus to think and thus to suffer, is what I do for Her who is in Pain at my Approach, and calls all my tender Sorrow Impertinence. You are now before my Eyes, my Eyes that are ready to flow with Tenderness, but cannot give Relief to my gushing Heart, that dictates what I am now saying, and yearns to tell you all its Achings. How art thou, oh my Soul, stoln from thy self! How is all thy Attention broken! My Books are blank Paper, and my Friends Intruders.[7] I have no hope of Quiet but from your Pity. To grant it would make more for your Triumph. To give Pain is the Tyranny, to make Happy the true Empire of Beauty. If you would consider aright, you'd find an agreeable Change in dismissing the Attendance of a Slave, to receive the Complaisance of a Companion. I bear the former in hopes of the latter Condition: As I live in Chains without murmuring at the Power which inflicts 'em, so I could enjoy Freedom without forgetting the Mercy that gave it.

> *Madam,*
> *I am,*
> *your most Devoted,*
> *most Obedient Servant.*"

[6] Tapestry hangings, with Biblical scenes, were now out of date, replaced by wall paper, and sometimes by Indian screens, with more worldly depictions, like the love stories from Greek mythology.

[7] He is so distracted by thoughts of her that he cannot attend to his usual affairs and associates.

Tho' I made him no Declarations in his Favour, you see he had hopes of Me when he writ this in the Month following.

"*Madam,*   *September 3, 1671.*

Before the Light this Morning dawned upon the Earth I awak'd, and lay in expectation of its return, not that it cou'd give any new Sense of Joy to me, but as I hop'd it would bless you with its chearful Face, after a Quiet which I wish'd you last Night. If my Prayers are heard, the Day appear'd with all the Influence of a Merciful Creator upon your Person and Actions. Let others, my lovely Charmer, talk of a Blind Being[8] that disposes their Hearts, I contemn their low Images of Love. I have not a Thought which relates to you, that I cannot with Confidence beseech the All-seeing Power to bless Me in. May he direct you in all your Steps, and reward your Innocence, your Sanctity of Manners, your prudent Youth, and becoming Piety, with the Continuance of his Grace and Protection. This is an unusual Language to Ladies; but you have a Mind elevated above the giddy Motions of a Sex insnared by Flattery, and mis-led by a false and short Adoration into a solid and long Contempt. Beauty, my fairest Creature, palls in the Possession, but I love also your Mind; your Soul is as dear to me as my own; and if the Advantages of a liberal Education, some Knowledge, and as much Contempt of the World,[9] join'd with the Endeavours towards a Life of strict Virtue and Religion, can qualify me to raise new Ideas in a Breast so well dispos'd as yours is, our Days will pass away with Joy; and old Age instead of introducing melancholy Prospects of Decay, give us hope of Eternal Youth in a better Life. I have but few Minutes from the Duty of my Employment to write in, and without time to read over what I have writ, therefore beseech you to pardon the first Hints of my Mind, which I have express'd in so little Order.

I am,
Dearest Creature,
your most Obedient,
most Devoted Servant."

The two next were Written after the Day for our Marriage was fix'd.

---

8 Cupid is usually represented as a winged boy, carrying a bow and arrows and wearing a blindfold.

9 I.e., some knowledge of the world and as much contempt for the world.

"*Madam,*   *September* 25, 1671.
It is the hardest thing in the World to be in Love, and yet attend Business. As for me, all that speak to me find me out, and I must lock my self up, or other People will do it for me.[10] A Gentleman ask'd me this Morning what News from *Holland,*[11] and I answer'd She's exquisitly handsome. Another desir'd to know when I had been last at *Windsor,* I reply'd She designs to go with me. Prethee allow me at least to kiss your Hand before the appointed Day, that my Mind may be in some Composure. Methinks I could write a Volume to you, but all the Language on Earth would fail in saying how much, and with what dis-interested[12] Passion,

                                                              I am ever Yours."

                                                      September 30, 1671.
"*Dear Creature,*   *Seven in the Morning.*
Next to the Influence of Heav'n, I am to thank you that I see the returning Day with Pleasure. To pass my Evenings in so sweet a Conversation, and have the Esteem of a Woman of your Merit, has in it a Particularity of Happiness no more to be express'd than return'd.[13] But I am, my Lovely Creature, contented to be on the oblig'd Side, and to employ all my Days in new Endeavours to convince you and all the World of the Sense I have of your Condescension in Chusing,
                                       Madam,

                                            Your most Faithful,
                                  Most Obedient Humble Servant."

He was, when he writ the following Letter, as agreeable and pleasant a Man as any in England.

"*Madam,*   *October* 20, 1671.
I beg Pardon that my Paper is not Finer, but I am forc'd to write from a Coffee-house where I am attending about Business. There is a dirty Croud of Busie Faces all around me talking of Mony, while all my Ambition, all my Wealth is Love: Love, which animates my Heart, sweetens my Humour, enlarges my Soul, and affects every Action of

[10] If he does not lock himself away from others, they will interpret his romantic distraction as madness and have him locked up.

[11] See *Tatler* No. 155, n. 4.

[12] Unselfish, virtuous.

[13] I.e., she makes him more happy that he can express and more happy than he can ever make her. This is why he declares himself "on the oblig'd Side."

my Life. 'Tis to my Lovely Charmer I owe that[14] many noble Ideas are continually affix'd to my Words and Actions: 'Tis the natural Effect of that Generous Passion to create in the Admirer some Similitude of[15] the Object admir'd; thus, my Dear, am I every Day to improve from so sweet a Companion. Look up, my Fair One, to that Heaven which made thee such, and join with me to implore its Influence on our tender innocent Hours, and beseech the Author of Love to bless the Rights he has ordain'd, and mingle with our Happiness a just Sense of our Transient Condition, and a Resignation to his Will, which only can regulate our Minds to a steady Endeavour to please him and each other.

> I am, for Ever,
> Your Faithful Servant."

I will not trouble you with more Letters at this time, but if you saw the poor withered Hand which sends you these Minutes, I am sure you would smile to think that there is one who is so gallant as to speak of it still as so welcome a Present, after forty Years Possession of the Woman whom he writes to.

"Madam,   June 20, 1711.
I heartily beg your Pardon for my Omission to write Yesterday. It was no Failure of my tender Regard for you; but having been very much perplexed in my Thoughts on the Subject of my last, made me determine to suspend speaking of it till I came my self. But, my lovely Creature, know it is not in the Power of Age, of Misfortune, or any other Accident which hangs over human Life, to take from me the pleasing Esteem I have for you, or the Memory of the bright Figure you appeared in when you gave your Hand and Heart to,

> Madam,
> Your most grateful Husband
> and obedient Servant."[16]

T

14 I.e., the fact that.

15 Similarity to.

16 Though it is doubtful that Steele was in any way insincere or ironic in presenting these letters, one can read elements of unintended humor. Notable are the Whig-like references to business; the ethereal quality of the sentiments, which contrast with Steele's too human character; and the fact that the addressee was Steele's second wife, whom he married within a year of the death of the first.

The Spectator, No. 159

Saturday, September 1.

[Addison]

————*Omnem quae nunc obducta tuenti*
Mortales hebetat visus tibi, & humida circum
Caligat, nubem eripiam————Virg.[1]

When I was at *Grand Cairo*[2] I picked up several Oriental Manuscripts, which I have still by me. Among others I met with one entituled, *The Visions of Mirzah*,[3] which I have read over with great Pleasure. I intend to give it to the Publick when I have no other Entertainment for them; and shall begin with the first Vision, which I have translated Word for Word as follows.

"On the fifth Day of the Moon,[4] which according to the Custom of my Forefathers I always keep holy, after having washed my self and offered up my Morning Devotions, I ascended the high Hills of *Bagdat,* in order to pass the rest of the Day in Meditation and Prayer. As I was here airing my self on the Tops of the Mountains, I fell into a profound Contemplation on the Vanity of humane Life; and passing from one Thought to another, Surely, said I, Man is but a Shadow and Life a Dream. Whilst I was thus musing, I cast my Eyes towards the Summit of a Rock that was not far from me, where I discovered one in the Habit[5] of a Shepherd, with a little Musical Instrument in his Hand. As I looked upon him he applied it to his Lips, and began

1 Virgil *Aeneid* 2. 604–606: "I will rend all the cloud that now, veiling your sight, dulls mortal vision and spreads a mist around."

2 See *Spectator* No. 1.

3 The title *Mirza* or *Mirzah,* meaning "son of a Prince," appeared regularly in Sir John Chardin's *Travels into Persia and the East Indies* (1686).

4 I.e., of the lunar month.

5 Garments.

to play upon it. The Sound of it was exceeding sweet, and wrought into a Variety of Tunes that were inexpressibly melodious, and altogether different from any thing I had ever heard. They put me in mind of those heavenly Airs that are played to the departed Souls of good Men upon their first Arrival in Paradise, to wear out the Impressions of their last Agonies, and qualify them for the Pleasures of that happy Place. My Heart melted away in secret Raptures.

"I had been often told that the Rock before me was the Haunt of a Genius;[6] and that several had been entertained with Musick who had passed by it, but never heard that the Musician had before made himself visible. When he had raised my Thoughts, by those transporting Airs which he played, to taste the Pleasures of his Conversation, as I looked upon him like one astonished, he beckoned to me, and by the waving of his Hand directed me to approach the Place where he sat. I drew near with that Reverence which is due to a superiour Nature; and as my Heart was entirely subdued by the captivating Strains I had heard, I fell down at his Feet and wept. The Genius smiled upon me with a Look of Compassion and Affability that familiarized him to my Imagination, and at once dispelled all the Fears and Apprehensions with which I approached him. He lifted me from the Ground, and taking me by the Hand, *Mirzah,* said he, I have heard thee in thy Soliloquies, follow me.

"He then led me to the highest Pinnacle of the Rock, and placing me on the Top of it, Cast thy Eyes Eastward, said he, and tell me what thou seest. I see, said I, a huge Valley and a prodigious Tide of Water rolling through it. The Valley that thou seest, said he, is the Vale of Misery, and the Tide of Water that thou seest is Part of the great Tide of Eternity. What is the Reason, said I, that the Tide I see rises out of a thick Mist at one End, and again loses it self in a thick Mist at the other? What thou seest, said he, is that Portion of Eternity which is called Time, measured out by the Sun, and reaching from the Beginning of the World to its Consummation. Examine now, said he, this Sea that is thus bounded with Darkness at both Ends, and tell me what thou discoverest in it. I see a Bridge, said I, standing in the Midst of the Tide. The Bridge thou seest, said he, is humane Life;[7] consider it attentively. Upon a more leisurely Survey of it, I found that it consisted of threescore and ten entire Arches,

6 A genie, a spirit.

7 The allegory is uncomplicated: The arches of the bridge reflect the normal seventy-year life span; the broken arches, the years beyond age seventy; and the trap-doors, premature death.

with several broken Arches, which added to those that were entire made up the Number about an hundred. As I was counting the Arches, the Genius told me that this Bridge consisted at first of a thousand Arches; but that a great Flood swept away the rest, and left the Bridge in the ruinous Condition I now beheld it.[8] But tell me further, said he, what thou discoverest on it. I see Multitudes of People passing over it, said I, and a black Cloud hanging on each End of it. As I looked more attentively, I saw several of the Passengers dropping thro' the Bridge, into the great Tide that flowed underneath it; and upon further Examination, perceived there were innumerable Trap-doors that lay concealed in the Bridge, which the Passengers no sooner trod upon, but they fell through them into the Tide and immediately disappeared. These hidden Pit-falls were set very thick at the Entrance of the Bridge, so that Throngs of People no sooner broke through the Cloud,[9] but many of them fell into them. They grew thinner towards the Middle, but multiplied and lay closer together towards the End of the Arches that were entire.

"There were indeed some Persons, but their Number was very small, that continued a kind of hobbling March on the broken Arches, but fell through one after another, being quite tired and spent with so long a Walk.

"I passed some Time in the Contemplation of this wonderful Structure, and the great Variety of Objects which it presented. My Heart was filled with a deep Melancholy to see several dropping unexpectedly in the Midst of Mirth and Jollity, and catching at every thing that stood by them to save themselves. Some were looking up towards the Heavens in a thoughtful Posture, and in the Midst of a Speculation stumbled and fell out of Sight. Multitudes were very busy in the Pursuit of Bubbles that glittered in their Eyes and danced before them, but often when they thought themselves within the Reach of them their Footing failed and down they sunk. In this Confusion of Objects, I observed some with Scymetars in their Hands, and others with Urinals, who ran to and fro upon the Bridge, thrusting several Persons on Trap-doors which did not seem to lie in their Way, and which they might have escaped had they not been thus forced upon them.[10]

[8] A literal reading of Genesis indicates that, before the flood, men lived up to 1000 years.

[9] The clouds at the entrance of the bridge suggest a concept of pre-existence.

[10] The suggestion is that doctors—like soldiers with scimitars (swords with a curved blade)—help to destroy men before their allotted time. See *Tatler* No. 240.

"The Genius seeing me indulge my self in this melancholy Prospect, told me I had dwelt long enough upon it: Take thine Eyes off the Bridge, said he, and tell me if thou yet seest any thing thou dost not comprehend. Upon looking up, What mean said I, those great Flights of Birds that are perpetually hovering about the Bridge, and settling upon it from Time to Time? I see Vultures, Harpyes, Ravens, Cormorants; and among many other feathered Creatures several little winged Boys, that perch in great Numbers upon the middle Arches.[11] These said the Genius, are Envy, Avarice, Superstition, Despair, Love, with the like Cares and Passions that infest humane Life.

"I here fetched a deep Sigh, Alass, said I, Man was made in vain! How is he given away to Misery and Mortality! tortured in Life, and swallowed up in Death! The Genius being moved with Compassion towards me, bid me quit so uncomfortable a Prospect: Look no more, said he, on Man in the first Stage of his Existence, in his setting out for Eternity; but cast thine Eye on that thick Mist into which the Tide bears the several Generations of Mortals that fall into it. I directed my Sight as I was ordered, and (whether or no the good Genius strengthened it with any supernatural Force, or dissipated Part of the Mist that was before too thick for the Eye to penetrate) I saw the Valley opening at the further End, and spreading forth into an immense Ocean, that had a huge Rock of Adamant[12] running through the Midst of it, and dividing it into two equal Parts. The Clouds still rested on one Half of it, insomuch that I could discover nothing in it; but the other appeared to me a vast Ocean planted with innumerable Islands, that were covered with Fruits and Flowers, and interwoven with a thousand little shining Seas that ran among them. I could see Persons dressed in glorious Habits, with Garlands upon their Heads, passing among the Trees, lying down by the Sides of Fountains, or resting on Beds of Flowers; and could hear a confused Harmony of singing Birds, falling Waters, humane Voices, and musical Instruments. Gladness grew in me upon the Discovery of so delightful a Scene. I wished for the Wings of an Eagle, that I might fly away to those happy Seats;[13] but the Genius told me there was no Passage to them, except through the Gates of Death that I saw open-

[11] Harpies are, in later Greek literature, hideous birds with heads of maidens; cormorants are sea-crows; the *little winged Boys* are, of course, Cupid figures.

[12] The hardest substance; originally the word referred to the diamond. The huge rock represents the eternal division in the after life, the separation of the blessed from the damned souls.

[13] Habitations.

ing every Moment upon the Bridge. The Islands, said he, that lie so fresh and green before thee, and with which the whole Face of the Ocean appears spotted as far as thou canst see, are more in Number than the Sands on the Sea-shore; there are Myriads of Islands behind those which thou here discoverest, reaching further than thine Eye or even thine Imagination can extend it self. These are the Mansions of good Men after Death, who according to the Degree and Kinds of Virtue in which they excelled, are distributed among these several Islands, which abound with Pleasures of different Kinds and Degrees, suitable to the Relishes and Perfections of those who are settled in them; every Island is a Paradise accommodated to its respective Inhabitants. Are not these, O *Mirzah*, Habitations worth contending for? Does Life appear miserable, that gives thee Opportunites of earning such a Reward? Is Death to be feared, that will convey thee to so happy an Existence? Think not Man was made in vain, who has such an Eternity reserved for him. I gazed with inexpressible Pleasure on these happy Islands. At length said I, shew me now, I beseech thee, the Secrets that lie hid under those dark Clouds which cover the Ocean on the other Side of the Rock of Adamant. The Genius making me no Answer, I turned about to address my self to him a second time, but I found that he had left me; I then turned again to the Vision which I had been so long contemplating, but instead of the rolling Tide, the arched Bridge, and the happy Islands, I saw nothing but the long hollow Valley of *Bagdat,* with Oxen, Sheep, and Camels, grazing upon the Sides of it.

   The End of the first Vision of Mirzah."[14]   C

   [14] Since this is called "the first Vision," it is probable that Addison intended a series. Despite the immense popularity of this Mirzah paper, no others were published.

The Spectator, No. 160

Monday, September 3.

[A d d i s o n]

————*Cui mens divinior, atque os*
Magna sonaturum, des nominis hujus honorem. Hor.[1]

There is no Character more frequently given to a Writer, than that of being a Genius. I have heard many a little Sonneteer called a *fine Genius.* There is not an Heroick Scribler[2] in the Nation, that has not his Admirers who think him a *great Genius;* and as for your Smatterers in Tragedy,[3] there is scarce a Man among them who is not cried up by one or other for a *prodigious Genius.*

My Design in this Paper is to consider what is properly a great Genius, and to throw some Thoughts together on so uncommon a Subject.

Among great Geniuss, those few draw the Admiration of all the World upon them, and stand up as the Prodigies of Mankind, who by the meer Strength of natural Parts,[4] and without any Assistance of Art or Learning, have produced Works that were the Delight of their own Times and the Wonder of Posterity. There appears something nobly wild and extravagant in these great natural Geniuss, that is infinitely more beautiful than all the Turn and Polishing of what the *French* call a *Bel Esprit,* by which they would express a Genius refined by Conversation, Reflection, and

1 Horace *Satires* 1. 4. 43–44: "Call him a poet, who has a divine nature and an eloquent voice."

2 An inferior writer of epics.

3 The work of such *Smatterers* was discussed in *Spectators* No. 39, 40, 42, and 44.

4 Talents.

the Reading of the most polite[5] Authors. The greatest Genius
which runs through the Arts and Sciences, takes a kind of Tincture from them, and falls unavoidably into Imitation.

Many of these great natural Geniuss that were never disciplined and broken by Rules of Art, are to be found among the
Ancients, and in particular among those of the more Eastern Parts
of the World. *Homer* has innumerable Flights that *Virgil* was not
able to reach, and in the Old Testament we find several Passages
more elevated and sublime than any in *Homer*. At the same Time
that we allow a greater and more daring Genius to the Ancients,
we must own that the greatest of them very much failed in, or, if
you will, that they were much above the Nicety and Correctness
of the Moderns. In their Similitudes and Allusions, provided
there was a Likeness, they did not much trouble themselves about
the Decency[6] of the Comparison: Thus *Solomon* resembles the
Nose of his Beloved to the Tower of *Libanon* which looketh
toward *Damascus;* as the Coming of a Thief in the Night, is a
Similitude of the same Kind in the New Testament.[7] It would be
endless to make Collections of this Nature: *Homer* illustrates one
of his Heroes encompassed with the Enemy, by an Ass in a Field
of Corn that has his Sides belaboured by all the Boys of the Village without stirring a Foot for it; and another of them tossing to
and fro in his Bed and burning with Resentment, to a Piece of
Flesh broiled on the Coals.[8] This particular Failure in the Ancients, opens a large Field of Raillerie to the little Wits, who can
laugh at an Indecency but not relish the Sublime in these Sorts
of Writings. The present Emperor of *Persia*,[9] conformable to this
Eastern way of Thinking, amidst a great many pompous Titles,
denominates himself the Sun of Glory and the *Nutmeg of Delight*.
In short, to cut off all Cavelling against the Ancients, and particularly those of the warmer Climates, who had most Heat and Life

[5] Refined, polished.

[6] Appropriateness.

[7] The "Tower" reference appears in the Song of Solomon 7:4. The "Thief"
image is from 2 Peter 3:10: "But the day of the Lord will come as a thief in
the night." The simile also appears in 1 Thessalonians 5:2.

[8] The first hero is Ajax (*Iliad* 2. 558–565); the second, Ulysses (*Odyssey* 20.
25–30).

[9] Husein (1675?–1729) was Shah of Persia from 1694 to 1722.

in their Imaginations, we are to consider that the Rule of observing what the *French* call the *Bienseance*[10] in an Allusion, has been found out of latter Years and in the colder Regions of the World; where we would make some Amends for our want of Force and Spirit, by a scrupulous Nicety and Exactness in our Compositions. Our Countryman *Shakespear* was a remarkable Instance of this first kind of great Geniuss.

I cannot quit this Head without observing that *Pindar* was a great Genius of the first Class, who was hurried on by a natural Fire and Impetuosity to vast Conceptions of things, and noble Sallies of Imagination. At the same time, can any thing be more ridiculous than for Men of a sober and moderate Fancy to imitate this Poet's Way of Writing in those monstrous Compositions which go among us under the Name of Pindaricks?[11] When I see People copying Works, which, as *Horace* has represented them, are singular in their Kind and inimitable; when I see Men following Irregularities by Rule, and by the little Tricks of Art straining after the most unbounded Flights of Nature, I cannot but apply to them that Passage in *Terence*.

> ———*incerta haec si tu postules*
> *Ratione certa facere, nihilo plus agas,*
> *Quàm si des operam, ut cum ratione insanias.*[12]

In short a modern pindarick Writer compared with *Pindar,* is like a Sister among the *Camisars* compared with *Virgil's* Sybil:[13] There is the Distortion, Grimace, and outward Figure, but nothing of that divine Impulse which raises the Mind above it self, and makes the Sounds more than humane.

There is another kind of Great Geniuss which I shall place in a second Class, not as I think them inferior to the first, but only for distinction's sake as they are of a different kind. This second

10 Propriety, decorum.

11 See *Spectator* No. 58, n. 25.

12 Terence *Eunuchus* 61–63: "You may as well pretend to be mad and sane at the same time, as to think of reducing these uncertainties into certainties by reason."

13 The Camisars—or Camisards—were French Calvinists, many of whom fled to England, where they were also called the French Prophets. The Cumaean Sibyl is a prophetess consulted by Aeneas before his journey into Hades (*Aeneid* 6. 42ff).

Class of great Genius's are those that have formed themselves by Rules, and submitted the Greatness of their natural Talents to the Corrections and Restraints of Art. Such among the *Greeks* were *Plato* and *Aristotle,* among the *Romans Virgil* and *Tully,*[14] among the *English Milton* and Sir *Francis Bacon.*

The Genius in both these Classes of Authors may be equally great, but shews it self after a different Manner. In the first it is like a rich Soil in a happy Climate, that produces a whole Wilderness of noble Plants rising in a thousand beautiful Landskips without any certain Order or Regularity. In the other it is the same rich Soil under the same happy Climate, that has been laid out in Walks and Parterres, and cut into Shape and Beauty by the Skill of the Gardener.

The great Danger in these latter kind of Geniuss, is, least they cramp their own Abilities too much by Imitation, and form themselves altogether upon Models, without giving the full Play to their own natural Parts. An Imitation of the best Authors, is not to compare with a good Original; and I believe we may observe that very few Writers make an extraordinary Figure in the World, who have not something in their Way of thinking or expressing themselves that is peculiar to them and entirely their own.

It is odd to consider what great Geniuss are sometimes thrown away upon Trifles.

I once saw a Shepherd, says a famous *Italian* Author,[15] who used to divert himself in his Solitudes with tossing up Eggs and catching them again without breaking them: In which he had arrived to so great a Degree of Perfection, that he would keep up four at a Time for several Minutes together playing in the Air, and falling into his Hand by Turns. I think, says the Author, I never saw a greater Severity than in this Man's Face; for by his wonderful Perseverance and Application, he had contracted the Seriousness and Gravity of a Privy-Councellour;[16] and I could not but reflect with my self, that the same Assiduity and Attention had they been rightly applied, might have made him a greater Mathematician than *Archimedes.*[17]

C

---

[14] See *Tatler* No. 167, n. 5.

[15] No editor has yet identified this author.

[16] See *Spectator* No. 106, n. 3.

[17] Famous Greek mathematician and inventor (287?–212 B.C.).

The Spectator, No. 165

Saturday, September 8.

[A d d i s o n]

————*Si forte necesse est,*
Fingere cinctutis non exaudita Cethegis,
Continget: labiturque licentia sumpta pudenter. Hor.[1]

I have often wished, that as in our Constitution there are several Persons whose Business it is to watch over our Laws, our Liberties and Commerce, certain Men might be set apart, as Superintendants of our Language, to hinder any Words of a Foreign Coin from passing among us; and in particular to prohibit any *French* Phrases from becoming Current in this Kingdom, when those of our own Stamp are altogether as valuable.[2] The present War has so Adulterated our Tongue with strange Words, that it would be impossible for one of our Great Grandfathers to know what his Posterity have been doing, were he to read their Exploits in a Modern News-Paper. Our Warriors are very Industrious in Propagating the *French* Language, at the same time that they are so gloriously successful in beating down their Power.[3] Our Soldiers are Men of strong Heads for Action, and perform such Feats as they are not able to express. They want[4] Words in their own Tongue to tell us what it is they Atchieve, and therefore send us

1 Horace *Ars Poetica* 48. 50–51: "If it is necessary, you can create words not current among the Cethegi and indulge a license until it becomes excessive."

2 In *Spectator* No. 45, Addison protested the importation of French fopperies; in No. 135, he decried the corruption of the English language.

3 At a time when Tories were seeking a negotiated settlement with France, the several references to the "gloriously successful" English campaigns suggest the author's Whig sympathies.

4 Lack.

over Accounts of their Performances in a Jargon of Phrases, which they learn among their Conquered Enemies. They ought however to be provided with Secretaries, and assisted by our Foreign Ministers, to tell their Story for them in plain *English,* and to let us know in our Mother-Tongue what it is our brave Countrymen are about. The *French* would indeed be in the right to Publish the News of the present War in *English* Phrases, and make their Campaigns unintelligible. Their People might flatter themselves that things are not so bad as they really are, were they thus palliated with Foreign Terms, and thrown into Shades and Obscurity. But the *English* cannot be too clear in their Narrative of those Actions, which have raised their Country to a higher Pitch of Glory than it ever yet arrived at, and which will be still the more admired the better they are explained.

For my part, by that Time a Siege is carried on two or three Days, I am altogether lost and bewildered in it, and meet with so many inexplicable Difficulties, that I scarce know which Side has the better of it, till I am informed by the Tower Guns that the Place is surrendred. I do indeed make some Allowances for this Part of the War,[5] Fortifications having been Foreign Inventions, and upon that Account abounding in Foreign Terms. But when we have won Battels which may be described in our own Language, why are our Papers filled with so many unintelligible Exploits, and the *French* obliged to lend us a part of their Tongue before we can know how they are Conquered? They must be made accessary to their own Disgrace, as the *Britains* were formerly so artificially wrought in the Curtain of the *Roman* Theatre,[6] that they seemed to draw it up, in order to give the Spectators an Opportunity of seeing their own Defeat celebrated upon the Stage: For so Mr. *Dryden* has translated that Verse in *Virgil*

> *Atque intertexti tollant aulaea Britanni.*[7]

> *Which interwoven* Britains *seem to raise,*
> *And show the Triumph that their Shame displays.*

---

[5] For the language describing battles won by siege.
[6] Figures of defeated Britons were woven in the curtains of the Roman theater.
[7] Virgil *Georgics* 3.25. The translation which follows is Dryden's.

The Histories of all our former Wars are transmitted to us in our Vernacular Idiom, to use the Phrase of a great Modern Critick.[8] I do not find in any of our Chronicles, that *Edward* the Third[9] ever reconnoitred the Enemy, tho' he often discover'd the Posture of the *French,* and as often vanquish'd them in Battel. The Black Prince[10] passed many a River without the help of Pontoons, and filled a Ditch with Faggots as successfully as the Generals of our Times do it with Fascines.[11] Our Commanders lose half their Praise, and our People half their Joy, by means of those hard Words and dark Expressions in which our News-Papers do so much abound. I have seen many a prudent Citizen, after having read every Article, enquire of his next Neighbour what News the Mail had brought.

I remember in that remarkable Year when our Country was delivered from the greatest Fears and Apprehensions, and raised to the greatest height of Gladness it had ever felt since it was a Nation, I mean the Year of *Blenheim,*[12] I had the Copy of a Letter sent me out of the Country, which was written from a young Gentleman in the Army to his Father, a Man of a good Estate and plain Sense: As the Letter[13] was very modishly checquered with this Modern Military Eloquence, I shall present my Reader with a Copy of it.

"*Sir,*

Upon the Junction of the *French* and *Bavarian* Armies they took Post behind a great Morass which they thought impracticable. Our General the next Day sent a Party of Horse to reconnoitre them from

8 Richard Bentley (1662–1742), English classical scholar. An adversary once complained of his use of the word "idiom."

9 Edward III, King of England (1327–1377), won many victories in France during the Hundred Years' War.

10 Edward, Prince of Wales (1330–1376), was the son of Edward III and fought victoriously in the same war.

11 The objection is to such corruptions as "reconnoitred," "Pontoons," and "Fascines." Fascines are faggots, sticks of wood used to fill up a ditch.

12 See *Spectator* No. 26, n. 16.

13 The letter reports that, after some preliminary communication between the Duke of Bavaria and "the General" (presumably Marlborough), the British forces defeated the French and Bavarian armies. The details are, of course, intentionally obscure.

a little Hauteur, at about a quarter of an Hour's distance from the Army, who return'd again to the Camp unobserved through several Defiles, in one of which they met with a Party of *French* that had been Marauding, and made them all Prisoners at Discretion. The Day after a Drum arrived at our Camp, with a Message which he would communicate to none but the General; he was followed by a Trumpet, who they say behaved himself very saucily, with a Message from the Duke of *Bavaria*. The next Morning our Army being divided into two Corps, made a Movement towards the Enemy: You will hear in the publick Prints how we treated them, with the other Circumstances of that glorious Day. I had the good Fortune to be in the Regiment that pushed the *Gens d'Arms.* Several *French* Battalions, who some say were a Corps de Reserve, made a Show of Resistance; but it only proved a Gasconade, for upon our preparing to fill up a little Fossé, in order to attack them, they beat the Chamade, and sent us *Charte Blanche.* Their Commandant, with a great many other General Officers, and Troops without number, are made Prisoners of War, and will I believe give you a Visit in *England,* the Cartel not being yet settled. Not questioning but these Particulars will be very welcome to you, I congratulate you upon them, and am your most dutiful Son, *&c."*

The Father of the young Gentleman upon the Perusal of the Letter found it contained great News, but could not guess what it was. He immediately communicated it to the Curate of the Parish, who upon the reading of it, being vexed to see any thing he could not understand, fell into a kind of Passion, and told him, that his Son had sent him a Letter that was neither Fish, Flesh, nor good Red Herring. I wish, says he, the Captain may be *Compos Mentis,*[14] he talks of a saucy Trumpet and a Drum that carries Messages: Then who is this *Charte Blanche:*[15] He must either banter us, or he is out of his Senses. The Father, who always look'd upon the Curate as a learned Man, began to fret inwardly at his Son's Usage, and producing a Letter which he had written to him about three Posts afore, You see here, says he, when he writes for Mony he knows how to speak intelligibly enough; there is no Man in *England* can express himself clearer, when he wants a new Furni-

---

[14] In his right senses.
[15] In the letter, *"Charte Blanche"* seems to be a hostage.

ture for his Horse. In short, the old Man was so puzzled upon the Point, that it might have fared ill with his Son, had he not seen all the Prints about three Days after filled with the same Terms of Art, and that *Charles* only writ like other Men.[16]   L

16 I.e., that his soldier son wrote like the newspaper writers.

The Spectator, No. 174

Wednesday, September 19.

[S t e e l e]

Haec memini & victum frustra contendere Thyrsin. Virg.[1]

There is scarce any thing more common than Animosities between Parties that cannot subsist but by their Agreement: This was well represented in the Sedition of the Members of the human Body in the old *Roman* Fable.[2] It is often the Case of lesser confederate States against a superior Power, which are hardly held together though their Unanimity is necessary for their common Safety: And this is always the Case of the landed and trading Interest of *Great Britain;* the Trader is fed by the Product of the Land, and the landed Man cannot be cloathed but by the Skill of the Trader; and yet those Interests are ever jarring.

We had last Winter an Instance of this at our Club, in Sir Roger de Coverly and Sir Andrew Freeport, between whom there is generally a constant, though friendly, Opposition of Opinions.[3] It happened that one of the Company, in an historical Discourse, was observing, that *Carthaginian* Faith was a proverbial Phrase to intimate Breach of Leagues.[4] Sir Roger said it could hardly be otherwise: That the *Carthaginians* were the greatest Traders in

---

[1] Virgil *Eclogues* 7. 69: "I remember these songs and how the defeated Thyrsis strove in vain."

[2] The fable, which appears in Livy (*History* 2. 32), was used five months earlier in Defoe's *Review* to make the same point: "Your Land might go a begging but for Trade; and for the Landed Men to rail at Trade, is like the Members Mutinying against the Belly" (May 1, 1711).

[3] See *Spectator* No. 126, n. 10.

[4] I.e., to describe a breach of contract or of loyalty.

the World; and as Gain is the chief End of such a People, they never pursue any other: The Means to it are never regarded; they will, if it comes easily, get Money honestly; but if not, they will not scruple to attain it by Fraud or Cosenage: And indeed what is the whole Business of the Trader's Accompt, but to over-reach him who trusts to his Memory? But were that not so, what can there great and noble be expected from him whose Attention is for ever fixed upon ballancing his Books, and watching over his Expences?[5] And at best, let Frugality and Parsimony be the Virtues of the Merchant, how much is his punctual Dealing below a Gentleman's Charity to the Poor, or Hospitality among his Neighbours?

Captain Sentry observed Sir Andrew very diligent in hearing Sir Roger, and had a Mind to turn the Discourse,[6] by taking Notice in general from the highest to the lowest Parts of humane Society, there was a secret, tho' unjust Way among Men, of indulging the Seeds of Ill-nature and Envy, by comparing their own State of Life to that of another, and grudging the Approach of their Neighbour to their own Happiness; and on the other Side, he who is the less at his Ease repines at the other who, he thinks, has unjustly the Advantage over him. Thus the civil and military List look upon each other with much Ill-nature; the Soldier repines at the Courtier's Power, and the Courtier rallies the Soldier's Honour; or to come to lower Instances, the private Men in the Horse and Foot of an Army, the Carmen and Coachmen in the City-streets, mutually look upon each other with Ill-will, when they are in Competition for Quarters or the Way[7] in their respective Motions.

It is very well, good Captain, interrupted Sir Andrew: You may attempt to turn the Discourse, if you think fit, but I must

---

[5] Sir Roger echoes the view expressed by Swift in *Examiner* No. 21 (December 28, 1710). Swift criticized the Whigs, who "come with the Spirit of *Shop-keepers* to frame Rules for the Administration of Kingdoms; or, as if they thought the whole Art of Government consisted in the Importation of *Nutmegs* and the Curing of *Herrings*."

[6] To leave this sensitive subject, by talking generally of the envy and division which separate men.

[7] Precedence in the street or on the road.

however have a Word or two with Sir Roger; who, I see, thinks he has paid me off,[8] and been very severe upon the Merchant. I shall not, continued he, at this Time remind Sir Roger of the great and noble Monuments of Charity and publick Spirit which have been erected by Merchants since the Reformation, but at present content my self with what he allows us, Parsimony and Frugality. If it were consistent with the Quality of so antient a Baronet as Sir Roger, to keep an Accompt or measure things by the most infallible Way, that of Numbers, he would prefer our Parsimony to his Hospitality. If to drink so many Hogsheads is to be hospitable, we do not contend for the Fame of that Virtue; but it would be worth while to consider, whether so many Artificers at work ten Days together by my Appointment, or so many Peasants made merry on Sir Roger's Charge, are the Men more obliged: I believe the Families of the Artificers will thank me, more than the Housholds of the Peasants shall Sir Roger. Sir Roger gives to his Men, but I place mine above the Necessity or Obligation of my Bounty. I am in very little Pain for the *Roman* Proverb upon the *Carthaginian* Traders; the *Romans* were their professed Enemies: I am only sorry no *Carthaginian* Histories have come to our Hands; we might have been taught perhaps by them some Proverbs against the *Roman* Generosity, in fighting for and bestowing other People's Goods. But since Sir Roger has taken Occasion from an old Proverb to be out of Humour with Merchants, it should be no Offence to offer one not quite so old in their Defence. When a Man happens to break[9] in *Holland,* they say of him that *he has not kept true Accompts.* This Phrase, perhaps, among us would appear a soft or humorous way of speaking, but with that exact Nation[10] it bears the highest Reproach; for a Man to be mistaken in the Calculation of his Expence, in his Ability to answer future Demands, or to be impertinently sanguine[11] in putting his Credit to too great Adventure, are all Instances of as much Infamy, as with gayer Nations to be failing in Courage or common Honesty.

Numbers are so much the Measure of every thing that is valu-

---

8 Convincingly dismissed me and my views.

9 Go bankrupt.

10 Dutch merchants were known for their scrupulosity in business matters.

11 Unduly confident.

able, that it is not possible to demonstrate the Success of any Action, or the Prudence of any Undertaking, without them. I say this in Answer to what Sir Roger is pleased to say, That little that is truly noble can be expected from one who is ever poring on his Cash-book or ballancing his Accompts. When I have my Returns from Abroad, I can tell to a Shilling by the Help of Numbers the Profit or Loss by my Adventure; but I ought also to be able to shew that I had Reason for making it, either from my own Experience or that of other People, or from a reasonable Presumption that my Returns will be sufficient to answer my Expence and Hazard; and this is never to be done without the Skill of Numbers. For Instance, if I am to trade to *Turkey,* I ought beforehand to know the Demand of our Manufactures there as well as of their Silks in *England,* and the customary Prices that are given for both in each Country. I ought to have a clear Knowledge of these Matters before-hand, that I may presume upon sufficient Returns to answer the Charge of the Cargo I have fitted out, the Freight and Assurance[12] out and home, the Customs to the Queen, and the Interest of my own Money, and besides all these Expences a reasonable Profit to my self. Now what is there of Scandal in this Skill? What has the Merchant done that he should be so little in the good Graces of Sir Roger? he throws down no Man's Enclosures, and tramples upon no Man's Corn;[13] he takes nothing from the industrious Labourer;[14] he pays the poor Man for his Work; he communicates his Profit with Mankind; by the Preparation of his Cargo and the Manufacture of his Returns, he furnishes Employment and Subsistance to greater Numbers than the richest Nobleman; and even the Nobleman is obliged to him for finding out foreign Markets for the Produce of his Estate, and for making a great Addition to his Rents; and yet 'tis certain that none of all these Things could be done by him without the Exercise of his Skill in Numbers.

This is the Oeconomy of the Merchant, and the Conduct of the

12 Insurance.

13 Where Sir Roger stereotyped all merchants as low shopkeepers, Sir Andrew tends to see all country squires as insensitive fox-hunters. See *Tatler* No. 89, n. 10.

14 Whereas a tenant had to sell his produce to pay the gentleman for the use of his land.

Gentleman must be the same, unless by scorning to be the Steward, he resolves the Steward shall be the Gentleman.[15] The Gentleman no more than the Merchant is able without the Help of Numbers to account for the Success of any Action, or the Prudence of any Adventure. If, for Instance, the Chace is his whole Adventure, his only Returns must be the Stag's Horns in the great Hall, and the Fox's Nose upon the Stable Door.[16] Without Doubt Sir Roger knows the full Value of these Returns; and if before-hand he had computed the Charges of the Chace, a Gentleman of his Discretion would certainly have hang'd up all his Dogs, he would never have brought back so many fine Horses to the Kennel, he would never have gone so often like a Blast over Fields of Corn. If such too had been the Conduct of all his Ancestors, he might truly have boasted at this Day that the Antiquity of his Family had never been sullied by a Trade; a Merchant had never been permitted with his whole Estate to purchase a Room for his Picture in the Gallery of the Coverlys, or to claim his Descent from the Maid of Honour.[17] But 'tis very happy for Sir Roger that the Merchant paid so dear for his Ambition. 'Tis the Misfortune of many other Gentlemen to turn out of the Seats of their Ancestors, to make Way for such new Masters as have been more exact in their Accompts than themselves; and certainly he deserves the Estate a great deal better who has got it by his Industry, than he who has lost it by his Negligence.   T

[15] I.e., unless the gentleman keeps careful accounts, he will lose his land to some exact merchant who does. Specifically, the steward was the servant who kept the accounts of an estate.

[16] In *Spectator* No. 115, Addison described Sir Roger's hunting trophies. Sir Andrew's comments on the hunt are ironical.

[17] In *Spectator* No. 109 by Steele Sir Roger showed the Spectator through his gallery of paintings, proudly pointing out—among other ancestors—one "Fair Lady, who was a Maid of Honour, and the greatest Beauty of her time," and one man who "left the Estate with ten thousand Pounds Debt upon it, but . . . was every way the finest Gentleman in the World." Next was the portrait of "a Citizen of our Name, but nothing at all a-kin to us," who relieved the Estate of the debt. The Knight reported Sir Andrew's facetious claim that the citizen was descended from the maid of honor.

The Spectator, No. 191

Tuesday, October 9.

[A d d i s o n]

———οὐλον ὄνειρον· Hom.[1]

Some ludicrous Schoolmen[2] have put the case, that if an Ass were placed between two bundles of Hay, which affected his Senses equally on each side, and tempted him in the very same degree, whether it would be possible for him to Eat of either. They generally determine this Question to the Disadvantage of the Ass, who they say would Starve in the midst of Plenty, as not having a single Grain of Free-will to determine him more to the one than to the other. The bundle of Hay on either side striking his Sight and Smell in the same proportion, would keep him in a perpetual Suspence, like the two Magnets which Travellers have told us, are placed one of them in the Roof, and the other in the Floor of *Mahomet's* Burying Place at *Mecca,* and by that means, say they, pull the Impostor's Iron Coffin with such an equal Attraction, that it hangs in the Air between both of them.[3] As for the Ass's Behaviour in such nice[4] Circumstances, whether he would Starve

1 Homer *Iliad* 2. 6: "A deluding dream."

2 The Aristotelian philosophers of the Middle Ages in Europe, who were commonly ridiculed for their theoretical precision. The problem of the ass and the bales of hay is popularly attributed to Jean Buridan (d. after 1358), a French scholastic philosopher.

3 In legend, Mahomet's coffin is in a room, the floors, walls, and ceiling of which are all faced with lodestone; because of the equal attraction from all sides, his iron shrine hangs in mid-air. As in *Spectator* No. 94, Addison refers to the prophet as "the Impostor."

4 Perplexing, requiring a careful discrimination.

sooner than violate his Neutrality to the two bundles of Hay, I shall not presume to determine; but only take Notice of the Conduct of our own Species in the same Perplexity.[5] When a Man has a mind to venture his Mony in a Lottery,[6] every Figure of it appears equally alluring, and as likely to succeed as any of its fellows. They all of them have the same Pretensions to good Luck, stand upon the same foot of Competition, and no manner of Reason can be given why a Man should prefer one to the other before the Lottery is drawn. In this Case therefore Caprice very often acts in the Place of Reason, and forms to it self some Groundless Imaginary Motive, where real and substantial ones are wanting. I know a well-meaning Man that is very well pleased to risque his good Fortune upon the Number 1711, because it is the Year of our Lord.[7] I am acquainted with a Tacker that would give a good deal for the Number 134.[8] On the contrary I have been told of a certain Zealous Dissenter who being a great Enemy to Popery, and believing that bad Men are the most fortunate in this World, will lay two to one on the Number 666 against any other Number, because, says he, it is the Number of the Beast.[9] Several would prefer the Number 12000 before any other, as it is the Number of the Pounds in the great Prize.[10] In short, some are pleased to find

[5] As Addison goes on to discuss "the Life of the Fool and the Superstitious" and to identify one such as "George Gosling," it becomes clear that the story of the ass is more than an introductory comparison.

[6] To relieve financial problems caused by the war, the Parliament of 1709–1710 revived the state lotteries. In 1711, two lotteries were held, one for prizes totalling 1,500,000 pounds and one for 2,000,000 pounds.

[7] I.e., the present year.

[8] In 1704, when a bill against Occasional Conformity was brought into the House of Commons, it was proposed to tack it to a money bill, that it might more surely pass the House of Lords. When the proposal was at length put to a vote, it was defeated by a large majority, with only 134 members voting for tacking.

[9] The Dissenters—i.e., Methodists, Baptists, Quakers, Independents, and other Protestant sects who dissented from the doctrines and forms of the Church of England—tended to be zealous enemies of Popery. Extreme Dissenters commonly identified the Pope with the Beast mentioned in Revelations 13:18: "Let him that hath understanding count the number of the beast: for it is the number of a man; his number is six hundred three-score and six."

[10] The largest prize was also called the great lot or the chief lot. There were lesser prizes as well.

their own Age in their Number; some that they have got a Number which makes a pretty Appearance in the Cyphers, and others because it is the same Number that succeeded in the last Lottery. Each of these, upon no other Grounds, thinks he stands fairest for the great Lot, and that he is possessed of what may not be improperly called the *Golden Number*.[11]

These Principles of Election are the Pastimes and Extravagances of Human Reason, which is of so busie a Nature, that it will be exerting it self in the meanest Trifles, and working even when it wants Materials. The wisest of Men are sometimes acted[12] by such unaccountable Motives, as the Life of the Fool and the Superstitious is guided by nothing else.

I am surprized that none of the Fortune-tellers, or as the *French* call them, the *Diseurs de bonne avanture,* who publish their Bills[13] in every Quarter of the Town, have not turned our Lotteries to their Advantage; did any of them set up for a Caster of Fortunate Figures, what might he not get by his pretended Discoveries and Predictions?

I remember among the Advertisements in the *Post-Boy*[14] of *September* the 27th, I was surprized to see the following one.

> *This is to give Notice, That Ten Shillings over and above the Market Price, will be given for the Ticket in the* 1500000 £. *Lottery, No* 132, *by Nath. Cliff*[15] *at the Bible and Three Crowns in Cheapside.*

This Advertisement has given great Matter of Speculation to Coffee-house Theorists.[16] Mr. *Cliff's* Principles and Conversation have been canvassed upon this Occasion, and various Conjectures made why he should thus set his Heart upon No 132. I have examined all the Powers in those Numbers, broken them into Fractions, extracted the Square and Cube Root, divided and multiplied them all ways, but could not arrive at the Secret till about three Days ago, when I received the following Letter from an un-

---

[11] The number of any year in the lunar cycle of nineteen years, used in establishing the date of Easter.

[12] Actuated.

[13] Advertise.

[14] See *Tatler* No. 18, n. 21.

[15] A London book-seller.

[16] Coffee-house regulars were commonly given to theoretical speculation.

known Hand; by which I find that Mr. *Nathaniel Cliff* is only the Agent, and not the Principal, in this Advertisement.

"*Mr.* Spectator,

I am the Person that lately advertised I would give ten Shillings more than the Current Price for the Ticket No 132 in the Lottery now Drawing, which is a Secret I have communicated to some Friends, who rally me incessantly upon that account. You must know I have but one Ticket, for which Reason, and a certain Dream I have lately had more than once, I was resolved it should be the Number I most approved. I am so positive I have pitched upon the great Lot, that I could almost lay all I am worth of it. My Visions are so frequent and strong upon this Occasion, that I have not only possessed the Lot, but disposed of the Money which in all probability it will sell for.[17] This Morning, in particular, I set up an Equipage which I look upon to be the gayest in the Town. The Liveries are very Rich, but not Gaudy.[18] I should be very glad to see a Speculation or two[19] upon Lottery Subjects, in which you would oblige all People concerned, and in particular

Your most humble Servant,
George Gossling.

P. S. Dear Spec, If I get the 12000 Pound I'll make thee a handsome Present."

After having wished my Correspondent good Luck, and thanked him for his intended Kindness, I shall for this time dismiss the Subject of the Lottery, and only observe that the greatest part of Mankind are in some degree guilty of my Friend *Gossling*'s Extravagance. We are apt to rely upon future Prospects, and become really expensive while we are only rich in Possibility. We live up to our Expectations, not to our Possessions, and make a Figure proportionable to what we may be, not what we are. We out-run our present Income, as not doubting to disburse[20] our selves out of the Profits of some future Place, Project or Rever-

---

[17] I.e., in his imagination he has already cashed in the ticket, and in real life, he has begun spending the money.

[18] The uniforms of his servants are described by the lines of Polonius (*Hamlet,* act 1, sc. 3).

[19] An essay or two in the *Spectator*.

[20] Reimburse.

sion, that we have in view. It is through this Temper of Mind, which is so common among us, that we see Tradesmen break, who have met with no Misfortunes in their Business, and Men of Estates reduced to Poverty, who have never suffered from Losses or Repairs, Tenants, Taxes or Law-suits. In short, it is this foolish sanguine Temper, this depending upon Contingent Futurities that occasions Romantick Generosity, Chymerical Grandure, Senseless Ostentation, and generally ends in Beggary and Ruin. The Man, who will live above his present Circumstances, is in great Danger of living in a little time much beneath them, or as the *Italian* Proverb runs, The Man who lives by Hope will die by Hunger.[21]

It should be an indispensable Rule in Life, to contract our Desires to our present Condition, and, whatever may be our Expectations, to live within the compass of what we actually possess. It will be time enough to enjoy an Estate when it comes into our Hands; but if we anticipate our good Fortune we shall lose the Pleasure of it when it arrives, and may possibly never possess what we have so foolishly counted upon.   L

21 From Orlando Pescetti's *Proverbi Italiani* (1629).

The Spectator, No. 221

Tuesday, November 13.

[Addison]

—————*ab Ovo*
Usque ad Mala—————Hor.[1]

When I have finished any of my Speculations, it is my Method to consider which of the Ancient Authors have touched upon the Subject that I treat of. By this means I meet with some celebrated Thought upon it, or a Thought of my own expressed in better Words, or some Similitude for the Illustration of my Subject. This is what gives Birth to the Motto of a Speculation, which I rather chuse to take out of the Poets than the Prose Writers, as the former generally give a finer Turn to a Thought than the latter, and by couching it in few Words, and in harmonious Numbers,[2] make it more portable to the Memory.

My Reader is therefore sure to meet with at least one good Line in every Paper, and very often finds his Imagination entertained by a Hint that awakens in his Memory some beautiful Passage of a Classick Author.

It was a Saying of an Ancient Philosopher,[3] which I find some of our Writers have ascribed to Queen *Elizabeth,* who perhaps might have taken occasion to repeat it, That a good Face is a Letter of Recommendation. It naturally makes the Beholders inquisitive into the Person who is the Owner of it, and generally prepos-

---

[1] Horace *Satires* 1. 3. 6–7: "From the egg-course to the fruit."

[2] In pleasant-sounding words.

[3] Diogenes Laertius *Vitae Philosophorum* 5. 18–19.

sesses them in his Favour. A handsom Motto has the same Effect. Besides that, it always gives a Supernumerary Beauty to a Paper, and is sometimes in a manner necessary when the Writer is engaged in what may appear a Paradox to vulgar Minds,[4] as it shews that he is supported by good Authorities, and is not singular in his Opinion.

I must confess the Motto is of little use to an unlearned Reader. For which Reason I consider it only as *a Word to the Wise.* But as for my unlearned Friends, if they cannot relish the Motto, I take care to make Provision for them in the Body of my Paper. If they do not understand the Sign that is hung out, they know very well by it, that they may meet with Entertainment in the House; and I think I was never better pleased than with a plain Man's Compliment, who upon his Friend's telling him that he would like the *Spectator* much better if he understood the Motto, replied, *That good Wine needs no Bush.*[5]

I have heard of a couple of Preachers in a Country Town, who endeavoured which should outshine one another, and draw together the greatest Congregation. One of them being well versed in the Fathers,[6] used to quote every now and then a *Latin* Sentence to his Illiterate Hearers, who it seems found themselves so edified by it, that they flocked in greater Numbers to this Learned Man, than to his Rival. The other finding his Congregation mouldering[7] every *Sunday,* and hearing at length what was the Occasion of it, resolved to give his Parish a little *Latin* in his turn; but being unacquainted with any of the Fathers, he digested into his Sermons the whole Book of *Quae Genus,*[8] adding however such Explications to it as he thought might be for the Benefit of his People. He afterwards entered upon *As in praesenti,* which he

---

[4] I.e., when the Spectator is expressing what may seem heterodox opinions.

[5] Addison illustrates the value of adages by employing two fairly common ones. "A Word to the Wise" is from Cervantes' *Don Quixote;* "That good Wine needs no Bush" is from Shakespeare's *As You Like It,* epilogue line 4.

[6] Christian writers of the early church, commonly cited as authorities.

[7] Diminishing.

[8] *"Que genus"* and *"As in praesenti"* are the initial words of particular rules in Lily's Latin grammar.

converted in the same manner to the Use of his Parishioners. This in a very little time thickned his Audience, filled his Church, and routed his Antagonist.

The natural Love to *Latin* which is so prevalent in our common People, makes me think that my Speculations fare never the worse among them for that little Scrap which appears at the Head of them; and what the more encourages me in the use of Quotations in an unknown Tongue is, that I hear the Ladies, whose Approbation I value more than that of the whole Learned World, declare themselves in a more particular manner pleas'd with my *Greek* Motto's.[9]

Designing this Day's Work for a Dissertation upon the two Extremities of my Paper, and having already dispatched my Motto, I shall, in the next place, discourse upon those single Capital Letters which are placed at the End of it, and which have afforded great Matter of Speculation to the Curious.[10] I have heard various Conjectures upon this Subject. Some tell us, that C is the Mark of those Papers that are written by the Clergyman, though others ascribe them to the Club in general. That the Papers marked with R were written by my Friend Sir Roger. That L signifies the Lawyer, whom I have described in my Second Speculation; and that T stands for the Trader or Merchant: But the Letter X,[11] which is placed at the End of some few of my Papers is that which has puzled the whole Town, as they cannot think of any Name which begins with that Letter, except *Xenophon* and *Xerxes*,[12] who can neither of them be supposed to have had any Hand in these Speculations.

In Answer to these inquisitive Gentlemen, who have many of them made Enquiries of me by Letter, I must tell them the Reply of an ancient Philosopher,[13] who carried something hidden under

[9] One recalls the character of Leonora from *Spectator* No. 37, whose library held "all the Classick Authors in Wood."

[10] See *Spectator* No. 1, n. 16.

[11] Papers signed "X" were by Eustace Budgell (1686–1737), who produced twenty-nine *Spectators*.

[12] Xenophon (434?–355 B.C.) was a Greek historian; Xerxes (519?–465 B.C.), king of Persia.

[13] Plutarch, "On Curiosity," *Moralia* 516E.

his Cloak. A certain Acquaintance desiring him to let him know what it was he covered so carefully; *I cover it,* says he, *on purpose that you should not know.* I have made use of these obscure Marks for the same purpose. They are, perhaps, little Amulets or Charms to preserve the Paper against the Fascination and Malice of Evil Eyes; for which Reason I would not have my Reader surprized, if hereafter he sees any of my Papers marked with a Q, a Z, a Y, an &c. or with the Word *Abracadabra.*[14]

I shall however so far explain my self to the Reader, as to let him know that the Letters C, L and X are Cabalistical,[15] and carry more in them than it is proper for the World to be acquainted with. Those who are versed in the Philosophy of *Pythagoras,* and swear by the *Tetrachtys,* that is, the number Four,[16] will know very well that the Number *Ten,* which is signified by the Letter X, (and which has so much perplexed the Town) has in it many particular Powers; that it is called by Platonick Writers the Compleat Number; that One, Two, Three and Four put together make up the Number Ten; and that Ten is all. But these are not Mysteries for ordinary Readers to be let into. A Man must have spent many Years in hard Study before he can arrive at the Knowledge of them.

We had a Rabbinnical Divine[17] in *England,* who was Chaplain to the Earl of *Essex* in Queen *Elizabeth's* Time, that had an admirable Head for Secrets of this Nature. Upon his taking the Doctor of Divinity's Degree he preached before the University of

---

14 In all, there were ten *Spectators* signed "Z," one of which is known to be by John Hughes (1677–1720); there was one signed "Q," which remains unidentified; there were no papers signed "Y," "&c," or "Abracadabra."

15 Related to occult mystery.

16 Dacier's Life of *Pythagoras,* which appeared in English translation in 1707, discussed the mysteries of the number four: "Now the Power of ten is four; for before we come to a compleat and perfect Decad, we discover all the Virtue and all the Perfection of the ten in the four." Addison's paragraph is intentionally obscure.

17 Doctor William Alabaster (d. 1640), rector of Thorfield, Hertfordshire, maintained that in Hebrew Adam meant "man," Seth "placed," and Enoch "misery," and therefore interpreted the first chapter of 1 Chronicles to mean that man is placed in misery. Doctor Alabaster's opinion is mentioned in *History of the Worthies of England* (1662) by Thomas Fuller. See *Tatler* No. 220, n. 14.

Cambridge, upon the *First* Verse of the *First* Chapter of the *First* Book of *Chronicles,* in which, says he, you will see the three following Words,

Adam, Sheth, Enosh.

He divided this short Text into many Parts, and by discovering several Mysteries in each Word, made a most Learned and Elaborate Discourse. The Name of this profound Preacher was Doctor *Alabaster,* of whom the Reader may find a more particular Account in Doctor *Fuller*'s Book of *English* Worthies. This Instance will, I hope, convince my Readers that there may be a great deal of fine Writing in the Capital Letters which bring up the Rear of my Paper, and give them some Satisfaction in that Particular. But as for the full Explication of these Matters, I must refer them to Time, which discovers all things.   C

The Spectator, No. 235

Thursday, November 20.

[A d d i s o n]

——————*Populares*
Vincentem strepitus————Hor.[1]

There is nothing which lies more within the Province of a Spectator than Publick Shows and Diversions; and as among these there are none which can pretend to vie with those Elegant Entertainments that are exhibited in our Theatres, I think it particularly Incumbent on me to take Notice of every thing that is remarkable in such numerous and refined Assemblies.[2]

It is observed, that of late Years, there has been a certain Person in the Upper Gallery of the Play-house, who when he is pleased with any thing that is acted upon the Stage, expresses his Approbation by a loud Knock upon the Benches, or the Wainscot,[3] which may be heard over the whole Theatre. This Person is commonly known by the Name of the *Trunk-maker*[4] *in the Upper-Gallery.* Whether it be, that the Blow he gives on these Occasions resembles that which is often heard in the Shops of such Artizans, or that he was supposed to have been a real Trunkmaker, who after the finishing of his Day's Work, used to unbend his Mind at these Publick Diversions with his Hammer in his Hand, I cannot certainly tell. There are some, I know, who have

1 Horace *Ars Poetica* 81–82: "Stilling the commotions of the pit."

2 Considering his earlier references to bear-baiting, puppet shows, and particular plays, the Spectator clearly intends the words *elegant* and *refined* as irony.

3 The railing in front of the box.

4 A maker of luggage-trunks, therefore a man accustomed to a hammer and pounding.

been foolish enough to imagine it is a Spirit which haunts the Upper-Gallery, and from time to time makes those strange Noises; and the rather, because he is observed to be louder than ordinary every time the Ghost of *Hamlet* appears. Others have reported, that it is a Dumb Man, who has chosen this way of uttering himself, when he is transported with any thing he sees or hears. Others will have it to be the Play-house Thunderer,[5] that exerts himself after this manner in the Upper-Gallery, when he has nothing to do upon the Roof.

But having made it my business to get the best Information I cou'd in a matter of this Moment, I find that the Trunk-maker, as he is commonly called, is a large black[6] Man, whom no body knows. He generally leans forward on a huge Oaken Plant[7] with great Attention to every thing that passes upon the Stage. He is never seen to Smile; but upon hearing any thing that pleases him, he takes up his Staff with both Hands, and lays it upon the next piece of Timber that stands in his way with exceeding Vehemence: After which he composes himself in his former Posture, 'till such time as something new sets him again at Work.

It has been observed his Blow is so well timed, that the most judicious Critick could never except against it. As soon as any shining Thought is expressed in the Poet, or any uncommon Grace appears in the Actor, he smites the Bench or Wainscot. If the Audience does not concur with him, he smites a second time; and if the Audience is not yet awaked, looks round him with great Wrath, and repeats the Blow a third time, which never fails to produce the Clap.[8] He sometimes lets the Audience begin the Clap of themselves, and at the Conclusion of their Applause ratifies it with a single Thwack.

He is of so great use to the Play-house, that it is said a former Director of it, upon his[9] not being able to pay his Attendance by

---

[5] A man employed to produce the sound of thunder by rolling weights across an iron ceiling over the stage. See *Spectator* No. 44 and n. 2.

[6] Presumably, dark-complexioned.

[7] A large stick made from a young oak plant.

[8] Applause. Addison must have known that a venereal pun could be read into this essay wherever the word "Clap" occurs. Both the word and the disease were common in eighteenth-century England.

[9] I.e., the Trunk-maker's.

reason of Sickness, kept one in Pay to officiate for him 'till such time as he recovered; but the Person so employed, tho' he laid about him with incredible Violence, did it in such wrong Places, that the Audience soon found out it was not their old Friend the Trunk-maker.

It has been remarked, that he has not yet exerted himself with Vigour this Season. He sometimes plies at the Opera; and upon *Nicolini's*[10] first Appearance, was said to have demolished three Benches in the Fury of his Applause. He has broken half a dozen Oaken Plants upon *Dogget*,[11] and seldom goes away from a Tragedy of *Shakespear,* without leaving the Wainscot extreamly shattered.

The Players do not only connive at this his obstreperous Approbation, but very chearfully repair at their own Cost whatever Damages he makes. They had once a Thought of erecting a kind of Wooden Anvil for his use, that should be made of a very sounding Plank, in order to render his Stroaks more deep and mellow; but as this might not have been distinguished from the Musick of a Kettle Drum,[12] the Project was laid aside.

In the mean while I cannot but take notice of the great use it is to an Audience, that a Person should thus preside over their Heads, like the Director of a Consort,[13] in order to awaken their Attention, and beat Time to their Applauses. Or to raise my Simile, I have sometimes fancied the Trunk-maker in the Upper Gallery to be like *Virgil's* Ruler of the Winds,[14] seated upon the Top of a Mountain, who, when he struck his Sceptre upon the side of it, roused an Hurricane, and set the whole Cavern in an Uproar.

It is certain the Trunk-maker has saved many a good Play, and brought many a graceful Actor into Reputation, who would not otherwise have been taken notice of. It is very visible, as the Audience is not a little abashed, if they find themselves betrayed into a Clap, when their Friend in the Upper-Gallery does not come into it; so the Actors do not value themselves upon the Clap, but

---

10 Nicola Grimaldi (1673–1732), a popular opera performer.

11 Thomas Doggett (d. 1721), a comic actor.

12 Which would have been heard in operatic productions.

13 Concert.

14 Aeolus, who caused the storm which wrecked the fleet of Aeneas (*Aeneid* 1. 52ff).

regard it as a meer *Brutum fulmen*,[15] or empty Noise, when it has not the Sound of the Oaken Plant in it. I know it has been given out by those who are Enemies to the Trunk-maker, that he has sometimes been bribed to be in the Interest of a bad Poet, or a vicious Player; but this is a Surmise, which has no Foundation; his Stroaks are always just, and his Admonitions seasonable; he does not deal about his Blows at Random, but always hits the right Nail upon the Head. The inexpressible Force wherewith he lays them on, sufficiently shews the Evidence and Strength of his Conviction. His Zeal for a good Author is indeed outragious, and breaks down every Force and Partition, every Board and Plank, that stands within the Expression of his Applause.

As I do not care for terminating my Thoughts in Barren Speculations, or in Reports of pure Matter of Fact, without drawing something from them for the Advantage of my Countrymen, I shall take the Liberty to make an humble Proposal, that whenever the Trunk-maker shall depart this Life, or whenever he shall have lost the Spring of his Arm by Sickness, Old Age, Infirmity, or the like, some able-bodied Critick should be advanced to this Post, and have a competent Salary settled on him for Life, to be furnished with Bamboos for Opera's, Crabtree-Cudgels for Comedies, and Oaken Plants for Tragedy,[16] at the publick Expence. And to the End that this Place should always be disposed of, according to Merit, I would have none preferred to it, who has not given convincing Proofs, both of a sound Judgment and a strong Arm, and who could not, upon Occasion, either knock down an Ox or write a Comment upon *Horace*'s Art of Poetry.[17] In short, I would have him a due Composition of *Hercules* and *Apollo*,[18] and so rightly qualify'd for this important Office, that the *Trunk-maker* may not be missed by our Posterity.   C

[15] Literally, a bolt of lightning striking blindly; here, it means "empty noise."

[16] Each wood is suited to its purpose. Bamboo, which is hollow, is suited to the airy nature of opera. Crab-tree cudgels, which produce a sharp snap, suit the vivacity of comedy. And solid oaken plants would befit the more substantial concerns of tragedy.

[17] I.e., write a critical commentary on Horace's treatise concerning poetry. See *Tatler* No. 163, n. 7.

[18] I.e., a blend of the powerful hero and the god of poetry.

The Spectator, No. 237

Saturday, December 1.

[Addison]¹

Visu carenti magna Pars Veri latet. Senec. in Oedip.²

It is very reasonable to believe, that part of the Pleasure which happy Minds shall enjoy in a future State, will arise from an enlarged Contemplation of the Divine Wisdom in the Government of the World, and a Discovery of the secret and amazing Steps of Providence, from the Beginning to the End of Time. Nothing seems to be an Entertainment more adapted to the Nature of Man, if we consider that Curiosity is one of the strongest and most lasting Appetites implanted in us, and that Admiration is one of our most pleasing Passions; and what a perpetual Succession of Enjoyments will be afforded to both these, in a Scene so large and various as shall then be laid open to our View in the Society of superior Spirits,³ who will perhaps joyn with us in so delightful a Prospect.

It is not impossible, on the contrary, that part of the Punishment of such as are excluded from Bliss may consist not only in their being denied this Privilege, but in having their Appetites at the same time vastly encreased, without any Satisfaction afforded to them. In these, the vain Pursuit of Knowledge shall, perhaps, add to their Infelicity, and bewilder them in Labyrinths of Error, Darkness, Distraction, and Uncertainty of every thing but their

---

1 Though this essay was unsigned, it has regularly been credited to Addison.
2 Seneca *Oedipus* 295: "From the man lacking sight, the greater part of the truth is hidden."
3 Angelic spirits.

own Evil State. *Milton* has thus represented the fallen Angels reasoning together in a kind of Respite from their Torments, and creating to themselves a new Disquiet amidst their very Amusements; he could not properly have described the Sports of condemned Spirits, without that Cast of Horror and Melancholy he has so judiciously mingled with them.

> *Others apart sate on a Hill retir'd,*
> *In Thoughts more elevate, and reason'd high*
> *Of Providence, Fore-knowledge, Will, and Fate,*
> *Fixt Fate, Free-will, Fore-knowledge absolute,*
> *And found no End, in wandring Mazes lost.*[4]

In our present Condition, which is a middle State,[5] our Minds are, as it were, chequered with Truth and Falshood; and as our Faculties are narrow and our Views imperfect, it is impossible but our Curiosity must meet with many Repulses. The Business of Mankind in this Life being rather to act than to know, their Portion of Knowledge is dealt to them accordingly.

From hence it is, that the Reason of the Inquisitive has so long been exercised with Difficulties, in accounting for the promiscuous Distribution of Good and Evil to the Virtuous and the Wicked in this World. From hence come all those Pathetical Complaints of so many Tragical Events, which happen to the Wise and the Good; and of such surprizing Prosperity, which is often the Reward of the Guilty and the Foolish; that Reason is sometimes puzzled, and at a loss what to pronounce upon so mysterious a Dispensation.[6]

Plato expresses his Abhorrence of some Fables of the Poets, which seem to reflect on the Gods as the Authors of Injustice; and lays it down as a Principle, that whatever is permitted to befal a Just Man, whether Poverty, Sickness, or any of those things which seem to be Evils, shall either in Life or Death conduce to his

---

[4] John Milton *Paradise Lost* 2. 557–561. Addison quoted the same passage in *Tatler* No. 114.

[5] I.e., man's nature, which combines both animal and spiritual characteristics.

[6] I.e., the fact that, in this life, the corrupt are dispensed from the punishment they deserve.

Good.[7] My Reader will observe how agreeable this Maxim is to what we find delivered by a greater Authority. *Seneca*[8] has written a Discourse purposely on this Subject, in which he takes Pains, after the Doctrine of the *Stoicks,* to shew, that Adversity is not in it self an Evil; and mentions a noble Saying of *Demetrius,* That *nothing wou'd be more Unhappy than a Man who had never known Affliction.* He[9] compares Prosperity to the Indulgence of a fond[10] Mother to a Child, which often proves his Ruin; but the Affection of the Divine Being to that of a Wise Father, who would have his Sons exercised with Labour, Disappointment and Pain, that they may gather Strength, and improve their Fortitude. On this Occasion the Philosopher rises into that celebrated Sentiment, that there is not on Earth a Spectacle more worthy for a Creator intent on his Works, than a brave Man superior to his Sufferings; to which he adds, that it must be a Pleasure to *Jupiter* himself to look down from Heaven, and see *Cato*[11] amidst the Ruins of his Country preserving his Integrity.

This Thought will appear yet more reasonable, if we consider Human Life as a State of Probation, and Adversity as the Post of Honour in it, assigned often to the best and most select Spirits.

But what I would chiefly insist on here, is, that we are not at present in a proper Situation to judge of the Counsels by which Providence acts, since but little arrives at our Knowledge, and even that little we discern imperfectly; or, according to the elegant Figure in Holy Writ, *we see but in part, and as in a Glass darkly.*[12] Since Providence therefore in its Oeconomy regards the whole System of Time and Things together, we cannot discover the beautiful Connexions between Incidents which lye widely separated in Time, and by losing so many Links of the Chain, our

7 Plato *Apology,* 41D.

8 Seneca *De Providentia* 3. 3 (the saying of Demetrius); 2. 5–6 ("he compares prosperity"); and 2. 9 ("that celebrated sentiment").

9 I.e., Seneca.

10 Foolish.

11 Cato the Younger (95–46 B.C.), the Roman statesman who committed suicide on learning of Caesar's decisive victory at Thapsus. Addison's tragedy *Cato* was produced in 1713.

12 1 Corinthians 13:12.

Reasonings become broken and imperfect. Thus those Parts in the Moral World which have not an absolute, may yet have a relative Beauty, in respect of some other Parts concealed from us, but open to his Eye before whom *Past, Present* and *To come,* are set together in one Point of View;[13] and those Events, the Permission of which seems now to accuse his Goodness,[14] may in the Consummation of Things, both magnifie his Goodness, and exalt his Wisdom. And this is enough to check our Presumption, since it is in vain to apply our Measures[15] of Regularity to Matters of which we know neither the Antecedents nor the Consequents, the Beginning nor the End.

I shall relieve my Readers from this abstracted Thought, by relating here a *Jewish* Tradition[16] concerning *Moses,* which seems to be a kind of Parable, illustrating what I have last mentioned. That great Prophet, it is said, was called up by a Voice from Heaven to the Top of a Mountain; where, in a Conference with the Supreme Being, he was permitted to propose to him some Questions concerning his Administration of the Universe. In the midst of this Divine Conference he was commanded to look down on the Plain below. At the Foot of the Mountain there issued out a clear Spring of Water, at which a Soldier alighted from his Horse to Drink. He was no sooner gone than a little Boy came to the same Place, and finding a Purse of Gold which the Soldier had dropped, took it up and went away with it. Immediately after this came an Infirm old Man, weary with Age and Travelling, and having quenched his Thirst, sat down to rest himself by the side of the Spring. The Soldier missing his Purse returns to search for it, and demands it of the old Man, who affirms he had not seen it, and appeals to Heaven in witness of his Innocence. The Soldier not believing his Protestations, kills him. *Moses* fell on his Face with Horror and Amazement, when the Divine Voice thus prevented his Expostulation, "Be not surprised, *Moses,* nor ask why

---

[13] I.e., the eye of a person enjoying "that Part of the Pleasure which happy Minds shall enjoy in a future State," as described at the beginning of the essay.

[14] I.e., those wicked events which, because God permits them to occur, cause some to doubt his goodness.

[15] Concepts.

[16] The anecdote concerning Moses appears in the Talmud.

the Judge of the whole Earth hath suffered this thing to come to pass; the Child is the Occasion that the Blood of the old Man is spilt; but know, that the old Man whom thou sawest was the Murderer of that Child's Father."[17]

17 See *Spectator* No. 519. That essay, together with this one, take up the major ideas which inform Pope's *Essay on Man* (1733).

The Spectator, No. 239

Tuesday, December 4.

[A d d i s o n]

———*Bella, horrida Bella!* Virg.[1]

I have sometimes amused my self with considering the several Methods of managing a Debate, which have obtained in the World.

The first Races of Mankind[2] used to dispute, as our ordinary People do now-a-days, in a kind of wild Logick, uncultivated by Rules of Art.

Socrates introduced a Catachetical Method of Arguing. He would ask his Adversary Question upon Question, till he had convinced him out of his own Mouth that his Opinions were wrong. This way of debating drives an Enemy up into a Corner, seizes all the Passes through which he can make an Escape, and forces him to surrender at Discretion.[3]

Aristotle changed this Method of Attack, and invented a great variety of little Weapons, called Syllogisms. As in the *Socratic* way of Dispute you agree to every thing which your Opponent advances, in the *Aristotelic* you are still denying and contradicting some part or other[4] of what he says. *Socrates* conquers you by Stratagem, *Aristotle* by Force: The one takes the Town by Sapp,[5] the other Sword in Hand.

---

1 Virgil *Aeneid* 6. 86: "Wars, grim wars!"

2 I.e., those preceding Socrates, Aristotle, etc.

3 Unconditionally.

4 I.e., challenging an undemonstrated premise, an ambiguous term, or an invalidly constructed syllogism.

5 By undermining the defensive works of a fortress.

The Universities of *Europe*,[6] for many Years, carried on their Debates by Syllogism, insomuch that we see the Knowledge of several Centuries laid out into Objections and Answers, and all the good Sense of the Age cut and minced into almost an Infinitude of Distinctions.

When our Universities[7] found that there was no End of wrangling this way, they invented a kind of Argument, which is not reducible to any Mood or Figure in *Aristotle*. It was called the *Argumentum Basilinum* (others write it *Bacilinum* and *Baculinum*) which is pretty well expressed in our *English* Word Club-Law. When they were not able to confute their Antagonist, they knock'd him down. It was their Method in these Polemical Debates first to discharge their Syllogisms,[8] and afterwards to betake themselves to their Clubs, till such time as they had one way or other confounded their Gainsayers. There is in *Oxford* a narrow Defilé,[9] (to make use of a Military Term) where the Partisans used to Encounter, for which Reason it still retains the Name of *Logic Lane*.[10] I have heard an old Gentleman, a Physician, make his Boasts, that when he was a young Fellow he marched several times at the Head of a Troop of *Scotists,* and Cudgell'd a Body of *Smiglesians*[11] half the length of *High-street;* till they had dispersed themselves for Shelter into their respective Garrisons.

This Humour, I find, went very far in *Erasmus's*[12] Time. For that Author tells us, That upon the Revival of *Greek* Letters, most of the Universities in *Europe* were divided into *Greeks* and *Trojans*. The latter were those who bore a mortal Enmity to the Language of the *Grecians,* insomuch that if they met with any who

6 For the concerns of the Schoolmen, see *Spectator* No. 191, n. 2.

7 I.e., the English universities.

8 I.e., to discharge them as if firing on an enemy.

9 Just as Addison was guilty of punning after he criticized the practice, he here uses one of the imported French words he objected to in *Spectator* No. 165.

10 Logic Lane runs off High Street by University College.

11 The battle pit the followers of John Duns Scotus (1265?–1308?), the Scotch theologian, against the followers of Martin Smiglecius (d. 1618), the Polish Jesuit.

12 Desiderius Erasmus (1466?–1536), noted Dutch scholar and Renaissance humanist.

understood it, they did not fail to treat him as a Foe. *Erasmus* himself had, it seems, the Misfortune to fall into the Hands of a Party of *Trojans*, who laid him on with so many Blows and Buffets, that he never forgot their Hostilities to his dying Day.

There is a way of managing an Argument not much unlike the former, which is made use of by States and Communities, when they draw up a hundred thousand Disputants on each side, and convince one another by dint of Sword. A certain grand Monarch[13] was so sensible of his Strength in this way of Reasoning, that he writ upon his great Guns――――*Ratio ultima Regum*. The Logick of Kings. But God be thanked he is now pretty well baffled at his own Weapons. When one has to do with a Philosopher of this kind, one should remember the old Gentleman's[14] Saying who had been engaged in an Argument with one of the *Roman* Emperors. Upon his Friend's telling him, That he wonder'd he would give up the Question, when he had visibly the better of the Dispute, *I am never ashamed,* says he, *to be Confuted by one who is Master of Fifty Legions.*

I shall but just mention another kind of Reasoning, which may be called Arguing by Poll;[15] and another which is of equal force, in which Wagers are made use of as Arguments, according to the celebrated Line in *Hudibras*.[16]

But the most notable way of managing a Controversie is that which we may call *Arguing by Torture*. This is a Method of Reasoning which has been made use of with the poor Refugees,[17] and

[13] King Louis XIV of France was known as *le grand Monarque*. His forces had suffered numerous defeats on the continent.

[14] The reference is to Favorinus, Greek Sophist of the second century A.D., and his dispute with Hadrian (76–138 A.D.), the Roman Emperor who commanded some 250,000 troops.

[15] Counting the number of people for and against a proposition and assuming the majority view is necessarily right.

[16] To argue by wager is to offer to bet a large sum that a particular statement is correct, a form of argument which favors the affluent. The practice is mentioned in Butler's *Hudibras* (2. 1. 297–298).

[17] The French Protestants who, after long sufferings in Catholic France, took refuge in England. They came in great numbers after 1685, when Louis XIV revoked the Edict of Nantes, the act which had allowed them freedom of worship.

which was so fashionable in our Country during the Reign of Queen *Mary,* that in a Passage of an Author quoted by Monsieur *Bayle,*[18] it is said, the Price of Wood was raised in *England,* by reason of the Executions that were made in *Smithfield.* These Disputants convince their Adversaries with a *Sorites*[19] commonly called a Pile of Faggots. The Rack is also a kind of Syllogism which has been used with good Effect, and has made multitudes of Converts. Men were formerly disputed out of their Doubts, reconciled to Truth by force of Reason, and won over to Opinions by the Candour, Sense and Ingenuity of those who had the Right of their Side; but this method of Conviction operated too slowly. Pain was found to be much more Enlightning than Reason. Every Scruple was looked upon as Obstinacy, and not to be removed but by several Engines invented for that purpose. In a Word, the Application of Whips, Racks, Gibbets, Gallies,[20] Dungeons, Fire and Faggot, in a Dispute, may be looked upon as Popish Refinements upon the old Heathen Logick.

There is another way of Reasoning which seldom fails, tho' it be of a quite different Nature to that I have last mentioned. I mean convincing a Man by ready Mony, or, as it is ordinarily called, Bribing a Man to an Opinion. This Method has often proved successful, when all the others have been made use of to no purpose. A Man who is furnished with Arguments from the Mint, will convince his Antagonist much sooner than one who draws them from Reason and Philosophy. Gold is a wonderful Clearer of the Understanding: It dissipates every Doubt and Scruple in an Instant: Accommodates it self to the meanest Capacities; Silences the Loud and Clamorous, and brings over the most Ob-

---

18 Queen Mary I (1516–1558) succeeded to the throne of England in 1553, established Roman Catholicism as the national religion in 1555, and persecuted recalcitrant Protestants. Pierre Bayle (1647–1706), French philosopher, wrote of Andrew Ammonius (d. 1517): "He has an Hyperbolical Expression in one of his Letters, wherein he says that so many Hereticks were daily burnt that it rais'd the price of Wood." Since this expression appeared in the reign of Henry VIII, before Mary became queen, it seems that Addison was quoting Bayle from memory.

19 A series of syllogisms, the conclusion of one forming the premise of the next.

20 Vessels which convicts were condemned to row.

stinate and Inflexible. *Philip* of *Macedon*[21] was a Man of most Invincible Reason this way. He refuted by it all the Wisdom of *Athens,* confounded their Statesmen, struck their Orators Dumb, and at length argued them out of all their Liberties.

Having here touched upon the several Methods of Disputing, as they have prevailed in different Ages of the World, I shall very suddenly give my Reader an Account of the whole Art of Cavilling; which shall be a full and satisfactory Answer to all such Papers and Pamphlets as have yet appeared against the *Spectator.*[22]

C

[21] Philip II (382–336 B.C.), King of Macedon and conqueror of Greece, from whom is derived the expression "a bridge of gold," i.e., a way out of difficulty secured by bribery.

[22] No such paper appeared. In No. 335, responding to critics of *The Spectator,* Addison explained why "I have never once turned out of my way to observe those little Cavils which have been made against it by Envy or Ignorance."

The Spectator, No. 242

Friday, December 7.

[S t e e l e]

Creditur ex medio quia res accersit habere
Sudoris minimum———Hor.[1]

"*Mr.* Spectator,
Your Speculations do not so generally prevail over Mens Manners, as
I could wish. A former Paper of yours,[2] concerning the Misbehaviour
of People, who are necessarily in each other's Company in travelling,
ought to have been a lasting Admonition against Transgressions of
that kind: But I had the Fate of your Quaker, in meeting with a rude
Fellow in a Stage-Coach, who entertain'd two or three Women of us
(for there was no Man besides himself) with Language as indecent as
ever was heard upon the Water.[3] The impertinent Observations
which the Coxcomb made upon our Shame and Confusion, were such,
that it is an unspeakable Grief to reflect upon them. As much as you
have declaimed against Duelling,[4] I hope you will do us the Justice
to declare, that if the Brute has Courage enough to send to the Place
where he saw us all alight together to get rid of him, there is not one
of us but has a Lover who shall avenge the Insult. It would certainly
be worth your Consideration, to look into frequent Misfortunes of
this kind, to which the Modest and Innocent are expos'd, by the li-

1 Horace *Epistles* 2. 1. 168–169: "It is believed that because comedy takes its
substance from ordinary life, it requires less effort." The "less effort" presumably relates to Richard Steele, who is shaping a witty *Spectator* out of contributed documents. The sentiment does not easily apply to the contents of the
letters.

2 *Spectator* No. 132 by Steele described a stage-coach journey during which
a Quaker had to berate a vain Captain for his offensive language.

3 The Thames boatmen were known for their violent language.

4 Steele had discussed the subject in *Spectators* No. 84 and 97.

centious Behaviour of such, as are as much Strangers to good Breeding as to Virtue. Could we avoid hearing what we do not approve, as
easily as we can seeing what is disagreeable, there were some Consolation; but since, at a Box in a Play, in an Assembly of Ladies, or even
in a Pew at Church, it is in the Power of a gross Coxcomb to utter
what a Woman cannot avoid hearing,[5] how miserable is her Condition who comes within the Power of such Impertinents? and how
necessary is it to repeat Invectives against such a Behaviour? If the
Licentious had not utterly forgot what it is to be modest, they would
know, that offended Modesty labours under one of the greatest Sufferings to which human Life can be exposed. If one of these Brutes
could reflect thus much, though they want[6] Shame, they would be
moved, by their Pity, to abhor an impudent Behaviour in the Presence of the Chaste and Innocent. If you will oblige us with a *Spectator*
on this Subject, and procure it to be pasted against every Stage-Coach
in *Great-Britain* as the Law of the Journey, you will highly oblige the
whole Sex, for which you have professed so great an Esteem; and, in
particular, the two Ladies, my late Fellow-Sufferers, and,

Sir,

Your most Humble Servant,

Rebecca Ridinghood."

"*Mr.* Spectator,
The Matter which I am now going to send you is an unhappy Story
in low Life,[7] and will recommend it self, so that you must excuse the
Manner of expressing it. A poor idle drunken Weaver in *Spittle-
Fields*[8] has a faithful laborious Wife, who by her Frugality and Industry had laid by her as much Money as purchased her a Ticket in
the present Lottery.[9] She had hid this very privately in the Bottom
of a Trunk, and had given her Number to a Friend and Confident,
who had promis'd to keep the Secret, and bring her News of the Success.[10] The poor Adventurer[11] was one Day gone abroad, when her
careless Husband, suspecting she had saved some Money, searches
every Corner, till at length he finds this same Ticket; which he im-

---

[5] I.e., when she cannot leave the place where such conversation prevails.
[6] Lack.
[7] I.e., of low-born, working people.
[8] A poor district in the north-eastern part of London, inhabited chiefly by
silk-weavers.
[9] See *Spectator* No. 191.
[10] The outcome.
[11] Speculator.

mediately carries abroad, sells, and squanders away the Money, without the Wife's suspecting any thing of the Matter. A Day or two after this, this Friend, who was a Woman, comes, and brings the Wife Word that she had a Benefit of five hundred Pounds. The poor Creature overjoy'd, flies up Stairs to her Husband, who was then at work, and desires him to leave his Loom for that Evening, and come and drink with a Friend of his and hers below. The Man received this chearful Invitation, as bad Husbands sometimes do; and after a cross Word or two told her he wou'dn't come. His Wife with Tenderness renewed her Importunity, and at length said to him, My Love! I have within these few Months, unknown to you, scrap'd together as much Money as has bought us a Ticket in the Lottery, and now here is Mrs. *Quick* comes to tell me, that 'tis come up this Morning a five hundred Pound Prize. The Husband replies immediately, You lie you Slut, you have no Ticket, for I have sold it. The poor Woman upon this faints away in a Fit, recovers, and is now run distracted. As she had no Design to defraud her Husband, but was willing only to participate in his good Fortune,[12] every one pities her, but thinks her Husband's Punishment but just. This, Sir, is Matter of Fact, and would, if the Persons and Circumstances were greater,[13] in a well wrought Play be call'd Beautiful Distress. I have only sketch'd it out with Chalk, and know a good Hand can make a Moving-Picture[14] with worse Materials.

Sir, &c."

"*Mr.* Spectator,
I am what the World calls a warm[15] Fellow, and by good Success in Trade I have raised my self to a Capacity of making some Figure[16] in the World; but no Matter for that: I have now under my Guardianship a Couple of Neices, who will certainly make me run mad; which you will not wonder at when I tell you they are female Virtuosos,[17] and during the three Years and a half that I have had them under my Care, they never in the least inclined their Thoughts towards any one single Part of the Character of a notable Woman. Whilst they should have been considering the proper Ingredients for

---

12 I.e., she assumed that any winnings would be his, that she would enjoy them only as his wife.

13 If the individuals were not low-born.

14 See *Tatler* No. 167, n. 16.

15 Affluent, comfortably off.

16 Reputation.

17 Amateur scientists. See *Tatler* No. 216.

a Sack-Posset,[18] you should hear a Dispute concerning the Magnetical Virtue of the Loadstone, or perhaps the Pressure of the Atmosphere: Their Language is peculiar to themselves, and they scorn to express themselves on the meanest Trifle, with Words that are not of a *Latin* Derivation. But this were supportable still, would they suffer me to enjoy an uninterrupted Ignorance; but, unless I fall in with their abstracted Ideas of Things (as they call them) I must not expect to smoak one Pipe in quiet. In a late Fit of the Gout I complained of the Pain of that Distemper, when my Neice *Kitty* begged leave to assure me, that whatever I might think, several great Philosophers, both Ancient and Modern, were of Opinion, that both Pleasure and Pain were imaginary Distractions; and that there was no such thing as either *in rerum Naturâ*.[19] I have often heard them affirm that the Fire was not hot; and one Day when I, with the Authority of an old Fellow, desired one of them to put my Blue Cloak on my Knees, she answered, Sir, I will reach the Cloak; but, take notice, I do not do it as allowing your Description, for it might as well be called Yellow as Blue; for Colour is nothing but the various infractions of the Rays of the Sun. Miss *Molly* told me one Day, That to say Snow is white, is allowing a vulgar Error;[20] for as it contains a great Quantity of Nitrous Particles, it may more seasonably be supposed to be Black. In short, the young Husseys would perswade me, that to believe ones Eyes, is a sure way to be deceived; and have often advised me, by no means, to trust any Thing so fallible as my Senses. What I have to beg of you now, is, to turn one Speculation[21] to the due Regulation of Female Literature, so far at least, as to make it consistent with the Quiet of such, whose Fate it is to be liable to its Insults; and to tell us the difference between a Gentleman that should make Cheescakes, and raise Paste, and a Lady that reads *Lock,* and understands the Mathematicks.[22] In which you will extremely oblige

Your hearty Friend and Humble Servant,

Abraham Thrifty."

T

[18] A hot drink of sweetened milk curdled with wine.

[19] I.e., as either pleasure or pain, in the nature of things.

[20] In *Spectator* No. 138 Steele described the kind of men who "will put you to prove that Snow is White, and when you are upon that Topick can say that there is really no such thing as Colour in Nature. . . ." In *Guardian* No. 24 Jack Lizard expresses the same kind of paradoxes.

[21] I.e., to write one *Spectator*.

[22] I.e., the difference between a gentleman who acts like a woman and a lady who—by reading the philosophy of John Locke, etc.—acts like a man.

The Spectator, No. 251

Tuesday, December 18.

[Addison]

———*Linguae centum sunt, oraque centum,*
Ferrea vox——— ———*Virg.*[1]

There is nothing which more astonishes a Foreigner, and frights a Country Squire, than the *Cries of London.* My good Friend Sir Roger often declares, that he cannot get them out of his Head, or go to sleep for them the first Week that he is in Town. On the contrary, Will. Honeycomb calls them the *Ramage de la Ville,*[2] and prefers them to the Sounds of Larks and Nightingales, with all the Musick of the Fields and Woods. I have lately received a Letter from some very odd Fellow upon this Subject, which I shall leave with my Reader, without saying any thing further of it.

"*Sir,*
I am a Man out of all Business,[3] and would willingly turn my Head to any thing for an honest Livelihood. I have invented several Projects for raising many Millions of Money without burthening the Subject, but I cannot get the Parliament to listen to me, who look upon me, forsooth, as a Projector;[4] so that despairing to enrich either my self or my Country by this Publick-spiritedness, I would make some Proposals to you relating to a Design which I have very much at

---

[1] Virgil *Aeneid* 6. 625–626: "There are a hundred tongues, a hundred mouths, and a voice of iron."

[2] The warbling of town birds.

[3] With no present occupation.

[4] I.e., a crack-brained person or a questionable promoter of impossible schemes.

Heart, and which may procure me an handsome Subsistance, if you will be pleased to recommend it to the Cities of *London* and *Westminster.*

"The Post I would aim at is to be Comptroller general of the *London* Cries, which are at present under no manner of Rules or Discipline. I think I am pretty well qualified for this Place, as being a Man of very strong Lungs, of great Insight into all the Branches of our *British* Trades and Manufactures, and of a competent Skill in Musick.

"The Cries of *London* may be divided into Vocal and Instrumental. As for the latter, they are at present under a very great Disorder. A Freeman[5] of *London* has the Privilege of disturbing a whole Street for an Hour together, with the Twancking[6] of a brass Kettle or a Frying-pan. The Watch-man's Thump[7] at Midnight startles us in our Beds, as much as the breaking in of a Thief. The Sow-gelder's Horn[8] has indeed something musical in it, but this is seldom heard within the Liberties.[9] I would therefore propose, that no Instrument of this Nature should be made use of, which I have not tuned and licensed, after having carefully examined in what manner it may affect the Ears of her Majesty's liege Subjects.

"Vocal Cries are of much larger Extent, and indeed so full of Incongruities and Barbarisms, that we appear a distracted City to Foreigners, who do not comprehend the Meaning of such enormous Outcries. Milk is generally sold in a Note above *Elah*,[10] and in Sounds so exceeding shrill, that it often sets our Teeth an edge.[11] The Chimney-sweeper is confined to no certain Pitch; he sometimes utters himself in the deepest Base, and sometimes in the sharpest Treble; sometimes in the highest and sometimes in the lowest Note of the Gamut. The same Observation might be made on the Retailers of Small-coal, not to mention broken Glasses or Brick-dust.[12] In these, therefore, and the like Cases, it should be my Care to sweeten and mellow the Voices of these itinerant Tradesmen, before they make their Appearance in our Streets; as also to accommodate their Cries to their respective

[5] One who enjoys the freedom of the borough and can vote in the election of representatives.

[6] A form of *twanging.*

[7] The sound of his staff as he walks his rounds. See *Tatler* No. 111.

[8] With which he advertises himself.

[9] The limits within which certain immunities are enjoyed.

[10] The highest note in the musical scale.

[11] A form of *on edge.*

[12] Brick dust was often mixed with soil which had too much clay in it.

Wares; and to take Care in particular that those may not make the most Noise, who have the least to sell, which is very observable in the Venders of Cardmatches,[13] to whom I cannot but apply that old Proverb of *Much Cry but little Wool*.

"Some of these last-mentioned Musicians are so very loud in the Sale of these trifling Manufactures, that an honest splenetick[14] Gentleman of my Acquaintance bargained with one of them never to come into the Street where he lived: But what was the Effect of this Contract? why, the whole Tribe of Cardmatch-makers which frequent that Quarter, passed by his Door the very next Day, in hopes of being bought off after the same manner.

"It is another great Imperfection in our *London* Cries, that there is no just Time nor Measure observed in them. Our News should indeed be published in a very quick Time,[15] because it is a Commodity that will not keep cold. It should not however be cried with the same Precipitation as *Fire:* Yet this is generally the Case: A bloody Battel alarms the Town from one End to another in an Instant. Every Motion of the *French* is published in so great an Hurry, that one would think the Enemy were at our Gates. This likewise I would take upon me to regulate in such a manner, that there should be some Distinction made between the spreading of a Victory, a March, or an Incampment, a *Dutch*, a *Portugal*, or a *Spanish* Mail.[16] Nor must I omit under this Head, those excessive Alarms with which several boisterous Rusticks infest our Streets in Turnip Season;[17] and which are more inexcusable, because these are Wares which are in no Danger of Cooling upon their Hands.

"There are others who affect a very slow Time, and are in my Opinion much more tuneable than the former; the Cooper[18] in particular swells his last Note in an hollow Voice, that is not without its Harmony; nor can I forbear being inspired with a most agreeable Melancholy, when I hear that sad and solemn Air with which the Publick is very often asked, if they have any Chairs to mend. Your own Memory may suggest to you many other lamentable Ditties of

13 Pieces of card dipped in sulphur and used for lighting fires. Because the vendors were loud and their product small, the old proverb was applicable.

14 Morose, subject to the spleen. See *Spectator* No. 3, n. 6.

15 Used in a musical sense.

16 See *Tatler* No. 155, n. 4.

17 The season when the turnip crop was for sale. The turnip is a vegetable which will keep for months.

18 The basket maker.

the same Nature, in which the Musick is wonderfully languishing and melodious.

"I am always pleased with that particular Time of the Year which is proper for the pickling of Dill and Cucumbers;[19] but alas this Cry, like the Song of the Nightingales, is not heard above two Months. It would therefore be worth while to consider whether the same Air might not in some Cases be adapted to other Words.

"It might likewise deserve our most serious Consideration, how far, in a well-regulated City, those Humourists are to be tolerated, who not contented with the traditional Cries of their Fore-fathers, have invented particular Songs and Tunes of their own: Such as was, not many Years since, the Pastry-man, commonly known by the Name of the Colly-Molly-Puff;[20] and such as is at this Day the Vender of Powder and Washballs,[21] who, if I am rightly informed, goes under the Name of 'Powder-Watt.'[22]

"I must not here omit one particular Absurdity which runs thro' this whole vociferous Generation, and which renders their Cries very often not only incommodious, but altogether useless to the Publick. I mean that idle Accomplishment which they all of them aim at, of Crying so as not to be understood. Whether or no they have learned this from several of our affected Singers, I will not take upon me to say; but most certain it is, that People know the Wares they deal in rather by their Tunes than by their Words; insomuch that I have sometimes seen a Country Boy run out to buy Apples of a Bellows-mender, and Gingerbread from a Grinder of Knives and Scissars. Nay, so strangely infatuated are some very eminent Artists of this particular Grace in a Cry, that none but their Acquaintance are able to guess at their Profession; for who else can know, that *Work if I had it,* should be the Signification of a Corn-Cutter.

"Forasmuch therefore as Persons of this Rank are seldom Men of Genius or Capacity, I think it would be very proper that some Man of good Sense and sound Judgment should preside over these publick Cries, who should permit none to lift up their Voices in our Streets,

[19] In the final lines of Etherege's *The Man of Mode,* Harriet Woodvill protests returning to the country: "Methinks I hear the hateful noise of rooks already—kaw, kaw, kaw! There's music in the worst cry in London—'My dill and cowcumbers to pickle!'" (act 5, sc. 2).

[20] The man carried a basket of pastry on his head and sang out "Colly-Molly-Puff," a phrase which was used as his name.

[21] Cakes of cosmetic for washing the face.

[22] Probably short for "Walter."

that have not tuneable Throats, and are not only able to overcome the Noise of the Croud, and the rattling of Coaches, but also to vend their respective Merchandizes in apt Phrases, and in the most distinct and agreeable Sounds. I do therefore humbly recommend my self as a Person rightly qualified for this Post, and if I meet with fitting Encouragement, shall communicate some other Projects which I have by me, that may no less conduce to the Emolument[23] of the Publick.

I am,

Sir, &c.

Ralph Crotchett."

C

23 Profit or advantage.

The Spectator, No. 266

Friday, January 4.

[Steele]

Id vero est, quod ego mihi puto palmarium,
Me reperisse, quomodo adolescentulus
Meretricum ingenia & mores possit noscere:
Mature ut cum cognorit perpetuo oderit. Ter.[1]

No Vice or Wickedness, which People fall into from Indulgence to Desires which are natural to all, ought to place them below the Compassion of the virtuous Part of the World; which indeed often makes me a little apt to suspect the Sincerity of their Virtue, who are too warmly provoked at other Peoples personal Sins. The unlawful Commerce of the Sexes is of all other the hardest to avoid; and yet there is no one which you shall hear the rigider Part of Womankind speak of with so little Mercy. It is very certain that a modest Woman cannot abhor the Breach of Chastity too much; but pray let her hate it for herself, and only pity it in others. Will. Honeycomb calls these over-offended Ladies, the outragiously virtuous.

I do not design to fall upon Failures in general, with Relation to the Gift of Chastity, but at present only enter upon that large Field, and begin with the Consideration of poor and publick Whores. The other Evening passing along near *Covent-Garden,* I was jogged on the Elbow as I turned into the Piazza, on the right Hand coming out of *James-street,*[2] by a slim young Girl of about

---

[1] Terence *Eunuchus* 930–933: "I honor myself that I have been able to show a young man the character and artifices of whores, so having learned of them early, he will despise them forever."

[2] James Street leads north from Covent Garden to Long Acre.

Seventeen, who with a pert Air asked me if I was for a Pint of Wine. I do not know but I should have indulged my Curiosity in having some Chat with her, but that I am informed the Man of the *Bumper*[3] knows me; and it would have made a Story for him not very agreeable to some Part of my Writings,[4] though I have in others so frequently said that I am wholly unconcerned in any Scene I am in, but merely as a Spectator. This Impediment being in my Way, we stood under one of the Arches by Twilight; and there I could observe as exact[5] Features as I had ever seen, the most agreeable Shape, the finest Neck and Bosom, in a Word, the whole Person of a Woman exquisitely beautiful. She affected to allure me with a forced Wantonness in her Look and Air; but I saw it checked with Hunger and Cold: Her Eyes were wan and eager, her Dress thin and tawdry, her Mein[6] genteel and childish. This strange Figure gave me much Anguish of Heart, and to avoid being seen with her I went away, but could not forbear giving her a Crown.[7] The poor Thing sighed, curtisied, and with a Blessing, expressed with the utmost Vehemence,[8] turned from me. This Creature is what they call *newly come upon the Town*, but who, I suppose, falling into cruel Hands, was left in the first Month from her Dishonour,[9] and exposed to pass through the Hands and Discipline of one of those Hags of Hell whom we call Bawds. But

3 Steele's friend, the actor Richard Estcourt (1668–1712), had advertised in *Spectators* No. 260, 261, and 263 that he would open the Bumper Tavern in James Street on January 1, and his letter announcing the opening appeared in No. 264. Estcourt's "Man" at the tavern, the one the Spectator feared would recognize him, was probably Anthony Aston.

4 I.e., which would not correspond to the moral views expressed in parts of my writings.

5 Regular.

6 Demeanor.

7 A coin worth five shillings.

8 Passion, sincerity.

9 In *Spectator* No. 182 by Steele appears a letter from Alice Threadneedle, explaining: "It is the ordinary Practice and Business of Life with a Set of idle Fellows about this Town, to write Letters, send Messages, and form Appointments with little raw unthinking Girls, and leave them after Possession of them without any Mercy to Shame, Infamy, Poverty, and Disease." Though she herself was enticed, corrupted, and deserted by her lover, Alice Threadneedle chose not "to go upon the Town, as the Phrase is. . . ."

least I should grow too suddenly grave on this Subject, and be my self outragiously good, I shall turn to a Scene in one of *Fletcher*'s Plays, where this Character is drawn, and the Oeconomy of Whoredom most admirably described. The Passage I would point to is in the third Scene of the second Act of the *Humorous Lieutenant*.[10] *Leucippe,* who is Agent for the King's Lust, and bawds at the same Time for the whole Court, is very pleasantly introduced, reading her Minutes as a Person of Business, with two Maids, her Under-Secretaries, taking Instructions at a Table before her. Her Women, both those under her present Tutelage, and those which she is laying Wait for,[11] are alphabetically set down in her Book; and she is looking over the Letter *C,* in a muttering Voice, as if between Soliloquy and speaking out, she says,

> *Her Maiden-head will yield me; let me see now;*
> *She is not Fifteen they say: For her Complexion—*
> Cloe, Cloe, Cloe, *here I have her,*
> Cloe, *the Daughter of a Country Gentleman;*
> *Her Age upon Fifteen. Now her Complexion,*
> *A lovely brown; here 'tis; Eyes black and rowling,*
> *The Body neatly built; she strikes a Lute well,*
> *Sings most enticingly: These Helps consider'd,*
> *Her Maiden-head will amount to some three hundred*
> *Or three hundred and fifty Crowns, 'twill bear in handsomly.*
> *Her Father's poor, some little Share deducted,*
> *To buy him a Hunting-Nag——*

These Creatures[12] are very well instructed in the Circumstances and Manners of all who are any Way related to the fair one whom they have a Design upon. As *Cloe* is to be purchased with 350 Crowns, and the Father taken off with a Pad; the Merchant's Wife next to her,[13] who abounds in Plenty, is not to have downright Money, but the mercenary Part of her Mind is engaged with a

---

[10] This reference has the nature of an advertisement. *The Humorous Lieutenant* (1619) by John Fletcher (1579–1625), which had not been acted for nearly three years, was scheduled to be revived at Drury Lane within the month. Steele quotes from act 2, sc. 3, lines 15–26.

[11] I.e., the ladies of the town, both present and prospective.

[12] I.e., bawds like Leucippe.

[13] I.e., the name following Cloe's in the book of whores.

Present of Plate and a little Ambition: She is made to understand that it is a Man of Quality who dies for her. The Examination of a young Girl for Business, and the crying down her Value for being a slight Thing, together with every other Circumstance in the Scene, are inimitably excellent, and have the true Spirit of Comedy; tho' it were to be wished the Author had added a Circumstance which should make *Leucippe*'s Baseness more odious.

It must not be Thought a Digression from my intended Speculation, to talk of Bawds in a Discourse upon Wenches; for a Woman of the Town is not thoroughly and properly such, without having gone through the Education of one of these Houses: But the compassionate Case of very many is, that they are taken into such Hands without any the least Suspicion, previous Temptation, or Admonition to what Place they are going. The last Week I went to an Inn in the City, to enquire for some Provisions which were sent by a Waggon out of the Country; and as I waited in one of the Boxes[14] till the Chamberlain had looked over his Parcels, I heard an old and a young Voice repeating the Questions and Responces of the Church-Catechism. I thought it no Breach of good Manners to peep at a Crevise, and look in at People so well employed; but who should I see there but the most artful Procuress in the Town, examining a most beautiful Country-Girl, who had come up in the same Waggon with my Things, *Whether she was well educated, could forbear playing the Wanton with Servants and idle Fellows, of which this Town,* says she, *is too full:* At the same Time, *Whether she knew enough of Breeding; as that if a Squire or a Gentleman, or one that was her Betters, should give her a civil Salute, she could curtsie and be humble nevertheless. Her innocent forsooths, yes's, and't please you's, and she would do her Endeavour,* moved the good old Lady to take her out of the Hands of a Country Bumkin her Brother, and hire her for her own Maid. I stay'd till I saw them all marched out to take Coach; the Brother loaded with a great Cheese, he prevailed upon her to take for her Civilities to Sister. This poor Creature's Fate is not far off that of her's whom I spoke of above; and it is not to

14 A compartment partitioned off in the public room of a coffee-house or tavern.

be doubted, but after she has been long enough a Prey to Lust she will be delivered over to Famine; the Ironical Commendation of the Industry and Charity of these antiquated Ladies. These Directors of Sin, after they can no longer commit it, makes up the Beauty of the inimitable Dedication to the *Plain Dealer*,[15] and is a Master-piece of Railery on this Vice: But to understand all the Purlues[16] of this Game the better, and to illustrate this Subject in future Discourses, I must venture my self, with my Friend Will, into the Haunts of Beauty and Gallantry; from pampered Vice in the Habitations of the Wealthy, to distressed indigent Wicked-ness expelled the Harbours of the Brothel.[17]   T

[15] Wycherley's play (1676) is dedicated "To My Lady B———" in a long ironical address. Mother Bennett was a well-known procuress during the reign of Charles II.

[16] The region forming the outlying part of something abstract, i.e., all the varying aspects and complications.

[17] Though the Spectator published letters relating to this essay in No. 276, no paper appeared reporting his and Will Honeycomb's investigations in this area.

The Spectator, No. 267

Saturday, January 5.

[A d d i s o n]

Cedite Romani Scriptores, cedite Graii. Propert.[1]

There is Nothing in Nature so irksome as general Discourses, especially when they turn chiefly upon Words. For this Reason I shall wave the Discussion of that Point which was started some Years since, Whether *Milton's Paradise Lost* may be called an Heroick Poem?[2] Those who will not give it that Title, may call it (if they please) a *Divine Poem.* It will be sufficient to its Perfection, if it has in it all the Beauties of the highest Kind of Poetry; and as for those who alledge it is not an Heroick Poem, they advance no more to the Diminution of it, than if they should say *Adam* is not *Aeneas,* nor *Eve Helen.*

I shall therefore examine it by the Rules of Epic Poetry, and see whether it falls short of the *Iliad* or *Aeneid,* in the Beauties which are essential to that Kind of Writing.[3] The first Thing to be consider'd in an Epic Poem, is the Fable,[4] which is perfect or imperfect, according as the Action which it relates is more or less so. This Action should have three Qualifications in it. First, It should be but one Action. Secondly, It should be an entire Action; and Thirdly, it should be a great Action. To consider the Action of the *Iliad, Aeneid,* and *Paradise Lost,* in these three several

---

1 Propertius *Elegies* 2. 34. 65: "Yield, Roman writers; yield, Greeks."

2 Dryden's *Discourse concerning Satire* (1693) argued that Milton's subject "is not that of an Heroic Poem, properly so called."

3 Addison used the same system in his analysis of *Chevy Chase* in *Spectators* No. 70 and 74.

4 I.e., the story.

Lights. *Homer* to preserve the Unity of his Action hastens into the Midst of Things, as *Horace* has observed:[5] Had he gone up to *Leda*'s Egg, or begun much later, even at the Rape of *Helen,* or the Investing of *Troy,* it is manifest that the Story of the Poem would have been a Series of several Actions. He therefore opens his Poem with the Discord of his Princes, and with great Art interweaves in the several succeeding Parts of it, an Account of every Thing material which relates to them, and had passed before that fatal Dissension. After the same Manner *Aeneas* makes his first Appearance in the *Tyrrhene* Seas, and within Sight of *Italy,* because the Action proposed to be celebrated was that of his settling himself in *Latium.*[6] But because it was necessary for the Reader to know what had happened to him in the taking of *Troy,* and in the preceding Parts of his Voyage, *Virgil* makes his Heroe relate it by Way of Episode in the second and third Books of the *Aeneid.* The Contents of both which Books come before those of the first Book in the Thread of the Story, tho' for preserving of this Unity of Action, they follow them in the Disposition of the Poem. *Milton,* in Imitation of these two great Poets, opens his *Paradise Lost,* with an infernal Council plotting the Fall of Man, which is the Action he proposed to celebrate; and as for those great Actions which preceded, in Point of Time, the Battle of the Angels, and the Creation of the World, (which would have entirely destroyed the Unity of his principal Action, had he related them in the same Order that they happened) he cast them into the fifth, sixth and seventh Books, by way of Episode to this noble Poem.

Aristotle[7] himself allows, that *Homer* has nothing to boast of as to the Unity of his Fable, tho' at the same Time that great Critick and Philosopher endeavours to palliate this Imperfection in the *Greek* Poet, by imputing it in some Measure to the very Na-

[5] Horace *Ars Poetica* 146–152. Horace, who based his critical doctrine on the practice of Homer, maintained that an epic should begin *in medias res,* i.e., in "the Midst of things." It was argued that the unity of the *Iliad* would have suffered had the story begun with the birth of Helen (from Leda's egg), with her abduction by Paris, or with the beginning of the siege of Troy.

[6] Latium was a region of central Italy bordering the area of the Mediterranean called the Tyrrhene Sea.

[7] Aristotle *Poetics* 26. 6.

ture of an Epic Poem. Some have been of Opinion, that the *Aeneid* labours also in this Particular, and has Episodes which may be looked upon as Excrescencies rather than as Parts of the Action. On the contrary, the Poem which we have now under our Consideration, hath no other Episodes than such as naturally arise from the Subject, and yet is filled with such a Multitude of astonishing Incidents, that it gives us at the same Time a Pleasure of the greatest Variety, and of the greatest Simplicity.

I must observe also, that as *Virgil* in the Poem which was designed to celebrate the Original of the *Roman* Empire, has described the Birth of its great Rival, the *Carthaginian* Commonwealth:[8] *Milton* with the like Art in his Poem on the Fall of Man, has related the Fall of those Angels who are his professed Enemies. Besides the many other Beauties in such an Episode, it's running parallel with the great Action of the Poem, hinders it from breaking the Unity so much as another Episode would have done, that had not so great an Affinity with the principal Subject. In short, this is the same Kind of Beauty which the Criticks admire in the *Spanish Fryar,* or the *Double Discovery,*[9] where the two different Plots look like Counterparts and Copies of one another.

The second Qualification required in the Action of an Epic Poem is, that it should be an *entire* Action: An Action is entire when it is compleat in all its Parts; or as *Aristotle* describes it, when it consists of a Beginning, a Middle, and an End.[10] Nothing should go before it, be intermix'd with it, or follow after it, that is not related to it. As on the contrary, no single Step should be omitted in that just and regular Process which it must be supposed to take from its Original to its Consummation. Thus we see the Anger of *Achilles* in its Birth, its Continuance and Effects, and *Aeneas*'s Settlement in *Italy,* carried on through all the Oppositions in his Way to it both by Sea and Land. The Action in *Milton* excels (I think) both the former in this Particular; we see it

8 Dido, whom Aeneas met and loved during his journey to Rome, was founder and queen of Carthage.

9 *The Spanish Friar; or, The Double Discovery* (1681) was a comedy by John Dryden.

10 Aristotle *Poetics* 33. 1.

contrived in Hell, executed upon Earth, and punished by Heaven. The Parts of it are told in the most distinct Manner, and grow out of one another in the most natural Method.

The third Qualification of an Epic Poem is its *Greatness.* The Anger of *Achilles* was of such Consequence, that it embroiled the Kings of *Greece,* destroy'd the Heroes of *Troy,* and engaged all the Gods in Factions. *Aeneas's* Settlement in *Italy* produced the *Caesars,* and gave Birth to the *Roman* Empire. *Milton's* Subject was still greater than either of the former; it does not determine the Fate of single Persons or Nations, but of a whole Species. The united Powers of Hell are joined together for the Destruction of Mankind, which they effected in Part, and would have completed, had not Omnipotence it self interposed. The principal Actors are Man in his greatest Perfection, and Woman in her highest Beauty. Their Enemies are the fallen Angels: The Messiah[11] their Friend, and the Almighty their Protector. In short, every Thing that is great in the whole Circle of Being, whether within the Verge of Nature, or out of it, has a proper Part assigned it in this noble Poem.

In Poetry, as in Architecture, not only the Whole, but the principal Members, and every Part of them, should be Great. I will not presume to say, that the Book of Games in the *Aeneid,* or that in the *Iliad,* are not of this Nature, nor to reprehend *Virgil's* Simile of a Top,[12] and many other of the same Nature in the *Iliad,* as liable to any Censure in this Particular; but I think we may say, without derogating from those wonderful Performances, that there is an unquestionable Magnificence in every Part of *Paradise Lost,*[13] and indeed a much greater than could have been formed upon any Pagan System.

But *Aristotle,* by the Greatness of the Action, does not only mean that it should be great in its Nature, but also in its Duration, or in other Words, that it should have a due Length in it, as well as what we properly call Greatness. The just Measure of this Kind of Magnitude, he explains by the following Similitude. An

[11] Christ.

[12] The epic games appear in the *Aeneid* 5, and in the *Iliad* 23; the simile of the top in *Aeneid* 7. 378–384.

[13] Emphasize "every."

Animal, no bigger than a Mite, cannot appear perfect to the Eye, because the Sight takes it in at once, and has only a confused Idea of the Whole, and not a distinct Idea of all its Parts; If on the contrary you should suppose an Animal of ten thousand Furlongs in Length, the Eye would be so filled with a single Part of it, that it could not give the Mind an Idea of the Whole. What these Animals are to the Eye, a very short or a very long Action would be to the Memory. The first would be, as it were, lost and swallowed up by it, and the other difficult to be contained in it. *Homer* and *Virgil* have shewn their principal Art in this Particular; the Action of the *Iliad,* and that of the *Aeneid,* were in themselves exceeding short, but are so beautifully extended and diversified by the Invention of *Episodes,* and the Machinery[14] of Gods, with the like poetical Ornaments, that they make up an agreeable Story sufficient to employ the Memory without overcharging it. *Milton's* Action is enriched with such a Variety of Circumstances, that I have taken as much Pleasure in reading the Contents of his Books, as in the best invented Story I ever met with. It is possible, that the Traditions on which the *Iliad* and *Aeneid* were built, had more Circumstances in them than the History of *the Fall of Man,* as it is related in Scripture. Besides it was easier for *Homer* and *Virgil* to dash the Truth with Fiction, as they were in no danger of offending the Religion of their Country by it. But as for *Milton,* he had not only a very few Circumstances upon which to raise his Poem, but was also obliged to proceed with the greatest Caution in every Thing that he added out of his own Invention. And, indeed, notwithstanding all the Restraints he was under, he has filled his Story with so many surprising Incidents, which bear so close an Analogy with what is delivered in Holy Writ, that it is capable of pleasing the most delicate Reader, without giving Offence to the most scrupulous.

The modern Criticks[15] have collected from several Hints in the *Iliad* and *Aeneid* the Space of Time, which is taken up by the Action of each of those Poems; but as a great Part of *Milton's*

---

14 Descriptions.

15 Notably Dryden, Bossu, and Dacier. (See *Tatler* No. 165, nos. 3 and 8.) Dacier maintained that the *Iliad* covered 47 days; the *Odyssey,* 8½ years; and the *Aeneid,* 7 years.

Story was transacted in Regions that lie out of the Reach of the Sun and the Sphere of Day, it is impossible to gratifie the Reader with such a Calculation, which indeed would be more curious than instructive; None of the Criticks, either Antient or Modern, having laid down Rules to circumscribe the Action of an Epic Poem with any determined Number of Years, Days or Hours.

This Piece of Criticism on Milton's Paradise Lost *shall be carried on in the following* Saturdays *Papers.*[16]   L

---

[16] The papers on *Paradise Lost* appeared on the seventeen succeeding Saturdays, ending with *Spectator* No. 369.

The Spectator, No. 273

Saturday, January 12.

[Addison]

⸺*Notandi sunt tibi* Mores. Hor.[1]

Having examined the Action of *Paradise Lost,* let us in the next Place consider the Actors. This is *Aristotle's* Method of considering; first the Fable, and secondly the Manners, or as we generally call them in *English,* the Fable and the Characters.

Homer has excelled all the heroic Poets that ever wrote, in the Multitude and Variety of his Characters. Every God that is admitted into his Poem, acts a Part which would have been suitable to no other Deity. His Princes are as much distinguished by their Manners as by their Dominions; and even those among them, whose Characters seem wholly made up of Courage, differ from one another as to the particular Kinds of Courage in which they excel. In short, there is scarce a Speech or Action in the *Iliad,* which the Reader may not ascribe to the Person that speaks or acts, without seeing his Name at the Head of it.

Homer does not only out-shine all other Poets in the Variety, but also in the Novelty of his Characters.[2] He has introduced among his *Grecian* Princes a Person, who had lived thrice the Age of Man, and conversed with *Theseus, Hercules, Polyphemus,* and the first Race of Heroes. His principal Actor is the Son of a God-

---

1 Horace *Ars Poetica* 156: "Note well the manners."

2 I.e., the singularity of the characters. The prince "thrice the Age of Man" is Nestor; the "principal Actor" is Achilles, son of Thetis; the "venerable Trojan Prince" is Priam, whose son Aeneas founded the Roman Empire. Vulcan, the husband of Venus, is the patron of cuckolds. Thersites is a scurrilous, deformed Greek officer.

dess, not to mention the Off-spring of other Deities, who have likewise a Place in his Poem, and the venerable *Trojan* Prince who
was the Father of so many Kings and Heroes. There is in these
several Characters of *Homer,* a certain Dignity as well as Novelty,
which adapts them in a more peculiar manner to the Nature of
an heroic Poem. Tho', at the same Time, to give them the greater
Variety, he has described a *Vulcan,* that is, a Buffoon among his
Gods, and a *Thersites* among his Mortals.

Virgil falls infinitely short of *Homer* in the Characters of his
Poem,[3] both as to their Variety and Novelty. *Aeneas* is indeed a
perfect Character, but as for *Achates,* tho' he is stiled the Hero's
Friend, he does nothing in the whole Poem which may deserve
that Title. *Gyas, Mnesteus, Sergestus* and *Cloanthus,* are all of
them Men of the same Stamp and Character,

Fortemque Gyan, fortemque Cloanthum: Virg.[4]

There are indeed several very natural Incidents in the Part of
Ascanius; as that of *Dido* cannot be sufficiently admired. I do not
see any Thing new or particular in *Turnus. Pallas* and *Evander*
are remote Copies of *Hector* and *Priam,* as *Lausus* and *Mezentius*
are almost Parallels to *Pallas* and *Evander.* The Characters of
Nisus and *Eurialus* are beautiful, but common. We must not forget the Parts of *Sinon, Camilla,* and some few others, which are
beautiful Improvements on the Greek Poet. In short, there is neither that Variety nor Novelty in the Persons of the *Aeneid,* which
we meet with in those of the *Iliad.*

If we look into the Characters of *Milton,* we shall find that he
has introduced all the Variety his Poem was capable of receiving.
The whole Species of Mankind was in two Persons at the Time to

---

[3] Achates, Gyas, Mnesteus, Sergestus, and Cloanthus are companions of
Aeneas. Ascanius is his son. Turnus is his enemy, the leader of the Rutulians.
Evander is the ruler of Pallanteum, who welcomes Aeneas and who sends his
son Pallas to aid the Trojans. Mezentius is the king of the Tyrrhenians; both
he and his son Lausus are killed by Aeneas. Nisus and Eurialus are young
Trojans who accompany Aeneas. Sinon is the Greek who persuaded the Trojans to receive the wooden horse; Camilla is the virgin queen of the Volscians,
who aided Turnus against Aeneas.

[4] Virgil *Aeneid* 1. 222: "Brave Gyas and brave Cloanthus."

which the Subject of his Poem is confined. We have, however, four distinct Characters in these two Persons. We see Man and Woman in the highest Innocence and Perfection, and in the most abject State of Guilt and Infirmity. The two last Characters are, indeed, very common and obvious, but the two first are not only more magnificent, but more new than any Characters either in *Virgil* or *Homer,* or indeed in the whole Circle of Nature.

Milton was so sensible of this Defect in the Subject of his Poem, and of the few Characters it would afford him,[5] that he has brought into it two Actors of a shadowy and fictitious Nature, in the Persons of Sin and Death,[6] by which Means he has interwoven in the Body of his Fable a very beautiful and well invented Allegory. But notwithstanding the Fineness of this Allegory may atone for it in some Measure; I cannot think that Persons of such a chymerical[7] Existence are proper Actors in an Epic Poem; because there is not that Measure of Probability annexed to them, which is requisite in Writings of this Kind, as I shall shew more at large hereafter.

Virgil has, indeed, admitted Fame as an Actress in the *Aeneid,*[8] but the Part she acts is very short, and none of the most admired Circumstances in that Divine Work. We find in Mock-Heroic Poems, particularly in the *Dispensary* and the *Lutrin,*[9] several allegorical Persons of this Nature, which are very beautiful in those Compositions, and may, perhaps, be used as an Argument, that the Authors of them were of Opinion, such Characters might have a Place in an Epic Work. For my own Part, I should be glad the Reader would think so, for the sake of the Poem I am now examining, and must further add, that if such empty unsubstantial Beings may be ever made Use of on this Occasion, there were never

---

5 I.e., that the story of the Fall gave him so few characters to portray.

6 Sin and Death are personified as the twin keepers of the gates of Hell. See *Spectator* No. 357.

7 Fantastic, imaginary.

8 Virgil *Aeneid* 4. 173–197.

9 *The Dispensary* (1699) was a satire on physicians and apothecaries, written by Sir Samuel Garth (1661–1719). *Le Lutrin* (1674–1683) was the mock-heroic description of a dispute between two church officials over the positioning of a choir lectern; the author is Nicolas Boileau (1636–1711).

any more nicely imagined, and employed in more proper Actions, than those of which I am now speaking.

Another principal Actor in this Poem is the great Enemy of Mankind.[10] The Part of *Ulysses* in *Homer*'s *Odyssey* is very much admired by *Aristotle*,[11] as perplexing that Fable with very agreeable Plots and Intricacies, not only by the many Adventures in his Voyage, and the Subtilty of his Behaviour, but by the various Concealments and Discoveries of his Person in several Parts of that Poem. But the crafty Being I have now mentioned, makes a much longer Voyage than *Ulysses,* puts in Practice many more Wiles and Stratagems, and hides himself under a greater Variety of Shapes and Appearances, all of which are severally detected, to the great Delight and Surprise of the Reader.

We may likewise observe with how much Art the Poet has varied several Characters of the Persons that speak in his infernal Assembly.[12] On the contrary, how has he represented the whole Godhead exerting it self towards Man in its full Benevolence under the Three-fold Distinction of a Creator, a Redeemer and a Comforter!

Nor must we omit the Person of *Raphael,* who amidst his Tenderness and Friendship for Man, shews such a Dignity and Condescention in all his Speech and Behaviour, as are suitable to a Superior Nature. The Angels are indeed as much diversified in *Milton,* and distinguished by their proper Parts, as the Gods are in *Homer* or *Virgil.* The Reader will find nothing ascribed to *Uriel, Gabriel, Michael* or *Raphael,* which is not in a particular manner suitable to their respective Characters.[13]

There is another Circumstance in the principal Actors of the *Iliad* and *Aeneid,* which gives a peculiar[14] Beauty to those two Poems, and was therefore contrived with very great Judgment. I mean the Authors having chosen for their Heroes Persons who were so nearly related to the People for whom they wrote. *Achilles*

---

[10] Satan.

[11] Aristotle *Poetics* 17. 5; 24. 10.

[12] Addison analyzed the characters of the fallen angels in *Spectator* No. 309.

[13] Raphael is discussed in *Spectator* No. 327; Michael in No. 363; and Gabriel and Uriel in No. 321.

[14] Particular.

was a *Greek,* and *Aeneas* the remote Founder of *Rome.* By this means their Countrymen (whom they principally proposed to themselves for their Readers) were particularly attentive to all the Parts of their Story, and sympathized with their Heroes in all their Adventures. A *Roman* could not but rejoice in the Escapes, Successes and Victories of *Aeneas,* and be grieved at any Defeats, Misfortunes or Disappointments that befel him; as a *Greek* must have had the same Regard for *Achilles.* And it is plain, that each of those Poems have lost this great Advantage, among those Readers to whom their Heroes are as Strangers, or indifferent Persons.

Milton's Poem is admirable in this respect, since it is impossible for any of its Readers, whatever Nation, Country or People he may belong to, not to be related to the Persons who are the principal Actors in it; but what is still infinitely more to its Advantage, the principal Actors in this Poem are not only our Progenitors, but our Representatives. We have an actual Interest in every Thing they do, and no less than our utmost Happiness is concerned, and lies at Stake in all their Behaviour.[15]

I shall subjoyn as a Corollary to the foregoing Remark, an admirable Observation out of *Aristotle,*[16] which hath been very much misrepresented in the Quotations of some Modern Criticks. "If a Man of perfect and consummate Virtue falls into a Misfortune, it raises our Pity, but not our Terror, because we do not fear that it may be our own Case, who do not resemble the Suffering Person." But as that great Philosopher adds, "If we see a Man of Virtues mixt with Infirmities, fall into any Misfortune, it does not only raise our Pity but our Terror; because we are afraid that the like Misfortunes may happen to our selves, who resemble the Character of the suffering Person."

I shall take another Opportunity to observe, that a Person of an absolute and consummate Virtue should never be introduced in Tragedy,[17] and shall only remark in this Place, that the foregoing Observation of *Aristotle,* tho' it may be true in other Occa-

15 I.e., since we are descendants of Adam and Eve, our lives and our ultimate destiny are involved in their actions.

16 Aristotle *Poetics* 13. 2–3.

17 It is difficult to square this critical opinion with the characterization in Addison's *Cato.*

sions, does not hold in this; because in the present Case, though the Persons who fall into Misfortune are of the most perfect and consummate Virtue, it is not to be considered as what may possibly be, but what actually is our own Case; since we are embark'd with them on the same Bottom, and must be Partakers of their Happiness or Misery.

In this, and some other very few Instances, *Aristotle*'s Rules for Epic Poetry (which he had drawn from his Reflections upon *Homer*) cannot be supposed to quadrate exactly with the heroic Poems which have been made since his Time; as it is plain his Rules would have been still more perfect, could he have perused the *Aeneid* which was made some hundred Years after his Death.[18]

In my next I shall go through other Parts of *Milton*'s Poem; and hope that what I shall there advance, as well as what I have already written, will not only serve as a Comment upon *Milton*, but upon *Aristotle*.   L

[18] Actually, Aristotle died in 322 B.C., and the *Aeneid* was first transcribed in 17 B.C.

The Spectator, No. 275

Tuesday, January 15.

[A d d i s o n]

————*tribus Anticyris caput insanabile*————Juv.[1]

I was Yesterday engaged in an Assembly of Virtuoso's,[2] where one of them produced many curious Observations, which he had lately made in the Anatomy of an humane Body. Another of the Company communicated to us several wonderful Discoveries, which he had also made on the same Subject, by the Help of very fine Glasses.[3] This gave Birth to a great Variety of uncommon Remarks, and furnished Discourse for the remaining Part of the Day.

The different Opinions which were started on this Occasion, presented to my Imagination so many new Ideas, that by mixing with those which were already there, they employed my Fancy all the last Night, and composed a very wild extravagant Dream.

I was invited, methought, to the Dissection of a *Beau's*[4] *Head,* and of a *Coquet's Heart,* which were both of them laid on a Table before us. An imaginary Operator opened the first with a great deal of Nicety, which, upon a cursory and superficial View, appeared like the Head of another Man; but, upon applying our Glasses to it, we made a very odd Discovery, namely, that what we

1 Actually, the line is from Horace *Ars Poetica* 300: "A head which three doses of hellebore cannot cure." Hellebore was a plant used as a specific for madness.

2 See *Tatler* No. 216, n. 2. The term could refer to more creditable scientists.

3 Microscopes.

4 A beau is a fop or dandy, one largely concerned with personal appearance and social gesture. For the coquette, see *Spectator* No. 66, n. 11.

looked upon as Brains, were not such in Reality, but an Heap of strange Materials wound up in that Shape and Texture, and packed together with wonderful Art in the several Cavities of the Skull. For, as *Homer*[5] tells us, that the Blood of the Gods is not real Blood, but only Something like it; so we found that the Brain of a Beau is not real Brain, but only Something like it.

The *Pineal Gland*,[6] which many of our Modern Philosophers suppose to be the Seat of the Soul, smelt very strong of Essence and Orange-Flower Water, and was encompas'd with a Kind of horny Substance, cut into a thousand little Faces[7] or Mirrours, which were imperceptible to the naked Eye; insomuch that the Soul, if there had been any here, must have been always taken up in contemplating her own Beauties.

We observed a large *Antrum* or Cavity in the *Sinciput*,[8] that was filled with Ribbons, Lace and Embroidery, wrought together in a most curious Piece of Network, the Parts of which were likewise imperceptible to the naked Eye. Another of these *Antrums* or Cavities was stuffed with invisible Billet-doux, Love-Letters, pricked Dances,[9] and other Trumpery of the same Nature. In another we found a Kind of Powder, which set the whole Company a Sneezing, and by the Scent discovered it self to be right *Spanish*.[10] The several other Cells were stored with Commodities of the same Kind, of which it would be tedious to give the Reader an exact Inventory.

There was a large Cavity on each Side of the Head, which I must not omit. That on the right Side was filled with Fictions, Flatteries and Falsehoods, Vows, Promises and Protestations; that on the left with Oaths and Imprecations. There issued out a *Duct* from each of these Cells, which ran into the Root of the Tongue, where both joined together, and passed forward in one common

[5] In the *Iliad* 5. 339–343, Homer writes of the "ichor" or ethereal juice which flows in the veins of gods.

[6] A gland in the brain once thought to be the seat of the soul, called "pineal" because it resembles a pine cone.

[7] I.e., a horn-like substance cut into a thousand facets.

[8] The fore part of the head.

[9] Dance programs marked with pin-pricks.

[10] Snuff.

Duct to the Tip of it. We discovered several little Roads or Canals running from the Ear into the Brain, and took particular Care to trace them out through their several Passages. One of them extended it self to a Bundle of Sonnets and little Musical Instruments.[11] Others ended in several Bladders which were filled either with Wind or Froth. But the large Canal entered into a great Cavity of the Skull, from whence there went another Canal into the Tongue. This great Cavity was filled with a Kind of spongy Substance, which the *French* Anatomists call *Galimatias,* and the *English* Nonsense.

The Skins of the Forehead were extreamly tough and thick,[12] and, what very much surpris'd us, had not in them any single Blood-Vessel that we were able to discover, either with or without our Glasses; from whence we concluded, that the Party when alive must have been entirely deprived of the Faculty of Blushing.

The *Os Cribriforme*[13] was exceedingly stuffed, and in some Places damaged with Snuff. We could not but take Notice in particular of that small Muscle, which is not often discovered in Dissections, and draws the Nose upwards, when it expresses the Contempt which the Owner of it has, upon seeing any Thing he does not like, or hearing any Thing he does not understand. I need not tell my learned Reader, this is that Muscle which performs the Motion so often mentioned by the *Latin* Poets,[14] when they talk of a Man's cocking his Nose, or playing the Rhinoceros.[15]

We did not find any Thing very remarkable in the Eye, saving only, that the *Musculi Amatorii,* or as we may translate it into *English,* the *Ogling Muscles,* were very much worn and decayed with Use; whereas on the contrary, the *Elevator* or the Muscle which turns the Eye towards Heaven, did not appear to have been used at all.

I have only mentioned in this Dissection such new Discoveries

11 I.e., the beau had been occupied with writing sonnets and playing musical instruments.

12 The thick skin indicates the impudence of the beau; he was not affected by social criticism.

13 The sieve-shaped bone of the nose.

14 E.g., Martial *Epigrams* 1. 3. 5–6.

15 I.e., turning up the nose, sneering.

as we were able to make, and have not taken any Notice of those Parts which are to be met with in common Heads. As for the Skull, the Face, and indeed the whole outward Shape and Figure of the Head, we could not discover any Difference from what we observe in the Heads of other Men. We were informed, that the Person to whom this Head belonged, has passed for *a Man*[16] above five and thirty Years; during which Time he eat and drank like other People, dressed well, talked loud, laught frequently, and on particular Occasions had acquitted himself tolerably at a Ball or an Assembly, to which one of the Company added, that a certain Knot[17] of Ladies took him for a Wit. He was cut off in the Flower of his Age, by the Blow of a Paring-Shovel,[18] having been surprised by an eminent Citizen, as he was tendring some Civilities to his Wife.

When we had thoroughly examin'd this Head with all its Apartments, and its several Kinds of Furniture, we put up the Brain, such as it was, into its proper Place, and laid it aside under a broad Piece of Scarlet Cloth, in order to be *prepared*,[19] and kept in a great Repository of Dissections, our Operator telling us that the Preparation would not be so difficult as that of another Brain, for that he had observed several of the little Pipes and Tubes which ran through the Brain were already filled with a Kind of mercurial Substance, which he looked upon to be true Quick Silver.[20]

He applied himself in the next Place to the *Coquet's Heart*, which he likewise laid open with great Dexterity. There occurred to us many Particularities in this Dissection; but being unwilling to burden my Reader's Memory too much, I shall reserve this Subject for the Speculation of another Day.[21]   L.

---

[16] Though he had impersonated a man, he was, in fact, only a beau.

[17] Group, circle.

[18] A flat spade used to pare turf.

[19] I.e., preserved as a medical specimen.

[20] Mercury was regularly prescribed for curing venereal disease.

[21] See *Spectator* No. 281.

The Spectator, No. 276

Wednesday, January 16.

[S t e e l e]

Errori nomen virtus posuisset honestum. Hor.[1]

"*Mr.* Spectator,

I hope you have Philosophy enough to be capable of bearing the Mention of your Faults. Your Papers which regard the fallen Part of the fair Sex,[2] are, I think, written with an Indelicacy which makes them unworthy to be inserted in the Writings of a Moralist who knows the World. I cannot allow that you are at Liberty to observe upon the Actions of Mankind with the Freedom which you seem to resolve upon; at least if you do so, you should take along with you the Distinction of Manners of the World, according to the Quality and Way of Life of the Persons concerned. A Man of Breeding speaks of even Misfortune among Ladies, without giving it the most terrible Aspect it can bear; and this Tenderness towards them, is much more to be preserved when you speak of Vices. All Mankind are so far related, that Care is to be taken, in Things to which all are liable, you do not mention what concerns one in Terms which shall disgust another.[3] Thus to tell a rich Man of the Indigence of a Kinsman of his, or abruptly inform a virtuous Woman of the Lapse of one who 'till then was in the same Degree of Esteem with her self, is in a Kind involving each of them in some Participation of those Disadvantages. It is therefore expected from every Writer, to treat his Argument in such a Manner, as is most proper to entertain the Sort of Readers to

1 Horace *Satires* 1. 3. 42: "Would that virtue had given error an honest name."

2 The reference is to *Spectators* No. 266 and 274.

3 Though Francis Courtly does object that the Spectator "should draw Vices which carry all the Horrour of Shame and Contempt," his main concern is civility of language.

whom his Discourse is directed. It is not necessary, when you write to the Tea-Table,[4] that you should draw Vices which carry all the Horrour of Shame and Contempt: If you paint an impertinent Self-love, an artful Glance, an assumed Complection, you say all which you ought to suppose they can possibly be guilty of. When you talk with this Limitation, you behave your self so as that you may expect others in Conversation may second your Raillery;[5] but when you do it in a Stile which every Body else forbears in Respect to their Quality, they have an easy Remedy in forbearing to read you, and hearing no more of their Faults. A Man that is now and then guilty of an Intemperance, is not to be called a Drunkard; but the Rule of polite Raillery, is to speak of a Man's Faults as if you loved him. Of this Nature is what was said by *Caesar:*[6] When one was railing with an uncourtly Vehemence, and broke out, What must we call him who was taken in an Intrigue with another Man's Wife? *Caesar* answered very gravely, *A careless Fellow.* This was at once a Reprimand for speaking of a Crime which in those Days had not the Abhorrence attending it as it ought, as well as an Intimation that all intemperate Behaviour before Superiours loses its Aim, by accusing in a Method unfit for the Audience. A Word to the Wise. All I mean here to say to you is, That the most free Person of Quality can go no further than being an unkind Woman; and you should never say of a Man of Figure worse, than that he knows the World.

I am

Sir,

Your most humble Servant,
Francis Courtly."

"*Mr.* Spectator,
I am a Woman of an unspotted Reputation, and know Nothing I have ever done which should encourage such Insolence; but here was one the other Day, and he was dressed like a Gentleman too, who took Liberty to Name the Words lusty Fellow in my Presence. I doubt not but you will resent it in Behalf of,

Sir,

Your humble Servant,
Celia."

---

[4] I.e., when you write for ladies of delicacy.

[5] If you confine yourself to discussing harmless follies, others will echo your gentle criticism.

[6] The story is included in Thomas Bayly's *Witty Apopthegms* (1658).

"*Mr.* Spectator,

You lately put out a dreadful Paper,[7] wherein you promise a full Account of the State of criminal Love; and call all the Fair who have transgressed in that Kind by one very rude Name which I do not care to repeat: But I Desire to know of you whether I am or I am not one of those? My Case is as follows. I am kept by an old Batchelour, who took me so young that I knew not how he came by me: He is a Bencher[8] of one of the Inns of Court, a very gay healthy old Man; which is a very lucky Thing for him, who has been, he tells me, a Scowrer, a Scamperer, a Breaker of Windows, and Invader of Constables,[9] in the Days of Yore, when all Dominion[10] ended with the Day, and Males and Females met helter-skelter, and the Scowrers drove before them all who pretended to keep up Order or Rule to the Interruption of Love and Honour. This is his Way of Talk, for he is very gay when he visits me; but as his former Knowledge of the Town has alarmed him into an invincible Jealousy, he keeps me in a Pair of Slippers, neat Boddice, warm Petticoats, and my own Hair woven in Ringletts, after a Manner, he says, he remembers.[11] I am not Mistress of one Farthing of Money, but have all Necessaries provided for me, under the Guard of one who procured for him while he had any Desires to gratify. I know Nothing of a Wench's Life, but the Reputation of it: I have a natural Voice, and a pretty untaught Step in Dancing. His Manner is to bring an old Fellow who has been his Servant from his Youth, and is grey-headed: This Man makes on the Violin a certain Jiggish Noise, to which I dance, and when that is over I sing to him some loose Air that has more Wantonness than Musick in it. You must have seen a strange windowed House near *Hide-Park*, which is so built that no one can look out of any of the Apartments; my Rooms are after that Manner, and I never see Man, Woman or Child but in Company with the two Persons[12] above mentioned. He sends me in all the Books, Pamphlets, Plays, Operas and Songs that come out; and his utmost Delight in me, as a Woman, is

[7] No. 266.

[8] See *Tatler* No. 132, n. 8.

[9] I.e., one of a group who raged through the streets, destroying property, attacking law-officers, and generally looking for trouble. For "a Breaker of Windows," see *Spectator* No. 105, n. 2.

[10] Law, civilized order.

[11] In the style fashionable during the Restoration.

[12] I.e., the woman who formerly procured for him, and his gray-haired servant.

to talk over all his old Amours in my Presence, to play with my Neck, say *the Time was*, give me a Kiss, and bid me be sure to follow the Directions of my Guardian, (the abovementioned Lady) and I shall never want. The Truth of my Case is, I suppose, that I was educated for a Purpose he did not know he should be unfit for when I came to Years. Now, Sir, what I ask of you, as a Casuist,[13] is to tell me how far in these Circumstances I am innocent, though submissive; he guilty, though impotent?

I am,

Sir,

Your constant Reader,

PUCELLA."

To the Man called the Spectator.

"*Friend,*

Forasmuch as at the Birth of thy Labour, thou didst promise upon thy Word, that letting alone the Vanities that do abound, thou would-est only endeavour to strengthen the crooked Morals of this our *Babylon*,[14] I gave Credit to thy fair Speeches, and admitted one of thy Papers, every Day, save *Sunday*, into my House; for the Edification of my Daughter *Tabitha*, and to the End that *Susanna* the Wife of my Bosom might profit thereby. But alas! my Friend, I find that thou art a Liar, and that the Truth is not in thee;[15] else why didst thou in a Paper which thou didst lately put forth, make Mention of those vain Coverings for the Heads of our Females, which thou lovest to liken unto Tulips, and which are lately sprung up among us?[16] Nay, why didst thou make Mention of them in such a Seeming, as if thou didst approve the Invention, insomuch that my Daughter *Tabitha* beginneth to wax wanton, and to lust after these foolish Vanities? Surely thou dost see with the Eyes of the Flesh. Verily therefore, un-less thou dost speedily amend and leave off following thine own Imaginations, I will leave off thee.

Thy Friend as hereafter thou dost demean thy self,

Hezekiah Broadbrim."

T

---

[13] A philosopher given to close reasoning on complex subjects.

[14] I.e., London, our depraved city.

[15] 1 John 2:4.

[16] In *Spectator* No. 265, Addison described "a little Cluster of Women sit-ting together in the prettiest coloured Hoods that I ever saw" and compared them to "a Bed of Tulips."

The Spectator, No. 281

Tuesday, January 22.

[Addison]

Pectoribus inhians spirantia consulit exta. Virg.[1]

Having already given an Account of the Dissection of a *Beau's Head,*[2] with the several Discoveries made on that Occasion; I shall here, according to my Promise, enter upon the Dissection of a *Coquet's Heart,*[3] and communicate to the Publick such Particularities as we observed in that curious Piece of Anatomy.

I should perhaps have waved[4] this Undertaking, had not I been put in Mind of my Promise by several of my unknown Correspondents, who are very importunate with me to make an Example of the Coquet, as I have already done of the Beau. It is therefore in Compliance with the Request of Friends, that I have looked over the Minutes[5] of my former Dream, in order to give the Publick an exact Relation of it, which I shall enter upon without further Preface.

Our Operator, before he engaged in this visionary Dissection, told us, that there was Nothing in his Art more difficult, than to lay open the Heart of a Coquet, by reason of the many Labyrinths and Recesses which are to be found in it, and which do not appear in the Heart of any other Animal.

He desired us first of all to observe the *Pericardium,* or outward Case of the Heart, which we did very attentively; and by the

---

1 Virgil *Aeneid* 4. 64: "Anxious, he consults the reeking entrails."
2 See Essay No. 275, which describes the first part of the Spectator's dream.
3 See *Spectator* No. 66, n. 11.
4 Waived, laid aside.
5 The jotted-down notes.

Help of our Glasses[6] discerned in it Millions of little Scars, which
seem'd to have been occasioned by the Points of innumerable
Darts and Arrows, that from Time to Time had glanced upon the
the outward Coat; though we could not discover the smallest Ori-
fice, by which any of them had entered and pierced the inward
Substance.

Every Smatterer in Anatomy knows, that this *Pericardium,* or
Case of the Heart, contains in it a thin reddish Liquor, supposed
to be bred from the Vapours which exhale out of the Heart, and
being stopt here, are condensed into this watry Substance. Upon
examining this Liquor, we found that it had in it all the Qualities
of that Spirit which is made Use of in the Thermometer,[7] to shew
the Change of Weather.

Nor must I here omit an Experiment one of the Company assured us he himself had made with this Liquor, which he found
in great Quantity about the Heart of a Coquet whom he had formerly dissected. He affirmed to us, that he had actually enclosed
it in a small Tube made after the manner of a Weather-Glass; but
that instead of acquainting him with the Variations of the Atmosphere, it showed him the Qualities[8] of those Persons who entered
the Room where it stood. He affirmed also, that it rose at the Approach of a Plume of Feathers, an embroidered Coat, or a Pair of
fringed Gloves; and that it fell as soon as an ill-shaped Perriwig, a
clumsy pair of Shooes, or an unfashionable Coat came into his
House: Nay, he proceeded so far as to assure us, that upon his
Laughing aloud when he stood by it, the Liquor mounted very
sensibly, and immediately sunk again upon his looking serious.
In short, he told us, that he knew very well by this Invention
whenever he had a Man of Sense or a Coxcomb in his Room.

Having cleared away the *Pericardium,* or the Case and Liquor
above-mentioned, we came to the Heart itself. The outward Surface of it was extremely slippery, and the *Mucro,* or Point so very

6 I.e., microscopes.

7 Addison uses the terms *thermometer, weather glass* and *barometer* loosely,
to indicate an instrument which records temperature and forecasts weather-
change. See *Tatlers* No. 214 and 220.

8 I.e., the social rank.

cold withal, that upon endeavouring to take hold of it, it glided through the Fingers like a smooth Piece of Ice.[9]

The Fibres were turned and twisted in a more intricate and perplexed Manner than they are usually found in other Hearts; insomuch, that the whole Heart was wound up together like a Gordian Knot,[10] and must have had very irregular and unequal Motions, whilst it was employed in its Vital Function.

One Thing we thought very observable, namely, that upon examining all the Vessels which came into it or issued out of it, we could not discover any Communication that it had with the Tongue.

We could not but take Notice likewise, that several of those little Nerves in the Heart which are affected by the Sentiments of Love, Hatred, and other Passions, did not descend to this before us from the Brain, but from the Muscles which lie about the Eye.

Upon weighing the Heart in my Hand, I found it to be extreamly light, and consequently very hollow; which I did not wonder at when upon looking into the Inside of it, I saw Multitudes of Cells and Cavities running one within another, as our Historians describe the Appartments of *Rosamond's* Bower.[11] Several of these little Hollows were stuffed with innumerable Sorts of Trifles, which I shall forbear giving any particular Account of, and shall therefore only take Notice of what lay first and uppermost, which upon our unfolding it and applying our Microscope to it appeared to be a Flame-coloured Hood.[12]

We were informed that the Lady of this Heart, when living, received the Addresses of several who made Love to her, and did not only give each of them Encouragement, but made every one she conversed with believe that she regarded him with an Eye of

[9] I.e., the heart could never be won by a lover or held to a promise.

[10] This knot, attached to the chariot of Gordius, the legendary king of Phrygia, was so cunningly fastened that no one could untie it; finally it was cut by Alexander the Great.

[11] The residence at Woodstock—where Rosamond Clifford (d. 1176?), mistress of Henry II, was kept—could be approached only through a variety of labyrinths. Addison's opera *Rosamond* appeared in 1707.

[12] See *Spectator* No. 276, n. 16.

Kindness; for which Reason we expected to have seen the Impression of Multitudes of Faces among the several Plaites and Foldings of the Heart, but to our great Surprize not a single Print of this Nature discovered it self till we came into the very Core and Center of it. We there observed a little Figure, which, upon applying our Glasses to it, appeared dressed in a very Fantastick Manner. The more I looked upon it, the more I thought I had seen the Face before, but could not possibly recollect either the Place or Time; when at length one of the Company, who had examined this Figure more nicely than the rest, shew'd us plainly by the Make of its Face, and the several Turns of its Features, that the little Idol that was thus lodged in the very Middle of the Heart was the deceased Beau, whose Head I gave some Account of in my last *Tuesday*'s Paper.

As soon as we had finished our Dissection, we resolved to make an Experiment of the Heart, not being able to determine among our selves the Nature of its Substance, which differed in so many Particulars from that of the Heart in other Females. Accordingly we laid it into a Pan of burning Coals, when we observed in it a certain salamandrine Quality,[13] that made it capable of living in the Midst of Fire and Flame, without being consum'd, or so much as sindged.

As we were admiring this strange *Phaenomenon,* and standing round the Heart in a Circle, it gave a most prodigious Sigh, or rather Crack, and dispersed all at once in Smoke and Vapour. This imaginary Noise, which methoughts was louder than the Burst of a Cannon, produced such a violent Shake in my Brain, that it dissipated the Fumes of Sleep, and left me in an instant broad awake.   L

[13] A salamander was thought capable of enduring in fire, without being consumed.

The Spectator, No. 285

Saturday, January 26.

[Addison]

Ne quicunque Deus, quicunque adhibebitur heros,
Regali conspectus in auro nuper & ostro,
Migret in Obscuras humili sermone tabernas:
Aut dum vitat humum, nubes & inania captet. **Hor.**[1]

Having already treated of the Fable, the Characters, and Sentiments in the *Paradise Lost,*[2] we are in the last Place to consider the *Language;* and as the learned World is very much divided upon *Milton,* as to this Point, I hope they will excuse me if I appear particular[3] in any of my Opinions, and encline to those who judge the most advantagiously of the Author.

It is requisite that the Language of an heroick Poem should be both perspicuous and sublime. In proportion as either of these two Qualities are wanting, the Language is imperfect. Perspicuity is the first and most necessary Qualification; insomuch, that a good-natured Reader sometimes overlooks a little Slip even in the Grammar or Syntax, where it is impossible for him to mistake the Poet's Sense. Of this Kind[4] is that Passage in *Milton,* wherein he speaks of *Satan.*

---

1 Horace *Ars Poetica* 227–230: "So that whatever god, whatever hero has been brought on the stage, whom we have just beheld in royal gold and purple, shall not shift with vulgar speech into dingy hovels, nor, while shunning the earth, clutch at clouds and emptiness."

2 *Spectators* No. 267, 273, and 279.

3 Biased, unwilling to accommodate both sides of the question.

4 The given examples of "a little Slip" are from *Paradise Lost,* 2. 678–679 and 4. 323–324.

————*God and his Son except,*
Created Thing Nought valu'd he nor shunn'd.

And that in which he describes *Adam* and *Eve.*

Adam *the goodliest Man of Men since born*
His Sons, the fairest of her Daughters Eve.

It is plain, that in the former of these Passages, according to the natural Syntax, the Divine Persons mentioned in the first Line are represented as created Beings; and that in the other, *Adam* and *Eve* are confounded with their Sons and Daughters. Such little Blemishes as these, when the Thought is great and natural, we should, with *Horace*,[5] impute to a pardonable Inadvertency, or to the Weakness of humane Nature, which cannot attend to each minute Particular, and give the last finishing to every Circumstance in so long a Work. The ancient Cricks therefore, who were acted by a Spirit of Candour, rather than that of Cavilling, invented certain Figures of Speech, on purpose to palliate little Errors of this Nature in the Writings of those Authors, who had so many greater Beauties to atone for them.[6]

If Clearness and Perspicuity were only to be consulted, the Poet would have Nothing else to do but to cloath his Thoughts in the most plain and natural Expressions. But, since it often happens, that the most obvious Phrases, and those which are used in ordinary Conversation, become too familiar to the Ear, and contract a Kind of Meanness by passing through the Mouths of the Vulgar, a Poet should take particular Care to guard himself against idiomatick Ways of Speaking. *Ovid* and *Lucan* have many Poornesses of Expression upon this Account, as taking up with the first Phrases that offered, without putting themselves to the Trouble of looking after such as would not only have been natural, but also elevated and sublime. *Milton* has but few Failings in this Kind, of which, however, you may meet with some Instances, as in the following Passages.[7]

---

[5] Horace *Ars Poetica* 351–353.

[6] I.e., in order to excuse questionable figures of speech, the "Ancient Cricks" gave them identifying names.

[7] The *Paradise Lost* passages reflecting "too familiar" speech are from 3. 474–476; 5. 395–397; and 10. 733–736.

> *Embrio's and Idiots, Eremites and Fryars*
> White, Black and Grey, *with all their* Trumpery,
> *Here Pilgrims roam*———
> ———*A while Discourse they hold,*
> No fear lest Dinner cool; *when thus began*
> *Our Author*———
> *Who of all Ages to succeed, but feeling*
> *The Evil on him brought by me, will curse*
> *My Head, ill fare our Ancestor impure,*
> For this we may thank *Adam*———

The great Masters in Composition know very well that many an elegant Phrase becomes improper for a Poet or an Orator, when it has been debased by common Use. For this Reason the Works of ancient Authors, which are written in dead Languages, have a great Advantage over those which are written in Languages that are now spoken. Were there any mean Phrases or Idioms in *Virgil* and *Homer,* they would not shock the Ear of the most delicate modern Reader, so much as they would have done that of an old *Greek* or *Roman,* because we never hear them pronounced in our Streets, or in ordinary Conversation.

It is not therefore sufficient, that the Language of an Epic Poem be perspicuous, unless it be also sublime. To this End it ought to deviate from the common Forms and ordinary Phrases of Speech. The Judgment of a Poet very much discovers it self in shunning the common Roads of Expression, without falling into such Ways of Speech as may seem stiff and unnatural; he must not swell into a false Sublime, by endeavouring to avoid the other Extream. Among the *Greeks, Eschylus,* and sometimes *Sophocles,* were guilty of this Fault; among the *Latins, Claudian* and *Statius;* and among our own Countrymen, *Shakespear* and *Lee.*[8] In these Authors the Affectation of Greatness often hurts the Perspicuity of the Stile, as in many others the Endeavour after Perspicuity prejudices its Greatness.

Aristotle[9] has observed, that the Idiomatick Stile may be

---

8 Claudian (d. 408?) and Statius (45?–96?) were Latin poets; Nathaniel Lee (*c.* 1652–1706), an English dramatist.

9 Aristotle *Poetics* 22. 1.

avoided, and the Sublime formed, by the following Methods. First, by the Use of Metaphors, like those in *Milton*.[10]

> Imparadised *in one anothers Arms,*
> ———*And in his Hand a Reed*
> *Stood waving* tipt *with Fire;*———
> *The grassie Clods now* calv'd.———

In these and innumerable other Instances, the Metaphors are very bold, but beautiful: I must however observe, that the Metaphors are not thick sown in *Milton,* which always savours too much of Wit; that they never clash with one another, which as *Aristotle*[11] observes, turns a Sentence into a Kind of an Enigma or Riddle; and that he seldom makes Use of them where the proper and natural Words will do as well.

Another Way of raising the Language, and giving it a poetical Turn, is to make Use of the Idioms of other Tongues.[12] *Virgil* is full of the *Greek* Forms of Speech, which the Criticks call *Hellenisms,* as *Horace* in his Odes abounds with them much more than *Virgil.* I need not mention the several Dialects which *Homer* has made Use of for this End. *Milton* in conformity with the Practice of the ancient Poets, and with *Aristotle*'s Rule, has infused a great many *Latinisms,* as well as *Graecisms,* and sometimes *Hebraisms,* into the Language of his Poem,[13] as towards the Beginning of it.

> Nor *did they* not *perceive the evil Plight*
> *In which they were,* or *the fierce Pains* not *feel.*
> *Yet to their Gen'ral's Voice they soon obey'd.*
> ———*Who shall tempt with wandring Feet*
> *The dark unbottom'd infinite Abyss,*
> *And through the* palpable Obscure *find out his Way,*
> *His uncouth Way, or spread his airy Flight*
> *Upborn with indefatigable Wings*
> *Over the* vast Abrupt!———
> ———*So both ascend*
> *In the Visions of God.*———   B. 2.

---

[10] The *Paradise Lost* metaphors are from 4. 506; 6. 579–580; and 7. 463.

[11] *Poetics* 22. 2.

[12] *Poetics* 22. 2–3. This is "*Aristotle's* Rule" mentioned later in the paragraph.

[13] The examples which follow are taken from 1. 335–337; 2. 404–409; and 11. 376–377.

Under this Head may be reckoned the placing the Adjective after the Substantive, the Transposition of Words, the turning the Adjective into a Substantive, with several other foreign Modes of Speech, which this Poet has naturalized to give his Verse the greater Sound, and throw it out of Prose.

The third Method mentioned by *Aristotle*,[14] is what agrees with the Genius of the *Greek* Language more than with that of any other Tongue, and is therefore more used by *Homer* than by any other Poet. I mean the length'ning of a Phrase by the Addition of Words, which may either be inserted or omitted, as also by the extending or contracting of particular Words by the Insertion or Omission of certain Syllables. *Milton* has put in Practice this Method of raising his Language, as far as the Nature of our Tongue will permit, as in the Passage above-mentioned, *Eremite*, for what is Hermite[15] in common Discourse. If you observe the Measure of his Verse, he has with great Judgment suppressed a Syllable in several Words, and shortned those of two Syllables into one, by which Method, besides the abovementioned Advantage, he has given a greater Variety to his Numbers.[16] But this Practice is more particularly remarkable in the Names of Persons and of Countries, as *Beelzebub, Hessebon,* and in many other Particulars, wherein he has either changed the Name, or made Use of that which is not the most commonly known,[17] that he might the better deviate from the Language of the Vulgar.

The same Reason recommended to him several old Words, which also makes his Poem appear the more venerable, and gives it a greater Air of Antiquity.

I must likewise take Notice, that there are in *Milton* several Words of his own Coining,[18] as *Cerberean, miscreated, Hell-doom'd, Embryon* Atoms, and many Others. If the Reader is offended at this Liberty in our *English* Poet, I would recommend

[14] *Poetics* 22. 4.

[15] I.e., Milton used "Eremite" for its sound, rather than the commoner word "hermit."

[16] Versification.

[17] *Beëlzebub* is the Latin form of the Hebrew *Baal-zebub; Hesebon,* the Greek form of the Hebrew *Heshbon*. The first name denotes the devil next in rank to Satan; the second (1, 408), a city whose destruction is celebrated in Numbers 21:25–31.

[18] The created words are from 2. 655, 683, 697, and 900.

him to a Discourse in *Plutarch*,[19] which shews us how frequently *Homer* has made Use of the same Liberty.

Milton, by the abovementioned Helps, and by the Choice of the noblest Words and Phrases which our Tongue would afford him, has carried our Language to a greater Height than any of the *English* Poets have ever done before or after him, and made the Sublimity of his Stile equal to that of his Sentiments.

I have been the more particular in these Observations of *Milton*'s Stile, because it is that Part of him in which he appears the most singular. The Remarks I have here made upon the Practice of other Poets, with my Observations out of *Aristotle,* will perhaps alleviate the Prejudice which some have taken to his Poem upon this Account; tho' after all, I must confess, that I think his Stile, tho' admirable in general, is in some Places too much stiffened and obscured by the frequent Use of those Methods, which *Aristotle* has prescribed for the raising of it.

This Redundancy of those several Ways of Speech which *Aristotle*[20] calls *foreign Language,* and with which *Milton* has so very much enriched, and in some Places darkned the Language of his Poem, was the more proper for his Use, because his Poem is written in blank Verse; Rhyme, without any other Assistance, throws the Language off from Prose, and very often makes an indifferent Phrase pass unregarded; but where the Verse is not built upon Rhymes, there Pomp of Sound, and Energy of Expression, are indispensably necessary to support the Stile, and keep it from falling into the Flatness of Prose.

Those who have not a Taste for this Elevation of Stile, and are apt to ridicule a Poet when he departs from the common Forms of Expression, would do well to see how *Aristotle*[21] has treated an ancient Author, called *Euclid,* for his insipid Mirth upon this occasion. Mr. *Dryden* used to call this Sort of Men his Prose-Criticks.[22]

I should, under this Head of the Language, consider *Milton*'s Numbers, in which he has made Use of several Elisions, that are

[19] *The Life and Poetry of Homer,* formerly attributed to Plutarch.

[20] *Poetics* 22. 1.

[21] *Poetics* 22. 5.

[22] I.e., those who complained his poetry was not prosaic enough.

not customary among other *English* Poets, as may be particularly observed in his cutting off the Letter *Y*, when it precedes a Vowel. This, and some other Innovations in the Measure of his Verse, has varied his Numbers in such a Manner, as makes them incapable of satiating the Ear, and cloying the Reader, which the same uniform Measure would certainly have done, and which the perpetual Returns of Rhime never fail to do in long narrative Poems. I shall close these Reflections upon the Language of *Paradise Lost*, with observing that *Milton* has copied after *Homer*, rather than *Virgil*, in the Length of his Periods, the Copiousness of his Phrases, and the running of his Verses into one another.   L

The Spectator, No. 297

Saturday, February 9.

[Addison]

———— ——— ———— ————*velut si*
Egregio inspersos reprendas corpore naevos. Hor.[1]

After what I have said in my last *Saturday*'s Paper,[2] I shall enter on the Subject of this without farther Preface, and remark the several Defects which appear in the Fable, the Characters, the Sentiments, and the Language of *Milton*'s *Paradise Lost;* not doubting but the Reader will pardon me, if I alledge at the same Time whatever may be said for the Extenuation of such Defects. The first Imperfection which I shall observe in the Fable is, that the Event of it is unhappy.

The Fable of every Poem is according to *Aristotle*'s Division either *Simple* or *Implex*.[3] It is called Simple when there is no Change of Fortune in it, Implex when the Fortune of the chief Actor changes from Bad to Good, or from Good to Bad. The Implex Fable is thought the most perfect; I suppose, because it is more proper to stir up the Passions of the Reader, and to surprize him with a greater Variety of Accidents.

The Implex Fable is therefore of two Kinds: In the first the

[1] Horace *Satires* 1. 6. 66–67: "As perfect beauties often have a mole."

[2] *Spectator* No. 291 discussed the characteristics of a responsible critic and concluded, "As I intend in my next Paper to shew the Defects in *Milton's Paradise Lost,* I thought fit to premise these few Particulars, to the End that the Reader may know I enter upon it, as on a very ungrateful Work, and that I shall just point at the Imperfections, without endeavouring to enflame them with Ridicule."

[3] Aristotle *Poetics* 10. 1.

chief Actor makes his way through a long Series of Dangers and
Difficulties, 'till he arrives at Honour and Prosperity, as we see in
the Story of *Ulysses*. In the second, the chief Actor in the Poem
falls from some eminent Pitch of Honour and Prosperity, into
Misery and Disgrace. Thus we see *Adam* and *Eve* sinking from a
State of Innocence and Happiness, into the most abject Condition
of Sin and Sorrow.

The most taking Tragedies among the Antients were built on
this last Sort of Implex Fable, particularly the Tragedy of *Oedipus*, which proceeds upon a Story, if we may believe *Aristotle,* the
most proper for Tragedy that could be invented by the Wit of
Man.[4] I have taken some pains in a former Paper[5] to shew, that
this Kind of Implex Fable, wherein the Event is unhappy, is more
apt to affect an Audience than that of the first Kind; notwithstanding many excellent Pieces among the Antients, as well as most of
those which have been written of late Years in our own Country,
are raised upon contrary Plans. I must however own, that I think
this Kind of Fable, which is the most perfect in Tragedy, is not so
proper for an Heroick Poem.

. *Milton* seems to have been sensible of this Imperfection in his
Fable, and has therefore endeavoured to cure it by several Expe-
dients; particularly by the Mortification which the great Adversary of Mankind meets with upon his Return to the Assembly of
Infernal Spirits, as it is described in a beautiful Passage of the
tenth Book; and likewise by the Vision, wherein *Adam* at the
Close of the Poem sees his Off-spring triumphing over his great
Enemy, and himself restored to a happier *Paradise* than that from
which he fell.[6]

There is another Objection against *Milton*'s Fable, which is indeed almost the same with the former, tho' placed in a different
Light, namely, That the Hero in the *Paradise Lost* is unsuccessful,
and by no means a Match for his Enemies. This gave Occasion to
Mr. *Dryden*'s Reflection, that the Devil was in reality *Milton*'s

4 *Poetics* 2. 2–3.
5 See *Spectator* No. 40.
6 Satan's mortification is described in *Paradise Lost,* 10. 504ff; Adam's vision in 12. 325ff.

Hero.[7] I think I have obviated this Objection in my first Paper.[8] The *Paradise Lost* is an Epic, or a Narrative Poem, he that looks for an Hero in it, searches for that which *Milton* never intended; but if he will needs fix the Name of an Hero upon any Person in it, 'tis certainly the *Messiah* who is the Hero, both in the Principal Action, and in the chief Episodes. Paganism could not furnish out a real Action for a Fable greater than that of the *Iliad* or *Aeneid*, and therefore an Heathen could not form a higher Notion of a Poem than one of that Kind, which they call an Heroick. Whether *Milton*'s is not of a sublimer Nature I will not presume to determine: It is sufficient that I shew there is in the *Paradise Lost* all the Greatness of Plan, Regularity of Design, and masterly Beauties which we discover in *Homer* and *Virgil*.

I must in the next Place observe, that *Milton* has interwoven in the Texture of his Fable some Particulars which do not seem to have Probability enough for an Epic Poem, particularly in the Actions which he ascribes to *Sin* and *Death*, and the Picture which he draws of the *Lymbo of Vanity*, with other Passages in the second Book.[9] Such Allegories rather favour of the Spirit of *Spencer* and *Ariosto*,[10] than of *Homer* and *Virgil*.

In the Structure of his Poem he has likewise admitted of too many Digressions. It is finely observed by *Aristotle*,[11] that the Author of an Heroick Poem should seldom speak himself, but throw as much of his Work as he can into the Mouths of those who are his principal Actors. *Aristotle* has given no Reason for this Precept; but I presume it is because the Mind of the Reader is more awed and elevated when he hears *Aeneas* or *Achilles* speak, than when *Virgil* or *Homer* talk in their own Persons. Besides that assuming the Character of an eminent Man is apt to fire the Imagi-

7 From the Dedication of *Aeneis* (1697). John Dennis expressed the same view of Milton's work: "The Devil is properly his Hero, because he gets the better" (*The Grounds of Criticism*, 1704).

8 I.e., in *Spectator* No. 267, in which he demonstrates that *Paradise Lost* is an epic.

9 Sin and Death appear in book 2. 648–889; the Limbo of Vanity in 3. 444–497.

10 Edmund Spenser (1552?–1599), author of *The Faerie Queene;* and Lodovico Ariosto (1474–1533), Italian poet, author of *Orlando Furioso*.

11 *Poetics* 24. 7.

nation, and raise[12] the Ideas of the Author. *Tully*[13] tells us, mentioning his Dialogue of Old Age, in which *Cato* is the chief Speaker, that upon a Review of it he was agreeably imposed upon, and fancied that it was *Cato,* and not he himself, who uttered his Thoughts on that Subject.

If the Reader would be at the pains to see how the Story of the *Iliad* and the *Aeneid* is delivered by those Persons who act in it, he will be surprized to find how little in either of these Poems proceeds from the Authors. *Milton* has, in the general Disposition of his Fable, very finely observed this great Rule; insomuch, that there is scare a third Part of it which comes from the Poet; the rest is spoken either by *Adam* and *Eve,* or by some Good or Evil Spirit who is engaged either in their Destruction or Defence.

From what has been here observed it appears, that Digressions are by no means to be allowed of in an Epic Poem. If the Poet, even in the ordinary Course of his Narration, should speak as little as possible, he should certainly never let his Narration sleep for the sake of any Reflections of his own. I have often observed, with a secret Admiration, that the longest Reflection in the *Aeneid* is in that Passage of the Tenth Book, where *Turnus* is represented as dressing himself in the Spoils of *Pallas,* whom he had slain. *Virgil* here lets his Fable stand still for the sake of the following Remark. *How is the Mind of Man ignorant of Futurity, and unable to bear prosperous Fortune with Moderation? The Time will come when* Turnus *shall wish that he had left the Body of* Pallas *untouched, and curse the Day on which he dressed himself in these Spoils.*[14] As the great Event of the *Aeneid,* and the Death of *Turnus,* whom *Aeneas* slew because he saw him adorned with the Spoils of *Pallas,* turns upon this Incident, *Virgil* went out of his way to make this Reflection upon it, without which so small a Circumstance might possibly have slipped out of his Reader's Memory. *Lucan,* who was an Injudicious Poet, lets drop his Story very frequently for the sake of his unnecessary Digressions, or his

---

12 Enhance, give power to.

13 Cicero *De Amicitia* 1. 4.

14 Virgil *Aeneid* 10. 501–505. For Turnus and Pallas, see *Spectator* No. 273, n. 3.

Diverticula, as *Scaliger* calls them.[15] If he gives us an Account of
the Prodigies which preceded the Civil War, he declaims upon
the Occasion, and shews how much happier it would be for Man,
if he did not feel his Evil Fortune before it comes to pass, and
suffer not only by its real Weight, but by the Apprehension of it.[16]
Milton's Complaint of his Blindness, his Panegyrick on Marriage,
his Reflections on *Adam* and *Eve's* going naked, of the Angels
eating,[17] and several other Passages in his Poem, are liable to the
same Exception, tho' I must confess there is so great a Beauty in
these very Digressions, that I would not wish them out of his
Poem.

I have, in a former Paper,[18] spoken of the *Characters* of *Milton's Paradise Lost,* and declared my Opinion, as to the Allegorical Persons who are introduced in it.

If we look into the *Sentiments,* I think they are sometimes defective under the following Heads; First, as there are several of
them too much pointed, and some that degenerate even into
Punns. Of this last Kind I am afraid is that in the First Book,
where, speaking of the Pigmies, he calls them

——————*The small* Infantry
Warr'd on by Cranes——————[19]

Another Blemish that appears in some of his Thoughts, is his
frequent Allusion to Heathen Fables, which are not certainly of
a Piece with the Divine Subject, of which he treats. I do not find
fault with these Allusions, where the Poet himself represents them
as fabulous, as he does in some Places, but where he mentions

[15] Julius Caesar Scaliger (1484–1558), Italian critic noted for his commen-
taries on Aristotle, Hippocrates, and others. The reference is to his *Poetices*
6. 6 (1561).

[16] Lucan *Pharsalia* 2. 1–15.

[17] Milton's digressions appear, respectively, in *Paradise Lost,* 3. 1–55; 4.
750–770; 4. 312–320; and 5. 404–433.

[18] See *Spectator* No. 273.

[19] The reference is to book 1. 575–576, in which Milton says that the army
of Devils in hell was so strong that, compared to them, the greatest human
army ever to exist would be no more than the legendary race of pygmies which
were said to ride goats and war on cranes. The objectionable pun relates
pygmy infantry to infants.

them as Truths and Matters of Fact. The Limits of my Paper will not give me leave to be particular in Instances of this Kind: The Reader will easily remark them in his Perusal of the Poem.

A third Fault in his Sentiments, is an unnecessary Ostentation of Learning, which likewise occurs very frequently. It is certain that both *Homer* and *Virgil* were Masters of all the Learning of their Times, but it shews it self in their Works after an indirect and concealed Manner. *Milton* seems ambitious of letting us know, by his Excursions on Free-Will and Predestination, and his many Glances upon History, Astronomy, Geography and the like, as well as by the Terms and Phrases he sometimes makes use of, that he was acquainted with the whole Circle of Arts and Sciences.

If, in the last Place, we consider the *Language* of this great Poet, we must allow what I have hinted in a former Paper, that it is often too much laboured, and sometimes obscured by old Words, Transpositions, and Foreign Idioms. *Seneca*'s Objection to the Stile of a great Author, *Riget ejus oratio, nihil in ea placidum nihil lene*,[20] is what many Criticks make to *Milton*: As I cannot wholly refute it, so I have already apologized for it in another Paper;[21] to which I may further add, that *Milton*'s Sentiments and Ideas were so wonderfully sublime, that it would have been impossible for him to have represented them in their full Strength and Beauty, without having Recourse to these Foreign Assistances. Our Language sunk under him, and was unequal to that Greatness of Soul, which furnished him with such glorious Conceptions.

A second Fault in his Language is, that he often affects a Kind of Jingle in his Words, as in the following Passages,[22] and many others:

> *And brought into the* World *a* World *of woe.*
> ———*Begirt th' Almighty throne*
> Beseeching *or* besieging———

20 Seneca the Elder's criticism of the orator Calvus appeared in *Controversies* 7. 4. 8: The "Objection," as altered by Addison: "His speech is stiff; nothing in it is pleasing or easy."

21 See *Spectator* No. 285.

22 The examples criticized for repetition of sound are respectively from book 9. 11; 5. 868–869; 1. 642; and 4. 181.

> *This* tempted *our* Attempt————
> *At one flight* Bound *high overleapt all* Bound.

I know there are Figures for this Kind of Speech, that some of the greatest Antient have been guilty of it, and that *Aristotle*[23] himself has given it a Place in his Rhetorick among the Beauties of that Art. But as it is in itself poor and trifling, it is I think at present universally exploded by all the Masters of polite Writing.

The last Fault which I shall take notice of in *Milton's* Stile, is the frequent Use of what the Learned call *Technical Words,* or Terms of Art. It is one of the great Beauties of Poetry, to make hard Things intelligible, and to deliver what is abstruse of it self in such easy Language as may be understood by ordinary Readers: Besides that the Knowledge of a Poet should rather seem born with him, or inspired, than drawn from Books and Systems. I have often wondered how Mr. *Dryden* could translate a Passage of *Virgil* after the following manner

> *Tack to the Larboard, and stand off to Sea.*
> *Veer Star-board Sea and Land.————*[24]

Milton makes use of *Larboard* in the same manner. When he is upon Building he mentions *Doric Pillars, Pilasters, Cornice, Freeze, Architrave.*[25] When he talks of Heavenly Bodies, you meet with *Ecliptic,* and *Eccentric,* the *Trepidation, Stars dropping from the Zenith, Rays culminating from the Equator.*[26] To which might be added many Instances of the like Kind in several other Arts and Sciences.

I shall in my next Papers give an Account of the many particular Beauties in *Milton,* which would have been too long to insert under those general Heads I have already treated of, and with which I intend to conclude this Piece of Criticism.   L

[23] Aristotle *Rhetoric* 3. 2. 7.

[24] Dryden's *Aeneis* 3. 526–527. "Larboard" means the port side, the left side of a ship; Milton used the term in book 2. 1019.

[25] The architectural terms are from book 1. 713–716.

[26] The astronomical references are, respectively, from book 3. 740; 3. 575; 3. 483; 1. 745; and 3. 616–617.

The Spectator, No. 305

Tuesday, February 19.

[Addison]

Non tali auxilio, nec defensoribus istis
Tempus eget———Virg.[1]

Our late News-Papers being full of the Project now on Foot in the Court of *France,* for establishing a Political Academy, and I my self having received Letters from several Vertuoso's among my foreign Correspondents, which give some Light into that Affair, I intend to make it the Subject of this Day's Speculation. A general Account of this Project may be met with in the *Daily Courant* of last *Friday* in the following Words, translated from the Gazette of *Amsterdam.*[2]

> *Paris, February 12.* " 'Tis confirmed, that the King has resolv'd to establish a new Academy for Politicks, of which the Marquess de *Torcy,*[3] Minister and Secretary of State, is to be Protector. Six Academicians are to be chosen, endow'd with proper Talents, for beginning to form this Academy, into which no Person is to be admitted under twenty five Years of Age: They must likewise have each an Estate of two thousand Livres a Year, either in Possession, or to come to 'em by Inheritance. The King will allow to each a Pension of a thousand Livres. They are likewise to have able Masters to teach 'em

1 Virgil *Aeneid* 2. 521–522: "The time does not require such aid or such defenders."

2 The passage quoted from the *Daily Courant* (See *Tatler* No. 18, n. 29) was headed "From the Amsterdam Gazette, dated Feb. 19 [N.S.]."

3 Jean-Baptiste Colbert, Marquis de Torcy (1665–1746), was well qualified for the appointment. He was at this time negotiating in secret with British Tories, seeking to win peace and the possible restoration of the Pretender.

the necessary Sciences, and to instruct them in all the Treaties of Peace, Alliance, and others which have been made in several Ages past. These Members are to meet twice a Week at the *Louvre*. From this Seminary are to be chosen Secretaries to Ambassies, who by Degrees may advance to higher Employments.

Cardinal *Richelieu*'s[4] Politicks made *France* the Terror of *Europe*. The Statesmen who have appeared in that Nation of late Years, have on the contrary rendered[5] it either the Pity or Contempt of its Neighbours. The Cardinal erected that famous Academy which has carried all the Parts of polite Learning to the greatest Height. His chief Design in that Institution was to divert the Men of Genius from meddling with Politicks, a Province in which he did not care to have any one else interfere with him. On the contrary, the Marquess de *Torcy* seems resolved to make several young Men in *France* as wise as himself, and is therefore taken up at present in establishing a Nursery of Statesmen.

Some private Letters[6] add, that there will also be erected a Seminary of Petticoat Politicians, who are to be brought up at the Feet of Madam de *Maintenon*,[7] and to be dispatched into Foreign Courts upon any Emergencies of State; but as the News of this last Project has not been yet confirmed, I shall take no farther Notice of it.

Several of my Readers may doubtless remember, that upon the Conclusion of the last War,[8] which had been carried on so successfully by the Enemy, their Generals were many of them transformed into Ambassadors; but the Conduct of those who have commanded in the present War, has, it seems, brought so little Honour and Advantage to their great Monarch, that he is re-

[4] Cardinal Richelieu (1585–1642), chief minister of France under Louis XIII, founded the Académie Française in 1635.

[5] Earned.

[6] Having grounded his essay on a genuine newspaper account, the Spectator goes on to present satirical speculation based on "private Letters."

[7] Madam de Maintenon (1635–1719), secretly married to Louis XIV since 1684, was thought to exercise notable political power.

[8] The Peace of Ryswick (1697) offered an interval between King William's War and the War of the Spanish Succession. The phrase "carried on so successfully" is intended as irony.

solved to trust his Affairs no longer in the Hands of those military Gentlemen.

The Regulations of this new Academy very much deserve our Attention. The Students are to have in Possession, or Reversion, an Estate of two thousand *French* Livres *per Annum,* which, as the present Exchange runs, will amount to at least one hundred and twenty six Pounds English. This, with the royal Allowance of a thousand Livres, will enable them to find themselves in Coffee and Snuff; not to mention News Papers, Pen and Ink, Wax and Wafers,[9] with the like Necessaries for Politicians.

A Man must be at least five and twenty before he can be initiated into the Misteries of this Academy, tho' there is no Question but many grave Persons of a much more advanced Age, who have been constant Readers[10] of the *Paris* Gazette, will be glad to begin the World a-new, and enter themselves upon this List of Politicians.

The Society of these hopeful young Gentlemen is to be under the Direction of six Professors, who, it seems, are to be speculative Statesmen, and drawn out of the Body of the Royal Academy. These six wise Masters, according to my private Letters, are to have the following Parts alloted them.

The first is to instruct the Students in *State Legerdemain,* as how to take off the Impression of a Seal, to split a Wafer, to open a Letter, to fold it up again, with other the like ingenious Feats of Dexterity and Art. When the Students have accomplished themselves in this Part of their Profession, they are to be delivered into the Hands of their second Instructor, who is a Kind of *Posture-master.*

This Artist is to teach them how to nod judiciously, to shrug up their Shoulders in a dubious Case, to connive with either Eye, and in a Word, the whole Practice of *political Grimace.*

The third is a Sort of *Language Master,* who is to instruct them in the Stile proper for a Foreign Minister in his ordinary Discourse. And to the End that this College of Statesmen may be

9 As a succeeding reference makes clear, one could split a wafer to conceal a secret message.

10 These would be the French equivalent of the English amateur politicians who frequented the coffee-houses.

thoroughly practised in the political Stile, they are to make use of it in their common Conversations, before they are employed either in Foreign or Domestick Affairs. If one of them asks another, what a Clock it is, the other is to answer him indirectly, and, if possible, to turn off[11] the Question. If he is desired to change a *Louis d'or,* he must beg Time to consider of it. If it be enquired of him, whether the King is at *Versailles* or *Marly,*[12] he must answer in a Whisper. If he be ask'd the News of the last *Gazette,* or the Subject of a Proclamation, he is to reply, that he has not yet read it: Or if he does not care for explaining himself so far, he needs only draw his Brow up in Wrinkles, or elevate the left Shoulder.

The fourth Professor is to teach the whole Art of political Characters and Hieroglyphicks; and to the End that they may be perfect also in this Practice, they are not to send a Note to one another (tho' it be but to borrow a *Tacitus* or a *Machiavel*)[13] which is not written in Cypher.

Their fifth Professor, it is thought, will be chosen out of the Society of Jesuits,[14] and is to be well read in the Controversies of probable Doctrines, mental Reservations, and the Rights of Princes. This learned Man is to instruct them in the Grammar, Syntax, and construing Part of *Treaty-latin;*[15] how to distinguish between the Spirit and the Letter, and likewise demonstrate how the same Form of Words may lay an Obligation upon any Prince in Europe, different from that which it lays upon his most Christian Majesty.[16] He is likewise to teach them the Art of finding Flaws, Loopholes and Evasions, in the most solemn Compacts,

---

11 Avoid.

12 Versailles was the royal palace; Marly referred to a chateau five miles away, to which the King retreated from time to time.

13 Cornelius Tacitus (55?–117?), Roman politician who wrote the history of the reigns of several emperors; and Niccolò Machiavelli (1469–1527), Florentine statesman and author of *The Prince.* Both could provide budding statesmen with precepts and examples of political duplicity and cunning.

14 Members of the Society of Jesus, thought to be given to intrigue and equivocation.

15 This essay had particular implications for contemporary readers: secret negotiations were then going on between Tory leaders and the French.

16 Louis XIV.

and particularly a great *Rabbinical Secret,* revived of late Years by the Fraternity of Jesuits, namely, that contradictory Interpretations of the same Article, may both of them be true and valid.

When our Statesmen are sufficiently improved by these several Instructors, they are to receive their last Polishing from one who is to act among them as *Master of the Ceremonies.*[17] This Gentleman is to give them Lectures upon those important Points of the *Elbow-Chair,* and the *Stair-Head;* to instruct them in the different Situations of the Right-Hand, and to furnish them with Bows and Inclinations of all Sizes, Measures and Proportions. In short, this Professor is to give the Society their *stiffening,* and infuse into their Manners that beautiful political Starch, which may qualifie them for Levees,[18] Conferences, Visits, and make them shine in what Vulgar Minds are apt to look upon as Trifles.[19]

I have not yet heard any further Particulars, which are to be observed in this Society of unfledged Statesmen; but I must confess, had I a Son of five and twenty, that shou'd take it into his Head at that Age to set up for a Politician, I think I shou'd go near to disinherit him for a Block-head. Besides, I should be apprehensive least the same Arts which are to enable him to negotiate between Potentates, might a little infect his ordinary Behaviour between Man and Man. There is no Question but these young *Machiavels* will, in a little Time, turn their College upside-down with Plots and Stratagems, and lay as many Schemes to circumvent one another in a Frog or a Sallad, as they may hereafter put in Practice to over-reach a neighbouring Prince or State.

We are told that the *Spartans,*[20] tho' they punish'd Theft in their young Men, when it was discovered, looked upon it as honourable if it succeeded. Provided the Conveyance was clean and unsuspected, a Youth might afterwards boast of it. This, say the Historians, was to keep them sharp, and to hinder them from being imposed upon, either in their publick or private Negociations.

[17] Master of protocol.

[18] State receptions.

[19] *Tatler* No. 86 and *Guardian* No. 137 both ridiculed the excessive concern with ceremonial precision.

[20] Plutarch "Ancient Customs of the Spartans" *Moralia* 273E; *Life of Lycurgus* 17. 3.

Whether any such Relaxations of Morality, such little *Jeux d'esprit*,[21] ought not to be allowed in this intended Seminary of Politicians, I shall leave to the Wisdom of their Founder.

In the mean Time we have fair Warning given us by this doughty Body of Statesmen; and as *Sylla* saw many *Marius's* in *Caesar,* so I think we may discover many *Torci's* in this College of *Academicians.*[22] Whatever we think of our selves, I am afraid neither our *Smyrna* or St. *James's* will be a Match for it.[23] Our Coffee-houses are, indeed, very good Institutions, but whether or no these our *British* Schools of Politicks may furnish out as able Envoys and Secretaries as an Academy that is set a-part for that Purpose, will deserve our serious Consideration; especially if we remember that our Country is more famous for producing Men of Integrity than Statesmen; and that, on the contrary, *French* Truth, and *British* Policy make a Conspicuous Figure *in* Nothing, as the Earl of *Rochester* has very well observed in his admirable Poem upon that barren Subject.[24]   L

[21] Play of the mind.

[22] Because Caesar's aunt married the great Marius and because Caesar himself wed Cornelia, daughter of a leader in the Marian party, the Roman general Sulla—commenting on the young Caesar and his future descendants—said they knew little who did not see in him many Mariuses (Plutarch *Life of Caesar* 1. 3). In the same way, the new Academy would produce generations of Torcys.

[23] Both St. James's Coffee-house (See *Tatler* No. 1, n. 3) and the Smyrna Coffee-house in Pall Mall were seats of political intrigue.

[24] The reference appears in stanza 16 of Rochester's "Upon Nothing" (*Poems,* 1705).

The Spectator, No. 335

Tuesday, March 25.

[A d d i s o n]

Respicere exemplar vitae morumque jubebo
Doctum imitatorem, & veras hinc ducere voces. Hor.[1]

My Friend Sir Roger de Coverly, when we last met together at
the Club, told me, that he had a great Mind to see the new Tragedy[2] with me, assuring me at the same Time, that he had not been
at a Play these twenty Years. The last I saw, says Sir Roger, was
the *Committee,*[3] which I should not have gone to neither, had not
I been told before-hand that it was a good Church of *England*
Comedy. He then proceeded to enquire of me who this Distress'd
Mother was, and upon hearing that she was *Hector*'s Widow, he
told me, that her Husband was a brave Man, and that when he
was a School-Boy he had read his Life at the end of the Dictionary.[4] My Friend asked me, in the next Place, if there would not be
some Danger in coming home late, in case the *Mohocks*[5] should

1 Horace *Ars Poetica* 317–318 (altered): "I would direct the skilled imitator
to study the life and manners of men, and thence to draw living voices."

2 *The Distressed Mother* by Ambrose Philips, was first acted on March 17,
1712 and ran to March 29. Steele wrote the prologue and praised the play, then
in rehearsal, in *Spectator* No. 290. The epilogue was written either by Addison
or Budgell.

3 Sir Robert Howard's drama (1662) satirizing the Commonwealth government. Sir Roger, a staunch Tory, would have approved the play.

4 At this time, biographical descriptions of famous people were given at the
end of the dictionary.

5 Bands of young men who wandered the streets at night, attacking both
men and women. They took their name from a tribe of North-American
Indians.

be abroad. I assure you, says he, I thought I had fallen into their Hands last Night, for I observ'd two or three lusty black[6] Men that followed me half way up *Fleetstreet,* and mended their Pace behind me, in Proportion as I put on to get away from them. You must know, continued the Knight with a Smile, I fancied they had a mind to *hunt* me; for I remember an honest Gentleman in my Neighbourhood, who was serv'd such a Trick in King *Charles* the Second's Time; for which Reason he has not ventured himself in Town ever since. I might have shown them very good Sport, had this been their Design, for as I am an old Fox-hunter, I should have turned and dodged, and have play'd them a thousand Tricks they had never seen in their Lives before. Sir Roger added, that if these Gentlemen had any such Intention, they did not succeed very well in it, for I threw them out, says he, at the End of *Norfolk-street,* where I doubled the Corner,[7] and got Shelter in my Lodgings before they could imagine what was become of me. However, says the Knight, if Captain Sentry will make one with us to Morrow Night, and if you will both of you call upon me about Four a-Clock, that we may be at the House[8] before it is full, I will have my own Coach in Readiness to attend you, for *John* tells me he has got the Fore-Wheels mended.

The Captain, who did not fail to meet me there at the appointed Hour, bid Sir Roger fear nothing, for that he had put on the same Sword which he made use of at the Battel of *Steenkirk*.[9] Sir Roger's Servants, and among the rest my old Friend the Butler, had, I found, provided themselves with good Oaken Plants,[10] to attend their Master upon this Occasion. When we had plac'd him in his Coach, with my self at his Left Hand, the Captain before him, and his Butler at the Head of his Footmen in the Rear, we convoy'd him in Safety to the Play-house; where, after having march'd up the Entry in good Order, the Captain and I went in with him, and seated him betwixt us in the Pit. As soon as the House was full, and the Candles lighted, my old Friend stood up

---

6 Dark complexioned.

7 I.e., he baffled them by getting round the corner, as a fox turns and twists to escape the hounds.

8 The Drury Lane playhouse.

9 A battle fought in 1692 between King William III and the French.

10 Stout oak cudgels.

and looked about him with that Pleasure, which a Mind seasoned with Humanity naturally feels in it self, at the Sight of a Multitude of People who seem pleased with one another, and partake of the same common Entertainment. I could not but fancy to my self, as the old Man stood up in the Middle of the Pit, that he made a very proper Center to a Tragick Audience. Upon the Entring of *Pyrrhus*,[11] the Knight told me, that he did not believe the King of *France* himself had a better Strut. I was indeed very attentive to my old Friend's Remarks, because I looked upon them as a Piece of Natural Criticism, and was well pleased to hear him at the Conclusion of almost every Scene, telling me that he could not imagine how the Play would end. One while he appear'd much concerned for *Andromache;* and a little while after as much for *Hermione;* and was extremely puzzled to think what would become of *Pyrrhus.*

When Sir Roger saw *Andromache*'s obstinate Refusal to her Lover's Importunities, he whispered me in the Ear, that he was sure she would never have him; to which he added, with a more than ordinary Vehemence, You can't imagine, Sir, what 'tis to have to do with a Widow. Upon *Pyrrhus* his[12] threatning afterwards to leave her, the Knight shook his Head, and muttered to himself, Ay, do if you can. This Part dwelt so much upon my Friend's Imagination, that at the Close of the Third Act, as I was thinking of something else, he whispered in my Ear, These Widows, Sir, are the most perverse Creatures in the World. But pray, says he, you that are a Critick, is this Play according to your Dramatick Rules,[13] as you call them? Should your People in Tragedy always talk to be understood? Why, there is not a single Sentence in this Play that I do not know the Meaning of.[14]

11 After the victory over Troy, Pyrrhus, the son of Achilles, was allotted Andromache, widow of Hector, "the distressed mother." Eventually he wed Hermione, daughter of Menelaus and Helen, who had earlier been promised to Orestes. When Orestes came to claim Hermione and found her married, he stirred up the Delphians against Pyrrhus, who was slain in the tumult.

12 I.e., Pyrrhus's.

13 See *Tatler* No. 165, n. 7.

14 Philips' play lacked the bombast common in heroic drama. Praising the work in *Spectator* No. 290, Steele wrote, "I congratulate to the Age, that they are at last to see Truth and humane Life represented in the Incidents which concern Heroes and Heroines."

The Fourth Act very luckily begun before I had Time to give the old Gentleman an Answer; Well, says the Knight, sitting down with great Satisfaction, I suppose we are now to see *Hector*'s Ghost.[15] He then renewed his Attention, and, from Time to Time, fell a praising the Widow. He made, indeed, a little Mistake as to one of her Pages, whom, at his first Entring, he took for *Astyanax*;[16] but he quickly set himself right in that Particular, though, at the same time, he owned he should have been very glad to have seen the little Boy, who, says he, must needs be a very fine Child by the Account that is given of him. Upon *Hermione*'s going off with a Menace to *Pyrrhus*,[17] the Audience gave a loud Clap, to which Sir Roger added, On my Word, a notable young Baggage.

As there was a very remarkable Silence and Stillness in the Audience during the whole Action, it was natural for them to take the Opportunity of these Intervals between the Acts, to express their Opinion of the Players, and of their respective Parts. Sir Roger hearing a Cluster of them praise *Orestes,* struck in with them, and told them, that he thought his Friend *Pylades* was a very sensible Man;[18] As they were afterwards applauding *Pyrrhus*, Sir Roger put in a second time, And let me tell you, says he, though he speaks but little, I like the old Fellow in Whiskers as well as any of them.[19] Captain Sentry, seeing two or three Waggs who sat near us, lean with an attentive Ear towards Sir Roger, and fearing lest they should smoak the Knight,[20] pluck'd him by the Elbow, and whispered something in his Ear, that lasted till the Opening of the Fifth Act. The Knight was wonderfully attentive to the Account which *Orestes* gives of *Pyrrhus* his Death, and at the Conclusion of it, told me it was such a bloody Piece of Work, that he was glad it was not done upon the Stage. Seeing afterwards *Orestes* in his raving Fit, he grew more than ordinarily serious, and took Occasion to moralize (in his Way) upon an evil Conscience, add-

[15] For the basis of this speculation, see *Spectator* No. 44.

[16] The son of Hector and Andromache, killed during the siege of Troy.

[17] I.e., as she leaves the stage threatening Pyrrhus.

[18] Orestes was the son of Agamemnon and Clytemnestra; Pylades was his friend.

[19] Phoenix, counsellor to Pyrrhus.

[20] Ridicule Sir Roger.

ing, that *Orestes, in his Madness, looked as if he saw something.*[21]

As we were the first that came into the House, so we were the last that went out of it; being resolved to have a clear Passage for our old Friend, whom we did not care to venture among the Justling of the Crowd. Sir Roger went out fully satisfy'd with his Entertainment, and we guarded him to his Lodgings in the same manner that we brought him to the Playhouse; being highly pleased, for my own Part, not only with the Performance of the excellent Piece which had been presented, but with the Satisfaction which it had given to the good old Man.   L

[21] Probably, a ghost.

The Spectator, No. 357

Saturday, April 19.

[A d d i s o n]

⁓⟋⟍⁓

————*quis talia fando*
Temperet à lacrymis?————Virg.[1]

The Tenth Book of *Paradise Lost* has a greater Variety of Persons in it than any other in the whole Poem.[2] The Author upon the winding up of his Action introduces all those who had any Concern in it, and shews with great Beauty the Influence which it had upon each of them. It is like the last Act of a well written Tragedy, in which all who had a Part in it are generally drawn up before the Audience, and represented under those Circumstances in which the Determination of the Action places them.

I shall therefore consider this Book under four Heads, in relation to the Celestial, the Infernal, the Human, and the Imaginary Persons, who have their respective Parts allotted in it.

To begin with the Celestial Persons: The Guardian Angels of *Paradise* are described as returning to Heaven upon the Fall of Man, in order to approve[3] their Vigilance; their Arrival, their Manner of Reception, with the Sorrow which appeared in them-

1 Virgil *Aeneid* 2. 6. 8.: "Who can forbear to weep at such a tale?"

2 After six essays of general criticism, Addison gave one paper to each of the twelve books of *Paradise Lost.* Book 10 shows the consequences of the Fall in Heaven and in Hell: the guardian angels report the news in Heaven; the Messiah flies to earth to pass judgment on the sinners; Satan returns to Hell triumphantly, only to find that he and the other devils have turned into serpents; Sin and Death advance on the world; God's angels make astronomical changes to afflict earth; Adam and Eve suffer, propose suicide, then try to retain a hopeful disposition.

3 Vindicate.

selves, and in those Spirits who are said to Rejoice at the Conversion of a Sinner, are very finely laid together in the following
Lines.

> *Up into Heav'n from Paradise in haste*
> *Th' angelick guards ascended, mute and sad*
> *For Man, for of his state by this[4] they knew,*
> *Much wond'ring how the subtle Fiend had stoln*
> *Entrance unseen. Soon as th' unwelcome news*
> *From Earth arriv'd at Heaven Gate displeas'd*
> *All were who heard, dim sadness did not spare*
> *That time Celestial visages, yet mixt*
> *With pity, violated not their Bliss.*
> *About the new-arriv'd, in multitudes*
> *Th' Aethereal People ran, to hear and know*
> *How all befell: They tow'rds the Throne supreame*
> *Accountable made haste to make appear*
> *With righteous plea, their utmost vigilance,*
> *And easily approv'd; when the most High*
> *Eternal Father from his secret Cloud*
> *Amidst in thunder utter'd thus his Voice.[5]*

The same Divine Person,[6] who in the foregoing Parts of this
Poem interceded for our first Parents before their Fall, overthrew
the Rebel Angels, and created the World, is now represented as
descending to *Paradise,* and pronouncing Sentence upon the three
Offenders.[7] The cool of the Evening, being a Circumstance with
which Holy Writ introduces this great Scene, it is Poetically described by our Author, who has also kept religiously to the Form
of Words, in which the three several Sentences were passed upon
Adam, Eve, and the Serpent. He has rather chosen to neglect the
Numerousness of his Verse than to deviate from those Speeches
which are recorded on this great Occasion.[8] The Guilt and Confusion of our first Parents standing naked before their Judge, is

[4] I.e., by this time.
[5] *Paradise Lost* 10. 17–33.
[6] Jesus Christ.
[7] Book 10. 85–102.
[8] I.e., he has altered the versification in order to retain the Biblical language describing the scene.

touched with great Beauty. Upon the Arrival of *Sin* and *Death* into the Works of the Creation, the Almighty is again introduced as speaking to his Angels that surrounded him.

> *See with what heat these Dogs of Hell advance*
> *To waste and havock yonder World, which I*
> *So fair and good Created,* &c.[9]

The following Passage is formed upon that glorious Image in Holy Writ, which compares the Voice of an innumerable Host of Angels, uttering Hallelujahs, to the Voice of mighty Thunderings, or of many Waters.

> *He ended, and the Heav'nly Audience loud*
> *Sung Hallelujah, as the sound of Seas,*
> *Through multitude that sung: Just are thy ways,*
> *Righteous are thy Decrees in all thy Works,*
> *Who can extenuate thee———*[10]

Though the Author in the whole Course of his Poem, and particularly in the Book we are now examining, has infinite Allusions to Places of Scripture, I have only taken Notice in my Remarks of such as are of a Poetical Nature, and which are woven with great Beauty into the Body of this Fable. Of this kind is that Passage in the present Book, where describing *Sin* and *Death* as marching through the Works of Nature, he adds,

> *———Behind her Death*
> *Close following pace for pace, not mounted yet*
> *On his pale Horse:———*[11]

Which alludes to that Passage in Scripture so wonderfully Poetical, and terrifying to the Imagination. *And I looked, and behold a pale Horse, and his Name that sat on him was* Death, *and* Hell *followed with him: and Power was given unto them over the fourth Part of the Earth, to kill with sword, and with Hunger, and with Sickness, and with the Beasts of the Earth.* Under this first Head of Celestial Persons we must likewise take Notice of the

---

[9] Book 10. 616–618.
[10] Book 10. 641–645. The passage echoes Revelations 19:6.
[11] Book 10. 588–590. The allusion is to Revelations 6:8.

Command which the Angels received, to produce the several Changes in Nature, and sully the Beauty of the Creation.[12] Accordingly they are represented as infecting the Stars and Planets with malignant Influences, weakning the Light of the Sun, bringing down the Winter into the milder Regions of Nature, planting Winds and Storms in several Quarters of the Sky, storing the Clouds with Thunder, and in short, perverting the whole Frame of the Universe to the Condition of its Criminal Inhabitants. As this is a noble Incident in the Poem, the Following Lines, in which we see the Angels heaving up the Earth, and placing it in a different Posture to the Sun from what it had before the Fall of Man, is conceived with that sublime Imagination which was so peculiar to this great Author.

> *Some say he bid his Angels turn ascance*
> *The Poles of earth twice ten degrees and more*
> *From the Sun's Axle; they with labour push'd*
> *Oblique the Centrick Globe.*————[13]

We are in the second Place, to consider the Infernal Agents under the View which *Milton* has given us of them in this Book. It is observed by those who would set forth the Greatness of *Virgil's* Plan, that he conducts his Reader thro' all the Parts of the Earth which were discovered in his Time. *Asia, Africk,* and *Europe* are the several Scenes of his Fable. The Plan of *Milton's* Poem is of an infinitely greater Extent, and fills the Mind with many more astonishing Circumstances. *Satan,* having surrounded the Earth seven times, departs at length from *Paradise.* We then see him steering his Course among the Constellations, and after having traversed the whole Creation, pursuing his Voyage thro' the *Chaos,* and entering into his own Infernal Dominions.[14]

His first Appearance in the Assembly of Fallen Angels, is work'd up with Circumstances which give a delightful Surprize to the Reader; but there is no Incident in the whole Poem which does this more than the Transformation of the whole Audience, that follows the Account their Leader gives them of his Expe-

12 Book 10. 649–667.
13 Book 10. 668–671.
14 Book 10. 325–349, 414–420.

dition. The gradual Change of *Satan* himself[15] is described after *Ovid*'s Manner, and may vie with any of those celebrated Transformations which are looked upon as the most Beautiful Parts in that Poet's Works. *Milton* never fails of improving his own Hints, and bestowing the last finishing Touches to every Incident which is admitted into his Poem. The unexpected Hiss which rises in this Episode, the Dimensions and Bulk of *Satan* so much superior to those of the Infernal Spirits who lay under the same Transformation, with the annual Change[16] which they are supposed to suffer, are Instances of this Kind. The Beauty of the Diction is very remarkable in this whole Episode, as I have observed in the Sixth Paper of these my Remarks[17] the great Judgment with which it was contrived.

The Parts of *Adam* and *Eve,* or the Humane Persons, come next under our Consideration. *Milton*'s Art is no where more shewn than in his conducting[18] the Parts of these our first Parents. The Representation he gives of them, without falsifying the Story, is wonderfully contrived to influence the Reader with Pity and Compassion towards them. Though *Adam* involves the whole Species in Misery, his Crime proceeds from a Weakness which every Man is inclined to pardon and commiserate, as it seems rather the Frailty of Humane Nature, than of the Person who offended. Every one is apt to excuse a Fault which he himself might have fallen into. It was the Excess of Love for *Eve* that ruin'd *Adam* and his Posterity. I need not add, that the Author is Justify'd in this Particular by many of the Fathers, and the most Orthodox Writers.[19] *Milton* has by this means filled a great part of his Poem with that kind of Writing which the *French* Criticks call the *Tender,* and which is in a particular manner engageing to all sorts of Readers.

Adam and *Eve,* in the Book we are now considering, are like-

[15] The transformation occurs in book 10. 504–515: Satan falls "A monstrous Serpent on his Belly prone, / Reluctant, but in vain."

[16] Book 10. 572–577. The infernal spirits must assume the serpent shape for a number of days each year.

[17] See *Spectator* No. 285, actually the fourth paper in the series.

[18] Treating, describing.

[19] St. Augustine quotes St. Paul to this effect: *City of God* 12.11.

wise drawn with such Sentiments as do not only interest the
Reader in their Afflictions, but raise in him the most melting
Passions of Humanity and Commiseration. When *Adam* sees the
several Changes in Nature produced about him, he appears in a
Disorder of Mind suitable to one who had forfeited both his In-
nocence and his Happiness: he is filled with Horror, Remorse,
Despair; in the Anguish of his Heart he expostulates with his Cre-
ator for having given him an unasked Existence.

> *Did I request thee, Maker, from my Clay*
> *To mould me Man, did I solicit thee*
> *From darkness to promote me, or here place*
> *In this delicious Garden? as my will*
> *Concurr'd not to my being, 'twere but right*
> *And equal to reduce me to my dust,*
> *Desirous to resign, and render back*
> *All I receiv'd———*[20]

He immediately after recovers from his Presumption, owns his
Doom[21] to be just, and begs that the Death which is threatned him
may be inflicted on him.

> *———Why delays*
> *His Hand to execute what his decree*
> *Fix'd on this day? Why do I overlive,*
> *Why am I mock'd with Death, and lengthen'd out*
> *To Deathless pain? how gladly would I meet*
> *Mortality my Sentence, and be Earth*
> *Insensible, how glad would lay me down*
> *As in my Mother's lap? there should I rest*
> *And sleep secure; his dreadful Voice no more*
> *Would thunder in my ears, no fear of worse*
> *To me and to my Off-spring, would torment me*
> *With cruel expectation.———*[22]

This whole Speech is full of the like Emotion, and varied with
all those Sentiments which we may suppose natural to a Mind so
broken and disturb'd. I must not omit that generous Concern

[20] Book 10. 743–750.
[21] Sentence.
[22] Book 10. 771–782.

which our first Father shews in it for his Posterity, and which is
so proper to affect the Reader.

> ———*Hide me from the Face*
> *Of God, whom to behold was then my height*
> *Of Happiness: yet well if here would end*
> *The Misery, I deserv'd it, and would bear*
> *My own deservings; but this will not serve;*
> *All that I eat, or drink, or shall beget,*
> *Is propagated Curse. O voice once heard*
> *Delightfully,* encrease *and* multiply,
> *Now Death to hear!*———[23]
> ———*In me all*
> *Posterity stands curst: Fair Patrimony*
> *That I must leave you, Sons: O were I able*
> *To waste it all my self, and leave you none!*
> *So disinherited how would you bless*
> *Me now your curse! Ah, why should all Mankind*
> *For one Man's fault thus guiltless be condemned*
> *If guiltless? But from me what can proceed*
> *But all corrupt*———[24]

Who can afterwards behold the Father of Mankind extended
upon the Earth, uttering his Midnight Complaints, bewailing his
Existence, and wishing for Death, without sympathizing with him
in his Distress?

> *Thus* Adam *to himself lamented loud*
> *Through the still night, not now, as e'er Man fell*
> *Wholesome and cool and mild, but with black Air*
> *Accompanied, with damps and dreadful gloom*
> *Which to his evil Conscience represented*
> *All things with double terrour: on the Ground*
> *Outstretch'd he lay, on the cold Ground, and oft*
> *Curs'd his Creation, Death as oft accus'd*
> *Of tardy execution.*———[25]

The Part of *Eve* in this Book is no less passionate, and apt to
sway the Reader in her Favour. She is represented with great Ten-

[23] Book 10. 723–731.
[24] Book 10. 817–825.
[25] Book 10. 845–853.

derness as approaching *Adam,* but is spurn'd from him with a
Spirit of Upbraiding and Indignation conformable to the Nature
of Man, whose Passions had now gained the Dominion over him.
The following Passage wherein she is described as renewing her
Addresses to him, with the whole Speech that follows it, have
something in them exquisitely moving and pathetick.

> *He added not, and from her turn'd: but* Eve
> *Not so repulst, with Tears that ceas'd not flowing,*
> *And Tresses all disorder'd, at his Feet*
> *Fell humble, and embracing them besought*
> *His peace, and thus proceeding in her plaint.*
>   *Forsake me not thus* Adam, *witness Heav'n*
> *What love sincere and reverence in my heart*
> *I bear thee, and unweeting have offended,*
> *Unhappily deceiv'd; thy Suppliant*
> *I beg, and clasp thy knees; bereave me not,*
> *Whereon I live, thy gentle looks, thy aid,*
> *Thy Cousel in this uttermost distress,*
> *My only strength and stay: Forlorn of thee*
> *Whither shall I betake me, where subsist?*
> *While yet we live, scarce one short hour perhaps,*
> *Between us two let there be peace,* &c.[26]

Adam's Reconcilement to her is work'd up in the same Spirit
of Tenderness. *Eve* afterwards proposes to her Husband, in the
Blindness of her Despair, that to prevent their Guilt from descending upon Posterity they should resolve to live Childless; or,
if that could not be done, they should seek their own Deaths by
violent Methods. As those Sentiments naturally engage the Reader
to regard the Mother of Mankind with more than ordinary Commiseration, they likewise contain a very fine Moral. The Resolution of dying to end our Miseries, does not shew such a degree of
Magnanimity as a Resolution to bear them, and submit to the
Dispensations of Providence. Our Author has therefore, with
great Delicacy, represented *Eve* as entertaining this Thought, and
Adam as disapproving it.

    We are, in the last Place, to consider the Imaginary Persons, or

[26] Book 10. 909–924.

Death and *Sin,* who act a large Part in this Book. Such beautiful extended Allegories are certainly some of the finest Compositions of Genius; but, as I have before observed, are not agreeable to the Nature of an Heroic Poem.[27] This of *Sin* and *Death* is very exquisite in its Kind, if not considered as a Part of such a Work. The Truths contained in it are so clear and open, that I shall not lose Time in explaining them; but shall only observe, that a Reader who knows the Strength of the *English* Tongue, will be amazed to think how the Poet could find such apt Words and Phrases to describe the Actions of those two imaginary Persons, and particularly in that Part where *Death* is exhibited as forming a Bridge over the *Chaos;*[28] a Work suitable to the Genius of *Milton.*

Since the Subject I am upon gives me an Opportunity of speaking more at large of such Shadowy and Imaginary Persons as may be introduced into Heroic Poems, I shall beg Leave to explain my self in a Matter which is curious in its Kind, and which none of the Criticks have treated of. It is certain *Homer* and *Virgil* are full of imaginary Persons, who are very beautiful in Poetry when they are just shewn without being engaged in any Series of Action. *Homer* indeed represents *Sleep* as a Person, and ascribes a short Part to him in his *Iliad;*[29] but we must consider that tho' we now regard such a Person as entirely shadowy and unsubstantial, the Heathens made Statues of him, placed him in their Temples, and looked upon him as a real Deity. When *Homer* makes use of other such Allegorical Persons, it is only in short Expressions, which convey an ordinary Thought to the Mind in the most pleasing Manner, and may rather be looked upon as Poetical Phrases than Allegorical Descriptions. Instead of telling us that Men naturally fly when they are terrified, he introduces the Persons of *Flight* and *Fear,* who, he tells us, are inseparable Companions. Instead of saying that the Time was come when *Apollo* ought to have received his Recompence, he tells us that the *Hours* brought him his Reward. Instead of describing the Effects which *Minerva*'s *Aegis* produced in Battel, he tells us that the Brims of it were en-

[27] Addison had made this criticism in *Spectators* No. 273, 297, 309, and 315.
[28] Book 10. 282–324.
[29] Homer *Iliad* 14. 231–291.

compassed by *Terrour, Rout, Discord, Fury, Pursuit, Massacre,* and *Death.* In the same Figure of speaking, he represents *Victory* as following *Diomedes; Discord* as the Mother of Funerals and Mourning; *Venus* as dressed by the *Graces; Bellona* as wearing Terrour and Consternation like a Garment.[30] I might give several other Instances out of *Homer,* as well as a great many out of *Virgil. Milton* has likewise very often made use of the same way of Speaking, as where he tells us, that *Victory* sat on the Right Hand of the Messiah when he marched forth against the Rebel Angels; that at the rising of the Sun the *Hours* unbarr'd the Gates of Light; that *Discord* was the Daughter of *Sin.* Of the same Nature are those Expressions, where describing the Singing of the Nightingale, he adds, *Silence was pleased;* and upon the Messiah's bidding Peace to the *Chaos, Confusion heard his Voice.*[31] I might add innumerable Instances of our Poet's writing in this beautiful Figure. It is plain that these I have mentioned, in which Persons of an imaginary Nature are introduced, are such short Allegories as are not designed to be taken in the literal Sense, but only to convey particular Circumstances to the Reader after an unusual and entertaining Manner. But when such Persons are introduced as principal Actors, and engaged in a Series of Adventures, they take too much upon them, and are by no means proper for an Heroic Poem, which ought to appear credible in its principal Parts. I cannot forbear therefore thinking that *Sin* and *Death* are as improper Agents in a Work of this Nature, as *Strength* and *Necessity* in one of the Tragedies of *Eschylus,* who represented those two Persons nailing down *Prometheus* to a Rock, for which he has been justly censured by the greatest Criticks.[32] I do not know any imaginary Person made use of in a more sublime manner of Thinking than that in one of the Prophets, who describing God as descending from Heaven, and visiting the Sins of Mankind, adds that dreadful Circumstance, *Before him went the Pes-*

[30] The preceding references are to *Iliad* 9. 1–3; 21. 450; 5. 738–742; 5. 835–841 (presumably); 4. 440; and 5. 338.

[31] The references appear in *Paradise Lost* 6. 762; 6. 4; 10. 707–708; 4. 604; and 3. 710.

[32] The allegorical figures appear in *Prometheus Bound* and are criticized by Aristotle in *Poetics* 14.

tilence.[33] It is certain this imaginary Person might have been described in all her purple Spots. The *Fever* might have marched before her, *Pain* might have stood at her Right Hand, *Phrenzy* on her Left, and *Death* in her Rear. She might have been introduced as gliding down from the Tail of a Comet, or darted upon the Earth in a Flash of Lightning: She might have tainted the Atmosphere with her Breath; the very Glaring of her Eyes might have scattered Infection.[34] But I believe every Reader will think, that in such sublime Writings the mentioning of her as it is done in Scripture, has something in it more just, as well as great, than all that the most fanciful Poet could have bestowed upon her in the Richness of his Imagination.   L

[33] Habakkuk 3:5.

[34] This example resembles the criticism of Cowley's "mixt wit," in *Spectator* No. 62.

The Spectator, No. 370

Monday, May 5.

[S t e e l e]

Totus mundus agit Histrionem.[1]

Many of my fair Readers, as well as very gay and well-received Persons of the other Sex, are extreamly perplexed at the *Latin* Sentences at the Head of my Speculations;[2] I do not know whether I ought not to indulge them with Translations of each of them: However, I have to Day taken down from the Top of the Stage in *Drury-Lane* a Bit of *Latin* which often stands in their View, and signifies that *the whole World acts the Player.* It is certain that if we look all round us, and behold the different Employments of Mankind, you hardly see one who is not, as the Player is, in an assumed Character. The Lawyer, who is vehement and loud in a Cause wherein he knows he has not the Truth of the Question on his Side, is a Player as to the personated Part,[3] but incomparably meaner than he as to the Prostitution of himself for Hire; because the Pleader's Falshood introduces Injustice, the Player feigns for no other End but to divert or instruct you. The Divine, whose Passions transport him to say any thing with any View but promoting the Interests of true Piety and Religion,[4] is a Player with a still greater Imputation of Guilt in Proportion to his depreciating a Character more sacred. Consider all the dif-

---

1 "The whole world acts the player."

2 See *Spectator* No. 221.

3 I.e., in his legal performance.

4 Presumably, this is a reference to Anglican clergymen, like the famous Henry Sacheverell (See *Spectator* No. 37, n. 12), who used the pulpit to express their political views.

ferent Pursuits and Employments of Men, and you will find half
their Actions tend to nothing else but Disguise and Imposture;
and all that is done which proceeds not from a Man's very self is
the Action of a Player. For this Reason it is that I make so frequent Mention of the Stage: It is, with me, a Matter of the highest Consideration what Parts are well or ill performed, what Passions or Sentiments are indulged or cultivated, and consequently
what Manners and Customs are transfused from the Stage to the
World, which reciprocally imitate each other. As the Writers of
Epick Poems introduce shadowy Persons and represent Vices and
Virtues under the Characters of Men and Women;[5] so I, who am
a Spectator in the World, may perhaps sometimes make use of the
Names of the Actors on the Stage, to represent or admonish those
who transact Affairs in the World. When I am commending
Wilks[6] for representing the Tenderness of a Husband and a Father in *Mackbeth,* the Contrition of a reformed Prodigal in *Harry
the Fourth,* the winning Emptiness of a young Man of Good-nature and Wealth in *the Trip to the Jubilee,* the Officiousness of
an artful Servant in *the Fox:* When I thus celebrate *Wilks,* I talk
to all the World who are engaged in any of those Circumstances.
If I were to speak of Merit neglected, misapplied, or misunder-
stood, might not I say *Eastcourt*[7] has a great Capacity? but it is
not the Interest of others who bear a Figure on the Stage that his
Talents were understood; it is their Business to impose upon him
what cannot become him, or keep out of his Hands any thing in
which he would shine. Were one to raise a Suspicion of himself[8]
in a Man who passes upon the World for a fine Thing, in order
to alarm him, one might say, if Lord *Foppington* were not on the
Stage, (*Cibber* acts the false Pretentions to a genteel Behaviour

---

5 See Addison's discussion of this technique, in *Spectator* No. 357.

6 Robert Wilks (1670–1732), celebrated actor and theater manager, had during the preceding two months played Macduff in *Macbeth,* Prince Hal in
Henry IV, and Mosca in *Volpone, or The Fox.* On the following evening, May
6, he played Sir Harry Wild-Air in Farquhar's *The Constant Couple, or a Trip
to the Jubilee* (1699).

7 Richard Estcourt (See *Spectator* No. 266, n. 3) was a celebrated mimic and
comic actor who, Steele argues, was capable of better roles and deserved a
grander reputation. Steele writes his obituary in *Spectator* No. 468.

8 Reveal a true picture of himself.

width:951px; height:1491px;

so very justly)[9] he would have in the generality of Mankind more
that would admire than deride him. When we come to characters
directly comical, it is not to be imagined what Effect a well regulated Stage would have upon Men's Manners. The Craft of an
Usurer, the Absurdity of a rich Fool, the awkard Roughness of a
Fellow of half Courage, the ungraceful Mirth of a Creature of
half Wit, might be for ever put out of Countenance by proper
parts for *Dogget*.[10] *Johnson*, by acting *Corbacchio* the other Night,
must have given all who saw him a through Detestation of aged
Avarice.[11] The petulancy of a pevish old Fellow, who loves and
hates he knows not why, is very excellently performed by the Ingenious Mr. *William Penkethman* in the *Fop's Fortune;* where,
in the Character of *Don Cholerick Snap Shorto de Testy,* he answers no Questions but to those whom he likes, and wants no Account of any thing from those he approves. Mr. *Penkethman* is
also Master of as many Faces in the Dumb-Scene, as can be expected from a Man in the Circumstances of being ready to perish
out of Fear and Hunger: He wonders throughout the whole Scene
very masterly, without neglecting his Victuals. If it be, as I have
heard it sometimes mentioned, a great Qualification for the World
to follow Business and Pleasure too, what is it in the Ingenious
Mr. *Penkethman* to represent a Sense of Pleasure and Pain at the
same time; as you may see him do this Evening?[12]

As it is certain that a Stage ought to be wholly suppressed, or
judiciously encouraged, while there is one in the Nation, Men
turned for regular Pleasure[13] cannot employ their Thoughts more
usefully for the Diversion of Mankind, than by convincing them
that it is in themselves to raise this Entertainment to the greatest
Height. It would be a great Improvement, as well as Embellish-

[9] Colly Cibber (1671–1757) played Lord Foppington in his own play *The
Careless Husband* (1704).

[10] See *Spectator* No. 235, n. 11.

[11] Benjamin Johnson (1665?–1742) had played old Corbaccio in *Volpone* a
week earlier at Drury Lane.

[12] William Penkethman played the role of Don Cholerick Snap Shorto de
Testy in Cibber's *Love Makes a Man; or, The Fop's Fortune* (1700) and was
repeating the performance on the evening of this essay. See *Tatler* No. 89, n.
18.

[13] I.e., those not given to dissolute or irregular courses.

ment to the Theatre, if Dancing were more regarded, and taught
to all the Actors. One who has the Advantage of such an agreeable
girlish Person as Mrs. *Bicknell*,[14] joyned with her Capacity of Imitation, could in proper Gesture and Motion represent all the decent Characters of Female Life. An amiable Modesty in one Aspect of a Dancer, an assumed Confidence in another, a sudden Joy
in another, a falling off with an Impatience of being beheld, a
Return towards the Audience with an unsteady Resolution to
approach them, and a well-acted Solicitude to please, would revive in the Company all the fine Touches of Mind raised in observing all the Objects of Affection or Passion they had before
beheld. Such elegant Entertainments as these, would polish the
Town into Judgment in their Gratifications; and Delicacy in
Pleasure is the first Step People of Condition take in Reformation
from Vice. Mrs. *Bicknell* has the only Capacity for this sort of
Dancing of any on the Stage; and I dare say all who see her Performance to Morrow Night, when sure the Romp[15] will do her
best for her own Benefit, will be of my Mind.[16]   T

[14] Mrs. Bicknell (1695?–1723) is mentioned by Steele in *Tatler* No. 11 and
in *Guardian* No. 50. She was to appear with Wilks in *The Constant Couple*
the following evening.

[15] The boisterous young lady.

[16] This essay is a companion to *Tatler* No. 182, in which Steele praised the
theater, not as a moral guide, but as a source of refined pleasure.

The Spectator, No. 394

Monday, June 2.

[Steele]

Bene colligitur haec Pueris & Mulierculis & Servis & Servorum simillimis Liberis esse grata. Gravi vero homini & ea quae siunt Judicio certo ponderanti probari posse nullo modo. Tull.[1]

I have been considering the little and frivolous things which give Men Accesses to one another, and Power with each other, not only in the common and indifferent Accidents of Life, but also in Matters of greater Importance. You see in Elections for Members to sit in Parliament, how far saluting[2] Rows of old Women, drinking with Clowns, and being upon a Level with the lowest Part of Mankind in that wherein they themselves are lowest, their Diversions, will carry a Candidate. A Capacity for prostituting a Man's self in his Behaviour, and descending to the present Humour of the Vulgar, is perhaps as good an Ingredient as any other for making a considerable Figure[3] in the World; and if a Man has nothing else, or better, to think of, he could not make his way to Wealth and Distinction by properer Methods, than studying the particular Bent or Inclination of People with whom he converses, and working from the Observation of such their Biass in all Matters wherein he has any Intercourse with them:[4] For his Ease and

[1] Cicero *De Officiis* 2. 16. 57 (altered): "It is well concluded that these things are pleasing to children, young women, slaves, and to such freeborn men as most resemble slaves; but the serious man who weighs such matters with thought and judgment cannot in any way approve of them."

[2] Greeting, either with a kiss or a bow.

[3] Reputation.

[4] I.e., condescending to them, taking advantage of their "Bent or Inclination."

Comfort he may assure himself, he need not be at the Expence of any great Talent or Virtue to please even those who are possessed of the highest Qualifications. Pride in some particular Disguise or other, (often a secret to the Proud Man himself) is the most ordinary Spring of Action among Men. You need no more than to discover what a Man values himself for; then of all things admire that Quality, but be sure to be failing in it your self in Comparison of the Man whom you court. I have heard, or read, of a Secretary of State in *Spain*,[5] who served a Prince who was happy in an elegant use of the *Latin* Tongue, and often writ Dispatches in it with his own Hand. The King shewed his Secretary a Letter he had written to a foreign Prince, and under the Colour of asking his Advice, laid a Trap for his Applause. The honest Man read it as a faithful Counsellor, and not only excepted against his tying himself down too much by some Expressions, but mended the Phrase in others. You may guess the Dispatches[6] that Evening did not take much longer Time. Mr. Secretary, as soon as he came to his own House, sent for his eldest Son, and communicated to him that the Family must retire out of *Spain* assoon as possible; for, said he, the King knows I understand *Latin* better than he does.

This egregious Fault in a Man of the World, should be a Lesson to all who would make their Fortunes: But a Regard must be carefully had to the Person with whom you have to do; for it is not to be doubted but a great Man of common Sense must look with secret Indignation, or bridled Laughter, on all the Slaves who stand round him with ready Faces to approve and smile at all he says in the Gross.[7] It is good Comedy enough to observe a Superior talking half Sentences, and playing an humble Admirer's Countenance from one thing to another, with such Perplexity

[5] The reference is probably to a story in *The Art of Prudence: or, a Companion to a Man of Sense* (a translation of Gracián's *Discreto*, 1646) which was published in 1702. There, however, the Spanish Lord is discredited for defeating the King at chess.

[6] "Dispatches" is probably a pun, referring to the outgoing messages and to the departure of the Secretary and his family.

[7] As a whole.

that he knows not what to sneer in Approbation of. But this kind of Complaisance is peculiarly the Manner of Courts; in all other Places you must constantly go farther in Compliance with the Persons you have to do with, than a meer Conformity of Looks and Gestures. If you are in a Country-Life, and would be a leading Man, a good Stomach, a loud Voice, and a rustick Chearfuless will go a great way, provided you are able to drink, and drink any thing. But I was just now going to draw the Manner of Behaviour I would advise People to practise under some Maxim, and intimated, that every one almost was governed by his Pride. There was an old Fellow about forty Years ago so peevish and fretful, tho' a Man of Business, that no one could come at him:[8] But he frequented a particular little Coffee-house, where he triumphed over every Body at Trick-track and Baggammon.[9] The way to pass his Office well, was first to be insulted by him at one of those Games in his leisure Hours; for his Vanity was to shew, that he was a Man of Pleasure as well as Business. Next to this sort of Insinuation, which is called in all Places (from its taking its Birth in the Housholds of Princes) making one's Court, the most prevailing way is, by what better bred People call a Present, the Vulgar a Bribe. I humbly conceive that such a thing is conveyed with more Gallantry in a *Billet-doux* that should be understood at the *Bank,* than in gross Money:[10] But as to stubborn People, who are so surly as to accept of Neither Note or Cash, having formerly dabbled in Chymistry,[11] I can only say that one Part of Matter asks one thing, and another another, to make it fluent; but there is nothing but may be dissolved by a proper Mean: Thus the Virtue[12] which is too obdurate for Gold or Paper, shall melt away very kindly in a Liquid. The Island of *Barbadoes* (a shrewd

---

8 I.e., do business with him.

9 Trick-track (or tick-tack) was a variety of backgammon.

10 A *billet-doux* is a love letter; but here it refers to an element of refined bribery, i.e., with a note of credit rather than with cash.

11 Though the Spectator made no previous mention of such interest, it is known that Richard Steele dabbled in alchemy.

12 Another pun: *Virtue* means either moral excellence or the quality or power of a physical element.

People) manage all their Appeals to *Great Britain* by a skilful Distribution of Citron-Water[13] among the Whisperers about Men in Power. Generous Wines do every Day prevail, and that in great Points where ten thousand times their Value would have been rejected with Indignation.

But to wave[14] the Enumeration of the sundry ways of applying by Presents, Bribes, Management of Peoples Passions and Affections, in such a Manner as it shall appear that the Virtue of the best Man is by one Method or other corruptible; let us look out for some Expedient to turn those Passions and Affections on the Side of Truth and Honour. When a Man has laid it down for a Position, that parting with his Integrity, in the minutest Circumstance, is losing so much of his very Self, Self-Love will become a Virtue. By this means Good and Evil will be the only Objects of Dislike and Approbation; and he that injures any Man, has effectually wounded the Man of this Turn as much as if the Harm had been to himself. This seems to be the only Expedient to arrive at an Impartiality; and a Man who follows the Dictates of Truth and right Reason, may by Artifice be led into Error, but never can into Guilt.   T

13 Brandy.
14 Waive.

The Spectator, No. 407

Tuesday, June 17.

[Addison]

——*abest facundis Gratia dictis.* Ov.[1]

Most Foreign Writers who have given any Character of the *English* Nation, whatever Vices they ascribe to it, allow in general, that the People are naturally Modest. It proceeds perhaps from this our National Virtue, that our Orators are observed to make use of less Gesture or Action than those of other Countries. Our Preachers stand stock-still in the Pulpit, and will not so much as move a Finger to set off the best Sermons in the World.[2] We meet with the same speaking Statues at our Bars, and in all publick Places of Debate. Our Words flow from us in a smooth continued Stream, without those Strainings of the Voice, Motions of the Body, and Majesty of the Hand, which are so much celebrated in the Orators of *Greece* and *Rome*. We can talk of Life and Death in cold Blood, and keep our Temper in a Discourse which turns upon every thing that is dear to us. Though our Zeal breaks out in the finest Tropes and Figures,[3] it is not able to stir a Limb about us. I have heard it observed more than once by those who have seen *Italy*, that an untravelled *Englishman* cannot relish all the Beauties of *Italian* Pictures, because the Postures which are expressed in them are often such as are peculiar to that Country.

1 Ovid *Metamorphoses* 13. 127: "Grace is absent from his fluent speech."

2 *Tatlers* No. 66 and 70 by Steele criticized English religious oratory. In *Spectator* No. 106 by Addison the Spectator watched Sir Roger's Clergyman read from his series of famous sermons and was "charmed with the Gracefulness of his Figure and Delivery."

3 Figures of speech.

One who has not seen an *Italian* in the Pulpit, will not know what to make of that noble Gesture in *Raphael*'s Picture of St. *Paul* preaching at *Athens*,[4] where the Apostle is represented as lifting up both his Arms, and pouring out the Thunder of his Rhetorick amidst an Audience of Pagan Philosophers.

It is certain, that proper Gestures and vehement Exertions of the Voice cannot be too much studied by a publick Orator. They are a kind of Comment to what he utters, and enforce every thing he says, with weak Hearers, better than the strongest Argument he can make use of. They keep the Audience awake, and fix their Attention to what is delivered to them, at the same time that they shew the Speaker is in earnest, and affected himself with what he so passionately recommends to others. Violent Gesture and Vociferation naturally shake the Hearts of the Ignorant, and fill them with a kind of Religious Horror. Nothing is more frequent than to see Women weep and tremble at the Sight of a moving Preacher, though he is placed quite out of their Hearing; as in *England* we very frequently see People lulled Asleep with solid and elaborate Discourses of Piety, who would be warmed and transported out of themselves by the Bellowings and Distortions of Enthusiasm.[5]

If Nonsense, when accompanied with such an Emotion of Voice and Body, has such an Influence on Mens Minds, what might we not expect from many of those admirable Discourses which are printed in our Tongue, were they delivered with a becoming Fervour, and with the most agreeable Graces of Voice and Gesture?

We are told, that the great *Latin* Orator very much impaired his Health by this *laterum contentio,* this Vehemence of Action, with which he used to deliver himself. The *Greek* Orator[6] was likewise so very Famous for this Particular in Rhetorick, that one of his Antagonists, whom he had banished from *Athens,* reading over the Oration which had procured his Banishment, and seeing

---

4 This was one of the seven tapestry cartoons by Raphael, then set up in a special gallery in Hampton Court.

5 The term usually refers to the emotional religious fervor of the dissenters.

6 The Latin orator is Cicero; the Greek, Demosthenes (385?–322 B.C.). The "one of his Antagonists" referred to is Aeschines (389–314 B.C.).

his Friends admire it, could not forbear asking them, if they were so much affected by the bare reading of it, how much more they would have been alarmed, had they heard him actually throwing out such a Storm of Eloquence?

How cold and dead a Figure, in Comparison of these two Great Men, does an Orator often make at the *British* Bar, holding up his Head with the most insipid Serenity, and stroaking the sides of a long Wigg that reaches down to his Middle? The Truth of it is, there is often nothing more ridiculous than the Gestures of an *English* Speaker; you see some of them running their Hands into their Pockets as far as ever they can thrust them, and others looking with great Attention on a piece of Paper that has nothing written in it; you may see many a smart Rhetorician turning his Hat in his Hands, moulding it into several different Cocks, examining sometimes the Lining of it, and sometimes the Button, during the whole course of his Harangue. A deaf Man would think he was Cheapning a Beaver,[7] when perhaps he is talking of the Fate of the *British* Nation. I remember, when I was a young Man, and used to frequent *Westminster-Hall*, there was a Counsellor who never pleaded without a Piece of Pack-thread in his Hand, which he used to twist about a Thumb, or a Finger, all the while he was speaking: The Waggs of those Days used to call it the Thread of his Discourse, for he was not able to utter a Word without it. One of his Clients, who was more merry than wise, stole it from him one Day in the midst of his Pleading, but he had better have let it alone, for he lost his Cause by his Jest.

I have all along acknowledged my self to be a dumb Man, and therefore may be thought a very improper Person to give Rules for Oratory;[8] but I believe every one will agree with me in this, that we ought either to lay aside all kinds of Gesture, (which seems to be very suitable to the Genius of our Nation) or at least to make use of such only as are graceful and expressive.   O

[7] Bargaining for a hat.
[8] This is true both for the Spectator and for Joseph Addison. Throughout his extensive political career, Addison was known as a reticent and inadequate public speaker.

The Spectator, No. 409

Thursday, June 19.

[Addison]

———*Musaeo contingere cuncta lepore.* Lucr.[1]

Gratian[2] very often recommends *the fine Taste,* as the utmost Perfection of an accomplished Man. As this Word arises very often in Conversation, I shall endeavour to give some Account of it, and to lay down Rules how we may know whether we are possessed of it, and how we may acquire that fine Taste of Writing, which is so much talked of among the Polite[3] World.

Most Languages make use of this Metaphor, to express that Faculty of the Mind, which distinguishes all the most concealed Faults and nicest Perfections in Writing. We may be sure this Metaphor would not have been so general in all Tongues,[4] had there not been a very great Conformity between that Mental Taste, which is the Subject of this Paper, and that Sensitive Taste which gives us a Relish of every different Flavour that affects the Palate. Accordingly we find, there are as many Degrees of Refinement in the intellectual Faculty, as in the Sense, which is marked out by this common Denomination.

I knew a Person who possessed the one in so great a Perfection, that after having tasted ten different Kinds of Tea, he would distinguish, without seeing the Colour of it, the particular Sort

---

[1] Lucretius *De Rerum Natura* 1. 934 (altered): "To grace each subject with wit."

[2] Baltasar Gracián (1601–1658), Spanish literary critic. The reference is to his *Arte de Ingenio* (1642).

[3] Learned, civilized.

[4] Again, Addison enjoys the "false Wit" of a pun.

which was offered him; and not only so, but any two Sorts of them that were mixt together in an equal Proportion; nay, he has carried the Experiment so far, as upon tasting the Composition of three different Sorts,[5] to name the Parcels from whence the three several Ingredients were taken. A Man of a fine Taste in Writing will discern after the same manner, not only the general Beauties and Imperfections of an Author, but discover the several Ways of thinking and expressing himself, which diversify him from all other Authors, with the several Foreign Infusions of Thought and Language, and the particular Authors from whom they were borrowed.

After having thus far explained what is generally meant by a fine Taste in Writing, and shewn the Propriety of the Metaphor which is used on this Occasion, I think I may define it to be *that Faculty of the Soul, which discerns the Beauties of an Author with Pleasure, and the Imperfections with Dislike*. If a Man would know whether he is possessed of this Faculty, I would have him read over the celebrated Works of Antiquity, which have stood the Test of so many different Ages and Countries; or those Works among the Moderns, which have the Sanction[6] of the Politer Part of our Contemporaries. If upon the Perusal of such Writings he does not find himself delighted in an extraordinary Manner, or if, upon reading the admired Passages in such Authors, he finds a Coldness and Indifference in his Thoughts, he ought to conclude, not (as is too usual among tasteless Readers) that the Author wants[7] those Perfections which have been admired in him, but that he himself wants the Faculty of discovering them.

He should, in the second Place, be very careful to observe, whether he tastes the distinguishing Perfections, or, if I may be allowed to call them so, the Specifick Qualities of the Author whom he peruses; whether he is particularly pleased with *Livy*[8] for his Manner of telling a Story, which *Sallust* for his entring into those internal Principles of Action which arise from the

---

5 I.e., a drink made with three different kinds of tea.

6 Approval, esteem.

7 Lacks.

8 Livy (59–17 B.C.) and Sallust (86–34 B.C.) were Roman historians. For Tacitus, see *Spectator* No. 305, n. 13.

Characters and Manners of the Persons he describes, or with *Tacitus* for his displaying those outward Motives of Safety and Interest, which give birth to the whole Series of Transactions which he relates.

He may likewise consider, how differently he is affected by the same Thought, which presents it self in a great Writer, from what he is when he finds it delivered by a Person of an ordinary Genius.[9] For there is as much difference in apprehending a Thought cloathed in *Cicero*'s Language, and that of a common Author, as in seeing an Object by the Light of a Taper, or by the Light of the Sun.

It is very difficult to lay down Rules for the Acquirement of such a Taste as that I am here speaking of. The Faculty must in some degree be born with us, and it very often happens, that those who have other Qualities in Perfection are wholly void of this. One of the most eminent Mathematicians of the Age[10] has assured me, that the greatest Pleasure he took in reading *Virgil*, was in examining *Aeneas* his Voyage by the Map; as I question not but many a Modern Compiler of History would be delighted with little more in that Divine Author, than in the bare Matters of Fact.

But notwithstanding this Faculty must in some measure be born with us, there are several Methods for Cultivating and Improving it, and without which it will be very uncertain, and of little use to the Person that possesses it. The most natural Method for this Purpose is to be conversant among the Writings of the most Polite Authors. A Man who has any Relish for fine Writing, either discovers new Beauties, or receives stronger Impressions from the Masterly Stroaks of a great Author every time he peruses him: Besides that he naturally wears himself into the same manner of Speaking and Thinking.

Conversation with Men of a Polite Genius is another Method for improving our Natural Taste. It is impossible for a Man of the greatest Parts to consider any thing in its whole Extent, and in all its variety of Lights. Every Man, besides those general Ob-

---

9 Capacity.
10 Critics have speculated that the mathematician may be Newton.

servations which are to be made upon an Author, forms several
Reflections that are peculiar to his own manner of Thinking; so
that Conversation will naturally furnish us with Hints which we
did not attend to, and make us enjoy other Mens Parts and Reflections as well as our own. This is the best Reason I can give for
the Observation which several have made, that Men of great Genius in the same way of Writing seldom rise up singly, but at certain Periods of Time appear together, and in a Body; as they did
at *Rome* in the Reign of *Augustus,* and in *Greece* about the Age
of *Socrates.* I cannot think that *Corneille, Racine, Moliere, Boileau, la Fontaine, Bruyere, Bossu,* or the *Daciers,*[11] would have
written so well as they have done, had they not been Friends and
Contemporaries.

It is likewise necessary for a Man who would form to himself a
finished Taste of good Writing, to be well versed in the Works of
the best *Criticks* both Ancient and Modern. I must confess that I
could wish there were Authors of this kind, who, beside the Mechanical Rules which a Man of very little Taste may discourse
upon,[12] would enter into the very Spirit and Soul of fine Writing,
and shew us the several Sources of that Pleasure which rises in
the Mind upon the Perusal of a noble Work. Thus altho' in Poetry it be absolutely necessary that the Unities of Time, Place and
Action,[13] with other Points of the same Nature, should be thoroughly explained and understood; there is still something more
essential to the Art, something that elevates and astonishes the
Fancy, and gives a Greatness of Mind to the Reader, which few
of the Criticks besides *Longinus* have considered.[14]

Our general Taste in *England* is for Epigram, turns of Wit,
and forced Conceits, which have no manner of Influence, either

[11] All are French authors of the seventeenth century. Pierre Corneille
(1606–1684), Jean Racine (1639–1699), and Molière (1622–1673) were dramatists. Jean de la Fontaine (1621–1680) and Jean de la Bruyère (1645–1696) were
prominent writers. For Boileau, see *Tatler* No. 158, n. 16. For Bossu and Dacier,
see *Tatler* No. 165, notes 3 and 8.

[12] This is illustrated in the description of Tom Folio in *Tatler* No. 158 and
of Sir Timothy Tittle in *Tatler* No. 165.

[13] See *Tatler* No. 165, n. 7.

[14] Dionysius Longinus (fl. 3rd century A.D.), Greek philosopher whose treatise *On the Sublime* discussed the sources of sublimity in literature.

for the bettering or enlarging the Mind of him who reads them, and have been carefully avoided by the greatest Writers, both among the Ancients and Moderns. I have endeavoured in several of my Speculations to banish this *Gothic* Taste, which has taken Possession among us. I entertained the Town for a Week together with an Essay upon Wit, in which I endeavoured to detect several of those false Kinds which have been admired in the different Ages of the World; and at the same time to shew wherein the Nature of true Wit consists. I afterwards gave an Instance of the great Force which lyes in a natural Simplicity of Thought to affect the Mind of the Reader, from such vulgar Pieces as have little else besides this single Qualification to recommend them. I have likewise examined the Works of the greatest Poet which our Nation or perhaps any other has produced, and particularized most of those rational and manly Beauties which give a Value to that Divine Work.[15] I shall next *Saturday* enter upon an Essay *on the Pleasures of the Imagination,*[16] which, though it shall consider that Subject at large, will perhaps suggest to the Reader what it is that gives a Beauty to many Passages of the finest Writers both in Prose and Verse. As an Undertaking of this Nature is entirely new, I question not but it will be received with Candour.   O

[15] In this paragraph, Addison recalls his essays on wit (Nos. 58–63), on ballads (Nos. 70, 74, 85), and on Milton (Nos. 267 and following).

[16] The essays on the pleasures of the imagination run from No. 411 to No. 421.

The Spectator, No. 410

Friday, June 20.

[S t e e l e]

———*Dum foris sunt, nihil videtur Mundius,*
Nec Magis compositum quidquam, nec magis elegans:
Quae, cum amatore suo cum coenant, Liguriunt,
Harum videre ingluviem, sordes, inopiam:
Quam inhonestae solae sint domi, atque avidae cibi,
Quo pacto ex Jure Hesterno panem atrum vorent.
Nosse omnia haec, salus est adolescentulis. Ter.[1]

Will. Honeycomb, who disguises his present Decay by visiting the Wenches of the Town only by Way of Humour,[2] told us, that the last rainy Night he with Sir Roger de Coverly was driven into the *Temple* Cloister,[3] whither had escaped also a Lady most exactly[4] dressed from Head to Foot. Will. made no Scruple to acquaint us, that she saluted[5] him very familiarly by his Name, and turning immediately to the Knight, she said, she supposed that was his good Friend Sir Roger de Coverly: Upon which nothing less could follow than Sir Roger's Approach to Salutation, with Madam the same at your Service. She was dressed in a black

1 Terence *Eunuchus* 934–940 (altered): "When they are abroad, none seem so elegant, modish, or genteel; when the ladies feast with their lovers, they sup with delicacy; but to see the filthy jades at home, their meanness, poverty, vulgarity, and greed, to see how they devour their black bread with yesterday's gravy: to know all this beforehand may be the saving of a young man."

2 I.e., he conceals his physical decay by soliciting the conversation of prostitutes.

3 A covered passage.

4 To perfection.

5 See *Spectator* No. 394, n. 2.

Tabby[6] Mantua and Petticoat, without Ribbonds; her Linnen striped Muslin, and in the whole in an agreeable Second-Mourning;[7] decent Dresses being often affected by the Creatures of the Town, at once consulting[8] Cheapness and the Pretension to Modesty. She went on with a familiar easie Air, Your Friend, Mr. Honeycomb, is a little surprised to see a Woman here alone and unattended; but I dismissed my Coach at the Gate, and tripped it down to my Council's Chambers, for Lawyers Fees take up too much of a small disputed Joynture to admit any other Expences but meer Necessaries.[9] Mr. Honeycomb begged they might have the Honour of setting her down,[10] for Sir Roger's Servant was gone to call a Coach. In the Interim the Footman returned, with no Coach to be had; and there appeared nothing to be done but trusting her self with Mr. Honeycomb and his Friend to wait at the Tavern at the Gate for a Coach, or be subjected to all the Impertinence she must meet with in that publick Place. Mr. Honeycomb being a Man of Honour determined the Choice of the first,[11] and Sir Roger, as the better Man,[12] took the Lady by the Hand, leading through all the Shower covering her with his Hat, and gallanting a familiar Acquaintance through Rows of young Fellows, who winked at *Sukey* in the State she marched off, Will. Honeycomb bringing up the Rear.

Much Importunity prevailed upon the Fair one to admit of a Collation,[13] where, after declaring she had no Stomach, and eaten a Couple of Chickens, devoured a Trusse of Sallet, and drunk a full Bottle to her Share, she sung the Old Man's Wish[14] to Sir Roger. The Knight left the Room for some Time after Supper, and writ the following Billet, which he conveyed to *Sukey,* and

6 A loose-fitting gown of waved or watered silk.

7 A style of dress worn after a period of strict mourning is over.

8 Seeking.

9 Throughout, the main characteristic of Sukey is an affected gentility.

10 Driving her to her destination.

11 I.e., the first alternative, waiting with them at the Tavern.

12 The man of higher rank.

13 To accept the offer of something to eat.

14 "The Old Man's Wish" (1685) is a poem by Walter Pope. This is not a bawdy song; it is Sukey's general behavior which disabuses Sir Roger.

Sukey to her Friend Will. Honeycomb. Will. has given it to Sir
Andrew Freeport, who read it last Night to the Club.

> "*Madam,*
> I am not so meer a Country-Gentleman, but I can guess at the Law-
> Business you had at the *Temple.* If you would go down to the Coun-
> try and leave off all your Vanities but your Singing, let me know at
> my Lodgings in *Bow-street, Covent-Garden,* and you shall be encour-
> aged by,[15]
>
> > *Your humble Servant,*
> > Roger de Coverly."

My good Friend could not well stand the Raillery which was
rising upon him; but to put a Stop to it I delivered Will. Honeycomb the following Letter,[16] and desired him to read it to the
Board.

> "*Mr.* Spectator,
> Having seen a Translation of one of the Chapters in the *Canticles*
> into English Verse inserted among your late Papers,[17] I have ven-
> tured to send you the 7th Chapter of the *Proverbs* in a poetical Dress.
> If you think it worthy appearing among your Speculations, it will be
> a sufficient Reward for the Trouble of
>
> > *Your constant Reader,*
> > A. B."[18]

> *My Son, th' Instruction that my Words impart,*
> *Grave on the living Tablet of thy Heart;*
> *And all the wholesome Precepts that I give,*
> *Observe with strictest Reverence, and live.*
> > *Let all thy Homage be to Wisdom paid,*
> *Seek her Protection, and implore her Aid;*
> *That she may keep thy Soul from Harm secure,*
> *And turn thy Footsteps from the Harlot's Door.*
> *Who with curs'd Charms lures the Unwary in,*

---

[15] I.e., if she would give up her city profession and begin life anew in the
country, he would assist her reformation.

[16] Note that the letter does not change the subject under discussion.

[17] *Spectator* No. 388 offered a poetic paraphrase of the second chapter of
the *Song of Solomon.*

[18] The translation of Proverbs 7:1–27 is by James Ward (d. 1736) who later
became the Lord Lieutenant of Ireland.

And sooths with Flattery their Souls to Sin.
    Once from my Window as I cast mine Eye
On those that pass'd in giddy Numbers by,
A Youth among the foolish Youths I spy'd,
Who took not sacred Wisdom for his Guide.

    Just as the Sun withdrew his cooler Light,
And Evening soft led on the Shades of Night,
He stole in covert Twilight to his Fate,
And pass'd the Corner near the Harlot's Gate;
When, lo, a Woman comes!————
Loose her Attire, and such her glaring Dress,
As aptly did the Harlot's Mind express:
Subtle she is, and practis'd in the Arts,
By which the Wanton conquer heedless Hearts:
Stubborn and loud she is; she hates her Home,
Varying her Place and Form, she loves to roam;
Now she's within, now in the Street do's stray,
Now at each Corner stands, and waits her Prey.
The Youth she seized, and laying now aside
All Modesty, the Female's justest Pride,
She said, with an Embrace, Here at my House
Peace-offerings are, this Day I paid my Vows.[19]
I therefore came abroad to meet my Dear,
And, Lo, in Happy Hour I find thee here.

    My Chamber I've adorn'd, and o'er my Bed
Are Cov'rings of the richest Tap'stry spread,
With Linnen it is deck'd from Egypt *brought,*
And Carvings by the curious Artist wrought,
It wants no Glad Perfume Arabia *yields*
In all her Citron Groves, and spicy Fields;
Here all her Store of richest Odours meets,
I'll lay thee in a Wilderness of Sweets.
Whatever to the Sense can grateful be
I have collected there—I want but Thee.
My Husband's gone a Journey far away,
Much Gold he took abroad, and long will stay, }
He nam'd for his Return a distant Day.
    Upon her Tongue did such smooth Mischief dwell,

---

[19] She has just sacrificed the fat and entrails of a beast at the altar, therefore has enough meat for a feast.

And from her Lips such welcome Flatt'ry fell.
Th' unguarded Youth, in Silken Fetters ty'd,
Resign'd his Reason, and with Ease comply'd.
Thus does the Ox to his own Slaughter go,
And thus is senseless of th' impending Blow.
Thus flies the simple Bird into the Snare,
That skilful Fowlers for his Life prepare.
But let my Sons attend, Attend may they
Whom Youthful Vigour may to Sin betray;
Let them false Charmers fly, and guard their Hearts
Against the wily Wanton's pleasing Arts.
With Care direct their Steps, nor turn astray
To tread the Paths of her deceitful Way;
Least they too late of Her fell Power complain,
And fall, where many mightier have been Slain.

T[20]

[20] According to Budgell (*The Bee*, No. 1, Feb. 1733), Addison was "so heartily vexed when he read this Paper, that he immediately called a Coach, went to his Friend Sir *Richard,* and never left him, till he had made him promise that he would meddle no more with Sir *Roger's* Character." In *Spectator* No. 544, after Sir Roger is dead, Steele had Captain Sentry explain that Sir Roger's meeting with Sukey was "an Instance of the Simplicity and Innocence of his Mind, which made him imagine it is a very easy thing to reclaim one of those Criminals. . . ."

The Spectator, No. 411

Saturday, June 21.

[A d d i s o n]

*Avia Pieridum peragro loca, nullius ante
Trita solo; juvat integros accedere fonteis;
Atque haurire:*———Lucr.[1]

Our Sight is the most perfect and most delightful of all our Senses. It fills the Mind with the largest Variety of Ideas, converses with its Objects at the greatest Distance, and continues the longest in Action without being tired or satiated with its proper Enjoyments. The Sense of Feeling can indeed give us a Notion of Extention, Shape, and all other Ideas that enter at the Eye, except Colours; but at the same time it is very much streightned[2] and confined in its Operations, to the Number, Bulk, and Distance of its particular Objects. Our Sight seems designed to supply all these Defects, and may be considered as a more delicate and diffusive Kind of Touch, that spreads its self over an infinite Multitude of Bodies, comprehends the largest Figures, and brings into our reach some of the most remote Parts of the Universe.

It is this Sense which furnishes the Imagination with its Ideas; so that by the Pleasures of the Imagination or Fancy (which I shall use promiscuously[3]) I here mean such as arise from visible Objects, either when we have them actually in our View, or when we call up their Ideas into our Minds by Paintings, Statues, De-

---

[1] Lucretius *De Rerum Natura* 1. 926–928: "I wander through the trackless places of the Muses, over ground never trod before. I like to pick fresh flowers and to approach virgin springs and drink."

[2] Limited.

[3] Interchangeably.

scriptions, or any the like Occasion. We cannot indeed have a single Image in the Fancy that did not make its first Entrance through the Sight; but we have the Power of retaining, altering and compounding those Images, which we have once received, into all the Varieties of Picture and Vision that are most agreeable to the Imagination; for by this Faculty a Man in a Dungeon is capable of entertaining himself with Scenes and Landskips more beautiful than any that can be found in the whole Compass of Nature.

There are few Words in the *English* Language which are employed in a more loose and uncircumscribed Sense than those of the *Fancy* and the *Imagination*. I therefore thought it necessary to fix and determine the Notion of these two Words, as I intend to make use of them in the Thread of my following Speculations,[4] that the Reader may conceive rightly what is the Subject which I proceed upon. I must therefore desire him to remember, that by the Pleasures of the Imagination, I mean only such Pleasures as arise originally from Sight, and that I divide these Pleasures in two Kinds: My Design being first of all to discourse of those Primary Pleasures of the Imagination, which entirely proceed from such Objects as are before our Eyes; and in the next place to speak of those Secondary Pleasures of the Imagination which flow from the Ideas of visible Objects, when the Objects are not actually before the Eye, but are called up into our Memories, or formed into agreeable Visions of Things that are either Absent or Fictitious.

The Pleasures of the Imagination, taken in their full Extent, are not so gross as those of Sense, nor so refined as those of the Understanding.[5] The last are, indeed, more preferable, because they are founded on some new Knowledge or Improvement in the Mind of Man; yet it must be confest, that those of the Imagination are as great and as transporting as the other. A beautiful Prospect delights the Soul, as much as a Demonstration;[6] and a Descrip-

4 I.e., in succeeding issues of the *Spectator*.

5 Addison makes a traditional distinction, discriminating between sensual pleasure, rational pleasure, and aesthetic pleasure ("the Pleasures of the Imagination").

6 I.e., a beautiful scene delights the mind as much as does a syllogistic proof or a solid philosophical discourse.

tion in *Homer* has charm'd more Readers than a Chapter in *Aristotle*. Besides, the Pleasures of the Imagination have this Advantage, above those of the Understanding, that they are more obvious, and more easie to be acquired. It is but opening the Eye, and the Scene enters. The Colours paint themselves on the Fancy, with very little Attention of Thought or Application of Mind in the Beholder. We are struck, we know not how, with the Symmetry of any thing we see, and immediately assent to the Beauty of an Object, without enquiring into the particular Causes and Occasions of it.

A Man of a Polite[7] Imagination is let into a great many Pleasures, that the Vulgar are not capable of receiving. He can converse with a Picture, and find an agreeable Companion in a Statue. He meets with a secret Refreshment in a Description, and often feels a greater Satisfaction in the Prospect of Fields and Meadows, than another does in the Possession. It gives him, indeed, a kind of Property[8] in every thing he sees, and makes the most rude uncultivated Parts of Nature administer to his Pleasures: So that he looks upon the World, as it were, in another Light, and discovers in it a Multitude of Charms, that conceal themselves from the generality of Mankind.

There are indeed, but very few who know how to be idle and innocent, or have a Relish of any Pleasures that are not Criminal; every Diversion they take is at the Expence of some one Virtue or another, and their very first Step out of Business[9] is into Vice or Folly. A Man should endeavour, therefore, to make the Sphere of his innocent Pleasures as wide as possible, that he may retire into them with Safety, and find in them such a Satisfaction as a wise Man would not blush to take. Of this Nature are those of the Imagination, which do not require such a Bent of Thought as is necessary to our more serious Employments, nor at the same Time, suffer the Mind to sink into that Negligence and Remissness, which are apt to accompany our more sensual Delights, but, like a gentle Exercise to the Faculties, awaken them from Sloth

---

7 Refined, cultivated.

8 Possession, a sense of ownership.

9 Normal procedures, customary activity.

and Idleness, without putting them upon any Labour or Difficulty.

We might here add, that the Pleasures of the Fancy are more conducive to Health than those of the Understanding, which are worked out by Dint of Thinking, and attended with too violent a Labour of the Brain. Delightful Scenes, whether in Nature, Painting, or Poetry, have a kindly Influence on the Body, as well as the Mind, and not only serve to clear and brighten the Imagination, but are able to disperse Grief and Melancholly, and to set the Animal Spirits in pleasing and agreeable Motions. For this Reason Sir *Francis Bacon,* in his Essay upon Health,[10] has not thought it improper to prescribe to his Reader a Poem or a Prospect, where[11] he particularly dissuades him from knotty and subtle Disquisitions, and advises him to pursue Studies, that fill the Mind with splendid and illustrious Objects, as Histories, Fables, and Contemplations of Nature.

I have in this Paper, by way of Introduction, settled the Notion of those Pleasures of the Imagination which are the Subject of my present Undertaking, and endeavoured, by several Considerations, to recommend to my Reader the Pursuit of those Pleasures. I shall, in my next Paper, examine the several Sources from whence these Pleasures are derived.   O

10 Francis Bacon "Of Regiment of Health," *Essays* (1625).
11 Whereas.

The Spectator, No. 412

Monday, June 23.

[Addison]

———*Divisum sic breve fiet Opus.* Mart.[1]

I shall first consider those Pleasures of the Imagination, which arise from the actual View and Survey of outward Objects: And these, I think, all proceed from the Sight of what is *Great, Uncommon* or *Beautiful.* There may, indeed, be something so terrible or offensive, that the Horrour or Loathsomeness of an Object may over-bear the Pleasure which results from its *Greatness, Novelty* or *Beauty;* but still there will be such a Mixture of Delight in the very Disgust it gives us, as any of these three Qualifications are most conspicuous and prevailing.

By *Greatness,* I do not only mean the Bulk of any single Object, but the Largeness of a whole View, considered as one entire Piece. Such are the Prospects of an open Champian[2] Country, a vast uncultivated Desart, of huge Heaps of Mountains, high Rocks and Precipicies, or a wide Expanse of Waters, where we are not struck with the Novelty or Beauty of the Sight, but with that rude kind of Magnificence which appears in many of these stupendous Works of Nature. Our Imagination loves to be filled with an Object, or to grasp at any thing that is too big for its Capacity. We are flung into a pleasing Astonishment at such unbounded Views, and feel a delightful Stillness and Amazement in the Soul at the Apprehension of them. The Mind of Man naturally hates every

---

1 Martial *Epigrams* 4. 82. 8: "Thus divided, this work will be made brief."
2 Champaign, flat and open.

thing that looks like a Restraint upon it, and is apt to fancy it self under a sort of Confinement, when the Sight is pent up in a narrow Compass, and shortned on every side by the Neighbourhood of Walls or Mountains. On the contrary, a spacious Horison is an Image of Liberty, where the Eye has Room to range abroad, to expatiate[3] at large on the Immensity of its Views, and to lose it self amidst the Variety of Objects that offer themselves to its Observation. Such wide and undetermined[4] Prospects are as pleasing to the Fancy, as the Speculations of Eternity or Infinitude are to the Understanding. But if there be a Beauty or Uncommonness joined with this Grandeur, as in a troubled Ocean, a Heaven adorned with Stars and Meteors, or a spacious Landskip cut out into Rivers, Woods, Rocks, and Meadows, the Pleasure still grows upon us, as it arises from more than a single Principle.

Every thing that is *new* or *uncommon* raises a Pleasure in the Imagination, because it fills the Soul with an agreeable Surprise, gratifies its Curiosity, and gives it an Idea of which it was not before possest. We are indeed so often conversant with one Sett of Objects, and tired out with so many repeated Shows of the same Things, that whatever is *new* or *uncommon* contributes a little to vary human Life, and to divert our Minds, for a while, with the Strangeness of its Appearance: It serves us for a Kind of Refreshment, and takes off from that Satiety we are apt to complain of in our usual and ordinary Entertainments. It is this that bestows Charms on a Monster, and makes even the Imperfections of Nature please us. It is this that recommends Variety, where the Mind is every Instant called off to something new, and the Attention not suffered to dwell too long, and waste it self on any particular Object. It is this, likewise, that improves what is great or beautiful, and makes it afford the Mind a double Entertainment. Groves, Fields, and Meadows, are at any Season of the Year pleasant to look upon, but never so much as in the opening of the Spring, when they are all new and fresh, with their first Gloss upon them, and not yet too much accustomed and familiar to the Eye. For

3 Range freely.
4 Unconfined.

this Reason there is nothing that more enlivens a Prospect than Rivers, Jetteaus,[5] or Falls of Water, where the Scene is perpetually shifting, and entertaining the Sight every Moment with something that is new. We are quickly tired with looking upon Hills and Vallies, where every thing continues fixt and settled in the same Place and Posture, but find our Thoughts a little agitated and relieved at the Sight of such Objects as are ever in Motion, and sliding away from beneath the Eye of the Beholder.

But there is nothing that makes its way more directly to the Soul than *Beauty,* which immediately diffuses a secret Satisfaction and Complacency through the Imagination, and gives a Finishing to any thing that is Great or Uncommon. The very first Discovery of it strikes the Mind with an inward Joy, and spreads a Chearfulness and Delight through all its Faculties. There is not perhaps any real Beauty or Deformity more in one piece of Matter than another, because we might have been so made, that whatsoever now appears loathsom to us, might have shewn it self agreeable; but we find by Experience, that there are several Modifications[6] of Matter which the Mind, without any previous Consideration, pronounces at first sight Beautiful or Deformed. Thus we see that every different Species of sensible[7] Creatures has its different Notions of Beauty, and that each of them is most affected with the Beauties of its own Kind. This is no where more remarkable than in Birds of the same Shape and Proportion, where we often see the Male determined in his Courtship by the single Grain or Tincture of a Feather, and never discovering any Charms but in the Colour of its Species.

> *Scit thalamo servare fidem, sanctasque veretur*
> *Connubii leges, non illum in pectore candor*
> *Sollicitat niveus; neque pravum accendit amorem*
> *Splendida Lanugo, vel honesta in vertice crista,*
> *Purpureusve nitor pennarum; ast agmina latè*
> *Faeminea explorat cautus, maculasque requirit*
> *Cognatas, paribusque interlita corpora guttis:*

5 From *jet d'eau,* a jet of water from a fountain, etc.
6 Forms.
7 Living.

Ni faceret, pictis sylvam circum undique monstris
Confusam aspiceres vulgò, partusque biformes,
Et genus ambiguum, & Veneris monumenta nefandae.
Hinc merula in nigro se oblectat nigra marito,
Hinc socium lasciva petit Philomela canorum,
Agnoscitque pares sonitus, hinc Noctua tetram
Canitiem alarum, & glaucos miratur ocellos.
Nempe sibi semper constat, crescitque quotannis
Lucida progenies, castos confessa parentes;
Dum virides inter saltus locosque sonoros
Vere novo exultat, plumasque decora Juventus
*Explicat ad solem, patriisque coloribus ardet.*8

There is a second Kind of *Beauty* that we find in the several Products of Art and Nature, which does not work in the Imagination with that Warmth and Violence as the Beauty that appears in our proper Species, but is apt however to raise in us a secret Delight, and a kind of Fondness for the Places or Objects in which we discover it. This consists either in the Gaiety or Variety of Colours, in the Symmetry and Proportion of Parts, in the Arrangement and Disposition of Bodies, or in a just Mixture and Concurrence of all together. Among these several Kinds of Beauty the Eye takes most Delight in Colours. We no where meet with a more glorious or pleasing Show in Nature, than what appears in the

8 The Latin verse was written by Addison. The *duodecimo* edition of the *Spectator* (1744) offered this translation:

The feather'd Husband, to his Partner true,
Preserves connubial Rites inviolate.
With cold Indifference every Charm he sees,
The milky Whiteness of the stately Neck,
The shining Down, proud Crest, and purple Wings:
But cautious with a searching Eye explores
The female Tribes, his proper Mate to find,
With kindred Colours mark'd: Did he not so,
The Grove with painted Monsters wou'd abound,
Th' ambiguous Product of unnatural Love.
The Black-bird hence selects her sooty Spouse;
The Nightingale her musical Compeer,
Lur'd by the well-known Voice: the Bird of Night,
Smit with his dusky Wings, and greenish Eyes,
Wo[o]s his dun Paramour. The beauteous Race
Speak the chaste Loves of their Progenitors;
When, by the Spring invited, they exult
In Woods and Fields, and to the Sun unfold
Their Plumes, that with paternal Colours glow.

Heavens at the rising and setting of the Sun, which is wholly made up of those different Stains of Light that shew themselves in Clouds of a different Situation. For this Reason we find the Poets, who are always addressing themselves to the Imagination, borrowing more of their Epithets from Colours than from any other Topic.

As the Fancy delights in every thing that is Great, Strange, or Beautiful, and is still more pleased the more it finds of these Perfections in the same Object, so is it capable of receiving a new Satisfaction by the Assistance of another Sense. Thus any continued Sound, as the Musick of Birds, or a Fall of Water, awakens every moment the Mind of the Beholder, and makes him more attentive to the several Beauties of the Place that lye before him. Thus if there arises a Fragrancy of Smells or Perfumes, they heighten the Pleasures of the Imagination, and make even the Colours and Verdure[9] of the Landskip appear more agreeable; for the Ideas of both Senses recommend each other, and are pleasanter together than when they enter the Mind separately: As the different Colours of a Picture, when they are well disposed, set off one another, and receive an additional Beauty from the Advantage of their Situation.   O

[9] Fresh greenness.

The Spectator, No. 416

Friday, June 27.

[Addison]

Quatenus hoc simile est oculis, quod mente videmus. Lucr.[1]

I at first divided the Pleasures of the Imagination, into such as arise from Objects that are actually before our Eyes, or that once entered in at our Eyes, and are afterwards called up into the Mind, either barely by its own Operations, or on occasion of something without us,[2] as Statues or Descriptions. We have already considered the first Division,[3] and shall therefore enter on the other, which, for Distinction sake, I have called the Secondary Pleasures of the Imagination. When I say the Ideas we receive from Statues, Descriptions, or such like Occasions, are the same that were once actually in our View, it must not be understood that we had once seen the very[4] Place, Action, or Person which are carved or described. It is sufficient, that we have seen Places, Persons, or Actions, in general, which bear a Resemblance, or at least some remote Analogy with what we find represented. Since it is in the Power of the Imagination, when it is once Stocked with particular Ideas, to enlarge, compound, and vary them at her own Pleasure.

1 Lucretius *De Rerum Natura* 4. 750: "Because the objects we fancy in our mind are similar to those we see with our eyes."

2 I.e., existing in the outer world.

3 After *Spectator* No. 411 discussed the nature of imaginative pleasure in general and No. 412 located it in objects which are "Great, Uncommon, or Beautiful," No. 413 speculated why God located pleasure in such qualities; No. 414 maintained that "the Works of Nature [are] still more pleasant, the more they resemble those of Art"; and No. 415 considered the quality of greatness (i.e., greatness in size and greatness in manner) as it appears in architecture.

4 Exact same.

Among the different Kinds of Representation, *Statuary* is the most natural, and shews us something *likest* the Object that is represented. To make use of a common Instance, let one who is born Blind take an Image in his Hands, and trace out with his Fingers the different Furrows and Impressions of the Chissel,[5] and he will easily conceive how the Shape of a Man, or Beast, may be represented by it; but should he draw his Hand over a *Picture,* where all is smooth and uniform, he would never be able to imagine how the several Prominencies and Depressions of a human Body could be shewn on a plain Piece of Canvas, that has in it no Unevenness or Irregularity. *Description* runs yet further from the things it represents than Painting; for a Picture bears a real Resemblance to its Original, which Letters and Syllables are wholly void of. Colours speak all Languages, but Words are understood only by such a[6] People or Nation. For this reason, tho' Mens Necessities quickly put them on finding out Speech, Writing is probably of a later Invention than Painting; particularly we are told, that in *America* when the *Spaniards* first arrived there, Expresses[7] were sent to the Emperor of *Mexico* in Paint, and the News of his Country delineated by the Strokes of a Pencil, which was a more natural Way than that of Writing, tho' at the same time much more imperfect, because it is impossible to draw the little Connexions of Speech, or to give the Picture of a Conjunction or an Adverb. It would be yet more strange, to represent visible Objects by Sounds that have no Ideas annexed to them, and to make something like Description in *Musick.* Yet it is certain, there may be confused, imperfect Notions of this Nature raised in the Imagination by an Artificial Composition of Notes; and we find that great Masters in the Art are able, sometimes, to set their Hearers in the heat and hurry of a Battel, to overcast their Minds with melancholy Scenes and Apprehensions of Deaths and Funerals, or to lull them into pleasing Dreams of Groves and Elisiums.[8]

In all these Instances, this Secondary Pleasure of the Imagina-

---

[5] I.e., made by the chisel.

[6] A particular.

[7] Messages.

[8] Elysium is the abode of the blessed in Greek mythology; more generally, Elysian Fields can refer to any area of delight and pleasure.

tion proceeds from that Action of the Mind, which compares the Ideas arising from the Original Objects, with the Ideas we receive from the Statue, Picture, Description, or Sound that represents them. It is impossible for us to give the necessary Reason, why this Operation of the Mind is attended with so much Pleasure, as I have before observed on the same Occasion,[9] but we find a great variety of Entertainments derived from this single Principle: For it is this that not only gives us a relish of Statuary, Painting and Description, but makes us delight in all the Actions and Arts of Mimickry. It is this that makes the several kinds of Wit pleasant, which consists, as I have formerly shewn, in the Affinity of Ideas:[10] And we may add, it is this also that raises the little Satisfaction we sometimes find in the different Sorts of false Wit; whether it consist in the Affinity of Letters, as in Anagram, Acrostick; or of Syllables, as in Doggerel Rhimes, Ecchos; or of Words, as in Puns, Quibbles; or of a whole Sentence or Poem, to Wings, and Altars. The *final Cause,* probably, of annexing Pleasure[11] to this Operation of the Mind, was to quicken and encourage us in our Searches after Truth, since the distinguishing one thing from another, and the right discerning betwixt our Ideas, depends wholly upon our comparing them together, and observing the Congruity or Disagreement that appears among the several Works of Nature.

But I shall here confine my self to those Pleasures of the Imagination, which proceed from Ideas raised by *Words,* because most of the Observations that agree with Descriptions, are equally Applicable to Painting and Statuary.

Words, when well chosen, have so great a Force in them, that a Description often gives us more lively Ideas than the Sight of Things themselves. The Reader finds a Scene drawn in stronger Colours, and painted more to the Life in his Imagination, by the help of Words, than by an actual Survey of the Scene which they describe. In this Case the Poet seems to get the better of Nature; he takes, indeed, the Landskip after her,[12] but gives it more vigorous Touches, heightens its Beauty, and so enlivens the whole Piece, that the Images which flow from the Objects themselves

9 I.e., in *Spectator* No. 413.
10 See *Spectator* No. 62.
11 I.e., of God's annexing pleasure.
12 Copies the landscape from her.

appear weak and faint, in Comparison of those that come from the Expressions. The Reason, probably, may be, because in the Survey of any Object we have only so much of it painted on the Imagination, as comes in at the Eye; but in its Description, the Poet gives us as a free View of it as he pleases, and discovers to us several Parts, that either we did not attend to, or that lay out of our Sight when we first beheld it. As we look on any Object, our Idea of it is, perhaps, made up of two or three simple Ideas; but when the Poet represents it, he may either give us a more complex Idea of it, or only raise in us such Ideas as are most apt to affect the Imagination.

It may be here worth our while to examine, how it comes to pass that several Readers, who are all acquainted with the same Language, and know the Meaning of the Words they read, should nevertheless have a different Relish of the same Descriptions. We find one transported with a Passage, which another runs over with Coldness and Indifference, or finding[13] the Representation extreamly natural, where another can perceive nothing of Likeness and conformity. This different Taste must proceed, either from the *Perfection of Imagination* in one more than in another, or from the *different Ideas* that several Readers affix to the same Words. For, to have a true Relish, and form a right Judgment of a Description, a Man should be born with a good Imagination, and must have well weighed the Force and Energy that lye in the several Words of a Language, so as to be able to distinguish which are most significant and expressive of their proper Ideas, and what additional Strength and Beauty they are capable of receiving from Conjunction with others. The Fancy must be warm, to retain the Print of those Images it hath received from outward Objects; and the Judgment discerning, to know what Expressions are most proper to cloath and adorn them to the best Advantage. A Man who is deficient in either of these Respects, tho' he may receive the general Notion of a Description, can never see distinctly all its particular Beauties: As a Person, with a weak Sight, may have the confused Prospect of a Place that lyes before him, without entering into its several Parts, or discerning the variety of its Colours in their full Glory and Perfection.   O

---

13 Or one finding.

The Spectator, No. 445

Thursday, July 31.

[A d d i s o n]

Tanti non es ais. Sapis, Luperce. Mart.[1]

This is the Day on which many eminent Authors will probably Publish their Last Words. I am afraid that few of our Weekly Historians, who are Men that above all others delight in War, will be able to subsist under the Weight of a Stamp,[2] and an approaching Peace.[3] A Sheet of Blank Paper that must have this new Imprimatur clapt upon it, before it is qualified to Communicate any thing to the Publick, will make its way in the World but very heavily. In short, the Necessity of carrying a Stamp, and the Improbability of notifying a Bloody Battel, will, I am afraid, both concur to the sinking of those thin Folios, which have every other Day retailed to us the History of *Europe* for several Years last past. A Facetious Friend of mine, who loves a Punn, calls this present Mortality among Authors, *The Fall of the Leaf.*

I remember, upon Mr. *Baxter*'s Death,[4] there was Published a Sheet of very good Sayings, inscribed, *The last Words of Mr.* Baxter. The Title sold so great a Number of these Papers, that about a Week after, there came out a second Sheet, inscribed, *More last*

1 Martial *Epigrams* 1. 117. 18: "You say you are not worth it? You are wise, Lupercus."

2 On August 1, 1712, a new Stamp Act went into effect which imposed a tax of one halfpenny on each halfsheet, and a shilling for each advertisement. The *Spectator* was forced to double its price, to twopence.

3 Since a peace treaty was pending with France, "Weekly Historians" with little to discuss except war news would have to issue "Blank Paper." See *Tatler* No. 18.

4 Richard Baxter (d. December 8, 1691).

Words of Mr. Baxter. In the same Manner, I have Reason to
think, that several Ingenious Writers, who have taken their Leave
of the Publick, in farewel Papers, will not give over so, but intend
to appear again, tho' perhaps under another Form, and with a
different Title. Be that as it will, it is my Business, in this place,
to give an Account of my own Intentions, and to acquaint my
Reader with the Motives by which I Act, in this great Crisis of
the Republick of Letters.

I have been long debating in my own Heart, whether I should
throw up my Pen, as an Author that is cashiered by the Act of
Parliament, which is to Operate within these Four and Twenty
Hours, or whether I should still persist in laying my Speculations,
from Day to Day, before the Publick. The Argument which prevails with me most on the first side of the Question is, that I am
informed by my Bookseller he must raise the Price of every single
Paper to Two-pence, or that he shall not be able to pay the Duty
of it. Now as I am very desirous my Readers should have their
Learning as cheap as possible, it is with great Difficulty that I
comply with him in this Particular.

However, upon laying my Reasons together in the Balance, I
find that those which plead for the Continuance of this Work
have much the greater Weight. For, in the first Place, in Recompence for the Expence to which this will put my Readers, it is to
be hoped they may receive from every Paper so much Instruction,
as will be a very good Equivalent. And, in order to this, I would
not advise any one to take it in, who, after the Perusal of it, does
not find himself Twopence the wiser, or the better Man for it; or
who, upon Examination, does not believe that he has had Two
penny-worth of Mirth or Instruction for his Mony.

But I must confess there is another Motive which prevails with
me more than the former. I consider that the Tax on Paper was
given for the Support of the Government; and as I have Enemies,
who are apt to pervert every thing I do or say, I fear they would
ascribe the laying down my Paper, on such an occasion, to a Spirit
of Malecontentedness, which I am resolved none shall ever justly
upbraid me with.[5] No, I shall glory in contributing my utmost to

---

[5] Despite the facetious nature of this "Motive," it is a fact that neither
Addison nor Steele was a friend of the existing Tory government.

the Weal Publick; and if my Country receives Five or Six Pounds a-Day by my Labours, I shall be very well pleased to find my self so useful a Member. It is a received Maxim, that no honest Man should enrich himself by Methods that are prejudicial to the Community in which he lives, and by the same Rule I think we may pronounce the Person to deserve very well of his Country-men, whose Labours bring more into the Publick Coffers, than into his own Pocket.

Since I have mentioned the Word Enemies, I must explain my self so far as to acquaint my Reader, that I mean only the insignificant Party Zealots on both sides; Men of such poor narrow Souls, that they are not capable of thinking on any thing but with an Eye to Whig or Tory. During the Course of this Paper, I have been accused by these despicable Wretches of Trimming, Time-serving,[6] Personal Reflection, secret Satire, and the like. Now, tho' in these my Compositions, it is visible to any Reader of Common Sense, that I consider nothing but my Subject, which is always of an Indifferent Nature; how is it possible for me to write so clear of Party, as not to lie open to the Censures of those who will be applying every Sentence, and finding out Persons and Things in it which it has no regard to?[7]

Several Paltry Scribblers and Declaimers have done me the Honour to be dull upon me in Reflections of this Nature; but not-withstanding my Name has been sometimes traduced by this con-temptible Tribe of Men, I have hitherto avoided all Animadver-sions upon 'em. The truth of it is, I am afraid of making them appear considerable by taking notice of them, for they are like those Imperceptible Insects which are discovered by the Micro-scope, and cannot be made the Subject of Observation without being magnified.[8]

Having mentioned those few who have shewn themselves the Enemies of this Paper, I should be very ungrateful to the Publick, did not I at the same time testifie my Gratitude to those who are its Friends, in which number I may reckon many of the most dis-

[6] Trimming is changing parties for reasons of expedience; time-serving is being obsequious to the wishes of those in power at the time. See *Tatler* No. 214.

[7] See *Spectators* No. 46 and 568 and *Guardian* No. 160, on "Personal Re-flection" and "secret Satire."

[8] The same attitude (and metaphor) is expressed in *Tatler* No. 229.

tinguished Persons of all Conditions,[9] Parties, and Professions in the Isle of *Great Britain*. I am not so vain as to think this Approbation is so much due to the Performance as to the Design.[10] There is, and ever will be, Justice enough in the World, to afford Patronage and Protection for those who endeavour to advance Truth and Virtue, without regard to the Passions and Prejudices of any particular Cause or Faction. If I have any other Merit in me, it is that I have new-pointed all the Batteries of Ridicule. They have been generally planted against Persons who have appeared Serious rather than Absurd; or at best, have aimed rather at what is Unfashionable than what is Vicious. For my own part, I have endeavoured to make nothing Ridiculous that is not in some measure Criminal. I have set up the Immoral Man as the Object of Derision: In short, if I have not formed a new Weapon against Vice and Irreligion, I have at least shewn how that Weapon may be put to a right use, which has so often fought the Battels of Impiety and Prophaneness.[11]   C

9 Social ranks.

10 Aim, ambition.

11 In Essay No. 488, Addison reported popular reaction to the more expensive *Spectator:* e.g., "*Eugenius* informs me very obligingly, that he never thought he should have disliked any Passage in my Paper, but that of late there have been two Words in every one of them, which he could heartily wish left out, *viz. Price Two-Pence.*"

The Spectator, No. 450

Wednesday, August 6.

[S t e e l e]

——————*Quaerenda pecunia primum*
Virtus post nummos.[1]

"*Mr.* Spectator,[2]

All Men, through different Paths, make at the same common thing, *Mony;* and it is to her we owe the Politician, the Merchant, and the Lawyer; nay, to be free with you, I believe to that also we are beholden for our *Spectator.* I am apt to think, that could we look into our own Hearts, we should see Mony ingraved in them in more lively and moving Characters than Self-Preservation; for who can reflect upon the Merchant hoisting Sail in a doubtful Pursuit of her, and all Mankind sacrificing their Quiet to her, but must perceive that the Characters of Self-Preservation, (which were doubtless originally the brightest) are sullied, if not wholy defaced; and that those of Mony (which at first was only valuable as a Mean to Security) are of late so brightened, that the Characters of Self-Preservation, like a less Light set by a greater, are become almost imperceptible? Thus has Mony[3] got the upper Hand of what all Mankind formerly thought most dear, *viz.* Security; and I wish I could say she had here put a Stop to her Victories; but, alas! common Honesty fell a Sacrifice to

---

[1] Horace *Epistles* 1. 1. 53–54: "Gold must be sought first, then virtue."

[2] In *Spectator* No. 442, Steele invited readers to submit essays for publication: "*The* Thesis *propos'd for the present Exercise of the Adventurers to write* Spectators, *is* MONEY, *on which Subject all Persons are desired to send in their Thoughts within Ten Days after the Date hereof.*" This letter, whether written by Steele or contributed by another, seems a response to that invitation.

[3] Here the coin imagery ("Characters . . . defaced . . . brightened") gives way to a metaphor of military conquest.

her. This is the Way Scholastick Men talk of[4] the greatest Good in
the World; but I, a Tradesman, shall give you another Account of this
Matter in the plain Narrative of my own Life. I think it proper, in the
first Place, to acquaint my Readers, that since my setting out in the
World, which was in the Year 1660, I never wanted[5] Mony; having
begun with an indifferent good Stock in the Tobacco Trade, to which
I was bred; and by the continual Successes it has pleased Providence to
bless my Endeavours with, am at last arrived at what they call a *Plumb*.[6]
To uphold my Discourse in the Manner of your Wits or Philosophers,
by speaking fine things, or drawing Inferences,[7] as they pretend, from
the Nature of the Subject, I account it vain; having never found any
thing in the Writings of such Men, that did not favour more of the
Invention of the Brain, or what is stiled Speculation, than of sound
Judgment, or profitable Observation. I will readily grant indeed, that
there is what the Wits call Natural in their Talk; which is the utmost
those curious Authors can assume to themselves, and is indeed all they
endeavour at, for they are but lamentable Teachers. And what, I pray,
is Natural? That which is Pleasing and Easie: And what are Pleasing
and Easie? Forsooth, a new Thought or Conceit dressed up in smooth
quaint Language, to make you smile and wag your Head, as being
what you never imagined before, and yet wonder why you had not;
meer frothy Amusements! fit only for Boys or silly Women to be
caught with.

  "It is not my present Intention to instruct my Readers in the Methods of acquiring Riches, that may be the Work of another Essay;[8] but
to exhibit the real and solid Advantages I have found by them in my
long and manifold Experience; nor yet all the Advantages of so worthy and valuable a Blessing, (for who does not know or imagine the
Comforts of being warm or living at Ease? and that Power and Pre-
heminence are their inseparable Attendants?) but only to instance
the great Supports they afford us under the severest Calamities and
Misfortunes; to shew that the Love of them is a special Antidote
against Immorality and Vice, and that the same does likewise natu-

---

4 I.e., debate what is.
5 Lacked.
6 100,000 pounds.
7 By offering elegant language and elaborate logical proofs.
8 No such essay appeared. In *Spectator* No. 509 by Steele, a letter from Mr.
Hezekiah Thrift charges "Mr. William Spectator" with "many Discourses on
the Subject of Money, which you have heretofore promised the Publick, but
have not discharged your self thereof."

rally dispose Men to Actions of Piety and Devotion: All which I can make out by my own Experience, who think my self no ways particular from the rest of Mankind, nor better nor worse by Nature than generally other Men are.[9]

"In the Year 1665, when the Sickness was,[10] I lost by it my Wife and two Children, which were all my Stock. Probably I might have had more, considering I was married between 4 and 5 Years; but finding her to be a teeming Woman, I was careful, as having then little above a Brace of thousand Pounds to carry on my Trade and maintain a Family with. I loved them as usually Men do their Wives and Children, and therefore could not resist the first Impulses of Nature on so wounding a Loss; but I quickly rouzed my self, and found Means to alleviate, and at last conquer my Affliction, by reflecting how that she and her Children having been no great Expence to me, the best Part of her Fortune[11] was still left; that my Charge being reduced to my self, a Journeyman and a Maid, I might live far cheaper than before; and that being now a childless Widower, I might perhaps marry a no less deserving Woman, and with a much better Fortune than she brought, which was but 800 *l*. And to convince my Readers that such Considerations as these were proper and apt to produce such an Effect, I remember it was the constant Observation at that deplorable Time, when so many Hundreds were swept away daily, that the Rich ever bore the Loss of their Families and Relations far better than the Poor; the latter having little or nothing beforehand, and living from Hand to Mouth, placed the whole Comfort and Satisfaction of their Lives in their Wives and Children, and were therefore inconsolable.

"The following Year happened the Fire;[12] at which Time, by good Providence, it was my Fortune to have converted the greatest Part of my Effects into ready Mony, on the Prospect of an extraordinary Advantage which I was preparing to lay Hold on. This Calamity was very terrible and astonishing, the Fury of the Flames being such, that whole Streets, at several distant Places, were destroyed at one and the same Time, so that (as it is well known) almost all our Citizens were burnt out of what they had. But what did I then do? I did not stand gazing on the Ruins of our noble Metropolis; I did not shake my

[9] The succeeding paragraphs are rich in irony. If they are indeed by Steele, they represent some of his finest writing.

[10] London was afflicted with the plague in 1664–1665.

[11] I.e., her dowry.

[12] The Great Fire of London occurred in 1666.

Head, wring my Hands, sigh and shed Tears; I considered with my self what could this avail; I fell a plodding what Advantages might be made of the ready Cash I had, and immediately bethought my self that wonderful Pennyworths[13] might be bought of the Goods that were saved out of the Fire. In short, with about 2000 *l.* and a little Credit, I bought as much Tobacco as raised my Estate to the Value of 10000 *l.* I then *looked on the Ashes of our City, and the Misery of its late Inhabitants, as an Effect of the just Wrath and Indignation of Heaven towards a sinful and perverse People.*

"After this I married again, and that Wife dying, I took another; but both proved to be idle Baggages, the first gave me a great deal of Plague and Vexation by her Extravagancies, and I became one of the By-words of the City. I knew it would be to no manner of Purpose to go about to curb the Fancies and Inclinations of Women, which fly out the more for being restrained; but what I could I did. I watched her narrowly, and by good Luck found her in the Embraces (for which I had two Witnesses with me) of a wealthy Spark of the Court-end of the Town; of whom I recovered 15000 Pounds, which made me Amends for what she had idly squandered, and put a Silence to all my Neighbours, taking off my Reproach by the Gain they saw I had by it. The last[14] died about two Years after I married her, in La-bour of three Children. I conjecture they were begotten by a Country Kinsman of hers, whom, at her Recommendation, I took into my Family, and gave Wages to as a Journey-man. What this Creature expended in Delicacies and high Diet with her Kinsman (as well as I could compute by the Poulterers, Fishmongers, and Grocers Bills) amounted in the said two Years to one hundred eighty six Pounds, four Shillings, and five Pence Half-penny. The fine Apparel, Brace-lets, Lockets and Treats, *&c.* of the other, according to the best Cal-culation, came in three Years and about three Quarters to seven hun-dred forty four Pounds, seven Shillings and nine Pence. After this I resolved never to marry more, and found I had been a Gainer by my Marriages, and the Damages granted me for the Abuses of my Bed, (all Charges deducted) eight thousand three hundred Pounds within a Trifle.

"I come now to shew the good Effects of the Love of Mony on the Lives of Men towards rendering them honest, sober, and religious. When I was a young Man, I had a Mind to make the best of my Wits,

13 Bargains.
14 The other wife.

and over-reached a Country Chap[15] in a Parcel of unsound Goods; to
whom upon his upbraiding, and threatning to expose me for it, I returned the Equivalent of his Loss; and upon his good Advice, wherein
he clearly demonstrated the Folly of such Artifices, which can never
end but in Shame, and the Ruin of all Correspondence, I never after
transgressed. Can your Courtiers, who take Bribes, or your Lawyers
or Physicians in their Practice, or even the Divines who intermeddle
in worldly Affairs, boast of making but one Slip in their Lives, and
of such a thorough and lasting Reformation? Since my coming into
the World I do not remember I was ever overtaken in Drink, save
nine times, one at the Christening of my first Child, thrice at our City
Feasts,[16] and five times at driving of Bargains. My Reformation I can
attribute to nothing so much as the Love and Esteem of Mony, for I
found my self to be extravagant in my Drink, and apt to turn Projector,[17] and make rash Bargains. As for Women, I never knew any,
except my Wives: For my Reader must know, and it is what he may
confide in as an excellent Recipe, That the Love of Business and
Mony is the greatest Mortifier of inordinate Desires imaginable, as
employing the Mind continually in the careful Over-sight of what
one has, in the eager Quest after more, in looking after the Negli-
gences and Deceits of Servants, in the due Entring and Stating of Accounts, in hunting after Chaps, and in the exact Knowledge of the
State of Markets; which Things whoever thoroughly attends, will find
enough and enough to employ his Thoughts on every Moment of the
Day: So that I cannot call to Mind, that in all the Time I was a Husband, which, off and on, was about twelve Years, I ever once thought
of my Wives but in Bed. And, lastly, for Religion, I have ever been
a constant Churchman, both Forenoons and Afternoons on *Sundays*,
never forgetting to be thankful for any Gain or Advantage I had had
that Day; and on *Saturday* Nights, upon casting up my Accounts, I
always was grateful for the Sum of my Weeks Profits, and at *Christmas* for that of the whole Year. It is true perhaps, that my Devotion
has not been the most fervent; which, I think, ought to be imputed
to the Evenness and Sedateness of my Temper, which never would
admit of any Impetuosities of any Sort: And I can remember, that in
my Youth and Prime of Manhood, when my Blood ran brisker, I
took greater Pleasure in Religious Exercises than at present, or many

[15] Chapman, customer.
[16] The Lord-Mayor's Day celebration.
[17] Speculator.

Years past, and that my Devotion sensibly declined as Age, which is dull and unwieldly, came upon me.

"I have, I hope, here proved, that the Love of Mony prevents all Immorality and Vice; which if you will not allow, you must, that the Pursuit of it obliges Men to the same Kind of Life as they would follow if they were really virtuous: Which is all I have to say at present, only recommending to you, that you would think of it, and turn ready Wit into ready Mony as fast as you can. I conclude,

Your Servant,

Ephraim Weed."

T

The Spectator, No. 465

Saturday, August 23.

[A d d i s o n]

Ouâ ratione queas traducere leniter aevum:
Nè te semper inops agitet vexetque cupido;
Nè pavor & rerum mediocriter utilium Spes. Hor.[1]

Having endeavoured in my last *Saturday*'s Paper to shew the great Excellency of Faith,[2] I shall here consider what are the proper Means of strengthning and confirming it in the Mind of Man. Those who delight in reading Books of Controversie, which are written on both sides of the Question in Points of Faith, do very seldom arrive at a fixed and settled Habit of it. They are one Day entirely convinced of its important Truths, and the next meet with something that shakes and disturbs them. The Doubt which was laid[3] revives again, and shews it self in new Difficulties, and that generally for this Reason, because the Mind which is perpetually tost in Controversies and Disputes, is apt to forget the Reasons which had once set it at rest, and to be disquieted with any former Perplexity, when it appears in a new Shape, or is started by a different Hand. As nothing is more laudable than an

1 Horace *Epistles* 1. 18. 97–99: "How can you pass your days in tranquillity, lest penniless greed ever drive and vex you, or fear and hope concerning things of little use."

2 In *Spectator* No. 459, Addison declared that "the Excellency of Faith" consists in clarifying points of morality; furnishing new motives for virtuous living; offering truer notions of the nature of God, of others, and of ourselves; in showing the deformity of vice; and in making morality effectual to salvation.

3 Put down, quelled; as one lays a ghost.

Enquiry after Truth, so nothing is more irrational than to pass
away our whole Lives, without determining our selves one way or
other in those Points which are of the last[4] Importance to us.
There are indeed many things from which we may with-hold our
Assent;[5] but in Cases by which we are to regulate our Lives, it is
the greatest Absurdity to be wavering and unsettled, without closing with that Side[6] which appears the most safe and the most
probable. The first Rule therefore which I shall lay down is this,
that when by Reading or Discourse we find our selves thoroughly
convinced of the Truth of any Article, and of the Reasonableness
of our Belief in it, we should never after suffer our selves to call
it into question. We may perhaps forget the Arguments which occasioned our Conviction, but we ought to remember the Strength
they had with us, and therefore still to retain the Conviction
which they once produced. This is no more than what we do in
every common Art or Science, nor is it possible to act otherwise,
considering the Weakness and Limitation of our intellectual Faculties. It was thus, that *Latimer*,[7] one of the glorious Army of
Martyrs who introduced the Reformation in *England,* behaved
himself in that great Conference which was managed between the
most Learned among the Protestants and Papists in the Reign of
Queen *Mary.* This venerable old Man knowing how his Abilities
were impaired by Age, and that it was impossible for him to recollect all those Reasons which had directed him in the Choice of
his Religion, left his Companions who were in the full Possession
of their Parts and Learning, to baffle and confound their Antagonists by the Force of Reason. As for himself he only repeated to
his Adversaries the Articles in which he firmly believed, and in
the Profession of which he was determined to die. It is in this manner that the Mathematician proceeds upon Propositions which
he has once demonstrated, and though the Demonstration may
have slipt out of his Memory, he builds upon the Truth, because

4 Utmost, ultimate.

5 See Addison's attitude concerning witches in *Spectator* No. 117.

6 Accepting that side of the argument.

7 Hugh Latimer (1485?–1555), Protestant prelate who was burned at the
stake. The account here is from Bishop Gilbert Burnet's *History of the Reformation of the Church of England* (1681).

he knows it was demonstrated. This Rule is absolutely necessary for weaker Minds, and in some measure for Men of the greatest Abilities; but to these last I would propose, in the second place, that they should lay up in their Memories, and all always keep by them in a readiness, those Arguments which appear to them of the greatest Strength, and which cannot be got over by all the Doubts and Cavils[8] of Infidelity.

But, in the third place, there is nothing which strengthens Faith more than Morality. Faith and Morality naturally produce each other. A Man is quickly convinced of the Truth of Religion, who finds it is not against his Interest that it should be true.[9] The Pleasure he receives at present, and the Happiness which he promises himself from it hereafter, will both dispose him very powerfully to give Credit to it, according to the ordinary Observation that *we are easie to believe what we wish*. It is very certain, that a Man of sound Reason cannot forbear closing with Religion upon an impartial Examination of it; but at the same time it is as certain, that Faith is kept alive in us, and gathers Strength from Practice more than from Speculation.

There is still another Method which is more Persuasive than any of the former, and that is an habitual Adoration of the Supreme Being, as well in constant Acts of Mental Worship, as in outward Forms. The Devout Man does not only believe but feels there is a Deity. He has actual Sensations of him; his Experience concurs with his Reason; he sees him more and more in all his Intercourses with him, and even in this Life almost loses his Faith in Conviction.[10]

The last Method which I shall mention for the giving Life to a Man's Faith, is frequent Retirement from the World, accompanied with religious Meditation. When a Man thinks of any thing in the Darkness of the Night, whatever deep Impressions it may make in his Mind, they are apt to vanish as soon as the Day breaks about him. The Light and Noise of the Day, which are perpetu-

8 Trivial objections.

9 This is dangerously like the prudential sentiments expressed by Ephraim Weed in *Spectator* No. 450.

10 "Faith" is belief in things one cannot see. In the next life, one will be convinced by the sight of God.

ally solliciting his Senses, and calling off his Attention, wear out of[11] his Mind the Thoughts that imprinted themselves in it, with so much Strength, during the Silence and Darkness of the Night. A Man finds the same difference as to himself in a Crowd and in a Solitude; the Mind is stunned and dazzled amidst that variety of Objects which press upon her in a great City: She cannot apply her self to the Consideration of those things which are of the utmost Concern to her. The Cares or Pleasures of the World strike in with every Thought, and a Multitude of vicious Examples give a kind of Justification to our Folly. In our Retirements every thing disposes us to be serious. In Courts and Cities we are entertained with the Works of Men, in the Country with those of God. One is the Province of Art, the other of Nature. Faith and Devotion naturally grow in the Mind of every reasonable Man, who sees the Impressions of Divine Power and Wisdom in every Object on which he casts his Eye. The Supream Being has made the best Arguments for his own Existence, in the Formation of the Heavens and the Earth, and these are Arguments which a Man of Sense cannot forbear attending to, who is out of the Noise and Hurry of human Affairs. *Aristotle* says, that should a Man live under Ground, and there converse with Works of Art and Mechanism, and should afterwards be brought up into the open Day, and see the several Glories of the Heav'n and Earth, he would immediately pronounce them the Works of such a Being as we define God to be.[12] The Psalmist has very beautiful Strokes of Poetry to this purpose, in that exalted Strain, *The Heavens declare the Glory of God: And the Firmament sheweth his handy Work. One Day telleth another: And one Night certifieth another. There is neither Speech nor Language: But their Voices are heard among them. Their Sound is gone out into all Lands: And their Words into the Ends of the World.*[13] As such a bold and sublime Manner of Thinking furnishes very noble Matter for an Ode, the Reader may see it wrought into the following one.

---

[11] Wear away from.

[12] Aristotle, in the lost treatise *De Philosophia*, which is quoted by Cicero in *Of the Nature of the Gods*, 2. 37. 95.

[13] Psalms 19:1–4 (Prayer Book version).

I.

The Spacious Firmament on high,
With all the blue Etherial Sky,
And spangled Heav'ns, a Shining Frame,
Their great Original proclaim:
Th' unwearied Sun, from Day to Day,
Does his Creator's Power display,
And publishes to every Land
The Work of an Almighty Hand.

II.

Soon as the Evening Shades prevail,
The Moon takes up the wondrous Tale,
And nightly to the listning Earth
Repeats the Story of her Birth:
Whilst all the Stars that round her burn,
And all the Planets, in their turn,
Confirm the Tidings as they rowl,
And spread the Truth from Pole to Pole.

III.

What though, in solemn Silence, all
Move round the dark terrestrial Ball?
What tho' nor[14] *real Voice nor Sound*
Amid their radient Orbs be found?
In Reason's Ear they all rejoice,
And utter forth a glorious Voice,
For ever singing, as they shine,
"The Hand that made us is Divine."

C

14 Neither.

The Spectator, No. 470

Friday, August 29.

[Addison]

Turpe est difficiles habere nugas,
Et stultus est labor ineptiarum. Mart.[1]

I have been very often disappointed of late Years, when upon examining the new Edition of a Classick Author, I have found above half the Volume taken up with various Readings.[2] When I have expected to meet with a Learned Note upon a doubtful Passage in a *Latin* Poet, I have only been informed, that such or such ancient Manuscripts for an *et* write an *ac*, or of some other notable Discovery of the like Importance. Indeed, when a different Reading gives us a different Sense, or a new Elegance in an Author, the Editor does very well in taking Notice of it; but when he only entertains us with the several ways of Spelling the same Word, and gathers together the various Blunders and Mistakes of twenty or thirty different Transcribers, they[3] only take up the Time of the learned Reader, and puzzle the Minds of the Ignorant. I have often fancied with my self how enraged an old *Latin* Author would be, should he see the several Absurdities in Sense and Grammar, which are imputed to him by some or other of these various Readings. In one[4] he speaks Nonsense; in another makes

---

[1] Martial *Epigrams* 2. 86. 9–10: "It is a disgrace to undertake a difficult trifle, and the labor of absurdities is fatuous."

[2] I.e., variant readings, as they have appeared in one or more manuscripts or in the succeeding editions of a text.

[3] The antecedents are "several ways of Spelling" and "various Blunders and Mistakes."

[4] I.e., in one reading.

use of a Word that was never heard of: And indeed, there is scarce
a Solecism[5] in Writing which the best Author is not guilty of, if
we may be at Liberty to read him in the Words of some Manuscript, which the laborious Editor has thought fit to examine in
the Prosecution of his Work.

I question not but the Ladies and pretty Fellows will be very
curious to understand what it is that I have been hitherto talking
of. I shall therefore give them a Notion of this Practice, by endeavouring to write after the manner of several Persons who make
an eminent Figure in the Republick of Letters. To this end we
will suppose, that the following Song is an old Ode which I present to the Publick in a new Edition, with the several various
Readings which I find of it in former Editions, and in Ancient
Manuscripts. Those who cannot relish the various Readings, will
perhaps find their Account[6] in the Song, which never before appeared in Print.

> *My Love was fickle once and changing,*
>   *Nor e'er would settle in my Heart;*
> *From Beauty still to Beauty ranging,*
>   *In ev'ry Face I found a Dart.*[7]
>
> *'Twas first a Charming Shape enslav'd me;*
>   *An Eye then gave the fatal Stroke:*
> *'Till by her Wit* Corinna *sav'd me,*
>   *And all my former Fetters broke.*
>
> *But now a long and lasting Anguish*
>   *For* Belvidera *I endure;*
> *Hourly I Sigh and hourly Languish,*
>   *Nor hope to find the wonted[8] Cure.*
>
> *For here the false unconstant Lover,*
>   *After a thousand Beauties shown,*
> *Does new surprising Charms discover,*
>   *And finds Variety in One.*
>
> *Various Readings.*

5 A grammatical blunder.
6 Find value or pleasure.
7 I.e., Cupid's dart.
8 Usual.

Stanza the First, Verse the First, *And changing.*] The *and* in some Manuscripts is written thus, *&,* but that in the *Cotton* Library writes it in three distinct Letters.

Verse the Second. *Nor e'er would.*] *Aldus*[9] reads it *ever would;* but as this would hurt the Metre, we have restored it to its genuine Reading, by observing that *Syraenesis*[10] which had been neglected by ignorant Transcribers.

Ibid. *In my Heart.*] *Scaliger,*[11] and others, *on my Heart.*

Verse the Fourth. *I found a Dart.*] The *Vatican* Manuscript for *I* reads *it,* but this must have been the Hallucination of the Transcriber, who probably mistook the Dash of the *I.* for a *T.*

Stanza the Second, Verse the Second. *The fatal Stroke.*] *Scioppius, Salmasius,*[12] and many others, for *the* read *a,* but I have stuck to the usual Reading.

Verse the Third. *'Till by her Wit.*] Some Manuscripts have it *his Wit,* others *your,* others *their Wit.* But as I find *Corinna* to be the Name of a Woman in other Authors, I cannot doubt but it should be *her.*

Stanza the Third, Verse the First. *A long and lasting Anguish.*] The *German* Manuscript reads *a lasting Passion,* but the Rhyme will not admit it.

Verse the Second. *For* Belvidera *I endure.*] Did not all the Manuscripts reclaim,[13] I should change *Belvidera* into *Pelvidera; Pelvis* being used by several of the Ancient Comick Writers for a Looking-Glass, by which means the Etymology of the Word is very visible, and *Pelvidera* will signifie a Lady who often looks in her Glass, as indeed she had very good reason, if she had all those Beauties which our Poet here ascribes to her.

Verse the Third. *Hourly I sigh and hourly languish.*] Some for the Word *hourly* read *daily,* and others *nightly;* the last has great Authorities of its side.

---

[9] See *Tatler* No. 158, n. 4.

[10] Contraction.

[11] See *Spectator* No. 297, n. 15.

[12] Caspar Schoppe (1576–1649), the German scholar; and Claude de Saumaise (1588–1653), the French classical scholar.

[13] Protest.

Verse the Fourth. *The wonted Cure.*] The Elder *Stevens*[14] reads *wanted Cure.*

Stanza the Fourth, Verse the Second. *After a thousand Beauties.*] In several Copies we meet with a *Hundred Beauties,* by the usual Error of the Transcribers, who probably omitted a Cypher, and had not taste enough to know, that the Word *Thousand* was ten Times a greater Compliment to the Poet's Mistress than an *Hundred.*

Verse the Fourth. *And finds Variety in one.*] Most of the Ancient Manuscripts have it *in two.* Indeed so many of them concur in this last Reading, that I am very much in doubt whether it ought not to take place. There are but two Reasons which incline me to the Reading, as I have Published it; First, because the Rhime, and, Secondly, because the Sense is preserved by it. It might likewise proceed from the Oscitancy[15] of Transcribers, who to dispatch their Work the sooner, used to write all Numbers in Cypher, and seeing the Figure 1 followed by a little Dash of the Pen, as is customary in old Manuscripts, they perhaps mistook the Dash for a second Figure, and by casting up both together composed out of them the Figure 2. But this I shall leave to the Learned, without determining any thing in a Matter of so great Uncertainty.   C

14 Robert Estienne, or Stephanus (1503–1559), French printer.
15 Drowsiness.

The Spectator, No. 473

Tuesday, September 2.

[S t e e l e]

Quid? si quis vultu torvo ferus & pede nudo
Exiguaeque togae simulet textore Catonem;
Virtutemne repraesentet moresque Catonis? Hor.[1]

To the Spectator.

"*Sir,*

I am now in the Country, and employ most of my Time in reading, or thinking upon what I have read. Your Paper comes constantly
down to me, and it affects me so much, that I find my Thoughts run
into your Way; and I recommend to you a Subject upon which you
have not yet touched, and that is the Satisfaction some Men seem to
take in their Imperfections, I think one may call it Glorying in their
Insufficiency; a certain great Author[2] is of Opinion it is the contrary
to Envy, tho' perhaps it may proceed from it. Nothing is so common,
as to hear Men of this sort speaking of themselves, add to their own
Merit (as they think) by impairing it, in praising themselves for their
Defects, freely allowing they commit some few frivolous Errors, in
order to be esteemed Persons of uncommon Talents and great Qualifications. They are generally professing an injudicious Neglect of
Dancing, Fencing and Riding, as also an unjust Contempt for Travelling and the modern Languages; as for their Part (say they) they
never valued or troubled their Head about them. This panegyrical
Satyr on themselves certainly is worthy of your Animadversion. I
have known one of these Gentlemen think himself obliged to forget

---

[1] Horace *Epistles* 1. 19. 12–14: "What? If a wild person with a savage face,
bare feet, and a scanty toga should impersonate Cato, would he represent the
virtue and moral of Cato?"

[2] Jean de la Bruyère (1645–1696), French satirist and social critic. The reference here is from chapter 10 of his most famous work *Les Caractères* (1688).

the Day of an Appointment, and sometimes even that you spoke to
him; and when you see 'em, they hope you'll pardon 'em, for they
have the worst Memory in the World. One of 'em started up t'other
Day in some Confusion, and said, Now I think on't, I'm to meet Mr.
Mortmain the Attorney about some Business, but whether it is to Day
or to Morrow, faith, I can't tell: Now to my certain Knowledge he
knew his Time to a Moment, and was there accordingly. These for-
getful Persons have, to heighten their Crime, generally the best Memories of any People, as I have found out by their remembring sometimes through Inadvertency. Two or three of them that I know can
say most of our modern Tragedies by Heart. I asked a Gentleman the
other Day that is famous for a good Carver, (at which Acquisition he
is out of Countenance, imagining it may detract from some of his
more essential Qualifications) to help me to something that was near
him;[3] but he excused himself, and blushing told me, Of all things he
could never carve in his Life; tho' it can be proved upon him, that
he cuts up, disjoints, and uncases with incomparable Dexterity. I
would not be understood as if I thought it laudable for a Man of
Quality and Fortune to rival the Acquisitions of Artificers, and endeavour to excel in little handy Qualities; No, I argue only against
being ashamed at what is really Praiseworthy. As these Pretences to
Ingenuity shew themselves several Ways, you'll often see a Man of
this Temper ashamed to be clean, and setting up for Wit only from
Negligence in his Habit.[4] Now I am upon this Head,[5] I can't help
observing also upon a very different Folly proceeding from the same
Cause. As these above-mentioned arise from affecting an Equality
with Men of greater Talents from having the same Faults, there are
others who would come at a Parallel with those above them, by possessing little Advantages which they want.[6] I heard a young Man not
long ago, who has Sense, comfort himself in his Ignorance of Greek,
Hebrew, and the Orientals:[7] At the same Time that he published his
Aversion to these Languages, he said that the Knowledge of 'em was
rather a Diminution than an Advancement of a Man's Character, tho'
at the same Time I know he languishes and repines he is not Master
of them himself. Whenever I take[8] any of these fine Persons, thus de-

[3] I.e., to cut a piece of meat for me.

[4] I.e., posing as an intellectual simply by neglecting his clothes.

[5] Subject.

[6] Among the "little Advantages" those above them lacked might be ignorance of languages.

[7] The Oriental languages.

[8] Encounter.

tracting from what they don't understand, I tell them I will complain
to you, and say I am sure you will not allow it an Exception against
a thing, that he who contemns it is an Ignorant in it.

I am,

Sir,

Your most humble Servant.

S. P."

"*Mr.* Spectator,
I am a Man of a very good Estate, and am honourably in Love. I
hope you will allow, when the ultimate Purpose is honest, there may
be, without Trespass against Innocence, some Toying by the Way.
People of Condition are perhaps too distant and formal on those
Occasions; but, however that is, I am to confess to you, that I have
writ some Verses to attone for my Offence. You profess'd Authors are
a little severe upon us, who write like Gentlemen: But if you are a
Friend to Love, you will insert my Poem. You cannot imagine how
much Service it will do me with my Fair one, as well as Reputation
with all my Friends, to have something of mine in the *Spectator.* My
Crime was, that I snatch'd a Kiss, and my Poetical Excuse as follows:

I.

Bellinda, see from yonder Flowers
The Bee flies loaded to its Cell;
Can you perceive what it devours?
Are they impair'd in Shew or Smell?

II.

So, tho' I robb'd you of a Kiss,
Sweeter than their Ambrosial Dew,
Why are you angry at my Bliss?
Has it at all impoverish'd you?

III.

'Tis by this Cunning I contrive,
In spight of your unkind Reserve,
To keep my famish'd Love alive,
Which you inhumanly would starve.[9]

I am,

Sir,

Your humble Servant,

Timothy Stanza."

[9] In Rae Blanchard's edition of Steele's *Occasional Verse* (1952), this is discussed among the "poems of doubtful authorship."

"*Sir,*   *Aug.* 23. 1712.
Having a little Time upon my Hands, I could not think of bestowing it better, than in writing an Epistle to the Spectator, which I now
do, and am,

Sir,

Your humble Servant,

Bob Short.

P. S. If you approve of my Stile, I am likely enough to become your
Correspondent. I desire your Opinion of it. I design it for that Way
of Writing called by the Judicious the *Familiar.*"   T

The Spectator, No. 475

Thursday, September 4.

[Addison]

————*quae res in se neque Consilium neque modum*
Habet ullum, eam consilio regere non potes. Ter.[1]

It is an old Observation, which has been made of Politicians who would rather ingratiate themselves with their Sovereign, than promote his real Service, That they accommodate their Counsels to his Inclinations, and advise him to such Actions only as his Heart is naturally set upon. The Privy-councellor[2] of one in Love must observe the same Conduct, unless he would forfeit the Friendship of the Person who desires his Advice. I have known several odd Cases of this Nature. *Hipparchus* was going to marry a common Woman,[3] but being resolved to do nothing without the Advice of his Friend *Philander,* he consulted him upon the Occasion. *Philander* told him his Mind freely, and represented his Mistress to him in such strong Colours, that the next Morning he received a Challenge for his Pains, and before Twelve a Clock was run through the Body by the Man who had asked his Advice. *Celia* was more prudent on the like Occasion; she desired *Leonilla* to give her Opinion freely upon a young Fellow who made his Addresses to her. *Leonilla,* to oblige her, told her with great Frankness, that she looked upon him as one of the most worthless —*Celia,* foreseeing what a Character she was to expect, begged her not to go on, for that she had been privately married to him

---

1 Terence *Eunuchus* 57–58: "A thing that in itself has neither measure nor consideration, reason cannot rule."

2 A member of the king's private council.

3 A harlot.

above a Fortnight. The Truth of it is, a Woman seldom asks Advice before she has bought her Wedding-Cloaths. When she has made her own Choice, for Form's Sake she sends a *Conge d'elire*[4] to her Friends.

If we look into the secret Springs and Motives that set People at Work in these Occasions, and put them upon asking Advice, which they never intend to take, I look upon it to be none of the least That they are incapable of keeping a Secret which is so very pleasing to them. A Girl longs to tell her Confident, that she hopes to be married in a little Time, and, in order to talk of the pretty Fellow that dwells so much in her Thoughts, asks her very gravely, what she would advise her to in a Case of so much Difficulty. Why else should *Melissa,* who had not a Thousand Pound in the World, go into every Quarter of the Town to ask her Acquaintance whether they would advise her to take *Tom Townly,* that made his Addresses to her with an Estate of Five Thousand a Year? 'Tis very pleasant, on this Occasion, to hear the Lady propose her Doubts, and to see the Pains she is at to get over them.

I must not here omit a Practice that is in Use among the vainer Part of our own Sex, who will often ask a Friend's Advice, in relation to a Fortune[5] whom they are never likely to come at. Will Honeycomb, who is now on the Verge of Threescore, took me aside not long since, and asked me in his most serious Look, Whether I would advise him to marry my Lady *Betty Single,* who, by the Way, is one of the greatest Fortunes about Town. I stared him full in the Face upon so strange a Question; upon which he immediately gave me an Inventory of her Jewels and Estate, adding, that he was resolved to do nothing in a Matter of such Consequence without my Approbation. Finding he would have an Answer, I told him, if he could get the Lady's Consent, he had mine. This is about the Tenth Match which, to my Knowledge, Will has consulted his Friends upon, without ever opening his Mind to the Party herself.

I have been engaged in this Subject by the following Letter,

4 "Permission to elect," a letter sent by the government giving permission to a religious body to fill a vacant see or abbacy by election. Actually, it was permission to accept the choice of the Sovereign.

5 A wealthy lady.

which comes to me from some notable young Female Scribe, who, by the Contents of it, seems to have carried Matters so far, that she is ripe for asking Advice; but as I would not lose her Good-will, nor forfeit the Reputation which I have with her for Wisdom, I shall only communicate the Letter to the Publick, without returning any Answer to it.

"*Mr.* Spectator,

Now, Sir, the Thing is this: Mr. *Shapely* is the prettiest Gentleman about Town. He is very tall, but not too tall neither. He dances like an Angel. His Mouth is made I don't know how, but 'tis the prettiest that I ever saw in my Life. He is always laughing, for he has an infinite Deal of Wit. If you did but see how he rolls his Stockings! He has a thousand pretty Fancies, and I am sure, if you saw him, you would like him. He is a very good Scholar, and can talk *Latin* as fast as *English*. I wish you could but see him dance. Now you must understand poor Mr. *Shapely* has no Estate; but how can he help that, you know? And yet my Friends are so unreasonable as to be always teizing me about him, because he has no Estate. But, I am sure, he has that that is better than an Estate; for he is a good-natured, ingenious, modest, civil, tall, well-bred, handsome Man, and I am obliged to him for his Civilities ever since I saw him. I forgot to tell you that he has black Eyes,[6] and looks upon me now and then as if he had Tears in them. And yet my Friends are so unreasonable, that they would have me be uncivil to him. I have a good Portion[7] which they cannot hinder me of, and I shall be Fourteen on the 29th Day of *August* next, and am therefore willing to settle in the World as soon as I can, and so is Mr. *Shapely*. But every Body I advise with here is poor Mr. *Shapely*'s Enemy. I desire therefore you will give me your Advice, for I know you are a wise Man, and if you advise me well, I am resolved to follow it. I heartily wish you could see him dance, and am,

Sir,

Your most humble Servant,

B. D.

He loves your *Spectators* mightily."

C

6 Dark eyes.
7 Estate, fortune.

The Spectator, No. 487

Thursday, September 18.

[A d d i s o n]

⁕

—————— —————— —————*Cum prostrata sopore*
Urget membra quies, & mens sine pondere ludit. Petr.[1]

Tho' there are many Authors, who have written on Dreams,
they have generally considered them only as Revelations of what
has already happened in distant Parts of the World, or as Presages
of what is to happen in future Periods of Time.

I shall consider this Subject in another Light, as Dreams may
give us some Idea of the great Excellency of an Human Soul, and
some Intimation of its Independency on[2] Matter.

In the first Place, our Dreams are great Instances of that Activity which is natural to the Humane Soul, and which it is not in
the Power of Sleep to deaden or abate. When the Man appears
tired and worn out with the Labours of the Day, this active Part
in his Composition is still busie and unwearied. When the Organs
of Sense want[3] their due Repose and necessary Reparations, and
the Body is no longer able to keep Pace with that spiritual Substance to which it is united, the Soul exerts her self in her several
Faculties, and continues in Action 'till her Partner is again qualified to bear her Company. In this Case Dreams look like the Relaxations and Amusements of the Soul, when she is disencum-

---

[1] Petronius Arbiter, from a poem found in one MS. of the *Satyricon:* "While
sleep oppresses the tired limbs, the weightless mind plays."

[2] Independence of.

[3] Lack.

bered of her Machine,[4] her Sports and Recreations, when she has
laid her Charge asleep.

In the Second Place, Dreams are an Instance of that Agility
and Perfection which is natural to the Faculties of the Mind,
when they are disengaged from the Body. The Soul is clogged and
retarded in her Operations, when she acts in Conjunction with a
Companion that is so heavy and unwieldy in its Motions. But in
Dreams it is wonderful, to observe with what a Sprightliness and
Alacrity she exerts her self. The flow of Speech make unpremedi-
tated Harangues, or converse readily in Languages that they are
but little acquainted with. The Grave abound in Pleasantries, the
Dull in Repartees, and Points of Wit. There is not a more painful
Action of the Mind, than Invention;[5] yet in Dreams it works with
that Ease and Activity, that we are not sensible when the Faculty
is employed. For Instance, I believe every one, some Time or
other, dreams that he is reading Papers, Books or Letters, in which
Case the Invention prompts so readily, that the Mind is imposed
upon, and mistakes its own Suggestions for the Compositions of
another.[6]

I shall, under this Head, quote a Passage out of the *Religio
Medici,*[7] in which the ingenious Author gives an Account of himself in his dreaming, and his waking Thoughts. *We are somewhat
more than our selves in our Sleeps, and the Slumber of the Body
seems to be but the Waking of the Soul. It is the Ligation*[8] *of
Sense, but the Liberty of Reason, and our waking Conceptions do
not match the Fancies of our Sleeps. At my Nativity my Ascendant
was the watery Sign of* Scorpius: *I was born in the Planetary Hour
of* Saturn, *and, I think, I have a Piece of that leaden Planet in me.*[9]
I am no way facetious, nor disposed for the Mirth and Galliard-

---

[4] I.e., the mechanical body which she operates.

[5] Creating new ideas.

[6] I.e., the sleeper dreams of reading an author's writing, which has really
been created by his own mind.

[7] A treatise (1643) by Sir Thomas Browne (1605–1682), the celebrated physician. The quotation is from part 2, paragraph 12.

[8] Binding fast.

[9] Browne uses the language of astrology to demonstrate that he is, while
awake, of a dull, leaden disposition. Scorpius is the sign for October, commonly

ize[10] *of Company; yet in one Dream I can compose a whole Comedy, behold the Action, apprehend the Jests, and laugh my self awake at the Conceits*[11] *thereof. Were my Memory as faithful as my Reason is then fruitful, I would never study but in my Dreams; and this Time also would I chuse for my Devotions; but our grosser Memories have then so little hold of our abstracted Understandings, that they forget the Story, and can only relate to our awaked Souls, a confused and broken Tale of that that has passed. —Thus it is observed that Men sometimes, upon the Hour of their Departure,*[12] *do speak and reason above themselves, for then the Soul beginning to be freed from the Ligaments of the Body, begins to reason like her self, and to discourse in a Strain above Mortality.*

We may likewise observe in the third Place, that the Passions affect the Mind with greater Strength when we are a-sleep, than when we are awake. Joy and Sorrow give us more vigorous Sensations of Pain or Pleasure at this Time, than at any other. Devotion likewise, as the excellent Author above-mentioned has hinted, is in a very particular Manner heightned and inflamed, when it rises in the Soul at a Time that the Body is thus laid at Rest. Every Man's Experience will inform him in this Matter, though it is very probable, that this may happen differently in different Constitutions. I shall conclude this Head[13] with the two following Problems, which I shall leave to the Solution of my Reader. Supposing a Man always happy in his Dreams, and miserable in his waking Thoughts, and that his Life was equally divided between them, whether would he be more happy or miserable? Were a Man a King in his Dreams, and a Beggar awake, and dreamt as consequentially, and in as continued unbroken Schemes,

---

a rainy month. Saturn, if in the ascendant—i.e., just rising above the eastern horizon at the moment of a child's birth—was thought to impart a gloomy, morose nature to the individual being born.

[10] Gaiety; from *galliard,* a lively dance.

[11] Fanciful ideas.

[12] Their death. It was traditionally believed that men spoke with sublimity —and even prophecy—in their last moments.

[13] Subject.

as he thinks when awake, whether he would be in Reality a King or Beggar, or rather whether he wou'd not be both?

There is another Circumstance which methinks gives us a very high Idea of the Nature of the Soul, in regard to what passes in Dreams, I mean that innumerable Multitude and Variety of Ideas which then arise in her. Were that active watchful Being only conscious of her own Existence at such a time, what a painful Solitude would her Hours of Sleep be? Were the Soul sensible of her being alone in her sleeping Moments, after the same Manner that she is sensible of it while awake, the Time would hang very heavy on her, as it often actually does when she dreams that she is in such a Solitude,

> ———*Semperque relinqui*
> *Sola sibi, semper longam incomitata videtur*
> *Ire viam!*———Virg.[14]

But this Observation I only make by the Way. What I would here remark is that wonderful Power in the Soul, of producing her own Company on these Occasions. She converses with numberless Beings of her own Creation, and is transported into ten thousand Scenes of her own raising. She is herself the Theatre, the Actors, and the Beholder. This puts me in Mind of a Saying which I am infinitely pleased with, and which *Plutarch* ascribes to *Heraclitus*, *That all Men whilst they are awake are in one common World; but that each of them, when he is asleep, is in a World of his own.*[15] The waking Man is conversant in the World of Nature, when he sleeps he retires to a private World that is particular to himself. There seems something in this Consideration that intimates to us a natural Grandeur and Perfection in the Soul, which is rather to be admired than explained.

I must not omit that Argument for the Excellency of the Soul, which I have seen quoted out of *Tertullian*,[16] namely, its Power

---

[14] Virgil *Aeneid* 4. 466–468: "She dreams of an unending solitude, of wandering alone in a lost land."

[15] Plutarch, "Of superstition" (*Moralia*, 166C). The reference is to Heraclitus of Ephesus, the Greek philosopher of the 6th–5th century B.C.

[16] Tertullian (160?–230? A.D.), one of the fathers of the church, discussed the power of prophecying in dreams in *De Anima,* 46.

of Divining in Dreams. That several such Divinations have been made, none can question who believes the Holy Writings,[17] or who has but the least Degree of a common historical Faith, there being innumerable Instances of this Nature in several Authors, both Ancient and Modern, Sacred and Prophane.[18] Whether such dark Presages,[19] such Visions of the Night proceed from any latent Power in the Soul, during this her State of Abstraction, or from any Communication with the Supreme Being, or from any Operation of Subordinate Spirits,[20] has been a great Dispute among the Learned; the Matter of Fact is I think incontestable, and has been looked upon as such by the greatest Writers, who have been never suspected either of Superstition or Enthusiasm.[21]

I do not suppose, that the Soul in these Instances is entirely loose and unfettered from the Body: It is sufficient, if she is not so far sunk, and immersed in Matter, nor intangled and perplexed in her Operations, with such Motions of Blood and Spirits, as when she actuates the Machine in its waking Hours. The corporeal Union[22] is slackened enough to give the Mind more Play. The Soul seems gathered within her self, and recovers that Spring[23] which is broke and weakened, when she operates more in concert with the Body.

The Speculations I have here made, if they are not Arguments, they are at least strong Intimations, not only of the Excellency of an Humane Soul, but of its Independance on the Body; and if they do not prove, do at least confirm these two great Points, which are established by many other Reasons that are altogether unanswerable.   O

[17] The Bible records the dreams of Laban, of Joseph, of Solomon, of St. Joseph, of Pilate's wife, etc. Joel 2:28 says explicitly: "And it shall come to pass afterward, that I will pour out my spirit upon all flesh; and your sons and daughters shall prophesy, your old men shall dream dreams, your young men shall see visions."

[18] Secular.

[19] Prophetic visions.

[20] Angelic spirits, ministers of the Supreme Being.

[21] See *Spectator* No. 407, n. 5.

[22] Union of the soul with the body.

[23] Liveliness, activity.

The Spectator, No. 494

Friday, September 26.

[Addison]

Aegritudinem laudare, unam rem maxime detestabilem, quorum est tandem Philosophorum? Cic.[1]

About an Age ago[2] it was the Fashion in *England,* for every one that would be thought religious, to throw as much Sanctity as possible into his Face, and in particular to abstain from all Appearances of Mirth and Pleasantry, which were looked upon as the Marks of a Carnal Mind. The Saint was of a sorrowful Countenance, and generally eaten up with Spleen[3] and Melancholy. A Gentleman, who was lately a great Ornament to the learned World, has diverted me more than once with an Account of the Reception which he met with from a very famous Independent Minister, who was Head of a College in those Times.[4] This Gentleman was then a young Adventurer in the Republick of Letters, and just fitted out for the University with a good Cargo of *Latin* and *Greek.* His Friends were resolved that he should try his Fortune at an Election which was drawing near in the College, of which the Independent Minister, whom I have before mentioned

---

[1] Cicero *Tusculan Disputations* 4. 25. 55: "To what sect of philosophers does it belong, pray, to extol melancholy, the most detestable thing in nature?"

[2] I.e., during the period of the Commonwealth (1649–1660) when Puritan ideals prevailed.

[3] Ill nature. See *Spectator* No. 3, n. 6.

[4] Commonly, the gentleman who was "a great Ornament to the Learned World" has been identified as Anthony Henley (1666–1711) and the "famous Independent Minister" as Dr. Thomas Goodwin (1600–1679). The latter identification is almost certainly correct.

was Governour. The Youth, according to Custom, waited on[5] him in Order to be examined. He was received at the Door by a Servant, who was one of that gloomy Generation that were then in Fashion. He conducted him, with great Silence and Seriousness, to a long Gallery which was darkned at Noonday, and had only a single Candle burning in it. After a short Stay in this melancholy Apartment, he was led into a Chamber hung with Black, where he entertained himself for some Time by the glimmering of a Taper, 'till at length the Head of the Colledge came out to him, from an inner Room, with half a Dozen Night-Caps upon his Head, and a religious Horror in his Countenance. The young Man trembled; but his Fears encreased, when, instead of being asked what Progress he had made in Learning, he was examined how he abounded in Grace. His *Latin* and *Greek* stood him in little stead; he was to give an Account only of the State of his Soul, whether he was of the Number of the Elect;[6] what was the Occasion of his Conversion; upon what Day of the Month, and Hour of the Day it happened; how it was carried on, and when compleated? The whole Examination was summed up with one short Question, Namely, *Whether he was prepared for Death?* The Boy, who had been bred up by honest Parents, was frighted out of his Wits at the Solemnity of the Proceeding, and by the last dreadful Interrogatory; so that upon making his Escape out of this House of Mourning he could never be brought a second Time to the Examination, as not being able to go through the Terrors of it.

Notwithstanding this general Form and Outside of Religion is pretty well worn out among us,[7] there are many Persons, who, by a natural Unchearfulness of Heart, mistaken Notions of Piety, or Weakness of Understanding, love to indulge this uncomfortable Way of Life, and give up themselves a Prey to Grief and Melancholy. Superstitious Fears, and groundless Scruples, cut them off from the Pleasures of Conversation, and all those social Entertainments which are not only innocent but laudable; as if Mirth

[5] Called upon.

[6] I.e., one of God's "elect," one of those destined for salvation.

[7] Though these external manifestations of religious belief are no longer popular or common.

was made for Reprobates, and Chearfulness of Heart denied those who are the only Persons that have a proper Title to it.

Sombrius is one of these Sons of Sorrow. He thinks himself obliged in Duty to be sad and disconsolate. He looks on a sudden Fit of Laughter, as a Breach of his Baptismal Vow. An innocent Jest startles him like Blasphemy. Tell him of one who is advanced to a Title of Honour, he lifts up his Hands and Eyes; describe a Publick Ceremony, he shakes his Head; shew him a gay Equipage, he blesses himself. All the little Ornaments of Life are Pomps and Vanities. Mirth is wanton, and Wit prophane. He is scandalized at Youth for being lively, and at Childhood for being playful. He sits at a Christening, or a Marriage-Feast, as at a Funeral; sighs at the Conclusion of a merry Story; and grows devout when the Rest of the Company grow pleasant. After all,[8] *Sombrius* is a religious Man, and would have behaved himself very properly, had he lived when Christianity was under a general Persecution.

I would by no Means presume to tax such Characters with Hypocrisie, as is done too frequently, that being a Vice which I think none but He, who knows the Secrets of Mens Hearts, should pretend to discover in another, where the Proofs of it do not amount to a Demonstration.[9] On the contrary, as there are many excellent Persons, who are weighed down by this habitual Sorrow of Heart, they rather deserve our Compassion than our Reproaches. I think, however, they would do well to consider, whether such a Behaviour does not deterr Men from a religious Life, by Representing it as an unsociable State, that extinguishes all Joy and Gladness, darkens the Face of Nature, and destroys the Relish of Being it self.

I have, in former Papers,[10] shewn how great a Tendency there is to Chearfulness in Religion, and how such a Frame of Mind is not only the most lovely, but the most commendable in a virtuous Person. In short, those who represent Religion in so unamiable a Light, are like the Spies sent by *Moses* to make a Discovery of the Land of *Promise,* when by their Reports they discouraged the

[8] In summary.

[9] Where a man is not self-evidently a hypocrite, no one but God should accuse him of being such.

[10] *Spectators* No. 381 and 387.

People from entering upon it.[11] Those who shew us the Joy, the Chearfulness, the good Humour, that naturally spring up in this happy State, are like the Spies bringing along with them the Clusters of Grapes, and delicious Fruits, that might invite their Companions into the pleasant Country which produced them.

An eminent Pagan Writer[12] has made a Discourse, to shew that the Atheist, who denies a God, does him less Dishonour than the Man who owns his Being,[13] but at the same Time believes him to be cruel, hard to please, and terrible to humane Nature. For my own Part, says he, I wou'd rather it shou'd be said of me, that there was never any such Man as *Plutarch,* than that *Plutarch* was ill-natured, capricious or inhumane.

If we may believe our Logicians, Man is distinguished from all other Creatures, by the Faculty of Laughter.[14] He has an Heart capable of Mirth, and naturally disposed to it. It is not the Business of Virtue to extirpate the Affections of the Mind, but to regulate them. It may moderate and restrain, but was not designed to banish Gladness from the Heart of Man. Religion contracts the Circle of our Pleasures, but leaves it wide enough for her Votaries to expatiate in.[15] The Contemplation of the Divine Being, and the Exercise of Virtue, are in their own Nature so far from excluding all Gladness of Heart, that they are perpetual Sources of it. In a Word, the true Spirit of Religion cheers, as well as composes the Soul: It banishes indeed all Levity of Behaviour, all vicious and dissolute Mirth, but in Exchange fills the Mind with a perpetual Serenity, uninterrupted Chearfulness, and an habitual Inclination to please others, as well as to be pleased in it self.   O

11 Numbers 13.

12 Plutarch, "Of Superstition," 10 (*Moralia*, 170A).

13 Admits God's existence.

14 In *Spectator* No. 249, Addison wrote, "Man is the merriest Species of the Creation, all above and below him are Serious."

15 I.e., the advocates and devotees of Religion can still move freely within the somewhat narrowed circle of pleasures.

The Spectator, No. 517

Thursday, October 23.

[Addison]

Heu pietas! heu prisca fides!————Virg.[1]

We last Night received a Piece of ill News at our Club, which very sensibly afflicted every one of us. I question not but my Readers themselves will be troubled at the hearing of it. To keep them no longer in Suspence Sir Roger de Coverly *is dead.*[2] He departed this Life at his House in the Country, after a few Weeks Sickness. Sir Andrew Freeport has a Letter from one of his Correspondents in those Parts, that informs him the old Man caught a Cold at the County Sessions,[3] as he was very warmly promoting an Address of his own penning, in which he succeded according to his Wishes. But this Particular comes from a Whig-Justice of Peace, who was always Sir Roger's Enemy and Antagonist. I have Letters both from the Chaplain and Captain *Sentry* which mention Nothing of it, but are filled with many Particulars to the Honour of the good old Man. I have likewise a Letter from the Butler, who took so much Care of me last Summer when I was at the Knight's House. As my Friend the Butler mentions, in the Simplicity of his Heart, several Circumstances the others have passed over in Silence, I

1 Virgil *Aeneid* 6. 878: "Alas for goodness, alas for old-world honor."
2 In *The Bee* No. 1 (February, 1733), Eustace Budgell wrote, "Mr. *Addison* was so fond of this Character, that a little before he laid down the *Spectator* (foreseeing that some nimble Gentlemen would catch up his Pen the Moment he quitted it) he said to an intimate Friend, with a certain *Warmth* in his Expression which he was not often guilty of, *By G*————*d, I'll* Kill *Sir* Roger, *that no Body else may* Murder *him*."
3 See *Spectator* No. 122.

shall give my Reader a Copy of his Letter, without any Alteration or Diminution.

"Honoured Sir,

Knowing that you was my old Master's good Friend, I could not forbear sending you the melancholy News of his Death, which has afflicted the whole Country,[4] as well as his poor Servants, who loved him, I may say, better than we did our Lives. I am afraid he caught his Death the last County Sessions, where he would go to see Justice done to a poor Widow Woman, and her Fatherless Children that had been wronged by a Neighbouring Gentleman; for you know, Sir, my good Master was always the poor Man's Friend. Upon his coming home, the first Complaint he made was, that he had lost his Roast-Beef Stomach, not being able to touch a Sirloin, which was served up according to Custom; and you know he used to take great Delight in it. From that Time forward he grew worse and worse, but still kept a good Heart to the last. Indeed we were once in great Hope of his Recovery, upon a kind Message that was sent him from the Widow Lady whom he had made Love to[5] the forty last Years of his Life; but this only proved a Light'ning before Death.[6] He has bequeathed to this Lady, as a Token of his Love, a great Pearl Necklace, and a Couple of Silver Bracelets set with Jewels, which belonged to my good old Lady[7] his Mother: He has bequeathed the fine white Guelding, that he used to ride a hunting upon, to his Chaplain, because he thought he would be kind to him, and has left you all his Books. He has, moreover, bequeathed to the Chaplain a very pretty Tenement[8] with good Lands about it. It being a very cold Day when he made his Will, he left for Mourning, to every Man in the Parish a great Frize Coat,[9] and to every Woman a black Riding-hood. It was a most moving Sight to see him take Leave of his poor Servants, commending us all for our Fidelity, whilst we were not able to speak a Word for weeping. As we

---

[4] Neighborhood.

[5] Courted.

[6] A last flicker of the flame of life before it goes out. Speaking over Juliet's body, Romeo says:

> How oft when men are at the point of death
> Have they been merry! which their keepers call
> A lightning before death.

(Romeo and Juliet act 5, sc. 3. 88–90)

[7] The good old mistress whom I served.

[8] Dwelling house.

[9] A coat made of a coarse woollen cloth.

most of us are grown gray-headed in our Dear Master's Service, he has left us Pensions and Legacies, which we may live very comfortably upon, the remaining Part of our Days. He has bequeathed a great Deal more in Charity, which is not yet come to my Knowledge, and it is peremptorily[10] said in the Parish, that he has left Money to build a Steeple to the Church; for he was heard to say some Time ago, that if he lived two Years longer *Coverly* Church should have a Steeple to it. The Chaplain tells every Body that he made a very good End, and never speaks of him without Tears. He was buried, according to his own Directions, among the Family of the *Coverly's*, on the left Hand of his Father Sir *Arthur*. The Coffin was carried by Six of his Tenants, and the Pall held up by Six of the *Quorum:*[11] The whole Parish followed the Corps with heavy Hearts, and in their Mourning-Suits, the Men in Frize, and the Women in Riding-hoods. Captain *Sentry*, my Master's Nephew, has taken Possession of the Hall-House, and the whole Estate. When my old Master saw him a little before his Death, he shook him by the Hand, and wished him Joy of the Estate which was falling to him, desiring him only to make a good Use of it, and to pay the several Legacies, and the Gifts of Charity which he told him he had left as Quit-rents[12] upon the Estate. The Captain truly seems a courteous Man, though he says but little. He makes much of those whom my Master loved, and shews great Kindness to the old House-dog, that you know my poor Master was so fond of. It wou'd have gone to your Heart to have heard the Moans the dumb Creature made on the Day of my Master's Death. He has ne'er joyed himself since; no more has any of us. 'Twas the melancholiest Day for the poor People that ever happened in *Worcestershire*. This being all from,

> Honoured Sir,
> Your most sorrowful Servant,
>   Edward Biscuit.

P. S. My Master desired, some Weeks before he died, that a Book which comes up to you by the Carrier should be given to Sir *Andrew Freeport* in his Name."

This Letter, notwithstanding the poor Butler's Manner of Writing it, gave us such an Idea of our good old Friend, that upon the Reading of it there was not a dry Eye in the Club. Sir *Andrew*

---

10 Confidently, positively.
11 See *Spectator* No. 2, n. 9.
12 Payments required by the heir to an estate.

opening the Book found it to be a Collection of Acts of Parliament. There was in Particular the Act of Uniformity,[13] with some Passages in it marked by Sir *Roger*'s own Hand. Sir *Andrew* found that they related to two or three Points, which he had disputed with Sir *Roger* the last Time he appeared at the Club.[14] Sir *Andrew,* who would have been merry at such an Incident on another Occasion, at the Sight of the old Man's Hand-writing burst into Tears, and put the Book into his Pocket. Captain *Sentry* informs me, that the Knight has left Rings and Mourning for every one in the Club.   O

[13] See *Spectator* No. 3, n. 4.
[14] This dispute was never recorded in the *Spectator*.

The Spectator, No. 519

Saturday, October 25.

[Addison]

Inde hominum, pecudumque genus, vitaeque volantum,
Et quae marmoreo fert monstra sub aequore pontus. Virg.[1]

Though there is a great deal of Pleasure in contemplating the Material World, by which I mean that System of Bodies into which Nature has curiously wrought the Mass of dead Matter, with the several Relations which those Bodies bear to one another; there is still, methinks, something more wonderful and surprizing in Contemplations on the World of Life, by which I mean all those Animals with which every Part of the Universe is furnished. The Material World is only the Shell of the Universe: The World of Life are its Inhabitants.

If we consider those Parts of the Material World which lie the nearest to us, and are therefore subject to our Observations and Enquiries, it is amazing to consider the Infinity of Animals with which it is stocked. Every part of Matter is peopled: Every green Leaf swarms with Inhabitants. There is scarce a single Humour in the Body of a Man, or of any other Animal, in which our Glasses do not discover Myriads of living Creatures. The Surface of Animals is also covered with other Animals, which are in the same manner the Basis of other Animals that live upon it;[2] nay, we find in the most solid Bodies, as in Marble it self, innumerable

---

[1] Virgil *Aeneid* 6. 728–729: "Thence the race of men and beasts, the life of flying creatures, and those monsters the ocean bears beneath its marble surface."

[2] See *Tatler* No. 229 in which Addison observed that "a Louse is itself a very lousy Creature."

Cells and Cavities that are crouded with such imperceptible Inhabitants, as are too little for the naked Eye to discover. On the other Hand, if we look into the more bulky Parts of Nature, we see the Seas, Lakes and Rivers teeming with numberless Kinds of living Creatures: We find every Mountain and Marsh, Wilderness and Wood, plentifully stocked with Birds and Beasts, and every part of Matter affording proper Necessaries and Conveniencies for the Livelihood of Multitudes which inhabit it.

The Author of the *Plurality of Worlds*[3] draws a very good Argument from this Consideration, for the *peopling* of every Planet, as indeed it seems very probable from the Analogy of Reason, that if no part of Matter, which we are acquainted with, lies waste and useless, those great Bodies which are at such a Distance from us should not be desart and unpeopled, but rather that they should be furnished with Beings adapted to their respective Situations.

Existence is a Blessing to those Beings only which are endowed with Perception, and is, in a manner, thrown away upon dead Matter, any further than as it is subservient to Beings which are conscious of their Existence. Accordingly we find, from the Bodies which lie under our Observation, that Matter is only made as the Basis and Support of Animals, and that there is no more of the one, than what is necessary for the Existence of the other.

Infinite Goodness is of so communicative a Nature, that it seems to delight in the conferring of Existence upon every degree of Perceptive Being. As this is a Speculation which I have often pursued with great Pleasure to my self, I shall enlarge farther upon it, by considering that part of the Scale of Beings which comes within our Knowledge.[4]

There are some living Creatures which are raised but just above dead Matter. To mention only that Species of Shell-fish, which are formed in the Fashion of a Cone, that grew to the Surface of several Rocks, and immediately die upon their being sev-

3 Bernard de Fontenelle (1657–1757), whose book *Entretiens sur la Pluralité des Mondes* (1686) offered a series of dialogues between a scientist and a countess concerning the possibility of life on other planets.

4 This discussion of the great chain of being exactly parallels that in Pope's *Essay on Man*. See *Spectator* No. 237 and n. 17.

ered from the Place where they grow. There are many other Creatures but one Remove from these, which have no other Sense besides that of Feeling and Taste. Others have still an additional one of Hearing; others of Smell, and others of Sight. It is wonderful to observe, by what a gradual Progress the World of Life advances through a prodigious Variety of Species, before a Creature is formed that is compleat in all its Senses, and even among these there is such a different degree of Perfection in the Sense, which one Animal enjoys beyond what appears in another, that though the Sense in different Animals be distinguished by the same common Denomination, it seems almost of a different Nature. If after this we look into the several inward Perfections of Cunning and Sagacity, or what we generally call Instinct, we find them rising after the same manner, imperceptibly one above another, and receiving additional Improvements, according to the Species in which they are implanted. This Progress in Nature is so very gradual, that the most perfect of an inferior Species comes very near to the most imperfect of that which is immediately above it.

The exuberant and overflowing Goodness of the Supream Being, whose Mercy extends to all his Works, is plainly seen, as I have before hinted, from his having made so very little Matter, at least what falls within our Knowledge, that does not Swarm with Life: Nor is his Goodness less seen in the Diversity than in the Multitude of living Creatures. Had he only made one Species of Animals, none of the rest would have enjoyed the Happiness of Existence;[5] he has, therefore, *specified* in his Creation every degree of Life, every Capacity of Being. The whole Chasm in Nature, from a Plant to a Man, is filled up with diverse Kinds of Creatures, rising one over another, by such a gentle and easie Ascent, that the little Transitions and Deviations from one Species to another, are almost insensible. This intermediate Space is so well husbanded[6] and managed, that there is scarce a degree of

[5] This is less tautological than it appears. Contemporary discussions of the concept of plenitude questioned why God did not make all kinds of beings equally perfect, speculated that—had He done this—there could be but one kind of being, and concluded that an infinitely fruitful God would not leave infinite kinds of life forever uncreated.

[6] Conserved.

Perception which does not appear in some one part of the World of Life. Is the Goodness or Wisdom of the Divine Being, more manifested in this his Proceeding?

There is a Consequence, besides those I have already mentioned, which seems very naturally deducible from the foregoing Considerations. If the Scale of Being rises by such a regular Progress, so high as Man, we may by a Parity of Reason[7] suppose that it still proceeds gradually through those Beings which are of a Superior Nature to him, since there is an infinitely greater Space and Room for different Degrees of Perfection, between the Supreme Being and Man, than between Man and the most despicable Insect. This Consequence of so great a Variety of Beings which are superior to us, from that Variety which is inferior to us, is made by Mr. *Lock,* in a Passage which I shall here set down,[8] after having premised, that notwithstanding there is such infinite room between Man and his Maker for the Creative Power to exert it self in, it is impossible that it should ever be filled up, since there will be still an infinite Gap or Distance between the highest created Being, and the Power which produced him.

That there should be more Species *of intelligent Creatures above us, than there are of sensible and material below us, is probable to me from hence; That in all the visible corporeal World, we see no Chasms, or no Gaps. All quite down from us, the descent is by easie steps, and a continued series of things, that in each remove, differ very little one from the other. There are Fishes that have Wings, and are not Strangers to the airy Region: and there are some Birds, that are Inhabitants of the Water; whose Blood is cold as Fishes, and their Flesh so like in Taste, that the scrupulous are allowed them on Fish-days. There are Animals so near of kin both to Birds and Beasts, that they are in the middle between both: Amphibious Animals link the Terrestrial and Aquatique together; Seals live at Land and at Sea, and Porpoises have the warm Blood and Entrails of a Hog, not to mention what is confidently reported of Mermaids, or Sea-men. There are some Brutes,*

---

[7] By analogy.

[8] The quotation is from John Locke's *Essay Concerning Human Understanding,* 3. 6. 12.

*that seem to have as much Knowledge and Reason, as some that
are called Men; and the Animal and Vegetable Kingdoms are so
nearly joyn'd, that if you will take the lowest of one, and the highest of the other, there will scarce be perceived any great difference
between them; and so on till we come to the lowest and the most
inorganical parts of Matter, we shall find every where that the
several Species are linked together, and differ but in almost insensible degrees. And when we consider the infinite Power and Wisdom of the Maker, we have reason to think, that it is suitable to
the magnificent Harmony of the Universe, and the great Design
and infinite Goodness of the Architect, that the Species of Creatures should also, by gentle degrees, Ascend upward from us
toward his infinite Perfection, as we see they gradually descend
from us downward: Which if it be probable, we have reason then
to be persuaded, that there are far more Species of Creatures above
us, than there are beneath; we being in degrees of perfection much
more remote from the infinite Being of God, than we are from
the lowest state of Being, and that which approaches nearest to
nothing. And yet of all those distinct Species, we have no clear distinct Ideas.*

In this System of Being, there is no Creature so wonderful in
its Nature, and which so much deserves our particular Attention,
as Man, who fills up the middle Space between the Animal and
Intellectual Nature, the visible and invisible World, and is that
Link in the Chain of Beings which has been often termed the
nexus utriusque mundi.[9] So that he, who in one Respect is associated with Angels and Arch-Angels, may look upon a Being of infinite Perfection as his Father, and the highest Order of Spirits as
his Brethren, may in another Respect say to *Corruption, thou art
my Father, and to the Worm, thou art my Mother and my Sister.*[10]

O

[9] The joining of both of two worlds.
[10] Job 17:14.

The Spectator, No. 521

Tuesday, October 28.

[S t e e l e]

Vera redit facies, dissimulata perit. Pe. Arb.[1]

"*Mr.* Spectator,

I have been for many Years loud in this Assertion, That there are very few that can see or hear, I mean that can report what they have seen or heard; and this through Incapacity or Prejudice, one of which disables almost every Man who talks to you from representing things as he ought. For which Reason I am come to a Resolution of believing nothing I hear; and I contemn the Men given to Narration under the Appellation of a Matter of Fact Man: And according to me, a Matter of Fact Man is one whose Life and Conversation is spent in the Report of what is not Matter of Fact.

I remember when Prince *Eugene* was here,[2] there was no knowing his Height or Figure, till you, Mr. Spectator, gave the Publick Satisfaction in that Matter. In Relations,[3] the Force of the Expression lies very often more in the Look, the Tone of Voice, or the Gesture, than the Words themselves; which being repeated in any other manner by the Undiscerning, bear a very different Interpretation from their original Meaning. I must confess, I formerly have turned this Humour of mine to very good Account; for whenever I heard any Narrations utter'd with extraordinary Vehemence, and grounded upon considerable Authority, I was always ready to lay any Wager that it was

1 Petronius Arbiter *Satyricon* 80 (altered): "The true face returns, the false one is gone."

2 Prince Eugene of Savoy (See *Tatler* No. 18, n. 16) had been in England from January 5 to March 18. Addison mentioned his arrival in *Spectator* No. 269, and Steele described his appearance in No. 340. The purpose of his visit was to persuade the English not to make peace with France.

3 In relating events and stories.

not so. Indeed I never pretended to be so rash, as to fix the Matter any particular Way in Opposition to theirs; but as there are an hundred Ways of any thing happening, besides that it has happen'd, I only controverted its falling out in that one Manner as they[4] settled it, and left it to the Ninety nine other Ways, and consequently had more Probability of Success. I had arrived at a particular Skill in warming a Man so far in his Narration,[5] as to make him throw in a little of the Marvelous, and then, if he has much Fire, the next Degree is the Impossible. Now this is always the Time for fixing the Wager. But this requires the nicest Management, otherwise very probably the Dispute may arise to the old Determination by Battel.[6] In these Conceits I have been very fortunate, and have won some Wagers of those who have professedly valued themselves upon Intelligence,[7] and have put themselves to great Charge and Expence to be misinform'd considerably sooner than the rest of the World.

"Having got a comfortable Sum by this my Opposition to publick Report, I have brought my self now to so great a Perfection in Inattention, more especially to Party Relations, that at the same time I seem with greedy Ears to devour up the Discourse, I certainly don't know one Word of it, but pursue my own Course of Thought, whether upon Business or Amusement, with much Tranquility: I say Inattention, because a late Act of Parliament has secur'd all Party-Lyars from the Penalty of a Wager,[8] and consequently made it unprofitable to attend them. However, good Breeding obliges a Man to maintain the Figure of the keenest Attention, the true Posture of which in a Coffee-house I take to consist in leaning over a Table, with the Edge of it pressing hard upon your Stomach; for the more Pain the Narration is received with the more gracious is your bending over: Besides that, the Narrator thinks you forget your Pain by the Pleasure of hearing him.

"Fort *Knock*[9] has occasioned several very perplexed and inelegant Heats and Animosities; and there was one t'other Day in a Coffee-

[4] I.e., those uttering narrations with extraordinary vehemence.

[5] In encouraging a man to become emotional and extravagant concerning his story.

[6] See *Spectator* No. 239.

[7] The reliability of their information.

[8] An act of Parliament had declared void all wagers relating to the war with France.

[9] Fort Knocke, an important position at the junction of the canals of Ypres and Furnes, had been taken by the Allied armies about a month earlier.

house where I was, that took upon him to clear that Business to me, for he said he was there. I knew him to be that sort of Man that had not Strength of Capacity to be informed of any thing that depended merely upon his being an Eye-Witness, and therefore was fully satisfied he could give me no Information, for the very same Reason he believed he could, for he was there. However, I heard him with the same Greediness as *Shakespear* describes in the following Lines:

> *I saw a Smith stand on his Hammer, thus,*
> *With open Mouth swallowing a Taylor's News.*[10]

"I confess of late I have not been so much amazed at the Declaimers in Coffee-houses as I formerly was, being satisfied that they expect to be rewarded for their Vociferations. Of these Liars there are two Sorts. The Genius of the first consists in much Impudence and a strong Memory; the others have added to these Qualifications a good Understanding and smooth Language. These therefore have only certain Heads,[11] which they are as eloquent upon as they can, and may be called Embellishers; the others repeat only what they hear from others as literally as their Parts or Zeal will permit, and are called Reciters. Here was a Fellow in Town some Years ago, who used to divert himself by telling a Lie at *Charing-Cross* in the Morning at eight of the Clock, and then following it through all Parts of the Town till eight at Night; at which time he came to a Club of his Friends, and diverted them with an Account what Censure it had at *Will's* in *Covent-Garden*, how dangerous it was believed to be at *Child's*, and what Inference they drew from it with Relation to Stocks at *Jonathan's*.[12] I have had the Honour to travel with this Gentleman I speak of in Search of one of his Falshoods; and have been present when they have described the very Man they have spoken to, as him who first reported it, tall or short, black or fair, a Gentleman or a Raggamuffin, according as they liked the Intelligence. I have heard one of our ingenious Writers of News say, that when he has had a Customer come with an Advertisement of an Apprentice or a Wife run away, he has desired the Advertiser to compose himself a little,

[10] *King John,* act 4, sc. 2, 193, 195.

[11] I.e., the Embellishers can speak and elaborate on only certain topics, presumably those which they have witnessed or been involved in.

[12] The three coffee-houses served different groups (See *Tatler* No. 1, n. 3; *Tatler* No. 220, n. 12; and *Spectator* No. 1, n. 12.). As the lie circulated, the wits censured it, the clergymen and physicians feared it, and the businessmen speculated about the effect of it.

before he dictated the Description of the Offender: For when a Person is put into a publick Paper by a Man who is angry with him, the real Description of such Person is hid in the Deformity with which the angry Man described him; therefore this Fellow always made his Customers describe him as he would the Day before he offended, or else he was sure he would never find him out. These and many other Hints I could suggest to you for the Elucidation of all Factions; but I leave it to your own Sagacity to improve or neglect this Speculation.

I am, Sir,

Your most Obedient

Humble Servant,

Postscript *to the* Spectator, *Numb.* 502.[13]

N. B. *There are in the Play of the* Self-Tormentor *of Terence's, which is allowed a most excellent Comedy, several Incidents which would draw Tears from any Man of Sense, and not one which would move his Laughter."*   T

---

[13] In *Spectator* No. 502 Steele praised Terence's play and criticized the insensitivity of contemporary dramatic audiences.

The Spectator, No. 523

Thursday, October 30.

[A d d i s o n]

————*nunc augur Apollo,*
Nunc Lyciae sortes, nunc & Jove missus ab ipso
Interpres Divûm fert horrida jussa per auras.
Scilicet is superis labor————Virg.[1]

I am always highly delighted with the Discovery of any rising Genius among my Countrymen. For this Reason I have read over, with great Pleasure, the late Miscellany published by Mr. *Pope*,[2] in which there are many excellent Compositions of that ingenious Gentleman. I have had a Pleasure, of the same kind, in perusing a Poem that is just published *on the Prospect of Peace*,[3] and which, I hope, will meet with such a Reward from its Patrons, as so noble a Performance deserves. I was particularly well pleased to find that the Author had not amused himself with Fables out of the Pagan Theology,[4] and that when he hints at any thing of this Nature, he alludes to it only as to a Fable.

Many of our Modern Authors, whose Learning very often ex-

---

[1] Virgil *Aeneid* 4. 376–379: "Now prophetic Apollo, now the Lycian oracles, now the courier of the gods sent by Jove himself carries the rough commands through the air. Indeed, that is work for the gods."

[2] *Miscellaneous Poems and Translations. By Several Hands* was advertised in *Spectator* No. 383 as "This Day . . . Published." Along with shorter pieces by Pope, it contained the first sketch of *The Rape of the Lock*, which seems to be complimented later in this essay.

[3] Tickell's "A Poem to his Excellency the Lord Privy-Sea, on the Prospect of Peace" was advertised two days earlier as "This Day . . . Published."

[4] I.e., Greek and Roman mythology.

tends no farther than *Ovid's Metamorphosis,* do not know how to
celebrate a great Man, without mixing a parcel of School-boy
Tales with the Recital of his Actions. If you read a Poem on a fine
Woman, among the Authors of this Class, you shall see that it
turns more upon *Venus* or *Helen,* than on the Party concerned. I
have known a Copy of Verses on a great Hero highly commended,
but upon asking to hear some of the beautiful Passages, the Admirer of it has repeated to me a Speech of *Apollo,* or a Description of *Polypheme.*[5] At other times when I have searched for the
Actions of a Great Man, who gave a Subject to the Writer, I
have been entertained with the Exploits of a River-God, or have
been forced to attend a Fury[6] in her mischievous Progress, from
one end of the Poem to the other. When we are at School it is
necessary for us to be acquainted with the System of Pagan Theology, and may be allowed to enliven a Theme, or point an Epigram with an Heathen God; but when we would write a manly
Panegyrick, that should carry in it all the Colours of Truth, nothing can be more ridiculous than to have Recourse to our *Jupiter's*
and *Juno's.*

No Thought is beautiful which is not just, and no Thought
can be just which is not founded in Truth, or at least in that
which passes for such.[7]

In Mock-Heroick Poems, the Use of the Heathen Mythology is
not only excusable but graceful, because it is the Design of such
Compositions to divert, by adapting the fabulous Machines of the
Antients to low Subjects, and at the same time by ridiculing such
kinds of Machinery in Modern Writers. If any are of Opinion,
that there is a Necessity of admitting these Classical Legends into
our Serious Compositions, in order to give them a more Poetical
Turn; I would recommend to their Consideration the Pastorals of
Mr. *Philips.*[8] One would have thought it impossible for this kind

---

[5] Since Polyphemus was a one-eyed, man-eating giant, it is interesting to
speculate how his description contributed to commending "a great Hero."

[6] In Greek mythology, one of the hideous women who pursued wrong-doers
seeking vengeance.

[7] See *Spectator* No. 62, where Addison referred to Bonhours and Boileau in
affirming this view.

[8] The *Pastorals* of Ambrose Philips (1675?–1749) had been commended by
Steele in *Spectator* No. 400. Such praise became irritating to Pope, whose *Pas-*

of Poetry to have subsisted without Fawns and Satyrs, Wood-Nymphs, and Water-Nymphs, with all the Tribe of Rural Deities. But we see he has given a new Life, and a more natural Beauty to this way of Writing, by substituting in the Place of these antiquated Fables, the superstitious Mythology which prevails among the Shepherds of our own Country.

Virgil and *Homer* might compliment their Heroes, by interweaving the Actions of Deities with their Atchievements; but for a Christian Author to write in the Pagan Creed, to make Prince *Eugene*[9] a Favourite of *Mars,* or to carry on a Correspondence between *Bellona* and the Marshal *De Villars*,[10] would be downright Puerility, and unpardonable in a Poet that is past Sixteen. It is Want of sufficient Elevation in a Genius to describe Realities, and place them in a shining Light, that makes him have Recourse to such trifling antiquated Fables; as a Man may write a fine Description of *Bacchus* or *Apollo,* that does not know how to draw the Character of any of his Contemporaries.

In order therefore to put a stop to this absurd Practice, I shall publish the following Edict, by Vertue of that Spectatorial Authority with which I stand invested.

"Whereas the Time of a General Peace is, in all Appearance, drawing near; being informed that there are several ingenious Persons who intend to shew their Talents on so happy an Occasion, and being willing, as much as in me lies, to prevent that Effusion of Nonsense, which we have good Cause to apprehend; I do hereby strictly require every Person, who shall write on this Subject, to remember that he is a Christian, and not to sacrifice his Catechism to his Poetry. In order to it, I do expect of him in the first Place, to make his own Poem, without depending upon *Phoebus*[11] for any part of it, or call-

---

torals had been published with Philips' in the same volume of Tonson's *Miscellany* (1709).

9 See *Tatler* No. 18, n. 16, and *Spectator* No. 521, n. 2.

10 Claude Louis Hector, Duc de Villars (1653–1734), the outstanding French general. (Bellona is the goddess of War.)

11 Addison refers to famous mythological figures: Phoebus is the god of Poetry; the Muses, goddesses identified with the arts; Mercury, the messenger; Minerva, the goddess of Wisdom; the Destinies, the three Fates who spin the thread of life; and Neptune, the god of the Sea. The latter would "have a great deal of Business on his Hands" because of the many sea engagements during the long war.

ing out for Aid upon any one of the Muses by Name. I do likewise positively forbid the sending of *Mercury* with any particular Message or Dispatch relating to the Peace, and shall by no means suffer *Minerva* to take upon her the Shape of any Plenipotentiary concerned in this Great Work. I do further declare, that I shall not allow the Destinies to have had an Hand in the Deaths of the several Thousands who have been slain in the late War, being of Opinion that all such Deaths may be very well accounted for by the Christian System of Powder and Ball. I do therefore strictly forbid the Fates to cut the Thred of Man's Life upon any Pretence whatsoever, unless it be for the sake of the Rhime. And whereas I have good Reason to fear that *Neptune* will have a great deal of Business on his Hands, in several Poems which we may now suppose are upon the Anvil, I do also prohibit his Appearance, unless it be done in Metaphor, Simile, or any very short Allusion, and that even here he be not permitted to enter, but with great Caution and Circumspection. I desire that the same Rule may be extended to his whole Fraternity of Heathen Gods, it being my Design to condemn every Poem to the Flames in which *Jupiter* thunders, or exercises any other Act of Authority which does not belong to him: In short, I expect that no Pagan Agent shall be introduced, or any Fact related which a Man cannot give Credit to with a good Conscience. Provided always, that nothing herein contained shall extend, or be construed to extend, to several of the Female Poets in this Nation, who shall be still left in full Possession of their Gods and Goddesses, in the same manner as if this Paper had never been written."[12]   O

[12] The implication is, of course, that female poets need all the help they can get.

The Spectator, No. 529

Thursday, November 6.

[Addison]

Singula quaeque locum teneant sortita decenter. Hor.[1]

Upon the hearing of several late Disputes concerning Rank and Precedence,[2] I could not forbear amusing my self with some Observations, which I have made upon the Learned World, as to this great Particular. By the Learned World I here mean at large, all those who are any way concerned in Works of Literature, whether in the Writing, Printing or Repeating Part. To begin with the Writers;[3] I have observed that the Author of a *Folio,* in all Companies and Conversations, sets himself above the Author of a *Quarto;* the Author of a *Quarto* above the Author of an *Octavo;* and so on, by a gradual Descent and Subordination, to an Author in *Twenty-Fours.* This Distinction is so well observed, that in an Assembly of the Learned, I have seen a *Folio* Writer place himself in an Elbow-chair, when the Author of a *Duodecimo* has, out of a just Deference to his superior Quality, seated

---

[1] Horace *Ars Poetica* 92: "Let every thing decently keep its place."

[2] In *Spectator* No. 481, Addison discussed "the present Controversie between Count *Rechteren* and Monsieur *Mesnager,* which employs the wise Heads of so many Nations, and holds all the Affairs of *Europe* in Suspense." The Dutch and French plenipotentiaries had met at Utrecht to arrange a peace settlement, then began to dispute concerning insults done to their servants.

[3] An author is ranked according to the physical size of his book. First place would be given to the author of a *folio,* then—in descending order—to those who had published a *quarto,* an *octavo,* a *duodecimo,* and a work "in *Twenty-Fours.*"

himself upon a Squabb.[4] In a Word, Authors are usually ranged in Company after the same manner as their Works are upon a Shelf.

The most Minute Pocket-Author hath beneath him the Writers of all Pamphlets, or Works that are only stitched. As for the Pamphleteer, he takes place of none but of the Authors of single Sheets, and of that Fraternity who publish their Labours on certain Days, or on every Day of the Week.[5] I do not find that the Precedency among the Individuals, in this latter Class of Writers, is yet settled.

For my own part, I have had so strict a Regard to the Ceremonial which prevails in the Learned World, that I never presumed to take Place of a Pamphleteer till my daily Papers were gathered into those two first Volumes, which have already appeared.[6] After which, I naturally jumped over the Heads not only of all Pamphleteers, but of every *Octavo* Writer in *Great-Britain,* that had written but one Book. I am also informed by my Bookseller, that six *Octavo's* have at all times been looked upon as an Equivalent to a *Folio,* which I take notice of the rather, because I would not have the Learned World surprized, if after the Publication of half a dozen Volumes I take my Place accordingly. When my scattered Forces are thus rallied, and reduced into Regular Bodies, I flatter my self that I shall make no despicable Figure at the Head of them.

Whether these Rules, which have been received time out of Mind in the Common-Wealth of Letters, were not originally established with an Eye to our Paper Manufacture, I shall leave to the Discussion of others, and shall only remark further in this Place, that all Printers and Booksellers take the Wall of one another,[7] according to the abovementioned Merits of the Authors to whom they respectively belong.

---

[4] A sofa or ottoman.

[5] The Spectator was the author of a single sheet, published every day of the week.

[6] Volumes 1 and 2 were published in January 1712; volumes 3 and 4 were already in the press. All were published in *octavo.*

[7] When two or more people walked along a street, the more distinguished individual took the position next to the wall, thus remaining less exposed to the dirt and mud from the road.

I come now to that Point of Precedency which is settled among the three Learned Professions, by the Wisdom of our Laws. I need not here take Notice of the Rank which is allotted to every Doctor in each of these Professions, who are all of them, though not so high as Knights, yet a Degree above 'Squires; This last Order of Men being the illiterate Body of the Nation,[8] are consequently thrown together into a Class below the three Learned Professions.[9] I mention this for the sake of several Rural 'Squires, whose Reading does not rise so high as to *the present State of England,*[10] and who are often apt to usurp that Precedency which by the Laws of their Country is not due to them. Their Want of Learning, which has planted them in this Station, may in some measure extenuate their Misdemeanour, and our Professors ought to pardon them when they offend in this Particular, considering that they are in a State of Ignorance, or as we usually say, do not know their Right Hand from their Left.

There is another Tribe of Persons who are Retainers to the Learned World, and who regulate themselves upon all Occasions by several Laws peculiar to their Body. I mean the Players or Actors of both Sexes. Among these it is a standing and uncontroverted Principle, that a Tragedian always takes Place of a Comedian; and 'tis very well known the merry Drolls who make us laugh are always placed at the lower end of the Table, and in every Entertainment give way to the Dignity of the Buskin.[11] It is a Stage Maxim, Once a King and always a King. For this Reason it would be thought very absurd in Mr. *Bullock,* notwithstanding the Height and Gracefulness of his Person, to sit at the Right Hand of an Hero, though he were but five Foot high.[12] The same Distinction is observed among the Ladies of the Theatre. Queens and Heroines preserve their Rank in private Conver-

[8] See *Tatler* No. 89, n. 10.

[9] I.e., lawyers, physicians, and clergymen.

[10] This is the subtitle of *Angliae Notitia,* an annual listing of knights, peers, members of parliament, etc. Such a book would be valuable in establishing social precedence.

[11] Tragedy. The word derives from the laced half boot worn by Greek and Roman tragic actors.

[12] The transition here is perhaps misleading. Just as a player who has once played a king always retains that rank, so Bullock (See *Tatler* No. 89, n. 18) who regularly played low comedy roles can never rise above that station.

sation, while those who are Waiting-Women and Maids of Honour upon the Stage, keep their Distance also behind the Scenes.

I shall only add, that by a Parity of Reason, all Writers of Tragedy look upon it as their due to be seated, served, or saluted[13] before Comick Writers: Those who deal in Tragi-Comedy usually taking their Seats between the Authors of either side. There has been a long Dispute for Precedency between the Tragick and Heroick Poets. *Aristotle* would have the latter yield the *Pas*[14] to the former, but Mr. *Dryden* and many others would never submit to this Decision.[15] Burlesque Writers pay the same Deference to the Heroick, as Comick Writers to their Serious Brothers in the Drama.

By this short Table of Laws, Order is kept up, and Distinction preserved in the whole Republick of Letters.　　　　　　　　O

[13] See *Spectator* No. 394, n. 2.

[14] Precedence, the right to go first.

[15] Aristotle's view appears in *Poetics*, 26; Dryden's in the *Apology for Heroic Poetry* (1677) and the Dedication of the *Aeneis* (1697).

The Spectator, No. 530

Friday, November 7.

[A d d i s o n]

Sic visum Veneri; cui placet impares
Formas atque animos sub juga ahenea
Saevo mittere cum joco. Hor.[1]

It is very usual for those who have been severe upon Marriage, in some part or other of their Lives to enter into the Fraternity which they have ridiculed, and to see their Raillery[2] return upon their own Heads. I scarce ever knew a Woman-hater that did not, sooner or later, pay for it. Marriage, which is a Blessing to another Man, falls upon such an one as a Judgment. Mr. *Congreve's Old Batchelor* is set forth to us with much Wit and Humour, as an Example of this kind.[3] In short, those who have most distinguished themselves by Railing at the Sex in general, very often make an honourable Amends, by chusing one of the most worthless Persons of it, for a Companion and Yoke-fellow. *Hymen*[4] takes his Revenge in kind, on those who turn his Mysteries into Ridicule.

My Friend *Will. Honeycomb,* who was so unmercifully witty upon the Women, in a couple of Letters, which I lately communi-

---

[1] Horace *Odes* 1. 33. 10–12: "Such the decree of Venus, whom it pleases in cruel sport to join ill-matched bodies and minds under her brazen yoke."

[2] Good-natured ridicule.

[3] In *Tatler* No. 9, Steele discussed Congreve's *Old Bachelor* (1693), saying it "excellently represented the Reluctance of a Batter'd Debauchee to come into the Trammels of Order and Decency."

[4] The god of marriage, usually represented as a youth carrying a torch and veil.

cated to the Publick,[5] has given the Ladies ample Satisfaction by marrying a Farmer's Daughter; a piece of News which came to our Club by the last Post. The *Templer* is very positive that he has married a Dairy-maid: But *Will,* in his Letter to me on this Occasion, sets the best Face upon the Matter that he can, and gives a more tollerable account of his Spouse. I must confess I suspected something more than ordinary, when upon opening the Letter I found that *Will* was fallen off from his former Gayety, having changed *Dear Spec.* which was his usual Salute at the Beginning of the Letter, into *My Worthy Friend,* and subscribed himself in the latter End of it at full length *William Honeycomb.* In short, the gay, the loud, the vain *Will Honeycomb,* who had made Love to every great Fortune that has appeared in Town for above thirty Years together, and boasted of Favours from Ladies whom he had never seen,[6] is at length wedded to a plain Country Girl.

His Letter gives us the Picture of a converted Rake. The sober Character of the Husband is dashed with the Man of the Town, and enlivened with those little Cant-phrases which have made my Friend *Will* often thought very pretty Company. But let us hear what he says for himself.

> *"My Worthy Friend,*
> I question not but you, and the rest of my Acquaintance, wonder that I, who have lived in the Smoak and Gallantries[7] of the Town for thirty Years together, should all on a sudden grow fond of a Country-life. Had not my Dog of a Steward run away as he did, without making up his Accounts, I had still been immersed in Sin and sea-Coal.[8] But since my late forced Visit to my Estate, I am so pleased with it, that I am resolved to live and die upon it. I am every Day abroad among my Acres, and can scarce forbear filling my Letter with

5 In *Spectators* No. 499 and 511, Addison presented letters from Will Honeycomb. The first described a dream in which the women of a besieged town were permitted to leave the city with whatever goods they deemed most valuable; almost every woman chose to take some good other than her husband. The second letter described a Persian auction at which men had to choose between ugly women with large fortunes and beautiful women with none.

6 See *Spectator* No. 475.

7 Amorous adventures.

8 Because his steward absconded with the money needed to pay his bills, Will has left the gallantry and smoke of London.

Breezes, Shades, Flowers, Meadows, and purling Streams.[9] The Simplicity of Manners, which I have heard you so often speak of, and which appears here in Perfection, charms me wonderfully. As an Instance of it, I must acquaint you, and by your means the whole Club, that I have lately married one of my Tenants Daughters. She is born of honest Parents, and tho' she has no Portion[10] she has a great deal of Virtue. The natural Sweetness and Innocence of her Behaviour, the Freshness of her Complection, the unaffected Turn of her Shape and Person, shot me through and through every time I saw her, and did more Execution upon me in Grogram,[11] than the greatest Beauty in Town or Court had ever done in Brocade. In short, she is such an one as promises me a good Heir to my Estate, and if by her means I cannot leave to my Children what are falsely called the Gifts of Birth; high Titles and Alliances: I hope to convey to them the more real and valuable Gifts of Birth; strong Bodies and healthy Constitutions. As for your fine Women, I need not tell thee that I know them. I have had my share in their Graces, but no more of that. It shall be my Business hereafter to live the Life of an honest Man, and to act as becomes the Master of a Family. I question not but I shall draw upon me the Raillery of the Town, and be treated to the Tune of *the Marriage-Hater matched*;[12] but I am prepared for it. I have been as witty upon others in my time. To tell thee truly, I saw such a Tribe of Fashionable young fluttering Coxcombs shot up, that I did not think my Post of an *homme de ruelle*[13] any longer tenable. I felt a certain Stiffness in my Limbs, which entirely destroyed that Jauntyness of Air I was once Master of. Besides, for I may now confess my Age to thee, I have been eight and forty above these twelve Years. Since my Retirement into the Country will make a Vacancy in the Club, I could wish you would fill up my Place with my Friend *Tom Dapperwitt*.[14] He has an infinite deal of Fire, and knows the Town. For my

[9] This is an impressive about-face for Will. In Essay No. 131 (Addison), he wrote the Spectator urging him to end his visit at Sir Roger's estate: "Thy Speculations begin to smell confoundedly of Woods and Meadows."

[10] Fortune.

[11] A coarse, loosely-woven fabric.

[12] This is the title of a comedy (1692) by Thomas D'Urfey.

[13] The custom of the *ruelle*, the morning visit in the boudoir, was satirized by Addison in *Spectator* No. 45 and by Pope in *The Rape of the Lock* 4. 35–38.

[14] Tom Dapperwit was mentioned in Will. Honeycomb's letters (*Spectators* No. 499 and 511), and he was described in No. 482 as one who considered "the married State" to be a kind of Purgatory.

own part, as I have said before, I shall endeavour to live hereafter
suitable to a Man in my Station, as a prudent Head of a Family, a
good Husband, a careful Father (when it shall so happen), and as
Your most Sincere Friend
and Humble Servant,
William Honeycomb."
O

The Spectator, No. 542

Friday, November 21.

[A d d i s o n]

Et sibi praeferri se gaudet————Ovid.[1]

When I have been present in Assemblies where my Paper has been talked of, I have been very well pleased to hear those who would detract from the Author of it observe, that the Letters which are sent to the *Spectator* are as good, if not better, than any of his Works. Upon this Occasion many Letters of Mirth are usually mentioned, which some think the *Spectator* writ to himself, and which others Commend because they fancy he received them from his Correspondents: Such are those from the *Valetudinarian;* the Inspector of the Sign-posts; the Master of the Fan Exercise: with that of the Hooped Petticoat; that of *Nicholas Hart* the annual Sleeper; that from Sir *John Envill;* that upon the *London* Cries;[2] with Multitudes of the same Nature. As I love nothing more than to mortifie the ill-natured, that I may do it effectually, I must acquaint them, they have very often praised me when they did not design it, and that they have approved my Writings when they thought they had derogated[3] from them. I have heard several of these unhappy Gentlemen proving, by undeniable Arguments, that I was not able to pen a Letter which I had written the Day before. Nay, I have heard some of them throwing out ambiguous Expressions, and

---

1 Ovid *Metamorphoses* 2. 430: "And rejoices to be preferred to himself."
2 The papers referred to—Nos. 25, 28, 102, 127, 184, 299, and 251, respectively—are all by Addison.
3 Detracted.

giving the Company Reason to suspect that they themselves did me the Honour to send me such or such a particular Epistle, which happened to be talked of with the Esteem or Approbation of those who were present. These rigid Criticks are so afraid of allowing me any thing which does not belong to me, that they will not be positive whether the Lion, the wild Boar, and the Flower-pots in the Playhouse did not actually write those Letters which came to me in their Names.[4] I must therefore inform these Gentlemen, that I often chuse this way of casting my Thoughts into a Letter, for the following Reasons; First, out of the Policy of those who try their Jest upon another,[5] before they own it themselves. Secondly, because I would extort a little Praise from such who will never applaud any thing whose Author is known and certain. Thirdly, because it gave me an Opportunity of introducing a great variety of Characters into my Work, which could not have been done, had I always written in the Person of the *Spectator*. Fourthly, because the Dignity Spectatorial would have suffered, had I published as from my self those several ludicrous Compositions which I have ascribed to fictitious Names and Characters. And lastly, because they often serve to bring in, more naturally, such additional Reflections as have been placed at the End of them.

There are others who have likewise done me a very particular Honour, though undesignedly. These are such who will needs have it, that I have translated or borrowed many of my Thoughts out of Books which are written in other Languages. I have heard of a Person, who is more famous for his Library than his Learning, that has asserted this more than once in his private Conversation.[6] Were it true, I am sure he could not speak it from his own Knowledge; but had he read the Books which he has collected, he would find this Accusation to be wholly groundless. Those who are truly learned will acquit me in this Point, in which I have

---

[4] In protesting the grotesqueness of stage presentations, Steele in *Spectator* No. 14 offered a letter from a man who performed as a lion; in No. 22, he published letters from a wild boar and a flower-pot.

[5] As if it came from another.

[6] Probably this refers to Mr. Thomas Rawlinson, whom Addison satirized as Tom Folio in *Tatler* No. 158.

been so far from offending, that I have been scrupulous perhaps to a Fault in quoting the Authors of several Passages which I might have made my own.[7] But as this Assertion is in reality an Encomium on what I have published, I ought rather to glory in it, than endeavour to confute it.

Some are so very willing to alienate from me that small Reputation which might accrue to me from any of these my Speculations, that they attribute some of the best of them to those imaginary Manuscripts with which I have introduced them.[8] There are others, I must confess, whose Objections have given me a greater Concern, as they seem to reflect, under this Head, rather on my Morality than on my Invention. These are they who say an Author is guilty of Falsehood, when he talks to the Publick of Manuscripts which he never saw, or describes Scenes of Action or Discourse in which he was never engaged. But these Gentlemen would do well to consider, there is not a Fable or Parable which ever was made use of, that is not liable to this Exception; since nothing, according to this Notion, can be related innocently which was not once Matter of Fact. Besides, I think the most ordinary Reader may be able to discover, by my way of writing, what I deliver in these Occurrences as Truth, and what as Fiction.

Since I am unawares[9] engaged in answering the several Objections which have been made against these my Works, I must take Notice that there are some who affirm a Paper of this Nature should always turn upon diverting Subjects, and others who find Fault with every one of them that hath not an immediate Tendency to the advancement of Religion or Learning.[10] I shall leave these Gentlemen to dispute it out among themselves, since I see one half of my Conduct patronized by each side. Were I serious on an improper Subject, or trifling in a serious one, I should de-

---

[7] In *Spectator* No. 546 Steele made the same point.

[8] See *Spectator* No. 159, which begins "When I was at *Grand Cairo* I picked up several Oriental Manuscripts, which I have still by me. Among others I met with one entituled, *The Visions of Mirzah. . . .*"

[9] Unexpectedly.

[10] In *Spectator* No. 179, Addison made the same distinction, adding "I must confess, were I left to my self, I should rather aim at Instructing than Diverting; but if we will be useful to the World, we must take it as we find it."

servedly draw upon me the Censure of my Readers; or were I conscious of any thing in my Writings that is not innocent at least, or that the greatest part of them were not sincerely designed to discountenance Vice and Ignorance, and support the Interest of true Wisdom and Virtue, I should be more severe upon my self than the Publick is disposed to be. In the mean while I desire my Reader to consider every particular Paper or Discourse as a distinct Tract by it self, and independant of every thing that goes before or after it.

I shall end this Paper with the following Letter, which was really sent me, as some others have been which I have published, and for which I must own my self indebted to their respective Writers.

"*Sir,*

I was this Morning in a Company of your Well-wishers, when we read over, with great Satisfaction, *Tully*'s Observations on Action adapted to the *British* Theatre:[11] Though, by the way, we were very sorry to find that you have disposed of another Member of your Club. Poor Sir *Roger* is dead, and the worthy Clergyman dying. Captain *Sentry* has taken Possession of a fair Estate, *Will Honeycomb* has married a Farmer's Daughter, and the *Templar* withdraws himself into the Business of his own Profession.[12] What will all this end in! We are afraid it portends no good to the Publick. Unless you very speedily fix a Day for the Election of new Members, we are under Apprehensions of losing the *British Spectator*. I hear of a Party of Ladies who intend to address you on this Subject, and question not, if you do not give us the Slip very suddenly, that you will receive Addresses from all Parts of the Kingdom to continue so useful a Work. Pray deliver us out of this Perplexity, and among the Multitude of your Readers you will particularly oblige,

Your most Sincere Friend
and Servant,
Philo-Spec."

O

---

[11] This was the subject of *Spectator* No. 541 by Hughes.

[12] These events relating to the dissolution of the Club were reported in Nos. 513, 517, 530, and 541. All but the last were by Addison.

The Spectator, No. 549

Saturday, November 29.

[Addison]

Quamvis digressu veteris confusus amici,
Laudo tamen——— ———Juv.[1]

I believe most People begin the World with a Resolution to withdraw from it into a serious kind of Solitude or Retirement, when they have made themselves easie in it. Our Unhappiness is, that we find out some Excuse or other for deferring such our good Resolutions till our intended Retreat is cut off by Death. But among all kinds of People there are none who are so hard to part with the World, as those who are grown old in the heaping up of Riches. Their Minds are so warped with their constant Attention to Gain, that it is very difficult for them to give their Souls another Bent, and convert them towards those Objects, which, though they are proper for every Stage of Life, are so more especially for the last. *Horace*[2] describes an old Usurer as so charmed with the Pleasures of a Country Life, that in order to make a Purchase he called in all his Mony; but what was the event of it? Why in a very few Days after he put it out again.[3] I am engaged in this Series of Thought by a Discourse which I had last Week with my worthy Friend Sir Andrew Freeport, a Man of so much natural Eloquence, good Sense, and Probity of Mind, that I always hear him with a particular Pleasure. As we were sitting together, being

---

[1] Juvenal *Satires* 3. 1–2: "Although confounded by the departure of my old friend, still I praise him."

[2] Horace *Epodes* 2. 67–70.

[3] I.e., he reinvested it.

the sole remaining Members of our Club,[4] Sir Andrew gave me an Account of the many busie Scenes of Life in which he had been engaged, and at the same time reckoned up to me abundance of those lucky Hits, which at another time he would have called pieces of good Fortune; but in the Temper of Mind he was then, he termed them Mercies, Favours of Providence, and Blessings upon an honest Industry. Now, says he, you must know, my good Friend, I am so used to consider my self as Creditor and Debtor, that I often state my Accounts after the same manner, with regard to Heaven and my own Soul. In this case, when I look upon the Debtor-side, I find such innumerable Articles, that I want Arithmetick to cast them up; but when I look upon the Creditor-side, I find little more than blank Paper.[5] Now tho' I am very well satisfied that it is not in my Power to ballance Accounts with my Maker, I am resolved however to turn all my future Endeavours that way. You must not therefore be surprized, my Friend, if you hear that I am betaking my self to a more thoughtful kind of Life, and if I meet you no more in this Place.

I could not but approve so good a Resolution, notwithstanding the Loss I shall suffer by it. Sir Andrew has since explained himself to me more at large in the following Letter, which is just come to my Hands.

"*Good Mr.* Spectator,
Notwithstanding my Friends at the Club have always rallied me, when I have talked of retiring from Business, and repeated to me one of my own Sayings, *that a Merchant has never enough till he has got a little more,* I can now inform you that there is one in the World who thinks he has enough, and is determined to pass the Remainder of his Life in the Enjoyment of what he has. You know me so well, that I need not tell you, I mean, by the Enjoyment of my Possessions, the making of them useful to the Publick. As the greatest Part of my Estate has been hitherto of an unsteady and volatile Nature, either tost upon Seas or fluctuating in Funds;[6] it is now fixt and setled in Substantial Acres and Tenements. I have removed it from the Un-

---

4 See *Spectator* No. 542 and n. 12.

5 I.e., God has loaned me more riches and blessings than I can calculate, so many that my repayments—in prayers and good works—amount to nothing.

6 Either in goods subject to loss or in speculative stocks.

certainty of Stocks, Winds and Waves, and disposed of it in a considerable Purchase. This will give me great Opportunity of being charitable in my way, that is in setting my poor Neighbours to Work, and giving them a comfortable Subsistence out of their own Industry. My Gardens, my Fishponds, my Arable[7] and Pasture Grounds shall be my several Hospitals, or rather Work-houses,[8] in which I propose to maintain a great many indigent Persons, who are now starving in my Neighbourhood. I have got a fine Spread of improveable Lands, and in my own Thoughts am already plowing up some of them, fencing others; planting Woods, and draining Marshes. In fine, as I have my Share in the Surface of this Island, I am resolved to make it as beautiful a Spot as any in Her Majesty's Dominions; at least there is not an Inch of it which shall not be cultivated to the best Advantage, and do its utmost for its Owner. As in my Mercantile Employment, I so disposed of my Affairs, that from whatever Corner of the Compass the Wind blew, it was bringing home one or other of my Ships; I hope, as a Husband-man,[9] to contrive it so, that not a Shower of Rain, or a Glimpse of Sunshine, shall fall upon my Estate without bettering some part of it, and contributing to the Products of the Season. You know it has been hitherto my Opinion of Life, that it is thrown away when it is not some way useful to others. But when I am riding out by my self, in the fresh Air on the open Heath that lies by my House, I find several other Thoughts growing up in me. I am now of Opinion, that a Man of my Age may find Business enough on himself,[10] by setting his Mind in order, preparing it for another World, and reconciling it to the Thoughts of Death. I must, therefore, acquaint you, that besides those usual Methods of Charity, of which I have before spoken, I am at this very Instant finding out a convenient Place where I may build an Alms-house,[11] which I intend to endow very handsomly, for a Dozen superannuated Husbandmen. It will be a great Pleasure to me to say my Prayers twice a Day with Men of my own Years, who all of them, as well as my self, may have their Thoughts taken up how they shall die, rather than how they shall live. I remember an excellent Saying that I learned at School, *Finis coronat opus*.[12]

[7] Tillable.

[8] Poor-houses.

[9] A farmer.

[10] In the commercial image, can fully occupy himself.

[11] A privately financed home for the poor, this one with prayer facilities.

[12] I.e., the end crowns the work. The saying appeared in Lehmann's *Florilegium Politicum* (1630).

You know best whether it be in *Virgil* or in *Horace,* it is my business to apply it. If your Affairs will permit you to take the Country Air with me sometimes, you shall find an Apartment fitted up for you, and shall be every Day entertained with Beef or Mutton of my own feeding; Fish out of my own Ponds; and Fruit out of my own Gardens. You shall have free Egress and Regress about my House, without having any Questions asked you, and in a Word such an hearty Welcome as you may expect from

Your most Sincere Friend
and humble Servant,
Andrew Freeport."

The Club of which I am a Member being entirely dispersed, I shall consult my Reader next Week, upon a Project relating to the Institution of a new one.   O

The Spectator, No. 550

Monday, November 30.

[Addison]

Quid dignum tanto feret hic promissor HIATU? Hor.[1]

Since the late Dissolution of the Club whereof I have often declared my self a Member, there are very many Persons who by Letters, Petitions, and Recommendations, put up for the next Election. At the same Time I must complain, that several indirect and underhand Practices have been made use of upon this Occasion. A certain Country Gentleman begun to *tapp*[2] upon the first Information he received of Sir Roger's Death, when he sent me up Word, that if I would get him chosen in the Place of the Deceased, he would present me with a Barrel of the best *October*[3] I had ever drank in my Life. The Ladies are in great Pain to know whom I intend to elect in the Room of Will. Honeycomb. Some of them indeed are of Opinion that Mr. Honeycomb did not take sufficient Care of their Interest in the Club, and are therefore desirous of having in it hereafter a Representative of their own Sex. A Citizen, who subscribes himself *Y. Z.*[4] tells me that he has one and twenty Shares in the *African* Company,[5] and offers to bribe me with the odd one in case he may succeed Sir Andrew Freeport, which he thinks would raise the Credit of that Fund. I have sev-

---

1 Horace *Ars Poetica* 138: "What will this maker of promises produce to fill so large a gap?"

2 To make offers, to "turn on the tap" of gifts.

3 October ale.

4 See *Spectator* No. 1, n. 16 and No. 221.

5 A joint-stock company which exported cloth, imported sugar, and sold African slaves to the new world.

eral Letters dated from *Jenny Man*'s,[6] by Gentlemen who are
Candidates for Captain Sentry's Place, and as many from a Coffee-
house in *Paul*'s Church-yard, of such who would fill up the Vacancy occasioned by the Death of my worthy Friend the Clergyman,[7] whom I can never mention but with a particular Respect.

Having maturely weighed these several Particulars, with the
many Remonstrances that have been made to me on this Subject,
and considering how invidious an Office I shall take upon me if
I make the whole Election depend upon my single Voice, and being unwilling to expose my self to those Clamours, which, on such
an Occasion, will not fail to be raised against me for Partiality,
Injustice, Corruption, and other Qualities which my Nature ab-
hors, I have formed to my self the Project of a Club as follows.

I have Thoughts of issuing out Writs to all and every of the
Clubs that are established in the Cities of *London* and *Westminster,* requiring them to chuse out of their respective Bodies a Person of the greatest Merit, and to return his Name to me before
Lady-day,[8] at which Time I intend to sit upon Business.

By this Means I may have Reason to hope, that the Club over
which I shall preside will be the very Flower and Quintescence of
all other Clubs. I have communicated this my Project to none but
a particular Friend of mine, whom I have celebrated twice or
thrice for his Happiness in that kind of Wit which is commonly
known by the Name of a Punn. The only Objection he makes to
it is, that I shall raise up Enemies to my self if I act with so regal
an Air; and that my Detractors, instead of giving me the usual
Title of Spectator, will be apt to call me the *King of Clubs*.

But to proceed on my intended Project: It is very well known
that I at first set forth in this Work with the Character of a silent
Man;[9] and I think I have so well preserved my Taciturnity, that
I do not remember to have violated it with three Sentences in the
Space of almost two Years. As a Monosyllable is my Delight, I
have made very few Excursions in the Conversations which I have

6 The Tiltyard Coffee-house, a popular meeting place for soldiers.

7 This is the first announcement of his death. The coffee-house referred to
is probably Child's.

8 The feast of the Annunciation, commonly celebrated on March 25.

9 See *Spectator* No. 1.

related beyond a Yes or a No. By this Means my Readers have lost many good things which I have had in my Heart, tho' I did not care for uttering them.

Now in order to diversify my Character, and to shew the World how well I can talk if I have a Mind,[10] I have Thoughts of being very loquacious in the Club which I have now under Consideration. But that I may proceed the more regularly in this Affair, I design upon the first Meeting of the said Club to have *my Mouth opened* in Form, intending to regulate my self in this Particular by a certain Ritual which I have by me, that contains all the Ceremonies which are practised at the opening of the Mouth of a Cardinal.[11] I have likewise examined the Forms which were used of old by *Pythagoras*,[12] when any of his Scholars, after an Apprenticeship of Silence, was made free of his Speech. In the mean Time, as I have of late found my Name in foreign Gazettes upon less Occasions, I question not but in their next Articles from *Great Britain,* they will inform the World that *the* Spectator*'s Mouth is to be opened on the twenty fifth of* March *next.* I may perhaps publish a very useful Paper at that Time of the Proceedings in that Solemnity, and of the Persons who shall assist at it.[13] But of this more hereafter. O

[10] I.e., if I cared to.

[11] At the consecration ceremony, the Pope closes the mouth of the cardinal to symbolize the discretion he must observe in his new office; then he opens it, to represent the man's new privilege and duty to express his opinion on religious matters. This is the kind of excessive religious ceremony Addison ridiculed in *Spectator* No. 201.

[12] This reference to the Greek philosopher (fl. ca. 530 B.C.) appears in Diogenes Laertius's *Vitae Philosophorum* 8. 10.

[13] The paper never appeared. *The Spectator* ceased publication on December 6.

The Spectator, No. 555

Saturday, December 6.

[S t e e l e]

Respue quod non es——— ———Pers.[1]

All the Members of the Imaginary Society, which were described in my First Papers, having disappeared one after another, it is high time for the *Spectator* himself to go off the Stage. But, now I am to take my Leave I am under much greater Anxiety than I have known for the Work of any Day since I undertook this Province. It is much more difficult to converse with the World in a real than a personated Character. That might pass for Humour, in the *Spectator,* which would look like Arrogance in a Writer who sets his Name to his Work. The Fictitious Person might contemn those who disapproved him, and extoll his own Performances, without giving Offence. He might assume a Mock-Authority;[2] without being looked upon as vain and conceited. The Praises or Censures of himself fall only upon the Creature of his Imagination, and if any one finds fault with him, the Author may reply with the Philosopher of old, *Thou dost but beat the Case of* Anaxarchus.[3] When I speak in my own private Sentiments, I cannot but address my self to my Readers in a more submissive

---

[1] Persius *Satires* 4. 51: "Lay aside the fictitious character."

[2] E.g., *Spectator* No. 523 by Addison criticized the use of pagan mythology in modern poems relating to the coming peace: "In order, therefore, to put a stop to this absurd Practice, I shall publish the following Edict, by Vertue of that Spectatorial Authority with which I stand Invested."

[3] Anaxarchus (fl. ca. 350 B.C.), the Greek philosopher, was condemned to be beaten to death with iron pestles, but he ridiculed his tormentors, saying "Pound, pound the bag containing Anaxarchus; ye pound not Anaxarchus."

manner, and with a just Gratitude, for the kind Reception which they have given to these Daily Papers that have been published for almost the space of Two Years last past.

I hope the Apology I have made as to the Licence allowable to a feigned Character, may excuse any thing which has been said in these Discourses of the *Spectator* and his Works; but the Impu-tation of the grossest Vanity would still dwell upon me, if I did not give some Account by what Means I was enabled to keep up the Spirit of so long and approved a Performance. All the Papers marked with a C, an L, an I, or an O,[4] that is to say, all the Papers which I have distinguished by any Letter in the Name of the Muse *Clio,* were given me by the Gentleman, of whose Assistance I for-merly boasted in the Preface and concluding Leaf of my *Tatlers.*[5] I am indeed much more proud of his long continued Friendship, than I should be of the Fame of being thought the Author of any Writings which he himself is capable of producing. I remember when I finished the *Tender Husband,* I told him there was noth-ing I so ardently wished, as that we might some time or other pub-lish a Work written by us both, which should bear the Name of *the Monument,* in Memory of our Friendship.[6] I heartily wish what I have done here, were as Honorary to that Sacred Name, as Learning, Wit and Humanity render those Pieces which I have taught the Reader how to distinguish for his.[7] When the Play abovementioned was last Acted, there were so many applauded Stroaks in it which I had from the same Hand, that I thought very meanly of my self that I had never publickly acknowledged them. After I have put other Friends upon importuning him to publish Dramatick, as well as other Writings he has by him,[8] I shall end

4 I.e., those by Addison. See *Spectator* No. 1, n. 16 and No. 221.

5 Steele praised Addison in the Preface to Vol. IV of the *Tatler,* as well as in *Tatler* No. 271.

6 Steele's *The Tender Husband* (1705) was dedicated to Addison, who wrote the Prologue. No work called *The Monument* ever appeared, possibly because the friendship did not endure.

7 I.e., I wish that what I have here said of Addison, honored his name as much as did his essays throughout the series, which were regularly superior to mine.

8 Addison's *Cato* was finally performed on April 14, 1713.

what I think I am obliged to say on this Head, by giving my Reader this Hint for the better judging of my Productions, that the best Comment upon them would be an Account when the Patron to the *Tender Husband* was in *England,* or Abroad.[9]

The Reader will also find some Papers which are marked with the Letter X, for which he is obliged to the ingenious Gentleman who diverted the Town with the Epilogue to the *Distressed Mother.*[10] I might have owned these several Papers with the free Consent of these Gentlemen, who did not write them with a design of being known for the Authors. But as a candid and sincere Behaviour ought to be preferred to all other Considerations, I would not let my Heart reproach me with a Consciousness of having acquired a Praise which is not my Right.

The other Assistances which I have had have been conveyed by Letter, sometimes by whole Papers, and other times by short Hints from unknown Hands. I have not been able to trace Favours of this kind, with any Certainty, but to the following Names, which I place in the Order wherein I received the Obligation, tho' the first I am going to Name can hardly be mentioned in a List wherein he would not deserve the Precedence.[11] The Persons to whom I am to make these Acknowledgments are Mr. *Henry Martin,* Mr. *Pope,* Mr. *Hughs,* Mr. *Carey* of *New-College* in *Oxford,* Mr. *Tickell* of *Queen's* in the same University, Mr. *Parnelle,* and Mr. *Eusden* of *Trinity* in *Cambridge.*[12] Thus to speak in the Language of my late Friend Sir Andrew Freeport, I have Ballanced my Accounts with all my Creditors for Wit and Learning. But as

9 I.e., the best way to judge my works is to consider whether or not I could have had Addison's assistance on them.

10 Eustace Budgell (See *Spectator* No. 221, n. 11). The Epilogue to the *Distressed Mother* was printed under his name, but there is evidence that Addison wrote it.

11 Steele must mean "the first I have named," i.e., Addison. The praise scarcely applies to Henry Martyn.

12 The contributors acknowledged are Henry Martyn (d. 1721), Alexander Pope (1688–1744), John Hughes (1677–1720), Mr. [probably Walter] Carey, Thomas Tickell (1685–1740), Thomas Parnell (1679–1718), and Laurence Eusden (1688–1730). At the end of the essay, Richard Ince of Grey's-Inn is acknowledged as a contributor.

these Excellent Performances would not have seen the Light without the means of this Paper, I may still arrogate[13] to my self the Merit of their being communicated to the Publick.

I have nothing more to add, but having swelled this Work to Five hundred and fifty five Papers, they will be disposed into seven Volumes, four of which are already published, and the three others in the Press. It will not be demanded of me why I now leave off, tho' I must own my self obliged to give an Account to the Town of my Time hereafter, since I retire when their Partiality to me is so great, that an Edition of the former Volumes of *Spectators* of above Nine thousand each Book is already sold off, and the Tax on each half Sheet has brought into the Stamp-Office one Week with another above 20 *l.* a Week arising from this single Paper,[14] notwithstanding it at first reduced it to less than half the Number that was usually Printed before this Tax was laid.

I humbly beseech the Continuance of this Inclination to favour what I may hereafter produce, and hope I have in many Occurrences of Life tasted so deeply of Pain and Sorrow, that I am Proof against much more prosperous Circumstances than any Advantages to which my own Industry can possibly exalt me.

> *I am,*
> *My Good-natured Reader,*
> *Your most Obedient,*
> *Most Obliged Humble Servant,*
>   Richard Steele.

> *Vos valete & plaudite.*   Ter.[15]

The following Letter[16] regards an ingenious Sett of Gentlemen, who have done me the Honour to make me one of their Society.

---

13 Appropriate.

14 See *Spectator* No. 445, n. 2.

15 This is the closing sentence in Terence's plays *Self-Tormentor, Eunuch,* and *Phormio:* "Farewell, and clap your hands."

16 In the folio sheets, this transition was less abrupt: "*P.S.* Give me leave, before I conclude, to insert a Letter which regards an Ingenious Sett of Gentlemen. . . ." The quotation from Terence followed the letter.

"*Mr.* Spectator,   *Dec.* 4. 1712.

The Academy of *Painting,* lately established in *London,* having done you, and themselves, the Honour to chuse you one of their Directors,[17] that Noble and Lovely Art, which before was entitled to your Regards, as a *Spectator,* has an additional Claim to you, and you seem to be under a double Obligation to take some care of her[18] Interests.

"The Honour of our Country is also concerned in the Matter I am going to lay before you; we (and perhaps other Nations as well as we) have a National false Humility as well as a National Vain-Glory; and tho' we boast our selves to excell all the World in things wherein we are out-done abroad; in other things we attribute to others a Superiority which we our selves possess. This is what is done, particularly, in the Art of *Portrait* or *Face-Painting.*

"*Painting* is an Art of a vast Extent, too great by much for any mortal Man to be in full Possession of, in all its Parts; 'tis enough if any one succeed in painting Faces, History, Battels, Landscapes, Seapieces, Fruit, Flowers, or Drolls,[19] &c. Nay no Man ever was excellent in all the Branches (tho' many in Number) of these several Arts, for a distinct Art I take upon me to call every one of those several Kinds of Painting.

"And as one Man may be a good Landscape-Painter, but unable to paint a Face or a History[20] tollerably well, and so of the rest; one Nation may excell in some kinds of Painting, and other kinds may thrive better in other Climates.

"*Italy* may have the Preference of all other Nations for History-Painting; *Holland* for Drolls, and a neat finished manner of Working; *France,* for Gay, Janty, Fluttering Pictures; and *England* for Portraits; but to give the Honour of every one of these kinds of Painting to any one of those Nations on account of their Excellence in any of these parts of it, is like adjudging the Prize of Heroick, Dramatick, Lyrick or Burlesque Poetry, to him who has done well in any one of them.

"Where there are the greatest Genius's and most Helps and Encouragements, 'tis reasonable to suppose an Art will arrive to the greatest Perfection: By this Rule let us consider our own Country

[17] The first Academy of drawing and painting from life was founded in England in 1711; Steele was invited to join in 1712.
[18] The antecedent is "that Noble and Lovely Art."
[19] Jesters, wags.
[20] I.e., a scene from history.

with respect to Face-Painting. No Nation[21] in the World delights so much in having their own, or Friends or Relations Pictures; whether from their National Good-Nature, or having a Love to Painting, and not being encouraged in that great Article of Religious Pictures, which the Purity of our Worship refuses the free use of, or from whatever other Cause. Our Helps are not inferior to those of any other People, but rather they are greater; for what the Antique Statues and Bas-reliefs which *Italy* enjoys are to the History-Painters, the beautiful and noble Faces with which *England* is confessed to abound, are to Face-Painters; and besides, we have the greatest number of the Works of the best Masters in that kind of any People, not without a competent number of those of the most Excellent in every other Part of Painting. And for Encouragement, the Wealth and Generosity of the *English* Nation affords that in such a degree, as Artists have no reason to complain.

"And accordingly in fact, Face-Painting is no where so well performed as in *England:* I know not whether it has lain in your way to observe it, but I have, and pretend to be a tolerable Judge. I have seen what is done Abroad, and can assure you that the Honour of that Branch of Painting is justly due to us. I appeal to the judicious Observers for the Truth of what I assert. If Foreigners have oftentimes, or even for the most part, excelled our Natives, it ought to be imputed to the Advantages they have met with *here,* join'd to their own Ingenuity and Industry, nor has any one Nation distinguished themselves so as to raise an Argument in favour of their Country; but 'tis to be observed, that neither *French* nor *Italians,* nor any one of either Nation, notwithstanding all our Prejudices in their Favour, have, or ever had, for any considerable time, any Character among us as Face-Painters.

"This Honour is due to our own Country; and has been so for near an Age: So that instead of going to *Italy,* or elsewhere, one that designs for Portrait Painting ought to Study in *England.* Hither such should come from *Holland, France, Italy, Germany,* &c. as he that intends to Practise any other kind of Painting, should go to those Parts where 'tis in greatest Perfection. 'Tis said the Blessed Virgin descended from Heaven, to Sit to St. *Luke;*[22] I dare venture to affirm, that if she should desire another *Madonna* to be Painted by the Life,

---

[21] I.e., no people.
[22] To sit for St. Luke to make a portrait of her. The source of the legend is Theodorus Lector's *Anagnostes* (c. 530).

she would come to *England;* and am of Opinion that your present President, Sir *Godfrey Kneller,*[23] from his Improvement since he Arrived in this Kingdom, would perform that Office better than any Foreigner living. I am, with all possible Respect,

Sir,

Your most Humble, and

most Obedient Servant, &c."

The Ingenious Letters sign'd the Weather-Glass, *with several others, were receiv'd, but came too late.*

Postscript.

It had not come to my Knowledge, when I left off the *Spectator,* that I owe several excellent Sentiments and agreeable Pieces in this Work to Mr. *Ince* of *Grey's-Inn.*

R. Steele.

[23] Kneller (1646–1723), the celebrated portrait painter. In 1715, Addison wrote a poem "To Sir Godfrey Kneller," praising his painting of King George.

The Continuation of The Spectator

The Spectator, No. 556

Friday, June 18. [1714]

[A d d i s o n]

Qualis ubi in lucem coluber, mala gramina pastus,
Frigida sub terra tumidum quem bruma tegebat;
Nunc positis novus exuviis, nitidusque juventa,
Lubrica convolvit sublato pectore terga
Arduus ad solem, et linguis micat ore trisulcis. Virg.[1]

Upon laying down the Office of Spectator, I acquainted the World with my Design of electing a new Club, and of opening my Mouth in it after a most solemn Manner.[2] Both the Election and the Ceremony are now past; but not finding it so easy as I at first imagined, to break through a fifty Years Silence, I would not venture into the World under the Character of a Man who pretends to talk like other People, 'till I had arrived at a full Freedom of Speech.[3]

I shall reserve for another time the History of such Club or Clubs of which I am now a Talkative, but unworthy Member; and shall here give an Account of this surprising Change which has been produced in me, and which I look upon to be as remarkable an Accident as any recorded in History, since that which hap-

---

[1] Virgil *Aeneid* 2. 471–475: "As when a snake, full fed on poisonous herbs during the winter, crawls into the light and, fresh with its old skin discarded, shines in youth, coiling its slippery body, raising its head to the sun, and flickering its forked tongue."

[2] See *Spectator* No. 550 and n 11.

[3] The opening of the mouth was scheduled for March 25, 1713. Noting that it has taken him fifteen months to learn to speak easily, the Spectator explains away the time interval between No. 555 and No. 556.

pened to the Son of *Croesus*,[4] after having been many Years as much Tongue-tied as my self.

Upon the first opening of my Mouth, I made a Speech consisting of about half a Dozen well-turned Periods;[5] but grew so very hoarse upon it, that for three Days together, instead of finding the use of my Tongue, I was afraid that I had quite lost it. Besides, the unusual Extension of my Muscles on this Occasion, made my Face ake on both Sides to such a Degree, that nothing but an invincible Resolution and Perseverance could have prevented me from falling back to my Monosyllables.

I afterwards made several Essays towards Speaking; and that I might not be startled at my own Voice, which has happen'd to me more than once, I used to read aloud in my Chamber, and have often stood in the Middle of the Street to call a Coach, when I knew there was none within hearing.

When I was thus grown pretty well acquainted with my own Voice, I laid hold of all Opportunities to exert it. Not caring however to speak much by my self, and to draw upon me the whole Attention of those I conversed with, I used, for some time, to walk every Morning in the *Mall*,[6] and talk in Chorus with a Parcel of *Frenchmen*. I found my Modesty greatly relieved by the communicative Temper of this Nation, who are so very sociable, as to think they are never better Company than when they are all opening at the same time.

I then fancied I might receive great Benefit from Female Conversation, and that I should have a Convenience of talking with the greater Freedom, when I was not under any Impediment of thinking: I therefore threw my self into an Assembly of Ladies, but could not for my Life get in a Word among them; and found that if I did not change my Company, I was in Danger of being reduced to my primitive Taciturnity.

The Coffee-houses have ever since been my chief Places of Resort, where I have made the greatest Improvements; in order to which I have taken a particular Care never to be of the same Opin-

4 Croesus (d. 546 B.C.), King of Lydia. The reference to his tongue-tied son is from Herodotus *History* 1. 85.

5 I.e., long, periodical sentences.

6 An enclosed walk in St. James's Park.

ion with the Man I conversed with. I was a Tory at *Button*'s and a Whig at *Childe*'s; a Friend to the *Englishman;* or an Advocate for the *Examiner,* as it best served my Turn:[7] Some fancy me a great Enemy to the *French* King, though, in reality, I only make use of him for a Help to Discourse. In short, I wrangle and dispute for Exercise; and have carried this Point so far, that I was once like to have been run through the Body for making a little too free with my Betters.

In a Word, I am quite another Man to what I was.

> ————*Nil fuit unquam*
> *Tam dispar sibi*————[8]

My old Acquaintance scarce know me; nay I was asked the other Day by a *Jew* at *Jonathan*'s,[9] whether I was not related to a dumb Gentleman, who used to come to that Coffee-house? But I think I never was better pleased in my Life than about a Week ago, when, as I was battling it across the Table with a young Templar,[10] his Companion gave him a Pull by the Sleeve, begging him to come away, for that the old Prig would talk him to Death.

Being now a very good Proficient in Discourse, I shall appear in the World with this Addition to my Character, that my Countrymen may reap the Fruits of my new acquired Loquacity.

Those who have been present at publick Disputes in the University, know that it is usual to maintain Heresies for Argument's sake. I have heard a Man a most impudent Socinian[11] for Half an Hour, who has been an Orthodox Divine[12] all his Life after. I have taken the same Method to accomplish my self in the Gift of Utterance, having talked above a Twelve-month, not so much for

7 Button's was a coffee-house which had opened since the first series of *Spectators* concluded; it catered to Whigs and received letters addressed to the *Guardian.* Child's (See *Tatler* No. 220, n. 12) was a Tory coffee-house. In both places, the Spectator spoke against the prevailing sentiment. The *Englishman* was a Whig paper published by Steele; the *Examiner* (See *Tatler* No. 229, n. 8) a Tory periodical written by Swift and others.

8 Horace *Satires* 1. 3. 18 (altered): "Nothing was ever so unlike itself."

9 See *Spectator* No. 1, n. 12.

10 See *Spectator* No. 2, n. 11.

11 An anti-Trinitarian.

12 Clergyman.

the Benefit of my Hearers as of my self. But since I have now
gained the Faculty, I have been so long endeavouring after, I intend to make a right Use of it, and shall think my self obliged, for
the future, to speak always in Truth and Sincerity of Heart. While
a Man is learning to fence, he practises both on Friend and Foe;
but when he is a Master in the Art, he never exerts it but on what
he thinks the right Side.

That this last Allusion may not give my Reader a wrong Idea
of my Design in this Paper, I must here inform him, that the Author of it is of no Faction, that he is a Friend to no Interests but
those of Truth and Virtue, nor a Foe to any but those of Vice and
Folly. Tho' I make more Noise in the World than I used to do, I
am still resolved to act in it as an indifferent Spectator. It is not
my Ambition to encrease the Number either of Whigs or Tories,
but of wise and good Men; and I could heartily wish there were
not Faults common to both Parties, which afford me sufficient
Matter to work upon, without descending to those which are peculiar to either.

If in a Multitude of Counsellors there is Safety,[13] we ought to
think our selves the securest Nation in the World. Most of our
Garrets are inhabited by Statesmen, who watch over the Liberties
of their Country, and make a Shift to keep themselves from starving, by taking into their Care the Properties of all their Fellow-
Subjects.

As these Politicians of both Sides have already worked the Nation into a most unnatural Ferment, I shall be so far from endeavouring to raise it to a greater Height, that, on the contrary,
it shall be the chief Tendency of my Papers, to inspire my Countrymen with a mutual Good-will and Benevolence.[14] Whatever
Faults either Party may be guilty of, they are rather inflamed than
cured by those Reproaches, which they cast upon one another.
The most likely Method of rectifying any Man's Conduct, is, by
recommending to him the Principles of Truth and Honour, Religion and Virtue; and so long as he acts with an Eye to these

13 Proverbs 11:14.
14 Addison repeats the promise of neutrality he made in *Spectator* No. 1.
Though the war was over, party spirit remained high because Queen Anne
was dying and the succession to the throne uncertain.

Principles, whatever Party he is of, he cannot fail of being a good *Englishman,* and a Lover of his Country.

As for the Persons concerned in this Work, the Names of all of them, or at least of such as desire it, shall be published hereafter: Till which time I must entreat the courteous Reader to suspend his Curiosity, and rather to consider what is written, than who they are that write it.[15]

Having thus adjusted all necessary Preliminaries with my Reader, I shall not trouble him with any more prefatory Discourses, but proceed in my old Method, and entertain him with Speculations on every useful Subject that falls in my Way.

[15] Though authors of the earlier *Spectators* were identified in No. 555, the new issues were published anonymously. There were no terminal initials.

The Spectator, No. 567

Wednesday, July 14.

[Addison]

————*Inceptus clamor frustratur hiantes.* Virg.[1]

I have received private Advice from some of my Correspondents, that if I would give my Paper a general Run,[2] I should take care to season it with Scandal. I have indeed observed of late, that few Writings sell which are not filled with great Names and illustrious Titles. The Reader generally casts his Eye upon a new Book, and if he finds several Letters separated from one another by a Dash, he buys it up and peruses it with great Satisfaction. An *M* and an *h*, a *T* and an *r*,[3] with a short Line between them, has sold many an insipid Pamphlet. Nay I have known a whole Edition go off by vertue of two or three well-written *&c*————'s.

A sprinkling of the Words *Faction, Frenchman, Papist, Plunderer,* and the like significant Terms, in an Italick Character,[4] have also a very good Effect upon the Eye of the Purchaser; not to mention *Scribler, Lier, Rogue, Rascal, Knave,* and *Villain,* without which it is impossible to carry on a Modern Controversie.

Our Party-writers are so sensible of the secret Virtue of an Innuendo to recommend their Productions, that of late they never mention the Q————n or P————t at length, tho' they speak of

1 Virgil *Aeneid* 6. 493: "They tried to shout, but their wide mouths only whimpered."

2 I.e., a larger sale.

3 The references are to Marlborough (See *Tatler* No. 1, n. 17) and to the Treasurer, Sidney, First Earl of Godolphin (1645–1712). Both fell from power in 1710.

4 I.e., printed in italics.

them with Honour, and with that Deference which is due to them
from every private Person. It gives a secret Satisfaction to a Pe-
ruser of these mysterious Works, that he is able to decipher them
without help, and, by the Strength of his own natural Parts, to fill
up a Blank-Space, or make out a Word that has only the first or
last Letter to it.

Some of our Authors indeed, when they would be more Satyrical than ordinary, omit only the Vowels of a great Man's Name,
and fall most unmercifully upon all the Consonants. This way of
writing was first of all introduced by *T—m Br—wn*,[5] of facetious
Memory, who, after having gutted a Proper Name of all its intermediate Vowels, used to plant it in his Works, and make as free
with it as he pleased, without any danger of the Statute.

That I may imitate these celebrated Authors, and publish a
Paper which shall be more taking than ordinary, I have here
drawn up a very curious Libel, in which a Reader of Penetration
will find a great deal of concealed Satyr, and if he be acquainted
with the present Posture of Affairs, will easily discover the Meaning of it.

"If there are *four* Persons in the Nation who endeavour to
bring all things into Confusion and ruin their native Country, I
think every honest *Engl—shm—n* ought to be upon his Guard.
That there are such every one will agree with me, who hears me
name *** with his first Friend and Favourite *** not to mention
*** nor ***. These People may cry Ch—rch, Ch—rch,[6] as long as
they please, but, to make use of a homely Proverb, The Proof of
the P—dd—ng is in the eating. This I am sure of, that if a *certain
Prince* should concur with a *certain Prelate,* (and we have Monsieur *Z—n*'s Word for it) our Posterity would be in a sweet
P—ckle. Must the *British* Nation suffer forsooth, because my
Lady *Q—p—t—s* has been disobliged? Or is it reasonable that our
English Fleet, which used to be the Terror of the Ocean, should
lie Wind-bound for the sake of a————.[7] I love to speak out and

---

[5] Thomas Browne (1663–1704) was an English writer of satirical verse, including "I do not love thee, Dr. Fell."

[6] See *Tatler* No. 220, n. 11.

[7] Though it is uncertain what the rest of the paragraph means, this
"————" is certainly no compliment to Lady Q—p—t—s. Several critical attempts to decipher "Q—p—t—s" have produced wicked conjectures.

declare my Mind clearly, when I am talking for the good of my Country. I will not make my Court to an ill Man, tho' he were a *B—y* or a *T—t*. Nay, I would not stick to call so wretched a Politician a Traitor, an Enemy to his Country, and a Bl—n—d—r-b—ss, *&c. &c.*"

The remaining part of this political Treatise, which is written after the manner of the most celebrated Authors in *Great Britain,* I may communicate to the Publick at a more convenient Season.[8] In the mean while I shall leave this with my curious Reader, as some ingenious Writers do their Enigmas, and if any sagacious Person can fairly unriddle it, I will print his Explanation, and, if he pleases, acquaint the World with his Name.

I hope this short Essay will convince my Readers, it is not for want of Abilities that I avoid State-tracts, and that if I would apply my Mind to it, I might in a little time be as great a Master of the Political Scratch as any the most eminent Writer of the Age. I shall only add, that in order to outshine all this Modern Race of *Syncopists,*[9] and thoroughly content my *English* Readers, I intend shortly to publish a Spectator that shall not have a single Vowel in it.

[8] The "remaining Part" of this treatise never appeared.
[9] A nonce word.

The Spectator, No. 568

Friday, July 16.

[Addison]

~~~~~~~~~~~~

——*Dum recitas, incipit esse Tuus.* Mart.[1]

I was Yesterday in a Coffee-House not far from the *Royal Exchange,* where I observed three Persons in close Conference over a Pipe of Tobacco; upon which, having filled one for my own use, I lighted it at the little Wax Candle that stood before them; and after having thrown in two or three Whiffs amongst them, sat down, and made one of the Company. I need not tell my Reader, that lighting a Man's Pipe at the same Candle, is looked upon among Brother-smokers as an Overture to Conversation and Friendship. As we here lay our Heads together in a very amicable Manner, being intrenched under a Cloud of our own raising, I took up the last Spectator,[2] and casting my Eye over it, *The* Spectator, says I, *is very witty to Day;* upon which a lusty lethargick[3] old Gentleman who sat at the Upper-end of the Table, having gradually blown out of his Mouth a great deal of Smoak, which he had been collecting for some Time before, *Ay,* says he, *more witty than wise I am afraid.* His Neighbour, who sat at his right Hand, immediately coloured, and being an angry Politician, laid down his Pipe with so much Wrath that he broke it in the Middle, and by that Means furnished me with a Tobacco-stopper. I took it up very sedately, and looking him full in the Face, made

1 Martial *Epigrams* 1. 38. 2 (altered): "When you recite my verse, it begins to be your own."

2 I.e., the latest one, *Spectator* No. 567.

3 I.e., emotional, but idle.

use of it from Time to Time all the while he was speaking: *This Fellow*, says he, *can't for his Life keep out of Politicks. Do you see how he abuses* four *great Men here?* I fix'd my Eye very attentively on the Paper, and asked him if he meant those who were repre- sented by Asterisks. *Asterisks*, says he, *do you call them? They are all of them Stars. He might as well have put Garters to 'em.*[4] *Then pray do but mind the two or three next Lines! Ch—rch and P—d- d—ng in the same Sentence!*[5] *Our Clergy are very much beholden to him.* Upon this the third Gentleman, who was of a mild Dispo- sition, and, as I found, a Whig in his Heart, desired him not to be too severe upon the Spectator neither; *For*, says he, *you find he is very cautious of giving Offence, and has therefore put two Dashes*[6] *into his Pudding. A Fig for his Dash*, says the angry Politician. *In his next Sentence he gives a plain Innuendo, that our Posterity will be in a sweet P—ckle. What does the Fool mean by his Pickle? Why does not he write it at length if he means honestly?* I have read over the whole Sentence, says I; *but I look upon the Paren- thesis in the Belly of it to be the most dangerous Part, and as full of Insinuations as it can hold.*[7] *But who*, says I, *is my Lady Q—p—t—s? Ay, Answer that if you can, Sir*, says the furious Statesman to the poor Whig that sat over-against him. But with- out giving him Time to reply, *I do assure you*, says he, *were I my Lady Q—p—t—s, I would sue him for* Scandalum Magnatum. *What is the World come to? Must every Body be allowed to————?* He had by this time filled a new Pipe, and applying it to his Lips, when we expected the last Word of his Sentence, put us off with a Whiff of Tobacco; which he redoubled with so much Rage and Trepidation, that he almost stifled the whole Company. After a short Pause, I owned that I thought the Spectator had gone too far in writing so many Letters of my Lady Q—p—t—s's

4 Stars and garters were emblems of knighthood. The Tory speaker is sen- sitive to possible criticism in this area.

5 See *Tatler* No. 220, n. 11. The speaker senses the implication that the An- glican clergy is less ascetic than its Puritan brethren.

6 A pun, recalling that in making up a recipe, one puts in a dash of this and a dash of that.

7 The deadly parenthesis read: "(and we have Monsieur Z—n's Word for it)."

Name; *but however,* says I, *he has made a little Amends for it in his next Sentence, where he leaves a blank Space without so much as a Consonant to direct us; I mean, says* I, *after those Words,* The Fleet, that used to be the Terrour of the Ocean, should be Windbound for the Sake of a————; *after which ensues a Chasm, that, in my Opinion, looks modest enough, Sir,* says my Antagonist, *you may easily know his Meaning by his gaping; I suppose he designs his Chasm, as you call it, for an Hole to creep out at, but I believe it will hardly serve his Turn. Who can endure to see the great Officers of State, the* B—y's *and* T—t's, *treated after so scurrilous a Manner? I can't for my Life,* says I, *imagine who they are the* Spectator *means? No!* says he,————*Your humble Servant Sir!*[8] Upon which he flung himself back in his Chair after a contemptuous Manner, and smiled upon the old lethargick Gentleman on his left Hand, who I found was his great Admirer. The Whig however had begun to conceive a Good-will towards me, and seeing my Pipe out, very generously offered me the use of his Box; but I declined it with great Civility, being obliged to meet a Friend about that Time in another Quarter of the City.

At my leaving the Coffee-house, I could not forbear reflecting with my self upon that gross Tribe of Fools who may be termed the *Over-wise,*[9] and upon the Difficulty of writing any thing in this censorious Age, which a weak Head may not construe into private Satyr and personal Reflection.

A Man who has a good Nose at an Innuendo, smells Treason and Sedition in the most innocent Words that can be put together, and never sees a Vice or Folly stigmatized, but finds out one or other of his Acquaintance pointed at by the Writer. I remember an empty pragmatical Fellow in the Country, who upon reading over *the whole Duty of Man,*[10] had written the Names of several Persons in the Village at the Side of every Sin which is mentioned

---

[8] I.e., the speaker introduces himself as either B—y or T—t.

[9] Addison made this point in *Tatler* No. 155 and *Spectator* No. 46. In *Spectator* No. 170, he wrote, "I believe no Men see less of the Truth and Reality of things, than these great Refiners upon Incidents, who are so wonderfully subtile and over-wise in their Conceptions."

[10] *The Whole Duty of Man* (1658), a popular religious work credited to Richard Allestree (1619–1681).

by that excellent Author; so that he had converted one of the best Books in the World into a Libel against the 'Squire, Church-wardens, Overseers of the Poor, and all other the most consider-able Persons in the Parish. This Book with these extraordinary marginal Notes fell accidentally into the Hands of one who had never seen it before; upon which there arose a current Report that Some-body had written a Book against the 'Squire and the whole Parish. The Minister of the Place having at that Time a Contro-versie with some of his Congregation upon the Account of his Tythes,[11] was under some Suspicion of being the Author, 'till the good Man set his People right by shewing them that the satyrical Passages might be applied to several others of two or three neigh-bouring Villages, and that the Book was writ against all the Sin-ners in *England*.

[11] See *Spectator* No. 112, n. 16.

The Spectator, No. 579

Wednesday, August 11.

[A d d i s o n]

———*Odora canum vis.* Virg.[1]

In the Reign of King *Charles* I, the Company of Stationers, into whose Hands the Printing of the Bible is committed by Patent, made a very remarkable *Erratum* or Blunder in one of their Editions: For instead of *Thou shalt not commit Adultery,* they printed off several thousands of Copies with *Thou shalt commit Adultery.*[2] Archbishop *Laud*[3] to punish this their Negligence, laid a considerable Fine upon that Company in the *Star-Chamber.*

By the Practice of the World, which prevails in this degenerate Age, I am afraid that very many young Profligates, of both Sexes, are possessed of this spurious Edition of the Bible, and observe the Commandment according to that faulty Reading.

Adulterers, in the first Ages of the Church, were excommunicated for ever, and unqualified all their Lives from bearing a part in Christian Assemblies, notwithstanding they might seek it with Tears, and all the Appearances of the most unfeigned Repentance.

I might here mention some antient Laws among the Heathens which punished this Crime with Death;[4] and others of the same

1 Virgil *Aeneid* 4. 132: "Keen-scented pack of hounds."

2 The so-called "Wicked Bible" was printed in 1631. Because the word "not" was omitted from the Seventh Commandment, the whole printing was called back.

3 William Laud (1573–1645), Archbishop of Canterbury from 1613. The Star-Chamber was a room in Westminster Palace, the ceiling of which bore gilt stars, wherein sat the arbitrary court of the early Stuarts.

4 Under Athenian law, for example, a man taken in adultery could be killed with impunity by the father, the husband, or the brother of the woman involved.

Kind, which are now in Force among several Governments that have embraced the Reformed Religion.[5] But because a Subject of this Nature may be too serious for my ordinary Readers, who are very apt to throw by my Papers, when they are not enlivened with something that is diverting or uncommon; I shall here publish the Contents of a little Manuscript lately fallen into my Hands, and which pretends to great Antiquity,[6] tho' by Reason of some modern Phrases and other Particulars in it, I can by no means allow it to be genuine, but rather the Production of a Modern Sophist.

It is well known by the Learned, that there was a Temple upon Mount *Aetna* dedicated to *Vulcan*,[7] which was guarded by Dogs of so exquisite a Smell, (say the Historians) that they could discern whether the Persons who came thither were Chast or otherwise. They used to meet and faun upon such as were Chast, caressing them as the Friends of their Master *Vulcan;* but flew at those who were polluted, and never ceased barking at them till they had driven them from the Temple.

My Manuscript gives the following Account of these Dogs, and was probably designed as a Comment upon this Story.[8]

"These Dogs were given to *Vulcan* by his Sister *Diana*, the Goddess of Hunting and of Chastity, having bred them out of some of her Hounds, in which she had observed this natural Instinct and Sagacity. It was thought she did it in Spight to *Venus*, who, upon her Return home, always found her Husband in a good or bad Humour, according to the Reception which she met with from his Dogs. They lived in the Temple several Years, but were such snappish Curs that they frighted away most of the Votaries.[9] The Women of *Sicily* made a solemn Deputation to the Priest, by which they acquainted him, that they would not come up to the Temple with their annual Offerings unless he muzzled his Mastiffs; and at last compromised the Matter with him, that the Offering should always be brought by a Chorus

5 Protestantism.

6 See *Spectator* No. 542 concerning "imaginary Manuscripts."

7 Vulcan was identified with the Greek artisan-god Hephaestus, the special patron of cuckolds.

8 The story is told in a second-century work *De Natura Animalism* by Claudius Aelianus.

9 I.e., the faithful.

of young Girls, who were none of them above seven Years old.[10] It was wonderful (says the Author) to see how different the Treatment was which the Dogs gave to these little Misses, from that which they had shown to their Mothers. It is said that a Prince of *Syracuse,* having married a young Lady, and being naturally of a jealous Temper, made such an Interest with the Priests of this Temple, that he procured a Whelp from them of this famous Breed. The young Puppy was very troublesome to the fair Lady at first, insomuch that she sollicited her Husband to send him away, but the good Man cut her short with the old *Sicilian* Proverb, *Love me, love my Dog.*[11] From which Time she lived very peaceably with both of them. The Ladies of *Syracuse* were very much annoyed with him, and several of very good Reputation refused to come to Court till he was discarded. There were indeed some of them that defied his Sagacity, but it was observed tho' he did not actually bite them, he would growle at them most confoundedly. To return to the Dogs of the Temple: After they had lived here in great Repute for several Years, it so happened, that as one of the Priests, who had been making a charitable Visit to a Widow who lived on the Promontory of *Lilybeum,*[12] returned home pretty late in the Evening, the Dogs flew at him with so much Fury, that they would have worried him if his Brethren had not come in to his Assistance: Upon which, says my Author, the Dogs were all of them hanged, as having lost their original Instinct."

I cannot conclude this Paper without wishing, that we had some of this Breed of Dogs in *Great Britain,* which would certainly do *Justice,* I should say *Honour,* to the Ladies of our Country, and shew the World the difference between Pagan Women and those who are instructed in sounder Principles of Virtue and Religion.[13]

[10] The same defensive measure was mentioned in *Guardian* No. 114, after Nestor Ironside (the Guardian) erected a lion's head to receive letters at Button's Coffee-house and the rumor circulated that the lion would bite the hands of unchaste ladies.

[11] The proverb (not Sicilian) has been traced back to a twelfth-century Latin version.

[12] A cape on the western extremity of Sicily.

[13] The reference is, of course, ironic.

The Spectator, No. 590

Monday, September 6.

[A d d i s o n]

———*Assiduo labuntur tempora motu*
Non secus ac flumen. Neque enim consistere flumen,
Nec levis hora potest: sed ut unda impellitur unda,
Urgeturque prior venienti, urgetque priorem,
Tempora sic fugiunt pariter, pariterque sequuntur;
Et nova sunt semper. Nam quod fuit ante, relictum est;
Fitque quod haud fuerat: momentaque cuncta novantur. Ov. Met.[1]

The following Discourse comes from the same Hand with the Essays upon Infinitude.[2]

We consider infinite Space as an Expansion without a Circumference: We consider Eternity, or infinite Duration, as a Line that has neither a Beginning nor an End. In our Speculations of infinite Space, we consider that particular Place in which we exist, as a kind of Center to the whole Expansion. In our Speculations of Eternity, we consider the Time which is present to us as the Middle, which divides the whole Line into two equal Parts. For this Reason, many witty[3] Authors compare the present Time to

---

[1] Ovid *Metamorphoses* 15. 179–185 (altered): "Time flows in a constant motion, like a river; for neither can the river stop, nor the swift hour. Wave is pushed by wave, and the one coming in both thrusts and is itself thrust, so time both flees and follows and is ever new. What once was vanishes, what was not is created, and all motions renew."

[2] *Spectators* No. 565, 571, 580, and this essay comprise Addison's four papers on "Infinitude."

[3] Ingenious.

an Isthmus or narrow Neck of Land, that rises in the midst of an Ocean, immeasurably diffused on either Side of it.[4]

Philosophy, and indeed common Sense, naturally throws Eternity under two Divisions; which we may call in *English,* that Eternity which is past, and that Eternity which is to come. The learned Terms of, *Aeternitas a Parte ante,* and *Aeternitas a Parte post,* may be more amusing to the Reader, but can have no other Idea affixed to them than what is conveyed to us by those Words, an Eternity that is past, and an Eternity that is to come. Each of these Eternities is bounded at the one Extream; or, in other Words, the former has an End, and the latter a Beginning.

Let us first of all consider that Eternity which is past, reserving that which is to come for the Subject of another Paper.[5] The Nature of this Eternity is utterly inconceivable by the Mind of Man: Our Reason demonstrates to us that it *has been,* but at the same Time can frame no Idea of it, but what is big[6] with Absurdity and Contradiction. We can have no other Conception of any Duration which is past, than that all of it was once present; and whatever was once present is at some certain Distance from us; and whatever is at any certain Distance from us, be the Distance never so remote, cannot be Eternity. The very Notion of any Duration's being past, implies that it was once present; for the Idea of being once present, is actually included in the Idea of its being past. This therefore is a Depth not to be sounded by human Understanding. We are sure that there has been an Eternity, and yet contradict our selves when we measure this Eternity by any Notion which we can frame of it.

If we go to the Bottom of this Matter, we shall find, that the Difficulties we meet with in our Conceptions of Eternity proceed from this single Reason, That we can have no other Idea of any kind of Duration, than that by which we our selves, and all other created Beings, do exist; which is a successive Duration, made up

---

[4] This image appears in Cowley's Pindaric ode "Life and Fame" (10–13). It is not unlike the bridge allegory in Addison's vision of Mirzah (*Spectator* No. 159).

[5] Tickell broached this subject in *Spectator* No. 628, but Addison never returned to it.

[6] Pregnant.

of past, present, and to come. There is nothing which exists after this Manner, all the Parts of whose Existence were not once actually present, and consequently may be reached by a certain Number of Years applied to it. We may ascend as high as we please, and employ our Being to that Eternity which is to come, in adding Millions of Years to Millions of Years, and we can never come up to any Fountain-head of Duration, to any Beginning in Eternity: But at the same time we are sure, that whatever was once present does lye within the Reach of Numbers, tho' perhaps we can never be able to put enough of 'em together for that Purpose. We may as well say,[7] that any thing may be actually present in any Part of infinite Space, which does not lie at a certain Distance from us, as that any Part of infinite Duration was once actually present, and does not also lie at some determined Distance from us. The Distance in both Cases may be immeasureable and indefinite as to our Faculties, but our Reason tells us that it cannot be so in it self. Here therefore is that Difficulty which human Understanding is not capable of surmounting. We are sure that something must have existed from Eternity, and are at the same Time unable to conceive that any thing which exists, according to our Notion of Existence, can have existed from Eternity.

It is hard for a Reader, who has not rolled this Thought in his own Mind, to follow in such an abstracted Speculation;[8] but I have been the longer on it, because I think it is a demonstrative Argument of the Being and Eternity of a God: And tho' there are many other Demonstrations which lead us to this great Truth, I do not think we ought to lay aside any Proofs in this Matter which the Light of Reason has suggested to us, especially when it is such a one as has been urged by Men famous for their Penetration and Force of Understanding, and which appears altogether conclusive to those who will be at the Pains to examine it.

Having thus considered that Eternity which is past, according to the best Idea we can frame of it, I shall now draw up those several Articles on this Subject which are dictated to us by the Light

[7] I.e., it is as unreasonable to say.

[8] Addison recognized that the preceding paragraphs would be difficult going for coffee-house and tea-table readers.

of Reason, and which may be looked upon as the Creed of a Philosopher in this great Point.

First, It is certain that no Being could have made it self; for if so, it must have acted before it was, which is a Contradiction.

Secondly, That therefore some Being must have existed from all Eternity.

Thirdly, That whatever exists after the manner of created Beings, or according to any Notions which we have of Existence, could not have existed from Eternity.

Fourthly, That this eternal Being must therefore be the great Author of Nature, *the Antient of Days,*[9] who, being at an infinite Distance in his Perfections from all finite and created Beings, exists in a quite different manner from them, and in a manner of which they can have no Idea.

I know that several of the School-men,[10] who would not be thought ignorant of any thing, have pretended to explain the Manner of God's Existence, by telling us, That he comprehends infinite Duration in every Moment; That Eternity is with him a *punctum stans,* a fixed Point; or, which is as good Sense, an *Infinite Instant;* that nothing with Reference to his Existence is either past or to come; To which the ingenious Mr. *Cowley* alludes in his Description of Heaven,

> *Nothing is there to come, and nothing past,*
> *But an Eternal* NOW *does always last.*[11]

For my own Part, I look upon these Propositions as Words that have no Ideas annexed to them; and think Men had better own their Ignorance, than advance Doctrines, by which they mean nothing, and which indeed are self-contradictory. We cannot be too modest in our Disquisitions, when we meditate on him, who is environed with so much Glory and Perfection, who is the Source of Being, the Fountain of all that Existence which we and his whole Creation derive from him. Let us therefore with the utmost

---

9 The Lord God, as described in Daniel's dream (Daniel 7:9, 13, and 22).
10 See *Spectator* No. 191, n. 2.
11 The quotation is from book I of Cowley's Biblical epic *Davideis* (1657).

Humility acknowledge, that as some Being must necessarily have existed from Eternity, so this Being does exist after an incomprehensible manner, since it is impossible for a Being to have existed from Eternity after our Manner or Notions of Existence. Revelation confirms these natural Dictates of Reason in the Accounts which it gives us of the Divine Existence, where it tells us, that he is the same Yesterday, to Day, and for Ever; that he is the *Alpha* and *Omega,* the Beginning and the Ending; that a thousand Years are with him as one Day, and one Day as a thousand Years;[12] by which, and the like Expressions, we are taught, that his Existence, with Relation to Time or Duration, is infinitely different from the Existence of any of his Creatures, and consequently that it is impossible for us to frame any adequate Conceptions of it.

In the first Revelation which he makes of his own Being, he intitles himself, *I am that I am;*[13] and when *Moses* desires to know what Name he shall give him in his Embassy to *Pharoah,* he bids him say that, *I am* hath sent you. Our great Creator, by this Revelation of himself, does in a manner exclude every thing else from a real Existence, and distinguishes himself from his Creatures, as the only Being which truly and really exists. The ancient Platonick Notion, which was drawn from Speculations of Eternity, wonderfully agrees with this Revelation which God has made of himself. There is nothing, say they,[14] which in Reality exists, whose Existence, as we call it, is pieced up of past, present, and to come. Such a flitting and successive Existence is rather a Shadow of Existence, and something which is like it, than Existence it self. He only properly exists whose Existence is intirely present; that is, in other Words, who exists in the most perfect manner, and in such a manner as we have no Idea of.

I shall conclude this Speculation with one useful Inference. How can we sufficiently prostrate our selves and fall down before our Maker, when we consider that ineffable Goodness and Wisdom which contrived this Existence for finite Natures? What

---

12 The allusions are to Revelations 21:6 and Psalms 90:4.

13 Exodus 3:14. The reference is discussed in some detail in *Guardian* No. 74.

14 The Platonic writers.

must be the Overflowings of that good Will, which prompted our Creator to adapt Existence to Beings, in whom it is not necessary?[15] Especially when we consider, that he himself was before, in the compleat Possession of Existence and of Happiness, and in the full Enjoyment of Eternity. What Man can think of himself as called out and separated from nothing, of his being made a conscious, a reasonable and a happy Creature, in short, of being taken in as a Sharer of Existence and a kind of Partner in Eternity, without being swallowed up in Wonder, in Praise, in Adoration! It is indeed a Thought too big for the Mind of Man, and rather to be entertained in the Secrecy of Devotion and in the Silence of the Soul, than to be expressed by Words. The Supreme Being has not given us Powers or Faculties sufficient to extol and magnifie such unutterable Goodness.

It is however some Comfort to us, that we shall be always doing what we shall be never able to do, and that a Work which cannot be finished, will however be the Work of an Eternity.

[15] See *Spectator* No. 519 and n. 5.

The GUARDIAN.

Proprium hoc effe prudentiæ, conciliare fibi animos hominum & ad ufus fuos adjungere.   Cicer.

Wednefday, September 16. 1713.

I Was the other Day in Company at my Lady *Lizard*'s, when there came in among us their Coufin *Tom*, who is one of thofe Country Squires that fet up for plain honeft Gentlemen who fpeak their Minds. *Tom* is in fhort a lively impudent Clown, and has Wit enough to have made him a pleafant Companion, had it been polifhed and rectified by good Manners. *Tom* had not been a Quarter of an Hour with us, before he fet every one in the Company a Blufhing, by fome blunt Queftion, or unlucky Obfervation. He asked the *Sparkler* if her Wit had yet got her a Husband; and told her eldeft Sifter fhe looked a little Wan under the Eyes, and that it was time for her to look about her, if fhe did not defign to lead Apes in the other World. The good Lady *Lizard*, who fuffers more than her Daughters on fuch an occafion, defired her Cofin *Thomas* with a Smile, not to be fo fevere on his Relations; to which the Booby replied, with a rude Country Laugh, if I be not miftaken Aunt, you were a Mother at Fifteen, and why do you expect that your Daughters fhould be Maids till Five and twenty? I endeavoured to divert the Difcourfe, when without taking Notice of what I faid, Mr. *Ironfide*, fays he, you fill my Cofins Heads with your fine Notions as you call them, can you teach them to make a Pudding? I muft confefs he put me out of Countenance with his Ruftick Raillery, fo that I made fome Excufe, and left the Room.

(Price Two Pence.)

This Fellow's Behaviour made me reflect on the Ufefulnefs of Complaifance, to make all Converfation agreeable. This, tho' in itfelf it be fcarce reckoned in the number of Moral Virtues, is that which gives a Luftre to every Talent a Man can be poffeft of. It was *Plato*'s Advice to an unpolifh'd Writer, that he fhould Sacrifice to the Graces. In the fame manner I would advife every Man of Learning, who would not appear in the World a meer Scholar, or Philofopher, to make himfelf Mafter of the Social Virtue which I have here mentioned.

Complaifance renders a Superior amiable, an Equal agreeable, and an Inferior acceptable. It fmooths Diftinction, fweetens Converfation, and makes every one in the Company pleafed with himfelf. It produces Good-nature and mutual Benevolence, encourages the Timorous, fooths the Turbulent, humanifes the Fierce, and diftinguifhes a Society of Civilifed Perfons from a Confufion of Savages. In a word, Complaifance is a Virtue that blends all Orders of Men together in a Friendly Intercourfe of Words and Actions, and is fuited to that Equality in Human Nature which every one ought to confider, fo far as is confiftent with the Order and OEconomy of the World.

If we could look into the fecret Anguifh and Affliction of every Man's Heart, we fhould often find, that more of it arifes from little imaginary Diftreffes,
                                                        fuch

such as Checks, Frowns, Contradictions, Expressions of Contempt, and (what *Shakespear* reckons among other Evils under the Sun,)

——————— *The poor Man's Contumely,*
The Insolence of Office, and the Spurns
That patient Merit of the unworthy takes,

than from the more real Pains and Calamities of Life. The only Method to remove these imaginary Distresses as much as possible out of Human Life, wou'd be the Universal Practice of such an Ingenuous Complaisance as I have been here describing, which, as it is a Virtue, may be defined to be *a constant Endeavour to please those whom we converse with, so far as we may do it Innocently.* I shall here add, that I know nothing so effectual to raise a Man's Fortune as Complaisance, which recommends more to the Favour of the Great, than Wit, Knowledge, or any other Talent whatsoever. I find this Consideration very prettily illustrated by a little wild *Arabian* Tale, which I shall here a-bridge, for the sake of my Reader, after having again warned him, that I do not recommend to him such an impertinent or vicious Complaisance as is not consistent with Honour and Integrity.

' *Schacabac* being reduced to great Poverty, and
' having eat nothing for two Days together, made
' a Visit to a noble *Barmecide* in *Persia*, who was
' very hospitable, but withal a great Humourist.
' The *Barmecide* was sitting at his Table that seem-
' ed ready covered for an Entertainment. Upon
' hearing *Schacabac*'s Complaint, he desired him to
' sit down and fall on. He then gave him an empty
' Plate, and asked him how he liked his Rice-Soup.
' *Schacabac*, who was a Man of Wit, and resolved
' to comply with the *Barmecide* in all his Humours,
' told him 'twas admirable, and, at the same time,
' in Imitation of the other, lifted up the empty
' Spoon to his Mouth with great Pleasure. The
' *Barmecide* then asked him, if he ever saw whiter
' Bread? *Schacabac* who saw neither Bread nor
' Meat, If I did not like it, you may be sure, says he,
' I should not eat so heartily of it. You oblige
' me mightily, reply'd the *Barmecide*, pray let me
' help you to this Leg of a Goose. *Schacabac* reach-
' ed out his Plate, and received nothing on it with
' great Chearfulness. As he was eating very heartily
' on this imaginary Goose, and crying up the Sauce
' to the Skies, the *Barmecide* desired him to keep a
' Corner of his Stomach for a roasted Lamb, fed
' with Pistacho-Nuts, and after having call'd
' for it, as tho' it had really been served up, Here
' is a Dish, says he, that you will see at no Body's
' Table but my own. *Schacabac* was wonderfully

' delighted with the Taste of of it, which is like
' nothing, says he, I ever eat before. Several
' other nice Dishes were served up in Idea,
' which both of them commended and feasted on
' after the same manner. This was followed by an
' invisible *Dissert*, no part of which delighted
' *Schacabac* so much as a certain Lozenge, which
' the *Barmecide* told him was a Sweet-meat of his
' own Invention. *Schacabac* at length, being cour-
' teously reproached by the *Barmecide*, that he had
' no Stomach, and that he eat nothing, and, at the
' same time, being tired with moving his Jaws up
' and down to no Purpose, desired to be excused,
' for that really he was so full he could not eat a
' Bit more. Come then, says the *Barmecide*, the
' Cloth shall be removed, and you shall taste of my
' Wines, which I may say, without Vanity, are
' the best in *Persia*. He then *filled* both their Glas-
' ses out of an empty Decanter. *Schacabac* would
' have excused himself from drinking so much at
' once, because he said he was a little Quarrelsome
' in his Liquor; however being prest to it, he pre-
' tended to take it off, having before-hand praised
' the Colour, and afterwards the Flavour. Being
' ply'd with two or three other imaginary Bumpers
' of different Wines, equally delicious, and a little
' vexed with this fantastick Treat, he pretended to
' grow flustred, and gave the *Barmecide* a good Box
' on the Ear, but immediately recovering himself,
' Sir, says he, I beg ten thousand Pardons, but I
' told you before, that it was my Misfortune to be
' Quarrelsome in my Drink. The *Barmecide* could
' not but smile at the Humour of his Guest, and in-
' stead of being angry at him, I find, says he, thou
' art a complaisant Fellow, and deservest to be en-
' tertained in my House. Since thou canst acco-
' modate thy self to my Humour, we will now
' eat together in good Earnest. Upon which, cal-
' ling for his Supper, the Rice-Soup, the Goose,
' the Pistacho-Lamb, the several other nice Dishes,
' with the *Dissert*, the Lozenges, and all the Varie-
' ty of *Persian* Wines, were served up successively,
' one after another; and *Schacabac* was feasted
' in Reality, with those very things which he had
' before been entertained with in Imagination.

ADVERTISEMENT.

The Guardian

Three months after the first series of *Spectators* ended, *The Guardian* appeared. Printed on folio half-sheets, the papers were published six days a week (Monday through Saturday) from March 12 to October 1, 1713. Each copy sold for twopence.

The papers were published anonymously, and authorship of particular essays remains uncertain. Steele established the periodical and wrote over eighty of the 175 issues. Addison, involved with his tragedy *Cato,* did not produce a *Guardian* until No. 67. And he did not make regular contributions until No. 96, when he took over for a month while Steele was busy campaigning for a seat in Parliament. Addison wrote more than fifty papers, almost all of which appeared in three sequences; with but two exceptions, he wrote Nos. 96–124, Nos. 134–140, and Nos. 152–167. Other contributors included the young philosopher George Berkeley—who is credited with eleven essays—Thomas Tickell, Alexander Pope, John Gay, Eustace Budgell, and John Hughes.

The fictitious author is Nestor Ironside, an elderly person who recalls Isaac Bickerstaff as "a Man nearly related to the Family of the Ironsides" and the Spectator as "a Gentleman of the same Family." Ironside acts as friend and guardian in the family of the deceased Sir Marmaduke Lizard at Lizard Hall in Northamptonshire. As such, he counsels Aspasia ("my lady Lizard"); her four sons (Sir Harry, Thomas, William, and John); and five daughters (Jane, Anabella, Cornelia, Betty, and Mary—who is called "the Sparkler"). The family is described in Guardians No. 2, 5, and 13, but, as with many of the characters established in *The Tatler* and *The Spectator,* relatively little is said of them thereafter.

The title of the new series suggested that Steele had serious intentions. While a tatler is socially frivolous and a spectator is reserved, a guardian—particularly one named Ironside—might be expected to exercise authority. The first paper expressed an intention "to confront the Impudent, the Idle, to contemn the Vain, the Cowardly, and to disappoint the Wicked and Prophane."

Where the Spectator, in his opening essay, had promised "to observe an exact Neutrality between the Whigs and Tories," Ironside declared, "As to these Matters, I shall be impartial, tho' I cannot be Neuter."

Nevertheless, a new note of stern admonition did not characterize *The Guardian*. The essays are not easily distinguishable from those of *The Tatler* and *The Spectator*. The papers continued to discuss duelling, clubs, God, charity, gallantry, and fashion. Saturday papers still treated subjects related to religion. Except for Tickell's five essays on pastoral poetry (Nos. 22, 23, 28, 30, 32) and Pope's famous ironic response (No. 40), there were no series papers. However, recurring topics included death, freethinkers, the Lizard family, the tucker, the lion's head at Button's, and *The Examiner*. The strongest attacks on the Tory journal were—it should be noted—never penned by the Guardian himself. All appeared as letters from correspondents, among them one who signed himself "Richard Steele."

Though Nestor Ironside admitted he could not be neuter on matters of church and state, *The Guardian* avoided political issues during its first month of publication. But when the ministry described the Treaty of Utrecht (signed April 11) as a Tory triumph and when its journal criticized Daniel Finch, the Earl of Nottingham, for opposing the Treaty, Steele dropped the pose of impartiality. *Guardian* No. 41 carried an unsigned letter accusing *The Examiner* of aggravating the disgraces of the brave and unfortunate, of trampling on the ashes of the dead. No. 53 printed a letter from Steele, acknowledging authorship of the earlier epistle and repeating its charges. No. 63 published a ribald letter from Steele, speculating whether the Examiner is male or female. And No. 90 carried an unsigned letter scoring *The Examiner* for criticizing a bishop and his anti-papal book.

Thus *The Guardian* was deeply embroiled in political controversy when Addison began writing regularly for the journal. To ease the situation, he produced a series of papers (Nos. 96–120, 122–124) notable for their charm and inoffensiveness. He discussed medals, the tucker, the art of flying, Tom Truelove's courtship, the Tall Club, etc. Steele returned to *The Guardian* with essay No. 128, a letter from "English Tory" which criticized Iron-

side for writing "too frivolously" and demanded, in accordance
with provisions of the Treaty of Utrecht, the demolition of the
French port at Dunkirk. While Addison continued to write un-
controversial essays, Steele included in his papers another letter
from English Tory (No. 131), a signed letter admitting he is English Tory (No. 168), and a passage praising *The Examiner* for
excelling in "The Art of Defamation" (No. 170).

The varying emphases of the two authors contributed to the
termination of *The Guardian*. Steele ended the paper on October 1 to free himself for more exclusively political writing. His
new periodical *The Englishman* appeared on October 6. In June
of the following year, Addison began the second series of *The
Spectator*.

The Guardian, No. 1

Thursday, March 12. 1713.

[S t e e l e]

———*Ille quem requiris.* Mart.[1]

There is no Passion so universal, however diversified or dis-
guised under different Forms and Appearances, as the Vanity of
being known to the rest of Mankind, and communicating a Man's[2]
Parts, Virtues or Qualifications to the World; this is so strong
upon Men of great Genius, that they have a restless Fondness for
satisfying the World in the Mistakes they might possibly be under, with relation even to their Physiognomy. Mr. *Airs,* that excellent Penman, has taken care to affix his own Image opposite to
the Title Page of his Learned Treatise, wherein he instructs the
Youth of this Nation to arrive at a flourishing Hand. The Author[3]
of *the Key to Interest, both Simple and Compound, containing
Practical Rules plainly expressed in Words at length for all Rates
of Interest, and Times of Payment, for what time soever,* makes up
to us the Misfortune of his living at *Chester,* by following the Example of the abovementioned *Airs,* and coming up to Town, over-
against his Title Page in a very becoming Periwig, and a flowing
Robe or Mantle, inclosed in a Circle of Foliages; below his Por-
traiture, for our farther Satisfaction, as to the Age of that useful
Writer, is subscribed *Johannes Ward de Civitat. Cestriae, Aetat.
suae* 58. *An. Dom.* 1706. The serene Aspect of these Writers, join'd

---

[1] Martial *Epigrams* 2. 1: "He, whom you seek."
[2] I.e., one's own.
[3] *The Key to Interest* . . . was the work of John Ward, a Director of the
Bank and of the East India Company.

with the great Encouragement I observe is given to another, or, what is indeed to be suspected, in which he indulges himself, confirmed me in the Notion I have of the prevalence of Ambition this way. The Author whom I hint at shall be nameless, but his Countenance is communicated to the Publick in several Views and Aspects drawn by the most eminent Painters, and forwarded by Engravers, Artists by way of Metsotinto,[4] Etchers, and the like. There was, I remember, some Years ago one *John Gale,* a Fellow that play'd upon a Pipe, and diverted the Multitude by Dancing in a Ring they made about him, whose Face became generally known, and the Artists employ'd their Skill in delineating his Features, because every Man was Judge of the Similitude of them. There is little else than what this *John Gale* arriv'd at in the Advantages Men enjoy from common Fame, yet do I fear it has always a Part in moving us to exert our selves in such things, as ought to derive their beginnings from nobler Considerations: But I think it is no great matter to the Publick what is the Incentive which makes Men bestow time in their Service, provided there be any thing useful in what they produce; I shall proceed therefore to give an Account of my intended Labours, not without some hope of having my Vanity, at the end of them, indulged in the Sort abovementioned.

I should not have assumed the Title of *Guardian,* had I not maturely considered, that the Qualities necessary for doing the Duties of that Character, proceed from the Integrity of the Mind, more than the Excellence of the Understanding: The former of these Qualifications it is in the Power of every Man to arrive at; and the more he endeavours that Way, the less will he want the Advantages of the latter; to be Faithful, to be Honest, to be Just, is what you will demand in the Choice of your Guardian; or if you find added to this, that he is Pleasant, Ingenious, and Agreeable, there will overflow Satisfactions which make for the Ornament, if not so immediately to the Use, of your Life. As to the Diverting Part of this Paper, by what Assistance[5] I shall be capacitated for that, as well as what Proofs I have given of my Be-

---

4 An engraving made from a copper plate.
5 Gifts.

haviour as to Integrity in former Life, will appear from my History to be delivered in ensuing Discourses. The main Purpose of the Work shall be to protect the Modest, the Industrious, to celebrate the Wise, the Valiant, to encourage the Good, the Pious, to confront the Impudent, the Idle, to contemn the Vain, the Cowardly, and to disappoint the Wicked and Prophane. This Work cannot be carried on but by preserving a strict Regard, not only to the Duties but Civilities of Life, with the utmost Impartiality towards Things and Persons. The unjust Application of the Advantages of Breeding and Fortune is the Source of all Calamity both Publick and Private; the Correction therefore, or rather Admonition, of a Guardian, in all the Occurrences of a various Being, if given with a benevolent Spirit, would certainly be of General Service.[6]

In order to contribute as far as I am able to it, I shall publish in respective Papers whatever I think may conduce to the Advancement of the Conversation of Gentlemen, the Improvement of Ladies, the Wealth of Traders, and the Encouragement of Artificers. The Circumstance relating to those who excel in Mechanicks,[7] shall be consider'd with particular Application. It is not to be immediately conceived by such as have not turned themselves to Reflections of that Kind, that Providence, to enforce and endear the Necessity of Social Life, has given one Man Hands to another Man's Head, and the Carpenter, the Smith, the Joiner[8] are as immediately necessary to the Mathematician, as my Amanuensis[9] will be to me, to Write much fairer than I can my self. I am so well convinced of this Truth, that I shall have a particular regard to Mechanicks, and to show my Honour for them, I shall place at their head[10] the Painter. This Gentleman is as to the Execution of his Work a Mechanick, but as to his Conception, his Spirit and Design, he is hardly below even the Poet, in Liberal Art. It will be from these Considerations useful to make the World

---

[6] I.e., just as a guardian corrects and admonishes the children of well-born families, so he will correct and admonish the excesses of the general public.

[7] Work done by hand.

[8] The cabinet-maker.

[9] The one who writes out the final copy of his essays.

[10] I.e., consider as the first among them.

see the Affinity between all Works which are beneficial to Mankind is much nearer, than the illiberal Arrogance of Scholars will, at all times allow. But I am from Experience convinced of the Importance of Mechanick Heads, and shall therefore take them all into my Care, from *Rowley,* who is improving the Globes of the Earth and Heavens in *Fleetstreet,*[11] to *Bat Pidgeon* the Hair Cutter in the *Strand.*

But it will be objected upon what Pretensions I take upon me to put in for the *prochain amy,* or nearest Friend of all the World. How my Head is accomplished for this Employment towards the Publick, from the long Exercise of it in a private Capacity, will appear by reading me the two or three next Days with Diligence and Attention. There is no other Paper in Being which tends to this Purpose. They are most of them Histories or Advices of Publick Transactions; but as those Representations affect the Passions of my Readers, I shall sometimes take Care, the Day after a Foreign Mail,[12] to give them an Account of what it has brought. The Parties among us are too violent to make it possible to pass them by without Observation. As to these Matters, I shall be impartial, tho' I cannot be Neuter.[13] I am, with Relation to the Government of the Church, a Tory, with Regard to the State, a Whig.

The Charge of Intelligence,[14] the Pain in compiling and digesting my Thoughts in proper Stile, and the like, oblige me to value my Paper an Half-peny above all other Half-Sheets.[15] And all Persons who have any thing to communicate to me, are desired to direct their Letters (Postage paid) to *Nestor Ironside,* Esq; at Mr. *Tonson's*[16] in the *Strand.* I declare before-hand, that I will at

---

[11] John Rowley (d. 1728) was quoted in *Spectator* No. 552, in which he proposed to construct two globes, one showing the geography of the earth and one the arrangement of heavenly constellations. Subscribers who paid him twenty-five pounds would receive the pair of globes, either for their own use or for the school or library of their choice.

[12] See *Tatler* No. 155, n. 4.

[13] To quote Calhoun Winston (*Captain Steele,* 1964), "Readers may have found Nestor's distinction between impartiality and neutrality a little hard to grasp. . . ."

[14] The expense involved in securing information.

[15] The original price of the paper was two pence.

[16] Jacob Tonson (1656?–1736), printer and bookseller.

no Time be conversed with any other ways than by Letter; for as I am an Antient Man, I shall find enough to do to give Orders proper for their Service, to whom I am by Will of their Parents Guardian,[17] tho' I take that to be too narrow a Scene for me to pass my whole Life in. But I have got my Wards so well off my Hands, and they are so able to act for themselves, that I have little to do but give an Hint, and all that I desire to be amended is altered accordingly.

My Design upon the whole is no less, than to make the Pulpit, the Bar, and the Stage, all act in Concert in the Care of Piety, Justice and Virtue. For I am past all the Regards of this Life, and have nothing to manage with any Person or Party, but to deliver my self as becomes an Old Man with one Foot in the Grave, and one who thinks he is passing to Eternity. All Sorrows which can arrive at me are comprehended in the Sense of Guilt and Pain; If I can keep clear of these two Evils, I shall not be apprehensive of any other. Ambition, Lust, Envy, and Revenge, are Excrescencies of the Mind which I have cut off long ago: But as they are Excrescencies which do not only deform, but also torment those on whom they grow, I shall do all I can to persuade all others to take the same Measures for their Cure which I have.

17 I.e., proper to the younger members of the Lizard family. See *Guardian* No. 5, n. 2.

The Guardian, No. 5

Tuesday, March 17.

[Steele]

Laudantur simili prole puerperae. Hor.[1]

I have in my second Paper mentioned the Family, into which I was retained by the Friend of my Youth; and given the Reader to understand, that my Obligations to it are such as might well naturalize me into the Interests of it.[2] They have, indeed, had their deserved Effect; and if it were possible for a Man, who has never entered into the State of Marriage, to know the Instincts of a kind Father to an Honourable and Numerous House, I may say I have done it. I do not know but my Regards,[3] in some Considerations, have been more useful than those of a Father; and as I wanted[4] all that Tenderness, which is the Byass of Inclination in Men towards their own Offspring, I have had a greater Command of Reason when I was to judge of what concerned my Wards, and consequently was not prompted, by my Partiality and Fondness towards their Persons, to transgress against their Interests.

[1] Horace *Odes* 4. 5. 23: "The parents' virtues are imaged in the children."

[2] *Guardian* No. 2 gave the history of Ironside's employment: An old college friend, Sir Ambrose Lizard, asked that he act as tutor and guardian to his only son, Marmaduke. Now, years later, with both Sir Ambrose and Sir Marmaduke dead, he lives with and counsels the remaining members of the family: Sir Ambrose's widow; Sir Marmaduke's forty-six year old widow, Aspasia, regularly referred to as My Lady Lizard; and Sir Marmaduke's nine children. The five daughters are introduced in this essay; the four sons—Sir Harry Lizard, Mr. Thomas, Mr. William, and Mr. John—in essays No. 6 and 13.

[3] I.e., my guardianly concern.

[4] Lacked.

As the Female Part of a Family is the more constant and immediate Object of Care and Protection, and the more liable to Misfortune or Dishonour, as being in themselves more sensible of the former, and from Custom and Opinion for less Offences more exposed to the latter; I shall begin with the more delicate part of my Guardianship, the Women of the Family of *Lizard*. The ancient and Religious Lady, the Dowager of my Friend Sir *Ambrose,* has for some time estranged her self from Conversation, and admits only of the Visits of her own Family. The Observation, That Old People remember best those things which entered into their Thoughts when their Memories were in their full Strength and Vigour, is very remarkably exemplified in this good Lady and my self when we are in Conversation: I chuse indeed to go thither, to divert any Anxiety or Weariness, which at any time I find grow upon me from any present Business or Care. It is said, that a little Mirth and Diversion are what recreate the Spirits upon those Occasions; but there is a kind of Sorrow, from which I draw a Consolation that strengthens my Faculties, and enlarges my Mind beyond any thing that can flow from Merriment. When we meet, we soon get over any Occurrence which passed the Day before, and are in a Moment hurried back to those Days which only we call good ones: The Passages of the Times when we were in Fashion, with the Countenances, Behaviour and Jollity, so much forsooth above what any appear in now, are present to our Imaginations, and almost to our very Eyes. This Conversation revives to us the Memory of a Friend, that was more than my Brother to me; of a Husband, that was dearer than Life to her: Discourses about that dear and worthy Man generally send her to her Closet,[5] and me to the Dispatch of some necessary Business, which regards the Remains, I would say the numerous Descendants, of my generous Friend. I am got, I know not how, out of[6] what I was going to say of this Lady; which was, that she is far gone towards a better World; and I mention her only (with Respect to this) as she is the Object of Veneration to those who are derived from her: Whose Behaviour towards her may be an Example to others, and make

[5] Her private apartment.
[6] I have digressed from.

the Generality of young People apprehend, that when the Ancient are past all Offices of Life, it is then the Young are to exert themselves in their most laudable Duties towards them.

The Widow of Sir *Marmaduke* is to be considered in a very different View. My Lady is not in the shining Bloom of Life, but at those Years, wherein the Gratifications of an ample Fortune, those of Pomp and Equipage, of being much esteemed, much visited, and generally admired, are usually more strongly pursued than in younger Days: In this Condition she might very well add the Pleasures of Courtship, and the grateful Persecution of being followed by a Croud of Lovers; but she is an excellent Mother and great Oeconomist;[7] which Considerations, joined with the Pleasure of living her own way, preserve her against the Intrusion of Love. I will not say that my Lady has not a secret Vanity in being still a fine Woman, and neglecting those Addresses, to which perhaps we in part owe her Constancy in that her Neglect.[8]

Her Daughter *Jane,* her eldest Child of that Sex, is in the Twenty third Year of her Age, a Lady who forms her self after the Pattern of her Mother; but in my Judgment, as she happens to be extremely like her, she sometimes makes her Court unskilfully, in affecting that Likeness in her very Mein, which gives the Mother an uneasie Sense, that Mrs. *Jane*[9] really is what her Parent has a mind to continue to be;[10] but 'tis possible I am too observing in this Particular, and this might be overlooked in them both, in respect to greater Circumstances: For Mrs. *Jane* is the Right hand of her Mother; it's her Study and constant Endeavour to assist her in the Management of her Houshold, to keep all idle Whispers from her, and discourage them before they can come at her from any other hand; to enforce every thing that makes for the Merit of her Brothers and Sisters towards her, as well as the Diligence and Chearfulness of her Servants. It's by Mrs. *Jane*'s Management, that the whole Family is governed, neither by Love nor Fear, but a certain Reverence which is composed of both. Mrs. *Jane* is what

7 One who practices economy.

8 By rejecting her suitors she remains "a fine Woman," i.e., one eligible for courtship.

9 At this time, "Mrs." meant simply adult, not wed.

10 I.e., unmarried.

one would call a perfect good young Woman; but neither strict
Piety, Diligence in Domestick Affairs, or any other Avocation,
have preserved her against Love, which she bears to a young Gentleman of great Expectation, but small Fortune; at the same time,
that Men of very great Estates ask her of her Mother. My Lady
tells her that Prudence must give way to[11] Passion, so that Mrs.
Jane, if I cannot accommodate the matter, must conquer more
than one Passion, and out of Prudence banish the Man she loves,
and marry the Man she hates.

The next Daughter is Mrs. *Annabella,* who has a very lively
Wit, a great deal of good Sense, is very pretty, but gives me much
trouble for her from a certain dishonest Cunning I know in her;
she can seem blind and careless, and full of her self only, and
entertain with twenty affected Vanities whilst she is observing all
the Company, laying up store for Ridicule; and, in a word, is
selfish and interested under all the agreeable Qualities in the
World.[12] Alas, what shall I do with this Girl!

Mrs. *Cornelia* passes her time very much in Reading, and that
with so great an Attention, that it gives her the Air of a Student,
and has an ill effect upon her as she is a fine young Woman; the
giddy part of the Sex will have it she is in Love; none will allow
that she affects so much being alone but for want of particular
Company. I have railed at Romances before her, for fear of her
falling into those deep Studies; she has fallen in with my Humour
that way for the time, but I know not how, my imprudent Prohi-
bition has, it seems, only excited her Curiosity; and I am afraid
she is better read than I know of, for she said of a Glass of Water
in which she was going to wash her Hands after Dinner, dipping
her Fingers with a pretty lovely Air, *It is Crystalin.*[13] I shall examine further, and wait for clearer Proofs.

Mrs. *Betty* is (I cannot by what means or methods imagine)
grown mightily acquainted with what passes in the Town; she
knows all that matter of my Lord such a one's leading my Lady

11 I.e., must take the place of.

12 While appearing light and frivolous, she is really self-concerned and
critical.

13 Presumably Mrs. Cornelia is enjoying the kind of romances displayed in
Leonora's library. See *Spectator* No. 37.

such a one out from the Play; she is prodigiously acquainted, all of a sudden, with the World, and asked her Sister *Jane* t'other Day in an Argument, *Dear Sister, how should you know any thing that hear nothing but what we do in our own Family?* I don't much like her Maid.

Mrs. *Mary,* the youngest Daughter, whom they rally and call Mrs. *Ironside,* because I have named her *the Sparkler,* is the very Quintescence of good Nature and Generosity; she is the perfect Picture of her Grandfather, and if one can imagine all good Qualities which adorn Human Life become Feminine; the Seeds, nay the Blossom of them, are apparent in Mrs. *Mary.* It is a weakness I cannot get over, (for how ridiculous is a regard to the bodily Perfections of a Man who is dead) but I cannot resist the Partiality to this Child, for being so like her Grandfather; how often have I turned from her to hide the melting of my Heart when she has been talking to me! I am sure the Child has no Skill in it, for Artifice could not dwell under that Visage; but if I am absent a Day from the Family, she is sure to be at my Lodging the next Morning to know what is the matter.

At the head of these Children, who have very plentiful Fortunes, provided they marry with mine and their Mother's Consent, is my Lady *Lizard;* who, you cannot doubt, is very well visited. Sir *William Oger,* and his Son almost at Age, are frequently at our House on a double Consideration. The Knight is willing (for so he very gallantly expresses himself) to marry the Mother, or he'll consent, whether that be so or not, that his Son *Oliver* shall take any one of the Daughters *Noll*[14] likes best.

Mr. *Rigburt* of the same County, who gives in[15] his Estate much larger, and his Family more antient, offers to deal with us for two Daughters.

Sir *Harry Pandolf* has writ Word from his Seat in the Country, that he also is much enclin'd to an Alliance with the *Lizards,* which he has declared in the following Letter to my Lady; she shewed me it this Morning.

---

[14] Short for "Oliver."
[15] Claims.

"Madam,

I have heard your Daughters very well spoken of; and tho' I have very great Offers in my own Neighbourhood, and heard the Small-Pox is very rife at *London,* I will send my eldest Son to see them, provided that by your Ladyships Answer, and your liking of the Rent-Roll which I send herewith, your Ladyship assures me he shall have one of them, for I don't think to have my Son refused by any Woman; and so, Madam, I conclude,

Your most Humble Servant,
Henry Pandolf."

The Guardian, No. 12

Wednesday, March 25.

[S t e e l e]

Vel quia nil rectum, nisi quod placuit sibi, ducunt:
Vel quia turpe putant parere minoribus————Hor.[1]

When a Poem makes its first Appearance in the World, I have always observed, that it gives Employment to a greater number of Criticks, than any other kind of Writing. Whether it be that most Men, at some time of their Lives, have try'd their Talent that way,[2] and thereby think they have a right to judge; or whether they imagine, that their making shrewd Observations upon the Polite Arts, gives them a pretty figure;[3] or whether there may not be some Jealousie and Caution in bestowing Applause upon those who write chiefly for Fame. Whatever the Reasons be, we find few discouraged by the Delicacy and Danger of such an Undertaking.

I think it certain, that most Men are naturally not only capable of being pleased with that which raises agreeable Pictures in the Fancy, but willing also to own it. But then there are many, who, by false Applications of some Rules ill understood, or out of Deference to Men whose Opinions they value, have formed to themselves certain Schemes and Systems of Satisfaction, and will not be pleased out of their own way. These are not Criticks themselves, but Readers of Criticks, who, without the Labour of perusing Authors, are able to give their Characters in general; and know just

---

1 Horace *Epistles* 2. 1. 83–84: "Either they think nothing is good unless they themselves have liked it, or they think it a weakness to yield to their juniors."

2 I.e., in writing poetry.

3 Reputation.

as much of the several Species of Poetry, as those who read Books of Geography do of the Genius[4] of this or that People or Nation. These Gentlemen deliver their Opinions sententiously, and in general Terms; to which it being impossible readily to frame compleat Answers, they have often the Satisfaction of leaving the Board in Triumph. As young Persons, and particularly the Ladies, are liable to be led aside by these Tyrants in Wit, I shall examine two or three of the many Stratagems they use, and subjoin such Precautions as may hinder candid Readers from being deceived thereby.

The first I shall take Notice of is an Objection commonly offered, *viz. That such a Poem hath indeed some good Lines in it, but it is not a regular Piece.* This for the most part is urged by those whose Knowledge is drawn from some famous *French* Criticks,[5] who have written upon the Epic Poem, the Drama, and the great kinds of Poetry, which cannot subsist without great Regularity; but ought by no means to be required in Odes, Epistles, Panegyricks, and the like, which naturally admit of greater Liberties. The Enthusiasm in Odes, and the Freedom of Epistles, is rarely disputed; But I have often heard the Poems upon Publick Occasions written in Heroic Verse, which I chuse to call Panegyricks, severely censured upon this Account; the Reason whereof I cannot guess, unless it be, that because they are written in the same kind of Numbers and Spirit as an Epic Poem, they ought therefore to have the same Regularity. Now an Epic Poem, consisting chiefly in Narration, it is necessary that the Incidents should be related in the same Order that they are supposed to have been transacted. But in Works of the above-mentioned kind, there is no more Reason that such Order should be observed, than that an Oration should be as methodical as an History. I think it sufficient that the great Hints, suggested from the Subject, be so disposed, that the first may naturally prepare the Reader for what follows, and so on; and that their Places cannot be changed with-

4 Character, temperament.

5 One recalls *Tatler* No. 165 by Addison in which Sir Timothy Tittle faults a young lady for laughing at a new comedy: "Madam, there are such People in the World as *Rapin, Dacier,* and several others, that ought to have spoiled your Mirth."

out Disadvantage to the whole. I will add further, that sometimes gentle Deviations, sometimes bold and even abrupt Digressions, where the Dignity of the Subject seems to give the Impulse, are Proofs of a noble Genius; as winding about, and returning artfully to the main Design, are Marks of Address and Dexterity.

Another Artifice made use of by Pretenders to Criticism, is an Insinuation, *That all that is good is borrowed from the Ancients.*[6] This is very common in the Mouths of Pedants, and perhaps in their Hearts too; but is often urged by Men of no great Learning, for Reasons very obvious. Now Nature being still[7] the same, it is impossible for any Modern Writer to paint her otherwise than the Ancients have done. If, for Example, I were to describe the General's Horse at the Battel of *Blenheim*,[8] as my Fancy represented such a noble Beast, and that Description should resemble what *Virgil* hath drawn for the Horse of his Hero,[9] it would be almost as ill-natured to urge that I had stolen my Description from *Virgil,* as to reproach the Duke of *Marlborough* for fighting only like *Aeneas.* All that the most exquisite Judgment can perform is, out of that great Variety of Circumstances, wherein natural Objects may be considered, to select the most beautiful; and to place Images in such Views and Lights, as will affect the Fancy after the most delightful manner.[10] But over and above a just Painting of Nature, a learned Reader will find a new Beauty superadded in a happy Imitation of some famous Ancient, as it revives in his Mind the Pleasure he took in his first reading such an Author. Such Copyings as these give that kind of double Delight which we perceive when we look upon the Children of a beautiful Couple; where the Eye is not more charm'd with the Symmetry of the Parts, than the Mind by observing the Resemblance transmitted

6 I.e., the ancient Greek and Roman writers.

7 Ever.

8 See *Spectator* No. 26, n. 16.

9 Virgil *Aeneid* 7. 280–283.

10 Steele is repeating a view expressed by Addison in *Spectator* No. 253: "It is impossible, for us who live in the later Ages of the World, to make Observations in Criticism, Morality, or in any Art or Science, which have not been touched upon by others. We have little else left us, but to represent the common Sense of Mankind in more strong, more beautiful, or more uncommon Lights."

from Parents to their Offspring, and the mingled Features of the Father and the Mother. The Phrases of Holy Writ, and Allusions to several Passages in the Inspired Writings, (though not produced as Proofs of Doctrine) add Majesty and Authority to the noblest Discourses of the Pulpit: In like manner an Imitation of the Air of *Homer* and *Virgil* raises the Dignity of modern Poetry, and makes it appear stately and venerable.

The last Observation I shall make at present is upon the Disgust taken by those Criticks, who put on their Cloaths prettily,[11] and dislike every thing that is not written *with Ease*. I hereby therefore give the genteel part of the learned World to understand, that every Thought which is agreeable to Nature, and exprest in Language suitable to it, is written with Ease. There are some Things which must be written with Strength, which nevertheless are easie. The Statue of the *Gladiator,* though represented in such a Posture as strains every Muscle, is as easie as that of *Venus;* because the one expresses Strength and Fury as naturally as the other doth Beauty and Softness. The Passions are sometimes to be rouzed, as well as the Fancy to be entertained; and the Soul to be exalted and enlarged, as well as soothed. This often requires a raised and figurative Stile; which Readers of low Apprehensions, or soft and lanquid Dispositions (having heard of the Words *Fustian*[12] and *Bombast*) are apt to reject as stiff and affected Language. But Nature and Reason appoint different Garbs for different Things; and since I write this to the Men of Dress, I will ask them if a Soldier, who is to mount a Breach,[13] should be adorned like a Beau, who is spruced up for a Ball?[14]

11 I.e., the beau-critics, whose main aesthetic concern is their fashionable appearance.

12 Fustian is pretentious writing.

13 To enter a gap in the enemy's defences.

14 The substance of this essay parallels portions of Pope's *Essay on Criticism,* published two years earlier, and of Addison's *Spectator* No. 253 which praised Pope's poem.

The Guardian, No. 17

Tuesday, March 31.

[S t e e l e]

———*Minimumque libidine peccant.* Juv.[1]

If it were possible to bear up against the Force of Ridicule, which Fashion has brought upon People for acknowledging a Veneration for the most Sacred things, a Man might say that the time we now are in[2] is set apart for Humiliation; and all our Actions should at present more particularly tend that way. I remember about thirty Years ago an eminent Divine,[3] who was also most exactly well-bred, told his Congregation at *Whitehall,* That if they did not vouchsafe to give their Lives a new Turn, they must certainly go to a Place which he did not think fit to name in that Courtly Audience. It's with me as with that Gentleman; I would, if possible, represent the Errors of Life, especially those arising from what we call Gallantry,[4] in such a manner as the People of Pleasure may read me. In this case I must not be rough to Gentlemen and Ladies, but speak of Sin as a Gentleman. It might not perhaps be amiss, if therefore I should call my present Precaution *a Criticism upon Fornication;*[5] and by representing the unjust Taste they have who affect that way of Pleasure, bring a Distaste

1 Juvenal *Satires* 6. 134: "Lust is the least sin they admit."

2 Holy Week, the final week of Lent.

3 Knightly Chestwood (1650–1720), Dean of Gloucester. Pope recalls this incident in his *Epistle to Burlington* 2. 149–150.

4 Amorous adventures.

5 Steele discussed the sordidness of gallantry in *Spectator* No. 266, then in No. 276 offered a letter from Francis Courtly complaining of his inelegant language: "A Word to the Wise. All I mean here to say to you is, That the most free Person of Quality can go no further than being an unkind Woman; and you should never say of a Man of Figure worse, than that he knows the World."

upon it among all those who are judicious in their Satisfactions. I will be bold then to lay down for a Rule, That he who follows this kind of Gratification, gives up much greater delight by pursuing it, than he can possibly enjoy from it. As to the Common Women and the Stews,[6] there is no one but will allow this Assertion at first sight; but if it will appear, that they who deal with those of the Sex who are less profligate descend to greater Basenesses than if they frequented Brothels, it should, methinks, bring this Iniquity under some Discountenance. The Rake, who without sense of Character or Decency, wallows and ranges in common Houses, is guilty no further than of prostituting himself, and exposing his Health to Diseases; but the Man of Gallantry cannot pursue his Pleasures without Treachery to some Man he ought to love, and making despicable the Woman he admires. To live in a continual Deceit, to reflect upon the Dishonour you do some Husband, Father or Brother, who does not deserve this of you, and whom you would destroy did you know they did the like towards you, are Circumstances which pall the Appetite, and give a Man of any Sense of Honour very painful Mortification. What more need be said against a Gentleman's delight, than that he 'himself thinks himself a base Man in pursuing it? When it is thoroughly considered, he gives up his very Being as a Man of Integrity, who commences Gallant. Let him or her who is guilty this way but weigh the matter a little, and the Criminal will find that those whom they most estemed are of a sudden become the most disagreeable Companions; nay, their good Qualities are grown odious and painful. It is said, People who have the Plague have a delight in communicating the Infection; in like manner, the Sense of Shame, which is never wholly overcome, inclines the Guilty this way to contribute to the Destruction of others. And Women are pleased to introduce more Women into the same Condition, tho' they can have no other Satisfaction from it, than that the Infamy is shared among greater Numbers, which they flatter themselves eases the burthen of each particular Person.

It is a most melancholy Consideration, that for momentary Sensations of Joy, obtained by stealth, Men are forced into a constraint of all their Words and Actions in the general and ordinary

6 Brothels.

Occurrences of Life. It is an Impossibility in this case to be faithful to one Person, without being false to all the rest of the World: The gay Figures in which Poetical Men of loose Morals have placed this kind of stealth are but feeble Consolations, when a Man is enclined to Soliloquy or Meditation upon his past Life; Flashes of Wit can promote Joy, but they cannot allay Grief.

Disease, Sickness and Misfortune are what all Men living are liable to, it is therefore ridiculous and mad to pursue, instead of shunning, what must add to our Anguish under Disease, Sickness or Misfortune. It is possible there may be those whose Bloods are too warm to admit of these Compunctions; if there are such, I am sure they are laying up Store for them: But I have better hopes of those who have not yet erazed the Impressions and Advantages of a good Education and Fortune; they may be assured, *that whoever wholly give themselves up to Lust, will soon find it the least Fault they are guilty of.*

Irreconcilable Hatred to those they have injured, mean Shifts to cover their Offences, Envy and Malice to the Innocent, and a general Sacrifice of all that is Good-natured or Praise-worthy when it interrupts them, will possess all their Faculties, and make them utter Strangers to the noble Pleasures which flow from Honour and Virtue. Happy are they, who, from the Visitation of Sickness, or any other Accident, are awakened from a Course which leads to an insensibility of the greatest Enjoyments in human Life.

A *French* Author, giving an Account of a very agreeable Man, in whose Character he mingles good Qualities and Infirmities, rather than Vices and Virtues, tells the following Story.

"Our Knight, says he, was pretty much addicted to the most fashionable of all Faults. He had a loose Rogue for a Lacquey, not a little in his Favour, though he had no other Name for him when he spoke of him but *the Rascal,* or to him but *Sirrah*.[7] One Morning when he was dressing, Sirrah, says he, be sure you bring home this Evening a pretty Wench. The Fellow[8] was a Person of Diligence and Capacity, and had for some time address'd himself to a decay'd[9] old Gentlewoman, who had a young Maiden to her Daughter, beauteous

[7] The form used to address an inferior, often implying contempt.
[8] I.e., the lackey.
[9] Impoverished.

as an Angel, not yet sixteen Years of Age. The Mother's extream Poverty, and the Insinuations of this artful Lacquey concerning the soft Disposition and Generosity of his Master, made her consent to deliver up her Daughter. But many were the Intreaties and Representations of the Mother to gain her Child's Consent to an Action, which she said she abhorred, at the same time she exhored her to it; but Child, says she, can you see your Mother die for Hunger? The Virgin argued no longer, but bursting into Tears, said she would go any where. The Lacquey conveyed her with great Obsequiousness and Secrecy to his Master's Lodging, and placed her in a commodious Apartment till he came home. The Knight, who knew his Man never failed of bringing in his Prey, indulged his Genius at a Banquet, and was in high Humour at an Entertainment with Ladies, expecting to be received in the Evening by one as agreeable as the best of them. When he came home, his Lacquey met him with a saucy and joyful Familiarity, crying out, She is as handsome as an Angel, (for there is no other Simile on these Occasions) but the tender Fool has wept till her Eyes are swelled and bloated; for she is a Maid and a Gentlewoman. With that he conducted his Master to the Room where she was, and retired. The Knight, when he saw her bathed in Tears, said in some surprize, Don't you know, young Woman, why you were brought hither? The unhappy Maid fell on her Knees, and with many Interruptions of Sights and Tears said to him, I know, alas! too well why I am brought hither; my Mother, to get Bread for her and my self, has sent me to do what you pleased; but wou'd it would please Heaven I could die, before I am added to the Number of those miserable Wretches who live without Honour! With this Reflection she wept anew, and beat her Bosom. The Knight stepping back from her, said, I am not so abandoned as to hurt your Innocence against your Will.

"The Novelty of the Accident surpriz'd him into Virtue; and covering the young Maid with a Cloak, he led her to a Relation's House, to whose Care he recommended her for that Night. The next Morning he sent for her Mother, and ask'd her if her Daughter was a Maid? the Mother assured him, that when she delivered her to his Servant she was a Stranger to Man. Are not you then, reply'd the Knight, a wicked Woman to contrive the Debauchery of your own Child? She held down her Face with Fear and Shame, and in her Confusion uttered some broken Words concerning her Poverty. Far be it, said the Gentleman, that you should relieve your self from Want by a much greater Evil: Your Daughter is a fine young Creature; do you know of none that ever spoke of her for a Wife? The Mother answer'd,

There is an honest Man in our Neighbourhood that loves her, who has often said he would marry her with Two Hundred Pounds.[10] The Knight ordered his Man to reckon out that Sum, with an Addition of Fifty to buy the Bride Cloaths, and Fifty more as an Help to her Mother."

I appeal to all the Gallants in Town, Whether possessing all the Beauties in *Great-Britain* could give half the Pleasure, as this young Gentleman had in the Reflection of having relieved a miserable Parent from Guilt and Poverty, an innocent Virgin from Publick Shame, and bestowing a Virtuous Wife upon an honest Man?

As all Men who are guilty this way have not Fortunes or Opportunities for making such Atonements for their Vices, yet all Men may do what is certainly in their Power at this good Season. For my Part I don't care how ridiculous the Mention of it may be, provided I hear it has any good Consequence upon the Wretched, that I recommend the most abandoned and miserable of Mankind to the Charity of all in prosperous Conditions under the same Guilt with those Wretches. The *Lock* Hospital in *Kent-Street, Southwark,* for Men, that in *Kingsland* for Women, is a Receptacle for all Sufferers mangled by this Iniquity.[11] Penitents should in their own Hearts take upon them all the Shame and Sorrow they have escaped; and it would become them to make an Oblation for their Crimes, by Charity to those upon whom Vice appears in that utmost Misery and Deformity; which they themselves are free from by their better Fortune, rather than greater Innocence. It would quicken our Compassion in this Case, if we considered there may be Objects there, who would now move Horror and Loathing, that we have once embraced with Transport; and as we are Men of Honour (for I must not speak as we are Christians) let us not desert our Friends for the Loss of their Noses.[12]

10 I.e., if she brought this amount as dowry.

11 Venereal disease.

12 Syphilis sometimes led to the loss of the nose. In *Tatler* No. 260, Addison told of an Italian doctor who at one time could make new noses for those who needed them, but Addison ended by warning the young men of the town to behave prudently, for "the Art of making new Noses is entirely lost."

The Guardian, No. 43

Thursday, April 30.

[S t e e l e]

Effutire leves indigna tragaedia versus,
Ut festis matrona moveri jussa diebus. Hor.[1]

I had for some Days observed something in Agitation, which
was carried by Smiles and Whispers, between my Lady *Lizard*
and her Daughters, with a professed Declaration that Mr. *Ironside*
should not be in the Secret. I would not trespass upon the Integrity of the *Sparkler*[2] so much as to sollicit her to break her Word
even in a Trifle; but I take it for an Instance of her Kindness to
me, that as soon as she was at Liberty she was impatient to let me
know it, and this Morning sent me the following Billet.

> "*Sir,*
> My Brother *Tom.* waited upon us all last Night to *Cato;*[3] we sat in
> the first Seats in the Box of the Eighteen-Penny Gallery; you must
> come hither this Morning, for we shall be full of Debates about the
> Characters.[4] I was for *Marcia* last Night, but find that Partiality was
> owing to the Awe I was under in her Father's Presence; but this Morn-
> ing *Lucia* is my Woman. You will tell me whether I am right or no

---

1 Horace *Ars Poetica* 231–232: "It is beneath the dignity of tragedy to bab-
ble trivial verse: like a matron bidden to dance on holy days."

2 Mrs. Mary, the youngest daughter. See *Guardian* No. 5.

3 Addison's play opened on April 14, 1713, two weeks before the date of this
paper.

4 In the drama, Marcia, Cato's daughter, refuses to answer Juba's declaration of love, while her father and Rome are threatened by Caesar's invasion.
Lucia, daughter of a Roman senator, vows never to accept Cato's son Portius,
whom she loves, because this would pain his brother, Marcus, who also loves
her.

when I see you; but I think it is a more difficult Virtue to forbear going into a Family, tho' she was in Love with the Heir of it, for no other Reason but because her Happiness was inconsistent with the Tranquillity of the whole House to which she should be ally'd, I say I think it a more generous Virtue in *Lucia* to conquer her Love from this Motive, than in *Marcia* to suspend hers in the present Circumstances of her Father and her Country; but pray be here to settle these Matters. *I am,*

> *Your most Obliged*
> *and Obedient Humble Servant,*
> Mary Lizard."

I made all the haste imaginable to the Family, where I found *Tom.* with the Play in his Hand, and the whole Company with a sublime Chearfulness in their Countenance, all ready to speak to me at once; and before I could draw my Chair, my Lady her self repeated,

> *'Tis not a Sett of Features or Complection,*
> *The Tincture of a Skin, that I admire;*
> *Beauty soon grows familiar to the Lover,*
> *Fades in his Eye, and palls upon the Sense.*
> *The Virtuous* Marcia *tow'rs above her Sex;*
> *True, she is fair, (Oh, how divinely Fair!)*
> *But still the lovely Maid improves her Charms*
> *With inward Greatness, unaffected Wisdom,*
> *And Sanctity of Manners.*[5]

I was going to speak when Mrs. *Cornelia* stood up, and with the most gentle Accent and sweetest Tone of Voice, succeeded her Mother.

> *So the pure limpid Stream, when foul with Stains*
> *Of rushing Torrents and descending Rains,*
> *Works it self clear, and as it runs refines,*
> *Till by Degrees the floating Mirrour shines,*
> *Reflects each Flow'r that on the Border grows,*
> *And a new Heav'n in its fair Bosom shows.*[6]

[5] The speech is Juba's praise of Marcia (act 1, sc. 5), whom my Lady Lizard prefers to Lucia.

[6] Mrs. Cornelia quotes Marcia's speech (act 1, sc. 6) assuring Lucia that their present wretched days may well give way to happy ones. It has little

I thought they would now have given me time to draw a Chair, but the *Sparkler* took hold of me, and I heard her with the utmost Delight pursue her Admiration of *Lucia,* in the Words of *Portius.*

> ————*Athwart the Terrors that thy Vow*
> *Has planted round thee, thou appear'st more fair,*
> *More amiable, and risest in thy Charms.*
> *Lovely'st of Women! Heav'n is in thy Soul,*
> *Beauty and Virtue shine for ever round thee,*
> *Bright'ning each other; thou art all Divine!*[7]

When the Ladies had done speaking, I took the Liberty to take my Place;[8] while *Tom,* who, like a just Courtier, thinks the Interest of his Prince and Country the same, dwelt upon these Lines.

> *Remember, O my Friends, the Laws, the Rights,*
> *The gen'rous Plan of Power deliver'd down*
> *From Age to Age, by your renown'd Fore-fathers,*
> *(So dearly bought, the Price of so much Blood)*
> *O let it never perish in your Hands!*
> *But piously transmit it to your Children.*[9]

Though I would not take Notice of it at that time, it went to my Heart that *Annabella,* for whom I have long had some Apprehensions, said nothing on this Occasion, but indulged her self in the Sneer of a little Mind, to see the rest so much affected. Mrs. *Betty* also, who knows forsooth more than us all, overlooked the whole Drama, but acknowledged the Dresses of *Syphax* and

---

relation to the Marcia-Lucia dispute, though it does demonstrate Marcia's eloquence.

7 Portius's praise of Lucia (act 3, sc. 2) after she has vowed to reject him, is quoted to reinforce the esteem for Lucia which Mrs. Mary spoke of in her letter.

8 I.e., to sit down.

9 Cato's speech to the counsellors, Sempronius and Lucius (act 3, sc. 5), illustrates the political ambiguity which contributed to make Addison's play a success. Taken literally, it would seem to favor the Jacobite position, that the English throne should go to James Stuart. But clearly Steele preferred the Whig reading, that "great Liberty" must be defended against despots like Caesar (or the Pretender).

Juba[10] were very prettily imagined. The Love of Virtue, which has been so warmly rouzed by this admirable Piece in all Parts of the Theatre, is an unanswerable Instance of how great Force the Stage might be towards the Improvement of the World, were it regarded and encouraged as much as it ought: There is no Medium in this Case, for the Advantages of Action, and the Representation of Vice and Virtue in an agreeable or odious manner before our Eyes, are so irresistably prevalent,[11] that the Theatre ought to be shut up, or carefully govern'd, in any Nation that values the Promotion of Virtue or Guard of Innocence among its People. Speeches or Sermons will ever suffer, in some Degree, from the Characters of those that make them; and Mankind are so unwilling to reflect on what makes for their own Mortification, that they are ever caviling against the Lives of those who speak in the Cause of Goodness, to keep themselves in Countenance, and continue in belov'd Infirmities.[12] But in the case of the Stage, Envy and Detraction are Baffled, and none are offended, but all insensibly won by personated Characters, which they neither look upon as their Rivals or Superiors; every Man that has any Degree of what is laudable in a Theatrical Character, is secretly pleased, and encouraged in the Prosecution of that Virtue, without fancying any Man about him has more of it. To this purpose I fell a Talking at the Tea-Table, when my Lady *Lizard,* with a Look of some Severity towards *Annabella* and Mrs. *Betty,* was pleased to say, that it must be from some trifling Prepossession of Mind that any one could be unmoved with the Characters of this Tragedy; nor do I yet understand to what Circumstance in the Family her Ladyship alluded, when she made all the Company look serious, and rehearsed, with a Tone more exalted, those Words of the Heroine,

> *In spight of all the Virtue we can boast,*
> *The Woman that Deliberates is lost.*[13]

[10] Both Juba and Syphax are Numidians of African descent, rather than Romans; hence they are garbed differently.

[11] I.e., one is not told the message of the author; one sees it.

[12] Steele discussed such cavilling in *Tatler* No. 271.

[13] Just as these lines from Marcia's speech to Lucia (act 4, sc. 1) are confusing in the context of the Lizard family, they have an uncertain meaning in Addison's play.

Whereas Bat. Pidgeon[14] *in the* Strand, *Hair-Cutter to the Family of the* Lizards, *has attained to great Proficience in his Art,* Mr. Ironside *advises all Persons of fine Heads, in order to have Justice done them, to repair to that industrious Mechanick.*

N. B. *Mr.* Pidgeon *has Orders to talk with, and examine into the Parts and Character of young Persons, before he thins the Covering near the Seat of the Brain.*

[14] See *Guardian* No. 1, in which Bat Pidgeon is praised, along with the whole order of "Mechanicks."

The Guardian, No. 94

Monday, June 29.

[Steele]

Ingenium sibi quod vacuas desumpsit Athenas,
Et studiis annos septem dedit, insenuitque
Libris & Curis; statuâ taciturnius exit
*Plerumque, & risu Populum quatit———*Hor.[1]

Since our Success in Worldly Matters may be said to depend upon our Education, it will be very much to the Purpose to enquire if the Foundations of our Fortune could not be laid deeper and surer than they are. The Education of Youth falls of Necessity under the Direction of those who, thro' fondness to us and our Abilities, as well as to their own unwarrantable Conjectures, are very likely to be deceived;[2] and the Misery of it is, that the poor Creatures, who are the Sufferers upon wrong Advances,[3] seldom find out the Errors till they become irretrievable. As the greater Number of all Degrees and Conditions have their Education at the Universities, the Errors which I conceive to be in those Places fall most naturally under the following Observations. The first Mismanagement in these Publick Nurseries, is the calling together a number of Pupils, of howsoever different Ages, Views

---

1 Horace *Epistles* 2. 2. 81–84: "Even in quiet Athens, if a gifted man who has studied seven long years and grown gray over books and ideas, walks through the streets—lost in thought and mute as a statue—he makes the people shake with laughter."

2 In *Guardian* No. 5, Ironside maintained that his particular excellence as a guardian lay in lacking "all that Tenderness, which is the Byass of Inclination in Men towards their own Offspring."

3 Through false counsel.

and Capacities, to the same Lectures: But surely there can be no Reason to think, that a delicate tender Babe, just wean'd from the Bosom of his Mother, indulg'd in all the Impertinences of his Heart's Desire, should be equally capable of receiving a Lecture of Philosophy, with a hardy Ruffian of full Age, who has been occasionally scourged thro' some of the great Schools, groaned under constant Rebuke and Chastisement, and maintain'd a ten Years War with Literature under very strict and rugged Discipline.

I know the Reader has pleas'd himself with an Answer to this already, *viz.* That an Attention to the particular Abilities and Designs of the Pupil, can't be expected from the trifling Salary paid upon such Account.[4] The Price indeed which is thought a sufficient Reward, for any Advantages a Youth can receive from a Man of Learning, is an abominable Consideration, the enlarging which, would not only increase the Care of Tutors, but would be a very great Encouragement to such as design'd to take this Province upon them, to furnish themselves with a more general and extensive Knowledge. As the Case now stands, those of the first Quality[5] pay their Tutors but little above half so much as they do their Footmen. What Morality, what History, what Taste of the Modern Languages, what, lastly, that can make a Man happy, or great, may not be expected in return for such an immense Treasure![6] 'Tis monstrous indeed, that the Men of the best Estates and Families, are more Sollicitous about the Tutelage of a favourite Dog or Horse, than of their Heirs Male. The next Evil is the Pedantical Veneration that is maintained at the University for *Greek* and *Latin,* which puts the Youth upon such Exercises as many of them are incapable of performing with any tolerable Success. Upon this Emergency they are succoured[7] by the allow'd Wits of their respective Colleges, who are always ready to befriend them with two or three hundred *Latin* or *Greek* Words thrown together, with a very small Proportion of Sense.

[4] I.e., to educators, tutors.
[5] Of the highest rank.
[6] Steele's use of irony here should not lead one to think that the remainder of the essay is ironical.
[7] Aided.

But the most establish'd Error of our University Education, is the general Neglect of all the little Qualifications and Accomplishments which make up the Character of a well-bred Man,[8] and the general Attention to what is called deep Learning. But as there are very few blessed with a Genius[9] that shall force Success by the Strength of it self alone, and few Occasions of Life that require the Aid of such Genius, the vast Majority of the unbless'd Souls ought to store themselves with such Acquisitions, in which every Man has Capacity to make a considerable Progress, and from which every common Occasion of Life may reap great Advantage. The Persons that may be useful to us in the making our Fortunes, are such as are already happy in their own; I may proceed to say, that the Men of Figure and Family are more superficial in their Education than those of a less Degree,[10] and, of Course, are ready to encourage and protect that Qualification in another which they themselves are Masters of. For their own Application implies the Pursuit of something commendable; and when they see their own Characters propos'd as imitable, they must be won by such an irresistible Flattery. But those of the University, who are to make their Fortunes by a ready Insinuation into the Favour of their Superiors, contemn this necessary Foppery so far, as not to be able to speak Common Sense to them, without Hesitation, Perplexity and Confusion. For want of Care in acquiring less[11] Accomplishments which adorn ordinary Life, he that is so unhappy as to be born poor, is condemned to a Method that will very probably keep him so.

I hope all the Learned will forgive me what is said purely for their Service, and tends to no other Injury against them, than admonishing them not to overlook such little Qualifications, as they every Day see defeat their greater Excellencies in the Pursuit both of Reputation and Fortune.

If the Youth of the University were to be advanced, according to their Sufficiency in the severe Progress of Learning; or *Riches*

---

8 In *Guardian* No. 34, Steele wrote, "Men of Courage, Men of Sense, and Men of Letters are frequent; but a true fine Gentleman is what one seldom sees."

9 I.e., intellect.

10 Of a lower rank.

11 I.e., the less profound.

*could be secured to Men of Understanding, and Favour to Men
of Skill;*[12] then indeed all Studies were solemnly to be defied, that
did not seriously pursue the main End: But since our Merit is to
be tried by the unskilful Many, we must gratifie the Sense of the
injudicious Majority, satisfying our selves that the Shame of a
trivial Qualification sticks only upon him that prefers it to one
more Substantial. The more Accomplishments a Man is Master
of, the better is he prepared for a more extended Acquaintance,
and upon these Considerations without doubt, the Author of the
Italian Book called *Il Cortegiano,* or the Courtier,[13] makes throwing the Bar, Vaulting the Horse, nay even Wrestling, with several
other as low Qualifications, necessary for the Man whom he Figures for a perfect Courtier; for this Reason no doubt, because his
End being to find Grace in the Eyes of Men of all Degrees, the
Means to pursue this End, was the furnishing him with such real
and seeming Excellencies as each Degree had its particular Taste
of. But those of the University, instead of employing their leisure
Hours in the Pursuit of such Acquisitions as would shorten their
way to better Fortune, enjoy those Moments at certain Houses in
the Town, or repair to others at very pretty distances out of it,
where *they drink and forget their Poverty, and remember their
Misery no more.* Persons of this Indigent Education are apt to
pass upon themselves and others for Modest, especially in the
Point of Behaviour; tho' 'tis easie to prove, that this mistaken
Modesty not only arises from Ignorance, but begets the Appearance of its Opposite, Pride. For he that is conscious of his own
Insufficiency to address his Superiors without appearing ridiculous, is by that betrayed into the same Neglect and Indifference
towards them, which may bear the Construction of Pride. From
this Habit they begin to argue against the base submissive Application from Men of Letters to Men of Fortune, and to be grieved
when they see, as *Ben. Johnson* says,

> ————*The Learned Pate*
> *Duck to the Golden Fool*————[14]

[12] The line is adapted from Ecclesiastes 9:11.

[13] Baldassare Castiglione (1478–1529) published *Il Cortegiano,* a dialogue
on the ideal courtly life, in 1528.

[14] Steele quotes from a faulty memory. The lines are from Shakespeare's
Timon of Athens, act 4, sc. 3, 17–18.

though these are Points of Necessity and Convenience, and to be esteem'd Submissions rather to the Occasion than to the Person. It was a fine Answer of *Diogenes,* who being ask'd in Mockery, why Philosophers were the Followers of Rich Men, and not Rich Men of Philosophers, replied, Because the one knew what they had need of, and the other did not. It certainly must be difficult to prove, that a Man of Business, or a Profession, ought not to be what we call a Gentleman, but yet very few of them are so. Upon this Account they have little Conversation with those who might do them most Service, but upon such occasions only as Application is made to them in their particular Calling; and for any thing they can do or say in such Matters have their Reward, and therefore rather receive than confer an Obligation: Whereas he that adds his being agreeable to his being serviceable, is constantly in a Capacity of obliging others. The Character of a Beau is, I think, what the Men that pretend to Learning please themselves in Ridiculing; and yet if we compare these Persons as we see them in Publick, we shall find that the Letter'd Coxcombs without good Breeding give more just Occasion to Raillery,[15] than the Unletter'd Coxcombs with it; as our Behaviour falls within the Judgment of more Persons than our Conversation, and a Failure therefore more visible. What pleasant Victories over the Loud, the Sawcy, and the Illiterate, would attend the Men of Learning and[16] Breeding, which Qualifications could we but join would beget such a Confidence, as, arising from good Sense and good Nature, would never let us oppress others, or desert our selves. In short, whether a Man intends a Life of Business or Pleasure, 'tis impossible to pursue either in an elegant manner, without the help of Good Breeding. I shall conclude with the Face at least of a Regular Discourse; and say, If 'tis our Behaviour and Address upon all common Occasions that Prejudice People in our Favour or to our Disadvantage, and the more Substantial Parts, as our Learning and Industry, can't possibly appear but to few; it is not justifiable to spend so much Time in that which so very few are Judges of, and utterly neglect that which falls within the Censure of so many.

[15] Ridicule.
[16] Emphasize the "and."

The Guardian, No. 97[1]

Thursday, July 2.

[A d d i s o n]

―――*Miserum est post omnia perdere Naulum.* Juv.[2]

"*Sir,*

    I was left a Thousand Pounds by an Uncle, and being a Man to my thinking very likely to get a Rich Widow, I laid aside all Thoughts of making my Fortune any other way, and without Loss of Time made my Applications to one who had buried her Husband about a Week before. By the help of some of her She Friends, who were my Relations, I got into her Company when she would see no Man besides my self and her Lawyer, who is a little, rivelled,[3] splindle-shanked Gentleman, and married to boot, so that I had no reason to fear him. Upon my first seeing her, she said in Conversation within my hearing, that she thought a pale Complexion the most agreeable either in Man or Woman: Now you must know, Sir, my Face is as white as Chalk. This gave me some Encouragement, so that to mend the Matter I bought a fine Flaxen long Wig that cost me thirty Guineas, and found an Opportunity of seeing her in it the next Day. She then let drop some Expressions about an Agate Snuff-Box. I immediately took the Hint and bought one, being unwilling to omit any

---

[1] This is the second in a long series of essays by Addison. After Steele had embroiled the paper in political controversy, Addison produced twenty-five consecutive papers (Nos. 96–120) notable for their charm and inoffensiveness. Peter Smithers (*The Life of Joseph Addison,* 1954) writes, "The purpose of this concentrated effort was probably to make sure that no quarrels were revived and to make it plain to the reading public that there had been a change in editorial policy."

[2] Juvenal *Satires* 8. 97: "After all else is lost, it is mad to throw away your passage-money."

[3] Shrivelled.

thing that might make me desireable in her Eyes. I was betrayed after the same manner into a Brocade Wastcoat, a Sword Knot, a pair of Silver fringed Gloves, and a Diamond Ring. But whether out of Fickleness, or a Design upon me, I can't tell; but I found by her Discourse, that what she liked one Day she disliked another: So that in six Months space I was forced to equip my self above a dozen times. As I told you before, I took her Hints at a distance, for I could never find an Opportunity of talking with her directly to the Point. All this time, however, I was allowed the utmost Familiarities with her Lapdog, and have played with it above an Hour together, without receiving the least Reprimand, and had many other Marks of Favour shown me, which I thought amounted to a Promise. If she chanced to drop her Fan, she received it from my Hands with great Civility. If she wanted any thing I reached it for her. I have filled her Tea-pot above an hundred times, and have afterwards received a Dish[4] of it from her own Hands. Now, Sir, do you judge if after such Encouragements she was not obliged to marry me. I forgot to tell you that I kept a Chair[5] by the Week, on purpose to carry me thither and back again. Not to trouble you with a long Letter, in the space of about a Twelvemonth I have run out of my whole Thousand Pound upon her, having laid out the last fifty in a new Suit of Cloaths, in which I was resolved to receive her final Answer, which amounted to this, That she was engaged to another; That she never dreamt I had any such thing in my Head as Marriage; and that she thought I had frequented her House only because I loved to be in Company with my Relations. This, you know, Sir, is using a Man like a Fool, and so I told her; but the worst of it is, that I have spent my Fortune to no purpose. All therefore that I desire of you is, to tell me whether upon exhibiting the several Particulars which I have here related to you, I may not sue her for Damages in a Court of Justice.[6] Your Advice in this particular will very much oblige

Your most humble Admirer,
Simon Softly."

Before I answer Mr. *Softly*'s Request, I find my self under a Necessity of discussing two nice Points: First of all, What it is, in Cases of this Nature, that amounts to an Encouragement; and Secondly, What it is that amounts to a Promise. Each of which

---

4 A cup.

5 Hired a sedan chair.

6 Though Simon Softly seeks a court of law, his case is more appropriate for Isaac Bickerstaff's Court of Honour. See *Tatler* No. 259, n. 2.

Subjects requires more Time to examine than I am at present Master of. Besides I would have my Friend *Simon* consider, whether he has any Council that would undertake his Cause in *Forma Pauperis,* he having unluckily disabled himself, by his own Account of the matter, from prosecuting his Suit any other way.

In answer however to Mr. *Softly*'s Request, I shall acquaint him with a Method made use of by a young Fellow in King *Charles* the Second's Reign, whom I shall here call *Silvio,* who had long made Love, with much Artifice and Intrigue, to a rich Widow, whose true Name I shall conceal under that of *Zelinda. Silvio,* who was much more smitten with her Fortune than her Person, finding a Twelve-month's Application unsuccessful, was resolved to make a saving Bargain of it, and since he could not get the Widow's Estate into his Possession, to recover at least what he had laid out of his own in the Pursuit of it.

In order to this he presented her with a Bill of Costs; having particularized in it the several Expences he had been at in his long perplexed Amour. *Zelinda* was so pleased with the Humour of the Fellow, and his frank way of dealing, that upon the Perusal of the Bill, she sent him a Purse of fifteen hundred Guineas, by the right Application of which the Lover, in less than a Year, got a Woman of a greater Fortune than her he had miss'd. The several Articles in the Bill of Costs I pretty well remember, tho' I have forgotten the particular Sum charged to each Article.

Laid out in Supernumerary Full-bottom Wiggs.

Fiddles for a Serenade, with a Speaking-trumpet.[7]

Gilt Paper in Letters, and Billetdoux with perfum'd Wax.

A Rheam of Sonnets and Love Verses, purchased at different Times of Mr. *Triplett* at a Crown a Sheet.

To *Zelinda* two Sticks of *May* Cherries.

Last Summer, at several times, a Bushel of Peaches.

Three Porters whom I planted about her to watch her Motions.[8]

The first who stood Centry[9] near her Door.

---

[7] A kind of megaphone.
[8] To spy on her activities.
[9] Sentry.

The second who had his Stand at the Stables where her Coach was put up.

The third who kept Watch at the Corner of the Street where *Ned Courtall*[10] lives, who has since married her.

Two additional Porters planted over her during the whole Month of *May*.

Five Conjurers kept in Pay all last Winter.

Spy-mony to *John Trott* her Footman, and Mrs. *Sarah Wheedle* her Companion.

A new *Conningsmark* Blade to fight *Ned Courtall*.

To *Zelinda*'s Woman (Mrs. *Abigal*) an *Indian* Fan, a dozen Pair of white Kid Gloves, a Piece of *Flanders* Lace, and fifteen Guineas in dry Mony.

Secret Service-mony to *Betty* at the Ring.[11]

Ditto, to Mrs. *Tape* the Mantua-maker.[12]

Loss of Time.

---

[10] Probably an allusion to Mr. Ned Courtall, hero of Etherege's comedy, *She Wou'd if She Cou'd* (1668).

[11] A fashionable area of Hyde Park.

[12] A mantua is a loose-fitting gown.

The Guardian, No. 98

Friday, July 3.

[A d d i s o n]

In sese redit——— ———Virg.[1]

The first who undertook to instruct the World in single Papers, was *Isaac Bickerstaff* of famous Memory; a Man nearly related to the Family of the Ironsides. We have often smoaked a Pipe together, for I was so much in his Books, that at his Decease he left me a Silver Standish,[2] a pair of Spectacles, and the Lamp by which he used to write his Lucubrations.

The venerable *Isaac* was succeeded by a Gentleman of the same Family, very memorable for the Shortness of his Face[3] and of his Speeches. This Ingenious Author published his Thoughts, and held his Tongue, with great Applause, for two Years together.

I Nestor Ironside have now for some Time undertaken to fill the Place of these my two renowned Kinsmen and Predecessors.[4] For it is observed of every Branch of our Family, that we have all of us a wonderful Inclination to give good Advice, though it is remarked of some of us, that we are apt on this Occasion rather to give than take.

However it be, I cannot but observe with some secret Pride,

---

[1] Virgil *Georgics* 4. 444: "He resumes himself."

[2] A stand for writing materials, an inkstand.

[3] Beginning with essays No. 17 and No. 19, the Spectator's short face was mentioned on a number of occasions. Richard Steele had a short face, i.e., one nearly as broad as it was long.

[4] By this time, the author of the *Guardian* was scarcely a secret. In papers No. 53 and No. 63, Steele had published politically controversial letters signed by himself.

that this way of Writing diurnal Papers[5] has not succeeded for any space of Time in the Hands of any Persons who are not of our Line. I believe I speak within compass, when I affirm that above a hundred different Authors have endeavoured after our Family-way of Writing. Some of which have been Writers in other kinds of the greatest Eminence in the Kingdom; but I do not know how it has happened, they have none of them hit upon the Art. Their Projects have always dropt after a few unsuccessful Essays. It puts me in mind of a Story which was lately told me by a pleasant Friend of mine, who has a very fine Hand on the Violin. His Maid Servant seeing his Instrument lying upon the Table, and being sensible there was Musick in it, if she knew how to fetch it out, drew the Bow over every part of the Strings, and at last told her Master she had tried the Fiddle all over, but could not for her Heart find whereabout the Tune lay.

But though the whole Burden of such a Paper is only fit to rest on the Shoulders of a *Bickerstaff* or an *Ironside;* there are several who can acquit themselves of a single Day's Labour in it with suitable Abilities. These are Gentlemen whom I have often invited to this Tryal of Wit,[6] and who have several of them acquitted themselves to my private Emolument,[7] as well as to their own Reputation. My Paper among the Republick of Letters is the *Ulysses* his Bow,[8] in which every Man of Wit or Learning may try his Strength. One who does not care to write a Book without being sure of his Abilities, may see by this means if his Parts and Talents are to the Publick Taste.

This I take to be of great Advantage to Men of the best Sense, who are always diffident of their private Judgement, 'till it receives a Sanction from the publick. *Provoco ad Populum,* I appeal to the People, was the usual Saying of a very excellent Dramatick Poet, when he had any Disputes with particular Persons about the Justness and Regularity of his Productions. It is but a melancholy Comfort for an Author to be satisfied that he has written up to

5 The *Guardian* appeared six days a week.

6 At this time, Berkeley, Pope, Gay, Budgell, Birch, Hughes, Parnell, and Wotton had contributed material to the series.

7 Advantage, profit.

8 Homer *Odyssey* 21.

the Rules of Art, when he finds he has no Admirers in the World besides himself. Common Modesty should, on this Occasion, make a Man suspect his own Judgment, and that he misapplies the Rules of his Art, when he finds himself singular in the Applause which he bestows upon his own Writings.

The Publick is always Even with[9] an Author who has not a just Deference for them. The Contempt is reciprocal. I laugh at every one, said an old Cynick, who laughs at me. Do you so? replied the Philosopher; then let me tell you, you live the merriest Life of any Man in *Athens*.

It is not therefore the least Use of this my Paper, that it gives a timorous Writer, and such is every good one, an Opportunity of putting his Abilities to the Proof, and of sounding the Publick before he launches into it. For this Reason I look upon my Paper as a kind of Nursery for Authors, and question not but some, who have made a good Figure here, will hereafter flourish under their own Names in more long and elaborate Works.

After having thus far inlarged upon this Particular, I have one Favour to beg of the Candid and Courteous Reader, that when he meets with any thing in this Paper which may appear a little dull or heavy, (tho' I hope this will not be often) he will believe it is the Work of some other Person, and not of Nestor Ironside.[10]

I have, I know not how, been drawn in to tattle of my self, *more Majorum,*[11] almost the length of a whole *Guardian.* I shall therefore fill up the remaining Part of it with what still relates to my own Person, and my Correspondents. Now I would have them all know that on the twentieth Instant it is my Intention to erect a Lion's Head in Imitation of those I have described in *Venice,* through which all the private Intelligence of that Commonwealth is said to pass.[12] This Head is to open a most wide and voracious

[9] Has a reciprocal attitude toward.

[10] Addison, it would seem, was trying to free Ironside from responsibility for any angry or tedious political commentary which had appeared or might appear in the paper.

[11] In the manner of my ancestors. He refers particularly to Bickerstaff.

[12] In *Guardian* No. 71, Addison wrote of "Lions," i.e., "any one that is a great Man's Spy." He mentioned the marble lions with gaping mouths which were erected near the doge's palace in Venice, noting that these were receptacles for "any private Intelligence of what passes in the City."

Mouth, which shall take in such Letters and Papers as are conveyed to me by my Correspondents, it being my Resolution to have a particular Regard to all such Matters as come to my Hands through the Mouth of the Lion. There will be under it a Box, of which the Key will be in my own Custody, to receive such Papers as are dropped into it. Whatever the Lion swallows I shall digest for the Use of the Publick. This Head requires some Time to finish, the Workman being resolved to give it several Masterly Touches, and to represent it as Ravenous as possible. It will be set up in *Button*'s Coffee-house[13] in *Covent-Garden,* who is directed to shew the Way to the Lion's Head, and to instruct any young Author how to convey his Works into the Mouth of it with Safety and Secrecy.

    13 See *Spectator* No. 556, n. 7. The "who" which follows suggests Addison was thinking more particularly of the proprietor, Daniel Button.

The Guardian, No. 100

Monday, July 6.

[A d d i s o n]

Hoc vos praecipuè, niveae, decet, hoc ubi vidi,
Oscula ferre humero, quà patet, usque libet. Ovid.[1]

There is a certain Female Ornament by some called a Tucker,[2] and by others the Neck-piece, being a slip of fine Linnen or Muslin that used to run in a small kind of ruffle round the uppermost Verge of the Womens Stays, and by that means covered a great part of the Shoulders and Bosom. Having thus given a Definition, or rather Description of the Tucker, I must take Notice, that our Ladies have of late thrown aside this Fig-Leaf, and exposed in its Primitive Nakedness that gentle Swelling of the Breast which it was used to conceal. What their Design by it is they themselves best know.

I observed this as I was sitting the other Day by a famous She Visitant at my Lady *Lizard*'s, when accidentally as I was looking upon her Face, letting my Sight fall into her Bosom, I was surprized with Beauties which I never before discovered, and do not know where my Eye would have run, if I had not immediately checked it. The Lady herself could not forbear blushing when she observed by my Looks, that she had made her Neck[3] too beautiful and glaring an Object, even for a Man of my Character and Grav-

1 Ovid *The Art of Love* 3. 309–310: "This becomes you expecially, you who have snowy skins; when I see this, how I wish to kiss that shoulder, wherever it is exposed."

2 See *Spectator* No. 113, n. 19.

3 The word "neck" is commonly used to mean bosom, as Addison makes clear in succeeding paragraphs.

ity. I could scarce forbear making use of my Hand to cover so unseemly a Sight.

If we survey the Pictures of our Great-Grandmothers in Queen *Elizabeth's* Time, we see them cloathed down to the very Wrists, and up to the very Chin. The Hands and Face were the only Samples they gave of their beautiful Persons. The following Age of Females made larger Discoveries of their Complection. They first of all tucked up their Garments to the Elbow, and notwithstanding the Tenderness[4] of the Sex, were content, for the Information of Mankind, to expose their Arms to the Coldness of the Air, and Injuries of the Weather. This Artifice hath succeeded to their Wishes, and betrayed many to their Arms, who might have escaped them had they been still concealed.

About the same time the Ladies considering that the Neck was a very Modest Part in a Human Body, they freed it from those Yoaks, I mean those monstrous Linnen Ruffs, in which the Simplicity of their Grandmothers had enclosed it. In proportion as the Age refined, the Dress still sunk lower, so that when we now say a Woman has a handsom Neck, we reckon into it many of the adjacent Parts. The disuse of the Tucker has still enlarged it, insomuch that the Neck of a fine Woman at present takes in almost half the Body.

Since the Female Neck thus grows upon us,[5] and the Ladies seem disposed to discover themselves to us more and more, I would fain have them tell us once for all how far they intend to go, and whether they have yet determined among themselves where to make a Stop.

For my own Part, their Necks, as they call them, are no more than *Busts* of Alablaster in my Eye. I can look upon

The yielding Marble of a snowy Breast[6]

with as much Coldness as this Line of Mr. *Waller* represents in the Object it self. But my fair Readers ought to consider, that all

---

4 Frailty.

5 A pun: to "grow upon" means to obtain increasing influence.

6 Waller, "On a Lady Passing Through a Crowd of People," line 11.

their Beholders are not *Nestors*.[7] Every Man is not sufficiently qualified with Age and Philosophy to be an indifferent Spectator of such Allurements. The Eyes of young Men are curious and penetrating, their Imaginations of a roving Nature, and their Passions under no Discipline or Restraint. I am in Pain for a Woman of Rank when I see her thus exposing her self to the Regards of every impudent staring Fellow. How can she expect that her Quality can defend her, when she gives such Provocation? I could not but observe last Winter, that upon the disuse of the Neckpiece (the Ladies will pardon me if it is not the fashionable Term of Art) the whole Tribe of Oglers gave their Eyes a new Determination, and stared the fair Sex in the Neck rather than in the Face. To prevent these sawcy familiar Glances, I would entreat my gentle Readers to sow[8] on their Tuckers again, to retreive the Modesty of their Characters, and not to imitate the Nakedness, but the Innocence of their Mother *Eve*.

What most troubles and indeed surprizes me in this Particular, I have observed that the Leaders in this Fashion were most of them married Women. What their Design can be in making themselves bare I cannot possibly imagine. No Body exposes Wares that are appropriated. When the Bird is taken the Snare ought to be removed. It was a remarkable Circumstance in the Institution of the severe *Lycurgus*.[9] As that great Law-giver knew that the Wealth and Strength of a Republick consisted in the Multitude of Citizens, he did all he could to encourage Marriage: In order to it he prescribed a certain loose Dress for the *Spartan* Maids, in which there were several Artificial Rents and Openings, that upon their putting themselves in Motion discovered several Limbs of the Body to the Beholders. Such were the Baits and Temptations made use of by that wise Law-giver, to incline the young Men of his Age to Marriage. But when the Maid was once sped she was not suffered to tantalise the Male Part of the Commonwealth: Her

---

[7] In Homer's *Iliad*, Nestor is the oldest and perhaps the wisest of the Greek generals fighting at Troy. Here, he is the writer as well.

[8] I.e., sew.

[9] According to tradition, a Spartan lawgiver of the ninth century B.C.

Garments were closed up, and stitched together with the greatest
Care imaginable. The Shape of her Limbs and Complexion of her
Body had gained their Ends, and were ever after to be concealed
from the Notice of the Publick.

I shall conclude this Discourse of the Tucker with a Moral
which I have taught upon all Occasions, and shall still continue
to inculcate into my Female Readers; namely, that nothing bestows so much Beauty on a Woman as Modesty. This is a Maxim
laid down by *Ovid* himself,[10] the greatest Master in the Art of
Love. He observes upon it, that *Venus* pleases most when she appears *(semi-reducta)* in a Figure withdrawing her self from the Eye
of the Beholder. It is very probable he had in his Thoughts the
Statue which we see in the *Venus de Medicis,* where she is represented in such a shy retiring Posture, and covers her Bosom with
one of her Hands. In short, Modesty gives the Maid greater Beauty
than even the bloom of Youth, it bestows on the Wife the Dignity
of a Matron, and reinstates the Widow in her Virginity.[11]

[10] Ovid *The Art of Love* 2. 13–15.

[11] References to the tucker appear in *Guardians* No. 109, 116, 121, 132, 134,
and 140.

The Guardian, No. 116

Friday, July 24.

[A d d i s o n]

——— ———*Ridiculum acri*
Fortius & melius——— ———Hor.[1]

There are many little Enormities in the World, which our Preachers would be very glad to see removed; but at the same time dare not meddle with them, for fear of betraying the Dignity of the Pulpit. Should they recommend the *Tucker*[2] in a Pathetick Discourse, their Audiences would be apt to laugh out. I knew a Parish, where the top-Woman[3] of it used always to appear with a Patch[4] upon some part of her Forehead: The good Man of the Place Preached at it with great Zeal for almost a Twelvemonth; but instead of fetching out the Spot which he perpetually aimed at, he only got the Name of Parson *Patch* for his Pains. Another is to this Day called by the Name of Doctor *Topknot*[5] for Reasons of the same Nature. I remember the Clergy, during the Time of *Cromwell*'s Usurpation, were very much taken up in reforming the Female World,[6] and showing the Vanity of those outward Ornaments in which the Sex so much delights. I have heard a

---

[1] Horace *Satire* 1. 10. 14–15: "Scornful ridicule is more effective and forceful."

[2] See *Guardian* No. 100.

[3] I.e., the ranking lady.

[4] See *Spectator* No. 37, n. 7.

[5] A topknot was a bow of ribbon which ladies wore on their heads.

[6] This refers to the excesses of Puritan preaching during the period of the Commonwealth.

whole Sermon against a White-wash,[7] and have known a coloured Ribbon made the Mark of the Unconverted. The Clergy of the present Age are not transported with these indiscreet Fervours, as knowing that it is hard for a Reformer to avoid Ridicule, when he is severe upon Subjects which are rather apt to produce Mirth than Seriousness. For this reason I look upon my self to be of great Use to these good Men; while they are employed in extirpating Mortal Sins, and Crimes of a higher Nature, I should be glad to rally the World out of Indecencies and Venial Transgressions.[8] While the Doctor is curing Distempers that have the Appearance of Danger or Death in them, the *Merry-Andrew* has his separate Packet for the Meagrims and the Tooth-ach.[9]

Thus much I thought fit to premise before I resume the Subject which I have already handled,[10] I mean the naked Bosomes of our *British* Ladies. I hope they will not take it ill of me, if I still beg that they will be covered. I shall here present them with a Letter on that Particular, as it was yesterday conveyed to me through the Lion's Mouth.[11] It comes from a Quaker,[12] and is as follows.

"Nestor Ironside,
    Our Friends like thee. We rejoice to find thou beginn'st to have a glimmering of the Light in thee: We shall pray for thee, that thou may'st be more and more enlightened. Thou givest good Advice to the Women of this World to Cloath themselves like unto our Friends, and not to expose their fleshly Temptations, for it is against the Record. Thy Lion is a good Lion; he roareth loud, and is heard a great way, even unto the Sink of *Babylon;* for the Scarlet Whore[13] is governed by the Voice of thy Lion. Look on his Order.
"Rome, July 8, 1713. *A Placard is published here, forbidding Women of whatsoever Quality, to go with naked Breasts; and the Priests are*

----

[7] A cosmetic wash used to cure a red or blotched complexion.

[8] In *Spectator* No. 34, Addison speculated "of the great Use this Paper might be of to the Publick, by reprehending those Vices which are too trivial for the Chastisement of the Law, and too fantastical for the Cognizance of the Pulpit."

[9] I.e., the clown has the less potent medicine needed for lesser ills.

[10] It is hardly conceivable that Addison did not intend this as a bold pun.

[11] See *Guardian* No. 98.

[12] A comparable letter from a Quaker zealot appears in *Spectator* No. 276.

[13] The reference is to Rome and to the Pope. See *Tatler* No. 190, n. 4.

ordered not to admit the Transgressors of this Law to Confession, nor to Communion; neither are they to enter the Cathedrals under severe Penalties.

"These Lines are faithfully copied from the nightly Paper, with this Title written over it, *The Evening Post,* from *Saturday, July* the 18th, to *Tuesday, July* the 21st.

"Seeing thy Lion is obeyed at this Distance, we hope the foolish Women in thy own Country will listen to thy Admonitions. Otherwise thou art desired to make him still Roar till all the Beasts of the Forest shall tremble. I must again repeat unto thee, Friend *Nestor,* the whole Brotherhood have great Hopes of thee, and expect to see thee so inspired with the Light, as thou mayest speedily become a great Preacher of the Word. I wish it heartily.

> *Thine,*
> *in every thing that is Praise-worthy,*
>
> Tom. Tremble."

Tom's *Coffee-house in* Birchin-lane *the* 23d *Day of the   Month called* July.[14]

It happens very oddly that the Pope[15] and I should have the same Thought much about the same Time. My Enemies will be apt to say that we hold a Correspondence together, and act by Concert in this Matter. Let that be as it will, I shall not be ashamed to join with his Holiness in those Particulars which are indifferent between us, especially when it is for the Reformation of the finer half of Mankind. We are both of us about the same Age, and consider this Fashion in the same View. I hope that it will not be able to resist his Bull[16] and my Lion. I am only afraid that our Ladies will take an Occasion from hence to show their Zeal for the Protestant Religion, and pretend to expose their naked Bosoms only in Opposition to Popery.

---

14 The Quakers preferred to avoid the pagan nomenclature which attended dating. (See *Tatler* No. 257, n. 21.) The correspondent in *Tatler* No. 72 dated his letter *"19th of the 7th month."*

15 Clement XI reigned from 1700 to 1721.

16 A papal letter secured with a lead seal called a *bulla.* See *Tatler* No. 25, n. 8.

The Guardian, No. 128

Friday, August 7.

[S t e e l e]

Delenda est Carthago———— ————[1]

It is usually thought, with great Justice, a very impertinent thing in a private Man to intermeddle in Matters which regard the State. But the Memorial[2] which is mentioned in the following Letter is so daring, and so apparently designed for the most Traiterous Purpose imaginable, that I do not care what Misinterpretation I suffer, when I expose it to the Resentment of all Men who value their Country, or have any Regard to the Honour, Safety, or Glory of their Queen. It is certain there is not much Danger in delaying the Demolition of *Dunkirk*[3] during the Life of his present most Christian Majesty, who is renowned for the most inviolable Regard to Treaties;[4] but that pious Prince is aged, and in case of his Decease, now the Power of *France* and *Spain* is in the same Family, it is possible an Ambitious Successor, (or his Ministry in a King's Minority) might dispute his being bound by the Act of his Predecessor in so weighty a Particular.

---

[1] Cato the Elder: "Carthage must be destroyed."

[2] The petitionary statement.

[3] One provision of the Treaty of Utrecht, signed March 1713, was that France should destroy the harbor and fortifications at Dunkirk. The port seemed a threat to English security, particularly if a Jacobite invasion were undertaken. Though the Treaty called for the destruction within five months of the signing, the first four months had produced nothing except this memorial from the magistrates of Dunkirk asking that the harbor be spared.

[4] For Steele's readers, who knew the history of King Louis XIV, the irony here was obvious.

"*Mr.* Ironside,

You employ your important Moments, methinks, a little too frivolously, when you consider so often little Circumstances of Dress and Behaviour, and never make mention of Matters wherein you and all your Fellow-Subjects in general are concerned.[5] I give you now an Opportunity, not only of manifesting your Loyalty to your Queen, but your Affection to your Country, if you treat an Insolence done to them both with the Disdain it deserves. The enclosed Printed Paper in *French* and *English* has been handed about the Town, and given *gratis* to Passengers in the Streets at Noon-Day. You see the Title of it is, *A most humble Address, or Memorial, presented to her Majesty the Queen of* Great Britain, *by the Deputy of the Magistrates of* Dunkirk. The nauseous Memorialist, with the most fulsom Flattery tells the Queen of her Thunder, and of Wisdom and Clemency adored by all the Earth, at the same time that he attempts to undermine her Power, and escape her Wisdom, by beseeching her to do an Act which would give a well-grounded Jealousie to her People.[6] What the Sycophant desires is, that the Mole and Dikes[7] of *Dunkirk* may be spared; and, it seems, the Sieur *Tugghe*,[8] for so the Petitioner is called, was Thunderstruck by *the Denunciation* (which he says) *the Lord Viscount* Bolingbroke[9] *made to him,* That her Majesty did not think to make any Alteration in the dreadful Sentence she had pronounced against the Town. Mr. Ironside, I think you would do an Act worthy your general Humanity, if you would put the Sieur *Tugghe* right in this Matter, and let him know That her Majesty has pronounced no Sentence against the Town, but his most Christian Majesty has agreed that the Town and Harbour shall be Demolished.

"That the *British* Nation expect the immediate Demolition of it.

"That the very Common People know, that within three Months after the signing of the Peace, the Works towards the Sea were to be demolished, and within three Months after it the Works towards the Land.

[5] Addison had been writing *Guardians* since the beginning of July and had resolutely kept the paper out of political controversy. Here, Steele seems to criticize his neutrality and returns to the fray.

[6] I.e., they would feel that Queen Anne is more concerned with French interests than with their own.

[7] The huge stone piers or breakwaters.

[8] Monsieur Tugghe, who represented the magistrates of Dunkirk.

[9] Henry St. John, Lord Bolingbroke (1678–1751), the Tory minister.

"That the said Peace was signed the last of *March,* O. S.[10]

"That the Parliament has been told from the Queen, that the Equivalent for it[11] is in the Hands of the *French* King.

"That the Sieur *Tugghe* has the Impudence to ask the Queen to remit the most material Part of the Articles of Peace between Her Majesty and his Master.

"That the *British* Nation received more Damage in their Trade from the Port of *Dunkirk,* than from almost all the Ports of *France,* either in the Ocean or in the Mediterranean.

"That Fleets of above thirty Sail have come together out of *Dunkirk,* during the late War, and taken Ships of War as well as Merchant Men.

"That the Pretender sailed from thence to *Scotland;*[12] and that it is the only Port the *French* have till you come to *Brest,* for the whole Length of St. *George*'s Channel,[13] where any considerable Naval Armament can be made.

"That destroying the Fortifications of *Dunkirk* is an inconsiderable Advantage to *England,* in Comparison to the Advantage of destroying the Mole, Dykes and Harbour, it being the Naval Force from thence which only can hurt the *British* Nation.

"That the *British* Nation expect the immediate Demolition of *Dunkirk.*

"That the *Dutch,* who suffered equally with us from those of *Dunkirk,* were probably induced to Sign the Treaty with *France* from this Consideration, That the Town and Harbour of *Dunkirk* should be destroyed.

"That the Situation of *Dunkirk* is such, as that it may always keep Runners to observe all Ships sailing on the *Thames* and *Medway.*

"That all the Suggestions, which the Sieur *Tugghe* brings concerning the *Dutch,* are false and scandalous.

"That whether it may be advantageous to the Trade of *Holland* or not, that *Dunkirk* should be demolished, it is necessary for the Safety, Honour, and Liberty of *England* that it should be so.

"That when *Dunkirk* is demolished, the Power of *France,* on that

10 See *Tatler* No. 1, n. 18.

11 A copy of the treaty.

12 In the futile Jacobite "invasion" of 1708, James Stuart fell ill with measles at Dunkirk, and then sailed all round Scotland and Ireland and back to Dunkirk without landing.

13 There may be a pun here. St. George's Channel is the strait between Ireland and Wales. And the Pretender's title was Chevalier de St. George.

Side, should it ever be turned against us, will be removed several hundred Miles further off of *Great Britain* than it is at present.

"That after the Demolition there can be no considerable Preparation made at Sea by the *French* in all the Channel but at *Brest;* and that *Great Britain* being an Island, which cannot be attacked but by a Naval Power, we may esteem *France* effectually removed by the Demolition from *Great Britain* as far as the Distance from *Dunkirk* to *Brest.*

"Pray, Mr. Ironside, repeat this last Particular, and put it in a different Letter,[14] *that the Demolition of* Dunkirk *will remove* France *many hundred Miles further off from us;* and then repeat again, *That the* British *Nation expects the Demolition of* Dunkirk.[15]

"I Demand of you, as you Love and Honour your Queen and Country, that you insert this Letter, or speak, to this Purpose, your own way; for in this all Parties must agree, that however bound in Friendship one Nation is with another, it is but prudent, that in case of a Rupture, they should be, if possible, upon equal Terms.

"Be Honest, old Nestor, and say all this; for whatever half-witted hot Whigs may think, we all value our Estates and Liberties, and every true Man of each Party must think himself concerned that *Dunkirk* should be Demolished.

"It lies upon all who have the Honour to be in the Ministry to hasten this Matter, and not let the Credulity of an honest brave People be thus infamously abused in our open Streets.

"I cannot go on for Indignation; but pray God that our Mercy to *France* may not expose us to the Mercy of *France.*

Your humble Servant,

English Tory."[16]

14 I.e., in italics for emphasis.

15 When Tory spokesmen responded to this essay, they commonly interpreted this thrice-repeated sentence as an insolent reminder to the Queen. Who was Steele, they asked, to tell her her duties? See *Guardian* No. 160 and n. 3.

16 Steele, a Whig, signed the letter "English Tory" to indicate that both parties should agree in so crucial an issue. *Guardian* No. 131 published another letter from "English Tory," which—under pretence of making a correction—repeats two paragraphs from this essay.

The Guardian, No. 137

Tuesday, August 18.

[A d d i s o n]

—————— —————— ——————*sanctus haberi*
Justitiaeque tenax, factis dictisque mereris?
Agnosco procerem—— ——————Juv.[1]

Horace, Juvenal, Boileau,[2] and indeed the greatest Writers in almost every Age, have exposed, with all the Strength of Wit and good Sense, the Vanity of a Man's valuing himself upon his Ancestors, and endeavoured to show that true Nobility consists in Virtue, not in Birth. With Submission however to so many great Authorities, I think they have pushed this matter a little too far. We ought in Gratitude to Honour the Posterity of those who have raised either the Interest or Reputation of their Country, and by whose Labours we our selves are more Happy, Wise or Virtuous than we should have been without them. Besides, naturally speaking, a Man bids fairer for Greatness of Soul, who is the Descendant of worthy Ancestors, and has good Blood in his Veins, than one who is come of an ignoble and obscure Parentage. For these Reasons I think a Man of Merit, who is derived from an Illustrious Line, is very justly to be regarded more than a Man of equal Merit who has no Claim to Hereditary Honours. Nay, I think those who are indifferent in themselves, and have nothing else to distinguish them but the Virtues of their Forefathers, are to be looked upon with a degree of Veneration even upon that account, and to be

---

1 Juvenal *Satires* 8. 24–26: "Prove yourself virtuous, one who holds to the right both in word and deed, and I acknowledge you as a lord."
2 See *Tatler* No. 158, n. 16.

more respected than the common Run of Men who are of low and vulgar Extraction.[3]

After having thus ascribed due Honours to Birth and Parentage, I must however take Notice of those who arrogate to themselves more Honours than are due to them on this Account. The first are such who are not enough sensible that Vice and Ignorance taint the Blood, and that an unworthy Behaviour degrades and disennobles a Man, in the Eye of the World, as much as Birth and Family aggrandize and exalt him.[4]

The second are those who believe a *new* Man of an elevated Merit is not more to be honoured than an insignificant and worthless Man who is descended from a long Line of Patriots and Heroes: Or, in other Words, behold with Contempt a Person who is such a Man as the first Founder of their Family was, upon whose Reputation they value themselves.

But I shall chiefly apply my self to those whose Quality sits uppermost in all their Discourses and Behaviour. An empty Man of a great Family is a Creature that is scarce conversible. You read his Ancestry in his Smile, in his Air, in his Eye-brow. He has indeed nothing but his Nobility to give Employment to his Thoughts. Rank and Precedency are the important Points which he is always discussing within himself. A Gentleman of this Turn begun a Speech in one of King *Charles*'s Parliaments: *Sir, I had the Honour to be born at a time*———upon which a rough honest Gentleman took him up short, *I would fain know what that Gentleman means, Is there any one in this House that has not had the Honour to be born as well as himself?* The good Sense which reigns in our Nation has pretty well destroyed this starched Be-

3 Though this essay expresses a Whig viewpoint, it is notable that the three Addison-Steele spokesmen were well-born. *Tatler* No. 111 and *Spectator* No. 1 made it clear that Isaac Bickerstaff and the Spectator were descended from ancient families. (*Tatler* No. 76 specified there had been a Sir Isaac Bickerstaff at King Arthur's round table.) Despite the exaggeration of Nestor's Aunt Martha, it is evident that the Ironside family has some claim to antiquity.

4 Two weeks earlier, in *Guardian* No. 123, Addison had printed a letter from a rural mother to a nobleman who had debauched her daughter. She asked, "Was it for this that the exalted Merits and godlike Virtues of your great Ancestor were honoured with a Coronet, that it might be a Pander to his Posterity . . . ?"

haviour among Men who have seen the World, and know that every Gentleman will be treated upon a Foot of Equality. But there are many who have had their Education among Women, Dependants or Flatterers, that lose all the Respect, which would otherwise be paid them, by being too assiduous in procuring it.[5]

My Lord *Froth* has been so educated in Punctilio, that he governs himself by a Ceremonial in all the ordinary Occurrences of Life. He Measures out his Bow to the degree of the Person he converses with. I have seen him in every Inclination of the Body, from a familiar Nod to the low Stoop in the Salutation-Sign. I remember five of us, who were acquainted with one another, met together one Morning at his Lodgings, when a Wag of the Company was saying, it wou'd be worth while to observe how he would distinguish us at his first Entrance. Accordingly he no sooner came into the Room, but casting his Eye about, *My Lord such a one,* says he, *your most humble Servant. Sir* Richard[6] *your humble Servant. Your Servant Mr.* Ironside. *Mr.* Ducker, *how do you do? Hah!* Frank *are you there?*

There is nothing more easie than to discover a Man whose Heart is full of his Family. Weak Minds that have imbibed a strong Tincture of the Nursery, younger Brothers that have been brought up to nothing,[7] Superannuated Retainers to a great House, have generally their Thoughts taken up with little else.

I had some Years ago an Aunt of my own, by Name Mrs[8] *Martha Ironside,* who would never Marry beneath herself, and is supposed to have died a Maid in the Fourscorth Year of her Age. She was the Chronicle of our Family, and past away the greatest part of the last Forty Years of her Life in recounting the Antiquity, Marriages, Exploits and Alliances of the *Ironsides.* Mrs. *Martha* conversed generally with a knot of old Virgins, who were likewise

----

[5] *Spectator* No. 299 recorded the aristocratic pretences of Lady Mary Oddly, who wed Jack Anvil, a *new* man who had made a fortune in iron and had been knighted. Anvil writes the Spectator, complaining that his wife treats him with disdain, has changed his name to Sir John Enville, and is educating their children with exaggerated accounts of their mother's family.

[6] Perhaps a reference to Sir Richard Steele.

[7] See the story of Will Wimble in *Spectator* No. 108.

[8] See *Guardian* No. 5, n. 9.

of good Families, and had been very cruel[9] all the beginning of the last Century. They were every one of 'em as proud as *Lucifer*, but said their Prayers twice a Day, and in all other respects were the best Women in the World. If they saw a fine Petticoat at Church, they immediately took to Pieces the Pedigree of her that wore it, and would lift up their Eyes to Heaven at the Confidence of the sawcy Minx when they found she was an honest Trades-man's Daughter. It is impossible to describe the pious Indignation that would rise in them at the sight of a Man who lived plentifully on an Estate of his own getting. They were transported with Zeal beyond measure, if they heard of a young Woman's matching into a great Family upon account only of[10] her Beauty, her Merit, or her Mony. In short, there was not a Female within ten Miles of them that was in Possession of a Gold Watch, a Pearl Necklace, or a Piece of *Mechlin Lace,* but they examined her Title to it. My Aunt *Martha* used to chide me very frequently for not sufficiently valuing my self. She would not eat a Bit all Dinner-time, if at an Invitation she found she had been seated below her self; and would frown upon me for an Hour together, if she saw me give place to any Man under a Baronet. As I was once talking to her of a wealthy Citizen whom she had refused in her Youth, she de-clared to me with great warmth, that she preferred a Man of Qual-ity in his Shirt to the richest Man upon the Change[11] in a Coach and Six. She pretended, that our Family was nearly related by the Mother's Side to half a dozen Peers; but as none of them knew any thing of the matter, we always kept it as a Secret among our selves. A little before her Death she was reciting to me the History of my Fore-fathers; but dwelling a little longer than ordinary upon the Actions of Sir *Gilbert Ironside,* who had a Horse shot under him at *Edghill* Fight,[12] I gave an unfortunate *Pish,* and asked, *What was all this to me?* upon which she retired to her Closet, and fell a Scribling for three Hours together, in which time, as I afterwards found, she struck me out of her Will, and left all she had to my Sister *Margaret,* a wheedling Baggage, that used to be asking Ques-

9 I.e., they were—as they tell it—very scornful to suing lovers.
10 With no qualifications other than.
11 The commercial exchange.
12 See *Tatler* No. 132, n. 17.

tions about her great Grandfather from Morning to Night. She now lies buried among the Family of the *Ironsides,* with a Stone over her, acquainting the Reader, that she died at the Age of Eighty Years, a Spinster, and that she was descended of the Ancient Family of the *Ironsides*————After which follows the Genealogy drawn up by her own Hand.

The Guardian, No. 158

Friday, September 11.

[Addison]

Gnossius haec Rhadamanthus habet durissima regna:
Castigatque, auditque dolos: subigitque fateri
Quae quis apud superos, furto laetatus inani,
Distulit in seram commissa piacula mortem. Virg.[1]

I was Yesterday pursuing the Hint which I mentioned in my last Paper, and comparing together the Industry of Man with that of other Creatures;[2] in which I could not but observe, that notwithstanding we are obliged by Duty to keep our selves in constant Employ, after the same manner as inferior Animals are prompted to it by Instinct, we fall very short of them in this Particular. We are here the more inexcusable, because there is a greater variety of Business to which we may apply our selves. Reason opens to us a large Field of Affairs, which other Creatures are not capable of. Beasts of Prey, and I believe of all other kinds, in their Natural State of Being, divide their time between Action and Rest. They are always at work or asleep. In short, their waking Hours are wholly taken up in seeking after their Food, or in consuming it. The Human Species only, to the great Reproach of our Natures, are filled with Complaints, that *the day hangs heavy on 'em,* that

---

[1] Virgil *Aeneid* 6. 566–569: "Here Rhadamanthus mercilessly rules, punishing wrongdoers and exacting confessions from any who on earth went guilty and gleefully undetected—but uselessly, since they only postponed their atonement till death."

[2] *Guardians* No. 156 and 157 carried "the Extract of a Letter upon [the behavior of ants], as it was published by Members of the French Academy, and since translated into English."

they do not know what to do with themselves, that *they are at a loss how to pass away their Time,* with many of the like shameful Murmurs, which we often find in the Mouths of those who are stiled Reasonable Beings.[3] How monstrous are such Expressions among Creatures, who have the Labours of the Mind, as well as those of the Body, to furnish them with proper Employments; who besides the Business of their proper Callings and Professions, can apply themselves to the Duties of Religion, to Meditation, to the Reading of useful Books, to Discourse; in a word, who may exercise themselves in the unbounded Pursuits of Knowledge and Virtue, and every Hour of their Lives make themselves wiser or better than they were before.

After having been taken up for some time in this course of Thought, I diverted my self with a Book, according to my usual Custom, in order to unbend my Mind before I went to Sleep. The Book I made use of on this occasion was *Lucian,* where I amused my Thoughts for about an Hour among the Dialogues of the Dead,[4] which in all probability produced the following Dream.

I was conveyed, methought, into the Entrance of the Infernal Regions, where I saw *Rhadamanthus,*[5] one of the Judges of the Dead, seated in his Tribunal. On his left Hand stood the Keeper of *Erebus,* on his Right the Keeper of *Elysium.* I was told he sat upon[6] Women that Day, there being several of the Sex lately arrived, who had not yet their Mansions assigned them. I was surprized to hear him ask every one of them the same Question, namely, *what they had been doing?* Upon this Question being proposed to the whole Assembly they stared one upon another, as not knowing what to Answer. He then Interrogated each of them separately. Madam, says he, to the first of them, you have been upon

---

[3] *Spectators* No. 317 and 323, both by Addison, gave the journals of a listless beau and a fashionably idle lady.

[4] Lucian (ca. 120–200 A.D.), the Greek wit and freethinker, wrote the famous satire, *Dialogues of the Dead.*

[5] In Greek mythology, Rhadamanthus, son of Jupiter and Europa, presided as one of the judges of the infernal regions. Erebus, son of Chaos, was darkness personified; his name was given to the gloomy cavern through which the shades had to walk on their way to Hades. Elysium is the abode of the blessed.

[6] Judged.

the Earth about Fifty Years: What have you been doing there all this while? Doing, says she, really I don't know what I have been doing: I desire I may have time given me to recollect. After about half an Hour's pause she told him, that she had been playing at Crimp;[7] upon which *Rhadamanthus* beckoned to the Keeper on his Left Hand, to take her into Custody. And you, Madam, says the Judge, that look with such a soft and languishing Air; I think you set out for this Place in your Nine and twentieth Year, what have you been doing all this while? I had a great deal of Business on my Hands, says she, being taken up the first Twelve Years of my Life, in dressing a Jointed Baby,[8] and all the remaining part of it in reading Plays and Romances. Very well, says he, you have employed your Time to good purpose. Away with her. The next was a plain Country Woman; Well Mistress, says *Rhadamanthus*, and what have you been doing? An't please your Worship, says she, I did not live quite Forty Years; and in that time brought my Husband seven Daughters, made him nine thousand Cheeses, and left my eldest Girl with him, to look after his House in my Absence, and who I may venture to say is as pretty a House-wife as any in the Country. *Rhadamanthus* smiled at the Simplicity of the good Woman, and order'd the Keeper of *Elysium* to take her into his Care. And you, fair Lady, says he, what have you been doing these Five and thirty Years? I have been doing no Hurt, I assure you, Sir, said she. That is well, says he, but what Good have you been doing? The Lady was in great Confusion at this Question, and not knowing what to answer, the two Keepers leaped out to seize her at the same time; the one took her by the Hand to convey her to *Elysium*, the other caught hold of her to carry her away to *Erebus*, But *Rhadamanthus* observing an ingenuous Modesty in her Countenance and Behaviour, bid them both let her loose, and set her aside for a Re-examination when he was more at Leisure.[9] An old Woman, of a proud and sower Look, presented her self next at the Bar, and being asked what she had been doing? Truly, says she, I lived threescore and ten Years in a very wicked World, and was so angry at the Behaviour of a parcel of young Flirts, that I past most

---

[7] A card game.

[8] I.e., playing with dolls.

[9] The dream ends before Rhadamanthus can undertake the reexamination.

of my last Years in condemning the Follies of the Times; I was
every Day blaming the silly Conduct of People about me, in order
to deter those I conversed with from falling into the like Errors
and Miscarriages. Very well, says *Rhadamanthus,* but did you
keep the same watchful Eye over your own Actions? Why truly,
says she, I was so taken up with publishing the Faults of others,
that I had no time to consider my own. Madam, says *Rhadamanthus,* be pleased to file off to the Left, and make Room for the
venerable Matron that stands behind you. Old Gentlewoman, says
he, I think you are fourscore? You have heard the Question, what
have you been doing so long in the World? Ah, Sir! says she, I
have been doing what I should not have done, but I had made a
firm Resolution to have changed my Life, if I had not been
snatched off by an untimely End. Madam, says he, you will please
to follow your Leader; and spying another of the same Age, interrogated her in the same Form. To which the Matron reply'd, I
have been the Wife of a Husband who was as dear to me in his old
Age as in his Youth. I have been a Mother, and very happy in my
Children, whom I endeavoured to bring up in every thing that is
good. My eldest Son is blest by the Poor,[10] and beloved by every
one that knows him. I lived within my own Family, and left it
much more wealthy than I found it. *Rhadamanthus,* who knew
the Value of the old Lady, smiled upon her in such a manner, that
the Keeper of *Elysium,* who knew his Office, reached out his Hand
to her. He no sooner touched her but her Wrinkles vanished, her
Eyes sparkled, her Cheeks glow'd with Blushes, and she appeared
in full Bloom and Beauty. A young Woman observing that this
Officer, who conducted the happy to *Elysium,* was so great a *Beau-
tifyer,* long'd to be in his Hands, so that pressing through the
Croud, she was the next that appeared at the Bar. And being
asked what she had been doing the five and twenty Years that she
had past in the World, I have endeavoured, says she, ever since I
came to Years of Discretion, to make my self Lovely and gain Admirers. In order to it I past my Time in bottling up May-dew,[11]

10 I.e., the gentlewoman's eldest son is the charitable lord of an estate.
11 Dew gathered during May was thought to have cosmetic and medicinal
properties.

inventing White-washes,[12] mixing Colours, cutting out Patches,[13] consulting my Glass, suiting my Complexion, tearing off my Tucker,[14] sinking my Stays—*Rhadamanthus,* without hearing her out, gave the Sign to take her off. Upon the Approach of the Keeper of *Erebus* her Colour faded, her Face was puckered up with Wrinkles, and her whole Person lost in Deformity.

I was then surprised with a distant Sound of a whole Troop of Females that came forward laughing, singing and dancing. I was very desirous to know the Reception they would meet with, and withal was very apprehensive, that *Rhadamanthus* would spoil their Mirth: But at their nearer Approach the Noise grew so very great that it awakened me.

I lay some time, reflecting in my self on the Oddness of this Dream, and could not forbear asking my own Heart, what I was doing? I answered my self, that I was writing *Guardians.* If my Readers make as good a Use of this Work as I design they should, I hope it will never be imputed to me as a Work that is vain and unprofitable.

I shall conclude this Paper with recommending to them the same short Self-Examination. If every one of them frequently lays his Hand upon his Heart, and considers what he is doing,[15] it will check him in all the idle, or, what is worse, the vicious Moments of Life, lift up his Mind when it is running on in a Series of indifferent Actions, and encourage him when he is engaged in those which are virtuous and laudable. In a Word, it will very much alleviate that Guilt which the best of Men have Reason to acknowledge in their daily Confessions, of *leaving undone those things which they ought to have done, and of doing those things which they ought not to have done.*

[12] See *Guardian* No. 116, n. 7. In *Spectator* No. 377, Addison included in a list of those who died for love, "Roger Blinko cut off in the Twenty First Year of his Age by a White-wash."

[13] See *Spectator* No. 37, n. 7.

[14] See *Guardians* No. 100 and 116.

[15] I.e., if one considers his own mortality.

The Guardian, No. 160

Monday, September 14.

[A d d i s o n]

Solventur risu tabulae, tu missus abibes. Hor.[1]

From Writing the History of Lions, I lately went off to that of Ants,[2] but to my great Surprise, I find that some of my good Readers have taken this last to be a work of Invention, which was only a plain Narrative of matter of Fact. They will several of them have it that my last *Thursday* and *Friday*'s Papers are full of concealed Satyr, and that I have attacked People in the shape of Pismires, whom I durst not meddle with in the shape of Men. I must confess that I write with Fear and Trembling ever since that ingenious Person the *Examiner*[3] in his little Pamphlet, which was to make way for one of his following Papers, found out Treason in the word *Expect*.

But I shall for the future leave my Friend[4] to manage the Controversie in a separate Work, being unwilling to fill with Disputes a Paper which was undertaken purely out of Good-will to my Country-men. I must therefore declare that those Jealousies and Suspicions, which have been raised in some weak Minds, by means of the two abovementioned Discourses concerning Ants or Pis-

[1] Horace *Satires* 2. 1. 86: "The court will laugh and you will be dismissed."

[2] Addison discussed the history of lions (along with the story of Androcles) in *Guardian* No. 139. In papers No. 156 and 157, he presented "the Extract of a Letter upon [the behavior of ants], as it was published by the Members of the French Academy, and since translated into English."

[3] See *Tatler* No. 229, n. 8. For the treasonable word *Expect*, see *Guardian* No. 128 and n. 15.

[4] I.e., "English Tory" from *Guardians* No. 128 and 131.

mires, are altogether Groundless. There is not an Emmit in all that whole Narrative who is either Whig or Tory; and I could heartily wish, that the Individuals of all Parties among us, had the Good of their Country at Heart, and endeavoured to advance it by the same Spirit of Frugality, Justice, and mutual Benevolence, as are visibly exercised by Members of those little Common-wealths.

After this short Preface, I shall lay before my Reader a Letter or two which occasioned it.

"*Mr.* Ironside,
I have laid a Wager, with a Friend of mine, about the Pidgeons that used to peck up the Corn which belonged to the Ants. I say that by these Pidgeons you mean the *Palatines.*[5] He will needs have it that they were the *Dutch.* We both agree that the Papers upon the Strings which frighted them away, were *Pamphlets, Examiners,* and the like. We beg you will satisfie us in this particular, because the Wager is very considerable, and you will much oblige two of your
Daily Readers."

"*Old* Iron,
Why so Rusty? Will you never leave your Innuendos? Do you think it hard to find out who is the Tulip in your last *Thursday*'s Paper? Or can you imagine that three Nests of Ants is such a Disguise, that the plainest Reader cannot see three Kingdoms[6] through it? The blowing up of the Neighbouring Settlement, where there was a Race of poor Beggarly Ants, under a worse Form of Government, is not so difficult to be explained as you imagine. *Dunkirk* is not yet Demolished. Your Ants are Enemies to Rain[7] are they! Old *Birmingham,* no more of your Ants, if you don't intend to stir up a Nest of Hornets.
Will. Waspe."

"*Dear* Guardian,
Calling in Yesterday at a Coffee-House in the City, I saw a very short Corpulent angry Man reading your Paper about the Ants. I observed that he redden'd and swell'd over every Sentence of it. After having perused it throughout he laid it down upon the Table, called the Woman of the Coffee-house to him, and asked her, in a magisterial Voice, if she knew what she did in taking in such Papers! The Woman

5 See *Tatler* No. 60, n. 17.
6 England, Scotland, and Wales were united politically in 1707.
7 Presumably, an anti-monarchial sentiment with a pun on the word *reign.*

was in such a Confusion, that I thought it a Piece of Charity to inter-
pose in her Behalf, and asked him whether he had found any thing in
it of dangerous Import. Sir, said he, it is a Republican[8] Paper from
one End to the other, and if the Author had his Deserts—He here
grew so exceeding cholerick and fierce, that he could not proceed;
'till after having recovered himself, he laid his Finger upon the following Sentence, and read it with a very stern Voice————*Tho' Ants are
very knowing, I don't take them to be Conjurers: And therefore they
could not guess that I had put some Corn in that Room. I perceived
for several Days that they were very much perplexed, and went a
great way to fetch their Provisions. I was not willing for some time to
make them more easie; For I had a mind to know, whether they would
at last find out the Treasure, and see it at a great Distance, and whether
Smelling enabled them to know what is good for their Nourishment.*
Then throwing the Paper upon the Table; Sir, says he, these things are
not to be suffered————I would engage out of this Sentence to draw
up an Indictment that[9]————He here lost his Voice a second time, in
the Extremity of his Rage, and the whole Company, who were all of
them Tories, bursting out into a sudden Laugh, he threw down his
Penny in great Wrath, and retir'd with a most formidable Frown.

"This, Sir, I thought fit to acquaint you with, that you may make
what Use of it you please. I only wish that you would sometimes diver-
sifie your Papers with many other Pieces of natural History, whether
of Insects or Animals; this being a Subject which the most common
Reader is capable of understanding, and which is very diverting in its
Nature; besides, that it highly redounds to the Praise of that Being
who has inspired the several Parts of the sensitive World with such
wonderful and different Kinds of Instinct as enable them to provide
for themselves, and preserve their Species in that State of Existence
wherein they are placed. There is no Party[10] concerned in Speculations of this Nature, which instead of enflaming those unnatural Heats
that prevail among us, and take up most of our Thoughts, may divert
our Minds to Subjects that are useful, and suited to reasonable Creatures. Dissertations of this kind are the more proper for your Purpose,
as they do not require any Depth of Mathematicks, or any previous
Science, to qualifie the Reader for the understanding of them. To this
I might add, that it is a Shame for Men to be ignorant of these Worlds

8 I.e., Whig.
9 The man's complaint is intentionally obscure. See *Tatler* No. 155, n. 11.
10 Political question.

of Wonders which are transacted in the midst of them, and not to be acquainted with those Objects which are every where before their Eyes. To which I might further add, that several are of Opinion, there is no other Use in many of these Creatures than to furnish Matter of Contemplation and Wonder to those Inhabitants of the Earth who are its only Creatures that are capable of it.

I am, Sir,
Your constant Reader,
and Humble Servant."

After having presented my Reader with this Sett of Letters, which are all upon the same Subject, I shall here insert one that has no Relation to it. But it has always been my Maxim never to refuse going out of my Way to do any honest Man a Service, especially when I have an Interest in it my Self.[11]

"*Most Venerable* Nestor,
As you are a Person that very eminently distinguish your self in the Promotion of the Publick Good, I desire your Friendship in signifying to the Town, what concerns the greatest Good of Life, *Health.* I do assure you, Sir, there is in a Vault, under the *Exchange* in *Cornhill,* over-against *Pope's-Head Alley,* a Parcel of *French* Wines, full of the Seeds of good Humour, Chearfulness and Friendly Mirth. I have been told, the Learned of our Nation agree, there is no such thing as Bribery in Liquors, therefore I shall presume to send you of it, lest you should think it inconsistent with Integrity to recommend what you do not understand by Experience. In the mean time please to Insert this, that every Man may judge for himself.

I am, Sir, &c."

11 I.e., when I stand to profit by it.

The Guardian, No. 162

Wednesday, September 16.

[A d d i s o n]

Proprium hoc esse prudentiae, conciliare sibi animos hominum & ad usus suos adjungere. Cicer.[1]

I was the other Day in Company at my Lady *Lizard*'s, when there came in among us their Cousin *Tom,* who is one of those Country Squires[2] that set up for plain honest Gentlemen who speak their Minds. *Tom* is in short a lively impudent Clown, and has Wit enough to have made him a pleasant Companion, had it been polished and rectified by good Manners. *Tom* had not been a Quarter of an Hour with us, before he set every one in the Company a Blushing, by some blunt Question, or unlucky Observation. He asked the *Sparkler* if her Wit had yet got her a Husband; and told her eldest Sister[3] she looked a little Wan under the Eyes, and that it was time for her to look about her, if she did not design to lead Apes in the other World.[4] The good Lady *Lizard,* who suffers more than her Daughters on such an Occasion, desired her Cousin *Thomas* with a Smile, not to be so severe on his Relations; to which the Booby replied, with a rude Country Laugh, If I be not mistaken Aunt, you were a Mother at Fifteen, and why do you expect that your Daughters should be Maids till Five and twenty? I endeavoured to divert the Discourse, when without taking Notice of what I said, Mr. *Ironside,* says he, you fill my Cous-

---

1 Cicero: "The art of prudence lies in gaining the esteem of the world, and turning it to a man's own advantage."

2 See *Tatler* No. 89, n. 10.

3 I.e., Jane, age twenty-three.

4 To be an old maid. Tom speaks euphemistically: the usual phrase is "to lead apes in hell."

in's Heads with your fine Notions as you call them, can you teach them to make a Pudding? I must confess he put me out of Countenance with his Rustick Raillery, so that I made some Excuse, and left the Room.

This Fellow's Behaviour made me Reflect on the Usefulness of Complaisance,[5] to make all Conversation agreeable. This, tho' in it self it be scarce reckoned in the number of Moral Virtues, is that which gives a Lustre to every Talent a Man can be possest of. It was *Plato's* Advice to an unpolish'd Writer,[6] that he should Sacrifice to the Graces. In the same manner I would advise every Man of Learning, who would not appear in the World a meer Scholar, or Philosopher, to make himself Master of the Social Virtue which I have here mentioned.[7]

Complaisance renders a Superior amiable, an Equal agreeable, and an Inferior acceptable. It smooths Distinction, sweetens Conversation, and makes every one in the Company pleased with himself. It produces Good-nature and mutual Benevolence, encourages the Timorous, sooths the Turbulent, humanises the Fierce, and distinguishes a Society of Civilised Persons from a Confusion of Savages. In a word, Complaisance is a Virtue that blends all Orders of Men together in a Friendly Intercourse of Words and Actions, and is suited to that Equality in Human Nature which every one ought to consider, so far as is consistent with the Order and Oeconomy of the World.

If we could look into the secret Anguish and Affliction of every Man's Heart we should often find, that more of it arises from little imaginary Distresses, such as Checks, Frowns, Contradictions, Expressions of Contempt, and (what *Shakespear* reckons among other Evils under the Sun,)

> ———*The poor Man's Contumely,*
> *The Insolence of Office, and the Spurns*
> *That patient Merit of the unworthy takes,*[8]

---

[5] The word is defined two paragraphs hence.

[6] Xenocrates (396–314 B.C.), a Greek philosopher. The advice is recorded in Diogenes' *Xenocrates*, 4, 2.

[7] Steele expressed the same view in *Guardian* No. 94.

[8] From *Hamlet*, act 3, sc. 1, 71–74. The first line should be "The *proud* Man's Contumely," i.e., his scornful insult.

than from the more real Pains and Calamities of Life. The only
Method to remove these imaginary Distresses as much as possible
out of Human Life, wou'd be the Universal Practice of such an
Ingenuous Complaisance as I have been here describing, which,
as it is a Virtue, may be defined to be *a constant Endeavour to
please those whom we converse with, so far as we may do it Innocently*. I shall here add, that I know nothing so effectual to raise
a Man's Fortune as Complaisance, which recommends more to the
Favour of the Great, than Wit, Knowledge, or any other Talent
whatsoever. I find this Consideration very prettily illustrated by
a little wild *Arabian* Tale, which I shall here abridge, for the sake
of my Reader, after having again warned him, that I do not recommend to him such an impertinent or vicious Complaisance as
is not consistent with Honour and Integrity.

"*Schacabac* being reduced to great Poverty, and having eat
nothing for two Days together, made a Visit to a noble *Barmecide*[9]
in *Persia,* who was very hospitable, but withal a great Humorist.
The *Barmecide* was sitting at his Table that seemed ready covered
for an Entertainment. Upon hearing *Schacabac*'s Complaint, he
desired him to sit down and fall on. He then gave him an empty
Plate, and asked him how he liked his Rice-Soup. *Schacabac,* who
was a Man of Wit, and resolved to comply with the *Barmecide* in
all his Humours, told him 'twas admirable, and, at the same time,
in Imitation of the other, lifted up the empty Spoon to his Mouth
with great Pleasure. The *Barmecide* then asked him, if he ever saw
whiter Bread? *Schacabac,* who saw neither Bread nor Meat, If I
did not like it, you may be sure, says he, I should not eat so heartily of it. You oblige me mightily, reply'd the *Barmecide,* pray let
me help you to this Leg of a Goose. *Schacabac* reached out his
Plate, and received nothing on it with great Chearfulness. As he
was eating very heartily on this imaginary Goose, and crying up
the Sauce to the Skies, the *Barmecide* desired him to keep a
Corner of his Stomach for a roasted Lamb, fed with Pistacho-Nuts,
and after having call'd for it, as tho' it had really been served up,
Here is a Dish, says he, that you will see at no Body's Table but
my own. *Schacabac* was wonderfully delighted with the Taste of

9 Prince.

it, which is like nothing, says he, I ever eat before. Several other nice Dishes were served up in Idea, which both of them commended and feasted on after the same manner. This was followed by an invisible *Dissert*, no part of which delighted *Schacabac* so much as a certain Lozenge, which the *Barmecide* told him was a Sweet-meat of his own Invention. *Schacabac* at length, being courteously reproached by the *Barmecide*, that he had no Stomach, and that he eat nothing, and, at the same time, being tired with moving his Jaws up and down to no Purpose, desired to be excused, for that really he was so full he could not eat a Bit more. Come then, says the *Barmecide*, the Cloth shall be removed, and you shall taste of my Wines, which I may say, without Vanity, are the best in *Persia*. He then *filled* both their Glasses out of an empty Decanter. *Schacabac* would have excused himself from drinking so much at once, because he said he was a little Quarrelsome in his Liquor; however being prest to it, he pretended to take it off,[10] having before-hand praised the Colour, and afterwards the Flavour. Being ply'd with two or three other imaginary Bumpers of different Wines, equally delicious, and a little vexed with this fantastick Treat, he pretended to grow flustred, and gave the *Barmecide* a good Box on the Ear, but immediately recovering himself, Sir, says he, I beg ten thousand Pardons, but I told you before, that it was my Misfortune to be Quarrelsome in my Drink. The *Barmecide* could not but smile at the Humour[11] of his Guest, and instead of being angry at him, I find, says he, thou art a complaisant Fellow, and deservest to be entertained in my House. Since thou canst accommodate thy self to my Humour, we will now eat together in good Earnest. Upon which, calling for his Supper, the Rice-Soup, the Goose, the Pistaco-Lamb, the several other nice Dishes, with the *Dissert*, the Lozenges, and all the Variety of *Persian* Wines, were served up successively, one after another; and *Schacabac* was feasted in Reality, with those very things which he had before been entertained with in Imagination."

10 Drink it down.
11 Whimsical attitude.

Selected Bibliography

Bibliographical Aids

Crane, Ronald S., and Kaye, F. B. *A Census of British Newspapers and Periodicals, 1620–1800*. Chapel Hill, 1927.

Crane, Ronald S., Bredvold, Louis I., Bond, Richmond P., Friedman, Arthur, and Landa, Louis A. *English Literature, 1660–1800: A Bibliography of Modern Studies Compiled for Philological Quarterly*. 2 vols. Princeton, 1950–52.

Morgan, William Thomas, and Morgan, Chloe Siner. *A Bibliography of British History (1700–1715), with Special Reference to the Reign of Queen Anne*. 5 vols. Bloomington, Ind. 1939–1942.

Weed, K. K., and Bond, R. P., *Studies in British Newspapers and Periodicals from their Beginning to 1800: a Bibliography*. Chapel Hill, 1946.

[Annual bibliographies in this area are published in *PMLA* and the *Philological Quarterly*.]

Primary Sources

The Tatler, edited by George A. Aitken. 4 vols. London, 1898–99.

The Spectator, edited by Donald F. Bond. 5 vols. Oxford, 1956.

The Guardian, Tonson 12mo. ed. London, 1745.

Addison, Joseph. *The Letters of Joseph Addison*. Edited by Walter Graham. Oxford, 1941.

———. *The Works of Joseph Addison*. Edited by George Washington Greene. 6 vols. Philadelphia, 1864.

Steele, Richard. *The Christian Hero*. Edited by Rae Blanchard. Oxford, 1932.

———. *The Correspondence of Richard Steele*. Edited by Rae Blanchard. Oxford, 1941.

———. *The Englishman*. Edited by Rae Blanchard. Oxford, 1955.

———. *The Occasional Verse of Richard Steele.* Edited by Rae Blanchard. Oxford, 1952.

———. *Richard Steele's Periodical Journalism, 1714–1716.* Edited by Rae Blanchard. Oxford, 1959.

———. *The Theatre, 1720.* Edited by John Loftis. Oxford, 1962.

———. *Tracts and Pamphlets by Richard Steele.* Edited by Rae Blanchard. Baltimore, 1944.

Swift, Jonathan. *Bickerstaff Papers.* Edited by H. Davis. Oxford, 1957.

———. *The Examiner and Other Pieces Written in 1710–11.* Edited by H. Davis. Oxford, 1957.

———. *Political Tracts, 1711–1713.* Edited by H. Davis. Oxford, 1951.

———. *Political Tracts, 1713–1719.* Edited by H. Davis and I. Ehrenpreis. Oxford, 1953.

Commentaries

Aiken, Lucy. *The Life of Joseph Addison.* 2 vols. London, 1843.

Aitkin, G. A. *The Life of Richard Steele.* 2 vols. London, 1889.

Ault, Norman. "Pope and Addison." *Review of English Studies* XVII (1941): 428–451.

Beljame, Alexandre. *Men of Letters and the English Public in the Eighteenth Century. . . .* Translated by E. O. Lorimer. Edited by Bonamy Dobrée. London, 1948.

Betz, A. E. "The Operatic Criticism of the *Tatler* and *Spectator.*" *Musical Quarterly* XXXI (1945): 318–330.

Blanchard, Rae. "Richard Steele and the Status of Women." *Studies in Philology* XXVI (1929): 325–355.

Bond, Donald F. "The Neo-classical Psychology of the Imagination." *Journal of English Literary History* IV (1937): 245–264.

Bond, Richmond P. *Contemporaries of the Tatler and Spectator.* Los Angeles, 1954.

———. "Isaac Bickerstaff, Esq." In *Restoration & 18th Century*

Literature. Edited by C. Camden, pp. 103–124. Chicago, 1963.

————. *Studies in the Early English Periodical.* Chapel Hill, 1957.

Broadus, Edmund K. "Addison's Influence on the Development of Interest in Folk-Poetry in the Eighteenth Century." *Modern Philology* VIII (1910–11): 123–134.

Clark, G. N. *The Later Stuarts: 1660–1714.* Oxford, 1934.

Connely, Willard. *Sir Richard Steele.* New York, 1934.

Courthope, W. J. *Addison.* New York, 1884.

Dobrée, Bonamy. *English Literature in the Early Eighteenth Century, 1700–1740.* London and New York, 1959.

————. "The First Victorian." In *Essays in Biography: 1680–1726,* pp. 201–357. London, 1925.

Elioseff, Lee Andres. *The Cultural Milieu of Addison's Literary Criticism.* Austin, Tex., 1963.

Ewald, W. B. *The Newsmen of Queen Anne.* Oxford, 1956.

Freeman, Phyllis. "Who was Sir Roger de Coverley?" *Quarterly Review* CCLXXXV (October 1947): 592–620.

Friedman, Albert B. "Addison's Ballad Papers and the Reaction to Metaphysical Wit." *Comparative Literature* XII (1960): 1–13.

Goldgar, Bertrand A. *The Curse of Party: Swift's Relations with Addison and Steele.* Lincoln, Nebr., 1961.

Graham, Walter. *English Literary Periodicals.* New York, 1930.

————. "Some Predecessors of the *Tatler*," *Journal of English and Germanic Philology* XXIV (1925): 548–554.

Hazlitt, William. "On the Periodical Essayists." In *Lectures on the English Comic Writers, with Miscellaneous Essays.* London, 1913.

Hodgart, M. J. C. "The Eighth Volume of the *Spectator*." *Review of English Studies,* n.s. V (1954): 367–387.

Humphreys, A. R. *Steele, Addison and their Periodical Essays.* London, 1959.

Johnson, Samuel. "Addison." In *Lives of the Poets,* edited by G. Birkbeck Hill. 3 vols. Oxford, 1905.

Lannering, Jan. *Studies in the Prose Style of Joseph Addison.* Uppsala, 1951.

Lewis, C. S. "Addison." In *Essays on the Eighteenth Century Presented to David Nichol Smith in Honour of His Seventieth Birthday* pp. 1–14. Oxford, 1945.

Lewis, Lawrence. *The Advertisements of the Spectator.* Boston, 1909.

Loftis, John. *Steele at Drury Lane.* Berkeley and Los Angeles, 1952.

Macaulay, Thomas Babington. *Essay on Addison,* edited by Herbert Augustine Smith. Boston, 1898.

Marr, George S. *The Periodical Essayists of the Eighteenth Century.* London, 1924.

McDonald, Daniel. "The 'Logic' of Addison's *Freeholder.*" In *Papers on Language & Literature* IV (1968): 20–34.

Nethercot, Arthur H. "The Reputation of the 'Metaphysical Poets' during the Age of Pope." *Philological Quarterly* IV (1925): 161–179.

Nicoll, Allardyce. "Italian Opera in England: the First Five Years." *Anglia* XVIV (1922): 257–281.

Smithers, Peter. *The Life of Joseph Addison.* Oxford, 1954.

Stephens, John C., Jr. "Addison as Social Critic." *Emory University Quarterly* XXI (1965): 157–172.

Todd, William B. "Early Editions of *The Tatler.*" *Studies in Bibliography* XV (1962): 121–133.

Trevelyan, George M. *England Under Queen Anne.* 3 vols. London, 1930–1934.

Walcott, Robert. *English Politics in the Early Eighteenth Century.* Oxford, 1956.

Winton, Calhoun. *Captain Steele: the Early Career of Richard Steele.* Baltimore, 1964.

———. "Steele and the Fall of Harley in 1714." *Philological Quarterly* XXXVII (1958): 440–447.

Woolf, Virginia. "Addison." In *The Common Reader,* pp. 98–108. New York, 1953.

Index